Eyewitness and Crusade Narrative

Crusading in Context

Series Editor
William J. Purkis

The crusading movement was a defining feature of the history of Europe, the Mediterranean and the Near East during the central and later Middle Ages. Ideas and practices associated with it touched the lives of people within and beyond Christendom and the Islamicate world, regardless whether they were ever directly engaged in, witnesses to, or victims of acts of crusading violence themselves.

This series aims to situate the medieval experience of the crusades and crusading societies in the broader social, cultural and intellectual contexts of the Middle Ages as a whole. Chronologically, its scope extends from the eleventh to the sixteenth century, and contributions from a range of disciplines are encouraged. Monographs and edited collections are both welcome; critical editions and translations of medieval texts will also be considered.

Proposals and queries should be sent in the first instance to the series editor or to Boydell and Brewer, at the addresses below.

Dr William J. Purkis, School of History and Cultures, University of Birmingham, Edgbaston, Birmingham, B15 2TT
w.j.purkis@bham.ac.uk

Boydell and Brewer Ltd, PO Box 9, Woodbridge, Suffolk, IP12 3DF
editorial@boydell.co.uk

Eyewitness and Crusade Narrative

Perception and Narration in Accounts of the Second, Third and Fourth Crusades

Marcus Bull

THE BOYDELL PRESS

First published 2018
The Boydell Press, Woodbridge
Paperback edition 2020

ISBN 978 1 78327 335 5 hardback
ISBN 978 1 78327 537 3 paperback

The Boydell Press is an imprint of Boydell & Brewer Ltd
PO Box 9, Woodbridge, Suffolk IP12 3DF, UK
and of Boydell & Brewer Inc.
668 Mt Hope Avenue, Rochester, NY 14620–2731, USA
website: www.boydellandbrewer.com

A CIP catalogue record for this book is available
from the British Library

Jonathan Riley-Smith
In memoriam

Contents

Acknowledgements

Over the course of the research for this book I have incurred a great many debts of gratitude. I have benefitted from exchanges with numerous colleagues. I shall not list names for fear of leaving some people out, but I think it is right to mention William Purkis, with whom it is always a great pleasure to discuss ideas.

I am appreciative of the ways in which the Department of History and the Medieval and Early Modern Studies programme at the University of North Carolina stimulate a creative atmosphere in which the synergies between teaching and research are fostered by opportunities to teach to one's evolving interests and to go in new research directions. I am therefore very grateful to my medievalist and other colleagues in Chapel Hill for contributing to a positive and energizing academic milieu. I would particularly like to thank the medieval postgraduate students in the Department of History. It is my very good fortune to have some small role in the academic formation of an exceptional group of talented and engaging young scholars. It is without question the best part of the job. They will recognize in this book many of the things that I have droned on about in recent years; but I hope that they will also get a sense of how much I learn from them.

I was fortunate to be awarded a fellowship at the National Humanities Center in the academic year 2014–15, during which time I did much of the reading that informs this book. I am very grateful to then Vice-President for Scholarly Programs Cassie Mansfield and her courteous staff for the wonderful scholarly ambience in which I found myself immersed at the Center. I am further grateful to Cassie and the Center for permitting me to retain my office there in the autumn of 2015, when I was in receipt of a Senior Faculty Research and Scholarly Leave from UNC.

I am extremely grateful to Caroline Palmer and Boydell and Brewer. It is always a great pleasure to work with such a professional and helpful team; and I am especially grateful for Caroline's gracious patience and keen insight. To inaugurate a new series for the press is a particular honour.

To my wife Tania and my daughter Sasha, my *hoofdklasse* team, no expression of gratitude is sufficient. In generously creating the conditions in which it is easy to work, they are effectively the co-authors of this book.

Finally, an acknowledgement of two scholars who made a big difference for me. I had always hoped that one day I might have the chance to register my appreciation of Rosalind Hill (1908–97) in some way; and although she is best known for her edition (with Sir Roger Mynors) and translation of the *Gesta Francorum*, a First Crusade text, and this book begins with the Second, this seems an opportune moment. In her late seventies and well into her eighties,

Rosalind would unfailingly attend the 'Crusades and the Latin East' seminars at the Institute of Historical Research; and what struck me at the time and remains an abiding memory is her great interest in and kindness towards the assembled postgraduate students, me included. British academic life is much the poorer for the passing of the generation whose values Professor Hill personified.

Jonathan Riley-Smith's death in 2016 was a loss keenly felt by many. It is a characteristic of unusually kind and generous people that they leave those around them in their debt, even though they would not for one minute dream of calling in that debt to their own advantage. Jonathan was such a person. This book is dedicated to his memory.

Chapel Hill, February 2018

Abbreviations

CCCM	Corpus Christianorum, Continuatio Mediaeualis
Conquête	Geoffrey of Villehardouin, *La conquête de Constantinople*, ed. and trans. E. Faral, 2nd edn, 2 vols (Les classiques de l'histoire de France au moyen âge, 18-19; Paris, 1961)
De expugnatione	*De expugnatione Lyxbonensi: The Conquest of Lisbon*, ed. and trans. C. W. David, rev. J. P. Phillips (New York, 2001)
De profectione	Odo of Deuil, *De profectione Ludovici VII in orientem*, ed. and trans. V. G. Berry (New York, 1948)
Estoire	Ambroise, *The History of the Holy War: Ambroise's Estoire de la Guerre Sainte*, ed. and trans. M. J. Ailes and M. C. Barber, 2 vols (Woodbridge, 2003)
MGH	Monumenta Germaniae Historica
MGH SS	*Monumenta Germaniae Historica, Scriptores in Folio et Quarto*, ed. G. H. Pertz *et al.* (Hanover, Weimar, Stuttgart, and Cologne, 1826–)
PL	*Patrologiae cursus completus, series Latina*, ed. J.-P. Migne, 221 vols (Paris, 1844–64)
RC	Robert of Clari, *La Conquête de Constantinople*, ed. and trans. P. Noble (British Rencesvals Publications, 3; Edinburgh, 2005)
RHGF	*Recueil des historiens des Gaules et de la France*, ed. M. Bouquet, rev. L. Delisle, 24 vols in 25 (Paris, 1840–1904)
RS	Rolls Series: Chronicles and Memorials of Great Britain and Ireland during the Middle Ages (London, 1838–96)

Introduction: Medieval and Modern Approaches to Eyewitnessing and Narratology as an Analytical Tool

There is a category of historical evidence that historians are wont to characterize, and indeed to essentialize, as 'eyewitness'. This is not just a technical term of art. The idea of being an eyewitness to something is deeply embedded in a wide range of cultural situations. We do not need to have a formal grounding in common law, for instance, to appreciate that the reliability of a witness who claims to have seen an event is normally greater than that of someone who is merely passing on hearsay. As is discussed in more detail below, sight and light are the basis of countless metaphors for understanding, realization and many other cognitive operations. So when we say that a historical source is 'eyewitness', we are making very large claims about it, even though the underlying assumptions about what we are saying have been surprisingly little studied relative to the importance of this category to the ways in which historians evaluate and deploy their evidence. All historical evidence that is the result or residue of human agency – as opposed to, say, tree-ring data and some types of archaeological deposit – has some experiential basis. But the particular appeal of eyewitness evidence is that, all other things being equal, it seems to close the gap between record and experience more than any other trace of the human past. It is through eyewitness evidence that we seem to get closest to validating the powerful instinct that people in the past must have led lives grounded in moment-by-moment sensory experience that was every bit as real to them as our lived experience is to us. In this way the category of eyewitness evidence seems to plug historical inquiry into basic human capacities that transcend cultural differences across time and space – or at least do so enough to grant us a meaningful point of entry into societies which in many respects can strike us as very dissimilar from our own. Eyewitnessing appears to be a powerful common denominator that permits us to understand and empathize with people in the past.[1]

[1] The most suggestive and theoretically informed discussion of premodern eyewitnessing is Andrea Frisch's *The Invention of the Eyewitness: Witnessing and Testimony in Early Modern France* (Chapel Hill, NC, 2004). See also her 'The Ethics of Testimony: A Genealogical Perspective', *Discourse*, 25 (2003), 36–54. Frisch seeks to challenge the dominant scholarly view that eyewitness experience acquired a new epistemological prestige in the early modern period as a result of European encounters with the New World. Frisch's attention to legal paradigms is interesting, if narrow in its scope. And her central argument that premodern eyewitness testimony should be seen as dialogic and performative, a social interaction charged with ethical meaning, rather than simply the articulation of knowledge gained from past experience, is

We need, therefore, to unpack the assumptions that we build into the category of evidence that we label 'eyewitness'. In order to do so, and to examine the mechanisms whereby the experiences of people who took part in a historical event are transposed into narratives about it, this study focuses on a selection of texts written in connection with the Second, Third and Fourth Crusades.[2] Individually and collectively, the chosen texts raise questions about the ways in which eyewitnessing informs substantial and detailed narratives that tell complex stories. The overall argument of this book is that, whereas we tend to appraise the eyewitness quality of a narrative source primarily in terms of the relationship of the source's author to the events that the source narrates, there is more to be gained from looking inwards into the workings of the eyewitness narrative as text. This is not to argue that the history of events, *histoire événementielle*, is trivial or unimportant, or that the reality of the past simply collapses

---

insightful. But her remarks about medieval conditions are based on too slender a body of evidence, and nudge too far towards caricature of (p. 83) the 'feudal mechanisms for establishing the credibility of testimony', to convince. For the scholarship with which Frisch takes issue, and which remains some of the most stimulating explorations of premodern eyewitnessing, see S. Greenblatt, *Marvelous Possessions: The Wonder of the New World* (Chicago, 1991), esp. pp. 128–45 on Bernal Díaz; A. Pagden, *Eyewitness Encounters with the New World: From Renaissance to Romanticism* (New Haven, 1993), esp. pp. 51–87 on the 'autoptic imagination'; *idem*, '*Ius et Factum*: Text and Experience in the Writings of Bartolomé de Las Casas', in S. Greenblatt (ed.), *New World Encounters* (Berkeley, 1993), pp. 85–100. See also R. Adorno, 'The Discursive Encounter of Spain and America: The Authority of Eyewitness Testimony in the Writing of History', *William and Mary Quarterly*, 3rd ser., 49 (1992), 210–28. For a thoughtful study of a medieval observer's reactions to a no-less unfamiliar world, see P. Jackson, 'William of Rubruck in the Mongol Empire: Perception and Prejudices', in Z. von Martels (ed.), *Travel Fact and Travel Fiction: Studies on Fiction, Literary Tradition, Scholarly Discovery and Observation in Travel Writing* (Brill's Studies in Intellectual History, 55; Leiden, 1994), pp. 54–71.

[2] The Latin eyewitness texts relating to the First Crusade are the subject of a valuable study: Y. N. Harari, 'Eyewitnessing in Accounts of the First Crusade: The *Gesta Francorum* and Other Contemporary Narratives', *Crusades*, 3 (2004), 77–99. Harari's definition of an eyewitness text as those (p. 77) 'whose main purpose is to narrate what their authors have seen and experienced and that accordingly privilege factual accuracy over skill of writing and breadth of interpretation' is too narrow, however, and his resultant taxonomy too rigid. For a long-term view, see the same author's 'Scholars, Eyewitnesses, and Flesh-Witnesses of War: A Tense Relationship', *Partial Answers: Journal of Literature and the History of Ideas*, 7 (2009), 213–28; 'Armchairs, Coffee, and Authority: Eye-witnesses and Flesh-witnesses Speak About War, 1100–2000', *Journal of Military History*, 74 (2010), 53–78. For a general survey of medieval eyewitness historiography, which, however, underestimates the amount and significance of such works before the later twelfth century, see P. Ainsworth, 'Contemporary and "Eyewitness" History', in D. M. Deliyannis (ed.), *Historiography in the Middle Ages* (Leiden, 2003), pp. 249–76.

into its textual representations. But it is to suggest that event-centred historical reconstructions that are substantially grounded in narratives such as those that feature in this study would do well to 'go the long way round', methodologically speaking, when validating their truth claims with reference to a given source's supposed eyewitness status. A fuller appreciation of the textual means by which this eyewitness, or 'autoptic', quality impresses itself upon narrative sources can deepen our understanding of both the past as lived experience and the means by which we are granted access to that experience.

A helpful point of entry into thinking about eyewitnessing is a well-known post-medieval narrative with a medieval setting. Kurosawa Akira's *Rashōmon* (1950) is, alongside the same director's *Seven Samurai* (*Shichinin no Samurai*, 1954), among the best-known Japanese period films in world cinema. Its setting and central plot device were inspired by two short stories by the popular writer Akutagawa Ryūnosuke (1892–1927).[3] It narrates from several viewpoints mutually exclusive versions of the story of the murder of a minor nobleman and the rape of his wife by a bandit in a remote forest clearing. Although the film's pared-down *mise-en-scène* does not mandate a precisely fixed period setting, the fact that some of the action takes place within the ruins of the Rashōmon, or Rajōmon, the gate that was the main southern entrance into Kyōto, Heian Japan's capital city, points to a time shortly after the collapse of the Heian political system and of Kyōto's importance in the mid 1180s.[4] The film's many ambiguities and subtleties are activated by placing what did, or did not, take place in the clearing within not one but two narrative frames. These are set off not only from the action in the forest but also from one another by means of starkly contrasting diegeses, or scenic settings: first, a courtyard-type space, characterized by clean geometric lines and bright sunlight, in which various of the characters, including the murder victim himself speaking through a medium, address an unseen and unspeaking judge; and second, the gloomy setting of the ruinous city gate that gives the film its name, under which a woodcutter who claims to have stumbled upon the scene of the crime and a priest who has also given evidence in the courtyard earlier that day are grilled by an inquisitive and aggressively cynical commoner – effectively the audience's surrogate in the search for answers about what really happened – as they shelter from pounding rain.[5]

[3] 'Rashōmon' and 'In a Bamboo Grove', in Ryūnosuke Akutagawa, *Rashōmon and Seventeen Other Stories*, trans. J. Rubin with an introduction by H. Murakami (London, 2006), pp. 3–19.

[4] For this process, see W. W. Farris, *Heavenly Warriors: The Evolution of Japan's Military, 500–1300* (Harvard East Asian Monographs, 157; Cambridge, MA, 1992), pp. 289–307; P. F. Souyri, *The World Turned Upside Down: Medieval Japanese Society*, trans. K. Roth (London, 2002), pp. 29–46.

[5] See D. Richie (ed.), *Focus on Rashomon* (Englewood Cliffs, NJ, 1972); D. Richie (ed.), *Rashomon: Akira Kurosawa, Director* (Rutgers Films in Print, 6; New Brunswick, NJ,

Rashōmon attracted a great deal of critical attention when it was released. It was awarded the Golden Lion, the top prize, at the 1951 Venice Film Festival, and it thus played a significant part in opening up Japanese cinema in particular and Japanese culture in general to global audiences after the isolation of the post-war years. *Rashōmon* inaugurated a brief but highly creative period during which Japanese filmmakers, principally Kurosawa himself and Mizoguchi Kenji, produced what is probably the richest corpus of filmic explorations of the premodern world in the history of cinema.[6] Interpretations of the film are many and varied. Viewed as a product of its particular time and place, it can be read as a parable about Japan's militaristic past, uncertain present and hoped-for future – this last element represented by the discordantly upbeat and sometimes criticized coda to the main action in which the woodcutter undertakes to care for an abandoned baby whom he, the priest and the commoner have chanced upon in the Rashōmon's ruins. The film can also be seen as a commentary on the Allied Occupation of Japan, or SCAP, still in place in 1950 and arguably represented by the unseen authority-figure in the courtyard scenes. It is noteworthy that the bandit, played by Mifune Toshirō, gestures in his wild and over-exuberant physical and vocal manner to Japanese stereotypes of Westerners, especially so when juxtaposed against the nobleman, who for the most part embodies the cold self-control of the Japanese warrior class. *Rashōmon* can be read as a critique of contemporary constructions of masculinity, and it is also about some of the different forms that sexual violence can assume. Kurosawa himself was generally reluctant to volunteer a definitive interpretation of his film; when pressed, he tended to suggest that it made an ethical point about the human propensity for egotistical mendacity and self-deceit.[7] The clichéd summary verdict on *Rashōmon*, however, has been that it concerns something called 'the relativity of truth'; that is to say, it captured a certain post-war anxiety about the absence of fixed points of moral reference in human affairs as well as presciently anticipating

1987); D. Richie, *The Films of Akira Kurosawa*, 3rd rev. edn (Berkeley, 1998), pp. 70–80; S. Prince, *The Warrior's Camera: The Cinema of Akira Kurosawa*, rev. edn (Princeton, 1999), pp. 127–35; M. Yoshimoto, *Kurosawa: Film Studies and Japanese Cinema* (Durham, NC, 2000), pp. 182–9; S. Galbraith IV, *The Emperor and the Wolf: The Lives and Films of Akira Kurosawa and Toshiro Mifune* (New York, 2001), pp. 127–42; B. Davis, R. Anderson and J. Walls (eds), *Rashomon Effects: Kurosawa,* Rashomon *and Their Legacies* (Routledge Advances in Film Studies, 44; Abingdon, 2016). Some of Kurosawa's own reflections on the film are to be found in his *Something Like an Autobiography*, trans. A. E. Bock (New York, 1983), pp. 180–9.

[6] For Mizoguchi's *jidai-geki*, or period films, in the four or five years up to his death in 1956, see M. Le Fanu, *Mizoguchi and Japan* (London, 2005), pp. 49–67, 105–10, 114–27; T. Sato, *Kenji Mizoguchi and the Art of Japanese Cinema*, trans. B. Tankha, ed. A. Vasudev and L. Padkaonkar (Oxford, 2008), pp. 101–29, 134–9.

[7] See *Something Like an Autobiography*, p. 183.

the later postmodernist insistence that objective knowledge of the world and of the past is in fact impossible.

Whatever the interpretive loading that the film is made to bear, however, two aspects of its foundational meaning-making project and the manner in which it invites responses from its audience are pertinent to the present study. The first is the basic plot artifice that grabs the viewer's interest; the presentation of multiple, irreconcilable versions of what happened violates our assumptions that eyewitnesses of an event are, or at least should be, reasonably accurate and reliable sources of information. True, we seldom insist on absolute uniformity among various witnesses to an event, and we typically tolerate minor discrepancies of detail and emphasis, but there is generally an expectation that different versions should converge on certain irreducible elements, what are sometimes termed plot cruxes or kernel events, which between them encapsulate and characterize what happened. This expectation is all the greater when an eyewitness is not simply someone placed in the role of observer but is her- or himself a protagonist in the action. The interactions of the three principals in the forest, the bandit, the nobleman and the woman, are in every version of events those of fully-engaged participants: this is *their* story, or rather stories. And while the woodcutter's role seems on the surface to be that of a passive and disinterested observer – a point-of-view shot during his second go at recalling his experience would seem to situate him just behind the tree line gazing through the leaves into the clearing – there is some suggestion in his exchanges with the commoner in the outer framing narrative that he may have played a more active role, at the very least purloining the nobleman's expensive dagger which was left at the scene and which may have been the actual murder weapon, and possibly even committing the murder himself.

We usually accept that a casual outside observer might miss or distort basic details, but how could people so intimately caught up in such memorable and personally consequential events seem to get it all so wrong? Indeed, the film itself plays with this very expectation in setting up a clear contrast between the principals, whose versions are full and circumstantial and focus on the all-important question of what happened in the clearing, and the minor contributions of other eyewitnesses, who can only flesh out brief and peripheral moments of little or no value as evidence. If these marginal scenes were excised from the film, their loss would scarcely affect the main plot. Thus, the constable who arrests the bandit is only in a position to recount the circumstances of the arrest. The priest, for his part, is an important figure in the outer framing narrative, complicating the antagonistic dynamic between the woodcutter and the commoner; but as a witness within the courtyard frame his contribution is self-highlighting in its triviality as he merely recalls fleetingly passing the nobleman and his wife on the forest path at some unspecified point before they encountered the bandit further down the road. If *Rashōmon* had been made as a film in which the audience is invited to solve a puzzle as it pieces together fragmentary clues volunteered by those people, such as the constable and the priest, on the margins of the action, it would conform to more familiar genre expectations, those of the detective story or murder mystery. But it would almost certainly have been a lesser achievement. For it is in getting the eyewitness-participant principals themselves to disagree in fundamental ways about their recent, vivid, physical and life-changing experiences that Kurosawa profoundly destabilizes our normally unexamined expectations: expectations, that is to say, about how we lock on to the world around us by means of our perceptions of it, how we remember and narrate our experiences, and how in our routine social interactions we tend to repose trust in the self-narration of others whose perceptual and mnemonic capacities, whose own purchase on the world, we presume to be very similar to our own.

In addition, and following on from this, the film resolutely refuses to steer the viewer towards one preferred version of events. Each main account is framed and narrated in the same ways and presented as entire unto itself as an ethical space, obeying its own logic of cause and effect and of character motivation within the parameters of the particular storyworld that it constructs. True, the fact that the nobleman speaks through a medium might give us pause as far as his testimony is concerned, even if we choose to suspend disbelief and tell ourselves that recourse to mediums was standard late Heian judicial practice. But his version of events stands or falls by the same criteria of belief or disbelief that apply to the others as long as we accept that his stated reason for killing himself, as he does in his telling, namely his shame at being dishonoured by the bandit's rape of his wife, is as plausible a motivation as those that inform the other accounts. There is no voiceover commentary to privilege one version over another, nor are significant differences present in the framing and sequencing of shots to nudge viewers in a particular direction. In addition, each of the three principal's tellings seems to enhance its plausibility by owning up to responsibility for the death of the nobleman, rather than trying to evade blame or point the finger at someone else, as one might expect: the bandit gleefully and defiantly confesses in the courtyard; the wife claims she plunged the dagger into her husband, although the nature of what would in common law parlance be called her *mens rea* is left open; and the nobleman admits to suicide, as we have seen.

The experience of showing the film to groups of students suggests that many viewers instinctively gravitate towards the woodcutter's second version of events in the clearing: it is placed last, thereby appearing to resolve the contradictions created by the competing versions that precede it; it is full of circumstantial detail, synthesizing in a seemingly plausible and coherent manner some of the motifs and diegetic bits and pieces, such as the dagger, that circulate within and between the three principals' accounts; and, on the surface at least, the woodcutter would seem to lack the principals' egotistical investment in spinning the story in a certain way. There are also built-in plausibilities, or reality effects, absent from the other renderings.[8] So, whereas in the bandit's telling the swordfight that he has with the nobleman is a demonstration of ultra-masculine skill and bravado in obvious keeping with his own self-image (as well as with the conventions then governing the stylized depiction of duelling in Japanese cinema), when the two men come to blows in the woodcutter's version, they are depicted as timorous, emasculated and rather pathetic figures, not only reduced to looking and acting like children but also brought down to the level of animals in their panicked, desperate scrambling around on the forest floor. This looks like what fighting someone to the death, shorn of its epic, masculine performativity, might actually be like.

But is the woodcutter such a privileged and reliable witness? After all, he is the only character who gets to tell his story twice, and he compromises his credentials in the process. His first version, as told to the unseen authority-figure in the courtyard, simply has him walking through the forest – a sequence shown in a famous montage – and literally stumbling over the nobleman's body after the fact; whereas it is only in his second version, which he is eventually goaded into volunteering by the commoner's cynicism, that he emerges as an eyewitness in the fuller sense of the word. Even then, as we have seen, doubts emerge as to the true nature and extent of his involvement in what took place. So, *pace* many students' instinct to search for a resolution and to attach their faith to that version of events which seems best able to provide it, a preference for the woodcutter's tale really comes down to the triumph of hope over reason – the desire or expectation that, somewhere in all this confusion, the truth will ultimately prove accessible after all because there was somebody there to witness it.

Rashōmon is only one among a number of works of art that in various ways exploit the device of conflicting perceptions, memories and narrativizations: other examples include Robert Browning's long poem 'The Ring and the Book' (1868–9), Fyodor Dostoyevsky's *The Brothers Karamazov* (1879–80), G. K. Chesterton's short story 'The Man in the Passage' (1914) and William Faulkner's *The Sound and the Fury* (1929). But in its formal structure and its unwillingness to offer the viewer the easy closure of a resolution – at least on the narrative level of the events in the forest – *Rashōmon* stages the problems of eyewitness perception and eyewitness narrative in particularly compelling, almost 'textbook', terms. This makes it an excellent point of entry into the questions that this book will

[8] The notion of the 'reality effect' (*l'effet du réel*) was introduced by Roland Barthes: see 'The Reality Effect', in his *The Rustle of Language*, trans. R. Howard (Berkeley, 1989), pp. 141–8. Cf. his remarks on 'indices' in his groundbreaking study 'Introduction to the Structural Analysis of Narratives', in his *Image, Music, Text*, trans. S. Heath (London, 1977), pp. 79–124, esp. 91–7. For a succinct overview, see R. Bensmaia, 'Reality Effect', in D. Herman, M. Jahn and M.-L. Ryan (eds), *Routledge Encyclopedia of Narrative Theory* (Abingdon, 2005), p. 492.

address. There are probably only a handful of examples of what has been termed the 'Rashōmon effect' in premodern history because the surviving sources seldom cluster in sufficient depth around events that were as compactly bounded in space and time and as readily observable as are the small-scale human confrontations played out in the clearing. And even when there are such source concentrations, they are more often than not derived from other written texts or are in conversation with oral traditions, not direct, independent and unmediated witnesses. Possible examples of the Rashōmon effect at work might include certain episodes during the First Crusade, the murder of Thomas Becket, and some of the more notorious incidents during the Spanish conquest of the New World such as the capture and execution of Atahualpa.[9] But it is important to stress that *Rashōmon*'s lessons extend far beyond the small number of recorded moments in premodern history for which we have multiple more or less discrepant and more or less independent sources that record, or are otherwise informed by, one or more eyewitnesses' perceptions.[10] Larger questions emerge. What do we think we mean when we describe someone as an eyewitness? What are the expectations and assumptions that we pack into the word eyewitness – that is to say, the very expectations and assumptions that are so profoundly destabilized in *Rashōmon*? What is an eyewitness source, and why are we so often disposed to privilege it over other sorts of historical evidence? Should eyewitness sources be read in particular ways, and what challenges of interpretation do they pose?

The once fashionable primers of historiographical method typically held up eyewitness evidence as a – sometimes *the* – privileged route into reconstructing the past.[11] And while more recent verdicts tend to be rather more guarded, eyewitness evidence, broadly conceived, retains its status as a central plank of historical research.[12] Much of the potency of the word eyewitness derives from

[9] On this last, my thanks to my former student Phillip Caprara, who wrote a very insightful paper for me on the autoptic quality of contemporary accounts of the arrest and murder of Atahualpa.

[10] For a striking modern-day example of the Rashōmon effect at work among numerous eyewitnesses, in this instance those present at a notorious *contretemps* between Ludwig Wittgenstein and Karl Popper during a seminar in Cambridge in 1946, see D. Edmonds and J. Eidinow, *Wittgenstein's Poker: The Story of a Ten-Minute Argument Between Two Great Philosophers* (London, 2001), esp. pp. 13–16.

[11] F. M. Fling, *The Writing of History: An Introduction to Historical Method* (New Haven, 1920), pp. 61–87; A. Nevins, *The Gateway to History* (Boston, 1938), pp. 173–7; G. J. Garraghan, *A Guide to Historical Method*, ed. J. Delanglez (New York, 1946), pp. 282–92; H. C. Hockett, *The Critical Method in Historical Research and Writing* (New York, 1955), pp. 44–50; L. Gottschalk, *Understanding History: A Primer of Historical Method*, 2nd edn (New York, 1969), pp. 53, 56, 141, 149–70. But cf. the rather more cautious approach to eyewitness testimony in A. Johnson, *The Historian and Historical Evidence* (Port Washington, NY, 1926), pp. 24–49.

[12] See e.g. R. J. Shafer (ed.), *A Guide to Historical Method*, 3rd edn (Homewood, IL,

the fact that when historians apply the term to their sources, they are stepping outside the technical and methodological boundaries of their discipline and plugging into much larger circuits of linguistic and cultural practice. The effect is to make the mobilization of eyewitness evidence seem simply a matter of common sense. The portmanteau word 'eyewitness' is first attested in English in the sixteenth century.[13] But the close combination of the two elements that the word captures goes back much further. Its equivalents in other European languages – for example, in the primary sense of the person who sees, *témoin oculaire*, *testigo ocular*, *Augenzeuge*, *ooggetuige*, *øyenvitne* – suggest that the tight and natural-seeming juxtaposition of the acts of seeing and of bearing witness transcends linguistic difference. Each of the two elements carries with it powerful associations that are magnified still further when they are combined.

One indication of the cultural importance of sight is that, in English as in many other languages, seeing is not confined to its literal semantic range. It extends figuratively into innumerable metaphors involving intangibles and abstractions, as well as mental actions of all kinds: 'I see what you mean', 'She glimpsed the truth', 'What is your perspective on what happened?', 'This changes his worldview', 'Watch yourself', and so on.[14] This is not intended as a 'sightist' observation at the expense of blind or visually-impaired people, simply a recognition of the fact that sight is much the most deeply sedimented and wide-ranging figurative resource among the five senses, especially so when

1980), pp. 153–62; M. C. Howell and W. Prevenier, *From Reliable Sources: An Introduction to Historical Methods* (Ithaca, NY, 2001), pp. 65–8; D. Henige, *Historical Evidence and Argument* (Madison, WI, 2005), pp. 44–50, 53–4, 58–64. In discussing the many discrepant eyewitness accounts of the assassination of Abraham Lincoln, Henige (p. 48) refers to 'the omnipresent Rashomon effect'. But it must be remembered that this remark better suits the richness of the modern historical record than the much thinner coverage of medieval eyewitness evidence. There were numerous witnesses to Lincoln's murder and what happened immediately afterwards: see *We Saw Lincoln Shot: One Hundred Eyewitness Accounts*, ed. T. L. Good (Jackson, MS, 1995). For an interesting example of another memorable modern event, in this instance one in which eyewitness accounts were confirmed or disconfirmed by subsequent scientific discoveries unimaginable at the time, see W. H. Garzke Jr, D. K. Brown, A. D. Sandiford, J. Woodward and P. K. Hsu, 'The *Titanic* and the *Lusitania*: A Final Forensic Analysis', *Marine Technology*, 33 (1996), 241–89; T. C. Riniolo, M. Koledin, G. M. Drakulic and R. A. Payne, 'An Archival Study of Eyewitness Memory of the *Titanic*'s Final Plunge', *Journal of General Psychology*, 130 (2001), 89–95.

[13] *The Shorter Oxford English Dictionary*, ed. C. T. Onions, 3rd edn rev. G. W. S Friedrichsen, 1 vol. in 2 (Oxford, 1978), *s.v.* 'eye-witness', suggesting a first attestation in 1539. The range of meaning would seem to have expanded from the witness her- or himself to the fact or product of her/his observation in the seventeenth century

[14] M. Jay, *Downcast Eyes: The Denigration of Vision in Twentieth-Century French Thought* (Berkeley, 1993), pp. 1–3. Cf. S. A. Tyler, 'The Vision Quest in the West, or What the Mind's Eye Sees', *Journal of Anthropological Research*, 40 (1984), 23–40.

we further factor in the many metaphorical applications of light and darkness. Sight is, alongside bodily orientation in space and physical motion, among the basic building blocks of what George Lakoff and Mark Johnson have termed the 'metaphors we live by'.[15] Indeed, it is closely bound up with questions of bodily situatedness and movement in that it typically seems the most responsive and versatile of the senses: to a large extent at least, the eye responds to the conscious will of the viewer, and attention can be purposefully directed towards a particular object. Sight is thus the sense that we tend to feel most effectively positions us as active subjects apprehending the world as opposed to passive recipients of the world's acting upon us. When historians use the term eyewitness evidence, they are implicitly appealing to these powerful associations, for the expectation is that in the act of generating the source to hand the historical observer has more or less seamlessly made a transition from simple sensory perception to cognitive apperception, in other words from the workings of physiology to cultural articulation. She or he has introduced into the source some expression of the understanding and interpretation that the metaphorical acceptations of sight and light capture.

Witnessing is such a resonant idea because it is flexible, adapting to a wide range of human situations and needs. In the section (#10) of his *An Enquiry Concerning Human Understanding* (first published in 1748) concerning miracles, David Hume observed that 'there is no species of reasoning more common, more useful, and even necessary to human life, than that which is derived from the testimony of men, and the reports of eye-witnesses and spectators'.[16] That is to say, much and probably most of our knowledge of the world and the beliefs that this knowledge subtends reach us from what others reveal to us about their own experiences. This pooling of information locks us into the world as we believe it is, given that our general day-to-day experiences of human interaction tend to reassure us that there is a tolerably close correspondence between the testimony we receive from others, unless we happen to suspect mendacity, incapacity or error on their part, and how we believe the world is or plausibly might be. In the helpful formulation of C. A. J. Coady, whose 1992 study of testimony remains the best philosophical exploration of the subject: 'The judgements of others constitute an important, indeed perhaps *the* most important, test of whether my own judgements reflect a reality independent of my subjectivity.'[17]

[15] See G. Lakoff and M. Johnson, *Metaphors We Live By*, rev. edn (Chicago, 2003).

[16] *An Enquiry Concerning Human Understanding: A Critical Edition*, ed. T. L. Beauchamp (Oxford, 2000), p. 84. On Hume's approaches to testimony, see C. A. J. Coady, *Testimony: A Philosophical Study* (Oxford, 1992), pp. 79–100.

[17] *Testimony*, p. 12. For the workings of 'natural' testimony in ordinary social interactions, as well as in more formal, especially legal and quasi-legal, settings, see pp. 27–48. As Coady points out, testifying can extend to the reporting of intangibles and abstractions such as mental states and moral positions: *ibid.*, pp. 63–75.

As Coady suggests, there may well be an egotistical or individualist slant within people's self-awareness that predisposes them to overestimate the extent to which their knowledge of the world derives from their own experience, and correspondingly to underestimate their reliance on what they learn from others.[18] In other words, we are prone to exaggerate the extent to which we feel, epistemologically speaking, masters of the world around us. This has important implications for our understanding of historical eyewitness evidence, for it is deceptively easy to project this same sort of epistemological over-confidence onto the historical observer. Such a projection is made all the easier by the fact that 'eyewitness evidence' is not a precise and technical term of art but a very large and baggy category that subsumes a wide variety of human experiences and observer-observed relationships. As Marc Bloch noted, eyewitness evidence is usually nothing of the sort on a strict understanding of the term. His example is that of a general whose official account of the victory recently won by his forces necessarily draws on much more than the memories derived from his own sensory experiences, even if he enjoyed a good view of the battlefield. In order to craft a coherent account of what happened, he must also have recourse to the testimonies of informants such as his lieutenants.[19] Bloch was here drawing upon the well-worn *topos*, familiar since Antiquity, to the effect that battles represent the limit case of individuals' inability to grasp the scale and complexity of what is going on around them.[20] But his larger point extends to all varieties of historical action and testimony. If anything, Bloch's claim that a 'good half of all we see is seen through the eyes of others' would seem to be an understatement.[21]

As we shall see, none of this study's chosen texts – in this respect they are broadly representative of medieval eyewitness narratives in general – are autobiographical memoirs in the sense that they consistently foreground the author's personal circumstances, perceptions and subjective reactions within the larger frame of the narrated action. In most of the sequences that our texts narrate, the eyewitness author is not 'there' at all in the sense of being overtly situated within the action *in propria persona*, still less precisely positioned relative to the action in such a way that he is able to bring an observant and tightly focused 'camera eye' to bear on what is happening. In some cases we can draw on external

[18] *Testimony*, pp. 6–14.

[19] M. Bloch, *The Historian's Craft*, trans. P. Putnam with an introduction by J. R. Strayer (Manchester, 1954), p. 49. See pp. 48–78 for Bloch's discussion of historical observation.

[20] Thucydides, *History of the Peloponnesian War*, VII.44, ed. and trans. C. Forster Smith, 4 vols (Loeb Classical Library, 108–10, 169; Cambridge, MA, 1928–30), iv, p. 86; trans. M. Hammond, *The Peloponnesian War*, with an introduction and notes by P. J. Rhodes (Oxford, 2009), p. 388. Cf. A. J. Woodman, *Rhetoric in Classical Historiography: Four Studies* (London, 1988), pp. 18–23.

[21] *Historian's Craft*, p. 49.

evidence to deduce that the author could not have been present at a given event or was at least unlikely to have been so. In other cases the physical proximity of the author to the narrated action may be suspected with greater or lesser degrees of confidence, but this is not expressly stated in the text. A minority of scenes or episodes include the sort of circumstantial detail that might seem to suggest that the author is recalling a direct eyewitness experience. But in some of these instances, perhaps the majority, we would probably do better to treat what we are reading as attempts to mimic the subjective texture of vivid recall rather than as direct evidence of the workings of eyewitness memory. When historians categorize a source as eyewitness, there is a tendency to allow this designation to blanket the material as a whole, whereas authorial autoptic perception may well inform only a small portion of the global content. We should always remember that when we label the authors of sources as eyewitnesses, we are for the most part simply saying that they found themselves placed in situations in which they were optimally exposed to the testimony of others, with intermittent opportunities for 'topping up' their knowledge with their own personal experience. Paradoxical as it might seem, being an effective historical eyewitness would normally seem to have had less to do with visual acuity or some happy knack of being in the right place at the right time, and more to do with being a good listener. But such is the resonance of the term eyewitness that when we apply it to a historical source, it can easily inflate our estimation of its unmediated experiential basis.

A good deal of medieval history-writers' understanding of the value of eyewitness experience, their own and that of informants whom they considered trustworthy, was inherited from their ancient Greek and Roman predecessors, although there were some differences of emphasis, as we shall see. It was stock etymological wisdom among ancient historiographers that the word *ἱστορία*/*historia* derived from the Greek verb *ἱστορεῖν*, 'to inquire', 'to observe', with the result that it was felt to be incumbent upon the historian to establish his personal credentials as a researcher in order to pronounce authoritatively and credibly upon his chosen subject. Often this involved rhetorical appeals to good character and impartiality, as well as references to the time, effort and expense involved and the difficulties overcome – more practical and logistical than conceptual and epistemological – in the process of researching and writing.[22] Where the historian's subject matter was the recent past, moreover, mention could also be made of his own perceptions or those of others, with the experience of sight assuming a standard, though not automatic, pride of place over hearing and the other senses.[23] It is noteworthy that Herodotus chose very early in his *Histories*

[22] J. Marincola, *Authority and Tradition in Ancient Historiography* (Cambridge, 1997), pp. 128–33, 148–74.

[23] Marincola, *Authority and Tradition*, pp. 63–87, 281–2; L. Pitcher, *Writing Ancient History: An Introduction to Classical Historiography* (London, 2009), pp. 57–64.

to illustrate the supposition that people believe the evidence of their eyes more readily than what they hear in his story of how Candaules, the king of Lydia, improvidently arranges for his favourite guard, Gyges, to spy on his naked wife in order to prove his boastful claims about her great beauty; Candaules's explanation to Gyges assumes the force of an obvious and incontestable cliché when he observes that 'it's true that people trust their ears less than their eyes'.[24]

Occasional notes of caution were sounded about the uncritical use of others' testimonies: as Thucydides observed, it could be very hard work to appraise evidence rigorously 'as eyewitnesses on each occasion would give different accounts of the same event, depending on their individual loyalties or memories'.[25] Thucydides stages the mutability of the eyewitness's gaze in a remarkable passage that forms part of his account of the Athenians' ill-starred campaign against Syracuse in 413 BC. The Athenian land forces look on helplessly from the harbour as they watch the progress of the naval battle that will decide their fate. Various groups have different lines of sight on the action, and their responses to what they think they see play out in their different cries and bodily movements, until a collective understanding of the disastrous Athenian defeat gradually emerges:

> For the Athenians everything depended on their ships, and their anxiety for the outcome was intense beyond words. Localized action varied throughout the theatre of battle, and so inevitably the men lining the shore had varying perspectives: the action was quite close in front of their eyes, and they were

---

See also G. Nenci, 'Il motivo dell'autopsia nella storiografia greca', *Studi classici e orientali*, 3 (1955), 14–46; G. Schepens, *L'autopsie dans la méthode des historiens grecs du Ve siècle avant J.-C.* (Verhandelingen van de Koninklijke Academie voor Wetenschappen, Letteren en Schone Kunsten van België. Klasse der Letteren, 93; Brussels, 1980). For the innovative quality of historical works that derived a substantial amount of their subject matter from the author's personal experiences, see J. Marincola, 'Genre, Convention, and Innovation in Greco-Roman Historiography', in C. S. Kraus (ed.), *The Limits of Historiography: Genre and Narrative in Ancient Historical Texts* (Leiden, 1999), pp. 309–20, esp. 316–17.

[24] Herodotus, [*The Histories*], I.6, ed. and trans. A. D. Godley, 4 vols (Loeb Classical Library, 117–20; Cambridge, MA, 1920–5), i, p. 10; trans. R. Waterfield, *The Histories*, with introduction and notes by C. Dewald (Oxford, 1998), p. 6. Cf. Polybius, *The Histories*, XII.27, ed. and trans. W. R. Paton, rev. F. W. Walbank and C. Habicht, 6 vols (Loeb Classical Library, 128, 137–8, 159–61; Cambridge, MA, 2010–12), iv, p. 444; trans. R. Waterfield, *The Histories*, with introduction and notes by B. McGing (Oxford, 2010), p. 443: 'We are naturally endowed with two instruments, so to speak, to help us acquire information and undertake research. Of the two, sight is, as Heraclitus [a predecessor of and probable influence on Herodotus] says, much more reliable, eyes being more accurate witnesses than ears.' See also Lucian, 'How To Write History', c. 29, in *Lucian: A Selection*, ed. and trans. M. D. MacLeod (Warminster, 1991), p. 224.

[25] Thucydides, *History*, I.22, i, p. 38; trans. Hammond, *Peloponnesian War*, p. 12.

> not all looking at the same arena. So if some saw their own side winning in their particular part of the battle, they would take instant encouragement and begin calling out to the gods not to deprive them of this hope of salvation; others who had witnessed an area of defeat turned to loud cries of lament, and from the mere sight of what was happening were in more abject terror than the actual combatants. Yet others, focused on a part of the battle which was evenly balanced, went through all the agonies of suspense: as the conflict lasted on and on without decisive result, their acute anxiety had them actually replicating with the movement of their bodies the rise and fall of their hopes – at any point throughout they were either on the point of escape or on the point of destruction. And as long as the battle at sea remained in the balance you could hear across the Athenian ranks a mixture of every sort of response – groans, cheers, 'we're winning', 'we're losing', and all the various involuntary cries let out by men in great danger.[26]

In general, however, even though there was a lively tradition in ancient philosophy of questioning the reliability of the senses and the status of the knowledge derived from them, among historians reservations about eyewitness testimony simply attached to questions of the witness's possible bias and partiality, not to more basic matters of human perception and cognition.[27] The result was that when historians, as they often did, sought to establish their credentials as impartial and scrupulous authorities in contrast to the shortcomings of others, they were implicitly assuring the reader that the evidence gathered from the experience of their own eyes was impeccably reliable.

The trust reposed in the historian's own sensory perceptions was magnified by an extension of 'autopsy' (*αὐτόπτης*) in the strict sense of direct visual apprehension of a given event (*ὄψις*) to include more wide-ranging personal experiences that aided a feeling of proximity to and understanding of the historical reality in question.[28] Public affairs such as politics, diplomacy and war were considered the proper stuff of written history, and it was therefore routinely assumed that only those with personal experience of such matters were equipped to pronounce upon them.[29] As Polybius, the ancient historian whose methodological remarks on this score are the most considered and developed, observed:

[26] Thucydides, *History*, VII.71, iv, pp. 142–4; trans. Hammond, *Peloponnesian War*, pp. 403–4.

[27] See Marincola, *Authority and Tradition*, pp. 64–6; G. Schepens, 'History and *Historia*: Inquiry in the Greek Historians', in J. Marincola (ed.), *A Companion to Greek and Roman Historiography* (Chichester, 2011), pp. 42–4.

[28] Marincola, *Authority and Tradition*, pp. 133–48. Cf. Schepens, 'History and *Historia*', pp. 39–55. See also M. G. Bull, 'Eyewitness and Medieval Historical Narrative', in E. S. Kooper and S. Levelt (eds), *The Medieval Chronicle 11* (Leiden, 2018), pp. 1–22.

[29] But for useful remarks cautioning against too homogenized a view of the backgrounds and circumstances of Greco-Roman historians as 'statesmen', see C. W. Fornara, *The*

> The point is that, just as it is impossible for someone who lacks military experience to write about warfare, it is impossible for someone who has never acted in the political sphere or faced a political crisis to write good political history. Nothing written by authors who rely on mere book-learning [Polybius is here particularly attacking his bookish *bête noire* Timaeus] has the clarity that comes from personal experience, and nothing is gained by reading their work.[30]

Such experience extended to visiting historically resonant locations such as battlefields.[31] One suspects that such a capacious understanding of autopsy, one that included the right sort of career path and opportunities for a kind of historical tourism as well as individual personal experiences and interviewing reliable third parties, was in part a self-serving way of justifying the fact that historiography was the preserve of a socially exclusive elite. There is some support for such a view: for example, the fourth-century BC writer Theopompus, whose historical works, including a history of Alexander the Great's father Philip of Macedon, are substantially lost, was believed to have had the leisure to devote much of his life to his work, to have been able to spend very large amounts of money in conducting research, and to have had the social *entrée* to cultivate personal connections with important politicians, generals and intellectuals.[32] But more seems to have been at stake than indulging the opportunities of privilege. As Polybius shrewdly remarked, because the answers one elicits from respondents are only as good as the framing of the questions one poses, appropriate life experience was necessary to be able to extract the most useful information from witnesses to events.[33]

Nature of History in Ancient Greece and Rome (Berkeley, 1983), pp. 48–56. And for a sense of the quite narrow parameters within which experience might be considered an aid to understanding, see Polybius, *Histories*, XII.25f, iv, pp. 420–2; trans. Waterfield, *Histories*, p. 436.

[30] Polybius, *Histories*, XII.25g, iv, p. 422; trans. Waterfield, *Histories*, p. 436. See also *ibid.*, XII.22, iv, p. 402; trans. Hammond, *Histories*, p. 431. Cf. Lucian, 'How To Write History', c. 37, pp. 230–2.

[31] Polybius, *Histories*, III.57–9, ii, pp. 148–56; XII.25e, iv, pp. 418–20; trans. Waterfield, *Histories*, pp. 173–5, 435; Lucian, 'How To Write History', c. 47, p. 238. But cf. Thucydides's remarks about the dangers of misreading historically resonant sites: *Histories*, I.10, i, p. 18; trans. Hammond, *Peloponnesian War*, p. 7; Marincola, *Authority and Tradition*, pp. 67–8. For ancient historians as travellers, see G. Schepens, 'Travelling Greek Historians', in M. G. Angeli Bertinelli and A. Donati (eds), *Le vie della storia: Migrazioni di popoli, viaggi di individui, circolazione di idee nel Mediterraneo antico. Atti del II Incontro Internazionale di Storia Antica (Genova 6–8 ottobre 2004)* (Serta antiqua et mediaevalia, 9; Rome, 2006), pp. 81–102.

[32] Fornara, *History in Ancient Greece and Rome*, p. 49; Marincola, *Authority and Tradition*, pp. 87, 148–9; Schepens. 'History and *Historia*', p. 49.

[33] Polybius, *Histories*, XII.28a, iv, pp. 452–4; trans. Waterfield, *Histories*, p. 445.

It has been convincingly argued that in relation to all the ancient works of history that once existed but are now lost or known only from fragments (sadly, the great majority), the surviving corpus of substantially intact texts over-represents the sort of historical writing that focused on recent political and military events and thereby particularly lent itself to authorial appeals to eyewitness evidence.[34] This was, nonetheless, an important strand among the strategies of authorial self-fashioning and validation that were bequeathed to medieval historians. Because ancient Greek historians tended to be more expansive about their methodologies and sources than their Latin counterparts, western medieval historiographical culture drew much of its inspiration from the works of authors such as Josephus and Eusebius that both cast themselves as continuations of Greek traditions of historical writing and were available in late antique Latin translations. In his *The Jewish War*, for example, Josephus positioned himself as the heir of Polybius in his insistence that participation in the events that one narrates lends one's account the important quality of vitality or vividness (*ἐνάργεια*), which enhances its credibility. His leaning towards autopsy also informed the temporal and geographical scope of his narrative. As he insisted, 'I shall relate the events of the war which I witnessed in great detail and with all the completeness of which I am capable, whereas events before my time will be run over in brief outline.'[35]

The influence of Greco-Roman models on medieval historical writing plays out in innumerable ways, but is especially visible in the many prologues and other forms of front matter in which the author, in referring to the example set by ancient writers, positions himself in relation to his predecessors in a spirit of emulation or the continuation of tradition.[36] There was, however, a shift in historians'

[34] Schepens, 'History and *Historia*', pp. 52–4.

[35] Josephus, *The Jewish War*, I.6, ed. and trans. H. St. J. Thackeray, 3 vols (Loeb Classical Library, 203, 210, 487; Cambridge, MA, 1997), i, p. 10; trans. G. A. Williamson, *The Jewish War*, rev. E. M. Smallwood (Harmondsworth, 1981), p. 29. See also *ibid.*, I.8, i, pp. 12–14; trans. Williamson, *Jewish War*, p. 30: 'Of the fate of the captured towns I shall give an exact account based on my own observations and the part I played.' For an indication of Josephus's influence upon medieval historical writers, see the approving reference to him by Rahewin, Otto of Freising's continuator, in *Gesta Frederici seu rectius Cronica*, ed. F.-J. Schmale, trans. A. Schmidt (Ausgewählte Quellen zur deutschen Geschichte des Mittelalters, 17; Darmstadt, 1965), p. 394; trans. C. C. Mierow, *The Deeds of Frederick Barbarossa* (Medieval Academy Reprints for Teaching, 31; Toronto, 1994), p. 171.

[36] Numerous such examples could be cited. See e.g. the *Chronica Adefonsi Imperatoris*, which is themed around the deeds of Alfonso VII of León-Castile (1126–57) and was probably written during his lifetime, perhaps (though this is uncertain) by Bishop Arnaldo of Astorga (1144–52): 'Forasmuch as the record of past events, which is composed by historians of old and handed down to posterity in writing, makes the memory of kings, emperors, counts, nobles and other heroes live anew, I have resolved that the best thing I can do is to describe the deeds of the Emperor Alfonso just as I

methodologies and self-presentation, in that the ancient extension of autopsy into authorial life experience in the round tended to recede somewhat. This was a subtle change: it is important not to paint a caricatured contrast between mobile and cosmopolitan ancient historiographers searching out their material in a spirit of active inquiry, and their more sedentary and passive medieval counterparts trapped in a less interconnected world and obliged to wait for news to come to them in dribs and drabs. When due allowance is made for their very different social, cultural, religious and intellectual circumstances, writers as diverse as, for example, Gregory of Tours, Einhard, Liudprand of Cremona, Aethelweard and Otto of Freising were in their various ways the medieval equivalents of the ancient type of the autoptic historian: educated, mobile, wealthy, well connected and completely at home in the world of the powerful.

Nonetheless, the purchase of medieval historians' own experiences and travels on the subject matter of their works is clearly more uneven in its application and relevance than it is within the (admittedly much smaller and less variegated) corpus of surviving ancient historiographical texts. When, for example, William of Malmesbury reached the point in his *Gesta Regum Anglorum* at which he began to narrate events during the reign of the king of his own day, Henry I (1100–35), and apologized to the reader that he was 'a man far distant from the mysteries of the court' ('homo procul ab aulicis misteriis remotus'), he was seeking to explain the selectivity of his treatment and the fact that he was, so he claimed, ignorant of some of the king's more important achievements, even as he also complained of the large amount of information that he still had to contend with. He was not making a point about how his limited experience meant he could not form an understanding of royal politics *per se*, nor that he was ill-equipped to picture what events played out in *aulae*, not just halls as such but all the privileged spaces of elite political action, looked like.[37]

learned and heard from those who witnessed them': 'Chronica Adefonsi Imperatoris', ed. A. Maya Sánchez, in E. Falque Rey, J. Gil and A. Maya Sánchez (eds), *Chronica Hispana saeculi XII* (CCCM 71; Turnhout, 1990), p. 149; trans. S. Barton and R. Fletcher, *The World of the Cid: Chronicles of the Spanish Reconquest* (Manchester, 2000), p. 162: translation slightly revised.

[37] William of Malmesbury, *Gesta Regum Anglorum*, ed. and trans. R. A. B. Mynors, R. M. Thomson and M. Winterbottom, 2 vols (Oxford, 1998–9), i, p. 708: translation slightly revised. William's disclaimer is somewhat disingenuous, for we know that he both had royal connections and travelled unusually widely around England in search of written materials for his historical projects, journeys that must have required him to get permission for lengthy absences from his abbey at Malmesbury: see R. M. Thomson, *William of Malmesbury* (Woodbridge, 1987), pp. 14–16. For the hall or palace as the metonym *par excellence* of the workings of elite power, cf. the remarks of the anonymous author conventionally known as the Astronomer that whereas for the first parts of his narrative of the reign of Louis the Pious he derived his information from a monk named Adhemar who had grown up with the emperor, the later

Similarly, William's close contemporary Orderic Vitalis seems to be making a straightforward point about the spatial reach of his competence as observer and researcher, not admitting to the wrong sort of life experience, when he states in the general prologue to his monumental *Ecclesiastical History*:

> For although I cannot explore Alexandrine or Greek or Roman affairs and many other matters worthy of the telling, because as a cloistered monk by my own free choice I am compelled to unremitting observance of my monastic duty, nevertheless I can strive with the help of God and for the consideration of posterity to explain truthfully and straightforwardly the things which I have seen in our own times, or know to have occurred in nearby provinces.[38]

Orderic's self-fashioning in this passage is quite subtle, for his construction 'res alexandrinas seu grecas uel romanas' cannot simply be read as a remark about the limitations of the geographical range of his work, even though it is set up in implied contrast to his secure grasp of events 'in nearby provinces' ('in uicinis regionibus'). If meant merely as samples of the numerous places that Orderic had never visited, the series seems oddly precise and eccentric relative to those parts of the world that Orderic knew best, the English marches of his childhood memories and the Norman-French borderlands where his monastery of St-Évroult was situated. Rather, Orderic is here gesturing towards the broad subject matter of ancient history and positioning himself in relation to it even as he implicitly acknowledges that, although his epistemological range, the reach of his autopsy, is more restricted than that of the ancient histories he implicitly evokes, this does not itself diminish his competence as an historian functioning within his tighter spatial boundaries. (The irony is, of course, that the

---

portions directly drew on what he had witnessed or been able to ascertain 'since I was in the midst of palace affairs' ('quia ego rebus interfui palatinis'): Astronomer, 'Vita Hludovici Imperatoris', in *Thegan, Die Taten Kaiser Ludwigs/Astronomus, Das Leben Kaiser Ludwigs*, ed. and trans. E. Tremp (MGH Scriptores rerum Germanicarum in usum scholarum, 64; Hanover, 1995), p. 284; trans. A. Cabaniss, *Son of Charlemagne: A Contemporary Life of Louis the Pious* (Syracuse, NY, 1961), p. 31. See also Wipo, 'Gesta Chuonradi II. Imperatoris', in *Die Werke Wipos*, ed. H. Bresslau, 3rd edn (MGH Scriptores rerum Germanicarum in usum scholarum, 61; Hanover, 1915), p. 3; trans. T. E. Mommsen and K. F. Morrison, 'The Deeds of Conrad II', in *Imperial Lives and Letters of the Eleventh Century*, ed. R. L. Benson (New York, 1962), p. 53, where the author argues that any errors that may have crept into his work must be the responsibility of those informants on whom he had to rely because he was frequently absent from his lord Conrad II's chapel due to illness.

[38] Orderic Vitalis, *Ecclesiastical History*, ed. and trans. M. Chibnall, 6 vols (Oxford, 1968–80), i, pp. 130–2; translation revised. Chibnall renders *alexandrinas* as 'Macedonian', which makes good sense but directs attention more to the geographical than the historiographical thrust of Orderic's remarks.

Ecclesiastical History spectacularly broke the geographical bounds of the sort of local history anticipated in this prologue, and that as a result Orderic found himself drawing upon a rich variety of sources including numerous narrative texts, charters, letters, inscriptions, oral reports and, to a limited degree, personal observation.)[39]

The contraction of the ancient understanding of autopsy meant that, if only by default, greater emphasis than before was placed on eyewitness observation in the specific sense of the visual perception of action and events.[40] Medieval history-writers were in particular nudged in this direction by the formulation of the most widely circulated and authoritative 'dictionary'-like definition of history available to them, that to be found in Isidore of Seville's *Etymologies*. According to Isidore:

> A history is a narration of deeds accomplished by means of which those things that occurred in the past are discerned. History is so called from the Greek term *ἀπό τοῦ ἱστορεῖν*, that is 'to see' [*videre*] or 'to know' [*cognoscere*]. Indeed, among the ancients no one would write a history unless he had been present and had seen what was to be written down, for we grasp with our eyes things that occur better than what we gather with our hearing. Indeed, what is seen is revealed without falsehood.[41]

In his sweeping, and to a large extent inaccurate, characterization of ancient historiographical practice, as well as in his significant narrowing of the semantic range of *ἱστορεῖν* to include only acts of visual perception and apperception, Isidore lost much of the sense of active inquiry and wide-ranging experience that ancient

[39] For Orderic's work and working methods, see M. Chibnall, *The World of Orderic Vitalis* (Oxford, 1984), esp. pp. 169–208. See also the important collection of studies in C. C. Rozier, D. Roach, G. E. M. Gasper and E. M. C. van Houts (eds), *Orderic Vitalis: Life, Works and Interpretations* (Woodbridge, 2016).

[40] But see the description by King Alfred's biographer Asser of the site of the battle of Ashdown ('which I have seen for myself with my own eyes'), fought about fifteen years before Asser first entered Alfred's service and more than twenty before Asser was writing: *Life of King Alfred*, c. 39, ed. W. H. Stephenson, rev. edn (Oxford, 1959), p. 30; trans. S. Keynes and M. Lapidge, *Alfred the Great: Asser's* Life of King Alfred *and Other Contemporary Sources* (Harmondsworth, 1983), p. 79.

[41] Isidore of Seville, *Etymologiarum sive Originum Libri XX*, I.41 [*De Historia*], ed. W. M. Lindsay, 2 vols (Oxford, 1911), i, sp; trans. S. A. Barney, W. J. Lewis, J. A. Beach and O. Berghof with M. Hall, *The Etymologies of Isidore of Seville* (Cambridge, 2006), p. 67: translation revised. For this passage, see the valuable study by A. Cizek, 'L'Historia comme témoignage oculaire: Quelques implications et conséquences de la définition de l'historiographie chez Isodore de Séville', in D. Buschinger (ed.), *Histoire et littérature au moyen âge: Actes du Colloque du Centre d'Études Médiévales de l'Université de Picardie (Amiens 20–24 mars 1985)* (Göppinger Arbeiten zur Germanistik, 546; Göppingen, 1991), pp. 69–84.

notions of autopsy had captured. The emphasis was instead placed on history conceived as the reflex of the mechanisms by means of which information reached the historian. And even though Isidore's ideal of historical writing based exclusively on the author's personal participation in events and his own eyewitness observations was very difficult to effect in practice, at least over anything more than brief bursts of autobiographical reminiscence, it easily commended itself as a rhetorical posture to enhance the historian's authority and the credibility of his narrative in the round.[42] One consequently finds in medieval historical writings numerous prologues, dedicatory epistles and other forms of prefatory utterance that ring the changes on the epistemological primacy of sight and articulate variations of the 'sooner by the eyes than by the ears' *topos*. For example, Einhard, whose *Life of Charlemagne* (probably composed in the 820s) was very widely read and copied, claimed that no one could write a more truthful account of those matters of which he had first-hand experience and knew 'with the faith of one's eyes' [*oculata fide*].[43] In the following century, in opening his *Antapodosis* Liudprand of Cremona apologized to his addressee, Bishop Recemund of Elvira, that for two years he had put off making good on Recemund's request that he write a history of all the rulers of Europe, 'not as one who, reliant on hearsay, can be doubted, but as one who is reliable, like one who sees'.[44]

[42] See Otto of Freising and Rahewin, *Gesta Frederici*, II.43, p. 370; trans. Mierow, *Deeds*, p. 159, where Otto of Freising gestures towards Isidore in invoking the 'custom of the ancients' (*antiquorum mos*) that those who experienced events were the ones who wrote about them. It is noteworthy that Otto enhances the status of eyewitness authority by retaining *videre* from Isidore's translation of the Greek root verb (*histeron* in his rendering) but not *cognoscere*: 'Unde et historia ab histeron, quod in Greco videre sonat, appellari consuevit.' See also M. Kempshall, *Rhetoric and the Writing of History, 400–1500* (Manchester, 2011), pp. 183–5.

[43] Einhard, *Vie de Charlemagne*, ed. and trans. M. Sot, C. Veyrard-Cosme *et al.* (Les classiques de l'histoire au moyen âge, 53; Paris, 2015), pp. 90–2; trans. D. Ganz, *Einhard and Notker the Stammerer: Two Lives of Charlemagne* (London, 2008), p. 17: translation revised. See also Wahlafrid Strabo's observation that in addition to reflecting his reputation for learning and honesty, the truth of Einhard's account was cemented by his having taken part in almost all the events that he narrated: *Vie de Charlemagne*, pp. 94–6; trans. Ganz, p. 15 (which understates the force of 'utpote qui his pene omnibus interfuerit'). Cf. Kempshall, *Rhetoric*, pp. 157–9.

[44] Liudprand of Cremona, 'Antapodosis', I.1, in *Die Werke Liudprands von Cremona*, ed. J. Becker, 3rd edn (MGH Scriptores rerum Germanicarum in usum scholarum, 41; Hanover, 1915), pp. 3–4 ('non auditu dubius, sed visione certus'); trans. P. Squatriti, *The Complete Works of Liudprand of Cremona* (Washington, DC, 2007), pp. 43–4; translation revised. See also *Encomium Emmae Reginae*, II.20, ed. and trans. A. Campbell with a supplementary introduction by S. Keynes (Cambridge, 1998), p. 36: 'For I will not speak of what he [King Cnut] did in separate places, but in order that what I assert may become more credible I will as an example tell what he did in the city of St Omer alone, and I place on record that I saw this with my own eyes.'

In a similar vein, Geoffrey Malaterra, who was a fairly recent arrival to southern Italy and Sicily when he wrote his history of Count Roger of Sicily and his brother Robert Guiscard in or soon after 1098, felt that he had to exculpate himself to his addressee Bishop Angerius of Catania by claiming that errors of chronology or omissions were to be ascribed not to the author himself but to his informants, in particular when it came to events that had taken place before he arrived in the area. His implication is that he would have been able to exercise much greater quality control had eyewitness participation in, or at least greater proximity to, the action been possible.[45] In offering a summary of the reasons why Prince John's intervention in Irish affairs in 1185 was a fiasco, Gerald of Wales, who had been in Ireland at that time, reasserts his eyewitness credentials by quoting John 3:11: 'We speak of what we know. We bear witness to what we have seen.'[46] And a similar epistemological leaning is evident in William of Malmesbury's contrasting treatments of two (on the face of it similarly impressive and politically significant) ecclesiastical councils that took place in England only a few months apart. Of the earlier council, that held at Winchester in April 1141, William expresses the belief that because he had taken part in the proceedings and his memory of them was very good, he is able to narrate the full truth of what had transpired ('integram rerum ueritatem'). But about the latter, at Westminster in December, he is much more guarded: 'I cannot relate the proceedings of that council with as much confidence as those of the earlier one because I was not present.'[47] As these and many similar remarks make plain, there was a clear tendency among medieval historians to believe that personal eyewitness was the single most secure and valuable resource at their disposal.[48]

[45] Geoffrey Malaterra, *De rebus gestis Rogerii Calabriae et Siciliae comitis et Roberti Guiscardi ducis fratris eius*, ed. E. Pontieri, 2nd edn (Rerum Italicarum Scriptores, 5:1; Bologna, 1927–8), p. 3; trans. K. B. Wolf, *The Deeds of Count Roger of Calabria and Sicily and of His Brother Duke Robert Guiscard* (Ann Arbor, MI, 2005), pp. 41–2.

[46] Gerald of Wales, *Expugnatio Hibernica: The Conquest of Ireland*, II.36, ed. and trans. A. B. Scott and F. X. Martin (Dublin, 1978), p. 238. Cf. the implication of remarks by Thietmar of Merseburg that personal experience creates a moral obligation to tell the truth about it: Thietmar of Merseburg, *Chronicon*, VI.78, ed. R. Holtzmann (MGH Scriptores rerum Germanicarum, ns 9; Berlin, 1935), p. 368; trans. D. A. Warner, *Ottonian Germany: The* Chronicon *of Thietmar of Merseburg* (Manchester, 2001), p. 289.

[47] William of Malmesbury, *Historia Novella*, ed. and trans. K. R. Potter (London, 1955), pp. 52, 62. Cf *ibid.*, pp. 26–7 for William's remarks concerning the Council of Oxford in June 1139 at which he tells us he was present.

[48] See Elisabeth van Houts's useful ranked taxonomy of the types of non-written evidence mobilized by medieval historians in 'Genre Aspects of the Use of Oral Information in Medieval Historiography', in B. Frank, T. Haye and D. Tophinke (eds), *Gattungen mittelalterlicher Schriftlichkeit* (ScriptOralia, 99; Tübingen, 1997), pp. 297–311; expanded in her *Memory and Gender in Medieval Europe, 900–1200* (Basingstoke,

In practice, however, writers understood that the sort of expectations as to accuracy, amplitude and coherence that William of Malmesbury encapsulated in the term *integra ueritas* could not always be met on the basis of authorial autopsy alone. Already in the ancient period historians had lamented the physical constraints under which they worked and had fantasized about being able to be everywhere all at once;[49] and their medieval successors likewise appreciated that, as was almost invariably the case, they needed to cast their net of sources as widely as possible if they were to write the history of public affairs in ways that suitably foregrounded the actions of third-party principals and aimed for a spatio-temporal reach greater than that of their own personal experience. The result was an often eclectic approach to the gathering of information that blended various types of sources of information in the interests of making the most of what were frequently acknowledged to be inadequate resources. An important exemplar was provided by Bede, himself following the lead of models such as Gregory the Great's *Dialogues* and Eusebius's *Ecclesiastical History*, which was available to him in Rufinus's Latin translation.[50] In the dedicatory epistle that begins his own *Ecclesiastical History*, Bede offers his addressee, Ceolwulf, king of the Northumbrians, a quite full and painstaking itemization of the sources (*auctores*) upon which he had drawn.[51] For the longer-range portions of his work, Bede states that he had consulted writings gathered 'here and there' (*hinc inde*): he does not mention the authors by name, but we know that he drew upon Orosius, Constantius, Gildas and others, in very large part thanks to the unusually rich library resources available to him in his twin monastery of Wearmouth-Jarrow.

Bede also drew on archival materials in Canterbury and Rome, in written copies or in oral summary, through the good offices of Albinus, the abbot of the monastery of SS Peter and Paul in Canterbury whom Bede acknowledges as a major source of encouragement to write the *Ecclesiastical History*, and of his go-between Nothhelm, a priest from London (and future archbishop of Canterbury) who conducted research on Bede's behalf during a visit to Rome. Once Bede reaches the all-important threshold moment of the arrival of Augustine's mission to the Anglo-Saxons in 597 – that is to say, a span of a little more than 130 years before

1999), pp. 19–39. Cf. S. John, 'Historical Truth and the Miraculous Past: The Use of Oral Evidence in Twelfth-Century Latin Historical Writing on the First Crusade', *English Historical Review*, 130 (2015), 263–301, esp. 287–91.

[49] See Polybius, *Histories*, XII.27, iv, p. 446; trans. Waterfield, *Histories*, p. 443: 'Ephorus [a fourth-century BC historian], for instance, remarks on what an outstanding experience it would be if we could be personally present at all events as they happen.'

[50] For Eusebius's use of sources, including writings, oral report, tradition and his own autopsy, in the context of his ambitions for his *Ecclesiastical History*, see Kempshall, *Rhetoric*, pp. 59–64.

[51] Bede, *Ecclesiastical History of the English People*, ed. and trans. B. Colgrave and R. A. B. Mynors (Oxford, 1969), pp. 2–6.

Bede was planning and writing the *Ecclesiastical History*, which he finished in 731 – his preface appeals to a kind of apostolic succession of elite ecclesiastical tradition as passed down from the time of the earliest evangelization of the English. Here named individuals and institutions are singled out, each typically dominating what Bede could discover of a part of the Anglo-Saxon world with which he was generally unfamiliar: thus Albinus himself for Kent and some other places; Bishop Daniel of Winchester for much of the south and south-west; the monastery of Lastingham, which although situated in Yorkshire preserved the memory of the evangelization of Mercia and Essex by its founders, Ched and Chad; an Abbot Esi, together with the writings and traditions of people in the past, for East Anglia; and Bishop Cyneberht, alongside other 'trustworthy men' (*fideles uiri*), for the kingdom of Lindsey (the area approximating to the later Lincolnshire).

This is not an exhaustive list, for there are many passages in the body of the text that must have been based on other sources of information. But its symmetries are meant to situate Bede's research within a clear three-way matrix: written sources; information supplied by individuals who stand out by virtue of being named and whose trustworthiness is a compound of their personal relationship to Bede himself, their elite status within the Anglo-Saxon Church, and their careful cultivation of memories of their predecessors; and behind these foregrounded figures a hazier but important body of memories, sometimes fixed within a specific institutional setting such as the monastery of Lastingham, but more often a freer-floating 'tradition of those in the past' (*traditio priorum*) that at its outer limits dissolved into an even more imprecise category of 'common report' (*fama uulgans*). When Bede's preface turns, however, to his home region of Northumbria, about which he knew much more and which duly enjoys a disproportionate amount of coverage in the *Ecclesiastical History*, he is aware that two shifts of emphasis come into play: he can draw on his own experience, and he has recourse to a much greater number, countless even, of informants.[52] As he notes: 'But what happened in the church of the various parts of the kingdom of Northumbria, from the time when they received the faith of Christ up to the present, apart from the matters of which I had personal knowledge, I have learned not from any one source but from the faithful testimony of innumerable witnesses, who either knew or remembered these things.'[53] Written texts continue to be important for the Northumbrian portions of the work, particularly what had been written about St Cuthbert at Lindisfarne. But the most important methodological lesson to be learned by those many later historians who looked to Bede for inspiration and whose projects were likewise set, in whole or substantial part, in their own localities, their own Northumbrias, was

[52] For a mapping of the place names supplied by the *Ecclesiastical History*, which reveals a clear weighting towards the north-east, see D. Hill, *An Atlas of Anglo-Saxon England* (Oxford, 1981), p. 30.

[53] Bede, *Ecclesiastical History*, p. 6.

the essential epistemological binary between the sort of knowledge that one could obtain directly (in Bede's phrase *per me ipsum*) and the indisputable testimony of reliable witnesses (*certissima fidelium uirorum adtestatio*).

Numerous examples of this binary appear in medieval historians' programmatic utterances. William of Malmesbury, for example, who was particularly conscious of following in Bede's footsteps, observes in the prologue to the first book of his *Gesta Regum Anglorum*, which serves as a general preface to the whole work, that whereas the reliability of his narrative, which begins with the end of Roman rule in Britain and the arrival of the Anglo-Saxons, substantially rests on that of his (written) authorities (*auctores*), his selection of material from more recent times is derived from what 'I either saw myself or heard from men who can be trusted'.[54] Similarly, Henry of Huntingdon, another self-conscious heir to the tradition of Bede, in the opening of the seventh book of his *Historia Anglorum*, flags up the transition from reliance on old books and *fama uulgans* to the means by which he knows of recent events (Book VII begins with the reign of William Rufus, 1087–1100, and was first written in the early 1130s). He announces that 'Now, however, the matters to be studied are those that I have either seen for myself or heard about from those who did see them.'[55] Formulations of this sight-report binary were not confined to those writers who deliberately fashioned themselves on Bede as their principal model. They appear in a wide variety of texts, for example in the remarks of two historians of the twelfth-century Mezzogiorno, Falco of Benevento[56] and the writer

[54] William of Malmesbury, *Gesta Regum Anglorum*, i, p. 16. The alliteration and assonance within William's formulation, 'uel ipse uidi uel a uiris fide dignis audiui', suggests that it expressed what he believed was an obvious and thus neatly compressible and catchy truism.

[55] Henry of Huntingdon, *Historia Anglorum*, VII.1, ed. and trans. D. E. Greenway (Oxford, 1996), p. 412. See also the similar statement in the general prologue, in which Henry states that having followed Bede and other authors he has brought the story 'down to the time of what we have heard and seen': *ibid.*, p. 6, where Greenway's translation, 'our own knowledge and observation', loses some of the force of the pairing of the senses in 'nostrum ad auditum et uisum'. For the complex chronology of the text's composition, see Greenway's discussion at pp. lxvi–lxxvi. For a rather different emphasis on Henry's part, see his observations towards the beginning of his *De contemptu mundi*, an epistolary meditation on the transience and moral pitfalls of earthly existence that he inserted into a revised version of the *Historia Anglorum* in the 1140s, and which draws many of its illustrative examples from recent events and the careers of prominent people known to Henry and his addressee Walter, probably the archdeacon of Leicester: 'Rather I shall speak with utter simplicity, so that it may be clear to the many … and I shall speak of events that you and I have witnessed' ['de his que tu et ego uidimus']: *ibid.*, p. 584.

[56] Falco of Benevento, *Chronicon Beneventanum: Città e feudi nell'Italia dei Normanni*, ed. and trans. E. D'Angelo (Testi mediolatini con traduzione, 9; Florence, 1998), p. 22; trans. G. A. Loud, *Roger II and the Creation of the Kingdom of Sicily* (Manchester,

conventionally but almost certainly incorrectly known as Hugo Falcandus;[57] in Eadmer's statement of purpose at the beginning of his *Historia Novorum in Anglia*;[58] Rodulfus Glaber's *Five Books of the Histories*;[59] Wipo's *Deeds of Emperor Conrad II*;[60] and Helmold of Bosau's *Chronicle of the Slavs*.[61]

In a similar vein to William of Malmesbury and Henry of Huntingdon, William of Jumièges, in the dedicatory letter of his *Gesta Normannorum Ducum* addressed to William I of England in about 1070, deployed the sight-informant binary in order to set up a contrast in relation to his written sources. He had relied on a guide text, the history of Dudo of St-Quentin, for the earlier portion of his narrative as far as the time of Duke Richard II of Normandy (996–1026); after this point, we are told, he had included material 'partly related by many persons trustworthy on account equally of their age and their experience, and partly based on the most assured evidence of what I have witnessed myself, from my own store'.[62] It is true that one encounters several instances of authors praying in aid written sources in addition to personal observation and the reports of informants: for example, in Lampert of Hersfeld's account of the foundation of the church of Hersfeld, written in the 1070s;[63] and John of Salisbury's *Historia Pontificalis*

2012), p. 142: 'testor, nihil aliud posuisse, preter quod viderim et audiverim, scripsisse'. For the extent of Falco's reliance on his own observations and the testimony of others, see G. A. Loud, 'The Genesis and Context of the Chronicle of Falco of Benevento', in M. Chibnall (ed.), *Anglo-Norman Studies XV: Proceedings of the XV Battle Conference and of the XI Colloquio Medievale of the Officina di Studi Medievali 1992* (Woodbridge, 1993), pp. 182–3.

57 Hugo Falcandus, *La Historia o Liber de Regno Sicilie e la Epistola ad Petrum Panormitane Ecclesie Thesaurium*, ed. G. B. Siragusa (Fonti per la storia d'Italia, 22; Rome, 1897), p. 4; trans. G. A. Loud and T. Wiedemann, *The History of the Tyrants of Sicily by 'Hugo Falcandus' 1154–69* (Manchester, 1998), p. 56: 'partim ipse vidi, partim eorum [qui in]terfuerunt veraci relatione cognovi'.

58 Eadmer, 'Historia Novorum in Anglia', in *Historia Novorum in Anglia et Opuscula Duo*, ed. M. Rule (RS 81; London, 1884), p. 1; trans. G. Bosanquet, *Eadmer's History of Recent Events in England* (London, 1964), p. 1: 'statui ea quae sub oculis vidi vel audivi ... commemorare'.

59 Rodulfus Glaber, 'The Five Books of the Histories', I.4, in *Opera*, ed. and trans. J. France, N. Bulst and P. Reynolds (Oxford, 1989), p. 8: 'prout certa relatione comperimus uel uisuri superfuimus'.

60 'Gesta Chuonradi', p. 8; trans. Mommsen and Morrison, *Imperial Lives*, p. 57: 'prout ipse vidi aut relatu aliorum didici'.

61 Helmold of Bosau, *Cronica Slavorum*, ed. B. Schmeidler (MGH Scriptores rerum Germanicarum in usum scholarum, 32; Hanover, 1937), p. 2; trans. F. J. Tschan, *The Chronicle of the Slavs* (New York, 1935), p. 44: 'quae aut longevis viris referentibus percepi aut oculata cognitione didici'.

62 William of Jumièges, Orderic Vitalis, and Robert of Torigni, *Gesta Normannorum Ducum*, ed. and trans. E. M. C. van Houts, 2 vols (Oxford, 1992–5), i, pp. 4–6.

63 Lampert of Hersfeld, 'Libelli de institutione Herveldensis ecclesiae quae supersunt', in *Lamperti monachi Hersfeldensis opera*, ed. O. Holder-Egger (MGH Scriptores rerum

from the mid twelfth century.[64] But more often than not the sight-reliable informant nexus was set up in contrast to the use of written authorities, not simply as a complement or amplification of it, and in terms that seem intended to suggest a qualitative shift of methodological orientation and epistemological ambition on the author's part. This is particularly evident in those cases in which, either by virtue of their choice of subject matter or because of some external factors beyond their control, writers had to concede that in the absence of written evidence on which to base their histories they had no choice but to become flexible and creative. A good case in point is Lethald of Micy's *Miracles of St Maximinus*, written in the early 980s, in which, confronted by the absence of adequate written records for the early history of the monastery of Micy, the author states that he directed his attention to the question of how best to deploy what he had himself seen and the truthful accounts of reliable informants.[65]

Does the frequent pairing of *visus* and *auditus* as complementary means to gain access to the past suggest that they were believed to be epistemologically equivalent, despite the recurrence of the trope about the superiority of the eyes that we have already noted? To some extent a projection of the perceptual and mnemonic capacities of the eyewitness onto third-party informants was implied by the semantic ranges of the Latin noun *testis* and verb *testificari* and their vernacular equivalents. In the same way that the English word 'witness' suggests both the experience of perception and the subsequent articulation of that experience, as in the bearing of witness, so the *testes* whose names, for example, appear in countless medieval documents were both witnesses to the transaction set out in the text and witnesses to the fact that the transaction had taken place; in this latter capacity their testimony could, potentially, be required to settle a legal dispute at some future date. The dual sense of being a witness would also have been very familiar from numerous reference to both witnessing-as-seeing and the bearing of witness in the Bible, especially the Gospels and Acts of the Apostles. It is reasonable to imagine that when medieval historians drew upon the *testimonium* of others, they were imaginatively projecting onto their interlocutors the same depth and acuity of eyewitness understanding that they would have expected to achieve had they been present themselves. In such cases, the informants were effectively autoptic surrogates. Thus, for example, Falco of Benevento invoked

Germanicarum in usum scholarum, 38; Hanover, 1894), pp. 344–5: 'quae olim me contigit … vel legisse vel a probissimis viris audisse, quae etiam ipse expertus sum'.

[64] John of Salisbury, *Historia Pontificalis*, ed. and trans. M. Chibnall (London, 1956), p. 4: 'quod uisu et auditu uerum esse cognouero, uel quod probalium uirorum scriptis fuerit et auctoritate subnixum'.

[65] Lethald of Micy, 'Liber miraculorum S. Maximini abbatis Miciacensis', *PL*, 137, cols. 795–6: 'quae vel ipse viderim, vel probatorum veridica relatione cognoverim'. For Lethald's text, see T. F. Head, *Hagiography and the Cult of the Saints: The Diocese of Orléans, 800–1200* (Cambridge, 1990), pp. 211–16.

the *testimonium* of those who had been present at the anointing of Prince Robert II of Capua in 1128 in support of his belief that 5,000 people had been present at the occasion.[66]

On the other hand, the kind of complete and explicit equivalence between seeing for oneself and having others seeing for you that one encounters in, for instance, Henry of Huntingdon's formulation that we have already noted, to the effect that his treatment of recent affairs would be based on what he himself had seen or what he had heard from those who had themselves been eyewitnesses ('uel ab his qui uiderant audiuimus'), was quite unusual.[67] More common was a studied imprecision about the exact relationship between one's informants and the material that they had to offer: it was often sufficient just to have 'been there', as in, for example, Hugo Falcandus's prefatory remarks that some of the events that he is going to recount he had seen himself, whereas others he had learned from the trustworthy reports of those who 'had taken part' ('[qui in]terfuerunt').[68] The criteria by which a witness was judged to be trustworthy were typically age, education, social status, moral reputation and familiarity with the author, not visual or mnemonic acuity as such. Moreover, to be 'present' at an event was necessarily an imprecise notion, less a case of being granted opportunities for camera-eye visual perception, and more a cultural immersion in a given moment and a receptivity to the back-and-forth, the 'buzz', of other participants' observations and reactions.

So, even as sight and hearing were often juxtaposed in historians' methodological remarks, there was nonetheless a built-in imbalance between the two perceptual modes. Personal observation was believed to entail greater precision, a quality that lent itself to being emphasized by means of pronouns, as in 'I myself saw', and by intensifying constructions such as 'with my own eyes' or 'with ocular trust'. This contrasted with the much baggier category of informants, some but not all of whom might themselves have been eyewitnesses to what they recounted. The use of phrases such as 'with my own eyes' suggests that the eyewitness historian was typically imagined close to but not caught up in the action: it is the role of observer that is highlighted, not participant. But exceptions to this sense of distance between observer and observed can be found, for example when the narrator presents himself as immersed in unusual or stressful collective situations in which his identification with other members of a beleaguered and threatened group is affirmed in acts of perception that assume a

[66] Falco of Benevento, *Chronicon Beneventanum*, p. 90; trans. Loud, *Roger II*, p. 177. Cf. *Chronicon Beneventanum*, p. 136; trans. Loud, *Roger II*, pp. 197–8 for a similar reference to 'the mouths of those who were there' in relation to the performance of Roger II of Sicily's forces at the Battle of Nocera in 1132.

[67] Henry of Huntingdon, *Historia Anglorum*, VII.1, p. 412.

[68] *La Historia o Liber*, p. 4; trans. Loud and Wiedemann, *History*, p. 56.

representative quality. That is to say, he casts himself as seeing on behalf of his co-sufferers. At the beginning of his account of the First Crusade, for example, Fulcher of Chartres, after drawing the reader's attention to his own eyewitness credentials ('oculis meis...perspexi'), emphasizes the sufferings and tribulations that the Franks had had to overcome during the expedition. Fulcher does so in order to invite the reader's wonder at the manner in which 'we, a few people' ('nos exiguus populus') prevailed against greatly superior opponents.[69] In the prologue to his account of the murder of Count Charles the Good of Flanders and its consequences, Galbert of Bruges expresses a similar sense of participating in a momentous collective experience when he recalls that the genesis of his text was his being caught up in the aftermath of Charles's death:

> Nor was there a good place or time to write when I turned my spirit to this work, for our place [*noster locus*: Galbert principally means Bruges but also Flanders more generally] was so upset then by fear and anxiety that all the clergy and the people, without exception, were in immediate danger of losing both their goods and their lives. It was there, surrounded by impediments and so narrowly confined, that I began to compose my mind, which was tossing as if it had been thrown into Euripus [a narrow, turbulent channel of water], and constrain it to the mode of writing...I rest secure in the knowledge that I speak a truth known to all those who endured the same danger with me, and I entrust it to our posterity to be remembered.[70]

This degree of narratorial immersivity in and identification with collectivities in times of particular peril is, however, fairly unusual. The typical eyewitness gaze presupposed a degree of detachment from the thick of the action; the eyewitness

[69] Fulcher of Chartres, *Historia Hierosolymitana (1095–1127)*, ed. H. Hagenmeyer (Heidelberg, 1912), pp. 116–17; trans. M. E. McGinty in E. Peters (ed.), *The First Crusade: The Chronicle of Fulcher of Chartres and Other Source Materials*, 2nd edn (Philadelphia, 1998), p. 48. For Fulcher, see esp. V. Epp, *Fulcher von Chartres: Studien zur Geschichtsschreibung des ersten Kreuzzuges* (Studia humaniora, 15; Düsseldorf, 1990). See also Harari, 'Eyewitnessing', 79–82.

[70] Galbert of Bruges, *De multro, traditione, et occisione gloriosi Karoli comitis Flandriarum*, ed. J. Rider (CCCM 131; Turnhout, 1994), p. 3; trans. J. Rider, *The Murder, Betrayal, and Slaughter of Glorious Charles, Count of Flanders* (New Haven, 2013), pp. 2–3. Cf. Galbert's related observations about his improvised working methods 'in the midst of such a great uproar of events and the burning of so many houses' while the siege of Charles's murderers was taking place around him in Bruges, in *De multro*, c. 35, p. 81; trans. Rider, *Murder*, pp. 65–6. For Galbert's circumstances and self-fashioning as a writer, see J. Rider, *God's Scribe: The Historiographical Art of Galbert of Bruges* (Washington, DC, 2001), esp. pp. 16–49; *idem*, '"Wonder with Fresh Wonder": Galbert the Writer and the Genesis of the *De multro*', in J. Rider and A. V. Murray (eds), *Galbert of Bruges and the Historiography of Medieval Flanders* (Washington, DC, 2009), pp. 13–35.

can step back, so to speak, and take it all in. This relative distancing seems to have been grounded in the belief that one's own autopsy, in theory at any rate, granted access to the sort of epistemological penetration and the confidence born of subjective personal experience that even the best informed and most reliable of third-party informants could never fully replicate.[71] In this connection, it is significant that even first-hand individual informants are not as a rule expressly named as sources. The exceptions tend to relate to stories about miracles and wonders or to a broader category of the unusual or coincidental, typically the stuff of arresting but tangential *obiter dicta*, not the 'routine' substance of public events in the political, military or ecclesiastical spheres.[72] *A fortiori*, longer chains of information are seldom traced out.[73] An exception that helps to prove the rule, atypical both in its featuring very well-known figures and as an example of what we would nowadays term the uncanny, is a story told by William of Malmesbury in anecdotal mode. This, he insists, is not idle chit-chat ('non friuolo auditu hausi') but a true account that had been passed on to him by someone who swore that he had heard the story from none other than Abbot Hugh of Cluny (who had been dead more than ten years when William was writing). The narrative concerns Hugh's first encounter with Hildebrand, the future Pope Gregory VII (1073–85), and turns on Hildebrand's apparent ability to read Hugh's mind, a knack so unnervingly acute that he is able to upbraid Hugh for the unfairly harsh first impressions that he had formed of him but had not articulated out loud.[74]

Guido Schepens has observed of ancient historians' attitudes to source criticism, in the basic sense of their categorization and evaluation of the material at their disposal, that they attached greater importance to the subjective process of discovery and less to the objective traces of the past in themselves. Research was principally a series of experiences, not an end product.[75] Much the same

[71] For the idea that personal experience created a surplus of historical material, see e.g. Falco of Benevento's statement of the commonplace view that it would be far too time-consuming and onerous to narrate everything of significance that one had seen oneself: *Chronicon Beneventanum*, p. 118; trans. Loud, *Roger II*, p. 189.

[72] But see Asser's explicit reference to the testimony of King Alfred himself concerning the reasons for the lesser status accorded to queens in Wessex compared with elsewhere, a situation that Asser characterizes as exceptional among the Germanic peoples: *Life of King Alfred*, c. 15, pp. 11–12; trans. Keynes and Lapidge, *Alfred the Great*, p. 71.

[73] Cf. John, 'Historical Truth', 279–81. For an example of a named witness to a miracle see Rodulfus Glaber, 'Five Books of the Histories', IV.19, p. 202, where Glaber reports Bishop Ulric of Orléans's particular experience of the miracle of the Holy Fire at the Holy Sepulchre while on pilgrimage to Jerusalem.

[74] *Gesta Regum Anglorum*, c. 263, i, p. 486. Cf. Orderic Vitalis, *Ecclesiastical History*, v, pp. 8–10, cited in John, 'Historical Truth', 281.

[75] G. Schepens, 'Some Aspects of Source Theory in Greek Historiography', in J. Marincola (ed.), *Greek and Roman Historiography* (Oxford, 2011), pp. 100–18.

can be said of medieval historians' approaches: what might seem to be their methodological leaning towards eyewitness evidence on pragmatic grounds is actually rooted in the idea that historical writing was the end result of various types of experience, among which the 'sightist' assumptions that we have noted are embedded in moment-by-moment perception and cognition as well as in language tended to assume pride of place. That said, there are of course many instances in which the circumstances in which the historian was writing or his distance from his subject matter made it prudent to downplay or simply ignore the question of autopsy. Not all history was about recent events in one's own part of the world. In the majority of such instances, the question of autopsy could simply be disregarded as irrelevant to the historian's purposes.

There were, moreover, liminal cases in which the writer chose as a matter of particularly assertive authorial self-fashioning, or in anticipation of his readers' suspicions about his methodology, to minimize, and even to rebut, the value of eyewitness evidence. A particularly clear example, remarks made by Guibert of Nogent, has been thoughtfully explored by Elizabeth Lapina in a study of the role of eyewitness authority in narratives of the First Crusade.[76] Guibert's *Dei Gesta per Francos* was a telling of the First Crusade that largely drew upon the anonymous first-hand account known as the *Gesta Francorum et aliorum Hierosolimitanorum* or a variant very close to the text as we now have it. As is well known, Guibert, alongside other learned historians of the crusade in northern France in the first decade or so after the fall of Jerusalem to the crusaders in 1099, was scornful of both the *Gesta*'s perceived lack of conceptual sophistication, in that it did not offer a sufficiently developed theological framework in which to situate the crusaders' achievements within the scheme of providential history, and, related to this, its supposedly crude style, which was regarded as unfitting for such an elevated subject.[77] Other writers who, like Guibert, did not participate in the crusade and also drew heavily upon the *Gesta*, Baldric of Bourgueil and Robert the Monk, made similar observations. But it is Guibert, the most methodologically self-conscious of the three, who works hardest to establish his trust in the truth value of the *Gesta*'s basic story matter while maintaining that his own retelling is superior. For Guibert, hearing (which subsumed the act of reading) was not necessarily inferior to seeing as a route to understanding, as attested by the many authoritative Lives of saints written by those who had not known their

[76] E. Lapina, '"Nec signis nec testis creditur…": The Problem of Eyewitnesses in the Chronicles of the First Crusade', *Viator*, 38 (2007), 117–39. This is an important and original contribution to our understanding of medieval history-writers' approaches to autopsy. In Lapina's discussion, however, there is some blurring of the important distinction between authorial eyewitness in itself and the historian's use of others' eyewitness testimony, oral or written.

[77] See J. S. C. Riley-Smith, *The First Crusade and the Idea of Crusading* (London, 1986), pp. 135–52.

subjects.[78] In Guibert's view, eyewitnesses such as the author of the *Gesta* could easily make mistakes and had difficulty in probing the motivations of others; they over-emphasized one dimension of their experience – in the *Gesta*'s case the military aspects of the crusade – to the detriment of a rounded understanding; and in perceiving only surface realities they missed more important transcendent truths.[79]

The relationship between Guibert and the recent events in the east amounted to a recasting in spatial terms of a sense of distance between author and subject matter that was more often expressed as temporal in nature. So, for example, Erchempert, whose history of the Lombards of Benevento was written around 889, admits that he is telling his story (which spans slightly more than a century) more on the basis of what he had heard than what he had seen. This he justifies with reference to the evangelists Mark and Luke, whose lack of eyewitness experience of what they narrated had not hindered them from basing their truthful and authoritative accounts (in the Middle Ages Luke was generally supposed to have authored the Acts of the Apostles in addition to his Gospel) on what they had heard from others.[80] Similarly, Agnellus of Ravenna, writing in the second quarter of the ninth century, appeals to the impeccable examples of Mark, who never followed Christ's footsteps in person or witnessed his miracles and thus drew on Peter's memories in order to compose his Gospel, and of Luke, whose Gospel was the fruit of his relationship after the fact with Paul. These are the models for his narrative, which he says he has based not only on what he has seen but also (and by necessary implication to a greater extent, for the story stretches back many centuries to the origins of Christianity in Ravenna) on what 'our elders' had told him.[81]

When a historian's evolving project brought him from the distant past to relatively recent events, it did not automatically follow that this was greeted

[78] Guibert of Nogent, *Dei Gesta per Francos*, ed. R. B. C. Huygens (CCCM 127A; Turnhout, 1996), p. 166; trans. R. Levine, *The Deeds of God through the Franks* (Woodbridge, 1997), p. 73.

[79] See Guibert's remarks in *Dei Gesta per Francos*, pp. 79–84, 350–2; trans. Levine, *Deeds*, pp. 24–6, 165–6. Cf. Lapina, '"Nec signis"', 125–6, 133–8. See also Kempshall, *Rhetoric*, pp. 392–408.

[80] Erchempert, 'Historia Langobardorum Beneventanorum', ed. G. H. Pertz and G. Waitz, *MGH Scriptores rerum Langobardicarum et Italicarum saec. VI–IX* (Hanover, 1878), pp. 234–5: 'non tantum ea quae oculis, set magis quae auribus ausi narrare me fateor, imitatus ex parte dumtaxat Marci Lucaeque euangelistarum preconiis, qui auditis potius quam uisis euangelia descripserunt'.

[81] Agnellus of Ravenna, *Liber pontificalis ecclesiae Ravennatis*, ed. D. M. Deliyannis (CCCM 199; Turnhout, 2006), pp. 145–6; trans. D. M. Deliyannis, *The Book of Pontiffs of the Church of Ravenna* (Washington, DC, 2004), pp. 99–100. Agnellus further cites the example of Gregory the Great, whose *Dialogues* similarly draw extensively on oral report.

with relief now that the narrative could be reinforced by appeals to eyewitness evidence. For example, when the mid-seventh-century chronicler known as Fredegar reached the end of his reliance on the work of Gregory of Tours (d. 594), and realized that he must now strike out on his own to bridge the approximately fifty-year gap to his own time, he reassured the reader that his narrative of royal politics and warfare remained securely based on what he had read and heard and even, almost as an afterthought, on what he had seen as well.[82] At work in these sorts of examples, as with Guibert, is the conviction that no, or minimal, autopsy was not a methodological impediment for the historian. On the other hand, it is noteworthy how these writers, again like Guibert, felt the need to position themselves in relation to eyewitnessing even as they sought to downplay its significance. This element of special pleading suggests that eyewitnessing did enjoy a privileged epistemic status, even as many historiographical projects did not, or could not, exploit it.

To a large extent, the important question is not what medieval historians thought about the value of eyewitness evidence in principle, but the ways in which their approaches fed through into their working methods. Most of the pronouncements that we have examined above are taken from prefatory statements that stage the author's circumstances, aims and credentials: they are moves in what Luke Pitcher, in the very similar context of ancient historiographical practice, has nicely termed 'author theatre'.[83] But to what extent did theory and practice match up? The potentially most revealing way in which to approach this question is to consider instances of the author doubling up as an agent within

[82] *The Fourth Book of the Chronicle of Fredegar with its Continuations*, ed. and trans. J. M. Wallace-Hadrill (London, 1960), pp. 2–3. Wallace-Hadrill's translation, 'read or heard or seen', dilutes the concessive nuance of the second conjunction in 'legendo simul et audiendo etiam et uidendo'.

[83] Pitcher, *Writing Ancient History*, pp. 34–44. For the medieval prologue and dedicatory letter as a form, see G. Simon, 'Untersuchungen zur Topik der Widmungsbriefe mittelalterlicher Geschichtsschreiber bis zum Ende des 12. Jahrhunderts', *Archiv für Diplomatik*, 4 (1958), 52–119; 5/6 (1959–60), 73–153; A. Gransden, 'Prologues in the Historiography of Twelfth-Century England', in D. T. Williams (ed.), *England in the Twelfth Century: Proceedings of the 1988 Harlaxton Symposium* (Woodbridge, 1990), pp. 55–81. There is an excellent collection of examples in translation in *Prologues to Ancient and Medieval History: A Reader*, ed. J. Lake (Readings in Medieval Civilizations and Cultures, 17; Toronto, 2013). See also J. A. Schultz, 'Classical Rhetoric, Medieval Poetics, and the Medieval Vernacular Prologue', *Speculum*, 59 (1984), 1–15; C. Marchello-Nizia, 'L'historien et son prologue: Forme littéraire et stratégies discursives', in D. Poirion (ed.), *La chronique et l'histoire au moyen âge: Colloque des 24 et 25 mai 1982* (Paris, 1984), pp. 13–25. For the Roman antecedents, see T. Janson, *Latin Prose Prefaces: Studies in Literary Conventions* (Studia Latina Stockholmiensia, 13; Stockholm, 1964), esp. pp. 64–83; E. Herkommer, *Die Topoi in den Proömien der römischen Geschichtswerke* (Stuttgart, 1968).

his own storyworld: that is to say, as we saw above in relation to *Rashōmon*, situations in which eyewitness perception is taken as read by virtue of its being subsumed within active participation in the events-as-narrated. For present purposes, we need to put to one side ego-texts in which the author-as-actor is the central protagonist for at least a substantial portion of the narrative as a whole, and which accordingly express much of the action in the first person singular or plural: for example, Liudprand of Cremona's embittered and vitriolic account of his unsuccessful embassy to Constantinople on behalf of Otto I of Germany in 968–9; [84] and two well-known texts inspired by St Augustine's *Confessions*, Guibert of Nogent's *Monodiae* (written in 1115) and Peter Abelard's *Historia Calamitatum* (*c*.1132), which have been central to the long-running debate about whether the twelfth century discovered, or rediscovered, the individual.[85] These sorts of texts have attracted a good deal of scholarly interest, but they are few in number compared with the large majority of historical works in which the narrative centre of interest is an individual who is not the author, an institution such as an abbey or bishopric, a polity such as a kingdom or self-governing city, or a miscellany of actors within an area that happens to correspond to the reach of the author's knowledge.

In such works, authors are for the most part sparing in their insertion of themselves into the action *in propria persona*. In many instances, there is no authorial intervention as a character at all within the storyworld; and in most of the cases in which there is some such presence, it tends to be occasional, brief and tangential to the main themes of the narrative, as when, for example, a personal reminiscence is cued by some name- or place-association. A good illustration is supplied by the twelfth-century chronicle of St-Maixent: when the author notes

[84] Liudprand of Cremona, 'Relatio de legatione Constantinopolitana', in *Die Werke Liudprands von Cremona*, ed. J. Becker, 3rd edn (MGH Scriptores rerum Germanicarum in usum scholarum, 41; Hanover, 1915), pp. 175–212; trans. P. Squatriti, *The Complete Works of Liudprand of Cremona* (Washington, DC, 2007), pp. 238–82. For the embassy, see H. Mayr-Harting, 'Liudprand of Cremona's Account of his Legation to Constantinople and Ottonian Imperial Strategy', *English Historical Review*, 116 (2001), 539–56.

[85] Guibert of Nogent, *Autobiographie*, ed. and trans. E.-R. Labande (Les classiques de l'histoire de France au moyen âge, 34; Paris, 1981); trans. P. J. Archambault, *A Monk's Confession: The Memoirs of Guibert of Nogent* (University Park, PA, 1996); Peter Abelard, *Historia Calamitatum*, ed. J. Monfrin, 4th edn (Paris, 1978); trans. B. Radice, *The Letters of Abelard and Heloise*, rev. M. T. Clanchy (London, 2003), pp. 3–43. The landmark publications in the debate concerning twelfth-century individualism are C. Morris, *The Discovery of the Individual 1050–1200* (Medieval Academy Reprints for Teaching, 19; Toronto, 1987), esp. pp. 64–95 (originally published in 1972); and the response to it in C. W. Bynum, 'Did the Twelfth Century Discover the Individual?', *Journal of Ecclesiastical History*, 31 (1980), 1–17, expanded in her *Jesus as Mother: Studies in the Spirituality of the High Middle Ages* (Berkeley, 1982), pp. 82–109.

that a new abbot of the monastery of Cormery, near Tours, was elected in 1082, this is followed by the throw-away remark that it was at this same monastery that he, the author, had once encountered a monk named Litier who exercised such remarkable self-control that over a period of ten years he never touched a drop of wine or water except during Mass.[86] Given that many authors grant themselves few or no 'walk-on parts' in their own storyworlds, it follows *a fortiori* that explicit references to autopsy or to conversations with informants that serve to validate a given assertion are also infrequent. For example, Henry of Huntingdon is typical of medieval historiographers in not routinely supplying the sources of his information; the narrative matter that constitutes his storyworld is for the most part delivered to the reader in the form of self-evident declarative statements. In a rare exception, however, he offers an intriguing glimpse of the temporal reach of oral tradition going back about a century when he reports the scheme hatched by King Aethelred II in 1002 to have all the Danes living in England seized and killed on St Brice's Day (13 November). Henry remarks that in his childhood (he was probably born around 1088) he had heard it told by very old men (who must themselves have heard the story from their parents' or grandparents' generation) that the king had coordinated the plot by means of letters sent to every town in the kingdom.[87] In many other cases, self-reference of this sort clusters around accounts of miracles, wonders and other unusual happenings. For example, although Rodulfus Glaber inserts himself into the 'routine' action of his *Five Books of the Histories* in a few passages of autobiographical reminiscence, the most sustained inclusion of individual agency on his own part comes in his account of various apparitions that he had experienced.[88] Similarly, one of the fairly few self-references within the action, as distinct from editorial comment on it, to be found in William of Malmesbury's *Historia Novella* concerns his learning about, though not apparently himself seeing, a solar eclipse in March 1140.[89]

In a minority of cases, however, a greater degree of authorial self-insertion is visible. This could take one of two forms. Either the author is positioned close to the action in the manner of a roving reporter but does not function as an actor within the storyworld, at least not as an identified individual with discrete agency; Galbert of Bruges is a case in point, the *locus classicus* of an observer placed very close to, but narratorially-speaking separate from, much of the action that he recounts. Or the author doubles up as an actor within the workings of the plot

[86] *La Chronique de Saint-Maixent 751–1140*, ed. and trans. J. Verdon (Les classiques de l'histoire de France au moyen âge, 33; Paris, 1979), p. 146.

[87] Henry of Huntingdon, *Historia Anglorum*, VI.2, p. 340. Cf. van Houts, 'Genre Aspects', pp. 305–7 for the suggestion that the chronological reach of reliable oral report for medieval historians was about one hundred years.

[88] Rodulfus Glaber, 'Five Books of the Histories', V.2–5, pp. 218–22. See also V.8, p. 226. Cf. III.12, p. 114; IV.7, p. 184; IV.11, p. 190.

[89] *Historia Novella*, pp. 42–3.

itself; a good example is provided by the chronicle of the polymath Odorannus of Sens, written in or shortly after 1032, which includes details of his personal involvement in events that took place in his monastery of St-Pierre-le-Vif in Sens, including a disagreement with some of his brethren that drove him into temporary exile in 1023, and his efforts to promote the cult of St Savinianus.[90] A revealing limit case with regard to the inclusion of autobiographical material within a narrative that is substantially about something or someone else, here the career of a king, is Suger's *Life* of Louis VI of France (1108–37).[91]

As is well known, Suger, abbot of St-Denis between 1122 and 1151, was one of the most active and important figures in the Capetian regime, a close adviser to Louis VI and to his son Louis VII (1137–80).[92] It would therefore not have seemed incongruent, an egregious distortion of political reality, for Suger to have included himself as a character in an account of the elder Louis's reign. Sure enough, there are sequences in the *Life* that imply that Suger was a regular companion of the king and moved easily among the great and the good at the royal court. In a famous passage, for example, he states that he used to overhear Philip I (1060–1108) complain to his son, the future Louis VI (the imperfect 'testabatur' suggests regular and easy intimacy with the king and his heir), about the trouble that had been regularly caused him by the castle of Montlhéry, a few miles south of Paris.[93] Suger also describes how he was one of the inner circle of close advisers ('intimi...et familiares') who in 1131 counselled the king to have his second son Louis crowned after his heir presumptive, Philip, had been killed in a riding accident; and he remarks that on one occasion Louis found him weeping in the royal chamber when he thought that the king was going to die.[94]

[90] Odorannus of Sens, *Opera Omnia*, ed. and trans. R.-H. Bautier, M. Gilles, M.-E. Duchez and M. Huglo (Sources d'histoire médiévale, 4; Paris, 1972), pp. 100, 102–6, 112. For Odorannus's chronicle within his wide and eclectic corpus, see *ibid.*, pp. 44–50. For another interesting insertion of autobiographical details, in this case into a royal biography, see Asser, *Life of King Alfred*, cc. 79, 81, pp. 63–6, 67–8; trans. Keynes and Lapidge, *Alfred the Great*, pp. 93–4, 96–7.

[91] Suger, *Vie de Louis VI le Gros*, ed. and trans. H. Waquet, 2nd edn (Les classiques de l'histoire de France au moyen âge, 11; Paris, 1964); trans. R. C. Cusimano and J. Moorhead, *The Deeds of Louis the Fat* (Washington, DC, 1992).

[92] The literature on Suger is vast. See, among many treatments, M. Bur, *Suger, abbé de Saint-Denis, régent de France* (Paris, 1991); L. Grant, *Abbot Suger of St-Denis: Church and State in Early Twelfth-Century France* (London, 1998); F. Gasparri, *Suger de Saint-Denis: Abbé, soldat, homme d'État au XIIe siècle* (Paris, 2015).

[93] *Vie de Louis*, c. 8, pp. 36–8; trans. Cusimano and Moorhead, *Deeds*, p. 40. Cf. c. 1, p. 12; trans. Cusimano and Moorhead, *Deeds*, p. 28, in which Suger states that, presumably in the royal court, he had often heard Walter Tirel, the man many blamed for the death of William Rufus in the New Forest in 1100, swear that he had not been present in that part of the forest on the fateful day.

[94] *Vie de Louis*, cc. 32, 33, pp. 266–8, 278; trans. Cusimano and Moorhead, *Deeds*, pp.

In a few places Suger permits himself the luxury of passages in which he is the main protagonist acting in his capacity as a senior figure in the French Church, most notably in a fairly full account of the circumstances in which he discovered that he had been elected abbot of St-Denis *in absentia* while on a visit to the papal curia.[95] But it is also noteworthy that his mentions of his meetings with Pope Gelasius II at Maguelone and Pope Calixtus II in Apulia, surely among the highpoints of his ecclesiastical career, make a point of noting that he had been sent there on royal business, as if to reassert his primary identity, for the purposes of the narrative at any rate, as a close royal confidant.[96]

Given that Suger's *Life*, which is by no means a comprehensive narrative of Louis's reign and is highly selective in its coverage, chiefly concerns itself with the king's military deeds – the frequent prosecution of just wars that cast him in the role of the defender of churches, the poor, widows and orphans – it is significant that the most extensive autobiographically-oriented sequence in the text concerns Suger's contributions to the king's campaigns against one of his most difficult opponents, Hugh III of Le Puiset, in 1111 and 1112. Hugh's reputation is that of an archetypal robber-baron, thanks in large part to Suger's lengthy excoriation of him in the *Life*, though in fact he was a member of an important kindred network with connections to the princely courts of northern France and to the Latin East. Hugh's *caput*, the castle of Le Puiset, was situated in the Beauce, an agriculturally rich area south-west of Paris where the abbey of St-Denis owned a cluster of valuable estates centred on Toury, about four miles from Le Puiset. Having received complaints about Hugh from Count Theobald of Blois and his mother Agnes, as well in response to the petition of a coalition of bishops and monasteries, including St-Denis, whose lands Hugh threatened, Louis moved against him in 1111. As part of his forward planning, Louis sent Suger – at this stage in his career an up-and-coming political fixer in the royal circle – to Toury with instructions to improve its defences and to station a force of knights there in anticipation of its serving as a base of operations against Le Puiset. It is noteworthy that Suger, in what amounts to a *mise-en-abyme* of the

149–51, 155. Cf. Suger's inclusion in the high-status party sent by Louis, in nearly his last act as king, to Aquitaine in order to arrange the soon-to-be Louis VII's marriage to Eleanor, the heiress of the recently deceased Duke William X: c. 34, pp. 280–2; trans. Cusimano and Moorhead, *Deeds*, pp. 156–7.

[95] *Vie de Louis*, c. 27, pp. 206–12; trans. Cusimano and Moorhead, *Deeds*, pp. 122–4.

[96] *Vie de Louis*, c. 27, pp. 200–2, 206; trans. Cusimano and Moorhead, *Deeds*, pp. 119–20, 121–2. Cf. c. 10, p. 52; trans. Cusimano and Moorhead, *Deeds*, p. 47, where Suger states that he was present when Paschal II consecrated the abbey of La-Charité-sur-Loire (in 1107); although, at least as Suger here implies, he was a sufficiently senior figure at St-Denis to use this occasion to argue, and win, a case against the bishop of Paris before Pope Paschal, he was most probably not yet a significant figure in royal court circles by that date.

ideological programme of the text as a whole, conflates his monastic and curial personae in insisting that he was sent to Toury, where he was already the abbey's *praepositus*, or estate-manager, by the king; his abbot, Adam, gave his consent but did not initiate this move. Suger's account of Louis's assault on Le Puiset is told as though by someone close to the action. Although an eyewitness gaze directed at the fighting is not explicitly evoked, Suger's substantial narrative, one of the longest military sequences in the text, includes the kinds of details, once it moves from generic evocations of the clash of arms to specifics such as a type of incendiary wagon pushed against the defenders' gate and the brave actions of a bald priest in command of a local levy, that suggest that Suger was close to the action at least some of the time and in a position to be well briefed by others on what he had not seen for himself.[97]

Hugh of Le Puiset was taken prisoner when his castle fell, but in due course he was released and became an even greater nuisance than before thanks to a realignment of regional alliances around Count Theobald of Blois, who had fought against Hugh in the 1111 campaign but now joined forces with him in opposition to the king. Louis therefore resumed his offensive against Le Puiset, which had been largely demolished but was still serviceable as a dangerous base of military operations, in 1112.[98] Because Toury was once again caught up in the unfolding action, Suger is able to work himself into the narrative of the second Le Puiset campaign as a prominent protagonist with a significant role to play in the plot, particularly in the early stages. Indeed, the action proper begins in Suger's telling as he is tricked by Hugh, newly reinstalled in Le Puiset, into leaving the area in order to find the king and intercede with him on Hugh's behalf, thereby freeing Hugh to launch an assault on Toury in his absence. Upbraided by Louis for falling for Hugh's tricks, Suger hastens back ahead of the forces that the king assembles.

[97] For the 1111 campaign against Hugh, see *Vie de Louis*, c. 19, pp. 128–42; trans. Cusimano and Moorhead, *Deeds*, pp. 84–90. For the vulnerability of St-Denis's possessions in the Beauce and the coalition against Hugh of Le Puiset, see also Suger, 'Gesta Suggerii Abbatis' [= *De Rebus in Administratione sua Gestis*], I.14–20, in *Oeuvres*, ed. and trans. E. Gasparri, 2 vols (Les classiques de l'histoire de France au moyen âge, 37 and 41; Paris, 1996–2001), i, pp. 74–90, esp. I.18, pp. 82–6. For the geopolitical context of Louis's actions against Hugh in this and subsequent campaigns, and the strategic significance of Toury and Suger's control of it, see Grant, *Abbot Suger*, pp. 91–6; É. Bournazel, *Louis VI le Gros* (Paris, 2007), pp. 112–17, 119–21, 138–9.

[98] For the 1112 campaign, a more complex and close-run affair than the assault on Le Puiset in 1111 because of the substantial princely forces arrayed against Louis, see Suger, *Vie*, c. 21, pp. 152–68; trans. Cusimano and Moorhead, *Deeds*, pp. 95–103. For the circumstances of Hugh of Le Puiset's release, which Suger spins as an illustration of his duplicity, perhaps to deflect criticism from Louis for allowing a known trouble-maker to go free, see c. 20, pp. 150–2; trans. Cusimano and Moorhead, *Deeds*, pp. 94–5.

In the meantime his men have been resolutely defending Toury, benefitting from the strengthening of the site that had been undertaken the previous year. At this point in the narrative there is a remarkable, and in its explicitness quite unusual, moment of authorial autopsy placed within the diegesis. As Suger nears Toury, we are told how he and his party scrutinize the scene that confronts them:

> Persistently peering ahead, we beheld from afar one sure sign that the fortress had not yet been taken. Its three-storied tower could still be seen [*apparebat*] dominating the entire plain, whereas, if the fortress had fallen, the enemy would have immediately destroyed it by fire.[99]

Suger-as-agent continues to serve as the narrative focus as he and his party boldly slip through the enemy positions and gain entry to Toury by means of a pre-arranged signal. The defenders' morale is restored, though in his inability to refrain his men from taunting their opponents Suger implies that his personal control of the situation is less than complete.

Thereafter, as first a royal advance party and then the king himself arrive on the scene, Suger drops away as an active protagonist within the storyworld. The plot now works itself through in four phases that are all centred on Louis's actions and reactions: a repulsed royal assault on Le Puiset in which Louis bravely covers his force's retreat but which causes the royal host to scatter; renewed royal pressure on Le Puiset aided by the use of a nearby motte as a siege castle; Louis's relocation of his forward base to Janville, closer to Le Puiset than Toury, and a royal victory won there; and the conclusion of the siege when Louis grants Theobald of Blois permission to slip away, leaving Hugh to be taken prisoner and Le Puiset to be razed once more. Although the narrative of these events is full and detailed, there is greater use of generic combat language and there are fewer circumstantial details than in the corresponding account of the fighting the year before. This would seem to suggest that Suger was not consistently positioned as an eyewitness close to the action, at least with respect to the combat sequences that account for much of the chapter, though he would have been well placed at Toury to keep abreast of developments. The remark that concludes the whole chapter, however, to the effect that when Le Puiset had been levelled, its walls shattered and it wells filled in, it resembled a scene of divine malediction, seems to evoke a moment of personal observation and reflection on the author's part.[100]

Suger's *Life* of Louis VI usefully highlights many of the challenges that attach to autoptic evidence and our reading of it. At first sight, the passages concerning the campaigns against Hugh of Le Puiset in 1111 and 1112 would appear to be textbook eyewitness evidence: the intersection of the author's personal

[99] *Vie*, c. 21, p. 156; trans. Cusimano and Moorhead, *Deeds*, p. 97.
[100] *Vie*, c. 21, p. 168; trans. Cusimano and Moorhead, *Deeds*, p. 103.

circumstances and political events contrive to place Suger at the right place at the right times; and what seem to result are two full and detailed narrative sequences which, if for the most part not the direct result of visual perception on Suger's part, at least capture his ability to keep up with sometimes fast-moving events and to correlate his experiences and impressions with those of informants who were likewise in or near the thick of the action. This quality seems to be confirmed by the fact that Suger's treatment of Louis's third and final campaign against Hugh, in 1118, is strikingly brief and undeveloped by comparison, no doubt in large part because Suger had ceased to be responsible for Toury in the intervening period. In the interests of reaching closure on Hugh, Suger is willing to break into his normal chronological structure in order to jump ahead to Hugh's final defeat and eventual departure for the Holy Land, but the contrast with the detailed and circumstantial narratives that precede this chapter is stark.[101] The autoptic quality of the accounts of the first two Le Puiset campaigns further emerges in a comparison with Suger's treatment of Louis's actions against Thomas of Marle, who is often paired with Hugh as a representative of the aggressive castellan class that Louis was committed to subduing. In Suger's presentation, the dynamics are in many ways the same: Louis is moved to act after learning of the complaints against Thomas raised by an ecclesiastical council at Beauvais in late 1114, and this enables Suger to position the king as a righteous protector of churches and the poor. The narrative of the royal campaign that results, and that of the second and final action against Thomas in 1130, likewise prompted by the 'lamentations of churches', are full and quite detailed, but they lack some of the circumstantial texture of the first two Le Puiset sequences, especially the first.[102]

It is possible that, as Lindy Grant has suggested, the attention that Suger devotes to Louis's actions against Thomas of Marle reflects the fact that he was personally involved in these events.[103] As a senior counsellor of the king, at least by the time of the second campaign, Suger doubtless contributed to Louis's

[101] *Vie*, c. 22, p. 170; trans. Cusimano and Moorhead, *Deeds*, p. 104.

[102] *Vie*, cc. 24, 31, pp. 172–8, 250–4; trans. Cusimano and Moorhead, *Deeds*, pp. 106–9, 142–4. For Louis's campaigns against Thomas of Marle, see Bournazel, *Louis VI*, pp. 132–4, 194, 312–13, 315–16. The importance that Suger's *Life* attaches to Thomas is suggested by the fact that it flags him up as a living embodiment of evil early on, in the scene-setting section that narrates various happenings before Louis becomes king and the story of his reign proper gets underway: *Vie*, c. 7, pp. 30–4; trans. Cusimano and Moorhead, *Deeds*, pp. 37–9. As is well known, Thomas was also bitterly attacked by Guibert of Nogent: see esp. *Autobiographie*, III.11, pp. 362–4; III.14, pp. 396–8, 402–4; trans. Archambault, *Monk's Confession*, pp. 166–8, 182–3, 184–5. But his reputation for evil was more widespread: see Henry of Huntingdon, *Historia Anglorum*, p. 602 (a passage in Henry's *De contemptu mundi*). See also Orderic Vitalis, *Ecclesiastical History*, vi, pp. 258, 290.

[103] Grant, *Abbot Suger*, pp. 40, 97, 109, 123–4.

strategizing and may have accompanied the king. But we need to be careful not to treat relative length and narrative density as unequivocal signs of authorial autopsy. Suger does not insert himself into the action in the Thomas sequences, in large part because, although St-Denis had many interests in the Laonnais, Thomas's main theatre of operations, there would seem to have been no equivalent to Toury to place Suger at the centre of the storyworld at key plot junctures. Moreover, given the great deal of selectivity that Suger brings to the *Life*, the driving force behind his choice of incidents to include and the narrative detail devoted to them should be seen as ideological in inspiration far more than autobiographical. The text's primary purpose is to construct an image of Louis's kingship as that of a just ruler willing to put his military might at the service of the Church, his close relationship with which is exemplified in particular by his deferential posture towards the abbey of St-Denis.[104] And, to this end, personal reminiscence is a useful resource, but one that surfaces only intermittently at those points in which it reinforces the ideological thrust of the text. The 'perfect storm' in the Le Puiset sections that aligns Suger's autobiographical circumstances and his text's principal thematic preoccupations is not typical of the narrative as a whole. Additionally, Suger's *Life* is itself unusual among medieval historical works in the degree to which authorial autopsy plays through into the specifics of the storyworld, as opposed to simply hovering over it in shadowy and imprecise ways. If, therefore, we take the *Life* as an example of what an 'eyewitness' source can deliver, we need to be aware that in long and complex narratives the texture of the author's autopsy will inevitably be uneven. *A fortiori*, this autoptic quality will vary considerably from one text to another.

The parameters within which authorial autopsy functions in Suger's *Life* may usefully be compared with the mobilization of eyewitness agency and authority in a text that at first glance one would expect to be free of real-world constraints but which in fact ends up largely reinstating them: the *Historia Turpini*, often

[104] For the *Life*'s ideological agenda, see now the excellent study by J. Führer, 'Französisches Königreich und französisches Königtum in der Wahrnehmung der zeitgenössischen Historiographie: Suger von Saint-Denis und Guillaume de Nangis', in N. Kersken and G. Vercamer (eds), *Macht und Spiegel der Macht: Herrschaft in Europa im 12. und 13. Jahrhundert vor dem Hintergrund der Chronistik* (Deutsches Historisches Institut Warshau, Quellen und Studien, 27; Wiesbaden, 2013), pp. 199–218. See also G. M. Spiegel, 'History as Enlightenment: Suger and the *Mos Anagogicus*', in her *The Past as Text: The Theory and Practice of Medieval Historiography* (Baltimore, 1997), pp. 163–77. James Naus makes a convincing case for believing that an important strand in Suger's programme was to reestablish Louis's prestige and political capital relative to those newly attaching to the several families in the royal orbit that had been well represented on the First Crusade: 'Negotiating Kingship in France at the Time of the Early Crusades: Suger and the *Gesta Ludovici Grossi*', *French Historical Studies*, 36 (2013), 525–41; *idem*, *Constructing Kingship: The Capetian Monarchs of France and the Early Crusades* (Manchester, 2016).

known as the *Pseudo-Turpin*. This curious text purports to narrate the history of Charlemagne's campaigns in the Iberian peninsula, the last of which involves a version of the battle of Roncesvalles different from that familiar from the tradition preserved in the Oxford *Chanson de Roland* and later tellings. This is not real history, of course, but it would have been generally accepted as such by medieval readers. The earliest extant copy of the *Historia* is in the famous twelfth-century manuscript known as the *Codex Calixtinus* preserved in Santiago de Compostela. This contains a miscellany of materials themed around the cult of St James; the *Historia*, together with three documents that form a coda to it, comprises Book IV.[105] The story told by the *Historia* is narrated by Archbishop Turpin of Reims, who claims eyewitness authority and is in a position to serve as narrator because, unlike his incarnation in the Oxford *Roland* tradition who is killed at Roncesvalles – he is in fact the last Frank to die before Roland[106] – he survives that battle by virtue of his being positioned with Charlemagne's main army down in the valley and away from the thick of the fighting.[107] Indeed, the Turpin of the *Historia* outlives Charlemagne – just.

There has been a great deal of debate about the origins of the *Historia* and its place within the *Codex Calixtinus*. Although, in its account of the privileges that Charlemagne grants to St-Denis after his return from the last of his Spanish wars, the text shows a good understanding of the more grandiose claims to political and ecclesiastical status within France that this abbey nurtured, the once common scholarly belief that it was written by a monk or monks from St-Denis is no longer generally supported.[108] A case can be made for a Cluniac connection, but

[105] 'Historia Turpini', in *Liber Sancti Jacobi: Codex Calixtinus*, ed. W. M. Whitehill, G. Prado and J. C. García, 3 vols (Santiago de Compostela, 1944), i, pp. 301–48; trans. K. R. Poole, *The Chronicle of Pseudo-Turpin* (New York, 2014).

[106] *The Song of Roland*, ll. 2233–45, ed. and trans. G. J. Brault, 2 vols (University Park, PA, 1978), ii, pp. 136–8.

[107] But there is some confusion, which we shall see is typical of the text. Turpin is named (in the third person, whereas elsewhere in the text he usually appears in the first person) among those few Franks, Roland included, who are still alive at the conclusion of the battle, and it is implied that he stays with Roland to the end, in that he is not among those who we are told flee the scene: 'Historia Turpini', c. 21, p. 329; trans. Poole, *Chronicle*, pp. 60–1. But in what follows, Roland's drawn-out death scene, some of the plot roles that are assigned to Turpin in the *Chanson de Roland* tradition are performed by surrogates, Roland's brother Baldwin, who fetches water for the dying Roland and blesses him (but then rides away), and Theoderic, who consoles Roland with the advice to make confession: pp. 332–4; trans. Poole, *Chronicle*, pp. 65–7. Theoderic is named as Turpin's source for the manner of Roland's death. For other appearances of Turpin in the third person, see c. 2, p. 304; c. 21, p. 329; trans. Poole, *Chronicle*, pp. 8, 60.

[108] 'Historia Turpini', c. 22, pp. 338–9, trans. Poole, *Chronicle*, pp. 74–5. See E. A. R. Brown, 'Saint-Denis and the Turpin Legend', in J. Williams and A. Stones (eds), *The* Codex Calixtinus *and the Shrine of St. James* (Jakobus-Studien, 3; Tübingen, 1992), pp. 51–88. The account of the genesis and diffusion of the *Pseudo-Turpin* in J.-P.

again this is open to debate. Perhaps the best that can be said is that the *Historia*, which is most probably to be dated to the 1140s, is a product of the many interactions between Spanish and French ecclesiastical culture that characterized the final decades of the eleventh century and the first half of the twelfth, in particular as they were energized by the growth of pilgrimage to Compostela. The *Historia* enjoyed enormous success; in its Latin original it survives, sometimes in abridged or expanded forms, in a very large number of manuscripts, about 170, the sort of total only achieved by the most conspicuous 'bestsellers' of medieval historiography; and from around the turn of the thirteenth century it was translated into several vernaculars and widely disseminated.[109] It is therefore highly likely that in its various guises the *Historia* was in fact the most widely read 'eyewitness' historical narrative in the later Middle Ages.

For our purposes, the problem of the text's origins is less important than the form in which it presents itself in its earliest surviving version. The *Historia* is an eclectic mix of generic influences. The sweeping narration of warfare on an epic scale is its principal concern. Indeed, in its evocation of rulers who can quickly mobilize implausibly large armies and effortlessly traverse great distances, and in its breezy disregard of logistics, physical obstacles and all the difficulties of warfare, it closely resembles Geoffrey of Monmouth's *History of the Kings of Britain*, which predates it by only about a decade.[110] But the text also contains many passages inspired by other genres, including vision and miracle literature, sermon *exempla* and moralizing commentary, religious polemic, royal biography, panegyric and chorography, or geographical description, which emerges in its listing of place names and its interest in local curiosities. There is even an excursus on the seven liberal arts cued by the claim that they were the subject of allegorical paintings that Charlemagne ordered to be made in his palace in Aachen.[111] In light of this pronounced composite quality, it is probably best to label the last person responsible for crafting the *Historia* in the earliest form in which it is preserved – if, as is likely, there was more than one creative agency at work in various places and at different times – as the 'author-compiler'.

Poly and É. Bournazel, *The Feudal Transformation 900–1200*, trans. C. Higgitt (New York, 1991), pp. 195–9, is too precise to be convincing. For an insightful examination of the text's mobilization of crusading ideas and motifs, see W. J. Purkis, *Crusading Spirituality in the Holy Land and Iberia c.1095–c.1187* (Woodbridge, 2008), pp. 150–65. See also K. Herbers, *Der Jakobuskult des 12. Jahrhunderts und der "Liber Sancti Jacobi": Studien über das Verhältnis zwischen Religion und Gesellschaft im hohen Mittelalter* (Historische Forschungen, 7; Wiesbaden, 1984), pp. 125–50.

[109] See G. M. Spiegel, *Romancing the Past: The Rise of Vernacular Prose Historiography in Thirteenth-Century France* (Berkeley, 1993), pp. 55–98.

[110] Geoffrey of Monmouth, *The History of the Kings of Britain*, ed. M. D. Reeve, trans. N. Wright (Woodbridge, 2007).

[111] 'Historia Turpini', c. 22, pp. 339–41; trans. Poole, *Chronicle*, pp. 75–9.

The *Historia* is only partly successful in synthesizing its various generic influences, with the result that it hovers in a space half way between an anthology of its constituent parts and a coherent military and political narrative. One sign of its rough-and-ready quality is the dissonance between the temporal logic of the device that governs the narrative as a whole – that the text is an exercise in near-contemporary history told by Turpin, a veteran of the Spanish wars and Charlemagne's close companion, very soon after Charlemagne's death – and individual passages that presuppose a much longer interval between what are sometimes termed the narrative now and the narratorial now, that is to say the when of the events in the storyworld and the when of the narrator's telling. For example, in one of the best-known set-pieces in the text, when some of Charlemagne's army plant lances in the ground on the eve of a battle, in the morning those who are destined to die a martyr's death later that day discover that overnight their lances have sprouted bark and leaves. The narrator states that from the stumps of these miraculous lances there grew great forests 'that are still visible in that place', which of course suggests that a substantial interval has elapsed in the meantime.[112] Similarly, in listing Charlemagne's noble companions, the narrator observes of Ogier the Dane that 'he is the subject of a song that is sung up to the present day, in that he performed countless wondrous deeds';[113] and the fact that Charlemagne freed from servitude those who gave particularly generously towards the construction of the church of St-Denis, earning each donor the title 'Frank [that is, free man] of St Dionysius', is said to lie behind the 'custom' (*mos*) of using the word *Francia* to refer to the area formerly known as *Gallia*.[114] These temporal inconsistencies, together with the many abrupt jumps between generic registers that are encountered throughout the text, reveal that the *Historia* is for the most part held together only very loosely.

Two elements, however, provide some cohesion and prevent the narrative from simply disintegrating into a collage of discrete sequences. One is the recurrent role of Charlemagne as central protagonist, in conjunction with the narrator's insistence on the high-minded sense of purpose that motivates his religious wars in the Iberian peninsula. The other is the bracketing of the action by means of passages in which Turpin's credentials as narrator are emphasized. To this extent, the *Historia* becomes a test case of the ability of authorial autopsy not only to validate what is stated but also to animate a narrative and to lend it coherence. The text's prologue seeks to emphasize Turpin's autoptic status in several ways. A sense of particular closeness to Charlemagne is communicated immediately by

112 'Historia Turpini', c. 8, p. 308: 'que adhuc in illo loco apparent'; trans. Poole, *Chronicle*, pp. 19–20: translation revised.

113 'Historia Turpini', c. 11, p. 312: 'De hoc canitur in cantilena usque in hodiernum diem, quia innumera fecit prodigia'; trans. Poole, *Chronicle*, p. 28: translation revised.

114 'Historia Turpini', c. 22, p. 339; trans. Poole, *Chronicle*, p. 75.

means of the address to a Leoprandus, dean of Aachen, in which Turpin announces himself not only with reference to his formal status, as archbishop of Reims, but also as Charlemagne's 'assiduous companion' ('sedulus...consocius').[115] After this, the circumstances in which the narrator claims to be writing are described with an unusual degree of attention to personal detail compared with the often cryptic or allusive self-presentations to be found in many historiographical prefaces and dedicatory epistles. This is done in terms, moreover, that insist that Turpin's recent experiences as imperial companion and eyewitness observer are so vivid and significant that they are even inscribed on his body:

> As I lay in Vienne not too long ago, suffering from the scars of my wounds, you ordered me to write down how our emperor, the most famous Charlemagne, liberated the Spanish and Galician lands from the infidel. So I have tried to write promptly, sending to your fraternal hands the most important of his admirable deeds and laudable triumphs over the Spanish Saracens, which I saw with my own eyes during the fourteen years that I spent at his side and with his armies traversing Spain and Galicia.[116]

Turpin's status as an eyewitness is further enhanced in his statement that Leoprandus had tried but failed to come by an adequate account of Charlemagne's actions in Spain in what is implied is a prestigious and authoritative written source, the 'royal chronicle of St-Denis'. Two reasons are suggested: either the chronicle's author was defeated by the sheer volume of material or, more bluntly, he had never been to Spain and was therefore ignorant of what had happened there. Turpin is careful to reassure Leoprandus that his own version of events does not contradict the telling, however insufficient, that is to be found in the chronicle. Eyewitnessing is therefore set up as the means to complement and enrich the knowledge that is anchored in the authority of writing; these are not competing, mutually exclusive epistemic resources.

Yet it is also implied that Turpin's autopsy ultimately grants him an authority superior to that of the chronicler, in the process equipping him to deliver a narrative that is full and sufficient unto itself, not a mere 'top up' of the shadowy royal text. The emphasis on Turpin's eyewitness evident at the beginning of the narrative is echoed in the long chapter that effectively, if not formally, concludes it with an account of Charlemagne's return to northern France at the end of his long Spanish adventures, his grants to St-Denis, and his death.[117] (Unsurprisingly,

[115] 'Historia Turpini', p. 301; trans. Poole, *Chronicle*, p. 3, where the translation as 'constant companion' downplays the sense of conscious diligence or solicitude on Turpin's part in his relationship with Charlemagne.

[116] 'Historia Turpini', p. 301; trans. Poole, *Chronicle*, p. 3.

[117] 'Historia Turpini', c. 22, pp. 338–43; trans. Poole, *Chronicle*, pp. 74–82. This chapter also includes the disquisition on the seven liberal arts mentioned above.

perhaps, the main body of the narrative – if we put to one side the three appended texts – contrives to frustrate any sense of closure by throwing in an extra chapter, implicitly still voiced by Turpin as narrator but set in time before the Spanish expeditions. This concerns the miraculous Jericho-like collapse of the walls of Grenoble, here oddly cast as a pagan city, after it had been besieged by Roland for seven years.)[118] Turpin inserts himself into the quasi-conclusion in two ways. First, there is a ring-narrative effect: in resuming the story of his homeward journey through southern France in Charlemagne's company with which he concludes the preceding chapter,[119] Turpin both picks up the motif of a sustained, immersive and deeply personal experience that has been inscribed on his body, and delivers himself to Vienne, the place where he has already told us in the preface he is writing his history: 'After all of this we proceeded together to Vienne, where I remained, fatigued by the scars of my wounds, the blows, the contusions, and the many misfortunes that I had suffered in Spain.'[120] Second, he recounts how he learns of Charlemagne's death in a vision. Only later does a human messenger, sent by the emperor just before he dies in accordance with an arrangement that the two men had made when they parted company in Vienne, arrive to fill in the details of Charlemagne's passing and burial.[121]

In the body of the narrative, however, the narrator's presence as a character is less in evidence than in the framing sections. Given the clear didactic purpose that runs through the text, it is unsurprising to find the narrator, sometimes in the 'editorial' first person plural, drawing out moral lessons from particular situations – though, in keeping with the rather cobbled-together quality of the text, the target audience for these uplifting *dicta* is not precisely fixed.[122] The narrator also occasionally nudges closer to the surface of the action by means of constructions that communicate inclusion in or identification with Charlemagne's forces: for example, *exercitus noster*, *tentoria nostra*, *omnes equites exercitus nostri*, and *nostri*. But these constructions are very few when set against the number of places in the text in which the actions of Charlemagne's army are narrated at some length; and, indeed, most of these references are concentrated in just one short

[118] 'Historia Turpini', c. 23, pp. 343–4; trans. Poole, *Chronicle*, pp. 83–4.

[119] 'Historia Turpini', c. 21, p. 338; trans. Poole, *Chronicle*, p. 73.

[120] 'Historia Turpini', c. 22, p. 338; trans. Poole, *Chronicle*, p. 74.

[121] 'Historia Turpini', c. 22, pp. 341–2; trans. Poole, *Chronicle*, pp. 79, 81.

[122] E.g. 'Historia Turpini', c. 7, p. 307; trans. Poole, *Chronicle*, pp. 17–18 (the proper distribution of alms for the dead); c. 8, p. 309; trans. Poole, *Chronicle*, pp. 20–1 (the need to cultivate virtues in order to fight sin); c. 13, p. 316; trans. Poole, *Chronicle*, pp. 34–5 (care for the poor and baptismal faith); c. 14, p. 317; trans. Poole, *Chronicle*, p. 37 (good works and correct belief: the first person is not used but is implied by the use of *Ecce* and the apostrophe in the second person to 'O Christian'); c. 15, p. 318; trans. Poole, *Chronicle*, p. 38 (religious who have left the world should not return to worldly affairs).

sequence.[123] Turpin appears as an actor within the storyworld at some points, but again this presence is muted. The narrator puts himself, *ego Turpinus*, in first place in his listing of the peers who accompany Charlemagne as his army sets out for Spain, but in doing so he draws particular attention to his episcopal function in preaching to the faithful, blessing, and granting absolutions, on top of which the statement that he also fought frequently with his own arms is almost in the nature of an afterthought.[124] Likewise, elsewhere in the narrative Turpin-as-character chiefly appears – particularly in the self-highlighting first person – performing actions that are both logically motivated by the immediate needs of the plot (such as it is) and congruent with his particular episcopal status: for example, his attendance at an ecclesiastical council, his consecration of a church, celebration of Mass, and burial of the dead.[125] It is noteworthy, therefore, that although the narrator invokes the *topos* of being unable to tell his story in all its great detail, he chooses not to compensate by padding out the narrative with a large number of personal appearances or reminiscences.[126]

In this way, the insistence on personal and physical experience, the fact of eyewitness, and easy proximity to the principal protagonist that is found in the bracketing passages is not translated into the body of the action-as-narrated. Two conclusions may be drawn. First, the concentration of autoptic reference within the framing passages, in a text that is, after all, confecting the past by mimicking, even caricaturing, historiographical tropes, points to the value of strategic placement; eyewitness warrant need not be invoked frequently in order for it to be effective, and for the author-compiler a little would seem to go a long way. Second, the extent to which the narrator grants himself agency within the storyworld emerges as a revealing but not decisive index of the impact of eyewitness on a text. Most of the action in the *Historia* is related in the third person as if by a very well-informed observer close to and familiar with, though not fully immersed within, the storyworld. But may Turpin the narrator be said to be 'there' in such moments, and, if so, in the same manner as he is in the minority of instances in which he announces himself overtly by means of the first person? The *Historia*, much like Suger's *Life* of Louis VI, reveals that the relationship between claimed authorial autopsy and the actions and gaze of the eyewitness-as-participant is fluid, capable of shifting many times over the course of a single narrative. This is an important lesson to carry forward into our analysis of our chosen texts.

What emerges from a consideration of eyewitness narratives such as these examples is that there is more to be gained from an examination of the workings

[123] 'Historia Turpini', c. 7, p. 307; c. 18, p. 324; trans. Poole, *Chronicle*, pp. 17, 50.

[124] 'Historia Turpini', c. 11, pp. 311–12; trans. Poole, *Chronicle*, p. 26.

[125] 'Historia Turpini', c. 19, p. 325; c. 21, pp. 334, 338; trans. Poole, *Chronicle*, pp. 53, 68, 73.

[126] 'Historia Turpini', c. 20, pp. 327–8; trans. Poole, *Chronicle*, pp. 57–8.

of the texts themselves than there is from trying to recreate the circumstances in which a historical actor might have witnessed events in the real world. We have seen with Suger's *Life* of Louis VI that there can be, or appear to be, moments of intersection between actual lived experience, Suger's personal memories, and the action narrated on the page. But we have also seen that there are many passages that recount events in which it is virtually certain, or at least highly probable, that Suger played some part, often in an important capacity, but which do not tell us so in so many words. Are there ways, then, in which we can approach eyewitness texts in a holistic manner that does not involve breaking them down into so many discrete sequences in which the role of autopsy can be judged, or guessed, episode by episode? There are as many possibilities as there are ways of subjecting a text to a close reading. In what follows, however, the favoured analytical approach is one inspired by the discipline of narratology. Narratology may be defined as the study of the poetics of narratives of all kinds or, to use a slightly imprecise but common formulation, their meaning-making operations.[127] Its origins lie in various schools of thought in linguistics, anthropology and literary study that culminated in the work of the French Structuralists in the 1960s and 70s.[128] Although the influence of structuralism as a governing intellectual framework has receded since that time, narratology has survived as a kind of useful residue. In its formative phase – the term narratology (*narratologie*) was coined by one of the leading French Structuralists, Tzvetan Todorov, in 1969 – it was an article of faith among the proponents of narratology that it was not concerned with the interpretation of texts.[129] This proved to be an unrealistically purist goal respected far more often in the breach than in the observance. And in recent years there has in any event been an expansion of scholarly attention away from what is now termed 'classical' narratology and towards narratology's

[127] The best introduction to narratology is the excellent H. P. Abbott, *The Cambridge Introduction to Narrative*, 2nd edn (Cambridge, 2008). This is a model of clarity. For another very good overview, see S. Keen, *Narrative Form*, 2nd edn (Basingstoke, 2015). See also L. Herman and B. Vervaeck, *Handbook of Narrative Analysis* (Lincoln, NE, 2005); and M. Fludernik, *An Introduction to Narratology*, trans. P. Häusler-Greenfield and M. Fludernik (Abingdon, 2009). D. Herman, M. Jahn and M.-L. Ryan (eds), *Routledge Encyclopedia of Narrative Theory* (Abingdon, 2005) is an invaluable work of reference. There are additionally several useful contributions in T. Kindt and H.-H. Müller (eds), *What Is Narratology? Questions and Answers Regarding the Status of a Theory* (Narratologia, 1; Berlin, 2003). For a clear and concise overview of the scope of narratology, see G. Prince, 'On Narrative Studies and Narrative Genres', *Poetics Today*, 11 (1990), 271–4.

[128] For the work of the French Structuralists, see J. Culler, *Structuralist Poetics: Structuralism, Linguistics and the Study of Literature* (London, 1975).

[129] See e.g. the remarks of one of the most forceful advocates of this position in G. Prince, 'Narrative Analysis and Narratology', *New Literary History*, 13 (1982), 179–88. Cf. Culler, *Structuralist Poetics*, pp. 137–9.

contribution to wider areas of interest to literary and cultural theorists such as post-colonialism and gender.[130]

This expanded engagement gets narratology away from the criticism that has often been levelled at its classical incarnation, that it is an exercise in formalist taxonomy for its own sake. It can strip down a car's engine and demonstrate how all the parts work individually and in combination, but the car never goes anywhere. Fortunately, however, this is not a problem as far as historians reading historical narratives are concerned because there *is* a destination, a purpose beyond the text, whether this is conceived in terms of the text's place in intellectual or cultural history, its contribution to a reconstruction of events, or some other goal. There is also much to be said for staying within the parameters of classical narratology. It may have been striving for interpretive neutrality largely in vain, but a consequence is that it never attached itself definitively to one theoretical fashion or school of thought. It has therefore never dated. This makes it a flexible analytical resource.[131] For the purposes of this book, the value of narratology is conceived in wholly pragmatic terms. Perhaps more than any other methodology favoured by scholars of literature in recent decades, it resonates with the ways in which historians have traditionally gone about the task of reading their narrative sources. Narratology can introduce greater precision into reading strategies that might otherwise be merely intuitive and common-sensical. It works with the grain of these strategies. And it is not intrinsically hostile or indifferent to historical inquiry in the way that some other literary approaches can seem to be.

This historian-friendly quality might at first glance seem surprising, given that narratology did not grow out of a scholarly interest in historiography at all but in fiction, in particular what Henry James termed 'loose, baggy monsters', that is nineteenth-century novels, as well as modernist and postmodernist works that subvert the norms of the traditional novel in ways that resonate with classical narratology's categories of analysis. Students of narratology have seldom given historical narrative its due.[132] In textbooks and overviews of the subject, it is striking how often historical narrative – curiously, given that a large proportion of

[130] For helpful accounts of the development of narratology and its intersections with various fields of inquiry, see D. Herman, 'Histories of Narrative Theory (I): A Genealogy of Early Developments', and M. Fludernik, 'Histories of Narrative Theory (II): From Structuralism to the Present', in J. Phelan and P. J. Rabinowitz (eds), *A Companion to Narrative Theory* (Oxford, 2005), pp. 19–35 and 36–59, respectively. See also D. Darby, 'Form and Context: An Essay in the History of Narratology', *Poetics Today*, 22 (2001), 829–52.

[131] See M. G. Bull, 'Narratological Readings of Crusade Texts', in A. J. Boas (ed.), *The Crusader World* (Abingdon, 2016), pp. 646–60.

[132] For a stimulating exception that draws to a considerable extent on narratological paradigms, see P. Carrard, *Poetics of the New History: French Historical Discourse from Braudel to Chartier* (Baltimore, 1992).

the stories told all over the world in many media and in innumerable cultures are, or purport to be, about the world as it was – is either ignored or parked in small and discrete sections. Where attempts are made to address historical writing, these sometimes consist of nothing more than summaries of the views of Hayden White, who is incorrectly termed an 'historian' or 'historiographer';[133] and what attention to history one does encounter is directed to historiographical discursive paradigms that have been current since the nineteenth century but which do not readily apply to ways of writing about the past that obtained before that time.[134] As Nicole Loraux observed in a famous article, Thucydides is not a colleague, and the same is equally true of medieval writers of history.[135]

Narratology's relative indifference to historiographical discourses contrasts, however, with the flourishing since the 1970s and 80s of the scholarly investigation of medieval historians and their texts: research that from a variety of disciplinary and methodological perspectives has deepened our understanding of medieval historical works as situated cultural artefacts which articulated discourses that neither rigidly separated what we would term 'history' and 'fiction' nor hopelessly conflated them, and which blended into many complementary areas of contemporary intellectual interest such as theology and the study of rhetoric.[136] The study of medieval historical writing is, therefore, a field

[133] See e.g. P. Cobley, *Narrative* (Abingdon, 2001), pp. 31–2.

[134] For the most comprehensive attempts to differentiate between fictional and (modern) historiographical narrative discourses, see D. Cohn, *The Distinction of Fiction* (Baltimore, 1999), esp. pp. 109–31; and L. Doležel, *Possible Worlds of Fiction and History: The Postmodern Stage* (Baltimore, 2010), esp. pp. 15–44. See also Keen, *Narrative Form*, pp. 115–23.

[135] N. Loraux, 'Thucydides Is Not a Colleague', in J. Marincola (ed.), *Greek and Roman Historiography* (Oxford, 2011), pp. 19–39 [French original published in 1980].

[136] Among many important studies, particular mention should be made of three groundbreaking works: N. F. Partner, *Serious Entertainments: The Writing of History in Twelfth-Century England* (Chicago, 1977); M. Otter, *Inventiones: Fiction and Referentiality in Twelfth-Century English Historical Writing* (Chapel Hill, NC, 1996); and Gabrielle Spiegel's collection of articles in her *The Past as Text: The Theory and Practice of Medieval Historiography* (Baltimore, 1997): see esp. 'History, Historicism, and the Social Logic of the Text', pp. 3–28. Although principally concerned with hagiographical texts, there is a great deal that is pertinent to medieval historiographers' understandings of the past in Amy Remensnyder's excellent *Remembering Kings Past: Monastic Foundation Legends in Medieval Southern France* (Ithaca, NY, 1995). Another important study is L. Ashe, *Fiction and History in England, 1066–1200* (Cambridge, 2007). For helpful discussions of many key issues, see S. Fleischmann, 'On the Representation of History and Fiction in the Middle Ages', *History and Theory*, 22 (1983), 278–310; P. Johanek, 'Die Wahrheit der mittelalterlichen Historiographen', in F. P. Knapp and M. Niesner (eds), *Historisches und fiktionales Erzählen im Mittelalter* (Schriften der Literaturwissenschaft, 19; Berlin, 2002), pp. 9–25; and S. Foot, 'Finding the Meaning of Form: Narrative in Annals and

sensitive to the value of interdisciplinary and methodological breadth; and the greater application to it of narratological approaches would complement that tradition.[137] In order to appreciate the potential gains, one has only to consider narratology's significant impact on the recent study of ancient Greek and Roman historiography. When reading some of the narratology-driven work done on ancient texts, one sometimes encounters a slippage between the ambition of the stated theoretical framework and the precision of its application to specifics, as the focus edges away from the internal workings of the text in question to considerations of what the author meant or knew, or how an event that the text narrates actually played out in practice. But the gains in understanding have nonetheless been considerable, and they offer a number of valuable pointers to those who work on medieval historiography.[138]

Chronicles', and M. Otter, 'Functions of Fiction in Historical Writing', in N. F. Partner (ed.), *Writing Medieval History* (London, 2005), pp. 88–108 and 109–30, respectively.

[137] The most valuable explorations of the narratology of medieval historiographical texts have been undertaken by Sophie Marnette: see esp. her *Narrateur et points de vue dans la littérature française médiévale: Une approche linguistique* (Bern, 1998), many of the conclusions of which are summarized in her 'Narrateur et points de vue dans les chroniques médiévales: une approche linguistique', in E. S. Kooper (ed.), *The Medieval Chronicle: Proceedings of the 1st International Conference on the Medieval Chronicle, Driebergen/Utrecht 13–16 July 1996* (Costerus New Series 120; Amsterdam, 1999), pp. 174–90. See also the same author's 'The Experiencing Self and the Narrating Self in Medieval Chronicles', in V. Greene (ed.), *The Medieval Author in Medieval French Literature* (Basingstoke, 2006), pp. 117–36. While the present book differs from Marnette's studies with respect to the definition and application of certain key narratological concepts, as well as in its thematic emphases, it is important to acknowledge the value of this body of work as a source of inspiration.

[138] A leading figure in the application of narratological approaches to ancient texts has been Irene de Jong: see her ground-breaking studies *A Narratological Commentary on the Odyssey* (Cambridge, 2001), and *Narrators and Focalizers: The Presentation of the Story in the* Iliad, 2nd edn (London, 2004). De Jong has written the best introduction to narratology's value for the study of ancient texts in *Narratology and Classics: A Practical Guide* (Oxford, 2014), esp. pp. 167–95 on historiography. (But note that some of her approaches, inspired by the work of theorist Mieke Bal, differ from those adopted here.) For an influential early study, see S. Hornblower, 'Narratology and Narrative Techniques in Thucydides', in S. Hornblower (ed.), *Greek Historiography* (Oxford, 1994), pp. 131–66. In addition to the treatment of narratological ideas in the useful overviews of ancient historiography by Marincola, *Authority and Tradition* and Pitcher, *Writing Ancient History*, see the in-depth applications in e.g. T. C. B. Rood, *Thucydides: Narrative and Explanation* (Oxford, 1998); C. J. Dewald, *Thucydides' War Narrative: A Structural Study* (Berkeley, 2005); E. Baragwanath, *Motivation and Narrative in Herodotus* (Oxford, 2008); and A. C. Purves, *Space and Time in Greek Narrative* (Cambridge, 2010). For insightful case studies, see C. S. Kraus, 'Caesar's Account of the Battle of Massilia (*BC* 1.34–2.22): Some Historiographical and Narratological Approaches', in J. Marincola (ed.), *A Companion to Greek and Roman Historiography* (Chichester, 2011), pp. 371–8; C. B. R. Pelling, 'Seeing Through

As the work on ancient historical texts makes clear, narratology is neither an analytical magic bullet nor an approach that excludes other complementary readings. Nor is it a zero-sum choice, something that must be applied whole cloth or not at all.[139] Narratology is, rather, a tool that lends itself to being used selectively. It suggests many possible approaches: for example, how does a narrative handle time, and by what means is the agency of characters, or actants, activated within the storyworld? This book, however, does not attempt to apply narratology across the board, although several of its concepts will crop up at various points. In the following discussion, three narratological categories of analysis in particular will be singled out as germane to an understanding of autopsy's contributions to medieval historiographical texts' meaning-making. The first and most fundamental is the figure of the narrator. The narrator may be defined as the proximate source of a narrative, that is to say the putative agent, sometimes termed the 'instance', that assumes responsibility for telling the story in the form in which it presents itself.[140] The narrator's brief extends beyond introducing the storyworld's actants and setting; he/she has epistemological and ethical control over the shaping of the story. Narrators come in numerous shapes and sizes, which means that it is unnecessary to go into the fine detail of the many sub-categories that have been identified. Several incarnations of the narrator figure that theorists

Caesar's Eyes: Focalisation and Interpretation', in J. Grethlein and A. Rengakos (eds), *Narratology and Interpretation: The Content of Narrative Form in Ancient Literature* (Berlin, 2009), pp. 507–26. For a robust reaction against the application of 'theory' to the study of Roman historiography – narratology would seem to represent one of its 'milder' forms – see J. E. Lendon, 'Historians Without History: Against Roman Historiography', in A. Feldherr (ed.), *The Cambridge Companion to the Roman Historians* (Cambridge, 2009), pp. 41–61. For an application of narratological insights to biblical narrative, and a remarkably insightful work in general, see M. Sternberg, *The Poetics of Biblical Narrative: Ideological Literature and the Drama of Reading* (Bloomington, IN, 1985).

[139] For an excellent demonstration of the ways in which narratological concepts may be selectively and productively combined with other approaches, see M. A. Flower, *Xenophon's* Anabasis, *or* The Expedition of Cyrus (Oxford, 2012). Flower's study is a model analysis of a premodern work of history that is much to be recommended. See also the interesting blend of methodological angles in A. M. Riggsby, *Caesar in Gaul and Rome: War in Words* (Austin, TX, 2006).

[140] For discussions of the narrator, see Abbott, *Cambridge Introduction*, pp. 68–77; Keen, *Narrative Form*, pp. 33–55; D. Herman, J. Phelan, P. J. Rabinowitz, B. Richardson and R. Warhol, *Narrative Theory: Core Concepts and Critical Debates* (Columbus, OH, 2012), pp. 29–56. For an excellent analysis of what the narrator is and does, see M.-L. Ryan, 'The Narratorial Functions: Breaking Down a Theoretical Primitive', *Narrative*, 9 (2001), 146–52. For quite different, and sceptical, approaches, see R. Walsh, 'Who Is the Narrator?', *Poetics Today*, 18 (1997), 495–513; G. Currie, *Narratives and Narrators: A Philosophy of Stories* (Oxford, 2010), esp. pp. 65–85.

have codified simply do not crop up in historical writing, ancient, medieval or modern, but certain types are clearly relevant.

For example, to apply the rather cumbersome but useful taxonomies that take their inspiration from one of the founding figures of narratology, Gérard Genette, narrators can be homodiegetic, situated within the world of the story that they narrate, or heterodiegetic, positioned outside it.[141] This distinction has obvious implications for our understanding of the interfaces between an author's experience and the manner of his or her telling of it. Is the narrator detached from the action, even though we might suspect that much of the author's knowledge of what happened is based on autopsy, or is the narrator immersed within the story-world, his or her perceptions of what is going on corresponding to or invoking the author's recollections of his or her eyewitness experiences? Narrators' epistemological reach into the storyworld, as evident, for example, in the extent to which they can drill into characters' minds and tell what they are thinking, or know what is happening simultaneously in more than one place, can be what is often called omniscient (though some theorists have queried the validity of this term).[142] Or it can replicate the perceptual and epistemological constraints of an individual engaged in normal human interaction. As we shall see, medieval historiographical narrators tend to occupy various intermediate positions, at least most of the time. And as we shall also see, narratorial positioning along the continuum between omniscience and situatedness has an important bearing on the extent to which eyewitness texts integrate the act of eyewitnessing itself into the narrated action, rather than simply drawing upon the author's memories of her or his experiences when constructing a version of events.

Up to this point, the discussion has mostly followed conventional usage in loosely applying the terms 'author' and 'authorial' to a range of historical and textual situations. Henceforth, we need to be more precise. The discussion above of Suger's *Life* of Louis VI in some places ran together the historical, flesh-and-blood Suger who was born in 1081, became abbot of St-Denis and died in 1151; the Suger who specifically authored the *Life* among the many other things that he did over the course of his lifetime; the Suger who is a protagonist in some, but not most, of the events that the *Life* recounts; and the Suger we 'hear' throughout the text telling us the story. All four are 'Suger', and to some extent, therefore, overlap.

[141] See G. Genette, *Narrative Discourse: An Essay in Method*, trans. J. E. Lewin (Ithaca, NY, 1980), pp. 212–59. The term 'intradiegetic' is usually applied to the situation of the narrator of a nested narrative vis-à-vis the narrator of the narrative that frames it; but in what follows it will be used as, in effect, an intensifier of 'homodiegetic' in relation to those situations in which the narrator-as-character is clearly situated in or very close to the action, as opposed to simply occupying some unspecified vantage point within the storyworld.

[142] For a thoughtful critique of the notion of omniscience, see J. Culler, *The Literary in Theory* (Stanford, 2007), pp. 183–201.

By appealing to the idea of the narrator, however, we can isolate the fourth Suger on this list. If we do so, several questions emerge. In the first place, is this a useful move? Some theorists query whether the narrator can meaningfully be detached from the figure of the author. And even if we concede that some formal distinction is helpful in certain cases, does not the distance between author and narrator shrink to vanishing point in those narratives that have an autobiographical dimension or speak, in some places at any rate, in the first person? In such instances, are we not simply in the presence of the flesh-and-blood author's experiences decanted onto the page, or a sort of transcription of what we would hear if the author were speaking to us face to face? Moreover, is not the figure of the narrator a critical sleight of hand, a way of talking in quasi-anthropomorphic terms about the signs of creative agency and authorial intentionality that one detects within a text while paying lip service to modern-day literary scholarship's aversion to the idea of the author as the point of origin of a work's meaning and aesthetic qualities? Even if one does not want to go as far as declaring the author dead, is not the narrator merely a device, interpretively speaking, to keep her or him at a safe distance while not falling into the trap of supposing that texts somehow write themselves?

All these objections have some merit. But in what follows it will be argued that the distinction between the figures of the author and the narrator has a practical value grounded in the ways in which our target texts actually go about the business of telling their stories – how, in other words, they make meaning.[143] The narrators of medieval eyewitness historiographical texts seldom achieve the subtle interplay between the self-as-character and the narratorial voice, the third and fourth Sugers, that Jonas Grethlein has identified in Xenophon's *Anabasis*: here Xenophon the character is distanced from the narrator (and by extension Xenophon the author, the equivalent of the second Suger) by being referred to in the third person and by using his several long speeches to recap and comment upon action that the narrator has already recounted.[144] The figure of the narrator

[143] In what follows, the word 'story' will mostly be used in its technical narratological sense as the basic, paraphraseable matter, the events 'as they happened', in contradistinction to the discursive packaging of its material by the narrative. This important distinction is not aided by the confusing range of terms that various theorists have proposed for story and related concepts: for a helpful clarification, see Keen, *Narrative Form*, pp. 74–83. The boundaries between the stories as they are present within historiographical texts such as ours and the extratextual reality that our sources globally permit us to reconstruct are fuzzy, and not always carefully policed by historians, but they are nonetheless central to an understanding of such texts as world-making, not simply world-reflecting, exercises.

[144] J. Grethlein, 'Xenophon's *Anabasis* from Character to Narrator', *Journal of Hellenic Studies*, 132 (2012), 23–40. For the narrator in this text, see also P. J. Bradley, 'Irony and the Narrator in Xenophon's *Anabasis*', in E. I. Tylawsky and C. G. Weiss (eds), *Essays in Honor of Gordon Williams* (New Haven, 2001), pp. 59–84; V. J. Gray, 'Xenophon', in I. J. F. de Jong, R. Nünlist and A. M. Bowie (eds), *Narrators,*

is nonetheless a fundamental part of the communicative techniques of this study's chosen texts. It is not a question of the author somehow pretending to be someone or something else. Nor is the narrator a *homuncula/us* at large somewhere inside the pages of a text. The narrator is simply, if pervasively, a textual effect, which is why some theorists prefer to apply depersonalizing labels such as 'narratorial voice' or 'narratorial instance' and to use the pronoun 'it'.

In what follows, such terms are sometimes used, but simply to ring the changes, not in a purist vein; for although the narrator is not a real person, the effects it achieves work *as if* it were the voice of a human interlocutor. Suger the narrator must be carefully distinguished from Suger the author and Suger the flesh-and-blood abbot. But he, or it, has an inescapable anthropomorphic quality that has a lot to do with our tendency to model written texts' illocutionary impact, in other words what we think makes them work as exercises in communication, on the experience of face-to-face conversation. This is the metaphorical connection we invoke when, for example, we ask of a particular passage 'What is Suger *saying* here?' It is also important to remember that the narrating instance does not need to be fixed over the course of a single narrative: it can shift back and forth between homodiegetic and heterodiegetic positions; and when in homodiegetic mode it can individuate itself by means of the first person singular, conjuring up the sense of a particular site of human agency and interiority looking out on the world around it, or it can immerse itself in a group by means of the first person plural. Most historical narratives – our sample texts included – are sufficiently coherent and internally consistent to allow us to postulate a single 'master-narrator' who presides over the whole telling, is always 'there', but can nonetheless shift narratorial modes. Such a narrator can align itself with the personal circumstances of the figure of the author in a prologue, but then abruptly switch to near-omniscient sweeps across space and time as soon as the action proper begins. It can even seem to delegate portions of the narration to other parties, as when a speech or letter is quoted directly.

The value of focusing our attention on our texts' narrators further emerges from the distinction between the narrator and another narratological category, the implied author. This latter term was first coined by Wayne Booth in his landmark study *The Rhetoric of Fiction* to express the 'second self' that a real author projects onto a text; it functions as the site of the values and norms that the author has selected to govern the world that the narrative fashions.[145] The concept has been the subject of much debate.[146] Is it something that the real author plants in a

Narratees, and Narratives in Ancient Greek Literature (Studies in Ancient Greek Narrative, 1; Leiden, 2004), pp. 129–46.

[145] W. C. Booth, *The Rhetoric of Fiction*, 2nd edn (Chicago, 1983), pp. 67–86, esp. 70–7.

[146] For perhaps the most effective defence of the concept of the implied author, see S. Chatman, *Coming to Terms: The Rhetoric of Narrative in Fiction and Film* (Ithaca,

text as a sort of *alter ego*, which is how Booth imagined it in at least some of his formulations, or is it an artefact of the reader's reception of the text, a complex of inferences that cumulatively suggest that a creative human agency of a particular sort is responsible for what one is reading? Either way – and because the implied author is present within the text and is not a real person, there is nothing to stop he/she/it from being both, depending on context – the notion of the implied author is valuable because it inserts itself between the real author and the narrator in the text's communicative chain.[147] It thereby helps to point up the biographist short-cuts to which readings of historiographical texts, eyewitness texts in particular, are prey. One often comes upon a statement to the effect that most or all of what we are in a position to know about a given author must be inferred from the text. One also encounters a form of shorthand along the lines of 'William of Tyre is our best source for the history of the twelfth-century Latin East'. That is to say, we look for real authors inside texts; and we anthropomorphize sources by treating them like people.

It is true that certain amounts of biographical information can be deduced from texts more often than not. But this is often pushed too far to become the basis of a circular argument in which an appeal is made to the putative circumstances and intentions of the real author, which assume the status of extra-textual points of reference, in order to explicate the nature of the text itself. A good case in point is the figure of the 'simple knight' that has long hung over discussion of the *Gesta Francorum et aliorum Hierosolimitanorum* that was mentioned earlier. The belief that this work – or perhaps a prior text very close to it – was written by a lower-level knight who went on the crusade gained traction in the nineteenth century thanks to the pioneering work of Heinrich von Sybel and Heinrich Hagenmeyer.[148] As is well known, and as we saw above, the *Gesta*, or a text very

NY, 1990), pp. 74–89. The debates surrounding the implied author are now comprehensively surveyed in T. Kindt and H.-H. Müller, *The Implied Author: Concept and Controversy* (Narratologia, 9; Berlin, 2006).

[147] For the classic application of a communication-theory paradigm to narrative, modelling a chain of communication from real author to real reader via intermediate quasi-anthropomorphic instances with a text, see S. Chatman, *Story and Discourse: Narrative Structure in Fiction and Film* (Ithaca, NY, 1978), pp. 147–51.

[148] H. von Sybel, *Geschichte des ersten Kreuzzugs* (Düsseldorf, 1841), pp. 22–32; *Anonymi Gesta Francorum et aliorum Hierosolimitanorum*, ed. H. Hagenmeyer (Heidelberg, 1890), pp. 1–10, 11–12, 21, 36–7, 39. This view of the author was popularized for English-speaking readers by Rosalind Hill's 1962 edition: see *Gesta Francorum et aliorum Hierosolimitanorum*, ed. and trans. R. M. T. Hill [with R. A. B. Mynors] (London, 1962), pp. xi–xvi. For an effective criticism of this position, see C. Morris, 'The *Gesta Francorum* as Narrative History', *Reading Medieval Studies*, 19 (1993), 55–71. Cf. K. B. Wolf, 'Crusade and Narrative: Bohemond and the *Gesta Francorum*', *Journal of Medieval History*, 17 (1991), 207–16, esp. 207–8. The old view continues, however, to receive support: see e.g. C. Kostick, 'A Further Discussion

like it, attracted the ire of Baldric of Bourgeuil, Robert the Monk and Guibert of Nogent for what they believed were its stylistic shortcomings, a deficiency which compounded its perceived lack of theological sophistication. This unusual and thus seemingly authoritative chorus of disapproval on the part of writers acting independently of one another (though this is debatable), when combined with the currency of the well-worn cliché (which the narrator of the *Gesta* does not in fact invoke) that a soldier-author's no-frills style is a sure sign of authenticity, made it seem obvious that the text was the work of a knight below the level of the crusade's aristocratic elite. True, he differed from Xenophon and Caesar – authors whose own 'simple' prose traditionally commended their war narratives to schoolteachers as starter texts for those learning Greek and Latin, respectively – in not being a commander figure. But his autoptic gaze on the action was no less direct than theirs. Thus the simple nature of the *Gesta* as a piece of writing was to be explained by its author's simple-knight-ness.

This has proved a tenacious view, and it still has adherents, despite the fact that the *Gesta* is a far more sophisticated text than its reputation would suggest. True, it is not grounded in a wide range of rhetorical techniques, though it neatly deploys the effects of *sermo facilis* such as alliteration, assonance and rhyme, as well as rhythmic *cursus*. But it is built on an extensive knowledge of biblical diction that seems to capture the level of routine, work-a-day Latinity, the mesolect, of middle-ranking clergy who seldom ventured into the realms of historiographical authorship and so did not routinely expose themselves to the sort of snobbish disapproval on the part of the literary elite that we find voiced by Baldric, Robert and Guibert. The key point is this: that the more one digs into the internal workings of the text of the *Gesta*, the less the question of the personal circumstances of the real author seems to matter. The real author of the *Gesta* (if it was in fact just one man) is simply the person – cleric, layman or someone whose experiences blended those two statuses – who was capable of writing that particular text, no more, no less. It was the implied author, or rather one possible version of him created in the image of their prior assumptions, that von Sybel and Hagenmeyer thought they were spotting when they persuaded themselves they had located traces of the flesh-and-blood author within the text. And the narrator, who actually gets to tell the story, is neither of these. What this distinction helps to show is that, as far as its application to medieval historical texts is concerned, the value of the narrator as a category of analysis does not reside in its being a vehicle for theoretical dogmatism, a way of corralling historiographical texts into a particular methodological or conceptual space. Rather, it is a pragmatic tool serving practical ends. It helps us to delve into the world-making, story-telling complexities of texts without sliding into biographism, that is to say the pull

on the Authorship of the *Gesta Francorum*', *Reading Medieval Studies*, 35 (2009), 1–14.

towards tracking everything one finds back to the (real) author and what she or he 'must have' meant or thought. Authors write texts, of course, and have intentions and aims for them, but narrators tell stories; and it is in the manner of the telling, not in what we can reconstruct or speculate about the author's actual circumstances, that we shall find most of the evidence for the impact of eyewitnessing on our so-called eyewitness texts.

The second important narratological concept is focalization.[149] This has generated a great deal of debate and controversy, and much about it remains obscure or confusing; but it is also, perhaps, the most significant category for an understanding of so-called 'eyewitness' texts. Definitions of focalization vary according to the positions on it taken by theorists. In essence, however, it comes down to the manner in which the narrator is granted access to information about the storyworld. Put another way, it is the extent of the narrator's mobilization of the intricate swirl of perceptions, ideas, motivations and feelings which can be imputed to the agents who inhabit the narrative's represented world. One such possible narratorial stance is what is sometimes termed omniscience and/or omnipresence; the narrator is equipped to traverse time and space at will and to penetrate the minds of characters. In practice the demands of narrative economy require the omniscient and omnipresent narrator to be sparing in her/his mobilization of these qualities. Nonetheless such a narrator is constantly implying that there are in principle no boundaries to her/his knowledge of what goes on in the storyworld and why it happens, even if the narrated action necessarily confines itself to small subsets of everything the narrator could in principle say and to delimited spatio-temporal co-ordinates. Access to such 'god-like' narratorial mastery of the storyworld, moreover, is not a zero-sum proposition, for a narrator is free to imply or explicitly acknowledge boundaries that limit what she/he can know but which still significantly exceed the capabilities of the agents inside the narrative universe.

Alternatively, the narrator's understanding of the world can be presented as if it were co-extensive with that of one or more of the characters, meaning that it is of necessity constrained by the limitations of human situatedness with which we are familiar from the experience of our day-to-day lives. We cannot traverse time and space at will, and we cannot drill into other people's heads, though we may draw inferences about their mindstuff with varying degrees of confidence. In this form of focalization, the character or characters through whose consciousness the narrator presents the world are seldom mere perceiving machines, for the

[149] See M. Jahn, 'Focalization', in D. Herman (ed.), *The Cambridge Companion to Narrative* (Cambridge, 2007), pp. 94–108 for a helpful discussion. See also Herman and Vervaeck, *Handbook*, pp. 70–80; Keen, *Narrative Form*, pp. 46–7; M. Jahn, 'Focalization', in Herman, Jahn and Ryan (eds), *Routledge Encyclopedia of Narrative Theory*, pp. 173–7.

act of perception almost always implies apperception – a level of self-awareness and understanding that is attained when raw sensory input is filtered through the various cognitive assumptions and cultural scripts that people use to make sense of the world, and which the narrator is in effect co-opting when focalization is routed through one or more characters' minds. One often encounters this form of focalization when first-person narrators are recounting what befell them as principals in their storyworld. But even in narratives that assume such an autobiographical form, unless the distance between the narrative now and the narrating now is collapsed by devices, such as constant use of the present tense, that are more at home in some modern fiction than in premodern historiographical discourses – 'I open the door, stop, look inside and call out' – there will always be some degree of dissonance or separation between the I-as-character focalizing within the action-as-narrated, and the narrating I who is subsequently reporting that act of focalization. This is so even when the stated or implied interval between the action and the narration is quite brief. An important question to be asked of the texts such as those studied in this volume is, therefore, the extent to which, when they are in overtly autobiographical mode (which is only a minority of the time), narrators deploy focalization to prioritize the experience of the first-person character in the narrative moment, or else use that experience as a kind of stepping-stone to a more capacious understanding of the narrated action that also draws on subsequent reflection and information that had not been available at the time. That is to say, how far do eyewitness narrators capture the quality of their moment-by-moment perceptions as an unfolding experience, or are they wise after the fact in ways that dilute the contribution of their personal eyewitness to their larger understanding of what they are narrating?

A third form of focalization attempts to sever the connection between perception and apperception by limiting the narrated action to the externals of what would be registered by, in effect, a movie camera pointed at the action, and by disavowing any narratorial knowledge or even inferences or guesses about what is going on inside characters' heads. Adverbs, relative clauses and other devices for making narratorial judgements and hinting at character motivation are stripped away. In practice, this narratorial posture of complete disinterest and disengagement is difficult to sustain for longer than a few sentences because the richness of language and behavioural schemata force their way up through the surface of the minimalistic affect. For example, the narrator's choice of one particular verb to denote a character's action as against various closely synonymous options may implicitly guide the reader's response, as will the facility for filling narrative gaps by appeal to scripts relevant to the situation in which the characters find themselves. Some sort of narratorial intervention, however camouflaged, must always be at work, it seems. Even very baldly articulated narratives, moreover, invite some reflection on the motivations and purposes of the characters within them.

In this connection, it is interesting to note that many studies have shown that test subjects routinely impute human-like states of mind to the movements of even very simple objects. In a famous early experiment, for example, Fritz Heider and Marianne Simmel showed their subjects a short animated film in which three shapes – two triangles and a circle – move around a mostly blank field. Not only did several viewers anthropomorphize the three shapes by imputing to them self-awareness, goals and desires, they also explained what they had seen in narrative terms.[150] The anthropomorphized shapes were given genders and backstories. Their interactions were sometimes described as the playing out of a love triangle in which the aggressive and covetous larger triangle, imagined as a male, tries but fails to assault the female circle, who is eventually rescued by her preferred partner, the smaller triangle. Similar effects are present in several of the pioneering experiments of Albert Michotte into the perception of causality: again, subjects often read human-like states of mind, behaviours and interactions into the movements of simple geometric shapes.[151] Our ability to construct narratives from such exiguous materials underpins the artifice of the detached narratorial posture that we are considering. It is typically associated with some modernist writing such as the work of Ernest Hemingway as well as mid-twentieth-century hard-boiled detective fiction. But it is also to be found in the very different discursive environment of medieval historiography, particularly when actions are narrated in a paratactic fashion with little or no subordination of ideas, narratorial judgements or even overt references to the actors' subjectivity and goal-directness. In such a narrative universe X happens, then Y happens, then Z, no more, no less. Typically associated with annalistic writing – though, as Sarah Foot has shown, the 'jerky', discontinuous feel of many annal sequences belies a greater degree of narrativity than might at first be apparent[152] – this type of focalization in fact crops up in all forms of historiographical texts, including those which we would categorize as eyewitness. The question therefore arises whether, in passages of stripped-down, 'camera eye' narration, the narrator of an eyewitness narrative is masking or bypassing the validating work of his/her autoptic gaze, or conversely whether this effect in fact seeks to capture something of the subjective experience of the perception of events.

The three forms of narratorial relationship to the storyworld discussed above correspond to the threefold schema proposed by Gérard Genette, the scholar

[150] F. Heider and M. Simmel, 'An Experimental Study of Apparent Behavior', *American Journal of Psychology*, 57 (1944), 243–59. Cf. B. J. Scholl and P. D. Tremoulet, 'Perceptual Causality and Animacy', *Trends in Cognitive Sciences*, 4 (2000), 299–309. See also B. Boyd, *On the Origin of Stories: Evolution, Cognition, and Fiction* (Cambridge, MA, 2009), pp. 132–58.

[151] A. Michotte, *The Perception of Causality*, trans. T. R. Miles and E. Miles (London, 1963).

[152] Foot, 'Finding the Meaning of Form', pp. 88–108.

whose work introduced the concept of focalization into narratological debate.[153] They are, respectively, what Genette termed zero- or non-focalization, internal focalization and external focalization. Genette's aim was to clarify a distinction that he argued had been confused by earlier theorists such as Wayne Booth between information about the storyworld that is mediated by a perceiving actor within the diegesis, and the work of the narrator. These functions can sometimes overlap, as when a first-person narrator makes a statement such as 'I saw her enter the room'. But Genette was right to insist on the formal distinction between what Seymour Chatman, one of Genette's most thoughtful followers, has termed 'slant', the narrator's attitudes towards the storyworld and the actors who populate it, and 'filter', the perceptions, emotions and other mental states that one or more characters experience in ways that inflect how the storyworld is presented.[154] In coining the term focalization Genette's principal focus was on the relationship that the narrator establishes with the information that the narrative communicates, not on the perceptual actions performed by narrative agents as such. But his elegant distinction between 'he who sees' and 'he who tells' has naturally drawn theorists' attention to the functions of perceiving characters, with the result that the idea of focalization is now generally applied not only to certain moves on the part of the narrator but also to the perceptions of characters: they themselves 'focalize' and may be termed 'focalizers'.[155] Although Genette's position is that such characters are simply the means by which the narrator achieves certain focalization effects, the extension of the concept of focalization along the lines of Chatman's slant/filter distinction is very helpful when considering texts such as ours in which, as we shall see, seeing and other forms of perception are among the most frequently reported actions that characters perform.

Since Genette, theorists have contested and revised his model in various ways. For example, Shlomith Rimmon-Kenan has made an important intervention in pointing out that if focalization is to mean anything more than mere sensory perception, it must be extended to include what she terms various 'facets', the focalizing agent's cognitive, psychological, emotional, ideological

[153] Genette, *Narrative Discourse*, pp. 185–98.

[154] See S. Chatman, 'Characters and Narrators: Filter, Center, Slant, and Interest-Focus', *Poetics Today*, 7 (1986), 189–204; *idem*, *Coming to Terms*, pp. 139–60.

[155] For a somewhat different approach, one that differentiates between focalization and the characters' 'gaze', see J. Davidson, 'The Gaze in Polybius' *Histories*', *Journal of Roman Studies*, 81 (1991), 10–24, esp. 10–11. For a succinct statement on this matter by Franz Stanzel, whose work remains influential among continental scholars, see his 'Teller-Characters and Reflector-Characters in Narrative Theory', *Poetics Today*, 2 (1981), 5–15. See also W. F. Edmiston, 'Focalization and the First-Person Narrator: A Revision of the Theory', *Poetics Today*, 10 (1989), 729–44.

and spatio-temporal orientations that govern his or her relationship to the narrated world.[156] Probably the most influential, but also most contentious, critic of Genette has been Mieke Bal.[157] For Bal, Genette's notions of zero- or non-focalization and the dispassionate, detached observational affect of external focalization are both misleading: focalization, as she understands it, informs every narrative utterance because it amounts to the logical corollary, perhaps even the enabling precondition, of the narrator's ability to narrate events in the first place. That is to say, all types of narrator, not just those placed homodiegetically inside the storyworld, should be imagined as perceiving what they are narrating from a kind of line-of-sight vantage point. They are always focalizing, and to narrate is to focalize. One can see some merit in this more expansive formulation because it responds to the sense conveyed by most verbal narratives most of the time that even the zero- or external focalizing narrator, to adopt Genette's terms, is situated in some sort of spatial relation to the diegesis; even if this 'viewing position' is only very hazily evoked, it feels more specific than the boundless sweep of an all-seeing, omnipresent eye.[158] This putative positioning is often fixed, even if only approximately, by what in linguistics are termed 'deictic shifters' – words and phrases with denotational meanings that can only be established with reference to the perceptual and situational context in which the speaker, who occupies the 'deictic centre', makes a given utterance. Examples include the pairs *here/there*, *this/that*, *bring/take* and *come/go*. Bal's approach also speaks to readers' instinctive anthropomorphization of the narratorial function: it seems as if some*one* is indeed addressing us in a written text, a response that does much to explain the frequent conflation of author and narrator that we have noted. If the narrator in some sense has, or at least approximates to, the attributes of a real person, it seems natural to

[156] S. Rimmon-Kenan, *Narrative Fiction: Contemporary Poetics*, 2nd edn (Abingdon, 2002), pp. 72–86.

[157] See M. Bal, *Narratology: Introduction to the Theory of Narrative*, 3rd edn (Toronto, 2009), pp. 145–65. For Genette's response to Bal's critique, see his *Narrative Discourse Revisited*, trans. J. E. Lewin (Ithaca, NY, 1988), pp. 72–8. For an excellent discussion of Genette's and Bal's respective views, which is broadly sympathetic to the former, see W. Nelles, 'Getting Focalization into Focus', *Poetics Today*, 11 (1990), 365–82. See also the insightful remarks, again broadly supportive of Genette as against Bal, in Rood, *Thucydides*, pp. 11–14, 294–6. Cf. W. Bronzwaer, 'Mieke Bal's Concept of Focalization: A Critical Note', *Poetics Today*, 2 (1981), 193–201; G. Nieragden, 'Focalization and Narration: Theoretical and Terminological Refinements', *Poetics Today*, 23 (2002), 685–97. The volume in the Narratologia series devoted to this question contains a number of useful studies: P. Hühn, W. Schmid and J. Schönert (eds), *Point of View, Perspective, and Focalization: Modeling Mediation in Narrative* (Narratologia, 17; Berlin, 2009). See esp. U. Margolin, 'Focalization: Where Do We Go from Here?', pp. 41–57; and T. Jesch and M. Stein, 'Perspectivization and Focalization: Two Concepts – One Meaning? An Attempt at Conceptual Differentiation', pp. 59–77.

[158] Cf. Chatman, *Story and Discourse*, pp. 101–7.

imagine her or him situated within or adjacent to, and engaged in perceiving, the storyworld.

As some critics have noted, however, Bal's generous understanding of focalization tends to treat verbal narratives as if they were pictures or films. Just because readers or listeners of verbal narratives often respond to what they are reading or hearing by visualizing elements of the diegesis and the actions of the characters within it – we speak of the 'mind's eye', after all – it does not follow that pictorial and verbal narratives are the same. More fundamentally, Bal's formulation can be accused of diluting the concept of focalization to the point of redundancy by making it simply co-extensive with, or wholly subsumed by, the act of narration.[159] In the discussion that follows, therefore, Bal's idea of a 'narrator-focalizer' will be adopted but applied only selectively in order to avoid this risk of superfluity. The concept comes into play most helpfully in those passages, to be found to a greater or lesser extent in all our target texts, in which the narrators narrate sequences of action (for example the impressive embarkation of a fleet) or describe scenes (such as the notable sights of Constantinople) in terms that nudge them closer than is typical of their routine narratorial register to the situated experience of a witness engaged in the act of perceiving. That is to say, even in passages in which the narratorial mode is zero- or external focalization, and the narrator is therefore, at least for the purposes of these sequences, heterodiegetic, the narrator may be said to be 'breaking cover' by speaking in terms redolent of a homodiegetic narrator drawing upon his or her memory of a given action or scene. In such circumstances, the narrator does not say 'I saw', but this is implied to a greater or lesser extent. Quasi-homodiegetic narration of this sort is evident in many places and in varying degrees of intensity over the course of all of our texts. Moreover, as we shall see, passages in which particular attention is drawn to the sights and sounds of the diegesis crop up often enough to suggest that they represent narratorial strategies. They therefore raise interesting questions about the extent to which the narrators in eyewitness texts are able to evoke or mimic autoptic experience without recourse to the obvious device of positioning themselves homodiegetically within the action and expressly placing themselves in perceptual situations. How far, in other words, can autopsy 'bleed out' out into narrative modes that hint at or gesture towards the operation of eyewitness memory but do not invoke it overtly?

A further criticism of Bal's critique of Genette is that her approach to internal focalization, that is to say the focalization performed by characters within the storyworld, comes close to saying that focalization is a quality or function that

[159] A point raised but not developed by Rimmon-Kenan, *Narrative Fiction*, p. 86. But see J. Phelan, 'Why Narrators Can Be Focalizers – and Why It Matters', in W. van Peer and S. Chatman (eds), *New Perspectives on Narrative Perspective* (Albany, NY, 2001), pp. 51–64.

attends every action performed by every character, not just when he or she is expressly described in the act of perceiving. Like Bal's approach to the narrator-focalizer, the opening up of the scope of agent focalization also has some merit, in that it chimes with the common-sense assumption that all human actions, with the exception of autonomic bodily operations such as breathing and blinking, physical reflexes, and the involuntary movements of people in states of unconsciousness, must be accompanied by some level of self-awareness on the agent's part. This consciousness need not amount to intense concentration directed towards the performance of the action in question; it might be nothing more than distracted inattentiveness, absent-mindedness or 'highway hypnosis'. But some measure of cognitive activity always implicitly attaches to the performance of actions, however superfluous or banal it would be for a narrator to say so. So when, for example, a text states that an army crossed over a bridge, we build into our understanding of this event not just a mental image of the soldiers' physical movements through space but also an assumption of self-awareness and sensory perception on their part. In Bal's terms, they focalize their way across the bridge.

As with Bal's running together of narration and focalization, however, the opening out of character focalization to become the accompaniment of all conscious action risks diluting the concept to the point of redundancy. In the following chapters, therefore, we shall limit discussion of focalizing characters to those cases in which the narrator either expressly states or clearly implies that one or more actors perceived, for the most part by means of sight, someone or something in the represented world. This approach might seem to limit our field of enquiry, but it in fact works nicely with the grain of our material, for the verb 'to see' – *videre* in Latin, *veoir* in Old French – and similar terms appear many times. It is quite possible, in fact, that they are the single most common action verbs in our target texts. Seeing, and to a lesser extent hearing, are actions performed by all sorts of characters, including central protagonists of whom the narrator's 'slant' approves, antagonists for whom the narrator has no sympathy, and more or less peripheral actors. It is also done by collectivities, though this raises interesting questions about whether focalization of this sort is qualitatively anything more than an economical way of expressing the idea that the individual members of a group each have the same or very similar focalizing experiences.

It might be argued, however, that the sheer frequency of verbs expressing the act of seeing and other forms of perception militates against their significance as markers of focalization. Are not seeing and hearing, and for that matter the workings of the other senses, just like the great many other things that agents get to do inside the storyworld, and so must some particular significance be sought in every reference to such actions?[160] The best way to meet this objection is not

[160] Cf. Rimmon-Kenan, *Narrative Fiction*, p. 86.

to treat focalization as a zero-sum proposition, and to consider each instance on a case-by-case basis. Sometimes characters may indeed simply see something incidentally, in a matter-of-fact way, and promptly move on to doing something else. The possibility, however, that character perception can assume particular significance as a form of focalization is suggested by the number of times in which the act of seeing is consequential in plot terms. Often characters discover that *seeing* leads immediately to *seeing that*. To cite a type of situation that crops up at several points in our sample texts, the battle scene, we are often informed that one group of belligerents 'sees' their opponents gaining some advantage and so runs away. That is to say, the act of perception serves as shorthand for the making of judgements and the emergence of emotional states that suffice to motivate the actors' resort to flight. Strictly speaking to say that the enemy saw what was happening is redundant: how else would they know to turn tail? But the act of seeing economically and effectively captures a complex of perceptual and apperceptual operations.

The apprehending gaze is not our narrators' only means of access to their characters' states of mind. But it is one of the most important devices for granting actors self-awareness and purchase on the world in which they move. In other words, sight plays a large role in granting our narratives' characters animacy, permitting them a human 'surplus' that transcends the base level of moment-by-moment cognitive functioning sufficient to perform the actions which occupy them in the immediate narrative now. This raises the interesting question whether the narrators of our target texts project or transpose their own originally autoptic memories onto third-party agents, co-opting them as surrogate focalizers of the storyworld, in order to extend and enrich the range of apperceiving gazes, and thereby to call up more effectively and evocatively than could a single homodiegetic character-narrator-focalizer composite, however perceptive and reflective, the richness and complexity of the experience of participating in a crusade.

The third narratological category of analysis to be singled out is something that has already cropped up several times in this discussion, the storyworld.[161] Associated in particular with the work of David Herman, the idea of a text's storyworld seeks to refine and deepen the familiar concept of story. Story might seem a commonplace and straightforward word, but, as noted earlier, it is in fact

[161] For a succinct formulation, see D. Herman, 'Storyworld', in D. Herman, M. Jahn and M.-L. Ryan (eds), *Routledge Encyclopedia of Narrative Theory* (Abingdon, 2005), pp. 569–70. Cf. M. J. Tolan, *Narrative: A Critical Linguistic Introduction* (London, 1988), pp. 103–6; J. B. Black and G. H. Bower, 'Story Understanding as Problem-Solving', *Poetics*, 9 (1980), 247–8. See also Y.-F. Tuan, 'Language and the Making of Place: A Narrative-Descriptive Approach', *Annals of the Association of American Geographers*, 81 (1991), 684–96.

a term of art in classical narratology. In brief, it refers to the things that happen in a narrative, as opposed to the text's discourse, which is the manner in which these happenings are presented. In effect, story is the event content that can be extracted from the discourse, and so itemized, summarized and paraphrased. Story, however, is not an idea that has attracted much interest from narrative theorists, largely because the story dimension of the fictional texts in which they are principally interested has no separate ontological status – it does not represent a different level of existence – and is of only limited value as an interpretive tool. So, for example, working out the actual chronological sequence of all the events shown in Quentin Tarantino's *Pulp Fiction* (1994) can aid an understanding of the film on some level, but in the end the playful breaking up of temporality in the film's discourse is precisely what makes it an interesting narrative exercise.[162]

Dissatisfied with the extent to which the notion of story fails to capture the space inhabited by the agents, actions, events and states upon which the discourse does its creative work, Herman has developed the notion of the storyworld. The concept is inspired by reader-centred, cognitivist approaches in asking how a reader (or listener but less so a viewer) processes a narrative by constructing a mental world to which she or he imaginatively relocates.[163] Many of the mental projections that a text invites involve the concretization of details that are stated or, more often than not, implied. So, for instance, a narrative's statement to the effect that someone entered the room triggers some sense of a space with walls and ceiling, an initial intimation of room-ness that may or may not be fleshed out further depending on what the narrator chooses to do with that space. The notion of the storyworld thus overlaps to a significant extent with two other useful terms, *mise-en-scène* and diegesis. These, however, refer in particular to the physical settings in which actions take place, whereas the storyworld reaches beyond the tangible to the ideas, assumptions, expectations and beliefs that govern what happens in a narrative.

It is important to note that, for the purposes of this book's discussion, the concept of storyworld is extended beyond its original grounding in cognitive theory in order for it to be approached from a more 'supply-side' perspective. The focus will not be on the reader's processing of a given narrative as much as on the ways in which a text communicates the information and cues the inferences out of which its storyworld is construed. In many medieval cases this process would have been supplemented by paratextual details as well as the text itself; for

[162] See D. Polan, *Pulp Fiction* (London, 2000), pp. 26–7.

[163] For valuable studies of reader response, see R. J. Gerrig, *Experiencing Narrative Worlds: On the Psychological Activities of Reading* (New Haven, 1993); C. Emmott, *Narrative Comprehension: A Discourse Perspective* (Oxford, 1997). See also M. Jahn, 'Frames, Preferences, and the Reading of Third-Person Narratives: Towards a Cognitive Narratology', *Poetics Today*, 18 (1997), 441–68.

example, a reader's mental construction of a narrative's storyworld might have been influenced by what was depicted in accompanying manuscript illuminations, what was stated in rubrics and marginalia, and other texts copied into the codex.[164] But for our purposes the focus will be on the work that the text itself does in this regard. In the formulation that we shall use, then, the storyworld is the universe of human action and possibility that a narrative part crafts, part presupposes in order for it to make complete sense. Put another way, it is the global ecology inhabited by the actors within a narrative. As with the other narratological terms that we have examined, the appeal of the idea of the storyworld for our purposes is simply its practical value. Just as the figure of the narrator helps to prevent us from short-circuiting our interpretations of a narrative by appealing to authorial circumstances and intentions as the privileged points of reference, so the notion of the storyworld helps us to keep in mind the important distinction between, on the one hand, the settings and contexts of the action as they might be reconstructed by a modern historian, and, on the other, the text's own culturally situated purchase on what it takes to be the world of the real for the purposes of its narration.

Why is this distinction important? It is not difficult to see how fictional texts, even the longest and most detailed, can only capture a small slice of the total potential reality of the storyworlds that they create.[165] They have more or less clear, and usually quite tight, boundaries. Thus, to invoke a well-worn cliché in literary scholarship, there is little to be gained from wondering how many children Lady Macbeth had, because this is not a matter that is addressed in Shakespeare's *Macbeth*. If one adopts an old-fashioned approach to fictional characters and treats them as fully-formed people who happen to be glimpsed through a text, then it might be arguable that the question of Lady Macbeth's experiences as a mother informed her behaviour, mental states and motivations as they are set forth or suggested in the play. But if Lady Macbeth the character is treated as the product of multiple story-telling moves on the play's part, not as a real person, the question of the number of her children is just one small demonstration among countless others of the enormous 'gappiness' of the narrative – a question so far removed from the play's storyworld that to build an interpretation around it would be far too speculative. There are, it is true, limit cases in the world of fiction. To cite another clichéd example, the Napoleon who is a character in Tolstoy's *War and Peace* is not the same Napoleon who is retrievable through the historical record, but it is an open question whether the novel invites readers to fill in the gaps that inevitably surround its Napoleon, in the same way that

[164] For paratexts in general, see the pioneering study by Gérard Genette, *Paratexts: Thresholds of Interpretation*, trans. J. E. Lewin (Literature, Culture, Theory, 20; Cambridge, 1997).

[165] See D. Herman, *Story Logic: Problems and Possibilities of Narrative* (Lincoln, NE, 2004), pp. 66–73.

there are gaps in the construction of wholly fictional characters such as Pierre and Natasha, by drawing on whatever knowledge they may have of the historical Napoleon. (Or should that be readers' knowledge of what well-educated Russians in the 1860s knew about Napoleon?)

Historians generally take a different approach to the gappiness of narratives that purport to narrate actual events. Here a text's storyworld – in the sense of the world that the reader summons up when reading – is sooner or later adapted to fit into a larger frame of reference that includes both what we know from independent evidence was happening within the same spatio-temporal coordinates as those of the storyworld but is not mentioned by the text, and what was happening beyond the reach of the storyworld. Between them these represent an extratextual reality that in principle if not in practice can by degrees extend outwards to touch any aspect of human experience across space and time. In other words, storyworlds called forth by historiographical texts are not treated as hermetically sealed 'bubbles' of human activity in the way that *Macbeth* occupies its own discrete narrative world, a full and complex bubble, to be sure, but certainly not one that is coextensive with eleventh-century Scotland. This makes a lot of sense; the world of the narrative source can and should contribute to the world of historical reconstruction whenever this is feasible. But, again, it is important to go the long way round, working through the ways in which a narrative constructs its universe on its own terms before converting aspects of its storyworld to forms congruent with modern historical analysis. To examine a text's storyworld, then, is to ask: what are at stake in its senses of place and space, its ideas about time, the understandings of cause and effect, the cultural scripts and conventions, the reach of the power granted to human agency, and all the other presuppositions that animate the narrative's meaning-making operations? What makes this world work for the purposes of effective narration?

This book examines eyewitness texts written in connection with the crusading movement between the middle of the twelfth century and the second decade of the thirteenth. It is not a comprehensive history of eyewitness crusade historiography in that period, but a series of case studies of some of the most significant works. The aim is simply to set up comparisons and contrasts and to suggest some pointers for future research. The book does not go back to the First Crusade. This is so for two reasons. First, there is currently a good deal of scholarly debate about the nature of the interrelationships between the various histories of the First Crusade that are traditionally labelled 'eyewitness'; and until greater clarity emerges on this issue it would be imprudent to showcase them on the basis of assumptions about their autoptic status that might subsequently prove to be untenable.[166] Some mention of one of the texts at issue, the *Gesta Francorum*,

[166] For the narrative histories of the First Crusade, the most comprehensive guide is J. Flori, *Chroniqueurs et propagandistes: Introduction critique aux sources de la*

has already been made, and it will also feature in Chapter 1 by way of illustrating particular points, on the traditional assumption that it is an eyewitness text of some sort. But it would be unwise to go much further than this. Second, it is a reasonable hypothesis that the success and cultural impact of the First Crusade made it a turning point in the status attached to eyewitness historical narratives. This is often assumed to have been the case. Witness Guibert of Nogent's resort to special pleading in order to establish his superior credentials as a writer as against his main source text. But it is important to avoid any appearance of teleology and simple linear development. More research is needed into eyewitness texts written before the time of the First Crusade, and also into the relationship between crusade histories and the wider historiographical culture of Latin Christendom, before the hunch that the First Crusade was a significant moment in the cultural prestige of autoptic historiography can be properly tested. In these circumstances, it seems a more satisfactory approach, for the purposes of this study, to jump into the material *in medias res*.

In doing so, what one finds is a rich body of material characterized by generic variety but also by significant substantive and thematic similarities. The two texts examined in Chapter 2, the anonymous *De expugnatione Lyxbonensi* and Odo of Deuil's *De profectione Ludovici VII in orientem*, are Latin prose campaign monographs similar in basic form to the majority of the written narratives of the First Crusade that were in circulation by the mid twelfth century. To this extent they fall within the then-current historiographical mainstream. But they are also interesting and distinctive narrative exercises in their own right, and they do much more than recycle tropes to be found in First Crusade models. In a sense, they resolve the problem that had exercised Guibert of Nogent, in that they are the work of well-educated writers who were themselves immersed in the very events that they recount.

The main text examined in Chapter 3, Ambroise's *Estoire de la Guerre Sainte*, is almost certainly – there is some lingering but ultimately minimal uncertainty about its status – our single most important eyewitness source for the contribution to the Third Crusade made by King Richard I of England and his forces. It is a ground-breaking work in the context of crusade historiography by virtue of its being in both Old French and in verse. A vogue for Old French

---

première croisade (Hautes études médiévales et modernes, 98; Geneva, 2010). For discussion of the most debated text within the corpus, the *Gesta Francorum*, see e.g. J. Rubenstein, 'What Is the *Gesta Francorum*, and Who Was Peter Tudebode?', *Revue Mabillon*, ns 16 (2005), 179–204; M. G. Bull, 'The Relationship between the *Gesta Francorum* and Peter Tudebode's *Historia de Hierosolymitano Itinere*: The Evidence of a Hitherto Unexamined Manuscript (St. Catherine's College, Cambridge, 3)', *Crusades*, 11 (2012), 1–17; S. Niskaken, 'The Origins of the *Gesta Francorum* and Two Related Texts: Their Textual and Literary Character', *Sacris Erudiri*, 51 (2012), 287–316.

verse historiography had been developing since the second quarter of the twelfth century, but it was still very unusual for such works to be written about closely contemporary events situated within compact temporal and spatial frames. The only surviving text that predates the *Estoire* and is a close point of comparison to it is Jordan Fantosme's account of the great rebellion against Henry II of England in 1173–4, with particular reference to events in the borderlands between England and Scotland. But even in this case, Jordan's and Ambroise's texts are very different narrative exercises in many respects, including their versification, plot structure and length. Ambroise's originality has invited a good deal of debate among literary scholars: simply put, is the *Estoire* a symptom of the florescence of vernacular literature which just happens to be about the Third Crusade, or is it a history of the Third Crusade which happens to appropriate features of *chansons de geste*, romances and other vernacular genres?[167] The obvious answer is, of course, that the *Estoire* is both these things, though in the discussion of it below we shall focus in particular on those aspects of its plot, storyworld construction, narratorial voice and use of focalization that invite comparisons and contrasts with our other sample texts.

The two texts discussed in Chapter 4, the accounts of the Fourth Crusade by Geoffrey of Villehardouin and Robert of Clari, likewise broke new generic ground – in their case the writing of substantial historiographical texts in Old French prose. Here the same methodological considerations apply as with Ambroise: we shall principally be looking for points of comparison and contrast with our other texts and so across generic boundaries, while also keeping in mind that Villehardouin and Clari were, as pioneers in a genre, necessarily taking baby steps in a narrative form that had many centuries of future development ahead of it.

These works, and some revealing supplementary narratives, will be examined through a narratological lens in order to identify the ways in which the eyewitness status of the author impresses itself on the text before us. The focus will be on the internal operations of the narratives' world-making operations, not because this is the only possible analytical route, but simply because it works best for these particular texts, and most probably many others like them. In other words, this study will not consider those discursive domains parallel to historiography that may have influenced educated understandings of eyewitnessing in the round. We have noted above that medieval historians were aware of the paradigms of witnessing and bearing witness that were suggested by the Bible, in particular the Gospels and Acts of the Apostles.[168] Similarly, the model of being a witness in

[167] Cf. M. J. Ailes, 'Early French Chronicle – History or Literature?', *Journal of Medieval History*, 26 (2000), 301–12.

[168] See A. A. Trites, *The New Testament Concept of Witness* (Society for New Testament Studies Monograph Series, 31; Cambridge, 1977).

legal contexts must sometimes have been in the back of our writers' minds. The influences of biblical and legal parallels on historical texts are certainly important questions. It is simply the case that in our sample texts, at any rate, such influences are seldom brought to the surface of the discourse by means of analogy, metaphor or allusion. For the same reason, this study will not consider the possible impact on eyewitness historiography of medieval understandings of optics.[169] What is at work within our chosen texts' storyworlds and in the fashioning of their narratorial voices is a 'vernacular', common-sense understanding of what the act of seeing comprises. This is not predicated on an understanding of the nature of light or the workings of the human eye, in much the same way that a witness giving evidence in a modern courtroom is not disqualified if not an expert in physics or physiology.

This last comparison is apt, for it invokes the forensic context that has inspired the large majority of research into the nature of eyewitnessing by modern-day scholars. Before we turn to our sample texts, then, Chapter 1 will go in a different but, it is hoped, complementary direction by reviewing some of this scholarship – research, that is, undertaken by cognitive and social psychologists into the workings of eyewitness perception and memory. This enormous body of work is the elephant in the room for any study of eyewitnessing; it has to be addressed, if only to establish the extent of the disciplinary discrepancies between it and the methods and aims of historical research. We shall find that there are indeed several significant methodological and conceptual dissonances, but also helpful lessons to be learned. For example, recent work has explored the ways in which eyewitnesses to events typically participate in a process of what is termed 'transactive memory'; they do not lock their memories in a private mental storehouse against the day that they might choose to narrate them in some more or less formal manner, but rather share and debate the details with others in a process of arriving at a memory that continues to feel subjectively personal and grounded in individual experience, but which in fact situates itself in conformity to, or sometimes in opposition to, an emergent group consensus. The potential implications of this research for the ways in which our authors formed memories and told them back are clear.

There are several other intriguing lessons to be drawn from the psychological research into eyewitnessing, as we shall see. It might be objected that we can never penetrate the psychological states of individual authors and historical actors as far back in time as the Middle Ages. The way to overcome this objection is to

[169] See D. C. Lindberg, *Studies in the History of Medieval Optics* (London, 1983); A. M. Smith, 'What Is the History of Medieval Optics Really About?', *Proceedings of the American Philosophical Society*, 148 (2004), 180–94; D. G. Denery II, *Seeing and Being Seen in the Later Medieval World: Optics, Theology and Religious Life* (Cambridge, 2005), esp. pp. 1–18.

note that a powerful thread that runs through almost all the psychological research literature is the close relationship between eyewitnessing and language. Much of the trust that we place in eyewitnessing flows from a sense that it constitutes a basic – indeed pre-linguistic – purchase on the world. But this trust is misplaced. As soon as we verbalize memories internally, and even more when we communicate them to others, they become enmeshed in language. Language is not a mere delivery vehicle for elemental memories of sensory experience; it profoundly affects the form and content of recall. The psychological research tradition is therefore relevant to our inquiry because it shows how eyewitnessing, our own and that of others, is something we can only access by means of discourse. In examining aspects of the discourses of our chosen texts, therefore, we shall in several respects be working with the grain of the research into the psychology of perception and memory.

1

Memory and Psychological Research into Eyewitnessing

This chapter explores the possible lessons for the study of our target texts of research into the psychological dimensions of eyewitnessing. Researchers in cognitive psychology and related fields have done an enormous amount of work on the nature of eyewitness perception and recall, and for this reason alone it merits our close attention, as much in order to establish where this research is not consonant with historians' methodologies and approaches as to find where there may be fruitful intersections. Before we examine some of the specifics of this research tradition, however, it is important to step back and consider the larger frames of reference within which psychological understandings of eyewitnessing operate. Because much of the research in this academic idiom is a subset of the large amount of work that scholars have done on memory, we need to establish what it is in various contexts that we understand by 'memory', an everyday but semantically slippery term. This will in turn allow us to align the thematic emphases of the present chapter in relation to those that follow it.[1]

In vernacular usage we principally take memory to mean one of two things: it is our minds' capacity to retain some parts our past experiences, or it is the

[1] Given that the word 'memory' has multiple acceptations and is of interest to scholars in a wide range of disciplines, it is not surprising that the literature on it is vast. For excellent introductions, see A. D. Baddeley, *Essentials of Human Memory* (Hove, 1995); and J. K. Foster, *Memory: A Very Short Introduction* (Oxford, 2009). A good point of entry into the subject is E. Tulving and F. I. M. Craik (eds), *The Oxford Handbook of Memory* (Oxford, 2000). Entries in this volume that bear upon questions addressed in the present chapter include H. L. Roediger III and K. B. McDermott, 'Distortions of Memory', pp. 149–62; K. Nelson and R. Fivush, 'Socialization of Memory', pp. 283–95; and U. Neisser and L. K. Libby, 'Remembering Life Experiences', pp. 315–32. See also A. D. Baddeley, *Human Memory: Theory and Practice*, rev. edn (Hove, 1997); G. Cohen and M. A. Conway (eds), *Memory in the Real World*, 3rd edn (Hove, 2008); S. Radstone and B. Schwarz (eds), *Memory: Histories, Theories, Debates* (New York, 2010); M. B. Howes and G. O'Shea, *Human Memory: A Constructivist View* (San Diego, 2014). There is much of interest in D. L. Schacter, *Searching for Memory: The Brain, the Mind, and the Past* (New York, 1996); and in the same author's *The Seven Sins of Memory: How the Mind Forgets and Remembers* (Boston, 2001). For the many interfaces between memory and historical understanding, see now the excellent synthesis in G. Cubitt, *History and Memory* (Manchester, 2007). For approaches to memory from the perspectives of literary and cultural studies, see A. Whitehead, *Memory* (London, 2009); A. Erll, *Memory in Culture*, trans. S. B. Young (Basingstoke, 2011).

product of our giving expression to these experiences. The process of expression may take place within the privacy of one's mind, but it is often outwardly articulated, typically but not necessarily in verbal modes. To be asked for one's memory for a particular experience is to be invited to retrieve that episode as preserved in some form in the mind, and then to give it communicative shape. (To this two-stage process, corresponding to the two main ways in which memory is popularly understood, we may perhaps add a third: an invitation to recall along such lines will also cue some awareness on the part of the person remembering with respect to the subjective quality of the act of recall. This feeling of correspondence between the memory and the experience-as-lived is often expressed in terms of 'confidence' or 'accuracy', and it accompanies the articulation of memories in the form of explicit indicators such as qualifications and metacommentary or implicitly in lexical choices, tone of voice, body language and facial expression, or other means.) Thanks to the cultural resonances of Freudian psychoanalysis and public interest in the workings of the mind, or at least in certain of its limitations and dysfunctions, modern-day folk psychology extends to some understanding of the sub- and unconscious and of the possibility of repressed memory. But for people's general day-to-day purposes, one's memory is principally manifested in acts of more or less conscious recollection as they seem to be subtended by the retentive abilities of the mind. This sort of memory is an important asset in our moment-by-moment navigation of the world, and it is deeply implicated in the individual's sense of self and the feeling of personal continuity through time. In an aging population many of us will have directly confronted the various forms of amnesia associated with Alzheimer's Disease and other neuropathologies. What is particularly upsetting and troubling about such conditions is that they not only demonstrate the vital importance of memory as a precondition of effective social interaction, they also mount vicious attacks on what seems to be the very identity and personhood of the sufferer.[2]

Just as a disease such as Alzheimer's affects the individual human organism, so the sort of memory that we have been considering foregrounds the individual as the primary mnemonic unit.[3] In this view, people are, as a matter of course,

[2] Cf. Oliver Sacks's case studies of patients whose ability to sustain a narrative sense of self is destroyed by neurological damage brought about by pathology or trauma: *The Man Who Mistook His Wife for a Hat* (London, 1986), esp. pp. 7–41. See also S. Engel, *Context is Everything: The Nature of Memory* (New York, 1999) for the relationship between memory and identity.

[3] See e.g. M. A. Conway, J. A. Singer and A. Tagini, 'The Self and Autobiographical Memory: Correspondence and Coherence', *Social Cognition*, 22 (2004), 491–529; M. A. Conway, 'Memory and the Self', *Journal of Memory and Language*, 53 (2005), 594–628. See also A. G. Greenwald's classic paper on the self's organization of knowledge in the interests of 'beneffectance' or a sense of control in the world, on account of which 'The past is remembered as if it were a drama in which the self

instinctively aware that others around them have cognitive capacities similar to their own, and many of their social interactions involve the articulation and pooling of recollections in various contexts; but the memory that makes such interactions possible is ultimately treated as a property and function of the individual, in the same sort of way that the fact of being in pain can easily be communicated to others whereas the subjective quality of the pain-as-experienced can only be present to the sufferer's internal awareness. Much of the research in the cognitive psychological and related domains has proceeded from the assumption that the individual is the paradigmatic site of memory. We shall see presently that this orientation, which is evident not only in 'pure' strains of the research tradition that examine the workings of the mind as a thing unto itself but also in 'applied' forms attentive to the functioning of cognition in real-world conditions, may be criticized for atomizing and de-socializing what we mean when we say that people have memories and that they remember. In some of its more extreme forms, this criticism extends to destabilizing the role of the individual within the workings of memory by arguing that cognition itself extends beyond the brain and nervous system, and beyond the body for that matter, to the environment in which the individual functions. Whatever the force of such criticisms might be, it is nonetheless helpful to review some of the understandings of memory that have emerged from the individual-centred research tradition. As was noted in the Introduction, the evaluative freight with which the idea of eyewitnessing has tended to be burdened in modern historical discourse has a clear individualistic slant. Eyewitness evidence seems like the contribution to the historical record *par excellence* that the individual in history has the capacity to make. We shall see that our sample narratives are voiced by narrators who sometimes position themselves as individual observers, but also identify and sympathize with various groups. It follows that the memories that the narrators articulate have both individual and collective dimensions. So we need to consider what aspects of memory underpin the individualistic strain within the psychological research tradition, as well as those approaches that favour a focus upon collectivities.

Needless to say, the considerable amount of research that has been undertaken into the neurology of the brain and the cognitive operations of the mind has generated many scholarly debates. But one way of schematizing individual memory, associated in large part with the work of Endel Tulving, has attained the status of a working scholarly orthodoxy, and, while aspects of it are contested, it supplies a helpful introductory framework for the non-specialist. This is particularly so for the historian insofar as it offers insights into those aspects of memory that have the most traction on both the circumstances in which a given piece of historical evidence is created and on the forms of human experience that are

---

was the leading player': 'The Totalitarian Ego: Fabrication and Revision of Personal History', *American Psychologist*, 35 (1980), 603–18, quotation at 604.

recorded by it.[4] In Tulving's schema various levels or functions of memory are identified. Leaving aside the question of how their relationship to one another should best be rendered diagrammatically as links between superordinate and subordinate elements, four principal functions are in evidence. Short-term memory, also known as working memory, is the mnemonic complement of the immediate horizon of consciousness that accompanies our moment-by-moment movement through the world. One commonly cited measure of the capacity of this form of memory in adults with normal cognitive functions is that it can typically hold seven digits, plus or minus two. Working memory is the mnemonic 'gateway', in that the material that finds its way into longer-term forms of memory must pass through it. The large majority of the stimuli that register in working memory are, however, lost to subsequent recollection, either because the brain creates a record of every stimulus but thereafter most of these become functionally inaccessible, or (the more commonly held position) most of the momentary stimuli that we receive from our environment are screened out at this stage. Working memory, then, is an important part of the mind's larger mnemonic operations. In practical terms, however, it has little discrete historical purchase, for it is effectively bound up in, and inseparable from, the actions and behaviours of the historical actors that we are able to observe through our evidence. A similar consideration applies to the second major level of memory in Tulving's schema, the procedural, which guides the performance of very well practised, instinctive or routine cognitive and motor tasks. This performance does not require deliberate attention and direction – it amounts to our mental and physical 'autopilot' – and for this reason the consciousness that accompanies it has been termed anoetic, or unknowing. Clearly this form of memory amounts to a significant part of the global cognitive equipment possessed by historical actors, but it is seldom, if ever, isolatable in the sorts of evidence at our disposal, certainly in the evidence left to us by premodern societies.

The two remaining levels of memory, together labelled explicit memory in contradistinction to the implicit, unknowing, nature of procedural memory, are

[4] See E. Tulving, *Elements of Episodic Memory* (Oxford Psychology Series, 2; Oxford, 1983), esp. pp. 34–57, 139–50; and the same author's 'Memory and Consciousness', *Canadian Psychology*, 26 (1985), 1–12. For a thoughtful study of the manner in which memories for events integrate the phenomenological, metacognitive judgements, attached emotional states, sensory perception, general knowledge, cultural scripts and other elements, see D. C. Rubin, 'The Basic Systems Model of Autobiographical Memory', in D. Bernsten and D. C. Rubin (eds), *Understanding Autobiographical Memory: Theories and Approaches* (Cambridge, 2012), pp. 11–32, esp. pp. 22–3 on the working value of Tulving's categories. See also M. A. Conway and L. Jobson, 'On the Nature of Autobiographical Memory', in *ibid.*, pp. 54–69. For a critique of Tulving's schema, which overstates the (in itself reasonable) argument that Tulving takes for granted the existence of universal psychological categories, see J. Fentress and C. Wickham, *Social Memory* (Oxford, 1992), pp. 20–1.

far more visible presences in the historical record. Semantic memory, sometimes known as generic or categorical memory, is memory for the facts, meanings and concepts that cumulatively make up our general knowledge of the world: for example, the fact that the chemical formula for water is H_2O, that Berlin is the capital of Germany, and that a given dog's behaviour will by and large reflect the general characteristics of the species *Canis lupus familiaris*. Although exceptions are possible, one routinely retrieves a piece of information such as these without calling to mind the occasion when it first lodged itself in long-term memory. The form of consciousness that accompanies semantic memory has therefore been termed noetic, or knowing; and it accounts for most of the content of explicit memory in normally functioning minds. Indeed, it is the basis of what most people vernacularly mean when they judge their own or someone else's memory to be 'good' or 'bad'; the ability to retain impersonal data about the world is treated as the stock measure of memory quality. Numerous types of historical evidence contain articulations of semantic memory, and they consequently form the main building blocks for many traditions of historical inquiry such as intellectual history, the history of science, and the history of theology – in fact, any branch of historical research in which the succession of events is not of primary interest. In the same way, cultural history may be understood as the study of those parts of shared semantic memory that members of a society elect to privilege in their various forms of self-representation.

In contrast, episodic memory has a close correlation with event-centred history, *histoire événementielle*. All forms of memory ultimately derive from stimuli in the experienced environment, but episodic memory best retains the traces of its experiential origin and subjective texture. It is the memory for what happened to someone earlier in her or his life: in the succinct and helpful distinction expressed by Tulving, it is what we believe we remember as opposed to what we think we know.[5] Episodic memory is accordingly, again in Tulving's formulation, characterized by autonoetic consciousness, the subjective, metacognitive awareness of one's self in the very act of recall.[6] The pertinence of this sort of memory to the expectations routinely placed upon an

[5] See Tulving, *Elements of Episodic Memory*, p. 48: 'Remembered events are felt by rememberers to be personal experiences that belong to the autogenous past, whereas "actualized" knowledge from semantic memory represents an impersonal experience bound to the present moment. Remembered past events somehow "belong" to the rememberer ... they tend to have a definite affective tone that is uniquely and unmistakably one of the salient attributes of recollective experiences. A similar feeling is missing in the actualization of knowledge of things we know about the world, even when these "things" refer to personally significant objects or people we know.'

[6] Cf. J. M. Gardiner, 'Episodic Memory and Autonoetic Consciousness: A First-Person Approach', in A. Baddeley, J. P. Aggleton and M. A. Conway (eds), *Episodic Memory: New Directions in Research* (Oxford, 2002), pp. 11–30.

eyewitness and upon eyewitness evidence is clear. Eyewitness texts can be, and regularly are, read as sources for cultural history, and the historical eyewitness author her- or himself, if observant and reflective, may well have brought to the act of perceiving some awareness of the larger trends, movements of ideas or patterns of representation which the perceived event instantiated or exemplified in some way. But such higher-order readings of an eyewitness text are typically possible on top of, not instead of, attention to the foundational *événementiel* content.

What exactly constitutes an 'episode' for the purposes of episodic memory is a delicate problem, for this sort of memory can extend from the one-off event to sequences and patterns of related experience that, in diluting the specificity of each constituent occurrence, begin to shade towards semantic memory.[7] A further problem emerges from the manner in which the world and the flow of experiences within it are divided up, or 'chunked'. While the placing of temporal and spatial boundaries around happenings in the natural world may have some objective basis in many cases, this is less true of human interactions, for here questions of cultural identity in general and of language in particular will always obtrude. Among the host of communicative misfires between European colonizers and their colonized subjects in the early modern and modern eras, for example, many were the result of incompatible assumptions about, and ways of describing, the ways in which the world of human action is broken down for the purposes of episodic perception and recall. As is well known, one of the principal strands of a body of criticism of traditional historical practice that began around the 1960s and peaked in the 80s and 90s, and which is principally associated with the work of Hayden White, is that historians impose a narrative order of beginning, middle and end on the fluid seamlessness that is held to characterize the flow of human action through time.[8] As is also well known, this is a view that has not gone unchallenged. But it at least sensitizes us to the fact that the episodes that form the basis of the episodic memories evidenced by our target texts are not, or at least not always, universal, self-evident and discrete units of human action; they are to a significant extent artefacts of the manner of their telling and of underlying cultural assumptions about the ordering of the world. What exactly, in a given cultural environment, does the eyewitness get to perceive as action unfolds

[7] See the useful comments on the relationship between episodic and semantic memory in M. Linton, 'Transformations of Memory in Everyday Life', in U. Neisser (ed.), *Memory Observed: Remembering in Natural Contexts* (New York, 1982), pp. 77–91.

[8] See H. White, 'The Historical Text as Literary Artifact', in his *Tropics of Discourse: Essays in Cultural Criticism* (Baltimore, 1978), pp. 81–100; *idem*, 'The Value of Narrativity in the Representation of Reality', in his *The Content of the Form: Narrative Discourse and Historical Representation* (Baltimore, 1987), pp. 1–25; *idem*, 'Historical Emplotment and the Problem of Truth in Historical Representation', in his *Figural Realism: Studies in the Mimesis Effect* (Baltimore, 1999), pp. 27–42.

around her or him, and what are the means by which perception is converted into apperception? What, in other words, is the epistemological and heuristic reach of the autoptic gaze?

Even if we take a common-sense and source-led approach to a working definition of episode, and say that it is whatever a given text at a given moment in its narrative construction of the represented world wants it to be, further challenges remain. As we shall see below, the understanding of episode that runs through much of the psychological research literature on eyewitnessing concentrates on the sort of short, vivid, emotionally charged and unexpected experience that befalls eyewitnesses to crimes. There is therefore a problem of scaling up to the sorts of episodes that are the building blocks of our target texts' plot architectures.[9] More generally, the boundaries between the categories of episodic and semantic memory are frequently blurred at source insofar as almost all recollection involves some combination of the two. It is, for example, very common in autobiographical recall for someone to fall back on deducing from inferences, analogy and contextual clues what she or he 'must have' been doing at a given time and place in the past, especially in the absence of the sort of mnemonic reinforcement that is supplied by subjectively experienced episodic recall. We must therefore allow for the probability that in our sample texts there will be passages of narrative that evoke the quality of episodic memory, and may even gesture towards its characteristic sensory aspects, but which actually derive from this kind of deductive and inferential reconstruction.

More fundamentally still, because language is the single most important carrier of semantic knowledge, it is impossible for any coherent and economical narrative sequence that seems to be grounded in eyewitness, episodic memory to be free of its influence. A brief passage in Robert of Clari's *La Conquête de Constantinople* serves as an illustration:

> The Venetians and the pilgrims sailed on until they came to Zara on the eve of the Feast of Saint Martin. When the people of Zara saw the ships [*nes*] and the great fleet arriving, they were very frightened; they shut the gates of the city and armed themselves as best they could making ready to defend themselves… Now the people of Zara knew perfectly well that the Venetians hated them. So they had acquired a letter from Rome stating that all who made war on them or did them any harm would be excommunicated.[10]

The narrator deploys many items of semantic knowledge in this passage, and the reader is expected to bring a matching body of knowledge to bear on his or her

[9] Cf. the helpful discussion of the relationship between experimentally contrived mini-events and real-world conditions in Tulving, *Elements of Episodic Memory*, pp. 144–6.

[10] RC, c. 14, pp. 16–18.

understanding: for example, the exact sort of vessel denoted by the word *nes*, what it is like to travel by sea, when in the year the Feast of St Martin happens to fall (11 November), the expectation that the frightened inhabitants of cities faced with the possibility of attack will take defensive measures, what a city gate looks like, the fact that 'Rome' can be used metonymically to mean the pope (here Innocent III) and the apparatus of papal authority, and the nature and consequences of excommunication. For good measure, semantic knowledge is on display within the storyworld as well: when we are told that the people of Zara know that they are hated by the Venetians, the implication is that this is a long-standing animus, not a momentary dislike reducible to a single episodic articulation. Just as semantic memory reinforces the episodic, so the reverse process, if less pervasive, is also possible: those who have sat exams, for example, may have had the experience of being able to visualize the relevant page of a book when retrieving a piece of (semantic) information, or recapturing the particular moment when the lecturer made a pertinent remark. There may be passages in our texts, therefore, that purport to capture a specific individual moment in the flow of experience, but which are really distillations of the semantic into episodic forms: illustrative stagings of motivations, ideas, moods, prejudices and other intangibles. Whether we are in a position to differentiate on the page between actual one-off episodes and such illustrative reifications of patterns and trends is, of course, another matter.

Up to this point our discussion of memory has been guided by the individualist orientation that characterizes much of the research into cognitive processes. If we look beyond the neural networks in the brain that are the physical basis of individuals' mnemonic faculties, however, we soon realize that all memory-as-expression has a social dimension. (There may even be a case for arguing that some of the neurological mechanisms of the brain are not themselves a trans-historical constant of human physiology but are instead configured to a degree by cultural influences, in particular the manner in which young children are socialized in certain ways of conceptualizing and talking about their past experiences as part of their language acquisition.) Even acts of private mental rehearsal typically centre upon memories for events in which the individual was involved in interactions with others; and outward remembering necessarily has a social quality, drawing upon shared social resources such as language and collectively understood symbols.

The social dimensions of memory have been the subject of an explosion of scholarly interest over the last forty or fifty years. With respect to the particular kinds of historical events and texts with which this book is concerned, and at the risk of some oversimplification, we may identify two significant strands within this large body of scholarship. They differ as to the levels of human scale and the physical and temporal reaches of memory that constitute their defaults, and they are shaped by different disciplinary traditions. Both, confusingly, use 'collective memory' as one of their principal terms of art.[11] The first emerges from research psychologists' interest in the social dimensions of cognition in general and the transactive nature of memory in particular. We shall see below that a good deal of research into the psychology of memory treats social interactions as potentially negative, contaminating influences on the individual's ability to recall fully and accurately. But a more positive approach, one that has gained some ground in recent years, emphasizes the social, communicative and collaborative basis of memory in real-world conditions.[12] Social interactions are not mere occasions or pretexts for individuals to summon up and articulate memories stored in the private world of their minds; they embed and to some degree even constitute the

[11] For a foundational study of the two concepts of collective memory and their points of divergence and intersection, see J. K. Olick, 'Collective Memory: The Two Cultures', *Sociological Theory*, 17 (1999), 333–48. See also W. Hirst and D. Manier, 'Towards a Psychology of Collective Memory', *Memory*, 16 (2008), 183–200; A. Coman, A. D. Brown, J. Koppel and W. Hirst, 'Collective Memory from a Psychological Perspective', *International Journal of Politics, Culture, and Society*, 22 (2009), 125–41; J. V. Wertsch, *Voices of Collective Remembering* (Cambridge, 2002), pp. 30–66; *idem*, 'Collective Memory', in P. Boyer and J. V. Wertsch (eds), *Memory in Mind and Culture* (Cambridge, 2009), pp. 117–37. Cf. M. S. Weldon, 'Remembering as a Social Process', in D. L. Medin (ed.), *The Psychology of Learning and Motivation: Advances in Research and Theory: Volume 40* (San Diego, 2001), pp. 67–120.

[12] See e.g. the valuable account of the various processes that inform conversational recall and aid the construction of agreed narrative articulations of shared memories in D. Edwards and D. Middleton, 'Joint Remembering: Constructing an Account of Shared Experience Through Conversational Discourse', *Discourse Processes*, 9 (1986), 423–59; and the same authors' 'Conversational Remembering: A Social Psychological Approach', in D. Middleton and D. Edwards (eds), *Collective Remembering* (London, 1990), pp. 23–45. See also C. B. Harris, H. M. Paterson and R. I. Kemp, 'Collaborative Recall and Collective Memory: What Happens When We Remember Together', *Memory*, 16 (2008), 213–30; R. G. Thompson, 'Collaborative and Social Remembering', in G. Cohen and M. A. Conway (eds), *Memory in the Real World*, 3rd edn (Hove, 2008), pp. 249–67; J. V. Wertsch and H. L. Roediger III, 'Collective Memory: Conceptual Foundations and Theoretical Approaches', *Memory*, 16 (2008), 318–26; G. Echterhoff, E. T. Higgins and J. M. Levine, 'Shared Reality: Experiencing Commonality with Others' Inner States About the World', *Perspectives on Psychological Science*, 4 (2009), 496–521; H. Blank, 'Remembering: A Theoretical Interface Between Memory and Social Psychology', *Social Psychology*, 40 (2009), 164–75; W. Hirst and G. Echterhoff, 'Creating Shared Memories in Conversation: Toward a Psychology of Collective Memory', *Social Research*, 75 (2008), 183–216; and the same authors' 'Remembering in Conversations: The Social Sharing and Reshaping of Memories', *Annual Review of Psychology*, 63 (2012), 55–79. Cf. the formulation of M. S. Weldon and K. D. Ballinger, 'Collective Memory: Collaborative and Individual Processes in Remembering', *Journal of Experimental Psychology: Learning, Memory, and Cognition*, 23 (1997), 1160: 'group memory is an emergent property of different individuals' recollections expressed within a social context'.

individual's act of recall, which may subjectively feel like it is simply emerging from within the self but is in fact significantly modulated by its social context.

To a large extent, this new attention to the environments in which memories are expressed and shared reflects wider shifts in the ways in which cognitive processes and the mind itself are conceived. It is argued by some that the workings of cognition are not a process confined to the human brain and central nervous system (or more accurately to those parts of them that are implicated in cognitive function). They extend to the rest of the body and, in a bolder conceptual move, to the world beyond the body.[13] An example that is often adduced is someone's use of a pencil and paper to be able to perform arithmetical tasks that she or he could not accomplish unaided. The pencil and paper are to be regarded as part of the cognitive apparatus that makes the performance of the task possible. Two ways of conceptualizing this sort of process are to be found in the literature. One, what we might term the common-sense, functionalist approach, treats the pencil and paper as one example of the enormous number of tools that are available in the environment to facilitate cognitive operations. In this view, the individual, and specifically the individual's cranial and neurological mechanisms, remain the essential locus of cognitive activity, while it is understood that this activity is realized by means of interactions with the outside world. A second view takes a more radical approach, however, in arguing that the mind itself extends into the world beyond the body. So, for example, various items used in the storage and retrieval of information, such as wax tablets, notebooks and computers, are not to be understood as mere adjuncts to the workings of memory but are on the contrary integral to it.[14] This line of argument is overstated, however. It does not adequately attend to the question where, if the mind extends beyond the cranium, it actually ends. And it falls prey to the fondness for reifying figurative language that one sometimes encounters in other theoretical discourses: what something is like or what it evokes is confused with what it is in itself.[15]

The common-sense approach to what has been termed distributed cognition is, however, persuasive, in particular when one considers that the environment with which the individual interacts includes other people, other loci of individual recollection, as well as inanimate objects such as a pencil and paper.[16] Distributed

[13] For a wide-ranging study of this question, see R. A. Wilson, *Boundaries of the Mind: The Individual in the Fragile Sciences: Cognition* (Cambridge, 2004).

[14] See the important study by A. Clark and D. Chalmers, 'The Extended Mind', *Analysis*, 58 (1998), 7–19. Cf. R. A. Wilson, 'Collective Memory, Group Minds, and the Extended Mind Thesis', *Cognitive Processing*, 6 (2005), 227–36; J. Sutton, 'Distributed Cognition: Domains and Dimensions', *Pragmatics & Cognition*, 14 (2006), 235–47.

[15] For a vigorous attack on the notion of extended cognition, see F. Adams and K. Aiziwa, *The Bounds of Cognition* (Malden, MA, 2008).

[16] See L. Marsh, A. J. Barnier, J. Sutton, C. B. Harris and R. A. Wilson, 'A Conceptual

cognition thus provides a useful way of thinking about the ways in which memory functions socially. In attending to immediate contextual environments, research in this vein favours looking at smaller types of groups, typically those such as families and groups of coworkers in which face-to-face exchanges are frequent. The memories that are articulated and shared in such group encounters tend to correspond to the private experiences of the various members, as opposed to public affairs, and the chronological reach of these memories is correspondingly shallow: it often relates to the recent past, and seldom extends back beyond the lifetimes of the group members. Extended cognition functioning in such more or less informal and intimate contexts is what has probably been the predominant experience of memory-as-lived for most historical actors most of the time, even though the sources at our disposal can seldom capture more than glimpses of its operations.

The second form of collective memory has attracted the interest of scholars in a wide range of social scientific and humanities disciplines. Whereas the psychological tradition we have just considered mostly sees collective memory as the aggregate of individuals' memories, even as these memories interact with one another in multiple and complex ways, the second approach regards the collective as the primary unit of analysis. Individuals within collectivities still possess cognitive capacities and have personal experiences, of course, but their senses of identity and the understandings of the past that subtend those identities are to be understood with direct reference to social and cultural frameworks.[17] People think, and remember, with the resources that the collectivities to which they belong make available to them.[18] The study of collective memory in this vein accordingly makes a metonymic move from the mental and perceptual functioning of a group's members to the collective representations that structure their ideas about themselves and the past: a far from exhaustive list would include political and legal institutions, the built environment, educational curricula and literary canons, museums, battlefields, the public calendar, public rituals, and shrines and monuments. A further dimension that has been the subject of

and Empirical Framework for the Social Distribution of Cognition: The Case of Memory', *Cognitive Systems Research*, 9 (2008), 33–51. Cf. J. Sutton, 'Between Individual and Collective Memory: Coordination, Interaction, Distribution', *Social Research*, 75 (2008), 23–48; A. Assmann, 'Transformations between History and Memory', *Social Research*, 75 (2008), 49–72.

[17] The work of Maurice Halbwachs was foundational in this regard: see his *On Collective Memory*, ed. and trans. L. A. Coser (Chicago, 1992). For two valuable studies, see Fentress and Wickham, *Social Memory*; and P. Connerton, *How Societies Remember* (Cambridge, 1989).

[18] For some of the distortions to which this kind of collective memory is vulnerable, see M. Schudson, 'Dynamics of Distortion in Collective Memory', in D. L. Schacter *et al.* (eds), *Memory Distortion: How Minds, Brains, and Societies Reconstruct the Past* (Cambridge, MA, 1995), pp. 346–64.

interesting research is the role of narratives and narrative templates within such frameworks. As with the debates on the extended mind, but on a larger scale and in a wider range of disciplinary idioms, some discussions of this conception of collective memory fall into the trap of hypostasizing their metaphorical language – treating the figurative as real – with the result that collectivities assume the guise of anthropomorphic entities capable of thinking, believing and remembering. This tendency has been vigorously, and persuasively, criticized.[19] But putting this anthropomorphism to one side, there can be no doubt as to the enormous impact that the study of collective memory, in this larger conception, has made. Indeed, it is what most scholars outside the neurological and cognitive psychological traditions usually take the word 'memory' to mean.

Research into collective memory in this vein favours larger units than the face-to-face groups studied for evidence of transactive memory: the modern nation state is paradigmatic in this regard. This form of collective memory also has a longer chronological reach, for it is not confined to the lived experiences of the individuals who comprise the collectivity at any given moment. A great deal of collective memory fixes on, for example, centuries-old migrations, battles, revolutions, invasions and perceived national injustices. It follows that although the smaller-scale forms of collective memory studied by psychologists may in many instances anticipate, and feed into the emergence of, longer-term cultural representations, for instance in formulating memories that simplify events, pegging the memories squarely to questions of identity, and eliminating space for qualifications and dissent, there are important experiential and functional differences between the two levels. This has significant implications for the study of our target texts, which occupy spaces somewhere between the two registers of collective memory that we have considered: they are more formal, structured and focused upon 'public' history than much of the stuff of small-group transactive memory; but they are also too close to events and too immersed in the historical specificity and the richness of detail embedded within their storyworlds to do anything more than gesture ahead to the streamlining and simplification that absorption into the matrices of longer-term collective memory entails.

With these remarks in mind, we may establish a working schema for the different forms, or phases, of memory at work within our target texts, and then

[19] See e.g. the valuable remarks by Sarah Foot in her discussion of the memory of the Viking raids in the ninth-century Anglo-Saxon kingdoms: 'Remembering, Forgetting and Inventing: Attitudes to the Past in England at the End of the First Viking Age', *Transactions of the Royal Historical Society*, 6th ser., 9 (1999), 185–200, esp. 187–8. Cf. the helpful discussion, taking Foot's comments as a point of departure, in Cubitt, *History and Memory*, pp. 9–12, 14–18, 66–117. From within the sociological tradition Olick observes that 'notions of collective memory as objective symbols or deep structures that transcend the individual risk slipping into a metaphysics of group mind': 'Collective Memory', 338.

relate this to the argument structure of what follows. A four-stage process is to be identified within which the pattern of relationships between the different stages may be likened to an a_1 b_1 a_2 b_2 rhyme scheme. (It should be emphasized that this process does not necessarily correspond to a clear-cut sequence of discrete phases in real time.) The first stage, a_1, represents the individual author's perceptions of actions and events around him, and the formation of episodic memories that draw upon both this experience and the semantic knowledge either brought to the events that the narrative recounts or formed during them. As we noted in the Introduction, it would be misleading to picture our eyewitness authors as lone, detached roving reporters: they were not just observing action but participating in it, and they were doing so in immersive and dislocating conditions that absorbed their attention for months or years on end. But as our discussion above of the various forms of memory suggests, we need to begin with the individual mnemonic dimension of their experience in order to proceed to its social ramifications.

The second stage, b_1, shifts the focus onto the author's articulations of his memories – and by obvious extension his exposure to the memories of others – in the sorts of transactive environments that forge the smaller-scale forms of collective memory. The texts are silent about this process, but we can be all but certain that it took place in each case, and that it began during the experience of the campaign rather than after it. In fact, it was probably most frequent and intensive in mid-experience, when episodic memories were fresh and outcomes were uncertain. We can make certain inferences about some of the social environments in which such exchanges might have occurred on the basis of the status of the authors – for example, the fact that Odo of Deuil was a well-connected senior ecclesiastic and Geoffrey of Villehardouin was a secular aristocrat at home in princely courts. But the sorts of opportunities or expectations to recount one's memories that we can surmise from the authors' status and circumstances must have been only the tip of the iceberg of numerous moments of transactive exchange within groups of various shapes and sizes, perhaps including people with whom high-status individuals such as our authors would not have routinely interacted back home in their familiar social environments. Crusading threw people together in unfamiliar and stressful situations and forced them out of their normal social routines and cultural comfort zones. It is important to remember that this second stage would have been in evidence even as the first was still ongoing, for our participant-authors would have been revisiting memories of earlier events in transactive situations even as new experiences presented themselves day to day.[20]

[20] For the manner in which the memory of an event may be influenced, and partly reinforced, by conversing with attentive and sympathetic interlocutors, see M. Pasupathi, L. M. Stallworth and K. Murdoch, 'How What We Tell Becomes What

This stage is particularly important in two respects. First, it marked the process whereby the author definitively embedded his memories in collective frames of reference. This would have started at an early point, for as we have seen the immediate formation of explicit memories is never innocent of the socially shared resources that give those memories verbal and visual form. Second, it was only in the back-and-forth of transactive memory that the author would have been able to situate his own recollections relative to those of others. This did not necessarily involve a simple pooling of memories to arrive at some lowest-common-denominator consensus, for the author would always have been free to retain some divergent postures vis-à-vis an emergent group narrative, for example concerning uncertain or contested details. But he would have needed to participate in multiple occasions of transactive memory to have been able to craft an extended, tightly plotted, and thematically coherent narrative of a complicated collective endeavour. Without this process, he would simply have been an individual with a mental scrapbook of discrete autobiographical anecdotes.

The third phase, a_2, represents the writing of the text, during which the individual focus reasserts itself, at least to a substantial degree. Leaving aside theoretical anxieties about the status, and death, of the author, in practical terms medieval authorship was seldom if ever a solitary undertaking. If one were writing in a religious institutional environment, the scriptorium amounted to a workshop in which suggestions could be made and ideas brainstormed, even as the author would attempt to retain ultimate editorial control of the emerging text. In the preface to his history of the First Crusade, written in about 1110, Robert the Monk bemoans the fact that, because he found himself in a remote priory that belonged to the abbey of St-Remi, Reims, he could not call upon the services of a scribe as he composed his text. In part this is just a grumpy complaint about personal inconvenience, but it also hints at a loss of the feeling of interactivity that was expected to accompany the process of writing.[21] Not all the authors of our target texts were writing in monastic or clerical institutions, but, especially given the physical logistics and costs of preparing writing materials and the considerable length of their works, it is highly likely that they sought out technical expertise and support, perhaps amongst clerics or professed religious, and in the process created informal and ad hoc but still interactive and collaborative variants of the working atmosphere of a scriptorium. In any event, wherever, and with whomever, a text assumed a definitive form, it probably went

---

We Know: Listener Effects on Speakers' Long-Term Memory for Events', *Discourse Processes*, 26 (1998), 1–25.

[21] Robert the Monk, *The Historia Iherosolimitana*, ed. D. Kempf and M. G. Bull (Woodbridge, 2013), p. 3; trans. C. Sweetenham, *Robert the Monk's History of the First Crusade: Historia Iherosolimitana* (Crusade Texts in Translation, 11; Aldershot, 2005), p. 75.

through more than one draft, and readers' comments would have been solicited. If, moreover, and as seems very likely, our authors began to assemble source materials, such as notes of their own making and other documents, before they embarked on the formal composition of their texts, this would have enlarged the pool of potential collaborators. Indeed, the transactive memory and writing phases would have bled into one another. For all these reasons, therefore, the individuality of our authors looks very fuzzy.

On the other hand, what in the end matters more than the particular biographical circumstances in which the author found himself during the time his history was taking shape is the manner in which his authorial role filters into the text. Our authors as historical actors in real time, perceiving events and discussing their memories of them, do in a sense 'die' once we turn our attention squarely to the texts before us and we are simply left with the projections of the authors that the texts call forth. As noted in the Introduction, narratological analysis offers two helpful concepts here: the implied author, which in one of its incarnations can be regarded as the impression of the author that the reader infers from the text; and the narrator, the agency behind the telling of the narrative. Each contributes to the sense that a text is the product of a consciousness situated within an individual brain, though, as we have seen, that directing consciousness is not to be conflated with what we might speculate was going through the real author's mind. So, it would not particularly matter if a text were actually written by committee as long as the implied author and narrator singly or in combination contrive to individuate what the reader takes to be the human agency responsible for it. For our immediate purposes it is immaterial whether in any given passage in our target texts it is the implied author, the narrator, or a combination of the two that is considered to be achieving this effect. As the Introduction argues, the narrator is ultimately the more important concept, but in this immediate context we do not need to overwork the distinction because both the narrator and the implied author are textual effects, artefacts of their host text's communicative functions and narrative strategies.

The key point is that an individuated implied authorial/narratorial persona seems to be present in all the texts that we shall be examining. This in itself might seem unremarkable, for a great many other texts from this and other periods, and in a wide variety of genres, fashion the implied author and narrator in similar ways. It is, however, noteworthy that in our target texts moments of individual participation in events, and also moments of perception, recognition and understanding, as well as remembering, are implicated in the larger project of implied authorial/narratorial construction. In other words, these are not simply narratives attributable to someone who just happened to be 'there', in the right place at the right time so to speak, nor is the eyewitness status of the author simply a badge of validation and authenticity (though these are important), something to prod the reader into calling to mind from time to time. Instead, as subsequent chapters will reveal, eyewitnessing is a motif central to most of our texts' meaning-making projects, though the ways in which it is mobilized and the intensity of its mobilization vary. For this reason it is useful to schematize this stage as a reversion to the individual orientation of the first phase, thus $a_1 > a_2$, even though in practice the individuality of the witness-rememberer would have blended into his ambient mnemonic environment.

The fourth phase, b_2, represents the reassertion of the social nexus, this time in the guise of the narrative templates, myths and various 'sites of memory' that would have supplied the substance of emergent collective memories in the larger sense. As our texts were read and copied, they would have contributed to a process of collective memory formation with respect to many subjects and themes. Possible examples of a more specific nature include the mythic reputations of Richard I and Saladin, the place of the Iberian peninsula in wider Mediterranean conflicts, what if anything 'went wrong' with the Fourth Crusade, and Latin Christians' prejudices about Greeks and Muslims. On more abstract levels, the texts would have contributed to the consolidation of collective understandings embedded in scripts and schemata such as 'what warfare is like', 'what a long journey involves', 'what it means to be afraid', and 'what risk entails'. The individual contributions of each of our texts to these processes are impossible to measure precisely. One partial index is the extent of the known or estimated manuscript transmission. But some caution is necessary, for while a text's wide manuscript dissemination might be *prima facie* evidence of its having made a significant contribution to the formation and reinforcement of collective memories, the reverse is not necessarily true: a little copied text is not for that reason alone an uninfluential one, and it might still drill narrowly but deeply into long-term collective representations. Some of the texts with which we are concerned in this study, in fact, survive in a single manuscript.

The reception and cultural impacts of our texts is, however, a large and diffuse subject beyond the scope of the present study. For this reason, the fourth phase will not occupy our attention, except in the important but limited sense of looking back to the pre-existing frameworks of collective memory that may have fed into our target texts via the various genres that influenced them: for example, epic songs, romances, pilgrimage and travel literature, deeds of rulers narratives, hagiography and sermons. A further reason why the fourth phase is less important to our immediate inquiry is that it is reasonable to suppose that each nexus of eyewitnessing that we shall identify – the author's particular biographical circumstances, autopsy as the basis of the text's claims for authority, the positioning of the narrator in relation to the diegesis, and eyewitnessing as something that animates action within its storyworld – would have mattered less and less to the text's reception and impact the further in time one moved from the events recounted, especially once these events passed from living memory. For these reasons, the focus of the remainder of this book will be on the first phases. Stage

a_2, the funnelling of the author's individually formed but transactively developed memories into the text, will be addressed in subsequent chapters. The remainder of the present chapter, in contrast, will focus on what was at stake during the formative stages of the creation of the texts as represented by the pair a_1-b_1. And here we are fortunate that a great deal of research, by cognitive psychologists and those in related fields, speaks to precisely this a_1-b_1 dynamic.

The study of eyewitnessing is a striking example of the disciplinary imbalances that can develop between various fields of scholarly inquiry. Whereas, as we have seen, historical scholarship has tended to rely upon the category of eyewitness more than it has tried to unpick it, it has been the subject of an enormous amount of research by cognitive and social psychologists in recent decades. A conservative estimate would be that over 5,000 articles on eyewitnessing, eyewitness memory and related topics have been published since the 1970s, when interest in the subject took off.[22] The sheer volume of this scholarly output is compelling, quite apart from the interdisciplinary curiosity that it naturally provokes. As this chapter will argue, the psychological research offers us numerous valuable insights, as much into the reasons why modern-day historians pack unspoken assumptions and expectations into their mobilization of eyewitness evidence as into the cognitive operations that subtended the creation of that evidence in the first place. We shall further see that the lessons to be drawn from the psychological literature are circumscribed by the limitations of disciplinary fit. The methodological and conceptual dissonances between psychological and historical approaches are themselves of interest, however, in that they throw into sharper relief the particular interpretive challenges that our eyewitness texts pose.

Given the very large amount of psychological research that has been published, it is only possible to provide an overview of some of the main trends and to highlight those individual studies that have been landmarks in the field or offer up particularly noteworthy points of comparison and contrast with the approaches of academic history. Some simplifications and loss of range and nuance are inevitable in such a survey. That said, one particularly prominent aspect of this research, and for this reason an excellent point of entry into it for the lay person, is its pronounced pragmatic orientation towards eyewitnessing in forensic and legal contexts. Many research projects frame their hypotheses and design their experimental procedures with express reference to the ways in which eyewitness evidence is handled in the American and other criminal justice systems, from the first contact made between a witness to a crime and the police, to the effects of

[22] This estimate is an extrapolation from the more than 2,000 bibliographical references assembled by a leading researcher in the field by the mid 1990s: see B. L. Cutler and S. D. Penrod, *Mistaken Identification: The Eyewitness, Psychology, and the Law* (Cambridge, 1995), pp. 67–9.

that same witness giving her or his evidence in court.[23] Even when studies do not overtly address themselves to matters of legal practice, this continues to be understood as the controlling paradigm and operative context of the research. In other words, 'eyewitness' and 'eyewitnessing' in an article's title usually amount to a conceptual and methodological alignment with research traditions that ground their academic value in their real-world forensic applications.[24]

To some extent, this has been a matter of professional self-fashioning on the part of the research psychologists. Especially in the early decades of research interest one finds in the literature a recurrent preoccupation that psychologists who study eyewitnessing should be called as expert witnesses in trials to speak to the pitfalls that attend eyewitness perception and memory, in much the same way as other kinds of scientific expertise are routinely presented to juries in order to help them weigh the evidence before them. The villains of the piece in this scenario are criminal prosecutors and judges who are either hostile towards the psychologists' scepticism about the accuracy of testimony or complacent about the rigour and fairness of the existing mechanisms for dealing with eyewitness evidence. To a large extent this antagonism replays a celebrated spat in the early twentieth century between Hugo Münsterberg, one of the founding figures of the modern study of psychology whose observations about eyewitness fallibility anticipated many of the conclusions of modern research, and John Henry Wigmore, a prominent jurist and the leading authority in the United States on the law of evidence.[25] Wigmore, though himself interested in psychological research

[23] For the role of witnesses and the status of eyewitness testimony in English law, see C. Tapper and R. Cross, *Cross and Tapper on Evidence*, 12th edn (Oxford, 2010), pp. 223–71, 296–9, 307–70, 551–666 (on hearsay).

[24] For a useful overview of the various intersections between the conduct of police cases and the problems addressed by the research literature, see B. W. Behrman and S. L. Davey, 'Eyewitness Identification in Actual Criminal Cases: An Archival Analysis', *Law and Human Behavior*, 25 (2001), 475–91. See also G. L. Wells, 'What Do We Know About Eyewitness Identification?', *American Psychologist*, 48 (1993), 553–71. For a discussion of the place of eyewitness research within the overall context of psychological research in general, see D. B. Wright, 'Causal and Associative Hypotheses in Psychology: Examples from Eyewitness Testimony Research', *Psychology, Public Policy, and Law*, 12 (2006), 190–213.

[25] For the nature and course of the dispute, see J. M. Doyle, *True Witness: Cops, Courts, Science, and the Battle Against Misidentification* (New York, 2005), pp. 9–34. Wigmore was reacting to Münsterberg's *On the Witness Stand: Essays on Psychology and Crime* (New York, 1908), a collection of essays pitched towards the general reader. Wigmore's notoriously robust and acidly satirical response to Münsterberg's belief that psychologists deserved to have an influential voice in the criminal legal process is found in 'Professor Muensterberg and the Psychology of Testimony: Being a Report of the Case of Cokestone *v.* Muensterberg', *Illinois Law Review*, 3 (1909), 399–445. For the lives and careers of the two protagonists generally, see W. R. Roalfe, *John Henry Wigmore: Scholar and Reformer* (Evanston, IL, 1977); M. Hale, *Human*

and open to some of its possible legal applications, was generally believed to have won their scholarly battle, and this helped to inhibit exchange between the two sides for several decades. In recent years, however, expert testimony by psychologists on the nature of eyewitness perception and memory has been allowed in ever greater numbers of cases, though in some jurisdictions more than others.[26]

In fairness to the many researchers in this field, however, something more was, and is, at stake than professional pride and the perceived relevance and impact of their academic interests. The research into eyewitnessing tackles issues of incontestable importance. Lay people may believe that they have an intuitive and healthily sceptical understanding of the fallibility and malleability of eyewitness evidence in some situations, and may recall news coverage of miscarriages of justice in which it has emerged that someone was falsely convicted on the basis of eyewitness testimony. But the scale of the problem is far greater than people generally suppose.[27] The statistics make sobering reading. Since DNA testing became available in the late 1980s, more than 300 wrongfully convicted people have been exonerated by it in the United States. Of these twenty had been sentenced to death; and the average length of time served before release was

---

Science and Social Order: Hugo Münsterberg and the Origins of Applied Psychology (Philadelphia, 1980). For further assessments of Münsterberg's importance relative to that of other pioneers in the field of applied psychology, see S. L. Sporer, 'Lessons from the Origins of Eyewitness Testimony Research in Europe', *Applied Cognitive Psychology*, 22 (2008), 937–57; B. H. Bornstein and S. D. Penrod, 'Hugo Who? G. F. Arnold's Alternative Approach to Psychology and Law', *Applied Cognitive Psychology*, 22 (2008), 759–68. Cf. M. A. Ash, 'Academic Politics in the History of Science: Experimental Psychology in Germany, 1879–1941', *Central European History*, 13 (1980), 255–86.

[26] See the remarks on the giving of expert testimony to be found in the relevant professional 'bible': E. F. Loftus, J. M. Doyle and J. E. Dysart (eds), *Eyewitness Testimony: Civil and Criminal*, 5th edn (New Providence, NJ, 2013), pp. 327–92. But see also S. R. Berkowitz and N. L. Javaid, 'It's Not You, It's the Law: Eyewitness Memory Scholars' Disappointment with *Perry v. New Hampshire*', *Psychology, Public Policy, and Law*, 19 (2013), 369–79 concerning a 2012 decision of the US Supreme Court to the effect that suggestive identification procedures violate a defendant's constitutional rights to due process only if the law enforcement officials themselves contrive the suggestive conditions. In other words, eyewitness testimony does not intrinsically merit pre-trial review, a position Berkowitz and Javaid interpret as tantamount to a rejection of the work of psychologists on the malleability of all eyewitness testimony. It is noteworthy that the sole dissenting opinion, by Justice Sonia Sotomayor, does expressly acknowledge this body of scholarship.

[27] For a negative assessment of popular understanding of the problems attaching to eyewitness memory, see A. D. Yarmey and H. P. Tresillian Jones, 'Is the Psychology of Eyewitness Identification a Matter of Common Sense?', in S. M. A. Lloyd-Bostock and B. R. Clifford (eds), *Evaluating Witness Evidence: Recent Psychological Research and New Perspectives* (Chichester, 1983), pp. 13–40.

over thirteen years. A study of the first 250 such cases suggests that 76 per cent involved mistaken eyewitness identification.[28] There are about 70,000 eyewitness identifications, by means of live identity parades ('lineups' in American parlance) or arrays of mugshot photographs, in the United States every year. And while only a small percentage of these will translate into a case tried in court, and a still smaller percentage will end in a conviction, it is always important to bear in mind that the safety net of exculpatory DNA evidence can only be applied to certain types of offences such as murder and sexual assault. If one extrapolates the exoneration figures to the general convict population, the majority of whom were found guilty of crimes in which DNA evidence has no place, and most of whom were convicted in whole or substantial part on the basis of eyewitness testimony, then it is statistically certain that there are currently many hundreds, probably several thousands, of men and women in US prisons who have been wrongfully convicted thanks to faulty eyewitness evidence. Although the American legal system is unusually large, sprawling and decentralized, and its prison population enormous, it would be unwise to assume that other common law jurisdictions, though more centralized and less punitive, have investigative and judicial mechanisms that are always sure proof against such miscarriages of justice.

A reforming zeal has consequently informed much of the research into eyewitnessing. A foremost example of this motivation and focus is provided by the work of Elizabeth Loftus. Since the 1970s and 80s Loftus has been the most visible and active public intellectual in the United States and elsewhere in the field of the psychology of memory.[29] Her research has engaged with several matters of

[28] B. L. Garrett, *Convicting the Innocent: Where Criminal Prosecutions Go Wrong* (Cambridge, MA, 2011), pp. 5–9, 45–83. Updated figures are available on the website of the Innocence Project based in Yeshiva University's School of Law, at <http://www.innocenceproject.org/about/> [Accessed 19 January 2015]. For similar organizations, see also the Center on Wrongful Convictions based in Northwestern University's School of Law: <http://www.law.northwestern.edu/legalclinic/wrongfulconvictions/issues/erroneousid/> [Accessed 19 January 2015]; and 'The National Registry of Exonerations' maintained by the University of Michigan Law School: <http://www.law.umich.edu/special/exoneration/Pages/about.aspx.> [Accessed 19 January 2015]. See especially, on the last of these sites, S. R. Gross and M. Shaffer, 'Exonerations in the United States, 1989–2012. Report by the National Registry of Exonerations', at <https://www.law.umich.edu/special/exoneration/Documents/exonerations_us_1989_2012_full_report.pdf>. An early groundbreaking study was P. M. Wall, *Eye-witness Identification in Criminal Cases* (Springfield, IL, 1965). See also Cutler and Penrod, *Mistaken Identification*; B. Scheck, P. J. Neufeld and J. Dwyer, *Actual Innocence: Five Days to Execution, and Other Dispatches from the Wrongly Convicted* (New York, 2000).

[29] For Loftus's career, see E. F. Loftus and K. Ketcham, *Witness for the Defense: The Accused, the Eyewitness, and the Expert Who Puts Memory on Trial* (New York, 1991); Doyle, *True Witness*, pp. 85–95; and the various appreciations in M. Garry

grave legal, social, cultural and individual consequence. One such was the wave of anxieties in the 1990s concerning the adult recovery, often under the guidance of zealous or manipulative psychotherapists, of what were taken to be repressed memories of childhood sexual abuse, some of it with allegedly satanic dimensions. A related scare around the same time involved accusations of the abuse of preschool children by care-givers in nurseries and kindergartens. One of the early pioneers of applied psychological research into eyewitnessing and memory, Alfred Binet, had demonstrated the ease with which children may form distorted and false memories of their own experiences.[30] So what was at stake in the preschool abuse allegations was the truthfulness of stories of malfeasance that were being teased out of the remarks of very young children, especially insofar as those remarks were elicited in conversations with adults who either brought strong ideological convictions to the task or were unaware of the deceptive ease with which a child's utterances can be innocently steered by prompts and hints embedded in the natural back-and-forth of dialogue. In the face of considerable hostility, and even personal threats, Loftus introduced a salutary note of rigorous scepticism into these debates.[31]

Loftus is best known, however, for her work on the problems of legal eyewitness testimony.[32] Her groundbreaking studies in the 1970s did much to reanimate the study of eyewitnessing, and they therefore provide a helpful point of entry into the wider body of research. Since Münsterberg's generation experimental psychologists had been able to demonstrate the inadequacies of eyewitness perception and memory by means of after-the-fact testing of the memories of unwitting witnesses to contrived and unexpected scenes such as staged classroom altercations or pretend robberies. Such demonstrations (many of which would now be considered unethically stressful on the involuntary subjects) were very good at exposing the exaggerated faith that the general public – and the legal profession – placed in the accuracy of eyewitness perception and

and H. Hayne (eds), *Do Justice and Let the Sky Fall: Elizabeth F. Loftus and Her Contributions to Science, Law, and Academic Freedom* (Mahwah, NJ, 2007).

[30] A. Binet, *La suggestibilité* (Paris, 1900).

[31] See E. F. Loftus, 'The Reality of Repressed Memories', *American Psychologist*, 48 (1993), 518–37; E. F. Loftus and K. Ketcham, *The Myth of Repressed Memory: False Memories and Allegations of Sexual Abuse* (New York, 1994).

[32] See her influential synthesis: E. F. Loftus, *Eyewitness Testimony*, rev. edn (Cambridge, MA, 1996). See also E. F. Loftus and K. Ketcham, 'The Malleability of Eyewitness Accounts', in S. M. A. Lloyd-Bostock and B. R. Clifford (eds), *Evaluating Witness Evidence: Recent Psychological Research and New Perspectives* (Chichester, 1983), pp. 159–71. A rather underrated study that was contemporary with Loftus's early research and touches on many similar questions is A. D. Yarmey, *The Psychology of Eyewitness Testimony* (New York, 1979). See also R. Buckhout, 'Eyewitness Testimony', *Scientific American*, 231:6 (1974), 23–31.

memory, but they could do little to explain the underlying psychological mechanisms at work.[33] This was the inspiration for Loftus's groundbreaking research.

In one of Loftus's experiments subjects were shown a film of a traffic accident and then immediately asked to state the speed of the cars 'when they smashed into each other'. Other subjects were asked the same question about speed, but it was rephrased with verbs such as 'collided', 'hit', 'contacted' and 'bumped'. Those who had been exposed to the notion of violent contact via the wording of the question offered higher estimates of the speed (though 'collided' and 'bumped', but not 'hit', generated similar figures). A week later, and without reviewing the film, the subjects were asked whether they had seen any broken glass. Although there was no such glass in the film, about one third of those who had responded to the 'smashed' question answered yes, while only about one in seven of the 'hit' group so responded – at the same rate, in fact, as a control group who had been exposed to no leading language at all.[34] In another test of the presumptions that can be introduced by the wording of a question after the fact, subjects were shown a film of cars colliding after one had failed to come to a proper halt at a stop sign. They were then asked about the speed of the offending car by means of a question that either did or did not expressly make mention of the sign. When also asked whether they remembered seeing the stop sign, 53 per cent of the group for whom the presence of the sign had been embedded in the phrasing of the earlier question answered in the affirmative but only 35 per cent of the group that had not received the implied confirmation did so.[35]

In a related experiment subjects were shown a film of a car accident involving a sports car on a country road. Some were then asked to give the speed of the car 'when it passed the barn'; others were asked without reference to a barn. There was no barn shown in the film. A week later the subjects were asked a new set of questions about the film, including 'Did you see a barn?'. Of those who had earlier been exposed to the suggestion that there had been a barn in the phrasing of the original round of questions, about 17 per cent replied yes, whereas fewer than 3 per cent of the control group did so.[36] In a further examination of this phenomenon which allowed subjects to nuance their responses rather than to confront a straight choice between yes and no, a slide sequence was shown depicting a pedestrian being knocked down by a red car. Part of the action involved a green car (shown

[33] See W. Stern, 'Realistic Experiments', in U. Neisser (ed.), *Memory Observed: Remembering in Natural Contexts* (New York, 1982), pp. 95–108.

[34] E. F. Loftus and J. C. Palmer, 'Reconstruction of Automobile Destruction: An Example of the Interaction Between Language and Memory', *Journal of Verbal Learning and Verbal Behavior*, 13 (1974), 585–9. For a helpful overview of these and related experiments, see Loftus, *Eyewitness Testimony*, pp. 56–60, 64–6, 71–2, 77–8, 95–7.

[35] E. F. Loftus, 'Leading Questions and the Eyewitness Report', *Cognitive Psychology*, 7 (1975), 560–72, esp. 563–5, 569–72.

[36] Loftus, 'Leading Questions', 566–7.

in just one slide) passing by the scene but not stopping. Immediately afterwards some of the participants in the experiment were asked whether the blue car that had passed by had had a ski rack on its roof; the others were asked this question without mention of a colour. In a recognition text administered some minutes later, the subjects were asked to identify the colour of the passing car on a colour wheel (in which the green and blue tones are adjacent and so shade into one another): those exposed to the presupposition that the car had in fact been blue tended to nudge towards the blue range or to choose compromise green-blue intermediate hues, whereas the responses of the control group, which had received no such complicating information, clustered more securely in the correct green range.[37]

In these experiments the subjects were distracted by dummy questions and filler tasks so as not to have their attention drawn unduly to the particular artifice at play within the wording of the questions that were directly at issue. Additionally, as we have seen, the complicating detail was smuggled into the presuppositions within questions that were overtly directed towards asking about other points of information. Loftus was here identifying a form of what has become known as the misinformation effect.[38] Its dangers in forensic settings are obvious, as when, for example, extraneous or erroneous details are introduced by the manner in which an investigating police officer frames a supportive remark to a witness or phrases the instructions in an identity parade; such distorting influences need not be malign in their intent or even consciously introduced for them to have a significant effect on the witness's subsequent recall.[39] There has been some debate over the cognitive mechanisms that allow such post-event information to exert an influence. Does it, as Loftus and many others would argue, replace the initial memory trace with a stronger version, so that the original memory is to all intents and purposes effaced? Does the new information simply fill gaps in the original memory trace? Or is the misinformation effect a failure of retrieval, which would imply that the original memory survives alongside the

[37] E. F. Loftus, 'Shifting Human Color Memory', *Memory & Cognition*, 5 (1977), 696–9. Cf. R. F. Belli, 'Color Blend Retrievals: Compromise Memories or Deliberate Compromise Responses?', *Memory & Cognition*, 16 (1988), 314–26.

[38] See E. F. Loftus, D. G. Miller and H. J. Burns, 'Semantic Integration of Verbal Information into a Verbal Memory', *Journal of Experimental Psychology: Human Learning and Memory*, 4 (1978), 19–31.

[39] See e.g. D. F. Hall, E. F. Loftus and J. P. Tousignant, 'Postevent Information and Changes in Recollection for a Natural Event', in G. L. Wells and E. F. Loftus (eds), *Eyewitness Testimony: Psychological Perspectives* (Cambridge, 1984), pp. 124–41; G. L. Wells and A. L. Bradfield, '"Good, You Identified the Suspect": Feedback to Eyewitnesses Distorts Their Reports of the Witnessing Experience', *Journal of Applied Psychology*, 83 (1998), 360–76; A. L. Bradfield, G. L. Wells and E. A. Olson, 'The Damaging Effect of Confirming Feedback on the Relation Between Eyewitness Certainty and Identification Accuracy', *Journal of Applied Psychology*, 87 (2002), 112–20.

intervening information and is potentially available, subject to the right stimulus, for subsequent recall free of the distorting detail? Is there a loss of awareness of the differences between the sources of information, a failure of what is referred to as 'source monitoring', such that a blend of inputs results which the subject believes is wholly based on the original perceptual experience? If this last, does revisualizing an event exacerbate the blurring of sources?[40]

Research has nuanced our understanding of the misinformation effect to some extent. One variable can be the perceived credibility and authority of the source of misinformation, and another is the extent to which the subject has made some extra mental commitment to the veracity of the original memory before the misinformation is introduced. The interval between the original event and the exposure to misinformation can also make a significant difference: longer delays can enhance the effect. And blatantly contradictory post-event information will often meet subject resistance.[41] Overall, however, the weight of research since Loftus's pioneering studies has confirmed the robustness of the misinformation effect hypothesis.[42] It can be shown at work in relation to

[40] For a helpful overview of the debates, co-authored by one of Loftus's former critics, see M. S. Zaragoza, R. F. Belli and K. E. Payment, 'Misinformation Effects and the Suggestibility of Eyewitness Memory', in Garry and Hayne (eds), *Do Justice*, pp. 35–63. Cf. D. A. Bekerian and J. M. Bowers, 'Eyewitness Testimony: Were We Misled?', *Journal of Experimental Psychology: Learning, Memory, and Cognition*, 9 (1983), 139–45; M. McCloskey and M. S. Zaragoza, 'Misleading Postevent Information and Memory for Events: Arguments and Evidence Against Memory Impairment Hypotheses', *Journal of Experimental Psychology: General*, 114 (1985), 1–16; D. S. Lindsay, 'Misleading Suggestions Can Impair Eyewitnesses' Ability to Remember Event Details', *Journal of Experimental Psychology: Learning, Memory, and Cognition*, 16 (1990), 1077–83; M. S. Zaragoza and S. M. Lane, 'Source Misattribution and the Suggestibility of Eyewitness Memory', *Journal of Experimental Psychology: Learning, Memory, and Cognition*, 20 (1994), 934–45; D. G. Payne, M. P. Toglia and J. S. Anastasi, 'Recognition Performance Level and the Magnitude of the Misinformation Effect in Eyewitness Memory', *Psychonomic Bulletin and Review*, 1 (1994), 376–82.

[41] Zaragoza, Belli and Payment, 'Misinformation Effects', 37–8; D. H. Dodd and J. M. Bradshaw, 'Leading Questions and Memory: Pragmatic Constraints', *Journal of Verbal Learning and Verbal Behavior*, 19 (1980), 695–704; V. L. Smith and P. C. Ellsworth, 'The Social Psychology of Eyewitness Accuracy: Misleading Questions and Communicator Expertise', *Journal of Applied Psychology*, 72 (1987), 294–300; L. A. Vornik, S. J. Sharman and M. Garry, 'The Power of the Spoken Word: Sociolinguistic Cues Influence the Misinformation Effect', *Memory*, 11 (2003), 101–9.

[42] See e.g. J. W. Schooler, D. Gerhard and E. F. Loftus, 'Qualities of the Unreal', *Journal of Experimental Psychology: Learning, Memory, and Cognition*, 12 (1986), 171–81, arguing that verbal descriptions of suggested visual details are typically longer, and contain more hedges and references to one's cognitive operations, than renderings of accurately recalled detail. This, however, runs up against the well-attested tendency of jurors to equate the amount of incidental detail in a piece of eyewitness testimony

a wide range of events, among different subject populations, and consequent upon various ways of introducing the post-event information.[43] The effect can prove remarkably robust even when subjects are reminded that the post-event information derives from a source other than their original perceptions; that is to say, people can almost wilfully persist in blending discrete sources of memory in the interests of securely assigning the resulting composite to the initial event alone.[44] At its further limits the misinformation effect can even be shown in the introduction of wholly false memories, a phenomenon that is of course pertinent to the problem of how suspects can sometimes come to believe that they have committed a crime of which they are in fact innocent, as well as to the controversy surrounding the supposed retrieval of buried childhood memories.[45] In one

---

with its credibility: see B. E. Bell and E. F. Loftus, 'Degree of Detail of Eyewitness Testimony and Mock Juror Judgments', *Journal of Applied Social Psychology*, 18 (1988), 1171–92.

43 E. F. Loftus, 'Planting Misinformation in the Human Mind: A 30-Year Investigation of the Malleability of Memory', *Learning and Memory*, 12 (2005), 361–6; A. B. Douglass and N. Steblay, 'Memory Distortion in Eyewitnesses: A Meta-Analysis of the Post-identification Feedback Effect', *Applied Cognitive Psychology*, 20 (2006), 859–69.

44 See P. A. Higham, 'Believing Details Known To Have Been Suggested', *British Journal of Psychology*, 89 (1998), 265–83. But see also the qualifications in D. S. Lindsay and M. K. Johnson, 'The Eyewitness Suggestibility Effect and Memory for Source', *Memory & Cognition*, 17 (1989), 349–58. For the dissociation that can occur between the memory for a source and the memory of its content, see L. L. Jacoby, C. Kelley, J. Brown and J. Jasechko, 'Becoming Famous Overnight: Limits on the Ability To Avoid Unconscious Influences of the Past', *Journal of Personality and Social Psychology*, 56 (1989), 326–38. For the general question of what is known as 'source monitoring', see M. K. Johnson, S. Hashtroudi and D. S. Lindsay, 'Source Monitoring', *Psychological Bulletin*, 114 (1993), 3–28; D. S. Lindsay, 'Autobiographical Memory, Eyewitness Reports, and Public Policy', *Canadian Psychology*, 48 (2007), 57–66. Cf. E. J. Marsh, M. L. Meade and H. L. Roediger III, 'Learning Facts from Fiction', *Journal of Memory and Language*, 49 (2003), 519–36. Many failures of source monitoring involve the filling of gaps, whereby what is unseen but inferred is later recalled as if directly experienced: see e.g. M. S. Greenberg, D. R. Westcott and S. E. Bailey, 'When Believing Is Seeing: The Effects of Scripts on Eyewitness Memory', *Law and Human Behavior*, 22 (1998), 685–94; M. R. Tuckey and N. Brewer, 'The Influence of Schemas, Stimulus Ambiguity, and Interview Schedule on Eyewitness Memory Over Time', *Journal of Experimental Psychology: Applied*, 9 (2003), 101–18; M. P. Gerrie, L. E. Belcher and M. Garry, '"Mind the Gap": False Memories for Missing Aspects of an Event', *Applied Cognitive Psychology*, 20 (2006), 689–96.

45 See Q. M. Chrobak and M. S. Zaragoza, 'Inventing Stories: Forcing Witnesses To Fabricate Entire Fictitious Events Leads to Freely Reported False Memories', *Psychonomic Bulletin and Review*, 15 (2008), 1190–5; Q. M. Chrobak and M. S. Zaragoza, 'When Forced Fabrications Become Truth: Causal Explanations and False Memory Development', *Journal of Experimental Psychology: General*, 142 (2013), 827–44.

set of revealing studies, for example, young adults could become convinced of a childhood memory that had no basis in fact when they were exposed to misinformation from parents or other family members who were in league with the experimenters.[46]

To what extent are the findings of recent research into eyewitnessing and eyewitness memory applicable to the study of the distant past and its historiographical cultures? Are there practical and theoretical limitations?[47] Certain dissonances between historical and psychological approaches emerge when one considers the constraints under which psychological researchers operate when they design and conduct their experiments, for these raise questions about the extent to which those who take part are representative of the rich variety of human experience in diverse times and places. The staple population pools from which experimental subject cohorts are typically drawn are university undergraduates. Some projects, such as investigations into memory in children and the old, obviously require that researchers look beyond their own institutional environments. But in almost every case in which the experiment's research questions do not highlight the sorts of variables, such as age, that would disqualify most students, this demographic tends to be treated as the default sample population with which to test hypotheses about human capacities in general. Sometimes the students are paid, modestly, for their time, but it is often the case that they are effectively a captive audience by virtue of their taking an introductory course on aspects of psychology and receiving class credit in return for their participation. This raises the possibility that subjects with some formal knowledge, however rudimentary, of the ways in which psychological research questions are framed, and of the procedures devised to answer those questions, are particularly susceptible to responding to what are termed an experiment's design demand characteristics. This is a phenomenon which has been understood for several decades whereby subjects make inferences from the nature of the experiment in which they are taking part about the sorts of responses that they believe the

[46] I. E. Hyman, T. H. Husband and F. J. Billings, 'False Memories of Childhood Experiences', *Applied Cognitive Psychology*, 9 (1995), 181–97; I. E. Hyman and J. Pentland, 'The Role of Mental Imagery in the Creation of False Childhood Memories', *Journal of Memory and Language*, 35 (1996), 101–17. Cf. M. Garry, C. G. Manning, E. F. Loftus and S. J. Sherman, 'Imagination Inflation: Imagining a Childhood Event Inflates Confidence That it Occurred', *Psychonomic Bulletin and Review*, 3 (1996), 208–14.

[47] For a helpful critique of eyewitness research, significantly from within the research tradition and at an early stage in its modern development, see B. Clifford, 'A Critique of Eyewitness Research', in M. M. Gruneberg, P. E. Morris and R. N. Sykes (eds), *Practical Aspects of Memory* (London, 1978), pp. 199–209. See also the robust and wide-ranging comments in C. A. J. Coady, *Testimony: A Philosophical Study* (Oxford, 1992), pp. 262–76.

experimenters expect of them.[48] The larger problem with this standard subject demographic, however, is one of cultural applicability. The majority of these student populations are North American; most of the remainder are western European. What has been termed experimental psychology's 'ethnocentric inertia' has recently been addressed by an increased interest in framing research questions in cross-cultural, comparative terms.[49] This research orientation qualifies some of the conclusions drawn from the use of Western undergraduate subject populations to a sufficient degree to suggest that one should be wary of making universalizing statements about the workings of human cognition and the attuning of the self to its ambient psychological environment not only laterally, with reference to diverse cultures in the present day, but also, and *a fortiori*, longitudinally with respect to people in the past.[50]

It is also important to remember that the sorts of experiments that we are considering seek to identify possible ways in which subjects respond in controlled conditions. They do not establish general laws that govern all human cognition and behaviour (a significant qualification that can sometimes get lost in syntheses of this research aimed at the non-specialist reader). Additionally, the legal orientation of much of the research into eyewitnessing means that the bar it sets for itself is quite low, for all that is needed is to be able to show that in a given set of circumstances eyewitness memory is often significantly less accurate than the demonstrably exaggerated faith placed in it by judges and jurors would seem to suggest. This is the source of much of the tension between trial lawyers and psychologists who serve as expert witnesses. The lawyers want the psychologists to be able to pronounce on whether a specific piece of eyewitness testimony is or is not reliable, whereas the psychologists can only point out the circumstances in which and the reasons why it *might* be unreliable.[51] For those psychologists

[48] Cf. Coady's rather harsh but not wholly unfair reference to 'university students who by now probably know what to expect when the [experimentally staged] "crime" occurs': *Testimony*, p. 276.

[49] The formulation is that of S. J. Heine, D. R. Lehman, H. R. Markus and S. Kitayama, 'Is There a Universal Need for Positive Self-Regard?', *Psychological Review*, 106 (1999), 785.

[50] Cf. M. B. Brewer and W. Gardner, 'Who Is This "We"? Levels of Collective Identity and Self–Representation', *Journal of Personality and Social Psychology*, 71 (1996), 83–93; M. D. Leichtman, Q. Wang and D. B. Pillemer, 'Cultural Variations in Interdependence and Autobiographical Memory: Lessons from Korea, China, India, and the United States', in R. Fivush and C. A. Haden (eds), *Autobiographical Memory and the Construction of a Narrative Self: Developmental and Cultural Perspectives* (Mahwah, NJ, 2003), pp. 73–97. It is noteworthy that much of the recent cross-cultural research nudges close to trading in stereotypes. This is especially evident in the recurrent contrasting of 'individualistic' American culture and the more 'collective' social systems found elsewhere, most notably in east Asia.

[51] The foundational study of this problem was G. L. Wells, 'Applied Eyewitness-Testimony

campaigning for their voices to be heard in the legal process, the calculation simply comes down to whether the doubts they raise about the accuracy of eyewitness evidence bite on the criminal burden of proof in common law, which requires that guilt be established beyond reasonable doubt. In this context, it is noteworthy that attempts to use discourse analysis to differentiate between accurate testimony and confabulation – for example, by looking for disfluencies and qualifications, references to sensory and emotional experience, and express mentions of the act of recall itself – are deeply unconvincing.[52] At best this research catalogues some of the means by which experienced interrogators and lawyers conducting cross-examinations instinctively spot the dishonest and mendacious witness, but it has practically no diagnostic value with respect to the sorts of situation with which the psychological research is predominantly concerned, which is when people have the subjective sense of telling the truth even though they are in fact volunteering distorted or false accounts of their eyewitness experience.

The dominance of the legal paradigm has had important implications for the types of questions that the psychological research has posed. In particular, and for obvious reasons, a good deal of attention has been paid to facial misrecognition.[53] While many of the factors that can influence false identification, such as the distorting effects of selective attention, simplification, stereotyping and failures of source monitoring, apply to other problems of eyewitness perception and recall, the recognition and reading of others' faces are so basic to all forms of human interaction that they make particular perceptual and cognitive demands.[54]

Research: System Variables and Estimator Variables', *Journal of Personality and Social Psychology*, 36 (1978), 1546–57. See also B. L. Cutler, S. D. Penrod and T. K. Martens, 'The Reliability of Eyewitness Identification: The Role of System and Estimator Variables', *Law and Human Behavior*, 11 (1987), 233–58. Cf. D. M. Bernstein and E. F. Loftus, 'How To Tell if a Particular Memory Is True or False', *Perspectives on Psychological Science*, 4 (2009), 370–4.

[52] See e.g. L. Haber and R. N. Haber, 'Criteria for Judging the Admissibility of Eyewitness Testimony of Long Past Events', *Psychology, Public Policy, and Law*, 4 (1998), 1135–59. It is perhaps significant that most of the interest in this approach is evident among scholars working in civil law jurisdictions, in which forensic procedures favour the inquisitorial piecing together of a master narrative of events, in contrast to the adversarial, all-or-nothing approach to the testing and evaluation of eyewitness testimony that characterizes the common law tradition. See e.g. B. Waubert de Puiseau, A. Assfalg, E. Erdfelder and D. M. Bernstein, 'Extracting the Truth from Conflicting Eyewitness Reports: A Formal Modelling Approach', *Journal of Experimental Psychology: Applied*, 18 (2012), 390–403. For an older such attempt, see A. Trankell, *Reliability of Evidence: Methods for Analyzing and Assessing Witness Statements* (Stockholm, 1972), esp. pp. 67–170.

[53] For a helpful overview, see Loftus, *Eyewitness Testimony*, pp. 134–52.

[54] See H. D. Ellis, 'Practical Aspects of Face Memory', in G. L. Wells and E. F. Loftus

Facial recognition and the ways in which it can misfire are thus to some extent *sui generis*. This is, moreover, a type of eyewitness perception that is seldom at issue in the sorts of historical evidence with which we are immediately concerned. Our target texts sometimes describe an individual's facial appearance but there are no situations, in these texts at least, in which the narrator expresses uncertainty about the facial recognition of a character or a plot sequence hinges on such misrecognition.

A further and related consequence of the orientation of the research towards forensic applications is that it privileges memories for the short, sharp shock, that is to say the sort of exposure to the world that an eyewitness has to a brief, sometimes violent and typically unexpected and upsetting event such as a serious crime or accident. The events to which experimental subjects are exposed, by means, for example, of films or sequences of still images, typically last from a few seconds to one or two minutes. Their brevity is, in a sense, the whole point. To what extent, however, may conclusions about eyewitness perception and recall based on the experience of such fleeting events be scaled outwards to larger and more complex slices of human action and interaction? For our purposes, a significant feature of all our texts, like most other medieval historiographical works, is that their main structuring device is the stringing together of more or less discrete sequences that narrate one episode or a tight cluster of episodes. As we shall see, this technique does not preclude generalization, abstraction, anachrony, gapping, elision and other means to break up the one-thing-after-another monotony of event-driven, paratactical narration. Nonetheless, the episode is for the most part the basic building block of the texts' plots, and to this extent the eyewitness research would seem to have some potentially valuable purchase on our material. There are, however, differences of scale to consider, for the temporal and spatial dimensions of the kinds of episodes that typically feature in our texts, such as conversations, diplomatic exchanges, military manoeuvres, battles and skirmishes, and one or more days' travel, are greater than the staple scenarios of eyewitness research. One of the questions that needs to be asked of the target texts, therefore, is the manner in which each divides the flow of narrated action into episodic units, and by extension whether these units are analogous to the sorts of experiences investigated by psychological research.

Within the psychological research tradition itself doubts have been raised about what is termed the 'ecological validity' of many of the experiments into eyewitnessing. To what extent do experimenters place subjects in situations within the laboratory that tidy up and simplify the sheer complexity and messiness of life in the outside world? It should be borne in mind that experimental protocols are as a matter of course designed precisely to filter out such complexity and messiness,

(eds), *Eyewitness Testimony: Psychological Perspectives* (Cambridge, 1984), pp. 12–37.

for the experimenter's imperative is to isolate a single variable so as to be able to measure its effects against a control that departs from the test conditions in just that one respect. There is too much 'noise' in the real world to be able to ascribe a given effect precisely to one particular antecedent factor. It is noteworthy that when researchers have sought out greater ecological validity, the picture drawn from laboratory experiments has sometimes stood in need of revision. For example, in a pioneering study along these lines Yuille and Cutshall tracked down and interviewed, after a delay of a few months, thirteen of the twenty-one witnesses who had originally supplied evidence to the police about an attempted armed robbery on a Canadian gun shop.[55] This had been a violent and shocking incident: the robber ended up being shot dead in the street outside the shop, while the shopowner, the one who shot him, was himself badly wounded. Yuille and Cutshall constructed a control version of events by means of a synthesis of the original witness statements to the police and other pieces of evidence, a process closely akin, that is, to historical reconstruction. When compared with this control, the memory of the thirteen re-interviewed witnesses proved on the whole to be remarkably robust. There was some loss of accuracy in such matters as the colour of clothing and estimates of the robber's age and height, but the overall quality of recall that had been evident in the witness statements made soon after the event was sustained in the subsequent interviews. Moreover, the memories of those who had been closest to the incident and had been most caught up in it were generally among the most accurate. Yuille and Cutshall wondered whether the persistence of the subjects' memories owed something to their having retold the incident many times in the intervening four or five months, for clearly the experience was such that it invited both frequent mental rehearsal and narration in conversational settings. They considered this a strong possibility, while also noting that some of the details that the subjects provided had not been volunteered in their police statements and were not necessarily of the sort that would be likely to appear in spontaneous and informal narrations of the event. In other words, the eyewitnesses' memories remained sufficiently detailed, and accurate, to be at least partial proof against the overlaying effects of mental rehearsal and retelling after the fact.[56]

As debates about the ecological validity of experimental paradigms have revealed, a key question is the extent to which experiments sufficiently capture

[55] J. C. Yuille and J. L. Cutshall, 'A Case Study of Eyewitness Memory of a Crime', *Journal of Applied Psychology*, 71 (1986), 291–301. See also P. J. van Koppen and S. K. Kochun, 'Portraying Perpetrators: The Validity of Offender Descriptions by Witnesses', *Law and Human Behavior*, 21 (1997), 661–85.

[56] Cf. the evidence of the persistence of broadly accurate, if generalized, memories over four decades discussed in W. A. Wagenaar and J. Groeneweg, 'The Memory of Concentration Camp Survivors', *Applied Cognitive Psychology*, 4 (1990), 77–87.

both the complexity of eyewitnessing as an experience and the self-construction of the eyewitness out in the real world of human interaction. It is sometimes argued that experimental procedures unduly detach the test subject from the material to which she or he is exposed. The subject has no ultimate stake in the exercise and its long-term consequences. Also, experimental inputs tend to be very simple. In part this is a consequence of the need to control variables, as discussed above, and to some extent it also comes down to constraints imposed by cost and logistics. But it has the effect of detaching the subject from personal investment in the human situation, such as a crime or accident, that the experiment calls forth. In part this makes perfect sense from the point of view of forensic application. Most legal eyewitnesses are not victims or suspects and their confederates; they are, instead, third-party bystanders who happened to find themselves unwillingly thrust into the role of observer. None of Yuille and Cutshall's subjects, for instance, knew the robber or the shopowner; their direct engagement with the robbery began and ended in the short period of time during which their attention was directed to the argument and exchange of gunfire on the pavement outside the gun shop. Here the dissonances with our historical eyewitnesses seem most pronounced, for the authors of our target texts were not bystanders in the wrong place at the wrong time, so to speak, but volunteers, more or less, who had placed themselves in unusual, stressful and immersive environments over long periods. Perhaps the most significant disanalogy to be noted, therefore, is that the psychological eyewitnessing research generally focuses on what happens when latent perceptual and cognitive capacities are briefly activated by occasional and unusual irruptions into the normal course of affairs, whereas the eyewitnessing of our authors was probably closer to a progressively developed and practised facility.[57] The eyewitnesses outside the gun shop would be forgiven for hoping that they would never be exposed to similar incidents in the future; they would have no desire to become *de facto* experts in the observation of violent crime. But this same sort of expertise, born of the sort of cumulative exposure and practice that naturalize the unusual, the unexpected and the shocking, was probably something to which our authors consciously aspired, especially those who had joined the crusade expedition with the preformed intention of writing an account of it. These eyewitnesses had the opportunity, the means and the motive to learn on the job.

Studies of eyewitnessing tend to share the strongly realist and materialist orientation that is evident in research psychology generally. That is to say, experiments contrive control points of reference, what are deemed to be the true or

[57] For a good overview of the factors attending the encoding, retrieval and articulation of memories of brief and unexpected events involving strangers, see R. N. Haber and L. Haber, 'Experiencing, Remembering and Reporting Events', *Psychology, Public Policy, and Law*, 6 (2000), 1057–97.

ideal conditions, against which subjects' responses are judged. As a corollary, the inevitable slippage, great or small, that experiments discover between the external reference point and the subject's recall of it is described in negative evaluative terms such as 'error', 'fallibility' and 'contagion'.[58] Again, the forensic context serves as a justification: it does not matter whether someone recalls information quite accurately almost all of the time if one of the few occasions on which she or he fails to do so results in an innocent person going to prison. This realist slant helps to explain the research's emphasis on the accurate recall of isolatable details. But ecological validity is thereby reduced on two counts. First, the *pointilliste* focus upon single details within an event strains out the associative texture of much recall. Suppose, for example, that a subject in Loftus's green car/blue car experiment had owned a car of that make and/or colour, or had been involved in a similar sort of accident. How might this influence her or his memory of the depicted event? Second, the stripping down of a witnessed episode to its basic propositional elements and the posing of yes/no recognition questions may correspond to certain forensic demands made of the eyewitness ('Is *this* the jacket the attacker was wearing?'), but it misses the essential narrative quality of recall in virtually all other circumstances. As a result, it fails to capture much of the richness of autobiographical memory, to which eyewitnessing substantially contributes.[59] As Tilmann Habermas has argued, the psychological researchers' emphasis upon the moment and its individual external details misses the complexity that psychoanalysis's attention to narrative introduces into the understanding of memory.[60] By extension, understandings of narrative other than those grounded in psychoanalysis, such as those suggested by narratology, also problematize the eyewitness research tradition's focus upon specific details and single events.

There are, therefore, good grounds for caution concerning the disciplinary synergies between the historical analysis of material such as our target texts and

[58] See e.g. M. L. Meade and H. L. Roediger III, 'Explorations in the Social Contagion of Memory', *Memory & Cognition*, 30 (2002), 995–1009.

[59] See e.g. the useful critique of cognitive psychology's attention to objective truthfulness in D. Edwards and J. Potter, 'The Chancellor's Memory: Rhetoric and Truth in Discursive Remembering', *Applied Cognitive Psychology*, 6 (1992), 187–215. This article builds in part on Ulric Neisser's classic study 'John Dean's Memory: A Case Study', *Cognition*, 9 (1981), 1–22.

[60] T. Habermas, 'Identity, Emotion, and the Social Matrix of Autobiographical Memory: A Psychoanalytic Narrative View', in D. Bernsten and D. C. Rubin (eds), *Autobiographical Memory: Theories and Approaches* (Cambridge, 2012), pp. 33–53. See also D. K. Thomsen, 'There Is More to Life Stories than Memories', *Memory*, 17 (2009), 445–57 on the relationship between specific memories, micro-narratives and temporally extended units of experience in the construction of a life story. For a similar approach, see S. Bluck and T. Habermas, 'The Life Story Schema', *Motivation and Emotion*, 24 (2000), 121–47.

psychological research into eyewitnessing. That said, the dissonances between the two are far from total, and certain suggestive interconnections are worth pursuing, subject to the caveats that have just been noted. The psychological literature cannot tell us how people in the Middle Ages 'must have' thought and acted, still less what went through the minds of the authors of our texts as they experienced events and wrote about them.[61] But it can help to guide the framing of questions about the authors' acts of eyewitnessing, their possible attitudes to their roles as observers, and the manner in which their experiences were articulated and communicated. The point to emphasize in this context is that the orientation towards real-world applications that we have seen animates much of the eyewitness research accentuates imbalances that characterize the investigative reach of psychological study in the round. Such imbalances are themselves grounded in the nature of memory itself. Memory is traditionally divided into three stages or functions. First a specific memory is formed, or encoded. It used to be believed that memory was a single, global capacity of the mind, which meant that the encoding of particular experiences involved the creation of a unitary memory trace, or engram, within which the totality of all that would be available for subsequent recall was compactly and efficiently stored. Much recent research has suggested that individual memory traces are in fact dispersed across the multiple sites within the brain that process various forms of stimulus, for example the visual and the verbal. In this way the encoding process, what in effect makes a particular memory, involves the creation of neural networks between the parts of the brain that are in play. Right from the moment of inception, therefore, a memory is a dynamic process, not a static state. The second stage or function of memory involves the persistence of memory traces. The metaphor of storage that is often used to denote this stage is too inert in its associations, for the retention phase is typically characterized by memory decay, a process familiar since Hermann Ebbinghaus's pioneering studies in the late nineteenth century into the rates at which he forgot sequences of nonsense syllables that he had made himself learn.[62]

The third stage is memory retrieval, an activation process that can assume many forms, from the awakening of what are believed to be repressed childhood memories in psychoanalytical therapy, and 'pop ups' cued by the associative links that surface in one's stream of consciousness, to memories activated by elements within the environment such as an evocative smell, and the sort of directed, conscious recollective effort one might make when sitting an exam or making a witness statement to the police. Obviously there is a heuristic mismatch built into the study of the three phases of memory, for the workings of the first and second can only be investigated by means of evidence supplied by the operation of the

[61] Cf. J. M. Zacks and B. Tversky, 'Event Structure in Perception and Cognition', *Psychological Review*, 127 (2001), 3–21.

[62] For Ebbinghaus's experiments, see Foster, *Memory*, pp. 8–11.

third. It is true that memory formation, like many and probably all cognitive processes, has physiological correlates that can be tracked by means of neuro-imaging techniques such as positron emission tomography (PET) and magnetic resonance imaging (MRI). But research has a very long way to go before it can make precise, predictive connections between fluctuations in neural activity and the detailed content of an encoded memory, still less capture the subjective texture of its subsequent recall. To all intents and purposes, therefore, the psychological investigation of memory must route itself through evidence generated by acts of retrieval. From the perspective of the retrieval process, the research gaze can be directed in one of two directions: back into the encoding and retention phases, or forward into the 'afterlife' of the retrieved memory, that is to say the mutations it undergoes and the effects that it has in the world of social interaction once it has left the privacy of the individual rememberer's mind. Whichever of these two emphases informs a given experiment's hypotheses, procedures and conclusions, in practical terms eyewitness research relies heavily on examination of manifestations of the latter. The result is that even studies that on the surface attend to questions of perception and memory encoding can also aid our understanding of eyewitness memory as something that is communicated between people and functions as a social resource.

A good example is Simons and Chabris's amusing but effective demonstration of the workings of change blindness, which is the well-known tendency to miss mutations in those parts of one's environment that are not the subject of focused attention.[63] It is easy to assume that the sheer amount of detail that becomes available to awareness when we self-consciously attend to what is in our visual field at a particular moment must translate into correspondingly rich and full mental representations. But our attentional selectivity, without which we would simply drown in all the detail of the world that we experience, severely limits what is apprehended and consequently what is available for later recall. In a striking exploration of this phenomenon, Simons and Chabris asked their subjects to direct their attention closely to a film of a group of people passing a basketball between themselves.[64] The degree of selective attention was enhanced by asking

[63] For studies of this phenomenon see U. Neisser and R. Becklen, 'Selective Looking: Attending to Visually Specified Events', *Cognitive Psychology*, 7 (1975), 480–94; R. Becklen and D. Cervone, 'Selective Looking and the Noticing of Unexpected Events', *Memory & Cognition*, 11 (1983), 601–8; R. A. Rensick, J. K. O'Regan and J. J. Clark, 'To See or Not To See: The Need for Attention to Perceive Changes in Scenes', *Psychological Science*, 8 (1997), 368–73; D. J. Simons and D. T. Levin, 'Failure to Detect Changes to People During a Real-World Interaction', *Psychonomic Bulletin and Review*, 5 (1998), 644–9. See also A. Mack and I. Rock, *Inattentional Blindness* (Cambridge, MA, 1998).

[64] D. J. Simons and C. F. Chabris, 'Gorillas in Our Midst: Sustained Inattentional Blindness for Dynamic Events', *Perception*, 28 (1999), 1059–74.

the subjects to count the number of passes. Incongruously, a woman holding an umbrella (the scene was played out indoors) or a person in a full-body gorilla suit was shown strolling through the middle of the group. Only about half of the subjects subsequently recalled having observed the umbrella-woman or the gorilla, even though they were prodded by an ascending scale of questions that went from innocently asking whether they had happened to see anything out of the ordinary to making explicit mention of the presence and appearance of the intrusive figure. When the monitoring task used to divert subjects' attention was made more intricate, the proportion of those who failed to notice the woman or the gorilla rose still higher.[65]

For our purposes, what is most compelling about this experiment is not its formal procedures, but what must have been its epilogue, when the subjects who had missed the woman or the gorilla were debriefed and shown, to their near-certain surprise, what had actually been visible in the film that they had only recently watched. True to the standard protocols of such experiments, the subjects would have been treated as isolated individuals, kept apart so that they could not contaminate their responses by conversationally swapping notes on what they had seen. They also, and unusually, were granted the opportunity to see an aspect of their experience played back and judged against an external record of 'how it really was'. But let us imagine that the observed scene had occurred in a natural human environment; that there were no external points of reference with which to gauge the accuracy of each observer's recollection of it after the fact; and that some or all of the observers knew one another and discussed what they had seen. What if one of these observers, someone whose original perception had missed an aspect of the episode that others had registered and considered noteworthy, decided to pen an account that omitted the detail in an act of self-assertive vindication of her or his own powers of observation and recollection as against what others claimed? What if, conversely, she or he acceded to the credibility of others by including the detail, or occupied some intermediate ground by means of qualifications and hedges? What if the author was one of those who *did* originally perceive the detail at issue but subsequently came to entertain doubts about its veracity? Whatever the particular permutation between observer, observation and telling, in each case the scene-as-narrated would be the result of negotiations and trade-offs between the individual observer's subjective convictions about what she or he did or did not see and a range of influences introduced in the course of social interactions.

If we return to Elizabeth Loftus's pioneering work on the post-event misinformation effect, we can see that one of its main contributions has been to highlight

[65] For countervailing evidence that people's memory for scenes can sometimes prove very robust, see A. Hollingsworth, 'Memory for Real-World Scenes', in J. R. Brockmole (ed.), *The Visual World in Memory* (Hove, 2009), pp. 89–116.

the intimate interplay between image and language in eyewitness memory. To take just one of the early experiments that we considered, that involving the planting of false suggestions about the presence of a barn, this neatly demonstrates the image-language binary that is a leitmotif of a great deal of eyewitness research. There are different views concerning the relationship between imagery and language within cognition and memory in general. One approach is that memory traces formed by visual and other sensory inputs are quickly effaced by their verbal representations, which then become the basis of subsequent recall. Recollection of the sensory dimensions of an experience is, in this view, a reconstitution, or back-formation, derived from the verbalization of the original non-verbal memory trace. The view that seems to enjoy general acceptance, however, is that both the verbal and the imagistic (and other sense-derived) elements of an experience are encoded in the mind, and that acts of autobiographical recall typically involve interactions between them.[66] The relative contributions of the imagistic and verbal components of a memory trace vary between individuals and from stimulus to stimulus; and they are also notoriously difficult to disentangle either experimentally or in private introspection. More often than not, however, the verbal element tends to have the greater impact on recall.

This effect, like many other aspects of current interest in psychological research, was observed by one of the founding figures in the field, Sir Frederic Bartlett, in his celebrated work *Remembering* (1932). Bartlett showed his subjects illustrations of the heads of individuals of various naval and military ranks; the experiment was conducted during the First World War and presupposed in the subjects a quite detailed knowledge of a wide range of service insignia and headwear. The subjects were then tested, after various intervals, for their memories of the depicted individuals' characteristics, as expressed in free description of the faces. Recall tended to be guided by judgements that had been made at the time of the viewing of the images, and drew upon stock characterizations such as 'grave', 'good-humoured', 'weather-beaten' and 'of a pleasant type'.[67] This process, sometimes known as verbal overshadowing, has subsequently been demonstrated in a wide variety of experimental conditions. For our purposes, two aspects of it are particularly noteworthy. First, verbal overshadowing is not simply, or mainly, in the nature of a complement or reinforcement of the visual memory of a stimulus. It can alter the memory, sometimes profoundly. In one study, for example, subjects were invited to verbalize their memories of the facial appearance of an individual whom they had seen in a film. In a subsequent

[66] Cf. A. Paivio, 'The Mind's Eye in Arts and Science', *Poetics*, 12 (1983), 1–18, esp. 6–11, 16–17.

[67] F. C. Bartlett, *Remembering: A Study in Experimental and Social Psychology* (Cambridge, 1932), pp. 47–62.

recognition test these subjects identified the person they had described less frequently than did members of a control group who had seen the film but had not articulated their memories of it.[68] Second, verbal overshadowing is evident even with very simple forms of verbalization. We would fully expect this sort of effect to be apparent in material such as our target texts if we were to focus on higher-order discursive registers such as the cultural scripts and schemata embedded in the narration of the action and the many subtleties and textures of literary language. But overshadowing begins at the basic lexical level; the verbal tagging of an aspect of experience, at the encoding stage or in subsequent mental rehearsals, can have a very significant impact on recall.[69]

The verbal dimension is, of course, the key to the communication of memories. Bartlett's subjects were not merely making individual and idiosyncratic personological judgements about the faces they had been shown; their assessments were informed, as Bartlett had expected, by socially current assumptions about naval and military 'types'. In other words, each subject's choices of characterizations implicitly anticipated the possibility that they might have occasion to communicate their impressions to others in a shared cultural environment sensitized by the mass experience of wartime conditions; Bartlett's testing of their memories was simply one occasion for this kind of social communication, albeit staged in unusually contrived circumstances. One of the greatest challenges posed by historical materials such as our target texts is to assess what happened to a given item of memory in the interval between the eyewitness experience and the act of committing it to writing. Even in the very unlikely event that our authors were socially detached figures, never sharing aspects of their experience orally during that interval, their verbal tagging and mental rehearsals would have sufficed to effect changes in the memory of events. And any articulation of the memory in social interactions would have accentuated this process of mutation. Various strands of research into eyewitnessing and related memory functions suggest some of the factors that might have been at play – that is to say, cognitive and social dimensions that we must suppose were as salient in our authors' worlds as they are in our own.

[68] J. W. Schooler and T. Y. Engstler-Schooler, 'Verbal Overshadowing of Visual Memories: Some Things Are Better Left Unsaid', *Cognitive Psychology*, 22 (1990), 36–71.

[69] Cf. a landmark study that was published in the same year as Bartlett's *Remembering*: L. Carmichael, H. P. Hogan and A. A. Walter, 'An Experimental Study of the Effect of Language on the Reproduction of Visually Perceived Form', *Journal of Experimental Psychology*, 15 (1932), 73–86. Subjects were shown simply drawn and deliberately ambiguous outline figures accompanied by one of a pair of verbal labels such as crescent moon/letter C and kidney bean/canoe. When asked to reproduce the figures from memory, the subjects tended to introduce additions and distortions in such a way that their rendering conformed more securely to the object designated by the label they had been given.

For example, the earliest and most formative occasions in which our authors discussed their experiences were probably not exercises in instruction for the benefit of those who had been absent, but rather the conversational sharing and comparing of recollections and impressions with fellow participants. Among the social psychological effects that such collective, and by extension collaborative, recall probably encouraged was convergence and transference, the tendency of an individual's memories to shift in the direction of conformity to an emergent consensus within a group to which the individual belongs or with which he or she identifies. A striking demonstration of this process is to be found in an analysis by Memon and Wright of the FBI's investigation of the Oklahoma City bombing in 1995.[70] The device that destroyed a large federal office building, killing 168 people and injuring many hundreds more, consisted of a truck packed with explosive materials. Three witnesses who worked at the car body shop from which the main culprit, Timothy McVeigh, rented the truck became convinced that he had visited the business accompanied by another man. This second suspect became known as 'John Doe 2'. John Doe 2 eventually turned out to be a phantom, but not before he had been the subject of a great deal of the FBI's investigative effort. (McVeigh did indeed have a confederate, Terry Nichols, but Nichols had not been involved in this part of their plan.) It transpired that one of the body shop witnesses had transposed into his memory of McVeigh's visit a (wholly innocent) customer who had visited the premises a day later. This type of error, that of conflation or transference, is one of the principal types of mistake to which eyewitness memory is prey.

Of further interest in this case is the experience of the two coworkers who had also been present at the body shop on the day of McVeigh's visit. At first their evidence to the authorities had been at best equivocal as to whether McVeigh had come on his own or with an accomplice, but when they learned of their colleague's version of events and of his confidence in his powers of recall, their own recollections substantially shifted to conform to his. One of the two even volunteered additional information about what John Doe 2 had been wearing. They also grew more confident in what they believed they remembered, the irony being that their initial, much more tentative, recollections subsequently proved to have had a far more secure basis in fact. It was precisely this new-found confidence, on top of the apparently large measure of correspondence between the three witnesses' versions of events, that confirmed the FBI in its efforts to pursue the mysterious second man. In a highly revealing coda to this episode, when, more than a year later, after the hunt for John Doe 2 had finally been abandoned as a wild goose chase, the employee who had made the initial transference was shown a photograph of the innocent customer, he willingly acceded to the suggestion that his

[70] A. Memon and D. B. Wright, 'Eyewitness Testimony and the Oklahoma Bombing', *The Psychologist*, 12 (1999), 292–5.

description of John Doe 2 had indeed derived from the appearance of that visitor to the body shop. But he remained wholly convinced that he had seen *a* second man with McVeigh. Why? Because he believed that his coworkers' recollections corroborated his own memory on that score![71]

The kind of effect seen in the case of the Oklahoma City body shop witnesses has also been demonstrated in many experimental studies of memory conformity.[72] The articulation of memories in social settings, such as when two or more people converse about a shared experience, can trigger what has been termed 'retrieval-induced forgetting', and repeated acts of recall can be shown to accentuate the gap between practised items that recur in a series of tellings and non-practised items that fall away into mnemonic oblivion. Common sense would seem to suggest that it would be details peripheral to a recalled experience that would be most likely to be forgotten, but there is evidence to suggest that the opposite is often the case. That is to say, the memory of elements that on

[71] For the manner in which an individual's memories can 'yield' so as to align with what are believed to be others' authoritative recollections, evaluative judgements, and the confidence with which these are expressed, see e.g. E. T. Higgins and W. S. Rhodes, '"Saying is Believing": Effects of Message Modification on Memory and Liking for the Person Described', *Journal of Experimental Social Psychology*, 14 (1978), 363–78; A. L. Betz, J. J. Skowronski and T. M. Ostrom, 'Shared Realities: Social Influence and Stimulus Memory', *Social Cognition*, 14 (1996), 113–40; F. Gabbert, A. Memon and K. Allan, 'Memory Conformity: Can Eyewitnesses Influence Each Other's Memories for an Event?', *Applied Cognitive Psychology*, 17 (2003), 533–43; E. Cowley, 'Remembering the Impressions of Others as Our Own: How Post-experience Decisions can Distort Autobiographical Memory', *Applied Cognitive Psychology*, 20 (2006), 227–38; G. E. Bodner, E. Musch and T. Azad, 'Reevaluating the Potency of the Memory Conformity Effect', *Memory & Cognition*, 37 (2009), 1069–76; A. Oeberst and J. Seidemann, 'Will Your Words Become Mine? Underlying Processes and Cowitness Intimacy in the Memory Conformity Paradigm', *Canadian Journal of Experimental Psychology*, 68 (2014), 84–96. For failures of source monitoring, the tagging of memories to their point of origin, see e.g. D. S. Lindsay, B. P. Allen, J. C. K. Chan and L. C. Dahl, 'Eyewitness Suggestibility and Source Similarity: Intrusions of Details from One Event into Memory Reports of Another Event', *Journal of Memory and Language*, 50 (2004), 96–111; R. Gordon, N. Franklin and J. Beck, 'Wishful Thinking and Source Monitoring', *Memory & Cognition*, 33 (2005), 418–29; J. S. Shaw III, L. M. Appio, T. K. Zerr and K. E. Pontoski, 'Public Eyewitness Confidence Can Be Influenced by the Presence of Other Witnesses', *Law and Human Behavior*, 31 (2007), 629–52.

[72] See e.g. D. B. Wright, G. Self and C. Justice, 'Memory Conformity: Exploring Misinformation Effects When Presented by Another Person', *British Journal of Psychology*, 91 (2000), 189–202; D. B. Wright and S. L. Schwartz, 'Conformity Effects in Memory for Actions', *Memory & Cognition*, 38 (2010), 1077–86. For the pressures that may be felt by a subject to mimic the perceived quality of others' recall, see M. B. Reysen, 'The Effects of Social Pressure on Group Recall', *Memory & Cognition*, 31 (2003), 1163–8.

any full and objective recounting of an episode would seem to be causally or thematically central to it can in fact disappear from the collective version of events that emerges from the back-and-forth of group recall.[73] As might be expected, the conformity and selectivity effects are often found among those who assume a relatively passive role as what is termed 'listeners' in the conversational rehearsals of memory. Their passivity may indicate a conscious or unconscious receptivity to the principle that their memories of an experience are contingent upon affirmation or modification by interlocutors whom they perceive to be more credible and knowledgeable, of a higher status, more intelligent or more adept in the art of narration.

A good deal of useful research, however, has indicated that these effects also influence the memories of 'narrators', those who take leading roles in the back-and-forth of group recollection.[74] For example, a study by Elizabeth Marsh and her colleagues suggests that recounting an experience in a way designed to entertain one's listener(s), as against the neutral recitation of factual detail, does not merely come down to a judgement about behaviour and impression-management in a given social setting, a one-off performance as it were, it can also influence what is retrievable in later acts of recall. Subjects who originally told a story in a lively and engaging manner did less well on recall of its substantive content, when subsequently asked to switch to a dry, informational telling, than did a control group who had only delivered the material in a factual mode.[75] In

[73] B. H. Basden, D. R. Basden, S. Bryner and R. L. Thomas III, 'A Comparison of Group and Individual Remembering: Does Collaboration Disrupt Retrieval Strategies?', *Journal of Experimental Psychology: Learning, Memory, and Cognition*, 23 (1997), 1176–89; B. H. Basden, D. R. Basden and S. Henry, 'Costs and Benefits of Collaborative Remembering', *Applied Cognitive Psychology*, 14 (2000), 497–507; M. Migueles and E. García-Bajos, 'Selective Retrieval and Induced Forgetting in Eyewitness Memory', *Applied Cognitive Psychology*, 21 (2007), 1157–72; A. Cuc, J. Koppel and W. Hirst, 'Silence Is Not Golden: A Case for Socially Shared Retrieval-Induced Forgetting', *Psychological Science*, 18 (2007), 727–33; C. B. Stone, A. J. Barnier, J. Sutton and W. Hirst, 'Building Consensus About the Past: Schema Consistency and Convergence in Socially Shared Retrieval-Induced Forgetting', *Memory*, 18 (2010), 170–84. Cf. D. B. Wright, E. F. Loftus and M. Hall, 'Now You See It; Now You Don't: Inhibiting Recall and Recognition of Scenes', *Applied Cognitive Psychology*, 15 (2001), 471–82. For the possible benefits of convergence and retrieval-induced forgetting as aids to sociability, see W. Hirst, A. Cuc and D. Wohl, 'Of Sins and Virtues: Memory and Collective Identity', in D. Bernsten and D. C. Rubin (eds), *Understanding Autobiographical Memory: Theories and Approaches* (Cambridge, 2012), pp. 141–57.

[74] See e.g. A. Cuc, Y. Ozuru, D. Manier and W. Hirst, 'On the Formation of Collective Memories: The Role of a Dominant Narrator', *Memory & Cognition*, 34 (2006), 752–62; A. D. Brown, A. Coman and W. Hirst, 'The Role of Narratorship and Expertise in Social Remembering', *Social Psychology*, 40 (2009), 119–29.

[75] N. M. Dudukovic, E. J. Marsh and B. Tversky, 'Telling a Story or Telling it Straight: The Effects of Entertaining Versus Accurate Retellings on Memory', *Applied Cognitive*

a similar and equally suggestive study by Marsh and Barbara Tversky, subjects read a story and were then asked to write a letter about one of its characters in either positively or negatively evaluative terms. On subsequent testing of the subjects' memory of the story, the substance and affective quality of what was recalled shifted towards the bias that the writing of the letter introduced.[76] Notions such as 'entertainment' and 'bias' are complex quantities – less clear cut, perhaps, than the experimenters investigating their effects acknowledge. They are also terms that have different resonances and associations in different cultures. But they at least begin to capture some of the key dynamics that are likely to be present in the usually informal settings in which groups share memories.[77]

The hypothesis that the act of telling affects the memory of the speaker, not just that of her or his listener, is thus well supported. But how, and how widely, does this effect operate? In the paradigm established by Loftus's early experiments, the subjects were explicitly or implicitly confronted with choices about some of the precise factual details of a perceived event, the memory for which might be probed by means of yes-no questions or simple choices between mutually exclusive alternatives. Once again the legal dimension is decisive, because in forensic situations the impact of eyewitness testimony can often turn upon such details. But if we were to map this sort of detail-centred approach onto the ways in which memories are narrated and shared in diverse real-world conditions, we would end up contriving scenes reminiscent of the dialogue in the song 'I Remember It Well' from the Lerner and Loewe musical *Gigi*, in which an elderly man and woman reminisce about a romantic relationship many years before by trading mutually contradictory recollections. There are, of course, many *Gigi*-esque exchanges in the course of daily life, arguments over precise factual details between parties whose versions of events are irreconcilable and whose investment in the veracity of their own memory is pronounced. In most real-world interactions, however, the cross-matching of mnemonic narratives is collaborative to a greater or lesser degree and does not reduce to the resolution of contests over particular facts. On the contrary, it can involve the making of generalizations in which detail is bleached out, as well as omissions, exaggerations and blendings, all driven by audience-tuning, which is to say the adjustment

Psychology, 18 (2004), 125–43. Cf. E. J. Marsh and B. Tversky, 'Spinning the Stories of our Lives', *Applied Cognitive Psychology*, 18 (2004), 491–503.

[76] B. Tversky and E. J. Marsh, 'Biased Retellings of Events Yield Biased Memories', *Cognitive Psychology*, 40 (2000), 1–38. See also E. J. Marsh, B. Tversky and M. Hutson, 'How Eyewitnesses Talk about Events: Implications for Memory', *Applied Cognitive Psychology*, 19 (2005), 531–44.

[77] For a good overview of the factors that shape conversational recounting of experience, see E. J. Marsh, 'Retelling Is Not the Same as Recalling', *Current Directions in Psychological Science*, 16 (2007), 16–20.

of content and delivery to judgements about the interests, needs and receptivity of one's interlocutors.[78]

In this context, it is noteworthy that some studies of the post-event information effect have pushed its operational range beyond the kind of overt and context-specific influences that feature in much of the research, as when, for example, a police officer conducting an identity parade turns to the witness and remarks, 'Good, you have identified the suspect'. The effect can also be found in the articulation of the sort of tonal emphases that accompany the exchange of eyewitness memories in social interactions which presuppose shared points of reference: less a case of 'Tell me what *you* saw for the record' and more 'So, how was *it* for you?'. In addition, the validation of an eyewitness's memory that he or she receives by means of conversational reinforcement is likely to feed into the degree of confidence with which the memories are held. If some of the authors of our target texts did not embark on their expeditions with the preformed intention of writing about it, the conversational affirmation of their eyewitness abilities most likely influenced their subsequent decision to do so. In this context, it is significant that conversational tuning has been shown to accentuate what has been termed the 'knew-it-all-along effect', when the benefit of hindsight permits someone to overstate the confidence with which she or he anticipated the consequences of an episode or action before it had run its full course, the underlying assumption being that the world, at least to a significant degree, is something that can be predicted.[79] It is arguable that much of the plot coherence and attention

[78] See e.g. G. Echterhoff, E. T. Higgins and S. Groll, 'Audience-Tuning Effects on Memory: The Role of Shared Reality', *Journal of Personality and Social Psychology*, 89 (2005), 257–76; R. Kopietz, G. Echterhoff, S. Niemeier, J. H. Hellmann and A. Memon, 'Audience-Congruent Biases in Eyewitness Memory and Judgment', *Social Psychology*, 40 (2009), 138–49; G. Echterhoff, S. Lang, N. Krämer and E. T. Higgins, 'Audience-Tuning Effects on Memory: The Role of Audience Status in Sharing Reality', *Social Psychology*, 40 (2009), 150–63.

[79] The foundational studies of what has been termed 'creeping determinism' were B. Fischhof, 'Hindsight ≠ Foresight: The Effect of Outcome Knowledge on Judgment Under Uncertainty', *Journal of Experimental Psychology: Human Perception and Performance*, 1 (1975), 288–99; and G. Wood, 'The Knew-It-All-Along Effect', *Journal of Experimental Psychology: Human Perception and Performance*, 4 (1978), 345–53. See also M. Snyder and S. W. Uranowitz, 'Reconstructing the Past: Some Cognitive Consequences of Person Perception', *Journal of Personality and Social Psychology*, 36 (1978), 941–50; E. Greene, 'Whodunit? Memory for Evidence in Text', *American Journal of Psychology*, 94 (1981), 479–96; M. R. Leary, 'Hindsight Distortion and the 1980 Presidential Election', *Personality and Social Psychology Bulletin*, 8 (1982), 257–63; S. A. Hawkins and R. Hastie, 'Hindsight: Biased Judgments of Past Events After the Outcomes Are Known', *Psychological Bulletin*, 107 (1990), 311–27; E. R. Hirt, H. E. McDonald and K. D. Markman, 'Expectancy Effects in Reconstructive Memory: When the Past Is Just What We Expected', in S. J. Lynn and K. M. McConkey (eds), *Truth in Memory* (New York, 1998), pp. 62–89; L.

to neat cause-effect dyads to be found in our target texts owes something to this phenomenon.

Many of the effects that we have noted are to be seen coming together in a valuable study by Coman, Manier and Hirst which asked whether the induced forgetting of information caused by communicative exchanges extends to the sorts of memories of important public events that people are likely to rehearse often and in emotionally charged ways. In other words, is the recollection of 'big' history proof against the sort of conformity effects and distorting influences that one might encounter in the telling of more private and trivial memories and in situations in which the inclusion of precise and maximal factual content is unlikely to be a priority for either the speaker or listener? Subjects were given a questionnaire concerning their recollection of 9/11, and were then asked to rehearse their memories either in an interview-type interaction with an experimenter or by means of somewhat more informal conversational recall conducted in subject pairs.[80] Subsequent testing of the subjects' memories as revealed by their response times in recognition tests suggested that some socially induced forgetting had occurred. The mnemonic 'silences' that emerged, moreover, extended to details that had occupied a significant place within the original memories as registered in the responses to the questionnaires. The importance of this study lies in the fact that 9/11 unquestionably belongs to a class of sudden, shocking and important public events that those who have experienced them – typically via media coverage – tend to believe are securely and immutably stored in their memories. Simply put, if the memories of 9/11 held by a group of American adults only a few years after 2001 proved as pliable and vulnerable as the study suggests, then we should expect the effects of conformity and tuning to be default expectations in every historical situation in which two or more eyewitnesses had occasion to discuss their experiences with one another.

Research into people's memories of events such as 9/11 has some intriguing lessons for our reading of eyewitness texts. Many people's recollections of 9/11 centre upon what have been termed 'flashbulb memories': particularly vivid and precise recollections of single moments that include a strong sensory dimension, such as what one could see and hear, as well as incidental, sometimes even trivial, circumstantial details that seem to anchor the reality of the whole scene in a manner reminiscent of Barthes's reality effects. The term 'flashbulb

---

S. Sanna, N. Schwarz and E. M. Small, 'Accessibility Experiences and the Hindsight Bias: I Knew It All Along Versus It Could Never Have Happened', *Cognition*, 30 (2002), 1288–96; E. M. Harley, K. A. Carlsen and G. R. Loftus, 'The "Saw-It-All-Along" Effect: Demonstrations of Visual Hindsight Bias', *Journal of Experimental Psychology: Learning, Memory, and Cognition*, 30 (2004), 960–8.

[80] A. Coman, D. Manier and W. Hirst, 'Forgetting the Unforgettable Through Conversation: Socially Shared Retrieval-Induced Forgetting of September 11 Memories', *Psychological Science*, 20 (2009), 627–33.

memory' was coined in 1977 by Brown and Kulik in a ground-breaking study that examined people's recollections of the circumstances in which they had first learned of noteworthy events such as the assassination of President John F. Kennedy in 1963.[81] Autobiographical memories of events that have taken place several years earlier are often constructed from inferences based on knowledge of where one was and what was doing at a given point in the past: in the terms of reference discussed above, they are substantially derived from semantic rather than episodic recall. But inspired by what seemed on the basis of anecdotal evidence to be a widespread experience, and building on work done at the end of the nineteenth century into people's long-term memories of the ways in which they learned about the assassination of Abraham Lincoln in 1865,[82] Brown and Kulik identified a particular species of intense and vivid episodic memory that seemed to require explanation. Despite some early criticism, their work has been largely corroborated and extended in subsequent research.[83] Studies have been conducted into the memories formed of numerous notable events, such as the fall of the Berlin Wall, the Hillsborough disaster and the death of Princess Diana.[84]

Brown and Kulik's attention to the circumstances in which someone first heard about the event remains the main research paradigm, and to this extent much of the research necessarily concerns the reach and effectiveness of modern forms of mass communication: those who recalled hearing of Lincoln's death back in the 1860s had effectively been on the cusp of enormous changes in the speed with which news could travel and in public consumption of that news, while Kennedy's assassination happened at a time when television was beginning to have a profound cultural impact in Western societies. There are, however, good grounds for believing that flashbulb memories are not merely artefacts of the reach of modern media. Research has shown that they can form around first-hand experiences as well as the learning of news that has happened elsewhere, and that they can relate to incidents in an individual's life that have a personal

[81] R. Brown and J. Kulik, 'Flashbulb Memories', *Cognition*, 5 (1977), 73–99.

[82] F. W. Colegrove, 'Individual Memories', *American Journal of Psychology*, 10 (1899), 228–55.

[83] For an important early critique see U. Neisser, 'Snapshots or Benchmarks?', in U. Neisser (ed.), *Memory Observed: Remembering in Natural Contexts* (New York, 1982), pp. 43–8. See the excellent overview of the main foundational studies in M. A. Conway, *Flashbulb Memories* (Hove, 1995). See also Schacter, *Searching for Memory*, pp. 195–201.

[84] D. B. Wright, 'Recall of the Hillsborough Disaster over Time: Systematic Biases of "Flashbulb" Memories', *Applied Cognitive Psychology*, 7 (1993), 129–38; J. N. Bohannon III, 'Flashbulb Memories for the Space Shuttle Disaster: A Tale of Two Theories', *Cognition*, 29 (1988), 179–96; S.-Å. Christianson, 'Flashbulb Memories: Special, But Not So Special', *Memory & Cognition*, 17 (1989), 435–43. See also D. B. Pillemer, 'Flashbulb Memories of the Assassination Attempt on President Reagan', *Cognition*, 16 (1984), 63–80.

but not a public resonance.[85] They can also be symptomatic of social groupings and forms of identity: Brown and Kulik's original study revealed a clear racial dimension within differential rates of flashbulb memory formation for culturally charged events such as the murder of Martin Luther King Jr in 1968; and subsequent research has revealed similar concentrations of flashbulb memories among particular populations, as when, for example, a nationally important politician has resigned or died.[86] Such concentrations of flashbulbs within a certain group may, indeed, indicate that multiple individuals' circumstantial memories will in due course blend into a master-narrative of the salience of that event within the group's frameworks of longer-term collective memory.[87]

Researchers have not for the most part concurred with Brown and Kulik's suggestion that the neurological basis of flashbulb creation is separate from the workings of the brain's routine mnemonic operations – what they termed a 'Now Print' process. It is now generally supposed that flashbulbs are grounded in the wider mechanisms of memory, although the exact processes are still debated.[88] For our purposes, the more interesting question is the psychological basis of flashbulb formation. Brown and Kulik proposed various contributory factors that are at play at the time of the event itself, including the element of surprise or novelty, the level of emotional arousal, and the subject's judgements as to importance and consequentiality. They also pointed to the effects of mental and

[85] See D. B. Pillemer, '"Hearing the News" versus "Being There": Comparing Flashbulb Memories and Recall of First-Hand Experiences', in O. Luminet and A. Curci (eds), *Flashbulb Memories: New Issues and New Perspectives* (Hove, 2009), pp. 125–40. Cf. D. C. Rubin and M. Kozin, 'Vivid Memories', *Cognition*, 16 (1984), 81–95; D. B. Pillemer, *Momentous Events, Vivid Memories: How Unforgettable Moments Help Us Understand the Meaning of Our Lives* (Cambridge, MA, 2000), esp. pp. 4–16, 25–62.

[86] E.g. A. Curci, O. Luminet, C. Finkenauer and L. Gisle, 'Flashbulb Memories in Social Groups: A Comparative Test-Retest Study of the Memory of French President Mitterand's Death in a French and a Belgian Group', *Memory*, 9 (2001), 81–101.

[87] Cf. D. Bernsten, 'Flashbulb Memories and Social Identity', in Luminet and Curci (eds), *Flashbulb Memories*, pp. 187–205; D. Páez, G. Bellelli and B. Rimé, 'Flashbulb Memories, Culture, and Collective Memories: Psychosocial Processes Related to Rituals, Emotions, and Memories', *ibid.*, pp. 227–45. Interesting work has been done on the persistence of flashbulb memories over long periods: see e.g. D. Bernsten and D. K. Thomsen, 'Personal Memories for Remote Historical Events: Accuracy and Clarity of Flashbulb Memories Related to World War II', *Journal of Experimental Psychology: General*, 134 (2005), 242–57. For the sense that some events seem to impose an ethical obligation upon the subject to retain a vivid memory of them, see G. Echterhoff and W. Hirst, 'Thinking About Memories for Everyday and Shocking Events: Do People Use Ease-of-Retrieval Cues in Memory Judgments?', *Memory & Cognition*, 34 (2006), 763–75.

[88] J. M. Talarico and D. C. Rubin, 'Flashbulb Memories Result from Ordinary Memory Processes and Extraordinary Event Characteristics', in Luminet and Curci (eds), *Flashbulb Memories*, pp. 79–97.

social rehearsals after the fact. Subsequent research has debated the relative importance of these factors; it is most probably the case that no one formula governs all forms of flashbulb memory formation, and that different kinds of noteworthy event trigger different permutations of response.[89] The categories of importance and consequentiality in principle differentiate between the degree to which the individual believes that she or he will personally be affected by the news, and the judgement that is reached as to its larger significance. In early criticism of Brown and Kulik, Neisser argued that consequentiality could not be regarded as an operative factor because people are not in a position to assess the longer-term significance of an event at the very moment in which they first learn of it.[90] Subsequent research, however, has confirmed the importance of what is in fact many people's experience of flashbulb-forming moments: that learning of the event is accompanied by some conscious apprehension of its likely future significance ('This will be big!').

In addition, the persistence of a flashbulb memory can owe something to the sense that one's initial judgement about the event was subsequently vindicated by other people's similar reactions and assessments of its future impact. It is arguable that the distinction between personal and public significances is usually not as hard and fast as some of the studies of flashbulb memory seem to suppose, and that subjects in these studies routinely conflate the two measures. Judgements as to consequentiality, moreover, may have different orientations, focusing on the foreseeable immediate effect or on the anticipated impact over the longer term, in other words the event's potential 'historical' importance. From this it follows that if we find evidence of flashbulb-like memories in our target texts, we shall need to situate them carefully within the dynamic interactions between individual focalization and collective perspective that we find there. Is a flashbulb memory in some sense the personal property of the narrator, or is its collective dimension and consequentiality emphasized? If the latter, to what extent do the texts reflect upon the future significance, anticipated or experienced, of the events that they narrate, or is the element of consequentiality downplayed?

Are there flashbulb memories in evidence in texts such as ours? A suggestive example is found in the *Gesta Francorum*'s account of the early stages of the First Crusade. In a well-known set-piece it narrates the moment when Bohemond of Taranto hears about the crusade message:

> For his part, the warlike Bohemond, who was at Ponte Scafati during the siege of Amalfi, upon hearing that a countless host of Christians, drawn from among the Franks, had arrived and was travelling to the Lord's Sepulchre, and was

[89] Conway, *Flashbulb Memories*, pp. 109–27; O. Luminet, 'Models for the Formation of Flashbulb Memories', in Luminet and Curci (eds), *Flashbulb Memories*, pp. 51–76.

[90] Neisser, 'Snapshots or Benchmarks?', pp. 43–8.

> ready to battle against the pagan peoples, began to enquire diligently about what weapons of war these people were carrying, and what sign of Christ they carried on the road, and what war-cry they made in battle. He was told the following in turn: 'They are carrying arms suitable for war, and they bear the cross of Christ on their right sides or between their shoulders; and their cry of "God wills, God wills, God wills!" they shout out in unison.' Promptly moved by the Holy Spirit, he ordered a very precious cloth that he had with him to be cut up, and he immediately used it all in making crosses. Then the majority of the knights who were taking part in that siege began enthusiastically to rush to Bohemond's side, in such a way that Count Roger [of Sicily] was left almost alone; and upon returning to Sicily he bewailed and bemoaned the loss of his people.[91]

There follows a list of the names of those who attached themselves to Bohemond's *famulatus* to go on the expedition.[92] In the overall context of the text's treatment of the preliminaries of the crusade, this passage draws particular attention to itself in several ways. It involves an analepsis, or flashback, within the broadly linear chronological flow of the narration: Bohemond has already been mentioned among those beginning their journey east, and the recounted action has got as far as delivering two of the other leaders of the crusade, Hugh of Vermandois and Godfrey of Bouillon, as far as Constantinople.[93] The passage also constructs an unrealistic image of Bohemond and his future followers as unaware of the crusade message as late as the summer of 1096, in order to emphasize Bohemond's quick thinking, charisma and control of the situation, whereas the text itself has already referred to southern Italians among those first-wave crusaders it says had reached Constantinople before Peter the Hermit arrived there on 1 August 1096. Taken at face value, this would imply that southern Italian recuitment for the crusade had begun some months before the Amalfi campaign was in full swing.[94] The passage is therefore fashioning one decisive, and visually striking, moment out of processes of news dissemination and crusade recruitment that were far more diffuse than one 'big bang' moment of attention-seeking reaction on Bohemond's part.

The specificity of the Bohemond scene, highlighted by the use of direct speech and anchoring reality-effect details such as the quality of the torn-up cloth, is

[91] *Gesta Francorum et aliorum Hierosolimitanorum*, ed. and trans R. M. T. Hill (London, 1962), p. 7: my translation. Hill's translation skips over the location, which was identified by Evelyn Jamison: 'Some Notes on the *Anonymi Gesta Francorum*, with Special Reference to the Norman Contingent from South Italy and Sicily in the First Crusade', in *Studies in French Language and Mediaeval Literature Presented to Professor Mildred K. Pope* (Manchester, 1939), pp. 188–91. Ponte Scafati, modern Scafati, is in Campania, very close to the (then undetected) site of Pompeii.

[92] *Gesta Francorum*, pp. 7–8.

[93] *Gesta Francorum*, pp. 2–7.

[94] *Gesta Francorum*, p. 2.

particularly worthy of emphasis. This is in sharp contrast to the beginning of the text, which evokes the initial papal preaching of the cross in language that seems deliberately crafted to evade temporal and spatial precision: there are no chronological markers beyond mention of the message's providential timeliness, and the enthusiastic response to Pope Urban II's appeal is located in areas that are designated only hazily by means of self-highlighting and distantly classicizing circumlocutions: *per uniuersas Galliarum regiones* and *per uniuersas regiones ac Galliarum patrias*.[95] It is sometimes stated that the author of the *Gesta Francorum* 'fails' to mention the launching of the crusade at the Council of Clermont, or at best refers to it elliptically. But this is to presuppose that at the time of writing, most probably late 1099 or early 1100, the council, and specifically Urban II's sermon to it, had already emerged as the inaugural motif and foundational occasion that it would become in some subsequent accounts of the crusade. Either the author of the *Gesta Francorum* was aware at some level of the council and Urban's sermon, or of other early set-piece pronouncements of the crusade message, and his passage on Bohemond is in the nature of a sublimation or displacement of such a scene to a more familiar setting and social environment. Or, more plausibly perhaps, the scene at Ponte Scafati stands for the various flashbulb memories of many in southern Italy and elsewhere, implicitly asking the reader, 'What were *you* doing when you first heard about the crusade message?'.

That something noteworthy did indeed take place during the siege of Amalfi is confirmed by a closely contemporary writer, Geoffrey Malaterra, who recounts essentially the same episode, though in terms less favourable to Bohemond.[96] We are told that Bohemond's participation in the Amalfi campaign, which had been at Count Roger's behest, ended up harming the interests of Bohemond's half-brother (and rival) Duke Roger Borsa of Apulia. In a rare direct narratorial aside, the text expresses the view that Bohemond's negative impact had not been premeditated (*ex industria*); but in so doing, of course, it implicitly invites the reader to reflect on the question of Bohemond's good faith and judgement. Unlike the scene evoked in the *Gesta Francorum*, in Malaterra's version Bohemond's eagerness to take part in the crusade is set against the background of his ambitions for conquest at the expense of the Byzantine empire (*Romania*); and the suggestion is made that his assumption of a leadership role in the upcoming

[95] *Gesta Francorum*, pp. 1–2.

[96] Geoffrey Malaterra, *De rebus gestis Rogerii Calabriae et Siciliae comitis et Roberti Guiscardi ducis fratris eius*, IV.24, ed. E. Pontieri (Rerum Italicarum Scriptores, 5:1; Bologna, 1927–8), p. 102; trans. K. B. Wolf, *The Deeds of Count Roger of Calabria and Sicily and of His Brother Duke Robert Guiscard* (Ann Arbor, MI, 2005), pp. 204–5. Cf. L. Russo, 'Oblia e memoria di Boemondo d'Altavilla nella storiografia normanna', *Bulletino dell'Istituto storico italiano per il medio evo*, 106 (2004), 137–65, esp. 151–65.

crusade was an opportunistic act. The same denuding of the Norman forces is noted, though Malaterra is more guarded than the author of the *Gesta Francorum* in his endorsement of the response to the crusade appeal, which is ascribed to the appetite for novelty that characterizes young warriors. In this version, both Count Roger of Sicily and Duke Roger Borsa of Apulia are abandoned by most of their men and return disconsolately to their respective territories. In Malaterra's telling, the significance of the episode lies not in its place within the story of the crusade but, more immediately and parochially, in the regrettable result that Amalfi was granted a reprieve just as it was on the point of falling to the Norman alliance. As the coda to the passage emphasizes by means of tersely phrased asyndeton and rhyme, 'Boamundus mare transiit; dux in Apuliam sucedit; comes Siciliam reuertitur; urbs obsessione gaudens liberatur'.[97] It is significant that up until this point – the passage occurs near the end of the text – Malaterra has made only a few and generally unenthusiastic mentions of Bohemond.[98] The inclusion of this episode therefore commands the reader's attention as it plays out rivalries within Bohemond's Hauteville kindred. For its part, the *Gesta Francorum* may likewise be showing a sensitivity to tensions within the Hauteville clan, as well as to the images of himself that Bohemond wished to project.

Whatever the exact role or roles of this passage within the *Gesta Francorum*'s overall narrative project, it is noteworthy that the narrator is not an overt presence in the scene. It is perfectly possible that the author was present at the siege of Amalfi and witnessed crusade recruitment happening there; but the scene-as-narrated is not routed through his acts of perception, nor validated by an appeal to his eyewitness status. Although, as we shall see, the narrators of our target texts generally insert themselves into their respective storyworlds more fully than is the case with the *Gesta Francorum*, it does not follow that any flashbulb-type scenes that we identify in them must invariably derive from moments of acute individual apperception and memory formation. On the contrary, and paradoxically perhaps given the anchoring of 'real' flashbulbs in the individual's personal episodic memory, scenes that seem to evoke flashbulb-like clarity may work to highlight collective perceptions and experiences. In this connection, it is noteworthy that research into flashbulb formation indicates that these sorts of memories form quickly; they are not, or at least not mainly, reconstructions after the fact motivated by an emergent sense of the significance of the original event. What makes flashbulb memories feel so distinctive is that they stand out in stark relief from the imprecision that characterizes most autobiographical memory. This mnemonic oasis-in-the-desert effect must have been experienced by many of Brown and Kulik's respondents given the fourteen-year interval since the

[97] 'Bohemond crossed the sea; the duke withdrew to Apulia; the count went back to Sicily; the city rejoiced in its liberation from the siege.'

[98] Geoffrey Malaterra, *De rebus gestis*, pp. 73, 77, 81, 82, 87, 90–1, 99.

death of John F. Kennedy, for example. But by virtue of forming immediately, flashbulbs also take shape when surrounding, contextualizing memories can still be fresh. In this way, they can insert themselves into fuller mnemonic landscapes that also have room for less vivid but nonetheless serviceable episodic memories as well as the varieties of semantic knowledge that regularly come into play as one navigates one's human environment. For example, being on a journey is, if nothing else, a constant reinforcement of one's being-on-a-journey script.

If, therefore, there are flashbulb-like moments in our target texts analogous to the crusade recruitment scene in the *Gesta Francorum*, they should be read, like it, as part of the texts' global meaning-making project, not simply as isolated moments of unusually rich detail. Flashbulbs contribute, often disproportionately, to people's beliefs about how their autobiographical memories hold together, as well as to their assumptions about the accuracy of eyewitness perception and memory in general. But it is impossible to construct a coherent and complex narrative covering events stretching over months or years simply by jumping from one vivid set-piece to another. One of the questions to be addressed in subsequent chapters is, therefore, the extent to which each text negotiates its eyewitness status in the balances its strikes between flashbulb-type moments of scenic pause and the demands of plot coherence and narrative pace, which can seldom limit themselves to the workings of the autoptic gaze alone.

What, then, are the applications of cognitive and social psychological research into eyewitnessing to the study of our target texts? One possible response is that it is of limited utility for the simple reason that we can seldom, if ever, establish sufficiently robust points of external reference against which to judge the accuracy of historical eyewitnesses' recollections. Nor can we drill into their minds to observe the various distorting influences at work on the operations of their memory. This is perfectly true, but in a sense trivially so, for historical reconstruction does not demand the standards of proof that obtain in criminal jurisprudence and in relation to which much of the psychological research literature situates itself. Another response might be to focus on the debate over the representative nature of psychological research's typical subject populations, and to argue that what pass for universal conclusions about the functioning of the human mind are in fact tightly culturally specific observations that cannot be projected back onto different societies in the past, especially the distant past. This is a serious objection, in particular because there is evidence to suggest that the human brain is physically adaptive to its environment, in other words to culture. But this objection can be overstated. While it is always important to emphasize the alterity of past cultures, this should not become a blanket excuse to shut down discussion couched in the language of similarity, equivalence or analogy. The psychological research literature does not tell us how the minds of twelfth- and thirteenth-century eyewitness authors worked, but it alerts us to many of the challenges that, *mutatis mutandis* within their own particular cultural environments, they would have faced when observing action around them, committing it to memory, listening to others' experiences, and crafting narratives of complex sequences of events. And insofar as cognitive psychology's terms of reference are ultimately grounded in the workings of human physiology and neurology, *pace* the evidence that there is some cultural inflection of the functioning of neural networks, the perspectives opened up by this body of research probably get us as close as we will ever get to the texture of lived experience for people in the past.

What of the criticism that a great deal of cognitive and social psychological research simply solemnizes the intuitions about the malleability and fragility of eyewitness memory that most lay people develop over the course of their lives, not least professional historians who have been trained to exercise caution about the evidence that they consult? Simple introspection regularly reminds us that our memories of our pasts are very patchy and full of gaps; and we are all familiar with the experience of recounting the same event in different ways over the course of repeated tellings, or else of finding our narration ossifying around clichéd language and familiar cultural scripts. Our memories – especially those we choose to share with others – are often exercises in conflation, simplification, exaggeration, wishful thinking and the tidying up of loose ends. We routinely exaggerate or over-estimate the extent to which our knowledge of the world is reached by means of direct and personal experience rather than from others. Are not historians alive to these sorts of problems at work in their sources? To a large extent, of course, yes. But, as was suggested in the Introduction, historical eyewitnesses are the nearest thing that historians have to surrogates at large in the slice of the past that they choose to study, and as such their evidence can be accepted too readily for fear that without it, and *faute de mieux*, imaginative access to that past, to its fine-grained specificity and experientiality, will be greatly impoverished. The great virtue of the forensic orientation of much of the psychological research into eyewitnessing, for all that it has certain limitations as noted earlier, is that, explicitly or implicitly, it returns us again and again to the exaggerated faith that we typically place in the accuracy and reliability of eyewitness testimony.

But where does this leave the historian using a piece of eyewitness evidence such as one of our texts in order to reconstruct a sequence of events? At what level of specificity, and with respect to which sorts of detail, do the distorting effects that the psychological research identifies begin to do their work? And, in the absence of an Archimedean external point of reference, and given that the difference between accurate recollection and confabulation is seldom if ever registered discursively, how is the historian to mobilize the substantive content of the source text, in particular those kinds of detail that look particularly vulnerable to the many forms of mnemonic error that the psychological research identifies? The good news is that mistakes at the level of the specific detail, the equivalent of Loftus's blue car/green car conundrum, seldom compound exponentially to bend a narrative sequence ever further from its factual reference. Although, as we shall see, narratives such as our target texts are substantially sequences of discrete episodic blocks, generally larger and more complex than, but not fundamentally dissimilar from, the micro-events confected by psychological researchers, and for this reason susceptible to the many sins of memory that we have considered, they nonetheless contrive to isolate most possible errors, distortions or exaggerations from long-term plot significance in such a way that their knock-on effects over the course of the narrative are contained.

The reasons for this lie both beyond and within the text. The eyewitness-author, confronted by the demands of crafting a complex narrative, would have been guided by memories of superordinate patterns of experience and understanding that transcended the details of individual moment-by-moment episodes, even as the resultant narrative substantially resorts to specific incidents to propel the action and to instantiate the text's various thematic preoccupations. This sort of superordinate mnemonic scaffolding, which would have shaded closer to the workings of semantic memory rather than episodic specificity, would have been much less vulnerable to the distorting influences we have been considering. Within the workings of the text, moreover, the needs of plot coherence would have had a complementary effect. It is arguable that the sorts of storyworlds that our target texts construct, involving travel over long distances, military conflict and cultural dislocation, especially favour this process. The chronotopes, the space-and-time co-ordinates, of mass movement in particular would seem to militate against small errors of detail obstructing or deflecting the inexorable narrative momentum generated by getting a large number of agents from A to B within a more or less precisely specified amount of time. But the same is probably true of all complex narratives featuring groups of people engaged in purposeful and goal-driven activities; teleology overrides mistakes in the fine detail even as it opens up the narrative spaces in which these sorts of mistakes are made possible.

One important lesson of the research into eyewitnessing is that it reminds us how daunting an undertaking and how impressive an achievement it would have been for our authors to produce long and detailed narratives of the crusade expeditions in which they had taken part. It is often claimed that the memories of fellow veterans would have exerted a powerful constraining influence on what historians such as our authors could and could not have said – what, in effect, they could get away with. But this supposed limiting effect is almost certainly overestimated; it amounts to the projection onto an author's contemporaries of the same sort of exaggerated faith in eyewitness evidence as proof against distortion and confabulation that one often finds voiced by modern judges and jurors. The author of a detailed and complex narrative would have enjoyed an enormous mnemonic advantage over his former comrades in the short term as well as in the longer run; conformity effects are very powerful, as we have seen. So the notion of a *vox populi* keeping eyewitness historians on the straight and narrow is simply a convenient contrivance for modern historians to justify their squeezing as much detail as they can from their eyewitness sources. The statement that one often encounters in ancient and medieval prefaces to the effect that writing is the best defence against oblivion is on one level a cliché subserving authorial self-fashionings; but it also captures a real anxiety about social forgetfulness that the super-abundance of mnemonic reinforcements in our modern culture makes it very difficult indeed for us to appreciate. So, as far as the near-contemporary memory of the Second, Third and Fourth Crusades was concerned, our texts represented significant and *sui generis* interventions, even if their manuscript traditions suggest that in most cases they were not widely read and copied. It is what they are that makes them stand out. Even a returning crusader with a penchant for telling vivid stories and a lively performance style could only have dipped here and there into the narrative richness and complexity that our written texts systematically achieve. In their sheer length, their sustained attention to plot coherence and consistency of character motivation, the subtleties of narratorial engagement, and the more or less even distribution of clearly realized diegetic detail across multiple episodes, our written texts represent a profound difference in kind, not just degree, from the collection of anecdotes that our putative veteran raconteur would have had at his disposal as he drew upon the recollected bits and pieces of his experience.

The complexity of our texts as narrative projects has important consequences. For the greater the story-telling ambition behind the narrativization of a drawn-out, collective enterprise such as a crusade, the more the narrator necessarily becomes detached from the constraints of autobiographical recall, even as he continues to appeal to it in order to validate his claims and, as we shall see, attempts to replicate the experiential quality of eyewitness perception by means of focalization, 'thick' scenic description and other devices. Does this mean that the actual participation of our authors in the crusade expeditions that their texts recount is to be treated as simply an incidental detail? If we suppose that our authors enjoyed some sort of epistemological privilege simply by virtue of being physically close to events, or at least to some of them, is this to fall prey to a variant of the biographism that was discussed in the Introduction? We would probably be right to imagine our authors exhibiting some intuitive understanding of the fragility of eyewitness recollection by scaffolding their memories by means of notes and jottings, copies or synopses of speeches and documents, even souvenir objects.[99] As suggested above, it is also possible that their decision to go to the considerable time and trouble of composing a long narrative of the campaign in which they

[99] For objects as foci of memories of participation in a crusade, see the important study by N. L. Paul, *To Follow in Their Footsteps: The Crusades and Family Memory in the High Middle Ages* (Ithaca, NY, 2012), pp. 90–133.

had taken part was prompted or confirmed by the apparent reinforcement of the accuracy of their perception and recall in conversations with others. Perhaps our authors believed they really *were* particularly good at seeing and remembering, though we can never know. Nor are their individual capacities ultimately what matters: for all we know, some of them may have had poor eyesight and were prone to absentmindedness. Perhaps the single most important lesson to emerge from research into the psychology of eyewitnessing and memory, then, is the importance of the transactive and collaborative quality of collective memory in the 'smaller' sense. We can only speculate about the circumstances in which our authors shared, revised, told and retold their experiences with others even as new experiences were presenting themselves mid-expedition; but we can be confident that transactive memory formation was the single most important factor at work in the transition from individual experience to fully crafted written narrative.

The cognitive and social psychological research into eyewitnessing suggests that historians should be very circumspect when pulling down details, especially those that are not independently attested, from an eyewitness source, and certainly very cautious indeed when certifying a claim with reference to that source's eyewitness status. But, though we may regret the unavoidable smudging of the detail that we find embedded in an eyewitness narrative, we gain a compensating appreciation of the importance of transactive memory. In the case of our authors, moreover, we can suspect that this pooling, sifting and streamlining of group memories took place not only among each author's immediate peers – the sort of people, in effect, with whom consensus would have been easiest to achieve – but also with others of different status or experience, even those who emerge as antagonists at certain junctures such as the Rhinelanders and Flemish in the account of the conquest of Lisbon that we shall consider in the next chapter, or the followers of the king of France in Ambroise's telling of the Third Crusade. For it was perhaps in their more challenging or destabilizing mnemonic exchanges that our authors cemented the trust in collective agency, purpose and perception that we shall see are potent themes in our target texts. Indeed, we shall find that the principal function of eyewitnessing in our texts is to offer the narrator a suite of narrative strategies with which to combine his individual narratorial autopsy and intradiegetic agency with a primary focus on the crusaders' collective actions – a substantive and thematic emphasis with which he is free to engage as part-evaluator, part-participant.

2

The Second Crusade: The *De Expugnatione Lyxbonensi* and Odo of Deuil's *De Profectione Ludovici VII in Orientem*

Although the reaction of western writers of history to the Second Crusade was a good deal more muted than to the First, we are fortunate in having two substantial monograph-type texts written by participants: an anonymous account of the Christian conquest of Lisbon in 1147, told largely from the perspective of the Anglo-Norman contingent of crusaders who – alongside others from north-western Europe – made a decisive contribution to the victory; and an account, written by Odo, monk and future abbot of St-Denis, of the progress of the expeditions to the east up to early 1148, with particular reference to the French contribution under the leadership of King Louis VII. The two texts have a good deal in common: in the main body of their narratives they cover similar stretches of time at comparable length; they are both cast in epistolary form; they are both the work of authors whose former scholarly reputations as literary mediocrities is now being revised by more positive evaluations of their learning and skill as writers; and the authors were well-situated participants in the events that their texts narrate. The two narratives therefore provide useful points of comparison and contrast in examining whether and in what ways eyewitnessing informs the content and presentation of their respective stories; the extent to which autopsy is invoked as a source of authority and a guarantee of accuracy; the construction of the narratorial voices; the nature of the narrators' homodiegetic presence within their storyworlds and the reach of their gazes; and the thematic emphases that undergird the narration.

The *De Expugnatione Lyxbonensi*

The work conventionally known as *De expugnatione Lyxbonensi* (*The Conquest of Lisbon*) serves as an excellent illustration of the ways in which a text's thematic, substantive and structural emphases can have a close bearing on questions of individual and group agency, which in turn influence the distribution and plot functions of acts of seeing and focalization.[1] The identities of those

[1] For the text, David's introduction to his edition and translation remains valuable (*De expugnatione*, pp. 3–51) but it should now be read in conjunction with Phillips's

within the text who are described perceiving aspects of the storyworld and of the action taking place within it, and just as importantly forming understandings based on those perceptions, are closely bound up with the narrator's plot choices and the forms of human interaction that are narrated. Focalization in its turn has a significant impact on the role played by seeing, in the form of both the narrator's gaze and characters' perceptions, within the text's larger operations.

The *De expugnatione* concerns a decisive intervention by crusaders from various parts of north-western Europe in the conflicts between Muslims and Christians in the Iberian peninsula. Specifically, it tells the story of the siege and capture of Muslim Lisbon in 1147 by a coalition of Christian forces, a signpost event in the emergence of an independent Portuguese polity under the first ruler of Portugal to style himself king, Afonso Henriques (1128–85).[2] The action begins with the assembly at Dartmouth of a large fleet comprising crusaders from the Rhineland, Flanders and the Anglo-Norman realm, the arrangements that are made to govern the conduct of their journey, and their departure on 23 May 1147. A quite long sequence, redolent of geographical and travel literature, some of it drawing upon the *Collectanea rerum mirabilium* of the late antique writer Solinus, brings the fleet to the Portuguese coast. Agreements are entered into with Afonso Henriques to co-ordinate with his forces in laying siege to Lisbon. The prosecution of the siege, which concludes with the defenders' capitulation towards the end of October, occupies the greater part of the narrative. Some attention is paid to recurrent and durative aspects of a process that lasted several months, but there are several sequences in which particular episodes are recounted, sometimes

---

preface to the revised reprint, pp. xi–xxxiii. See also the wide-ranging introduction, by M. J. V. Branco, in *A Conquista de Lisboa aos Mouros: Relato de um Cruzado*, ed. and trans. A. A. Nascimento with an introduction by M. J. V. Branco (Lisbon, 2001), pp. 9–51. The title is a nineteenth-century coinage.

[2] The best and fullest modern account of the conquest of Lisbon is J. P. Phillips, *The Second Crusade: Extending the Frontiers of Christendom* (New Haven, 2007), pp. 136–67. For the events of 1147 in their Portuguese context, see S. Lay, *The Reconquest Kings of Portugal: Political and Cultural Reorientation on the Medieval Frontier* (Basingstoke, 2009), pp. 71–102; *idem*, 'The Reconquest as Crusade in the Anonymous *De expugnatione Lyxbonensi*', in J.-J. López-Portillo (ed.), *Spain, Portugal and the Atlantic Frontier of Medieval Europe* (The Expansion of Latin Europe, 1000–1500, 8; Farnham, 2013), pp. 123–30. See also W. J. Purkis, *Crusading Spirituality in the Holy Land and Iberia c.1095–c.1187* (Woodbridge, 2008), pp. 171–2. For the siege as a military operation, see R. Rogers, *Latin Siege Warfare in the Twelfth Century* (Oxford, 1992), pp. 182–8; M. Bennett, 'Military Aspects of the Conquest of Lisbon, 1147', in J. P. Phillips and M. Hoch (eds), *The Second Crusade: Scope and Consequences* (Manchester, 2001), pp. 71–89. For an insightful study of the *De expugnatione* as a source for the crusaders' ritualistic behaviour, see S. A. Throop, 'Christian Community and the Crusades: Religious and Social Practices in the *De expugnatione Lyxbonensi*', *Haskins Society Journal*, 24 (2012), 95–126.

in considerable detail; these are especially clustered towards the end of the text, as the siege reaches its climax in elaborately planned and hard-pressed Christian assaults on the city walls. With the entry of the Christians into the city, the text's main narrative arc reaches a natural point of closure. The last dating reference is to 1 November. A coda, however, describes the miserable plight of the defeated Muslims, beset by pestilence, in the aftermath of the siege. The implication, therefore, is that the text, or at least a first draft of it, was composed over the winter of 1147–8.

The *De expugnatione* is substantially the longest and most detailed narrative source for the conquest of Lisbon, and consequently it has dominated historians' reconstructions of events and the debates that surround them. The principal supplementary piece of evidence is a grouping of closely related texts collectively known as the 'Teutonic source' or 'Lisbon Letter', which most probably originated in one of the extant variants, a letter written by a participant in the siege named Winand to Archbishop Arnold I of Cologne.[3] The Lisbon Letter is valuable on two counts. It broadly corroborates the sequence of events reported in the *De expugnatione*, while it introduces a different perspective from within the crusade army's mix of nationalities. It also supplies additional information: for example, one variant, that written by Duodechin to Abbot Cuno and the monastic community of Disibodenberg, includes a form of closure notably absent from the *De expugnatione* in concluding with the remark that the crusaders spent the following winter in Lisbon until 1 February, after which they sailed away and reached the Holy Sepulchre in performance of their vows. Interestingly, we are told that they sailed off in separate groups, which suggests that the co-ordination and co-operation that had characterized the fleet's voyage out from England to Portugal were no longer in evidence.[4] Like the Lisbon Letter, the narration of events in the *De expugnatione* is presented within an epistolary frame, but in its

[3] See S. B. Edgington, 'The Lisbon Letter of the Second Crusade', *Historical Research*, 69 (1996), 328–39. Winand's letter is edited at 336–9. There are two other versions, both somewhat fuller, written by participants and similarly addressed to high-ranking ecclesiastical correspondents in Germany, as well as reworkings inserted into annals from Cologne and Magdeburg and a fragment from Trier that is related to the extant Magdeburg version. The portions of text common to all three eyewitness variants, as well as the passages specific to each, are helpfully translated in S. B. Edgington, 'Albert of Aachen, St Bernard and the Second Crusade', in J. P. Phillips and M. Hoch (eds), *The Second Crusade: Scope and Consequences* (Manchester, 2001), pp. 61–7. For a useful overview of other texts that contribute to our understanding of the conquest of Lisbon and its effects, see G. Constable, 'A Further Note on the Conquest of Lisbon in 1147', in M. G. Bull and N. J. Housley (eds), *The Experience of Crusading I: Western Approaches* (Cambridge, 2003), pp. 39–44. See also Phillips, *Second Crusade*, p. 142 for reactions to the conquest of Lisbon on the part of various contemporary chroniclers.

[4] 'Annales Sancti Disibodi', ed. G. Waitz, *MGH SS*, 17, p. 28; trans. Edgington, 'Albert of Aachen', p. 67.

length and its range of intertextual reference it breaks free of the letter form to become a full-blown historiographical narrative, redolent of tellings of the First Crusade and with a pronounced homiletic dimension. It is noteworthy that after the salutation that begins the text, the addressee is expressly mentioned only once in the body of the text, and then in a minor aside concerning the quality of the fish found in the Tagus, which we are told does not fluctuate according to the seasons 'as happens with you'.[5]

The text survives in a single manuscript which dates from the third quarter of the twelfth century.[6] The only direct clue that it provides as to the identity of the author is its abbreviated opening address, 'Osb. de Baldr. R sal'.[7] The text's editor, Charles Wendell David, identified the addressee as Osbert of Bawdsey, a cleric from Suffolk with connections to the Glanvills, one of whom, Hervey, features prominently in the narrative. The identity of the author, 'R', defeated David, however. Subsequently, in an impressive piece of historical detective work, Harold Livermore made a good case for identifying the author as a priest named Raol, who is attested granting to the Augustinian community of Santa Cruz, Coimbra, a cemetery which his charter states he had founded for the English who had fallen during the siege – an operation in which he recalled taking an active part 'with my own bow' and 'not omitting to go daily to the siege'. The charter of donation, dated April 1148, suggests that Raol was an important figure in the emergent Christian establishment in and around Lisbon after the conquest, for he states in it that he had given the canons 200 marks of silver in addition to the cemetery itself, and his grant was witnessed by none other than King Afonso Henriques, his *alcaide* or royal governor in the city, and five bishops including John, archbishop of Braga.[8] It has been suggested that Raol had some formal position within the expedition as papal legate or representative of Bernard of Clairvaux, the dominant figure in the preaching of the Second Crusade.[9] It is perhaps more realistic, if the identification of Raol as the author is accepted, to see him as a chaplain in Hervey de Glanvill's household. This would seem to be confirmed by two references in the text to Hervey's tent as a focal point of the narrator's sense of group identification.[10] In this connection, it is useful to recall that two of the eyewitness accounts of the First Crusade, those by Raymond of

[5] *De expugnatione*, p. 90: 'ut aput vos est'.

[6] Cambridge, Corpus Christi College MS 470, fols 125r–146r.

[7] *De expugnatione*, pp. 43–5, 52.

[8] H. Livermore, 'The "Conquest of Lisbon" and its Author', *Portuguese Studies*, 6 (1990), 4–5. For the Latin text see also *A Conquista de Lisboa*, ed. Nascimento, pp. 202–4. An interesting absentee from the list of episcopal witnesses is Gilbert of Hastings, the new bishop of Lisbon whose election had followed closely upon the conclusion of the siege, as noted in *De expugnatione*, pp. 178–80.

[9] Livermore, 'The "Conquest of Lisbon"', 7; Phillips, *Second Crusade*, pp. 142, 162.

[10] See *De expugnatione*, pp. 96, 126.

Aguilers and Fulcher of Chartres, were written by clerics attached to lords on the campaign, and it is possible that the author of the *Gesta Francorum* was in a similar position.

Livermore's case for identifying the author as Raol is ingenious and imaginative, and it has generally been supported by other scholars, but it is only suggestive. It is important to bear in mind that, because Livermore's argument largely turns on perceived correspondences between the circumstances and interests of Raol as revealed by the 1148 charter and those of the implied author suggested by the *De expugnatione*, there is, in fact, little value added that such an identification can bring to an analysis of the text. We are, however, on firmer ground when we look for clues concerning the level of education and range of textual reference that contemporary readers would have detected. Here recent scholarship has substantially revised earlier judgements that the author was, in Giles Constable's formulation, a 'simple crusader', someone who, according to David, had had a limited education but was 'a priest of the virile fighting type'.[11] On the contrary, the author has been shown to have had a very good knowledge of some of the authorities that appear in the treatment of justified violence in Gratian's *Decretum* (*c*.1140), and it is likely that he knew the *Decretum* itself or an earlier compilation of canon law such as that by Ivo of Chartres.[12] There are good grounds for supposing that the author was familiar with the terms in which the Second Crusade had been preached, as expressed both by Eugenius III's bull *Quantum praedecessores* and the language of Bernard of Clairvaux's sermons and letters. Some awareness of the First Crusade as a historical precedent and of the manner of its representation in written accounts – insofar as these two things were separable after fifty years – emerges at several points in the text. For example, when one of the expedition's leaders, Arnold, count of Aerschot, is introduced, he is immediately glossed as the nephew of Godfrey of Bouillon, who is referred to simply and allusively as 'Godfrey the duke' by way of reinforcing the connection. Likewise, the image of the bishop of Oporto addressing the newly arrived northern crusaders in the open air, because the numbers were too great to be accommodated in his cathedral, recalls the stock *mise-en-scène* of Urban II's sermon at Clermont in November 1095. Additionally, the pairing of this occasion

[11] *De expugnatione*, pp. 40, 45–6; G. Constable, 'The Second Crusade as Seen by Contemporaries', *Traditio*, 9 (1953), 221. It is noteworthy that in the revised version of this seminal paper that appears in his *Crusaders and Crusading in the Twelfth Century* (Farnham, 2008), p. 236, Constable drops the mention of a simple crusader and, without qualification, endorses the identification with Raol.

[12] For the text's thematic sophistication and intertextual range, especially as revealed by its speeches, see J. P. Phillips, 'Ideas of Crusade and Holy War in *De expugnatione Lyxbonensi* (The Conquest of Lisbon)', in R. N. Swanson (ed.), *The Holy Land, Holy Lands, and Christian History* (Studies in Church History, 36; Woodbridge, 2000), pp. 123–41.

with an echoing sermon by an unnamed priest before the decisive assault on Lisbon's walls recalls the inclusion by Baldric of Bourgueil of a sermon purportedly delivered, again by an unnamed priest, before the first crusaders' final assault on Jerusalem in July 1099.[13]

The most compelling evidence for the author's sophistication and craft is, however, a series of interconnected passages of direct speech that cumulatively offer the reader one of the most reflective and subtle articulations of crusading's ethical, pastoral, legal and political dimensions to appear in any twelfth-century narrative history. In addition to the sermons of the bishop of Oporto and the unnamed priest, which are the two longest sequences of direct discourse and effectively bookend the other such passages, the text purports to quote King Afonso Henriques's address to the northerners when they first meet; an impassioned speech made by Hervey de Glanvill to talk down those who are unwilling to serve alongside the king and want to press on to Jerusalem; and an exchange of speeches in a parley between the archbishop of Braga and a Muslim elder.[14] In addition, there are several passages of extended indirect speech, as well as paraphrased or quoted oaths and documents.[15] All together these passages make up between a quarter and a third of the whole text. They provide a series of reflections and interpretive pointers to guide the reader's understanding of the action sequences that surround them. Although delivered by different people at different times, and in different rhetorical registers to reflect the status and purposes of the speaker, the sermons and speeches pick up on and complement one another in a deft interweaving of commentary on the crusade's theological and canonical underpinnings, the devotional and penitential demands that were made of the individual crusader, the need for ideological inflections that accommodated local conditions and priorities – here the long-standing rivalries between Christians and Muslims in the Iberian peninsula and the historical grievances that fed them – and crusading's ability to co-opt reinforcing value systems, as in the theme of Norman pride that appears in Hervey's speech.[16]

Scholars have pondered the extent to which the sermons and speeches as given in the text are accurate records of actual utterances. A marginal remark in the manuscript to the effect that Hervey's speech simply captures the gist of what was

[13] *De expugnatione*, pp. 52, 68–70, 146–58; Baldric of Bourgueil, *The Historia Ierosolimitana*, ed. S. Biddlecombe (Woodbridge, 2014), pp. 107–9. Phillips, *Second Crusade*, pp. 161–2 assumes that the priest who delivered the sermon was Raol himself. If so, the narrator's reluctance to insert himself into the action *in propria persona* at this juncture and thereby to take centre stage, if only briefly, is especially noteworthy.

[14] *De expugnatione*, pp. 98–100, 104–10, 114–22.

[15] *De expugnatione*, pp. 56, 68, 102, 110–12, 130–2.

[16] See below, pp. 143–4.

said might suggest, if this comment originated in the author's own reflections on his memories and notes, that some of the other passages were considered to be more faithful renderings.[17] Some support for this possibility is provided by the fact that most of the sermons and speeches are well motivated with immediate reference to the movement of the plot and the needs and perspectives of the characters within it; with the possible exception of the exchange between the archbishop of Braga and the Muslim elder, they are not 'soap box' narratorial asides ventriloquized by convenient mouthpieces. That said, these passages should not be regarded as points in the text in which authorial eyewitness – or earwitness – is especially at play. The sermons and speeches are principally devices to embed reflections on the significance of the events of the siege within the self-awareness of certain representative figures or types operating inside the storyworld.

A bone of contention in recent scholarship has been the extent to which the attack on Lisbon was planned as an integral part of the suite of campaigns that modern historians subsume under the term 'The Second Crusade', or was more in the nature of an adventitious supplement to the main crusade project, something that was made possible by Afonso Henriques's exploitation of the arrival of a large fleet in Portuguese waters to raise his sights towards a major strategic goal that would otherwise have been beyond his resources to achieve.[18] There are suggestions in the *De expugnatione* that Afonso Henriques and his lieutenant the bishop of Oporto had some advance warning of the northerners' arrival, but the text is reticent – characteristically so, as we shall see – about the expedition's direct antecedents. As a result we cannot tell whether this means that there had been long-range planning or simply that the Portuguese had had a reaction time measured in days and weeks rather than months.[19] This is a debate that will

[17] *De expugnatione*, p. 104 n. b. Phillips, *Second Crusade*, p. 151 argues that the note is the author's own addition.

[18] For arguments in favour of prior planning and co-ordination, which fold into the larger debate concerning the overall conceptualization and scope of the Second Crusade, see Livermore, 'The "Conquest of Lisbon"', 8–12; J. P. Phillips, 'St Bernard of Clairvaux, the Low Countries and the Lisbon Letter of the Second Crusade', *Journal of Ecclesiastical History*, 48 (1997), 485–97. For the contrary view, see A. J. Forey, 'The Siege of Lisbon and the Second Crusade', *Portuguese Studies*, 20 (2004), 1–13. Several of Forey's objections are effectively addressed in Phillips, *Second Crusade*, esp. pp. 137–44. Cf. S. B. Edgington, 'The Capture of Lisbon: Premeditated or Opportunistic?', in J. T. Roche and J. M. Jensen (eds), *The Second Crusade: Holy War on the Periphery of Latin Christendom* (Outremer, 2; Turnhout, 2015), pp. 257–72. For a somewhat different approach, see J. France, 'Logistics and the Second Crusade', in J. H. Pryor (ed.), *Logistics of Warfare in the Age of the Crusades: Proceedings of a Workshop held at the Centre for Medieval Studies, University of Sydney, 30 September to 4 October 2002* (Aldershot, 2006), pp. 87–93.

[19] See the reference in *De expugnatione*, p. 98 to the fact that five vessels that had pushed

probably never be resolved definitively unless new evidence comes to light. The point to stress is that, like the uncertainty concerning the identity of the author of the *De expugnatione*, it is substantially fed by the text's silences. These silences, however, even though they are problematic with respect to specific questions that we would like answered, should not be viewed negatively as omissions or oversights on the narrator's part, but as devices to highlight certain thematic emphases. As we shall see, this has, in turn, a significant bearing on the text's construction of its narratorial voice, and by extension on the function of eyewitness perception within the text's global meaning-making.

A number of preoccupations, including the importance of right intention, the corrosive effects of greed, and the penitential nature of the crusader's vocation, emerge from the sermons and speeches.[20] The single most important motif is the ideal of Christian collective unity, for this more than any other value or theme extends outwards from the set-piece utterances into what transpires in the storyworld, the workings of the plot, the language used to express the crusaders' agency, the selection of flashbulb-like episodes that are narrated in particular detail, and the narrator's evaluative remarks. The central importance of unity is emphasized at the very beginning of the action, after the opening epistolary salutation; the reader is abruptly plunged *in medias res* with the statement that 'peoples of diverse nations, customs and languages' gathered at Dartmouth in 164 ships.[21] The antecedent of the bridging connective after the salutation, 'igitur', 'and so it was that', is hinted at but left unstated. As Jonathan Phillips has argued, a rendezvous on this scale involving disparate contingents would only have been possible after months of planning and co-ordination, irrespective of whether or not an attack on Lisbon was anticipated at that stage.[22] But the text's aim is to call forth the image of what amounts to a spontaneous coming together on the part of a variety of participants in pursuit of a shared purpose.

This contrived spontaneity is subsequently reinforced by the remark that the crusaders had, in effect, self-recruited under the impulse of the Holy Ghost and without a preaching campaign ('nullo predicante'); this claim is lent extra force by being made by none other than the bishop of Oporto in his sermon to

on ahead of the main fleet had given the king a week's warning. On the other hand, a greater degree of forward planning is suggested by the Lisbon Letter's observations that the bishop of Oporto had been instructed by the king to meet the crusaders and that the king had made arrangements for markets to be available to them: 'Lisbon Letter', 337; trans. Edgington, 'Albert of Aachen', p. 63.

[20] France, 'Logistics and the Second Crusade', pp. 90–1 suggests that the text was written to rebut accusations that the crusaders at Lisbon had primarily been motivated by greed, but this is to exaggerate one theme at the expense of others in a complex work that is as much reflective and celebratory as it is apologetic.

[21] *De expugnatione*, p. 52: translation revised.

[22] Phillips, *Second Crusade*, pp. 142–3.

the crusaders on their arrival in Portugal, an event which assumes the status of a Clermont-like foundational moment even though the northerners are by this stage, of course, well into their pilgrimage.[23] We know that the Flemish and Rhenish crusaders came from areas of intensive crusade preaching, including that by Bernard of Clairvaux himself.[24] And while the situation with respect to the recruitment of Anglo-Norman crusaders is less well documented,[25] it is inconceivable that there had been no preaching to recruit and organize such a substantial force; there are clues in the *De expugnatione* to suggest that the Anglo-Norman contingent numbered between 4,000 and 5,000, probably only slightly fewer than the Flemish-Rhenish forces.[26] For the purposes of the narrative arc, however, the Dartmouth rendezvous is the originary event: all the action that follows effectively becomes a series of moments, or movements, in which the initial collective unity that is exemplified at Dartmouth is variously sustained, threatened or reaffirmed. The text's detailed mention of the so-called 'Dartmouth Rules', the sworn regulations governing the coalition's operations, reinforces the theme of unity in diversity: 'Among the people of so many different tongues the firmest guarantees of peace and friendship were taken.'[27] The text's foregrounding of the Dartmouth Rules is significant in that it underscores that the crusaders themselves are to be understood as consciously attaching particular importance to the ideal of unity; in other words, the text's insistence on this point is not to be seen as merely a narratorial interpretation projected back onto events.

A particularly sensitive index of the text's insistence on the value of collective unity is its treatment of individual leaders within the crusade forces as initiators of or reactors to events. The narratives of the First Crusade had, to different extents congruent with their chosen emphases, achieved working balances between attending to the actions and interactions of the crusade's leaders as plot drivers, and granting agency to the crusade army as the embodiment of a collective endeavour.[28] In the case of the leaders, more was at stake than placing them in plot situations in which their social status and command roles would happen to find expression as a matter of course. They could also function as focalizers, that is to say characters who, as we saw in the Introduction, serve as privileged perceivers of the storyworld around them, their reading of situations extending some way into the space between the level of knowledge and self-awareness

[23] *De expugnatione*, p. 72.

[24] See Phillips, *Second Crusade*, pp. 137–8.

[25] Cf. C. Tyerman, *England and the Crusades 1095–1588* (Chicago, 1988), p. 32.

[26] Phillips, *Second Crusade*, pp. 143, 156; Bennett, 'Military Aspects', p. 74.

[27] *De expugnatione*, p. 56. For the regulations governing the expedition, see Phillips, *Second Crusade*, pp. 143–4.

[28] M. G. Bull, 'The Eyewitness Accounts of the First Crusade as Political Scripts', *Reading Medieval Studies*, 36 (2010), 32–3; *idem*, 'The Historiographical Construction of a Northern French First Crusade', *Haskins Society Journal*, 25 (2013), 48–54.

routinely demonstrated by the narrator and the typically reactive, temporally shallow consciousness of those characters, the majority, who are simply caught up in the moment-by-moment flow of the action.[29] To take just one example, in the *Gesta Francorum*'s account of the opening stages of the Battle of Dorylaeum on 1 July 1097, Bohemond of Taranto brings heightened individual perception and understanding to bear at a moment of acute collective danger (while the singling out of his perceptual acuity is emphasized still further by a rare express disavowal of interpretive ability on the narrator's part):

> On the third day the Turks launched a fierce attack upon Bohemond and those who were were him. Immediately the Turks began to screech and babble and scream, raising their voices and making a devilish racket in their own tongue – how I do not know. Seeing [*uidens*] countless Turks in the distance, screeching and screaming with their devilish cries, that wise man Bohemond promptly ordered all the knights to dismount and to put up the tents with all dispatch.[30]

In view of the familiarity with the narrative tradition of the First Crusade that is in evidence in the *De expugnatione*, what balance between leadership and collective agency does it try to effect? The fact that, as we have seen, Godfrey of Bouillon, who by the mid twelfth century had emerged in Latin Europe's collective memory as *the* defining leader of the First Crusade, is mentioned in passing close to the beginning of the work suggests that the narrator is gesturing towards a paradigm of individual heroism as a possible organizational strategy and thematic emphasis for the narrative that follows. In the event, however, this strategy is not pursued. The closest that we come to a Bohemond- or Godfrey-like individual agent and dominant focalizer is Hervey de Glanvill: he is listed first among the four constables who direct subdivisions of the Anglo-Norman contingent; it is Hervey who delivers a vigorous and effective speech when a group of Norman and English crusaders propose to sail away early; and he is one of those who take charge of five Moorish hostages when negotiations for the surrender of Lisbon get under way.[31] The importance that the narrator attaches to Hervey's tent has already been noted, and this, in conjunction with the identification of the work's addressee as Osbert of Bawdsey, would seem to suggest that the author had close connections to East Anglia, the region where the Glanvill family was powerful.[32] It is significant that the clearest moment of

[29] For focalization, see above, pp. 57–64.

[30] *Gesta Francorum*, p. 18: my translation.

[31] *De expugnatione*, pp. 54–6, 104–10, 164.

[32] Hervey is introduced as the constable of the 'Norfolcenses et Sudfolcenses': *De expugnatione*, pp. 54–6. Cf. the mention of the brave actions of seven youths from 'the province of Ipswich' ('de provintia Gipeswicensi'), probably a reference to the southerly parts of Suffolk: p. 160.

focalization on Hervey's part, highlighting the text's principal thematic concern and thereby aligning Hervey closely with the narratorial slant, occurs when, at the beginning of his speech outside Lisbon, he recalls having borne witness ('me vidisse recolo') to the crusaders' unity as recently as their time in Oporto.[33]

It is further noteworthy, however, that Hervey is never portrayed as being wholly on top of events. His speech to those intending to leave is a reaction to the initiative of others, and its aim is to repair the first fracture in the unity of the Anglo-Norman contingent. The occasion is a collective gathering ('in concilio venimus'), in which Hervey has to fight to assert himself over the babel of raised voices ('Hinc illinc acclamantibus cunctis'). At the end of his speech, he resorts to a desperate gambit by offering to abase himself at the feet of his principal antagonist, William Viel, having already indicated his willingness to invert their social relationship by submitting to the lordship of William and his party.[34] Hervey's gesture has the desired effect, but at the expense of a potential loss of prestige and authority.[35] In a similar vein, the fact that Hervey is of sufficient importance to be given some of the responsibility for the Muslim hostages rebounds on him, for, in sharing custody of the hostages with Afonso Henriques's military commander Fernando Captivo, he opens himself up to suspicion of collusion with the king, and so becomes a target for those crusaders who are mistrustful of the king's good faith.[36] We are told that a mob of 400 armed crusaders, under the leadership of a rabble-rousing priest from Bristol, rampages through the camp in an attempt to track Hervey down. The narrator clearly sides with Hervey and condemns the rioters' motivations. But for all that, Hervey's last appearance in the narrative amounts to an ignominious non-appearance, as, presumably somewhere in hiding, he is pursued in vain by a mob branding him a wicked traitor.[37]

[33] *De expugnatione*, p. 104: 'Pie recordationis memoria qua tot nationum populos pieque eruditionis viros cruce dominica insignitos pridie aput Portugalam me vidisse recolo ...'

[34] *De expugnatione*, pp. 104, 108–10. See Throop 'Christian Community', 117–19 for an interesting interpretation of the abasement.

[35] But cf. the assured and effective intervention by 'Herueus de Glamuyle', most probably our Hervey, recorded in a fifteenth-century text preserving the narrative of a legal case discussed in the Suffolk shire court *c.*1150: H. M. Cam, 'An East Anglian Shire-Moot for Stephen's Reign', *English Historical Review*, 39 (1924), 570–1. If the Hervey in this document is the Hervey of the *De expugnatione*, it would suggest he was a practised public speaker, for in it he refers to forty years' experience of participating in hundred and shire courts.

[36] *De expugnatione*, pp. 164, 166–70. In view of the importance of the *concordia/discordia* binary in the text's general ethical scheme, the terms in which the narrator frames his judgement of the effects of the handing over of the hostages ('quod fere maximum discordie seminarium fuerat') are perhaps meant to imply that the criticism of Hervey had some merit: p. 164.

[37] *De expugnatione*, p. 168.

A second Anglo-Norman lord to feature in the narrative, Saher of Archelle, emerges as a somewhat more proactive figure. He is accorded the title *dominus* in four places, unlike Hervey who is never so termed.[38] He is also granted a measure of focalization and initiative when he takes charge of the first raid ashore after the crusaders arrive at Lisbon, in the process preventing the Christians from being lured by their initial success into a vulnerable position.[39] Similarly, during a later Christian assault on the suburbs outside Lisbon's walls, Saher improvises a change of plan when he perceives that the attack has reached the point where it should be pressed forward rather than that he order a withdrawal, which is what the king and the other constables have instructed him to do.[40] In this way, Saher is that individual in the text whose sharp perceptions, quick thinking and qualities of command come closest to those shown by the princes in the First Crusade narrative tradition. But these two quite brief sequences of action account for most of his contribution to the overall plot of the narrative. And, tellingly, his final appearance is in a more passive mode, not in charge of events but acting at the behest of others when he is sent by 'the Normans and English and those who were encamped with us on our side' on a retaliatory raid across the Tagus towards Almada.[41]

It is arguable that the author of the *De expugnatione* felt himself constrained by the social status of the human material at his disposal, especially among the Anglo-Norman crusaders who were his principal concern. Hervey and Saher were members of land-owning families of local substance in East Anglia and Lincolnshire, respectively, but they were one or two notches below the level of the Anglo-Norman baronial elite. (Hervey's son Ranulf, however, would rise to become Henry II's chief justiciar. Significantly, he too went on crusade, dying at Acre in 1190.) At one point in the *De expugnatione*, the narrator, vexed by the Muslim defenders' mockery of the cross, declares that God had ordained 'that vengeance should be wrought upon the enemies of the cross through the most insignificant men'; this remark seems to be making a social point that goes beyond a conventional expression of humility.[42] There is, moreover, evidence that the relative social obscurity of even the most prominent of the Anglo-Norman crusaders was subsequently folded into the myth of their

[38] *De expugnatione*, pp. 126, 128

[39] *De expugnatione*, p. 96. Bennett, 'Military Aspects', p. 75 interprets this action as an initial statement of intent and display of bravado directed towards the enemy.

[40] *De expugnatione*, pp. 126–8. Note, however, that the construction of the act of perception of the danger is ambiguous and does not single out Saher's focalization: 'Comperto vero quod'.

[41] *De expugnatione*, p. 140.

[42] *De expugnatione*, p. 132: 'sub qualibuscumque homunciis'. For the correlation between vengeance and imagery of the cross in this and other crusade texts, see S. A. Throop, *Crusading as an Act of Vengeance, 1095–1216* (Farnham, 2011), pp. 97–107.

achievements.[43] Writing no more than seven years after the Lisbon campaign, Henry of Huntingdon praised the actions of a fleet made up of men who were lacking in power ('exercitus naualis uirorum non potentum'), who had had no leader other than God Himself, and who had conducted themselves humbly; these poor men (*pauperes*), most of them English, had been able to resist all the mighty forces arrayed against them.[44]

These comments are all the more interesting in that Henry probably knew, and may even have got some of his information about the Lisbon expedition from one or both of, the two men who stood to lose the most from Henry's levelling remarks about the composition of the crusade host: Henry belonged to a senior branch of Hervey's family; and Saher was a benefactor of churches, including Lincoln cathedral, with which Henry was closely connected.[45] It is, however, important to set Henry's observations about the Lisbon campaign in their immediate context, for his aim in this passage was to point a sharp contrast with the utter failure of the expeditions to the east led by Kings Louis VII of France and Conrad III of Germany, disasters which Henry ascribed to divine punishment for the armies' pride and sinfulness.[46] The participation in the Second Crusade of the two most powerful monarchs in western Europe raised the stakes of crusade leadership to a new level; compared with these two any other crusaders would automatically seem inferior. It is therefore likely that Henry was exaggerating the social contrast for rhetorical effect. For its part, the *De expugnatione* seems very considered in its handling of the balance between individual and collective agency: it includes just enough episodes in which individual leaders feature to imply that it could have made more of them had it so wished, and that the emphasis on the crusaders' collective agency is in consequence not only, or mainly, a reflection of the actual social composition of the crusade army but also a considered narratorial strategy.[47]

[43] See the equivocal, even evasive, response given by the crusaders when Afonso Henriques, quite reasonably, asks them who is in charge, which suggests that decisions concerning leadership had been deferred or fudged at the Dartmouth rendezvous: *De expugnatione*, p. 98, 'breviter responsum est nos primates habere hos et hos, et quorum precipue actus et consilia preminerent, sed nondum deliberatum cui responsionis officia committerent'.

[44] Henry of Huntingdon, *Historia Anglorum*, X.27, ed. and trans. D. E. Greenway (Oxford, 1996), p. 752. Cf. J. Gillingham, 'Henry of Huntingdon and the Twelfth-Century Revival of the English Nation', in his *The English in the Twelfth Century: Imperialism, National Identity and Political Values* (Woodbridge, 2000), pp. 123–44, esp. 133–4, 139–40, placing Henry's remarks in the context of his dislike of a noble and snobbishly elitist faction that had been politically dominant in England since 1139.

[45] See Greenway's comments in *Historia Anglorum*, pp. xxiii–xxviii, xcix–c; cf. *De expugnatione*, p. 57 n. 3. See also R. Mortimer, 'The Family of Ranulf de Glanville', *Bulletin of the Institute of Historical Research*, 54 (1981), 1–16, esp. 2–3.

[46] *Historia Anglorum*, X.27, p. 752.

[47] See the various imprecise references to leaders, interestingly concentrated towards the

The text's attention to the corporate character of the Lisbon expedition is embedded in its lexis, grammatical constructions and rhetorical effects as well as in its plot dynamics. For example, the unity of purpose in evidence when all those crusaders who are first to arrive at Oporto gather to hear Bishop Peter Pitões's sermon is reinforced by the repetition of *omnes* in the account of the scene.[48] Similarly, when the northerners first encounter King Afonso Henriques, their solidarity is highlighted by the dense repetition of forms of *nos* and *noster*.[49] The sequences in the text in which the fleet sails from Dartmouth to Lisbon are marked by the dominant use of verbs in the first person plural, with repetitions reinforcing the effect.[50] The manner in which the text expresses acts of collective decision-making is also noteworthy, for this speaks to a low-level but insistent and cumulatively significant form of focalization that runs through the plot and motivates the action at several important junctures. The tone is set with the verb ('sanxerunt', 'they ordained') that is used to denote the act of agreeing to the Dartmouth Rules: the subject is not stated, implicitly leaving

---

end of the text, by which point a narrative framework that does not foreground their agency has already been securely established, in *De expugnatione*, pp. 124 (*optimates nostre partis*), 164 (*constabularii nostri una cum senioribus*), 166 (*duces nostri*), 166 (*primates*), 170 (*seniores nostri*), 170 (*domini*), 172 (*duces nostri*), 174 (*duces nostri*).

[48] *De expugnatione*, pp. 68–70: 'Summo mane ex **omnibus** navibus in summitate montis in cimiterio epyscopii coram episcopo **omnes** convenimus; nam ecclesia pro quantitate sui **omnes** non caperet. Indicto ab **omnibus** silentio, episcopus sermonem coram **omnibus** lingua Latina habuit, ut per interpretes cuiusque lingue sermo eius **omnibus** manifestaretur'. But note that immediately after the sermon we are informed that some of the fleet still had to join the rest, having been dispersed in a storm in the Bay of Biscay: *De expugnatione*, p. 84. See Throop, 'Christian Community', 117, who notes the conjunction of *omnimodum* and *omnibus* with multiple instances of the adjective *singulus* in the text's account of the Dartmouth Rules (*De expugnatione*, p. 56) as a device to stress the theme of unity in diversity. Cf. Afonso Henriques's wish that his offer of terms to the northerners be explained to everyone so that all might give their consent, 'in commune coram omnibus explicetur, ut omnibus deinde utrimque assensum prebentibus': *De expugnatione*, p. 100.

[49] *De expugnatione*, pp. 96–8: 'Episcopi vero qui **nobiscum** advenerant regem suum adeunt, ut, sicut **nobiscum** constituerant, eum **nobis** obviam facerent. Qui brevi cum eo redeunt, nam per dies plus octo in provintia commoratus **nostrum** adventum existimans expectaverat. Audierat enim per **nostros** de **nostro** adventu, qui, in navibus V. a **nostra** societate segregati...advenerant ante dies VIII.'

[50] Such verbs are principally in evidence in the most extended travel sequence in the text, which is the voyage between Dartmouth and Oporto narrated in *De expugnatione*, pp. 58–68: see e.g. 'velificare incepimus' (p.58), 'feliciter applicuimus' (p. 60), 'pervenimus' (p. 62), 'devenimus' (p. 64), 'pervenimus' (p. 64), 'venimus' (p. 66), 'pervenissemus' (p. 68). The narrative rhythm is resumed in the passage narrating the journey from Oporto to Lisbon at pp. 86–8: see esp. the repetition of the construction 'velificare incepimus, iter prosperum agentes' at pp. 86, 88. For further instances of the first person plural see e.g. 'pernoctassemus' (p. 88), 'venissemus' (p. 96).

the unspecified 'they' to relate back to the 'peoples of many different tongues' who have just been described exchanging pledges of concord and friendship.[51] The same sort of capacity for seemingly spontaneous and unanimous decision-making reappears once the northerners have reached Portugal and must navigate both their relationship with the Portuguese Christians and the challenges of the siege. From this point depersonalizing passive verb constructions do much of the work: for example, the immediate response to the bishop of Oporto's sermon is a corporate decision ('deliberatum est ab omnibus') to wait for those leaders who are still out to sea.[52]

A key moment during the siege, perhaps the critical turning point, was the besiegers' discovery of what appear to have been very large caches of food supplies that the defenders had stored outside the city. Again, this action is depersonalized by means of the passive 'Inventum est' so as to highlight the significance of the discovery for all the crusaders, even though it was made on the side of the city where the Anglo-Norman forces were concentrated.[53] Likewise, we are told that two churches 'are built' ('construuntur') as burial places for the Christian dead.[54] On one level the churches, by simple dint of there being two of them, are emblematic of the divisions that had, as we shall see, opened up within the crusaders' ranks: one was built close to the Flemish-Rhenish zone of operations to the east of the city, and the other served the Anglo-Normans concentrated on the western side. But if we accept Livermore's identification of the author with the priest Raol, this would suggest that the author had a strong, personal attachment to the latter foundation, Santa Maria dos Mártires, for Raol's charter of 1148 speaks of his having built this cemetery church 'with my own money, toil and sweat'.[55] If Raol was indeed our author, the tone of detachment and lack of precision conveyed by the text's account of the churches' foundation would be all the more striking: the formulation 'a Francis construuntur' almost has the force of a reflexive or a verb in the middle voice, as if the churches contrived to build themselves once the crusaders en masse, the *Franci*, had collectively so willed.[56]

The text's insistence on the primary importance of collective unity and agency

[51] *De expugnatione*, p. 56.

[52] *De expugnatione*, p. 84: note also that the construction 'deliberatum est' is almost immediately repeated in the context of the subsequent decision to take the local bishops with the fleet to Lisbon and to hear the king in person.

[53] *De expugnatione*, p. 130.

[54] *De expugnatione*, p. 132.

[55] Livermore, 'The "Conquest of Lisbon"', 4–5.

[56] Cf. the use of the passive in the account of the election of Gilbert of Hastings as bishop of Lisbon (p. 178): 'Electus est...ex nostris Gislebertus Hastingensis'. For further passives that detach the action from the specific identity of the agent, see e.g. pp. 110: 'Electi sunt ex optimatibus nostris'; 114: 'communi omnium consilio decretum est'; 140: 'Dum hec aput nos geruntur'; 146: 'Indictum [est]'.

raises the question of the optimal human level or levels at which this unity might operate. The narrator explores this issue with reference to various national and religious binaries; indeed, over the course of the text, the working through of these binaries becomes the principal means by which the narratorial voice and slant are established. At the highest level is the unity of humanity itself, seldom acknowledged in crusade narratives but here articulated by the archbishop of Braga when addressing the besieged within Lisbon.[57] His speech opens by evoking the concord-discord duality that is central to the text's whole programmatic, and in offering peace to the Muslim defenders of the city he appeals to a sense of shared humanity. It is noteworthy that the metaphors put into the archbishop's mouth to express the idea of commonality, a 'compact of human association' ('federe societatis humane') and 'bonds of concord from the mother of all' ('vincule matris omnium concordie'), closely recall the language used of the sworn agreement to the Dartmouth Rules and subsequent expressions of the crusaders' unity. The archbishop does not develop this theme more fully, and his arguments quickly move on to more traditional, oppositional tropes. But the very fact that the theme of common humanity is introduced at all is intriguing. It would be stretching a point to suggest that its inclusion, and the robust response made by a Muslim elder to the archbishop's speech, are evidence of authorial misgivings about the rectitude of the siege.[58] It is more likely an argument *a fortiori*: if a case, albeit defeasible, could be made for *concordia* as the governing principle informing the relationship between two deeply antagonistic groups such as Christians and Muslims, then it should of necessity apply to collectivities that are not separated by the same kinds of religious differences and senses of historical grievance that divide the archbishop of Braga and his interlocutor.

At another level, there is the shared Christian identity of the crusaders and their Portuguese hosts. Once the bishop of Oporto and Afonso Henriques have articulated the rationale for the crusaders' participation in the operations against Lisbon, the Portuguese do not feature prominently in the narration of the siege itself. It is possible that the author made a conscious decision to play down the Portuguese contribution, but we should perhaps be wary of argument from silence.[59] The *De expugnatione* tells us that Afonso Henriques and his forces set up their own camp; this was to the north of the besieged city. They thereby detached themselves both physically and figuratively from what we shall see is the text's central plot binary, the dynamic between the Anglo-Norman and

[57] *De expugnatione*, pp. 114–18.

[58] *De expugnatione*, pp. 120–2.

[59] The Lisbon Letter similarly downplays the contribution made by Afonso Henriques and the Portuguese forces, at one point suggesting that the local soldiers showed little fortitude. It is acknowledged, however, that the king bore the cost of one of the siege towers: 'Lisbon Letter', 338, 339; trans. Edgington, 'Albert of Aachen', pp. 64, 65.

the Flemish-Rhenish crusade contingents. Later, we are informed that the king redeployed most of his resources elsewhere, leaving behind just a rump force which is further marginalized in the remaining parts of the narrative.[60] But if the Portuguese play only a limited role in the action itself, they are disproportionately important with regards to the definition and reinforcement of the crusaders' collective sense of identity – even more so, perhaps, than the Muslim enemy. The two main clusters of unifying language that were noted above occur in the sequences in which the crusaders first encounter the bishop of Oporto and then Afonso Henriques himself. In a contrastive but also complementary vein, the first discordant note of division within the northerners' ranks, which the narrator introduces abruptly and without warning after another by now formulaic and almost routine expression of collective unity ('Ad hec omnes responsuri una in concilium veniunt'), is sounded immediately after the king has made his offer for the crusaders to stay and help.[61] In other words, the Portuguese both set up the conditions in which the collective agency of the crusaders can find effective expression, and catalyze the tensions that threaten their unity.[62] In this connection, it is striking that a note of separation and cultural distance is sounded at the very first formal moment of encounter between the crusaders and the Portuguese, and in a context of apparent cordiality and conjunction: when the fleet reaches Oporto, the bishop, accompanied by a clerical welcoming party, comes down to meet the new arrivals and greets them 'in the manner of his own people'.[63] It is a small moment, and precisely how the cultural distinctiveness registered itself is left unstated, but in invoking both custom and nationality in one compact phrase the remark establishes a mood of detachment between the local Christians and the northerners that will run underneath all that follows.

The Anglo-Norman contingent functions as the core element of the narrator's sense of loyalty and group identity. Once the unanimity and shared purpose that have characterized the early stages of the expedition break down, the Anglo-Normans become the text's principal referent when it uses *nos* and *nostri*, verbs expressing collective agency, and other group markers.[64] Although

[60] *De expugnatione*, p. 140. Bennett, 'Military Aspects', p. 80 suggests that these forces had come to the end of their term of service. If so, it would lend support to the argument that the Portuguese soldiers, or at least most of them, did not take the cross themselves and fight alongside their northern European allies as fellow crusaders: see on this point Purkis, *Crusading Spirituality*, pp. 171–2.

[61] *De expugnatione*, p. 100.

[62] See also the reaction to the handling of the Muslim hostages, which turns from distrust of the king to hostility towards Hervey de Glanvill: *De expugnatione*, p. 164.

[63] *De expugnatione*, p. 68: 'ex more gentis sue'. My translation. The text has earlier made reference to various contacts between locals and the crusaders as they sail south, but this is the first set-piece meeting.

[64] See e.g. *De expugnatione*, pp. 110: 'Electi sunt ex optimatibus nostris una cum

the text notes the presence at the siege of some groups, Bretons and Scots (or perhaps Irish), who were more likely to have attached themselves to the Anglo-Norman contingent than the Flemish-Rhenish party, the narrator clearly treats the English and the Normans themselves as the constituent elements that define their half of the crusade host.[65] Although differentiated, they always function as a collective unit.[66] It is important to remember that the term 'Anglo-Norman' is a modern convention, and in other contexts scholars have queried its value. John Gillingham, for example, has argued that 'English' rather than 'Anglo-Norman' better captures the identity and self-perception of those who began to settle in Ireland in the final third of the twelfth century.[67] The relationships during the Lisbon campaign between the unambiguously English, those from England who claimed Norman and other French roots, and the Normans from Normandy were probably complex, but the narrator does not burrow into this nexus. Instead, at a moment of particular vulnerability, as the first fissures within the contingent appear in the disagreements triggered by Afonso Henriques's invitation to contribute to the siege, those dissenting from the majority view are presented as hailing from both southern English coastal towns and Normandy.[68] Indeed, it is possible to glimpse in this group representatives of cross-Channel maritime interests who more than any other population in this period actually lived the routine reality of contacts between England and Normandy, and thus qualify better than anyone for the label 'Anglo-Norman'.

One slightly discordant note is sounded, however, in Hervey de Glanvill's speech to the dissenters, when, in appealing to the memory of ancestral virtues, he evokes 'the praise and glory of our race', 'us who are united in the same blood and race', and 'brothers' who 'all share one mother'; in addition, he explicitly refers to the Normans and their military prowess, and warns of the shame

---

Colonensibus et Flandrensibus'; 124: 'constabularii nostri et optimates nostre partis'; 124: 'garciones nostri'; 130: 'contra nos tres portas habentes'; 134: 'Turris...nostra'; 142: 'nostri...intendentes operi'; 162: 'machina nostra'. Note that this contraction of the referential range of *nos* in fact begins just before the first fracturing of the crusade's unity, with the foray ashore upon reaching Lisbon and the night spent in an exposed advance position by a small group under Hervey de Glanvill and Saher of Archelle: *De expugnatione*, p. 96.

[65] *De expugnatione*, pp. 104, 106, 140.

[66] *De expugnatione*, pp. 128: 'Nostri...Normanni scilicet et Angli'; 132: 'ab Anglis et a Normannis'; 140: 'Normanni igitur et Angli et qui nobiscum ex nostra parte manebant'; 142: 'Normanni et Anglici et qui cum eis erant'; 146: 'Normanni vero atque Angli'; 170: 'Normanni quoque et Angli'; 176: 'Normanni vero atque Angli'.

[67] J. Gillingham, 'The English Invasion of Ireland', in his *The English in the Twelfth Century: Imperialism, National Identity and Political Values* (Woodbridge, 2000), pp. 145–60, esp. 150–7.

[68] *De expugnatione*, pp. 102: 'omnes fere Hamtunenses et Hastingenses'; 104: 'quasi navibus octo Normannorum, Hamtonensium et Bristowensium'.

that 'Normandy, the mother of our race' would have to bear if the dissenters abandoned the expedition.[69] On the face of it, the effect of this sort of rhetoric would have been to alienate those among Hervey's listeners who identified themselves as English. But Hervey clearly intends the Norman memory to be a focal point of unity, not a source of further division, and there is no hint that the narrator is suggesting that this was a misjudgement on his part. On the contrary, the force of Hervey's remarks for the contemporary reader would have been that they sublimated discourses of racial or national pride into the sort of devotional frame of reference that was appropriate to participation in a crusade: in addition to recalling the terms of the bishop of Oporto's appeal to the 'worthy sons of the mother Church' and 'brothers', Hervey was evoking the emphasis on familial memory and example in *Quantum praedecessores* and the preaching of the cross built around it, as well as the more general use of metaphors of maternity and fraternity in crusade rhetoric.[70] The best explanation for the seeming divisiveness of Hervey's appeal, therefore, is that the evocation of Norman glory reflected the ideological asymmetry between the Normans and English as victors and vanquished after 1066, while also nudging towards an emergent sense of unitary identity among people of Hervey's class, landowners of largely Norman descent who nonetheless did not have cross-Channel estates and for whom England was their normal field of operation and locus of loyalty.[71] Hervey's emphasis is redolent of the sentiments found in closely contemporary texts from similar cultural milieux such as Aelred of Rievaulx's *Relatio de Standardo*, in which Walter of Espec's oration before the Battle of the Standard in 1138, recalling past Norman glories, precedes a victory over the Scots that is largely achieved by English soldiers.[72]

[69] *De expugnatione*, pp. 104–8: my translations.

[70] *De expugnatione*, pp. 78–80. Cf. the familial imagery in Baldric of Bourgueil's version of Urban II's sermon at Clermont: *Historia Ierosolimitana*, pp. 6–10.

[71] See Gillingham, 'Henry of Huntingdon', pp. 139–40. (As Gillingham notes, the Lisbon Letter always refers to this grouping as the 'English'.) For a different emphasis, see H. M. Thomas, *The English and the Normans: Ethnic Hostility, Assimilation, and Identity 1066–c.1220* (Oxford, 2003), pp. 74–81.

[72] Aelred of Rievaulx, 'Relatio de Standardo', ed. R. Howlett, *Chronicles of the Reigns of Stephen, Henry II, and Richard I*, vol. 3 (RS 82:3; London, 1886), pp. 185–9; trans. J. P. Freeland, *Aelred of Rievaulx: The Historical Works*, ed. M. L. Dutton (Cistercian Fathers Series, 56; Collegeville, MN, 2008), pp. 251–7. For the speech, see J. R. E. Bliese, 'Aelred of Rievaulx's Rhetoric and Morale at the Battle of the Standard, 1138', *Albion*, 20 (1988), 543–56. Cf. Henry of Huntingdon's account of the same battle, in which Ralph, bishop of the Orkneys, addresses his oration to 'Proceres Anglie, clarissimi Normannigene', and the speech is acclaimed by 'omnis populus Anglorum', while the subsequent battle is fought by the 'gens Normannorum et Anglorum in una acie circum Standard conglobata': *Historia Anglorum*, X.7–9, pp. 712–18. See also Gillingham, 'Henry of Huntingdon', pp. 129–30.

The principal binary around which the narrator develops the theme of unity is that between the Anglo-Normans and the crusaders from Flanders and the Rhineland. The German crusaders are first introduced as coming from 'the Roman Empire' and forming a separate force, in such a way that they, the Flemish and the Anglo-Normans represent a three-way coalition at the Dartmouth rendez-vous.[73] Thereafter the narrator uses Cologne as a synecdoche of the group's regional identity in consistently referring to the *Colonenses*.[74] A group from Boulogne associated with the Flemish and German party is mentioned twice in the text, but its role as a discrete element is little developed.[75] Although there are some hints that the narrator has a particular suspicion of the Flemings, the initial tripartite schema quickly resolves into a binary opposition, in that the Flemings and the men of Cologne largely function as a single plot entity, thereby mirroring to some extent the pairing of the English and Normans. The geography of the siege, with the two northern forces encamped on opposite sides of the city and thus detached from each other in much of their day-to-day operations, permits the narrator to highlight their interactions, when they do come into collision, for contrastive purposes.[76] It is significant, for example, that although the narrator emphasizes the first fissures within the crusade host by dwelling on the arguments within the Anglo-Norman forces, as we have seen, this comes immediately after the Flemings have introduced an initial note of disunity by precipitously and unilaterally agreeing to accept Afonso Henriques's offer of financial support and the obligations that go with it.[77]

Thereafter the Flemish-Rhenish bloc serves as a foil to the Anglo-Normans in situations that highlight two of its vices, envy and greed. Envy (*invidia*) first surfaces in the early stages of the siege when the English and Normans are successful in attacking the extramural suburbs on their side of the city.[78] And it reappears when the Flemish-Rhenish contingent fails to participate in a raid

[73] *De expugnatione*, pp. 52–4.

[74] *De expugnatione*, pp. 104, 106, 110, 132, 134, 136, 140, 142, 144, 146, 164, 170, 174, 176. The Lisbon Letter also refers to a group of Lotharingians: 'Lisbon Letter', 339; trans. Edgington, 'Albert of Aachen', p. 65.

[75] *De expugnatione*, pp. 54, 104.

[76] S. Lay, 'Miracles, Martyrs and the Cult of Henry the Crusader in Lisbon', *Portuguese Studies*, 24 (2008), 11, 14–17, 30 makes the interesting suggestion that the Anglo-Normans and the Flemings and Germans were divided by competing visions of the crusade vocation, the former adhering to a more old-fashioned emphasis on pilgrimage to Jerusalem, and the latter embracing St Bernard's vision of holy war on multiple fronts. This may push the evidence further than it warrants, however, and presupposes an absence of Bernardine influence on the preaching of the cross in the Anglo-Norman world that is difficult to imagine.

[77] *De expugnatione*, p. 100.

[78] *De expugnatione*, p. 128: note the open-ended reference to 'omnium ceterorum invidia'.

across the Tagus to Almada in retaliation for the abduction of five Bretons.[79] The Flemings and men of Cologne are portrayed as resentful and jealous of honourable Anglo-Norman offers of assistance, and as innately covetous; and it is therefore unsurprising that, at the climax of the siege, their greed (*cupiditas*) leads them to break the terms of the agreement that is meant to govern the orderly seizure of Lisbon and the distribution of the booty to be found in it, whereas the Normans and English remain guided by high-minded respect for their sworn obligations.[80] Perhaps the most striking indication of the text's hostility towards the other northern force, specifically here the Flemings, is its inclusion of a portent in which, one Sunday, bread blessed for the Mass is found to be suffused with blood.[81] Rather than seeking to place a positive interpretation on the omen, which the Eucharistic context might seem to invite, the narrator firmly, if a little indirectly, nudges in the opposite direction by stating that some thought this meant that the fierce and indomitable Flemings, ever greedy for others' belongings, remained thirsty for human blood despite their status as pilgrims.[82] Collectively, therefore, the Flemings and Rhinelanders embody a functional failure of right intention, one of the text's thematic priorities, as this manifests itself outwardly in the strains placed on the corporate cohesion of the crusade army.

In spite of the centrifugal forces that he bemoans, the narrator nonetheless retains the hope that divine clemency can reimpose *concordia* and overcome the devil's malice.[83] It is noteworthy that a clustering of the word *omnes* recurs at the climactic moment of the siege, as the crusaders rejoice at the sight of the formal entry into Lisbon of the king, their leaders and the bishops bearing a banner of the sign of the cross.[84] Although at this stage the Flemings and Rhinelanders still have one more divisive intervention to make, greedily pillaging the city and mistreating its inhabitants, they are soon depicted coming to their senses and

[79] *De expugnatione*, p. 140.

[80] *De expugnatione*, pp. 146, 170–6. For the fraught nature of the events surrounding the surrender and occupation of Lisbon, see Phillips, *Second Crusade*, pp. 163–5.

[81] *De expugnatione*, p. 134. This would have been blessed bread, *eulogia*, distributed to members of the army, not the consecrated host. Lay, 'Miracles', 15 overreads this passage to suggest that it expresses a critique of the idea that warfare against the Muslims was intrinsically meritorious. For interesting remarks on this episode in the context of the crusade's devotional regimen, see Throop, 'Christian Community', 105–6.

[82] This incident is reported at greater length, and with a more positive slant, in an account of the foundation of the monastery of S. Vicente, Lisbon, written in the 1180s: 'Indiculum Fundationis Monasterii Beati Vincenti Vlixbone', c. 9, in *A Conquista de Lisboa*, p. 186.

[83] *De expugnatione*, p. 166.

[84] *De expugnatione*, p. 174: 'O quanta omnium leticia! O quanta omnium specialis gloria!'

making their peace with the Anglo-Normans.[85] At the culmination of the siege the narrator also revisits the theme of unity by stressing the motif of a pan-Frankish identity that binds the northerners together. Up to this point, the word *Franci* has been used sparingly and without an ideological charge, interestingly so given the author's probable familiarity with narratives of the First Crusade; we have seen it used to denote the northerners as a single entity in the context of the construction of their two mortuary churches, but otherwise it mostly appears in Portuguese Christian and Moorish utterances, drawing attention to the idea that 'Frankish' was a label applied to the crusaders by outsiders rather than a self-generated and especially resonant expression of group belonging.[86] Now, however, while retaining the element of focalization by outsiders, the narrator states that after the conclusion of the siege and mopping-up operations against nearby castles, the Franks' renown (*Francorum nomen*) was magnified throughout Spain, with the result that terror seized the Moors when news of the defeat reached them. This remark represents the limit of the narrator's exploration of the wider ramifications of the siege – his concluding remarks on its aftermath are direct observations concerning its human effects in and around Lisbon itself – and to the extent, therefore, that this offers a summation of the expedition's achievement, it does so by emphasizing the idea of unity one final and definitive time.[87]

The text's insistence on the theme of unity has a direct impact on its construction of the narrator. As we shall see, the narratorial gaze is typically de-particularized in collective acts of perception and cognition, and the narrator seldom speaks in the first person singular. There is, however, one passage that bucks this trend in a self-highlighting manner and therefore merits attention. It occurs at the single most critical moment in the trajectory of the plot, when the crusaders' unanimity dissolves as a consequence of competing reactions to Afonso Henriques's offer to take part in the attack on Lisbon:

> To frame a reply to this we all assembled in council. But what on this occasion everyone said in proportion as he abounded in cocksureness and glibness of tongue, and in so saying profitted nothing except to beat the air, I think (*puto*) may not inconveniently be passed over, for there is no authority in talk. But when a large number had put forward many superfluities, the decision as to what course it were preferable to take was put off until after lunch. But in the

[85] *De expugnatione*, p. 176.

[86] *De expugnatione*, pp. 68 (letter of Afonso Henriques to Bishop Peter Pitões), 110 (charter of Afonso Henriques setting out his agreement with the crusaders), 132 (a reference to the building of churches by the crusaders), 136 (intercepted letter from the besieged to the emir of Évora). Cf. p. 170 where the 'Franks' are divided over the question whether to storm the city or agree terms.

[87] For the narrator's observations about conditions after the siege, see *De expugnatione*, pp. 180–2.

> meantime, by what agreement and through what intermediaries I know not (*nescio*), the Flemings acquiesced in the king's proposal – because, as I suppose (*ut estimo*), those who were feeling the pinch of want the hope of money-snatching reduced the more easily to its sway.[88]

Verb forms such as *puto*, *nescio* and *estimo* are often little more than routine and formulaic markers of a narrator's epistemological positioning in relation to the action and as such can be more akin to adverbial qualifiers than indicators of a distinctive and considered exercise of judgement. But their unusual concentration in this passage seems purposeful and emphatic, reinforcing the abruptness of the appearance of discord and, in immediate plot terms, its apparently unmotivated nature. By partly surrendering both his normally full knowledge of events and his ability to read agents' purposes and states of mind in their actions, the narrator shows himself to the reader wrestling with this confusing and consequential moment.[89]

This staging of confusion and ignorance on the narrator's part implies that this is his reaction as a character within the scene as it plays out *and* remains so in the act of recalling the moment from the vantage point of the narratorial now. That is to say, hindsight has not shed fuller light on the matter. Such a posture is all the more striking in that elsewhere in the text the narrator is at some pains to establish himself as a scrupulous, inquisitive and discriminating observer whose judgements resonate with, and are informed by an empathy towards, the collective experience of the crusade army, in particular the Anglo-Norman contingent. This assertive narratorial self-positioning is first established in the opening address to Osbert of Bawdsey: 'Accordingly we shall show forth in writing whatever events on our journey were worth telling, the successes and the setbacks, and all that was done or said or seen or heard during it.'[90] Such a knowledgeable stance is reinforced over the course of the text by numerous unobtrusively introduced reality effects. Some involve precision in counting or measuring: we are informed, for example, that about 164 ships gathered at Dartmouth;[91] that the

[88] *De expugnatione*, p. 100.

[89] The narrator uses the first person singular in only one further instance, but one that amounts to a restaging of the initial moment of communal discord, when the Flemings and Germans refuse to co-operate with the Anglo-Normans on a raid to Almada 'invidia vel timore, vel qua causa nescio': *De expugnatione*, p. 140.

[90] *De expugnatione*, p. 52. My translation: 'Itineris ergo nostri vel prospera vel adversa vel que interim facta vel dicta vel visa vel audita, relatu digna fuerint quecumque scripto manifestabimus.'

[91] *De expugnatione*, p. 52. Cf. the Lisbon Letter's rounding up to 'around 200' vessels, a figure that excludes those ships that carried the Rhinelanders: 'Lisbon Letter', 336; trans. Edgington, 'Albert of Aachen', p. 63.

depth of the water off Brittany was at least seventy-five cubits;[92] that the first siege tower built by the Anglo-Normans was ninety-five feet tall and the second eighty-three, while the Flemish-Rhenish mine under Lisbon's walls extended forty cubits.[93] Small, anchoring details are introduced within larger scenes: for example, the remark that, as the Anglo-Norman tower was moved towards the wall in the final assault, one of the attackers was killed by a sling shot; and the information that the seven youths from the area around Ipswich who took part in this assault were sheltered by a covered siege device known as a 'Welsh cat' (*cattus Waliscus*).[94]

Although the macro-chronology of the five or six months covered by the narrative is uneven – some dating precisions are introduced by references to the ecclesiastical calendar but not every event is so situated and there are some substantial jumps forward in time – there are numerous micro-chronological references to the time of day, again reinforcing the image of the narrator as a careful and accurate observer of individual scenes in their moment-by-moment lived actuality.[95] In a similar vein, sources of information are mentioned quite rarely, but when they are introduced they implicitly emphasize the narrator's access to high-status and knowledgeable informants: for example, the bishop of Oporto concerning the therapeutic properties of sand in his city's harbour; and the Muslim *alcaide* of Lisbon, after the city's fall, on the number of people who had been besieged (though the figure quoted, 154,000 excluding women and children, must be too high by a factor of twenty or thirty).[96] As with precise details, so with the bigger picture: the narrator is able to offer generalizations about the actions, responses and attributes of the crusaders and speak to their collective mood.[97] In addition, at several points in the text the narrator gestures towards a wider field of episodic and semantic knowledge than he is willing to share with

[92] *De expugnatione*, p. 58.

[93] *De expugnatione*, pp. 134, 142.

[94] *De expugnatione*, pp. 158–60.

[95] E.g. *De expugnatione*, pp. 68 (tenth hour), 96 (after lunch), 124 (about the ninth hour), 126 (sunset), 146 (until the first hour). For jumps in the temporal sequence, see *De expugnatione*, pp. 86 (ten days between the bishop of Oporto's speech and sailing away from the city), 136 (a jump from an unspecified earlier point to six weeks into the siege), 142 (an acceleration in the pace of the narration of the siege).

[96] *De expugnatione*, pp. 68, 94. Cf. the somewhat more guarded endorsement of a prophecy concerning the appearance of an ancient 'bridge' on the coast at Corunna which is nonetheless validated by being told by a very old local man ('a quodam gentis illius antiquissimo'): p. 64.

[97] E.g. *De expugnatione*, pp. 60 (multiple similar reactions to the danger of a storm at sea), 86 (we land on the island of Peniche *feliciter*), 98 (the usual behaviour of crowds), 170 (the innate covetousness of the Rhenish-Flemish contingent).

the reader, thereby implying that what is included is the result of a thoughtful process of reflection and selection on his part.[98]

Given the care with which the narrator's individual competence is constructed, it is noteworthy how far he permits his purchase on the storyworld to be subsumed within collective acts of perception and apprehension. The group emphasis is established early, in the sequences narrating the fleet's voyage south.[99] The 'travelogue' sections of the text have not attracted much scholarly attention since the work of David, whose notes carefully map the fleet's movements onto the hydrography and geography of the Spanish and Portuguese Atlantic littoral. They can seem a mere warm-up before the narrative gets down to its main business with the crusaders' arrival at Lisbon. But these sections account for about one seventh of the text, and the importance that the author attached to them may be gauged by the fact that after the first travelogue sequence, which delivers the crusaders to Oporto, and the introduction of a concomitant note of anticipation and change of mood by means of the bishop's lengthy sermon, the text reverts to its earlier discursive mode in a second extended travel section that gets the fleet down to Lisbon and concludes with a detailed pen-picture of Lisbon itself.[100]

The principal purpose of the travel sequences is to set up the Iberian landscape itself as compelling evidence of the justice of the crusaders' cause. The greater emphasis is on space rather than time, on geography more than history, though the two are closely linked. The text makes some references to past conflicts between Christians and Muslims in the peninsula – complete with seemingly precise but in fact inaccurate reality effects such as the claim that Oporto had been destroyed by the Moors and Almoravids about eighty years earlier, and the statement that the Moors had been in possession of Christian cities and lands for 358 years.[101] Beyond this chronological horizon lies the peninsula's early Christian history, as principally evidenced by its relics and saints' cults; and still further back a hazy Greco-Roman world of legend, as revealed by the remark that

[98] E.g. *De expugnatione*, pp. 56 (not all the Dartmouth Rules are specified), 60 (it is observed that it would be tedious to relate in detail the visions experienced during a bad storm at sea), 62 (an allusive, undeveloped reference to the negative qualities of the inhabitants of an area near Oviedo), 68 (the bishop of Oporto's claims about the harbour sands are corroborated by unspecified 'histories of the Romans'), 100 (the narrator passes over the vacuous remarks made at the first divisive council).

[99] *De expugnatione*, pp. 58–68, 86–96.

[100] See *De expugnatione*, pp. 84–96.

[101] *De expugnatione*, pp. 66–8, 116. The Almoravids first entered Spain in 1086, sixty-one years earlier; and the year 789 does not seem to have any obvious significance as a foundational moment in the Arab conquest, which began in 711, unless, at a stretch, this is an allusive reference to the death of the ruler of Muslim Spain 'Abd ar-Rahmān I in 788. See also *De expugnatione*, p. 118 for some knowledge of the Visigothic Church and the career of Isidore of Seville.

Julius Caesar first built the lighthouse at Corunna to aid maritime traffic between the British Isles and Spain, and the belief, found in Solinus and elsewhere, that Lisbon was founded by Ulysses.[102] The centre of gravity of the text's temporal reach nudges, however, towards very recent events. The bishop of Oporto, for example, tells the crusaders that his cathedral had been sacked by the Moors and its vessels, vestments, ornaments and bells had been carried off just seven years before, and that Santiago de Compostela had been threatened around the same time.[103]

The most significant piece of the past in terms of plot and character motivation is an earlier collaborative campaign against Lisbon, probably in 1142, about which little is known, but which seems to have ended in acrimony. This would seem to have formed the historical basis of much of the northerners' mistrust of Afonso Henriques. The narratee is expected to understand the significance of the earlier expedition as a point of comparison and contrast, to judge from the allusive character of the various references made to it.[104] In contrast, the travel sequences set up Iberian space as a secure site of knowledge and learning, by means of which the crusaders are able to insert themselves into the just cause of the Lisbon expedition. It is significant that the very first landfall on Iberian soil, probably at Gozón, presents the crusaders with a monastery that has recently been destroyed by the Moors; and their journey is bookended, immediately before the text picks up the story of the siege proper with the first disembarkation of the Anglo-Norman contingent, by the mention of the scene at the site of a church near Lisbon which had been razed by the Moors but where three stones remained

[102] *De expugnatione*, pp. 62–4, 66, 88, 92, 94–6. The belief that the city was founded by Ulysses is also recorded by the Lisbon Letter: 'Lisbon Letter', 337; trans. Edgington, 'Albert of Aachen', p. 63.

[103] *De expugnatione*, pp. 76–8, translating *signa* as bells, not insignia.

[104] *De expugnatione*, pp. 96 (during the very first engagement of the siege Saher of Archelle recalls the experiences of 'predecessors who had come here previously'), 102 (some of the leading Anglo-Norman dissenters were among those 'who had come to besiege Lisbon five years before this'). Cf. Hervey de Glanvill's reference to the dissenters' belief that Afonso Henriques had behaved reprehensibly in the past, which may be a further recollection of the 1142 campaign: *De expugnatione*, p. 108. The terms of the king's oath to the crusaders, not to practise deceit on them, may have been born of the earlier experience, while the Muslim elder's statement to the archbishop of Braga that the Christians had attacked them there in the past 'cum peregrinis et barbaris' may also evoke the previous attempted assault on Lisbon: *De expugnatione*, pp. 114, 120. For the 1142 campaign, see L. Villegas-Aristizábal, 'Revisiting the Anglo-Norman Crusaders' Failed Attempt to Conquer Lisbon *c.* 1142', *Portuguese Studies*, 29 (2013), 7–20. The principal source for this event is the late twelfth-century *Historia Gothorum*, which refers to the adventitious arrival of ships 'de partibus Galliarum' carrying 'armatis uiris uotum habentes ire in Jerusalem': 'Chronica Gothorum', *Portugaliae Monumenta Historica, Scriptores*, vol. 1 (Lisbon, 1856), pp. 13–14.

'as a sign of its ruin'.[105] The notion that Iberia is a place for learning by means of direct experience is reinforced in the bishop of Oporto's sermon to the crusaders. While he acknowledges that some knowledge of the aggression of the Moors and Almoravids will have reached the crusaders' own countries, they are, he claims, now in a far better position to judge for themselves because they are confronting the visual evidence:

> But these matters, of which a knowledge was brought to you by fame only, now most certainly lie open to your view more clear than day [*luce clarior certius...visibus patent*]. Alas, that in all Galicia and the kingdom of Aragon and in Numantia, of the numberless cities, castles, villages and saints' shrines there should now remain virtually nothing except the traces of ruins and marks of the desolation that has been wrought. Even this city of ours that you see [*cernitis*], once among the most populous, now reduced to the appearance of a tiny village, has within our memory been despoiled by the Moors many times... Indeed, what does the coast of Spain offer to your gaze [*vestris...obtutibus*] other than a remembrance of its own desolation and the signs of its downfall? How many cities and churches have you discovered to be in ruins upon it, either by your own observation or the reports of local people [*visu et indigenarum indiciis*]?[106]

As noted above, the travel sequences draw upon the late antique writer Solinus's work of chorography, the *Collectanea rerum mirabilium* or *Polyhistor*, specifically its section (c. 23) on Hispania.[107] The borrowings are particularly evident in the description of Lisbon and the natural resources of its hinterland, extending to the adaptation of whole constructions and sequences of ideas that in the source text refer to the peninsula in its entirety.[108] Other borrowings are briefer, involving the transposition of motifs from one setting to another and mentions of ancient toponyms.[109] The *ne plus ultra* of the author's embrace

[105] *De expugnatione*, pp. 60, 94–6.

[106] *De expugnatione*, pp. 76–8: translation revised.

[107] For the date of the work, which is much debated, see K. Brodersen, 'Mapping Pliny's World: The Achievement of Solinus', *Bulletin of the Institute of Classical Studies*, 54 (2011), 63–88, esp. 64–7, 87; Z. von Martels, 'Turning the Tables on Solinus' Critics: The Unity of Contents and Form of the *Polyhistor*', in K. Brodersen (ed.), *Solinus: New Studies* (Heidelberg, 2014), pp. 10–23, esp. 21–3. Solinus was himself heavily reliant on Pliny the Elder's *Historia Naturalis*.

[108] *De expugnatione*, pp. 90–2; Solinus, *Collectanea rerum mirabilium*, 23.1–7, ed. T. Mommsen (Berlin, 1895), pp. 103–4.

[109] *De expugnatione*, pp. 64–6, concerning the island of Tamba in the bay of Pontevedra, picks up the references to rabbits and snakes in Solinus's account of the Cassiterides, the fabled 'Tin Islands', and the Fortunatae, that is the Canaries: *Collectanea rerum mirabilium*, 23.10–12, pp. 104–5. The account of the island of Peniche and the Burlings (Berlengas) in *De expugnatione*, p. 86 borrows from the toponymical

of Solinus is his inclusion of the statement that mares in the region of Lisbon conceive thanks to the action of the wind as well as impregnation by their mates.[110] This seemingly gratuitous observation is perhaps motivated by the fact that Solinus explicitly relates this phenomenon to the area around Lisbon (*in proximis Olisiponis*), whereas most of the other remarks that the text adapts refer to Hispania in general. It is, in other words, Lisbon's 'signature' marvel. The *De expugnatione*'s use of Solinus raises interesting questions about its author's eyewitness credentials. Does it derogate from the text's construction of an observant narrator engaging in an unmediated manner with the storyworld and the events that take place within it? Solinus's work was very widely read and copied in the Middle Ages.[111] It therefore lent the *De expugnatione* considerable authority by conforming to an image of the Iberian peninsula that many of its readers would already have formed in their imaginations. In addition, a particular advantage of drawing upon Solinus for inspiration was that it enabled the narrator to extend the range of his attention beyond what would simply have presented itself to the crusaders' gaze as their fleet sailed along the coast. In this way, references to Oviedo, Lugo and Iria push the boundaries of the narrator's knowledge inland; these are places more or less close to the sea, but they also evoke a larger Iberian space and so affirm the narrator's competence to speak to the whole peninsula's past and present.[112]

A second advantage was that Solinus's framework was not tightly prescriptive: it established a descriptive idiom that could be added to and extended. Some of the categories that the *De expugnatione* brings to bear on its characterizations of places and spaces, such as distinctive fauna, the fertility of the land, mineral resources, hunting opportunities and toponymy, are directly derived from Solinus; Solinus would also seem to be the inspiration behind the text's particular interest in islands. But the framework could accommodate changes to the human landscape that had emerged since the Roman period, most obviously

---

remarks of *Collectanea rerum mirabilium*, 23.12, p. 105. The reference to a palace and workshops on the Burlings (of which there is nowadays no trace) may be a blending of Solinus's mention of 'plurimis monumentis' and an early version of the legend that the last Visigothic king of Spain, Rodrigo, fled to an Atlantic island when the Moors invaded: see *Conquista de Lisboa*, ed. Nascimento, n. 77 at p. 162.

[110] *De expugnatione*, p. 92; *Collectanea rerum mirabilium*, 23.7, p. 104. Solinus follows Pliny, *Historia Naturalis,* IV.116 and VIII.166. For this belief, see R. M. Rosado Fernandes, 'O vento, as éguas de Lusitânia e os autores grecos e latinos', *Euphrosyne*, 12 (1984), 53–77.

[111] See the list of the more than 250 extant manuscripts in K. Brodersen, 'A Revised Handlist of Manuscripts Transmitting Solinus' Work', in K. Brodersen (ed.), *Solinus: New Studies* (Heidelberg, 2014), pp. 201–8. See also Brodersen, 'Mapping Pliny's World', 67–9.

[112] *De expugnatione*, pp. 60–2, 64.

so in the text's mentions of churches, saints' cults and diocesan boundaries, but also evident in references to castles.[113] Moreover, something more subtle and blended is at stake than simply the superimposition of two discrete experiential registers, the direct autoptic gaze and the world as imagined through a source text. The bridge with twenty-four arches (a nicely precise reality effect) that is mentioned extending into the sea at Corunna is, on one obvious level, a Solinus-esque curiosity; but it is brought into the immediate present and granted greater meaning by the narrator's comment that the arches had only become visible over the previous two years, as well as by his inclusion of a prophecy to the effect that this signified the end of heathendom and idolatry in Spain.[114] It is significant that one of the text's first overt mentions of an act of collective perception, one in which sight is reinforced by other sensory experience, concerns a ray-like fish encountered in the mouth of the Tambre: 'We saw [*vidimus*] there, marvellous to relate, a fish that stuns the hand of the person holding it; it looks like a ray and has two very sharp points on the top of its back.'[115] No further significance is attached to the creature and its attributes – the following sentence cuts to Solinus-like remarks about the neighbouring area's wildlife and produce – but the effect of this passage is to drop the crusaders into a world in which their own experience affirms the sorts of expectations on the reader's part that are cued by recognizing Solinus's influence on the text.[116]

The sighting of the ray sets up a dynamic that surfaces at various later points. As noted above, verbs of movement and arrival in the first person plural drive much of the action in the opening travel sequences. Importantly, however, the

[113] *De expugnatione*, pp. 60–2, 64, 66, 86–8, 94–6. See also p. 180.

[114] *De expugnatione*, p. 64. The suggestion by France, 'Logistics and the Second Crusade', p. 91 that this is evidence that the text was written in 1149, two years after the author first saw the 'bridge', or jetty, is intriguing but ultimately unconvincing, for the implication of the wording of the passage is that the narrator is repeating what he learned from local people at the time of his voyage, namely that the jetty had appeared around 1145. The 'iam' of 'iam apparent' simply has the effect of foreshortening the distance between the narrative now and narratorial now – consistent, perhaps, with the narrator writing less than a year or so after the fact – rather than implying that there is a two-year interval between them.

[115] *De expugnatione*, p. 64: my translation. The text's first references to collective perception concern the crusaders' view of Brittany and soon thereafter their initial encounter with Spain as they sight (*comperimus*) the 'Pyrenees', probably in actuality the Picos de Europa, from aboard ship in the Bay of Biscay: *De expugnatione*, p. 58.

[116] Cf. the narrator's claim that the therapeutic qualities of the sands in the harbour entrance at Oporto, about which he says he learned from the local bishop, are also noted in works of Roman history: *De expugnatione*, p. 68. See also the blending of direct (and collective) experience with Solinus-like attention to a given place's produce in the remark that the area around Lisbon so abounded with figs that 'we could hardly eat a fraction of them': *De expugnatione*, p. 92. This comment occurs within the passage in which the debt to Solinus is most in evidence.

collective agency extends to perception. Its most developed expression occurs as the crusade fleet nears Lisbon and is presented with a portent in the form of a collision between white clouds blowing in from the sea and black clouds coming from inland.[117] The narrator describes this meteorological clash at some length, making full use of similes of human combat, and concludes by emphasizing the collective response of the onlookers, who cry out 'Behold, our cloud has conquered!'. It is arguable that the passive constructions used of the sighting of the cloud battle – 'Nobis...signum admirabile in aere visum est', 'nubes... concurrere vise sunt', 'ut...videretur', 'visa est confugere' – introduce a note of narratorial distance, in that the passive has earlier been used in this measured vein ('Audite sunt') of the crusaders' encounter with the horrible sounds supposedly made by Sirens during a storm in the Bay of Biscay.[118] But the sheer repetition of the verb *videre* and the direct reference to the onlookers' eyes ('nunc ab oculis in sublime ferri') suggest that the narrator means this to be understood as a real event perceived and understood by the crusaders collectively at a suitably liminal moment in their odyssey – at a point, moreover, when their sense of unity is still intact.

Thereafter, the narrator does not routinely appeal to the collective gaze as the action unfolds, but, significantly, it reappears at moments in which the Christian identity and devotional purpose of the crusaders are reasserted in the face of the *discordia* that divides them.[119] The narrator notes that, during the siege, the Moors would taunt the besiegers (*nostri*) from the walls of Lisbon with various insults; this included the desecration of crosses, which we are told was tantamount to seeing Christ actually relive his Passion. As a result 'it was fitting that we should become more bitter against the enemies of the cross'.[120] In a similar manner, at the climax of the siege, as the city is opened to the Christians and the clergy enter bearing a banner of the cross, the narrator emphasizes the universal joy and pride felt when all see ('ab omnibus videretur') the banner mounted on the highest point of the citadel.[121] Likewise, in the days that follow the defeated

[117] *De expugnatione*, pp. 88–90.

[118] *De expugnatione*, p. 60.

[119] Cf. the scene in which the Moors see eighty of their comrades' heads mounted on spears and are moved to beg the besiegers for them, a moment that the narrator marks as a turning-point in both the enemy's and the Flemish-Rhenish contingent's attitudes towards the Anglo-Normans: *De expugnatione*, pp.140–2.

[120] *De expugnatione*, pp. 130–2: 'Videbatur vero iterum Christus actualiter ab incredulis blasphemari, falsa genuflexione salutari, malignantium sputis rigari, vinculis affligi, fustibus illidi, crucis affigi opprobrio. Cuius ut decebat nos compassione in crucis adversarios acriores fieremus.'

[121] *De expugnatione*, p. 174. The sensory emphasis is extended by mention of the jubilant intonation that characterized the singing of the *Te Deum*, *Asperges me* and devout prayers. But cf. the contrastive negative tone introduced immediately afterwards by

Muslims do not simply leave the city, they are observed doing so.[122] Thus, just as the collective gaze is in evidence in the early stages of the expedition, so it becomes prominent once more at its conclusion. The narrator observes, a shade cryptically, that what he has said about the Muslims' religion received visual confirmation by the collective sight (*vidimus*) of almost two hundred corpses and more than eight hundred sick people in squalid conditions in their 'temple'.[123] And in the sermon-like coda to the main narrative, in which the narrator introduces a tone of compassion redolent of the archbishop of Braga's earlier appeal to a shared humanity, he notes the pestilence that struck the local inhabitants in the aftermath of the siege by emphasizing its visible effects. The condition of their devastated human landscape is affirmed by the victors' gaze: 'we see (*conspicimus*) the city in ruins and the castle overthrown, the fields depopulated, the land reduced to solitude, with no inhabitant in the fields'.[124] The narrator concludes by remarking that the workings of God's judgement may be seen but not understood, and that further divine punishment is no longer necessary.[125] As these passages indicate, the narrator has emphasized moments of collective perception in which his own narratorial persona is subsumed within the agency of the crusaders as a whole – especially so when they are not, or ought not to be, internally divided. The collective gaze and the text's treatment of sight and sensory perception within the storyworld thus align fully with, and reinforce, the thematic preoccupation with unity that we have observed.

Odo of Deuil's *De profectione Ludovici VII in orientem*

As noted earlier, the *De expugnatione Lyxbonensi* is the dominant source for our understanding of the siege of Lisbon. Without it our knowledge of events would be hugely diminished. As we shift from the Iberian theatre of the Second Crusade to the eastern Mediterranean, however, we enter a more crowded evidentiary landscape: papal bulls, charters, tracts, letters and historical narratives of various sorts, as well as eastern Christian and Muslim sources, help to build up a substantially fuller picture of the expeditions to the east led by the western emperor-elect Conrad III of Germany and King Louis VII of France.[126] This is

the Flemish-Rhenish contingent's greedy gaze upon Lisbon's riches ('visis in urbe tot adminiculis cupiditatis'): *De expugnatione*, p. 176.

[122] *De expugnatione*, p. 178: 'exeuntes visi sunt tanta gentium multitudo'.

[123] *De expugnatione*, p.178. What the narrator misses or forbears to mention, of course, is that the mosque must have been used as a hospital and makeshift mortuary during the siege.

[124] *De expugnatione*, p. 182.

[125] *De expugnatione*, p. 184.

[126] The fullest treatment of the crusade to the east is now Phillips, *Second Crusade*: see

so despite the fact that the Second Crusade contrasts strongly with the First in not occasioning a spate of stand-alone histories. Clearly, the ignominious outcome of the eastern campaigns was the main reason for this relative historiographical neglect. It is noteworthy that the person who was probably best equipped to have written a monograph-type treatment of the crusade, the scholarly and high-born Bishop Otto of Freising, who himself commanded a substantial portion of the German host, included observations about the crusade in his historical writings, but remarked that its outcome meant that he preferred to leave a full retelling to others.[127] No doubt other potential historians of the crusade were similarly deterred.

Against such a relatively thin historiographical background, the *De profectione Ludovici VII in orientem* by Odo of Deuil stands out as the sole dedicated narrative treatment of the eastern expeditions, in particular that led by Louis of France.[128] Other sources help us to track Louis's crusade, such as letters that the king wrote home to his regent Abbot Suger of St-Denis, and through them we encounter reactions to events significantly different from those of Odo;[129] but it is Odo's text that has traditionally done the main work of carrying the story of the crusade in modern reconstructions, and in consequence it has arguably contributed to an over-emphasis on the French expedition as against the German

esp. pp. 185–206 for the progress of the French expedition between the summer of 1147 and early 1148, the substance of Books II–VII of the *De profectione*. See also G. A. Loud, 'Some Reflections on the Failure of the Second Crusade', *Crusades*, 4 (2005), 1–14.

[127] Otto of Freising and Rahewin, *Gesta Frederici seu rectius Cronica*, I.47, ed. F.-J. Schmale, trans. A. Schmidt (Ausgewählte Quellen zur deutschen Geschichte des Mittelalters, 17; Darmstadt, 1965), p. 218; trans. C. C. Mierow, *The Deeds of Frederick Barbarossa* (Medieval Academy Reprints for Teaching, 31; Toronto, 1994), p. 79.

[128] For a helpful assessment, see J. P. Phillips, 'Odo of Deuil's *De profectione Ludovici VII in Orientem* as a Source for the Second Crusade', in M. G. Bull and N. J. Housley (eds), *The Experience of Crusading I: Western Approaches* (Cambridge, 2003), pp. 80–95. See also R. P. Lindner, 'Odo of Deuil's *The Journey of Louis VII to the East*: Between *The Song of Roland* and Joinville's *Life of Saint Louis*', in J. Glenn (ed.), *The Middle Ages in Text and Texture: Reflections on Medieval Sources* (Toronto, 2011), pp. 165–76. Aspects of the text's style, in particular its use of rhythmic *cursus*, are perceptively analysed in C. A. Cioffi, 'The Epistolary Style of Odo of Deuil in his "De Profectione Ludovici VII in Orientem"', *Mittellateinisches Jahrbuch*, 23 (1988), 76–81.

[129] See 'Epistolae Sugerii abbatis S. Dionysii', nos. 12–13, 36, *RHGF*, 15, pp. 487–8, 495–6. See esp. no. 36, pp. 495–6 for an upbeat account of the king's reception at Constantinople that is at variance with Odo's version of events, though the letter subsequently nudges closer to Odo's anti-Greek sentiments in its reference to the effects of imperial *fraus* on the army's progress in Asia Minor. Letter no. 13, p. 488 includes a reference to Odo 'quem pro reverentia beati Dionysii honorifice nobiscum habemus'.

contribution.[130] The *De profectione* is not in fact a full telling of events even within its chosen thematic and substantive parameters: it ends with the remnants of the French army making their way from the south coast of Asia Minor to Antioch in early 1148, leaving unchronicled the failed siege of Damascus in July 1148 and Louis's extended stay in the Latin East, which lasted until the summer of 1149. Within its temporal boundaries, however, the text offers itself as a full and coherent narrative of events and, as we shall see, it aims at a sense of closure even as the action breaks off in mid-expedition.

Like the *De expugnatione*, the *De profectione* is cast in an epistolary form: its salutation is addressed to Abbot Suger by Odo, 'the least of his monks'.[131] As the prefactory letter states matters, Odo is still engaged in the hardships of the crusade (he remarks that he is 'adhuc in agone itineris'), during which he has served as a chaplain and confidant of King Louis. Odo recalls the fact that Suger had written about Louis's father, a reference to the *Life* of Louis the Fat that was discussed above in the Introduction,[132] and suggests that he write a companion piece on the life of the son, beginning not with the crusade (Louis VII was in his twenties when he went east) but in his boyhood years, which is when his virtue first became evident and about which Suger is well informed, having served as the prince's tutor.[133] Odo claims that he is lacking in literary style but offers by ways of compensation a knowledge of events, thanks to his routine proximity to Louis's person; his stated aim is, therefore, to provide a succinct statement of the truth which Suger can then stylistically embellish.[134] It is sometimes supposed on the basis of these remarks that Odo was fulfilling a specific commission from Suger, who we know began, but was unable to complete, a *Life* of Louis VII. The thrust of Odo's prefatory remarks suggests that he had left St-Denis for the east in 1147 aware of Suger's aim to write a *Life*, though it is unclear whether this had got very far beyond the planning stage, for no fewer than three times in the prefatory section Odo alludes to the project as a moral obligation on Suger's part, as if to nudge him into following through on an unrealized ambition.[135] What

130 Cf. Phillips, 'Odo of Deuil's *De profectione*', p. 94.

131 *De profectione*, p. 2.

132 Above, pp. 35–40.

133 *De profectione*, pp. 2–4. It is perhaps significant that the narrator makes explicit reference to Louis's age at the very beginning of the main body of the text: *De profectione*, p. 6.

134 *De profectione*, p. 4: the contrast is between *veritas* expressed *summatim* and adornment by means of *litteralis eloquentia*.

135 *De profectione*, pp. 2: 'it will be a crime to cheat posterity of knowing the son' ('criminis erit fraudare posteros notitia filii'); 4: '[you] to whom is justly due the honour of writing about the son' ('cui iure debetur reverentia scribendi de filio'); 'And do you not be reluctant to do perform your duty' ('Nec ideo vos pigeat exsequi quod debetis').

remains of Suger's *Life* of Louis does not permit us to speculate about what use he might have made of Odo's text had he written up Louis's participation in the crusade.[136] But if we switch our focus from Suger-as-recipient to Odo-as-author in the prefatory letter, two important points emerge concerning the role that Suger plays in Odo's authorial self-construction.

First, the binary that is set up between eyewitness knowledge expressed in a simple manner and its literary refashioning directly replays the dynamic that had informed several narratives of the First Crusade, as most obviously evident in the disparaging remarks about the literary quality of their source text (the *Gesta Francorum* or a text very close to it), in conjunction with implicit or explicit trust in its underlying factual content, made by Robert the Monk, Baldric of Bourgueil and Guibert of Nogent.[137] There are several clues in the *De profectione* that Odo was sensitive to the precedent of the First Crusade; and it is possible that he took at least one (unfortunately unspecified) history of it with him on the expedition.[138] In the prefatory letter Odo is thus staking out for his work a status akin to that of texts that his readers would have known had been superseded by reworkings but which were nonetheless important in anchoring the collective memory of the First Crusade in what was trusted to be knowledge of the truth.[139] By extension, he is affirming that knowledge of the truth is indeed possible when gained in the sort of circumstances that he describes.

Second, more was clearly at stake in the writing of the *De profectione* than simply supplying Suger with detailed and reliable information. This could have been done orally on Odo's return or in note form. Moreover, Book I, of seven, which narrates the origins and organization of Louis's crusade up to his departure from northern France, would have been redundant on a strict reading of Odo's supposed brief, for this part of the narrative is structured around a sequence of significant encounters between Christmas 1145 and June 1147 in which Suger took part and about which he himself could be presumed to know much more

[136] The surviving fragment is edited as 'De glorioso rege Ludovico, Ludovici filio', in Suger, *Oeuvres*, ed. and trans. E. Gasparri, 2 vols (Les classiques de l'histoire de France au moyen âge, 37 and 41; Paris, 1996–2001), i, pp. 156–77.

[137] See above, pp. 30–1.

[138] William of St-Denis, 'Le dialogue apologétique du moine Guillaume, biographe de Suger', ed. A. Wilmart, *Revue Mabillon*, 32 (1942), 103.

[139] For St-Denis's role in preserving and inflecting the memory of the First Crusade, see Phillips, 'Odo of Deuil's *De profectione*', pp. 83–4. A codex containing a miscellany of eyewitness texts relating to the First Crusade and the Latin East, including the histories of Raymond of Aguilers and Fulcher of Chartres, had been presented to Louis by a knight named William Grassegals at some point before the Second Crusade: see J. Rubenstein, 'Putting History to Use: Three Crusade Chronicles in Context', *Viator*, 35 (2004), 131–68.

than Odo.[140] Book I therefore reveals that Odo's principal aim was to effect a full telling of the expedition (as far as it went) that was inspired by the traditions of narrativization of the First Crusade while remaining sensitive to his own chosen emphases. Its account of Bernard of Clairvaux's preaching of the cross at Vézelay resembles the scene of the bishop of Oporto's preaching in the *De expugnatione* in its unstated but unambiguous evocation of Urban II's preaching at Clermont; again, such a large crowd assembles that the sermon must be delivered in the open air.[141] Unlike Clermont in the versions of the First Crusade by Robert, Baldric, Guibert and others, however, Vézelay is not the sole originary moment, just as the bishop of Oporto is depicted preaching to crusaders who are already in motion. For although the statement that Louis took the cross at Vézelay opens the text, and this declaration is solemnized by the inclusion of the year of the Incarnation and the kings's formal *intitulatio* as 'illustrious king of the French and duke of the Aquitanians, Louis, son of King Louis', an analepsis immediately moves the action back three months to the Christmas court at Bourges, during which the king responds with enthusiasm to a sermon by Bishop Godfrey of Langres about the fall of Edessa (which had been captured by the ruler of Mosul, Zengi, at Christmas time one year earlier, in 1144).[142]

The Bourges court has been the crux of a long-running scholarly debate about whether there was sufficient time for Louis and his court to have known about Pope Eugenius III's bull launching the crusade, *Quantum praedecessores*, which was issued from Vetralla near Viterbo in central Italy on 1 December 1145. Was Godfrey's sermon and Louis's endorsement of it a staged response to news of the papal crusade appeal, or at least an anticipation of it, or a spontaneous expression of royal enthusiasm to travel to the east that then got overtaken by fast-moving events?[143] Odo's account is imprecise on this very point, most probably deliberately so in order to highlight Louis's own active zeal for the faith (*zelus fidei*) as a major motif that will inform much of the action to follow. The Louis constructed by the *De profectione* is not without ambiguities, a somewhat semi-detached king as much carried along by circumstances and easily swayed by others' opinions

[140] *De profectione*, pp. 6–18. The key structuring events are the royal Christmas court at Bourges (pp. 6–8), St Bernard's preaching of the crusade and the taking of the cross by Louis and many others at Vézelay (pp. 8–10), the meeting at Étampes that discussed campaign strategy and the arrangements for the government of the kingdom in Louis's absence (pp. 12–14), and the royal departure via St-Denis (pp. 14–18).

[141] *De profectione*, p. 8.

[142] *De profectione*, p. 6.

[143] For a review of this problem, see Phillips, *Second Crusade*, pp. 62–6. For the framing of the debate see e.g. J. G. Rowe, 'The Origins of the Second Crusade: Pope Eugenius III, Bernard of Clairvaux and Louis VII of France', in M. Gervers (ed.), *The Second Crusade and the Cistercians* (New York, 1992), pp. 79–89; G. P. Ferzoco, 'The Origins of the Second Crusade', in *ibid.*, pp. 91–9.

as he is in charge of events.[144] But his virtue is emphasized as a constant and secure point of reference, the opening scene having primed the reader's ethical evaluation of the king.

When Odo wrote the *De profectione* has been the subject of some debate. In the text there is virtually no anticipation of future events beyond the timeframe of the narrated action. The one important but cryptic exception is an allusive remark that appears in the account of the worst reverse suffered by the French army over the course of the crusade, a severe mauling by the Turks in the area of Mount Cadmus in January 1148.[145] Lamenting the deaths of lords who had perished protecting their servants, and likening this to Christ's sacrifice, the narrator observes that 'the flowers of France withered before they could bear fruit in Damascus'.[146] Unless the bearing of fruit is an ironic reference to the further frustrations that awaited the crusaders in their poorly executed and abortive siege of Damascus in July 1148, the implication would seem to be that the text was written, or at least completed, in the earlier part of the summer of 1148, after the crusaders had reached Antioch and the decision to attack Damascus had been made, but before the expedition itself in July.[147] This has been the general scholarly consensus. Henry Mayr-Harting has argued, however, for a date in early 1150, suggesting that the text was both implicated in the internal power politics of the abbey of St-Denis as the reign of Abbot Suger drew towards its end – Odo was to be elected his successor as abbot in 1151 – and, in its pronounced anti-Greek tone, served as a position piece in support of plans for a renewed crusade effort that some leading figures were mooting in the first few months of 1150.[148] In this view, the statement that Odo was still caught up in the agony of the journey is to be understood as a figurative reference to his state of mind as he looked back on its rigours from the relative comfort of northern France after his return.

This is an intriguing hypothesis to the extent that it is a useful reminder that the figure of the narrator within a historical text need not be tied closely to the

[144] See below, pp. 186–7.

[145] For the Mount Cadmus debacle, see Phillips, *Second Crusade*, pp. 199–201.

[146] *De profectione*, p. 118: 'Marcescunt flores Franciae antequam fructum faciant in Damasco.'

[147] The suggestion that the text was written in Antioch receives support from the narrator's knowledge of the recent history of Byzantine claims on the city: *De profectione*, pp. 68–70. For the campaign against Damascus, see Phillips, *Second Crusade*, pp. 216–26; A. J. Forey, 'The Failure of the Siege of Damascus in 1148', *Journal of Medieval History*, 10 (1984), 13–23; M. Hoch, 'The Choice of Damascus as the Objective of the Second Crusade: A Re-Evaluation', in M. Balard (ed.), *Autour de la première croisade* (Byzantina Sorboniensia, 14; Paris, 1996), pp. 359–69.

[148] H. Mayr-Harting, 'Odo of Deuil, the Second Crusade and the Monastery of Saint-Denis', in M. A. Meyer (ed.), *The Culture of Christendom: Essays in Medieval History in Commemoration of Denis L. T. Bethell* (London, 1993), pp. 225–41.

circumstances of the author at the time of writing, as biographist approaches to historiographical works typically assume. Odo the author was at liberty to write *as if* he were still in the Latin East about twenty months earlier, and in doing so he would not have been transgressing some rigid generic boundary between 'straight' historical reporting and the more elastic, even playful relationships between author and narrator to be found in contemporary works of imaginative literature. On the other hand, recent research into the crusade plan of 1150 has suggested that it was conceived as support for the Latin East, which had suffered further setbacks after the departure of the Second Crusade forces, rather than as a mission of vengeance against the Byzantines for their supposed sabotaging of the crusaders' efforts in 1147-8.[149] If so, this would suggest that the narrator's pronounced hellenophobia was less of the moment in early 1150 than Mayr-Harting proposes. In addition, as we shall see, a metaphorical refrain running through the text is the idea that the act of writing parallels the journey itself, which would suggest that we should take the reference to Odo's still experiencing the pain of the journey at face value, and thus date the text to mid 1148. Perhaps a copy was sent back to France in the summer sailing of that year. Whether a second instalment was planned or begun is unknown. To a certain extent, a dating range of less than two years does not make a great difference to our reading of the text, but an earlier date, in placing Odo still in the thick of the action, has the effect of accentuating the significance of the learning trajectory that, as we shall see, underpins the *De profectione*'s construction of the narrator.[150]

[149] T. Reuter, 'The "Non-Crusade" of 1149–50', in J. P. Phillips and M. Hoch (eds.), *The Second Crusade: Scope and Consequences* (Manchester, 2001), pp. 150–63. See also J. P. Phillips, *Defenders of the Holy Land: Relations Between the Latin East and the West, 1119–1187* (Oxford, 1996), pp. 112–18; G. Constable, 'The Crusading Project of 1150', in B. Z. Kedar, J. S. C. Riley-Smith and R. Hiestand (eds), *Montjoie: Studies in Crusade History in Honour of Hans Eberhard Mayer* (Aldershot, 1997), pp. 67–75.

[150] For an attempt to suggest that the *De profectione* was written much later than the events it narrates, see the somewhat confused argument in B. Schuster, 'The Strange Pilgrimage of Odo of Deuil', in G. Althoff, J. Fried and P. J. Geary (eds), *Medieval Concepts of the Past: Ritual, Memory, Historiography* (Cambridge, 2002), pp. 253–78. Schuster proposes, on the basis of shared motifs, ideas and language found in later texts such as Otto of Freising's *Gesta Frederici*, John of Salisbury's *Historia pontificalis* and Gerhoh of Reichersberg's *De investigatione Antichristi*, that the author of the *De profectione*, whom she argues was not Odo but someone assuming his authorial persona, must have drawn upon these sources. While Schuster thereby indirectly identifies a potentially important question, which is how memories of an experience such as the Second Crusade might attach to certain mnemonic 'hooks' that lent themselves to repeated retelling, for example the ineptitude of Geoffrey of Rançon that contributed to the disaster at Mount Cadmus and the self-sacrifice of Bernhard of Plötzkau in covering a German rout, the similarities between the *De profectione* and the texts that she cites are in fact much less pronounced than she supposes. In the end, Schuster's over-ambitious argument is defeated by the fact that she undercuts her

How, then, does the text fashion the narratorial voice? The narrator refers to himself in both the first person singular and plural.[151] In addition to conventional expressions of narratorial ignorance and calculation, as well as when searching for the *mot juste*,[152] the singular is favoured at those points where matters of judgement are defended, the limits of the narrator's competence acknowledged, emotional reactions registered, or reflections on the challenges of narration volunteered.[153] The plural generally features in more neutral moments of story management such as summaries, resumptions and the signposting of transitions.[154] Though less common than the singular, the narratorial first person plural is nonetheless significant because its specific range in the context of the narrator's self-reference helps to establish that when the first person plural appears elsewhere – often in verbs of perception, discovery and understanding – we are not dealing with a narratorial 'royal we' but an opening out towards collective perceptual agency. This has important implications for the narrator's development of what we shall see is a major motif running through the text, namely the crusaders' emergent understanding of the Greeks' true attitudes towards them.

The narrator presents himself as shrewd and well informed: he is observant but does not need to clutter up the narrative with reality effects, which are deployed fairly sparingly;[155] and although he mostly concentrates on specific events as

---

own position that the author and narrator of the *De profectione* are distinct entities by treating the narrator as an historical actor whose knowledge and experience of the crusade extended into extratextual conditions not overtly mentioned or alluded to in the text. To add to the confusion, the editors' remarks about Schuster's chapter in their 'Introduction', p. 15 bear scant resemblance to the piece itself.

[151] See e.g. *De profectione*, p. 24 for the close juxtaposition of *dicimus* and *dico* in relation to narratorial utterances.

[152] E.g. *De profectione*, p. 64 ('nescio'), 64 ('sicut aestimo'), 94 ('non possum describere'), 118 ('non dicam').

[153] See e.g. *De profectione*, pp. 26: the narrator partly disavows the ability (*non possum*) to understand Greek documents; 56: the narrator defends his verdict on the Greeks as based on what 'I have seen' ('vidi'); 64: the beauty of the interior of the Blachernae palace surpasses what 'I can say' ('dixero') on the subject; 66: the narrator expresses the belief ('credo') that the Greeks' ingratiating demeanour masked their treacherous intentions; 112: the narrator is guarded ('ego nec fallere vellem nec falli') about reports that a celestial white knight appeared during a battle in the Maeander valley; 118: the narrator grieves ('suffundor lacrimis, et de visceribus intimis ingemisco') in the act of recounting the French nobility's losses on Mount Cadmus; 134: the narrator defends his judgement ('credo autem') that the French suffered at Adalia more than at any earlier point in their journey.

[154] E.g. *De profectione*, pp. 28, 50, 56, 68, 82–4, 96. See also the reference to the text as *nostra pagina*: *De profectione*, p. 56.

[155] See e.g. *De profectione*, pp. 26 (details of Greek clothing), 74 (the golden gleam of Greek moneychangers' tables), 100 (the bishop of Metz's translation of Conrad III's speech into French), 106 (the situation of St John's tomb at Ephesus). See also p. 50,

singularities, he is able to extrapolate patterns from recurrent experiences.[156] He also emerges as ethically sensitive, suitably selective and discreet: he states, for example, that he has chosen not to set down the laws that were agreed to regulate the French crusade army because in the event they were not well respected.[157] Indeed, the narratorial presence within the *De profectione* is the most self-aware and reflective of all those in the texts that we are considering, with the possible exception of those found in the biographies of Saladin discussed in the next chapter.[158] While some of the indications of narratorial self-consciousness run to the conventional, such as the fear of boring the narratee,[159] a more considered note is sounded in the analogy that is claimed between the act of writing and the experience of the journey itself. This first emerges at the liminal moment represented by the beginning of Book II, when the action moves from the preliminaries of the crusade, which have been played out in the Capetian heartland and have climaxed in Louis VII's departure from St-Denis, to the journey proper. The king is first delivered to Metz, where the army musters, then in a brief analepsis to Verdun; with respect to both places the narrator overtly flags the sense of dislocation by stating that Louis was now outside the reach of his royal authority, his *ius dominii*, even though this is mitigated (for now) by the local people's willingness to treat him as if they were his subjects.[160] As the crusaders gradually move beyond their comfort zone, however, the narrator registers a concomitant shift in mood, as if the mostly upbeat treatment of the events narrated in Book I has become an unsustainable self-indulgence in light of what is to follow:

> I was engrossed in happy affairs, and, while, writing the words connected with my native land and while remembering its affairs, unweariedly I recalled for too long a time what I had seen when a happy man; for pleasant events do not soon cause fatigue. Now, however, at this new beginning I gird myself for difficult tasks, intending to enter strange lands in my description, just as we

where the number of Germans who crossed the Bosphorus is specified as 900,566 – a figure strangely close to Kinnamos's no less fantastic figure of 900,000 for those, either the Germans or the Germans and French combined, whom officials counted entering Byzantine territory at the Danube frontier: see John Kinnamos, *Epitome rerum ab Ioanne et Alexio Comnenis gestarum*, II.12, ed. A. Meineke (Corpus Scriptorum Historiae Byzantinae, 23; Bonn, 1836), p. 69; trans. C. M. Brand, *Deeds of John and Manuel Comnenus by John Kinnamos* (New York, 1976), p. 60.

156 See e.g. *De profectione*, p. 24 for observations concerning conditions on the march.

157 *De profectione*, p. 20. Cf. the remark that although many things suggest themselves for inclusion in the text, the discourse (*oratio*) should not become cluttered by a multiplicity of details (*rerum multiplicitas*): *De profectione*, p. 32.

158 See below, pp. 209–19.

159 *De profectione*, p. 20.

160 *De profectione*, p. 20.

> did in fact, and accordingly I shall bring to a swifter conclusion the hardships which ensued.[161]

The figurative relationship between writing and journeying is reinforced by the narrator's insistence that he is at the service of his story, the proper narrating of which he may best effect if he scrupulously respects the order in which events took place: as he observes, 'Many events happen at the same time, but in discourse one must observe a sequence.'[162] In practice, the declared adherence to strict chronological sequence proves an artful posture, for there are several anachronies in the narrative, principally cut-aways to accommodate mentions of the German army, which was marching several weeks ahead of the French, as well as to include stand-alone anecdotes.[163] The extent to which the challenges faced by the narrator are sublimated within the difficulties experienced by the crusaders is brought out most clearly in a moment staged as a limit case of comprehension and narrativization. German survivors of their grave defeat at the hands of the Turks, in October 1147, reach the French camp and report the bad news; and the reaction of the dumbfounded and grief-stricken French is rhetorically emphasized.[164] Then the Germans are asked for details – in terms consonant with precisely those analytical categories that would aid a lucid narration of their defeat in tune with the narrator's professed organizational preferences – but coherence eludes them as they confront the sheer incomprehensibility of recent and raw experience:

> They were asked about the order, means and cause of so great a reverse; but it is likely that all these questions were asked in an inappropriate way given that confusion respects no order, nor the exceptional means, and cause does not extend to what surpasses reason.[165]

Nonetheless, the narrator goes on to state that what happened is recoverable if one carefully attends to sequence, and a full and tightly plotted account of the German

[161] *De profectione*, p. 20.

[162] *De profectione*, p. 32: 'Collateraliter incedunt causae, sed oportet servari consequentiam in sermone.' See the anticipations of the narration of future events in *De profectione*, pp. 50, 98. See also the reference to the principal subject matter of the text as *nostra materia*: *De profectione*, p. 102.

[163] See e.g. the narrator's switch from an account of the death of Bishop Alvisus of Arras at Philippopolis to the progress of the Germans through the Balkans: *De profectione*, p. 46: 'Now, after this brief interruption ('His autem paululum intermissis'), I want to describe how the Germans were led to Constantinople, nay, even beyond the sea.' For the progress and fate of Conrad's expedition, see Phillips, *Second Crusade*, pp. 168–84. See also J. T. Roche, 'Conrad III and the Second Crusade: Retreat from Dorylaion?', *Crusades*, 5 (2006), 85–97.

[164] *De profectione*, p. 90: 'Audientes hoc nostri cum stupore dolent et cum dolore stupent'.

[165] *De profectione*, p. 90: my translation.

defeat duly follows.[166] The narrator's greatest acknowledged challenge has been surmounted, and his credentials as a skilful shaper of his story stuff (*materia*) are thereby reaffirmed.

In large measure, the narrator emerges in apposition to the text's narratee(s). These figures are much more in evidence than in the *De expugnatione Lyxbonensi*, where we have seen Osbert of Bawdsey plays very little role after the opening salutation. To a considerable degree, the body of the text delivers on the promise of its opening address to Abbot Suger: the dedicatory epistle's intercutting of statements beginning with 'Ego' and 'Vos' sets up the expectation of a form of dialogue in what follows, and although this surfaces only intermittently as the narration proceeds, Suger is sufficiently present as the putative interlocutor to inflect several of the narrator's positions.[167] It is significant that one of the few occasions in which Odo himself breaks into the storyworld as an individual agent in the first person singular concerns his lobbying of Louis VII about the unjust possession, by Conrad III and Frederick of Swabia, the future Emperor Frederick Barbarossa, of German properties claimed by the abbey of St-Denis.[168] In addition, 'You, Father Suger' is apostrophized when the narrator recalls the moment at Étampes when Bernard of Clairvaux evoked the two swords of Luke 22:38 with reference to the regency team that was originally proposed, Suger himself and Count William of Nevers; and a narratee clearly to be identified with Suger is called forth when the narrator asks what 'you wish' (*vultis*) to be put on record about the changes to the regency regime during the supposedly uneventful period in France after Louis's departure.[169] Further apostrophes to Suger occur in an apology for the author's loquaciousness and a statement of King Louis's devotion to the abbot.[170] Subsequent invitations in the second person singular to picture and assess events do not cite Suger by name, and they concern episodes during the crusade proper where obviously he was not present, so to some extent they represent an opening out of the narratee beyond Suger alone.[171] But the fact that 'Father Suger' is once more apostrophized near the very end of the text, as the narrator confirms that Louis is safe and well at the point at which the story concludes, reveals that Suger's role as primary narratee is to be assumed throughout the narrative.[172]

[166] *De profectione*, pp. 90–6.

[167] *De profectione*, pp. 2–4: 'Ego igitur… Vos tamen… Vos… Vos igitur… Ego vero… Nec ideo vos…'.

[168] *De profectione*, p. 102.

[169] *De profectione*, pp. 14, 20.

[170] *De profectione*, pp. 20, 102.

[171] *De profectione*, pp. 26: 'Videas iuvenes fixo gressu, reclino capite, in propriis dominis erectis aspectibus cum silentio'; 136: 'ut crederes eum nihil antea expendisse'. Cf. the invitation in the second person plural to recall an earlier point in the story at p. 40: 'debetis enim iam dicta reminisci'.

[172] *De profectione*, p. 142.

There are, however, several moments in the *De profectione* that suggest that the narrator is looking beyond Suger to a second-order narratee who takes a critical view of the conduct of the expedition. This putative interlocutor is not named and is referred to only by means of the pronoun *aliquis* or an allusive mention of 'the ignorant' (*ignari*): he/she/it is less a specific individual or group than the shadowy embodiment of potential counter-arguments that the narrator must address in order to validate his own reading of events. This note of defensiveness is first sounded in justifying a passage in which the narrator uses harsh language of the Greeks, and in the process asserts the value of eyewitness experience: 'Let no one think ['Nec me putet aliquis'] that I am taking vengeance on a race of men hateful to me and that because of my hatred I am inventing someone I have not seen.'[173] It reappears in discussions of strategic decisions made during the difficult march through Asia Minor, setting up the narrator as an informed observer of logistical practicalities in contradistinction to someone who would hastily advocate a full-blown conquest of the Byzantine cities and fortresses that the crusaders encounter. This perhaps reflects discussions within the crusade leadership during the march itself, but if so the text transposes the debate from the storyworld to an exchange between narrator and narratee. When narrating the army's passage along the western coast of Asia Minor, the narrator again sets up an opponent lacking direct experience, 'someone who was not present' ('aliquis qui non interfuit'), who might argue that the crusaders should have seized the cities that they passed and taken the supplies to be found within them. This, the narrator remarks, fails to appreciate the realities of their situation.[174] In a similar vein, towards the end of the text, as the crusaders are making arrangements to sail from Adalia to Antioch, the narrator remarks that those who are ignorant in such matters might suggest that the city should have been captured: this, however, would be to disregard the crusaders' lack of food, the strength of the city's fortifications and the close proximity of Turkish forces, as well as Louis's honourable scruples.[175]

The narrator's insistence on his experience and the lessons derived from them also informs remarks directed to future crusaders. As the narrator states, 'For never will there fail to be pilgrims to the Holy Sepulchre'.[176] Indeed, it is sometimes claimed that providing helpful advice to those who would follow in the crusaders' footsteps was one of Odo's main reasons for writing the *De profectione*.[177] Remarks in this vein, however, appear only intermittently and would have seemed very anodyne indeed to anyone with any experience either

[173] *De profectione*, p. 56: translation revised.
[174] *De profectione*, p. 106.
[175] *De profectione*, p. 134.
[176] *De profectione*, p. 28: 'Nunquam enim deerunt sancti Sepulchri viatores'.
[177] Phillips, *Second Crusade*, pp. 186, 188.

of military logistics or of long-distance pilgrimage – as in, for example, the rather bland and obvious observations concerning the difficulties presented by transporting supplies in carts.[178] Similarly, passages which list the sequence of and distances between major towns in Germany and the Byzantine Balkans are not road itineraries for the benefit of future travellers, but economical ways of dropping briefly into travelogue or chorographic mode in order to move the narrative briskly through certain phases of the crusade, thereby freeing the narrator to linger on events at other points.[179] In other words, the narrator's gesturing towards the offering of practical advice is to be read as a device to reassert his emphasis upon the experiential foundation of his recounting of the crusade, and by extension the legitimacy of the judgements grounded in such experience.

The narrator's attention to experience further emerges in his willingness to relate specific incidents and details to emerging patterns of understanding. This is particularly evident in his strident and vituperative treatment of the Byzantines in general and of Emperor Manuel Komnenos in particular. Older generations of scholars read Odo's anti-Greek rhetoric as evidence of the deep cultural antipathy that had developed between eastern and western Christendom by the mid twelfth century, while Odo's offering of a platform in his text for Bishop Godfrey of Langres to advocate the seizing of Constantinople seemed an uncanny foretaste of the attitudes that would lead to the diversion of the Fourth Crusade nearly sixty years later.[180] More recent interpretations have sought to modify this view: Odo's hellenophobia is seen as qualified to a degree by his remarks to the effect that the crusaders' actions contributed towards their difficult relations with the Byzantines, while he also has positive things to say about one or two Byzantine

[178] *De profectione*, p. 24. Cf. Mayr-Harting, 'Odo of Deuil', p. 231, pointing to the remark in *De profectione*, p. 104 'I advise you to keep to the shore route and preserve your knights' strength'. But this is in fact voiced in direct speech by Conrad III in comments made to the French crusade leadership in the light of his own recent defeat by the Turks, and it thus bears upon the specific strategic choices that were faced at that moment, not upon general conditions. The narrator's observations on the pros and cons of the various routes from Nicomedia [*recte* Nicaea] through Asia Minor (*De profectione*, p. 88) are framed in rather more general terms, but they too relate specifically to the now of the storyworld in anticipating what will become an important crux in the plot to follow.

[179] *De profectione*, pp. 30, 32.

[180] *De profectione*, pp. 68–70. For the Byzantine regime's reaction to the Second Crusade and its handling of it, see P. Magdalino, *The Empire of Manuel I Komnenos, 1143–1180* (Cambridge, 1993), pp. 46–53; R.-J. Lilie, *Byzantium and the Crusader States 1096–1204*, trans. J. C. Morris and J. E. Ridings (Oxford, 1993), pp. 148–62; P. Stephenson, *Byzantium's Balkan Frontier: A Political Study of the Northern Balkans, 900–1204* (Cambridge, 2000), pp. 214–22; J. Harris, *Byzantium and the Crusades* (London, 2003), pp. 94–6, 100–1.

individuals; and there is also a passage in which he applauds the contribution made by Greek clergy to the celebration of the feast of St Dionysius, an observation to be read in light of the fact that at St-Denis, unusually for a western church, Greek chant had been used in the celebration of the mass at Pentecost since the Carolingian period.[181] It is now clear that the text's anti-Greek position was not as representative as used to be supposed of opinion either within the crusade leadership or among intellectual circles back in western Europe. Indeed, the narrator himself seems to acknowledge as much in his staging of debates between anti- and pro-Greek (or at least guardedly non-committal) voices in the crusade hierarchy. An attempt is made to render these debates asymmetrical in favour of the position that the narrator favours by naming Bishop Godfrey of Langres, who had some patronal relationship to Odo, as the forceful and perspicacious voice of mistrust of the Byzantines, while those arguing against him are not identified.[182] But even so the narrator has in the end to concede that the opposing opinion carried the day.

Some nuance has thus been introduced into our understanding of the extratextual context of Odo's anti-Greek invective. Nonetheless the hellenophobic dimension within the text remains inescapable. For our immediate purposes, it does not matter whether the anti-Greek prejudices of Odo the flesh-and-blood author resonated with contemporary educated opinion or were regarded as extreme and eccentric, for within the workings of the narrative such views clearly amount to a dominant theme, both as it is played out and apprehended by the actors in the storyworld and as it is articulated by the narrator in much of his commentary upon the action. Moreover, it is possible to see the nuances that the text introduces as aligned with the ultimate purpose of denigrating the Byzantines, for the narrator builds the gradual emergence of his full understanding of the Greeks' true qualities into the experiential trajectory of the journey itself. In other words, the full force of the text's hellenophobic sentiment emerges piece by piece in a series of moments of discovery and in response to both the narrator-as-character's

[181] Phillips, 'Odo of Deuil's *De profectione*', pp. 85–90. For the celebration of the feast of St Dionysius, see *De profectione*, p. 68. Cf. M. Huglo, 'Les chants de la *missa Greca* de Saint-Denis', in J. Westrup (ed.), *Essays Presented to Egon Wellesz* (Oxford, 1966), pp. 74–83, esp. 75–6. Suger is apostrophized in this sequence so as to emphasize still further its particular interest to an abbot of St-Denis. It should be noted, however, that this passage is immediately followed by a statement of the dissonance between the Byzantine emperor's appearance of friendship towards the French and his true murderous intentions, a juxtaposition surely designed to undercut the image of cosy liturgical togetherness. See also the more dismissive reference to Greek clerical culture in *De profectione*, p. 44, describing *adventus*-type processions that emerge from cities to meet Louis and are led by clerics bearing icons and 'the other Greek stuff' ('et alio Graeco apparatu').

[182] *De profectione*, pp. 68–72, 78–80.

and other crusaders' experiences, meaning that there is space along the story arc to introduce minor concessions and localized points of sympathetic engagement – as when anticipating the obvious interest value of Greek chant on the feast of St Dionysius for a St-Denis readership – in order to seem to qualify, but ultimately to reinforce, the cumulative anti-Greek message. Indeed, an evolving understanding of what the Byzantines are really like, and how low they go in their treacherous dealings with the crusaders, amounts to *the* key structuring motif at work within the text, to the extent that the modulation of the narratorial voice is largely driven by it. That is to say, to explicate the true nature of the Greeks, and to ground that explanation securely in observation, experience and reflection, is what the narrator-as-constructed is principally there to do. By extension, this emphasis informs the narrator's wider approaches to eyewitness perception and understanding, as we shall see.

The denigration of the Byzantines builds over the course of the narrative in parallel with an unfolding process of discovery and realization on the narrator's and the crusaders' parts. The result is an ascending scale of vices and faults that culminates at the conclusion of the narrated action, as the wealthier crusaders escape their difficult situation at Adalia by sailing to Antioch. The central importance of anti-Greek sentiment as a structuring device is signalled at the start of the text by means of ominous prolepses that intrude into the otherwise positive tone of the account of the preparations for the French expedition and Louis's departure that occupies Book I. In a passage dealing with Louis's diplomatic exchanges in the interval between the taking of the cross at Vézelay and the council at Étampes in February 1147, the narrator off-handedly remarks that the king wrote to the 'emperor of Constantinople', 'whose name I ignore because it is not written in the book of life'.[183] We are then told that the emperor's prolix and flattering reply – the verbose unctuousness of Byzantine diplomatic discourse is a theme that will be resumed later in the text – made many promises that in the event were not honoured. The narrator draws attention to the fact that he is aware that his prolepsis has broken the strict sequence of the story by glancing ahead – 'But of these things another time!' – but this only serves to reinforce still further the ethical priming of the reader that this passage has initiated.

Its significance is immediately reinforced in the text's attention to the theme of experience in its account of the council at Étampes, where a debate takes place about the best route that the French forces should take: overland and thus

[183] *De profectione*, p. 10. The narrator makes good on this initial position throughout the remainder of the text, never supplying Emperor Manuel's name. Instead, damning metaphors and vituperative terms reinforced by deixis become the norm: e.g. *De profectione*, pp. 76 ('cum idolo'), 76 ('profanus ille'), 76 ('serpens ille'), 76 (like an asp), 78 ('Ecce impius'), 78 (equivalence to an infidel), 82 ('Ille sacrilegus'), 90 ('Constantinopolitanum idolum').

through Byzantine territory, or by sea on ships supplied by King Roger II of Sicily, whose representatives are at the meeting.[184] We are informed that some of those in attendance – who they were is not specified – stated that they had learned both from books and experience ('lectione et experientia') that the Greeks were deceitful, a view immediately endorsed by the narrator's regretful remark that the king and his followers should have been wary of deception. When the land route is chosen, King Roger's envoys depart in a state of confusion and grief, foretelling the Greek trickery which 'we later experienced' ('postea sumus experti'). This is a critical foundational moment in the unfolding of the story. The narrative arc of the remainder of the action will effectively comprise a working through and vindication of the envoys' prediction by means of the same two routes to understanding that the narrator has introduced into this scene in the anti-Greek interjections of some of those present; the crusaders and the reader will over the course of the narrative arrive at the same full appreciation courtesy of experience and reading, respectively.

The anti-Greek message is thereafter developed cumulatively by means of a step-wise intensification of what is at stake for the crusaders and, running in parallel, the steady lexical accumulation of condemnatory abstract nouns. As the crusade gets underway, the motif of discovery and emergent comprehension with respect to the Byzantines is first introduced as Louis meets a party of imperial ambassadors at Regensburg.[185] A note of separation is initially sounded in a seemingly off-the-cuff manner, as the narrator remarks of the fact that the ambassadors' retinue remained standing during the meeting that this was something which 'we afterwards learned was a Greek custom'. But this is followed by blunter condemnation of the vacuously flattering language used by the imperial envoys and the documents they bore: a prolepsis anticipates that, though on this occasion King Louis did not know what to make of the overblown manner of the Byzantine embassy, by the time he reached Byzantine territory repeated exposure to such diplomatic bombast had made him impatient of it, on one occasion to such an extent that Bishop Godfrey of Langres irritably interjected to tell some imperial messengers to cut to the chase.[186]

What begins, however, as ridicule of diplomatic grandiloquence, an easy marker of cultural separation, shades into darker hues as the crusaders' journey progresses. The narrator signals a decided change of mood, both in the manner of his narration and in the participants' experience of the storyworld, at the point at

[184] *De profectione*, pp. 12–14.

[185] *De profectione*, pp. 24–6. It is noteworthy that this is one of the most fully realized scenes, visually speaking, in the narrative.

[186] Cf. *De profectione*, p. 56 (by which point the French are in Byzantine territory): 'The Greeks always reported good news, but they never showed any proof of it, and they were the less believed because on every occasion all used the same prefatory flattery.'

which the army enters Byzantine territory.[187] From this moment onwards various encounters with the Byzantines and news of their dealings with the German army instantiate a growing list of vices and misdeeds. For example, immediately the French are in Byzantine lands, their need to use the local currency at what they believe are unfavourable rates of exchange, as well as the local inhabitants' wariness of dealing with the crusaders face to face, contrary to earlier Greek promises about fair access to markets, is interpreted as perjury (*periurium*) on the Greeks' part;[188] the Greeks' fraught dealings with the German forces outside Constantinople, though the narrator concedes that the Germans were partly responsible, demonstrates their haughty arrogance (*fastus*);[189] a French embassy to the emperor is shocked to discover that he has concluded a twelve-year truce with the Turks, which reveals his treachery (*perfidia*), on top of which are then heaped accusations of blasphemy (*blasphemia*), wickedness (*scelus*) and heresies (*haereses*) when it is learned that the Greek regarded altars on which Latin clergy had celebrated mass as having been defiled, and that Latins entering into a marriage with a Greek were rebaptized;[190] while the theme of heresy is resumed by Bishop Godfrey of Langres in an impassioned plea for the French to storm Constantinople.[191]

The trajectory of escalating Greek culpability is sustained after the French have crossed into Asia Minor and find that the Byzantines are spreading false rumours and manipulating the provision of supplies, conduct that illustrates their scheming (*versutiae*) and malice (*malitia*).[192] We are further informed that the crushing German defeat near Dorylaeum in October 1147 was brought about by the Greeks' mournful misdeeds (*dolorosa facinora*);[193] and that the deaths of numerous French and German crusaders were contrived by the emperor's treacherous cruelty (*dolosa crudelitas*).[194] By the end of the narrative even basic human interaction with the Greeks has become impossible thanks to their disregard of fundamental points of shared cultural reference in the form of right, reason and honour.[195] The apotheosis is reached at Adalia, once the wealthier crusaders

[187] *De profectione*, p. 40.
[188] *De profectione*, p. 40.
[189] *De profectione*, p. 48.
[190] *De profectione*, pp. 54–6, where, almost in a spirit of completeness for completeness's sake, the remarks concerning heresy cue mention of the stock differences between the Latin and Greek Churches concerning the use of unleavened bread in the host and the procession of the Holy Ghost. Cf. the later reference to the emperor's evil intent (*dolus*), p. 68. For the twelve-year truce, see Phillips, *Second Crusade*, pp. 189–90.
[191] *De profectione*, pp. 68–70.
[192] *De profectione*, p. 72. The Greeks' malice is reiterated later, p. 132.
[193] *De profectione*, p. 98.
[194] *De profectione*, p. 136.
[195] *De profectione*, p. 138: 'nec illos iure, ratione, vel honestate vicerunt'.

have sailed off, leaving behind the poor – the dispensable remnant who in the narrator's implausible estimation are very sanguine and gracious about being abandoned![196] The narrator has already noted that the local Greeks collaborated with the Turks at points during the crusaders' march through Asia Minor.[197] Now the Greeks not only brief the Turks on the crusaders' weaknesses, they collude with them to frustrate Louis's arrangements to provide for those left behind.[198]

Moreover, in a remarkable inversion of relative values, after the remaining crusaders are overcome by a Turkish force, the Turks sympathetically provide alms for the sick and the poor, while the Greeks force the stronger survivors into servitude and offer them nothing but violence. Those who went with the Turks are not forced to convert, the narrator supposes, and so, paradoxically, they end up better off than those mistreated by their cruel coreligionists.[199] This flipping of the ethical status of the Turks and Greeks close to the very end of the narrated action, when read in conjunction with a summative review of King Louis's qualities as they have been illustrated by his conduct during the campaign,[200] strongly suggests that the end of the text as we have it shows the narrator striving for full closure, not an interim conclusion pending a possible resumption of the action in a second instalment. Now that the Greeks have been shown to be even worse than the Turks, the prognosis of Roger II's ambassadors back at Étampes has been more than vindicated experientially. The difference between the Greeks and the French has been essentialized, and gendered, as that between servitude (*servitium*) and manly virtue (*virtus*);[201] the text's programmatic wish for the future, that vengeance be visited upon the Greeks by French and Germans alike, has been openly stated;[202] and in a sense, therefore, the narrator has nowhere further to go.[203]

[196] See the conveniently obliging speech by a delegation of the poor to Louis, accepting their fate and, for good measure, reminding him of Greek treachery: *De profectione*, p. 136.

[197] *De profectione*, pp. 114, 116, 126.

[198] *De profectione*, pp. 134, 136–8.

[199] *De profectione*, p. 140.

[200] *De profectione*, p. 142.

[201] *De profectione*, p. 88; cf. the earlier feminization of the Greeks, p. 56: 'and then the Greeks dissolved entirely into women, setting aside all manly vigour in both word and spirit': translation revised.

[202] *De profectione*, p. 98.

[203] Modern scholarly assessments of the degree of responsibility that Byzantine policy bore for the failures of the crusade expeditions in Asia Minor, while varying in their emphases, suggest that, even allowing for Odo's exaggerations of the extent and reach of Manuel's power and his over-simplifications of complex processes, his apportioning of blame was not wholly unjustified: see Magdalino, *Empire of Manuel I*, pp. 51–2; Lilie, *Byzantium*, pp. 158–61; Harris, *Byzantium*, pp. 98–100; Phillips, *Second Crusade*, pp. 205–6. For a more exculpatory approach, see S. Neocleous,

We have already noted the moment at which French envoys to Constantinople learn of Emperor Manuel's truce with the Turks, which seems to subvert earlier promises of military co-operation that he had made to Louis. This is one of several moments in the narrative in which the act of perception and the framing of understandings are brought to the fore. Two tracks are pursued. One, the more straightforward, is to go with the flow of the evidence as it presents itself to the observer within the storyworld. So, for example, in commenting on the chronic inability of the Greeks to maintain their position against Turkish pressure in Asia Minor, the narrator notes that it was the dilapidation of Nicomedia, clearly evident to the eye, that first made this plain: 'set among thorns and brambles, her lofty ruins prove [*probat*] her former glory and her present masters' inactivity'.[204] In a similar vein, the perspicacious bishop of Langres, in urging the crusaders to attack Constantinople, proves by appeal to the evidence [*comprobabat*] that the city walls, part of which had collapsed 'before our eyes', presented no insurmountable obstacle.[205] The second and more challenging approach, which is only made possible by experience, is to penetrate beyond surface appearance to an underlying reality. It is significant that this theme is first taken up by the narrator at the point where the collision of French and Greek cultures reaches a climax with Louis's arrival at Constantinople and his personal encounter with Emperor Manuel.[206] On the surface all is decorous diplomatic courtesy between two rulers whose physical similarities the narrator makes a point of noting, while his mention of their seating arrangements stresses their equality – in contrast to the note of hierarchy introduced into his description of the same scene by Manuel's encomiast John Kinnamos.[207] But Manuel's expressions of concern and interest are possibly insincere. As the narrator observes, perhaps hinting at direct eyewitness experience of the scene, and formalizing his remarks by drawing on the language of logical disputation:

> If his gestures, his liveliness of expression, and his words had been a true indication of his inner thoughts, those who stood nearby would have attested that he cherished the king with great affection; but such evidence is only plausible, not conclusive [*sed tale argumentum probabile est, non necessarium*].[208]

True to the inflationary trajectory that we have just noted, what begins as an intuitive heuristic soon becomes a studied penetration beyond surface appearance,

'Byzantine-Muslim Conspiracies against the Crusades: History and Myth', *Journal of Medieval History*, 36 (2010), 259–65.

[204] *De profectione*, p. 88: translation revised.

[205] *De profectione*, p. 68.

[206] *De profectione*, pp. 58–60.

[207] John Kinnamos, *Epitome rerum*, II.17, pp. 82–3; trans. Brand, *Deeds of John and Manuel*, p. 69. See Phillips, *Second Crusade*, p. 191.

[208] *De profectione*, p. 60.

a facility born of sustained and cumulative experience. In his account of a banquet laid on for Louis by the emperor, and again hinting at eyewitness knowledge and invoking the language of formal proofs, the narrator suggests that the sensory delights of the occasion for the eye, ear and mouth were really evidence of the Greeks' trying too hard:

> Although the Greeks furnished us no proof that they were treacherous [*nullum argumentum perfidiae*], I believe that they would have not exhibited such unremitting servitude if they had had good intentions. Actually, they were concealing the wrongs which were to be avenged after we crossed the Arm [Bosphorus].[209]

This tension between the immediately visible and the underlying reality is mapped onto the narrator's assessment of Constantinople itself. Book IV opens with what appears at first blush to be a laudatory description of the city, 'the glory of the Greeks', which is conventional in its language but gestures towards a grounding in eyewitness experience. The narrator applauds Constantinople's situation, the construction and fine workmanship of the Blachernae palace, the resources available to the city's inhabitants, and the marvellous beauty and relic collection of the church of Hagia Sophia.[210] But this positive image is immediately subverted by the comment that the city is 'squalid and fetid and in many places harmed by permanent darkness'; it is the filthy haunt of the murderous, the lawless and the uncontrolled.[211] To counterbalance the more positive remarks in this passage at the start of Book IV, moreover, Book V opens with an unambiguously negative judgement that projects human vices onto the personified city: 'Constantinople is arrogant in her wealth, treacherous in her practices, corrupt in her faith.'[212]

The text's hellenophobia principally emerges in narratorial commentary or, if it is articulated within the storyworld, it is energetically ventriloquized by the narrator's trusted surrogate and perspicacious focalizer Bishop Godfrey. But the simple trajectory of the plot – Constantinople is not in the event attacked and some form of *modus operandi* is indeed reached between the French and the Greeks at various junctures to the point that it is Byzantine shipping that finally

[209] *De profectione*, p. 66; cf. p. 68 for the belief that the emperor feigned friendship while harbouring murderous intentions.

[210] *De profectione*, pp. 62–4, 64–6.

[211] *De profectione*, p. 64. Cf. R. Macrides, 'Constantinople: The Crusaders' Gaze', in R. Macrides (ed.), *Travel in the Byzantine World: Papers from the Thirty-Fourth Spring Symposium of Byzantine Studies, Birmingham, April 2000* (Society for the Promotion of Byzantine Studies Publications, 10; Aldershot, 2002), pp. 194, 196–7, which slightly understates the acuity of Odo's gaze.

[212] *De profectione*, p. 86.

rescues the better-off crusaders from their predicament at Adalia – means that there are limits to the extent to which the narrator can claim general assent to his anti-Greek position. Counter-arguments within the crusade leadership are therefore acknowledged, as we have seen.[213] Nonetheless, it is a clear aim of the narrator's project to universalize his sentiments, and thus the experiences and perceptions that ground them, as far as plot constraints will tolerate. Thus, in a passage that scoops up all the available reasons to regard the Greeks as heretics – their treating of a mass in the Latin rite as a pollution of the altar and the forced rebaptism of Latin would-be spouses of Greeks, as well as the stock Eucharistic and doctrinal differences – the narrator is at pains to emphasize that these were not simply slights to educated Latin sensitivities but a cause for mass anger. At first sight, the people's stated reaction might seem extreme, but as the narrator expresses matters it is presented simply as an appropriate and commensurate, or at least understandable and logically motivated, position:

> Actually it was for these reasons that they [the Greeks] had incurred the hatred of our people, for their error had become known even among the lay people. For this reason they were judged not to be Christians, and they [the French] regarded killing them as a matter of no importance, and they could be restrained from pillage and plundering only with greater difficulty.[214]

Similarly, in defending himself from the accusation of personal vindictiveness, the narrator insists that anyone (*quicumque*) who has known the Greeks will come to the view that they act in a despicably self-debasing manner when afraid, but become haughtily oppressive towards those in their power when they enjoy the upper hand.[215] In a further evocation of the critical or sceptical second-order narratee, we are told that although some claim ('dictum est a pluribus') that the Byzantines' manipulative treatment of the French once they had crossed into Asia Minor was a case of revenge for earlier clashes rather than a spontaneously malicious act, this is an assessment so incomplete that it is defeasible on general principles akin to the manner in which a legal judgement is reached, not just with reference to the specific circumstances in which the crusaders found themselves at that particular juncture: 'The man who knows a case partially makes a partial judgement, but the man who does not know the entire case cannot make a just

[213] See *De profectione*, pp. 70, 72. Cf. the concessions that the crusaders were in part responsible for some of the friction with the Greeks, though typically when forced into a reaction by their mistreatment: *De profectione*, pp. 48 (both the Germans and Greeks act arrogantly), 106 (the local inhabitants' greed is set against the insolence of the French 'multitude').

[214] *De profectione*, p. 56: translation revised.

[215] *De profectione*, pp. 56–8.

judgement.'[216] Towards the end of the French army's grind through Asia Minor, moreover, we are informed that 'many of our men' complained that the local people were acting treacherously in refusing to sell grain for the horses, even though they gestured to the barrenness of the terrain and claimed, probably truthfully, that they had none for sale.[217] By the time of the text's last staged discussion of strategy between Louis and his counsellors, at Adalia, the fraudulence of the Greeks has assumed the status of an undisputed point of shared reference, a given so fundamental, in fact, that it is said to differentiate the experiences of the current crusaders from those of their predecessors on the First Crusade, whose march through Asia Minor had been characterized by a more direct, and more manageable, collision with Turkish military might uncomplicated by Greek guile.[218]

The narrator's desire to distribute his anti-Byzantine sentiments among as large a number of his fellow-crusaders as possible, and to justify his views with reference to the emergence of such a consensus, is the principal driver of the text's larger project of narratorial construction. For if the narrator is to fashion the crusade as a learning curve propelled by direct experience of relations with the Greeks, he needs to establish correspondences of scale between action and reaction that integrate him within the crusaders' group perceptions, not isolate him as an idiosyncratic mis- or over-reader of the evidence. It is significant that the one passage in which the narrator's identity is implicitly distilled down to specific characteristics that detach him from the mass of the crusaders around him – as he knowledgeably observes the Greek clergy contributing to the liturgy of the feast of St Dionysius as one among what must have been a very select group of those crusaders who were either monks from St-Denis or western religious with direct experience of blended Latin-Greek liturgical practice – is the one moment in which something approaching empathetic appreciation of the Byzantines emerges in the text, although it is swiftly problematized, as we have seen.[219] In contrast, the popular anti-Greek mood must, by definition, be grounded in larger acts of perception. Accordingly, the manner in which the crusaders apprehend the storyworld around them is made to correspond to their ability to understand what the Greeks do to them and why.

The connection between general perceptive acuity and specific appreciation of the Greeks is enacted in two remarkable moments in the text, arguably *the* defining moments. In them Manuel undergoes a twofold transformation. In allowing Turks who were fleeing a defeat at the hands of the French to seek refuge in the

[216] *De profectione*, p. 72.
[217] *De profectione*, p. 128.
[218] *De profectione*, pp. 128, 132. It should be recalled that the army was moving through Asia Minor in the winter months. For the contrast with the First Crusade, see Phillips, *Second Crusade*, pp. 203–4.
[219] Above, pp. 168–70.

imperially-controlled town of Antiochetta, the emperor abandons the pretence that has hitherto cloaked his dealings with the French: 'In so doing, that man switched from being a deceitful traitor and came out into the open as our enemy.'[220] And earlier, in an even more remarkable mutation made all the more striking for being visible to the naked eye, when Louis's envoys to the imperial court, Bishop Arnulf of Lisieux and Bartholomew the royal chancellor, are finally admitted to Manuel's presence, their attempts at renewed negotiation are thwarted when they are confronted by a changed man: 'but deaf and swollen with poison like an asp, he mutated from the person whom they had seen before; or, rather, the man stood revealed whom previously they had not recognized beneath the surface of his guile.'[221]

As this last passage indicates, the narrator-as-character's own gaze is not necessarily at play in the selection, narration and interpretation of important plot junctures. Throughout the text, the reported actions are accompanied by a broad range of perceptual correlates. This is facilitated by the fact that the motif of journey-as-experience, though substantially directed towards the emergent understanding of the Byzantines' true character and intentions, as we have seen, can extend to other contexts. For example, when the French reach Worms, a violent scuffle breaks out between some of their number and local people ferrying supplies over the Rhine: 'Here we first perceived', the narrator remarks in anticipation of what will prove to be a pattern of behaviour, 'the foolish arrogance of our people.'[222] Similarly, when the army sees an ominous partial eclipse of the sun as it marches through Asia Minor, its first reaction is to worry that Louis, delayed by negotiations with Manuel, has been betrayed in some way; only later is the truer meaning of the 'celestial prodigy' revealed, when news of the defeat of the German army emerges and the half-covered, half-visible sun is retrospectively taken to symbolize Louis and Conrad's combination of shared faith but contrasting circumstances.[223] The verb that here expresses the acquisition of truer understanding is in the first person plural, *didicimus*, reflecting the narrator's ambitions to subsume his personal perceptions within acts of collective experience whenever the plot so permits.

The emphasis upon the collective quality of the crusade-as-experience is further evident in the narrator's reluctance to drop Odo-as-character overtly

[220] *De profectione*, pp. 110–12: 'In quo ille de doloso proditore se in apertum transtulit inimicum': my translation. As this passage illustrates, much of the narrator's evidence for the reach of Manuel's malevolence towards the crusaders rests on the assumption that imperial authority extended deep into Asia Minor and the emperor was thus in a position to dictate the reactions of local people to the passing French army, even though the text at one point also acknowledges the uncertain boundaries between areas of Byzantine and Turkish control: *De profectione*, p. 112.

[221] *De profectione*, p. 76: my translation.

[222] *De profectione*, p. 22: the verb of perception is *sensimus*.

[223] *De profectione*, pp. 82–4.

into the storyworld, with the result that the narrative is only fitfully and briefly autobiographical in the full sense. We have already noted Odo's most developed appearance in the action, when he petitions Louis VII regarding some of the abbey of St-Denis's possessions in Germany.[224] It is significant that in this instance the narrator acknowledges that mention of this exchange deflects from his main subject matter (*nostra materia*); and as if to validate the diversion he resorts to an unusually explicit cue to guide the narratee's response in suggesting to Suger that he should pray for Louis in return for the king's continuing support of the abbot's interests. Apart from this scene, there is only one occasion in which Odo fully enters the diegesis, though in this instance his actions are integrated within the larger dynamics of the plot around him. As the French army approaches and begins to ascend Mount Cadmus, the vanguard allows itself to become detached from the baggage train behind it, thereby exposing the main body of the army to Turkish attacks. In what amounts to his fifteen minutes of fame as far as the military history of the crusade is concerned, Odo is sent forward to the vanguard, which has by now pitched camp, to report what is happening, whereupon everyone rushes to arms.[225] Clearly, Odo-as-character is pitched into a moment of great peril and may be presumed to have made an important contribution to the French salvaging their position, at least as the narrator presents matters.

But even here there is a note of apology for the personal intrusion into the narrative in the statement that 'I, who as a monk could only call upon the Lord and summon others to battle, was sent to the camp'. And while the narrator does a good job of communicating a sense of speed, urgency and purposefulness in his use of the present tense and asyndeton,[226] his treatment of the framing action that contextualizes Odo's intervention lacks some of the assured handling of time and space that characterizes much of the rest of the narrative. The account of the assaults launched against the central column of the army reaches the point where night has fallen and the killing has stopped, but then Odo's mission is introduced as an analepsis cutting back to some unspecified point during the day, while the intervention of those who respond to his message is not developed before we abruptly cut once more to the king in the rearguard, again at some point in

[224] *De profectione*, p. 102.

[225] *De profectione*, p. 116. Phillips, *Second Crusade*, p. 200 has Odo sent *back* to the rearguard, where Louis VII was positioned. But the narrator states that those who responded to his news quickly retraced their steps ('festinarent regredi') and found themselves impeded by those coming in the opposite direction ('occursu venientium') – presumably elements of the central part of the army scrambling to catch up with the vanguard. The action then cuts to Louis, back in the rear, by means of a disjunctive ('Rex vero…').

[226] 'Ego…mittor ad castra. Rem refero. Turbati currunt ad arma…'

the course of that day.[227] The narrator's relative confusion with regards to the temporal and spatial co-ordination of the various moving parts in the French army not only, or mainly, evokes the uncertainty and panic that must have been widely felt at a critical time, but also suggests tentativeness on his part as to the true significance of Odo's out-of-character intervention. What difference, the question seems to be, did he really make?

As noted earlier, the text for the most part fashions a narrator who is assured and well informed with respect to events, a knowledgeable guide whose reading of the action is to be taken as anchored in a full understanding of the truth. The qualification of narratorial verdicts is consequently very rare.[228] The means by which this secure knowledge is gained is, however, seldom stated. The narrator is generally coy about his informants, though we can make educated guesses in a number of cases – typically sequences involving cut-away action that takes place away from the main crusade host and which must have been reported back by one or more of those who took part.[229] There is a similar reticence in those instances where we can surmise that Odo-the-author was recalling direct personal experience. The text makes a handful of interesting references to the workings of memory, but these are not developed into reflections on the nature and difficulties of recall. Where the narrator does speak to the challenges that he faces, he is pondering how best to arrange his story (*materia*) so as to both retain a clear chronological sequence and include concurrent events happening in various places; such remarks amount to self-highlighting gestures towards his narrative craft, for the text mostly handles sequence and anachrony very deftly. But how the narrator calls this material to mind in the first place is not at issue.

Significantly, the most direct reference to memory involves an incidental detail triggered by very obvious and immediate cues that say little about the narrator's more general mnemonic strategies. When the army reaches Laodicea (in January 1148), the narrator observes that he is reminded, in the narratorial now ('Nunc venit in memoriam'), of the Count Bernard who sacrificed himself for his brethren – a reference to Bernhard of Plötzkau, who was killed covering

[227] *De profectione*, pp. 116–18.

[228] The principal exception is the narrator's handling of the delicate question of who was responsible for allowing the vanguard to become dangerously detached from the rest of the army on Mount Cadmus. The crusaders condemn Geoffrey of Rançon, but the narrator speculates whether the fact that the king's uncle also bore some responsibility for the debacle, but was untouchable, allowed Geoffrey to escape punishment: *De profectione*, p. 122. The uncle, whom the narrator discreetly does not name, was Count Amadeus II of Maurienne.

[229] See e.g. the account of the Byzantines' mistreatment of the separate force under Bishop Stephen of Metz, his brother Count Renald of Monçon and Bishop Henry of Toul which had detached itself from the Germans and subsequently joined Louis's army: *De profectione*, pp. 50–2.

the German retreat from Dorylaeum – by the fact that it was there that another German count of the same name (Bernhard of Carinthia), a member of the force led by Otto of Freising, died in an ambush, like his namesake the victim of Greek treachery.[230] Similarly, in the context of reflecting on the difficulty of juggling accounts of the simultaneous actions of discrete agents, the narrator remarks that in the act of writing about Louis VII's arrival at Regensburg (which has already been narrated some pages earlier) he was reminded of Conrad III, whose formal departure on the crusade had been from that city. The aim is to contrive a link that can cue a cut-away to an account of the passage of the German army into Hungary ahead of the French.[231] A similar hitching of a particular personal memory to a larger structural or thematic emphasis – here the experience of the journey as an exercise in growing understanding – informs the narrator's remark that as the army was marching from Klosterneuburg towards Hungary, he was struck by the rugged and mountainous terrain, whereas he has now revised this initial impression in light of his experience of the more imposing mountains of Asia Minor.[232]

The text's only other direct references to memory occur in a passage that we have already noted, when the narrator signals to his narratee at the beginning of Book II that this transition marks a shift of tone: he apologizes for having lingered in Book I over happy events that had taken place in his own homeland and which he himself had gladly witnessed, and concedes that he must now direct his narrative towards foreign lands and the hardships that the crusaders experienced there.[233] This is the text's fullest and clearest reference to a connection between narratorial eyewitness and recall, but it does not amount to a programmatic statement suggesting that the narrator's gaze will feature conspicuously thereafter. In fact, direct references to individual acts of perception on the narrator's part are few. As a result, there are correspondingly few passages that it might be argued capture some form of flashbulb recall. The nearest that the narrator comes to such a moment concerns Louis VII's visit to a house of lepers outside the gates of Paris and then his presence at St-Denis as part of the rituals of departure on crusade. Even here, however, the narrator hints at his autopsy without committing to specifics. Of the visit to the leper colony, the narrator notes:

[230] *De profectione*, p. 112. For the two Bernhards, see Phillips, *Second Crusade*, pp. 179, 182, 184.

[231] *De profectione*, pp. 32–4: 'Ecce enim rex et imperator occurrerunt mihi memoriae pariter Ratisbonae.'

[232] *De profectione*, p. 30. The reference may be to the Kahlenberg range.

[233] *De profectione*, p. 20: 'Intereram laetis rebus, et patriae meae nomina scribens et rerum reminiscens quod laetus videram sine taedio diutius recolebam.' Berry's translation of *intereram* as 'I was engrossed' would suggest that the narrator is recalling his being absorbed during the act of writing, but the reference may also be to the narrator's full and active participation in events as a character in the narrative now.

> ...having first visited some monks in Paris, he [Louis] at length moved outside and went to the buildings occupied by the lepers. There I definitely saw that he had gone in, accompanied by just two others, and had shut out the rest of his crowd of followers while he remained there a long time.[234]

The narrator's use of past infinitives (*intrasse*, *exclusisse*) suggests that he is not stressing direct eyewitness of this event on his part, simply that he was presented with evidence that this is what had happened – seeing, in other words as seeing *that*.

Once Louis has moved on to St-Denis, there follows a quite detailed account of the king's actions, as he first meets Pope Eugenius III, Abbot Suger and the monks (Odo presumably among them), prostrates himself, venerates the relic of St Dionysius, receives a banner (the standard of the abbey's advocate which was in due course conflated with the *oriflamme* that featured in legends of Charlemagne), is given the pilgrim's scrip and is blessed by the pope, before withdrawing to the monks' dormitory to spend time away from the throng.[235] Given the careful elaboration of the various elements of a complex ritual sequence, one feels that this *ought* to be tagged as an eyewitness scene, but it is not. While some of the incidental details that are supplied, particularly that the king's wife and mother were overcome by grief and the stifling heat as they waited for Louis to return from the dormitory, have a ring of autoptic specificity and authenticity, others do not; the observation that the relic of St Dionysius that was offered to Louis was in a silver reliquary housed behind a gold aperture in the altar would have been routine knowledge to Odo.[236] Likewise, the narrator does not tell us, as seems highly likely, that he was present when Louis concluded his visit to the abbey by dining with the monks in the refectory.[237]

It might be argued that the narrator did not need to labour his autoptic gaze in this instance because his narratee Suger was himself a witness, and a very

[234] *De profectione*, p. 16: my translation: 'nam cum prius religiosos quosque Parisius visitasset, tandem foras progrediens leprosorum adiit officinas. Ibi certe vidi eum cum solis duobus arbitris intrasse et per longam moram ceteram suorum multitudinem exclusisse.' Berry's translation has the narrator directly witness Louis's entry and his exclusion of all but two companions, but this reading would be more secure if present infinitives or present participles had been used.

[235] *De profectione*, pp. 16–18. For the ritualistic resonance of Louis's visit to St-Denis, see G. Koziol, 'England, France, and the Problem of Sacrality in Twelfth-Century Ritual', in T. N. Bisson (ed.), *Cultures of Power: Lordship, Status, and Process in Twelfth-Century Europe* (Philadelphia, 1995), pp. 128–9.

[236] Cf. the narrator's description of Bernard of Clairvaux which at first blush might seem to be based on direct observation but in fact simply resumes the clichéd contrast found in many contemporary texts between Bernard's physical frailty and his boundless spiritual energy: *De profectione*, p. 10.

[237] *De profectione*, p. 18.

well-placed one, of at least the St-Denis phase of the proceedings. But it is noteworthy that there is no shift to a greater reliance on overt eyewitness recall once the action moves beyond what Suger would have been in a position to remember on his own account. There are only two subsequent references to the act of seeing in the first person singular, and both serve to reinforce certain of the narrator's thematic strategies rather than evoke flashbulb-like recalled moments. In one the narrator seeks to justify his anti-Greek rhetoric, in the face of the possible objection on the part of a putative critic that he was merely motivated by vengefulness, by denying that he is constructing a bogey figure whom he has not seen ('quem non vidi'): in other words, his position is grounded in multiple acts of perception, and anyone else with the same experience of the Greeks would come to the same conclusion.[238] The second justifies the narrator's reticence about naming those crusaders who crossed the Bosphorus behind Louis by evoking the grief that was later caused him by witnessing them meet untimely deaths.[239] This, however, simply reinforces the remark that a listing of names would be tedious for the reader, a standard narratorial shortcut, and the particular deaths that would have been the basis of this remark are not in fact recounted in the remainder of the narrative; in other words, a submerged register of personal affect and response is hinted at but not allowed to work its way up onto the surface of the plot.

There are several sequences in the text where it is reasonable to suspect that the narrator is drawing in whole or substantial part on his own eyewitness recollection: one notes, for example, the reference to the fact that the envoys of Roger II of Sicily at Étampes were shocked by the council's rejection of their king's offer of help and 'went away confounded, like men in grief, showing clearly enough their love for their master';[240] the narrator's attention to the landscapes through which the army passes;[241] the mention of the appearance of the interior of Greek chapels;[242] the account of the meeting between the emperor Manuel Komnenos and Louis VII, where the narrator observes that the two men were the same age and height but unlike in dress and demeanour;[243] the narrator's description of the city of Constantinople, and the particular attention he pays to the Blachernae palace, where we know the French leadership was quartered;[244] the detail that attends the account of the Greek clergy's contribution to the

[238] *De profectione*, pp. 56–8.

[239] *De profectione*, p. 80: 'quia mortes eorum immaturas aspexi'.

[240] *De profectione*, p. 15: 'confusi abeunt, dolentium habitu, domini sui satis expresse monstrantes affectum'.

[241] *De profectione*, pp. 30–2, 86, 104.

[242] *De profectione*, pp. 54–6.

[243] *De profectione*, pp. 58–60.

[244] *De profectione*, pp. 62–6. It is difficult to imagine, however, that the narrator's remarks (p. 64) about Constantinople's squalid and crime-infested *demimonde* were based on street-level observation of the city's seedier districts.

celebration of the feast of St Dionysius, which we are informed was a source of pleasure for those who witnessed it;[245] and the remark that the bishop of Metz acted as the interpreter when Conrad III gave a moving *mea culpa* speech to the French that acknowledged that he was at fault for his defeat by the Turks.[246] It is noteworthy, however, that in none of these or similar passages does the narrator make any direct reference to individual eyewitness experience and personal recollection.

It is important to remember that density of narrative detail does not always constitute *prima facie* evidence of eyewitness recall, just as its absence is not clear proof of authorial reliance on second-hand information. Consequently, the inclusion of the sort of thicker description that we might superficially take as evidence of autopsy tends in fact to reinforce one or more of the text's thematic preoccupations or to point up the narrator's skilful interweaving of connections between various strands in the story. Two visually rich vignettes in the *De profectione* help to illustrate this point. One is a marginal case of possible autopsy in the sense that Odo-the-historical-actor may have witnessed some parts of the action, but if this were so it is not mentioned. This anecdote concerns a claimant to the Hungarian throne, Boris, who secretly attaches himself to Louis VII's army as it passes through Hungary but is discovered by his enemy, King Geisa II. Boris is roused from his bed and forced to flee. Having vainly attempted to steal a horse, he is seized and dragged before Louis 'beaten, soiled with mud, and naked except for his breeches'. He is, however, able to overcome the language barrier to make his identity clear. Louis subsequently refuses to hand him over to Geisa despite the diplomatic awkwardness that this causes.[247] The point of this story, which is told at some length, is, then, Louis's high-minded scruple in protecting the fugitive, a decision duly endorsed by the judgement of the French bishops and magnates; and the anecdote thus forms part of the narrator's larger construction of Louis over the course of the narrative.[248]

The second, no less vivid and well-told, anecdote cannot have been based on direct eyewitness observation, for it involves members of the German army when it was marching through the Balkans some weeks ahead of the French. The Germans reach Philippopolis, where there is an established settlement of Latins servicing the needs of passing travellers. In one of the taverns an entertainer (*ioculator*) starts to perform a snake-charming act as well as various

[245] *De profectione*, pp. 66–8: 'iocunditatem visibus offerebant'.

[246] *De profectione*, pp. 98–100.

[247] *De profectione*, pp. 34–8. For the incident, see Phillips, *Second Crusade*, pp. 187–8. See generally Z. Hunyadi, 'Hungary and the Second Crusade', *Chronica*, 9–10 (2011), 55–65.

[248] Cf. the story of a Flemish thief whose punishment serves to demonstrate Louis's stern and implacable justice, and by extension the effectiveness of his discipline of the army: *De profectione*, p. 74.

other tricks. The German spectators, however, the worse for drink, interpret the snake as an 'evil portent' (*prodigium*) and lay violent hands on the entertainer, who is killed. A riotous confrontation ensues between the Byzantine authorities and a drunken German mob, whose misreading of the Greeks' intentions only serves to escalate the violence. Many of the Germans are killed, whereupon the survivors rally and in retaliation set fire to whatever they can find outside the city walls.[249] This vignette plugs into the text's larger concerns in a number of ways. It sets up the narrator's subsequent remark that the Germans could also aggravate the French; this is then illustrated by the account of a brawl between Germans and French over supplies at an unspecified location.[250] Additionally, the snake anticipates the language (*serpens*, *aspis*) that will later be used of Manuel at the key moment of perception when Louis's envoys Arnulf of Lisieux and Bartholomew the chancellor see the emperor's true nature emerge before their eyes.[251]

Unlike the Germans in the inn, however, Arnulf and Bartholomew read their snake correctly. The scene also neatly folds back into comments that the narrator has made a little earlier, at the beginning of Book III, to the effect that when the crusaders first entered Byzantine territory the light-hearted mood that had characterized their passage up to that point now darkened as they became prey to injuries and deceit. The narrator's ludic metaphor, 'Up to this juncture we were playing' ('Hucusque lusimus'), a phrase which evokes both the mood of the crusaders on the march and the narrator's judgement as to the manner in which the journey has been narrated thus far, is picked up in the term used of the entertainer's various trickeries, 'ceteris lusibus ioculatoriis'.[252] The fact that the text explicitly mentions the presence of a Latin community at Philippopolis might suggest that the *ioculator* was presumed to be an expatriate westerner – given that he could not understand German, perhaps even a Frenchman. But the narrative aligns him with the local authorities that end up fighting the German rioters, and he thus stands for the world into which the crusaders abruptly and rudely intrude. As he discovers to his cost, there is precious little playfulness when it comes to the true nature of the interactions between the Greeks and the westerners.[253]

[249] *De profectione*, p. 42.

[250] *De profectione*, pp. 42–4. Cf. the manner in which the account of a brawl at Worms between the French crusaders and local people selling supplies both realizes for the first time what had hitherto only been an evil foreboding (*malum praesagium*) about the people's conduct, and implicitly anticipates future difficulties between the crusaders and the populations of areas through which they travel: *De profectione*, p. 22.

[251] *De profectione*, p. 76; see above, p. 178.

[252] *De profectione*, pp. 40 (my translation), 42.

[253] For other examples of vividly narrated incidents which could not have been based on authorial autopsy, see *De profectione*, pp. 44–6 (the death of Bishop Alvisus of Arras), 46–8 (the flooding which badly affects the German army in the Choirobacchoi plain in

The narrator's unwillingness to focalize the action through his individual gaze contributes to a wide distribution of focalizing roles among a variety of actors. While it is true that Louis VII assumes this role more than any other character, he does not do so often enough to dominate perceptions. Indeed, one could argue that, in light of the narrator's declared aim in the prefatory epistle of attending to the king's role in the crusade, the body of the narrative does not fully deliver on this promise: Louis retreats into the middle distance at several junctures after Book I, at the point, in effect, at which he leaves behind the ritual spaces where his regality can be routinely and visibly performed. The narrative's one moment of individual derring-do on Louis's part, as he scrambles onto a rock and fends off the enemy during the fighting on Mount Cadmus, stands out as an exception to the rule, as if this were the only incident available to the narrator in which to show off Louis's personal knightly qualities.[254] Moreover, although the narrator, again in the prefatory epistle, establishes his credentials by stating that as a chaplain he was routinely physically close to Louis, with him when he rose in the morning and again when he retired at night, this does not play out as a plot device in what follows; Louis is not the narrator's surrogate, nor does the narrator confront the action on the king's shoulder.

Although the title conventionally given to the work, foregrounding as it does Louis's individual agency, is that supplied by the one surviving manuscript, we cannot be certain in the absence of Odo's autograph copy that this was its original designation; if anything, *De profectione Ludovici VII in orientem* reads like the sort of summative description that a St-Denis scribe, institutionally predisposed to

September 1147), 92–4 (the self-sacrifice and death of Bernhard of Plötzkau), 118–20 (Louis VII's single-handed resistance against numerous Turkish opponents during the debacle on Mount Cadmus).

[254] There is one other moment in which Louis-as-warrior features, during the French engagement with the Turks in the Maeander valley at the end of December 1147. Their success in breaking through the Turkish forces deployed to obstruct their progress means that this was in fact the military highlight of the French performance during the crusade. Louis is mentioned riding against the Turks: *De profectione*, p. 110. But the text's restraint is noteworthy, for Louis's appearance is by way of an addendum ('Rex quoque…') after the narrator has emphasized the whirlwind-like charge into a hail of arrows by the 'excellent counts' Henry, the son of Theobald of Champagne, Thierry of Flanders and William of Mâcon. For this battle, which shows that the French could prove an effective fighting force when conditions favoured massed cavalry charges, see Phillips, *Second Crusade*, pp. 197–8. In addition to the account in *De profectione*, pp. 108–10, 112, this battle is narrated at some length by Niketas Choniates writing several decades later, which suggests that some memory of its significance persisted even in non-Latin circles: Niketas Choniates, *Historia*, ed. J. L. van Dieten, 2 vols (Corpus Fontium Historiae Byzantinae, Series Berolinensis, 11; Berlin, 1975), pp. 67–71; trans. H. J. Magoulias, *O City of Byzantium, Annals of Niketas Choniates* (Detroit, 1984), pp. 39–42. For Odo's treatment of the military aspects of the crusade generally, see Phillips, 'Odo of Deuil's *De profectione*', pp. 90–1, 92–4.

enhance the image of the French kings, might have introduced early in the text's transmission. In any event, the narrative does not amount to a *Gesta Ludovici* in which the action is represented as a series of projections outwards from Louis's personal achievement. It would probably be stretching a point to suggest that the narrator is dropping hints that Louis's performance on the crusade was less than exemplary, though this is not out of the question;[255] but there is clearly an element of strategic selectivity in the text's presentation of the king.[256] It follows that there is no clear pattern to Louis's focalizations, though some instances contribute towards an image of him as a careful and sympathetic observer of what is happening around him, especially as it affects the poorer crusaders.[257] In a similar fashion, Louis functions as the 'soul' of the expedition, its ethical centre more than the primary driver of the action, in demonstrating some appreciation of historical context when he evokes the precedent of the First Crusade – in this way responding literally and high-mindedly to the manner in which *Quantum praedecessores* and much of the preaching of the Second Crusade had set up the first crusaders as models to emulate.[258]

Many of the other focalizing roles played out in the narrative serve to reinforce the central theme of the journey as shared experience. For example, the narrator's evocation of the size and precipitousness of Mount Cadmus seems to recall the impression that it made on the crusaders generally in the act of scrambling up it, not just his individual recollection after the fact: 'The mountain was steep and rocky, and we had to climb along a ridge so lofty that its summit seemed to

[255] It is, however, arguable that the figure of Conrad III is used to deflect or absorb criticisms that could potentially have been made of Louis also, notably in Conrad's self-reproving speech: *De profectione*, pp. 98–100.

[256] See the implied marginalization of the king, effectively relegated to command of a tactical support group, in the Templars' reorganization of the army after the setback on Mount Cadmus: *De profectione*, pp. 124–6; Phillips, *Second Crusade*, p. 202. For hints as to Louis's ineffectiveness, pliability and naivety, see *De profectione*, pp. 12, 66, 80, 104.

[257] See e.g. *De profectione*, pp. 8 (Louis longs for the inauguration of the crusade at Vézelay), 20 (he finds the inhabitants of Verdun and Metz willing to act as if they were his subjects), 114 (he sees the Turks' battle lines and the bodies of their recent German victims), 130 (he observes the shortage of good horses at Adalia). For Louis's care for the poor, as well as for the nobles and *mediocres*, see *De profectione*, pp. 44, 124, 136, 142. Cf. Louis's rather impractical suggestion that it should be the poor who benefit from the ships available at Adalia, and the barons' prompt and uncompromising rejection of this idea: *De profectione*, pp. 130–2.

[258] See *De profectione*, pp. 58 (which, in evoking the example of what Franks in the past had done, may also imply that Louis was looking beyond the First Crusade to the legend of Charlemagne's pilgrimage to Constantinople), 130; but cf. p. 132, where the barons' response to the king points out the differences between the experience of their forebears on the First Crusade and their current situation.

touch heaven and the stream in the hollow valley below to descend to hell.'[259] Similarly, when Bishop Godfrey of Langres argues that the French should attack Constantinople, he points to the evidence of the weakness of the city wall, a large stretch of which is visibly ruinous.[260] The narrator is generous with his focalization, allowing the action to be filtered through multiple subjectivities – both those of individuals and of groups big and small.[261] Those opposed to the crusaders are included. Indeed one of the most developed scenes in which the act of seeing features concerns the emperor Manuel's and the Greeks' impotent gazes from within Constantinople upon the *spectaculum* unfolding before them as the German army pillages the Philopation, the imperial palace, game reserve and pleasure park outside the city walls.[262] A similar sense of outsiders looking inwards upon the crusade emerges from the narrator's comment that as the French forces struggle up Mount Cadmus, they are hard pressed by Turks and Greeks who harass them with arrows and 'rejoice at such a spectacle'.[263] Similarly, the Turks' gaze betokens vulnerability and threat when they appraise the exposed position of those crusaders who have been left behind to fend for themselves at Adalia: 'They saw their enemies densely packed together between two kinds of enemies [the Greeks within the city and the Turks outside] and walls, just like sheep in a fold, and they realized that they could fire arrows at them because they dared not move one way or the other.'[264]

The narrator also makes use, albeit very sparingly, of a device that we shall see is exploited more fully by some of our other texts, notably Ambroise's history of the Third Crusade, namely the intensification of the visual quality of a given

[259] *De profectione*, p. 116.

[260] *De profectione*, p. 68: 'ante nostros oculos'. Cf. the statement that the camp of a group of crusaders catching up with the main French force was visible to 'conspectu nostro': *De profectione*, p. 78. See also the whole army's witnessing of an eclipse: *De profectione*, p. 82.

[261] E.g. *De profectione*, pp. 18 (the crowds that have assembled at St-Denis, as well as Louis VII's mother and wife, are upset by the delay and the heat while the king tarries in the monks' dormitory), 22 (the people of Worms rush to arms when they see that a quarrel has broken out with the crusaders), 42 (the Germans perceive – 'oculus Alemannorum...videt' – those rushing towards them as the snake incident escalates), 74 (a Flemish thief sees the great wealth on display on Byzantine moneychangers' tables and is 'blinded' by greed), 90–2 (German standard-bearers first see that their treacherous guide has abandoned them, then observe that the Turks occupy threatening positions nearby), 96 ('our people' cannot bear to see the abundance of supplies in the countryside of Asia Minor while they remain in want), 122 (parties of knights see Louis VII returning from the fighting on Mount Cadmus 'alone, bloody and tired').

[262] *De profectione*, p. 48. Cf. the amazement of natives in Asia Minor at the French army's happy knack of crossing rivers just before they flood: *De profectione*, p. 106.

[263] *De profectione*, p. 116: 'de tali spectaculo...gratulantur': my translation.

[264] *De profectione*, p. 138: my translation.

scene, and by extension the significance that the reader is invited to attach to that moment, by means of adding the narratee's invited gaze to those of one or more agents within the diegesis, thereby creating a criss-cross effect of mutually reinforcing lines of sight. Although there is only one instance of this device in the *De profectione*, it highlights an encounter that is very important both thematically and in plot terms, as Louis and the French first run up against Byzantine diplomatic and political culture when they are met by the imperial ambassadors, Demetrios and Mauros, at Regensburg. As argued above, this is the moment that inaugurates the narratorial project of gradually closing the gap between the appearance and reality of the Greeks' attitudes towards the crusade. Note the implied invitation to linger on this scene in the inclusion of the reality effect-like detail that the ambassadors provided their own seating, and the opening out of the specifics of the moment to remarks of a more general nature concerning the Greeks' customs. In this way, by picturing this particular encounter the narratee is asked to imagine similar occasions at other times; and the narrator's blending of tenses helps to elide this one incident into a pattern of behaviour. Note also the congruence of the narrator's gaze, embedded in collective action, with that of the narratee as they witness this scene as a whole, and by implication imagine others like it, while the Byzantines' gaze is contrastively directed inwardly only at themselves:

> Then, after camp has been pitched and the king housed, the emperor's ambassadors are summoned and come. When they have greeted the king and delivered their letters, they stand waiting for his reply, for they will not sit unless ordered to do so; when so commanded, however, they sat on the chairs they had brought with them. We saw there what we subsequently learned is the Greeks' custom, which is that the entire retinue remains standing while their lords are seated. You would see [*Videas*] the young men standing stock still, their heads bowed, their eager gaze directed in silence upon their lords, ready to obey them at the merest nod. They do not wear cloaks, but the rich are clad in silken clothes that are short, tight all around and sewn up at the sleeves, and they always go around unimpeded like boxers. The poor dress themselves in a similar way only more cheaply.[265]

In light of the text's emphasis on collective apprehension, it is unsurprising that there are several references to group visual perception.[266] It is important to

[265] *De profectione*, pp. 24–6: my translation, here observing Odo's signature cutting between the past and present tenses. The ambassadors' names are supplied a little later: *De profectione*, p. 28.

[266] See the use of *vidimus* in e.g. *De profectione*, pp. 24, 46, 104. Cf. the statement that Louis's taking of the banner of St-Denis was done 'in the sight of all' ('visus ab omnibus'): *De profectione*, p. 16. See also the passive *visum est* with respect to

note, however, that seeing is not the dominant apperceptual mode in the narrator's schema, although there are many occasions in which it is implied that sight contributes to a character or characters' understanding. Greater emphasis is placed lexically on acts of discovery and the forming of verdicts (*invenimus*, *sensimus*, *didicimus*, *novimus*, *putavimus*) in terms that imply considered reflection of the evidence supplied by a variety of visual and non-visual markers. Likewise, the crusaders tend to hear about situations (*audivimus*) more than they directly perceive them visually.[267] The narrator is constructed so as to exploit a constant tension in his positioning relative to events: on the one hand, he occupies a narratorial now that puts him in advance of the state of knowledge of the characters as they move through the storyworld, as his ominous and ironic prolepses reveal; but on the other he also chooses to participate immersively in the drawn-out and often painful process of collective discovery. Accordingly, individual eyewitness is not foregrounded because it is not routinely needed to authenticate details or to privilege personal flashbulbs, though both of these approaches are present at a few points in the text. The narrator's principal goal is to explain how the crusaders came to a true understanding of the Greeks' malevolence towards them, a journey of discovery that structures the story of the crusade and is reinforced by the narrator's complementary emphases on experience and sequence.

In the *De expugnatione Lyxbonensi* and the *De profectione Ludovici VII in orientem* we encounter distinct but broadly similar approaches to the value of authorial autopsy and the construction of the narratorial persona. While both texts ground much of their authority on their authors' participation in events, and indeed accentuate this quality by means of mentions of their closeness to principal actors, neither foregrounds the theme of autobiographical recall. As we have seen, the *De profectione* inserts Odo as a character into its storyworld only sparingly: the conversation with Louis VII about St-Denis's German properties is in the nature of a tangent to the main action, as much as anything an aside for the benefit of Abbot Suger as narratee. And while Odo's role in the Mount Cadmus debacle grants him agency during one of the plot's kernel events, this looks like the narrator making the most of a rare opportunity for meaningful homodiegetic intervention in a moment of particularly acute crisis, almost as if to jolt the reader by permitting himself an unexpected walk-on part. Likewise with the *De expugnatione*, the simple fact that it is anonymous and the debates that have attached

collective understanding of the Germans' responsibility for souring relations with the Greeks: *De profectione*, p. 40.

[267] E.g. *De profectione*, pp. 22, 24–6, 30, 34, 40–2, 48, 50, 56, 96, 106, 110, 136. See also the remark that, at the liminal moment when the crusaders first enter Byzantine territory, 'for the first time wrongs began to arise and to be noticed [*inveniri*]': *De profectione*, p. 40.

to the identity of the author are largely functions of the narrator's reticence in matters of autobiographical self-insertion into the storyworld. The fact that in neither text is the narrator routinely situated inside the action as the locus of an individual gaze means that the 'live' autoptic perception of unfolding events is relatively downplayed. These are not eye-of-the-camera narratives. Odo's text in particular offers up salutary reminders that one cannot read unusually vivid or detailed scenes as *prima facie* evidence of authorial autopsy. The episode with the Germans and the snake at Philippopolis is a case in point: whatever its underlying messages might be, for example about the Germans' lack of discipline and the serpentine quality of the Greek emperor, the reason why the text devotes a significant amount of space to this single and in itself fairly minor incident is not that Odo was there. He was not. This is a flashbulb-like moment without any basis in actual flashbulb memory.

It is important to remember that Odo was one participant in an army of thousands that for much of the period covered by his text was strung out along many miles of road; opportunities for the camera-eye capture of key events would therefore have been limited, hence perhaps the narrative's particular attention to diplomatic exchanges, debates and other stagey, static encounters. Indeed, one might say of the exceptional moment of autobiographical inclusion in the Mount Cadmus sequence that this occurs precisely when the fact that the French army is strung out along the line of march matters as a plot device, for Odo just happens to be at the right place at the right moment when there was an especially urgent need to join up the army's various moving parts. For his part, the author of the *De expugnatione* would have been comparatively static once the crusaders had arrived at Lisbon; he must have been effectively confined to the area of the Anglo-Norman siege operations to the west of the city. But this does not translate into richly realized vignettes in which individual authorial autopsy is either expressly asserted or strongly implied.

The *De expugnatione*, moreover, alerts us to a further complicating factor, in that the borrowings from Solinus demonstrate how even when a text seems to be narrating what on the surface looks like unmediated experience, we need to consider the play of intertextual reference. In an important sense, the contemporary reader who spotted the text's borrowings from Solinus and its gestures towards his taxonomies would have interpreted these as validations of the author's and his fellow crusaders' experiences; in conforming to expectations as to what the Iberian peninsula was like and what in particular merited the viewer's attention, the acuity, directedness and accuracy of the crusaders' gaze would have been authenticated to a greater extent than appeals to direct experience alone could have achieved. The Solinus-inspired sequences in the *De expugnatione* stage this blending of seeing-as-visual-confrontation and seeing-through-text more than at any other point in our sample of sources; but they are a salutary reminder that for both authors and readers references to the act of seeing could invite responses that extended beyond easy familiarity with sight's immediate perceptual, experiential quality.

For all their relative downplaying of the homodiegetic narratorial gaze, however, both texts merit their designation as 'eyewitness' sources, and demonstrate, moreover, that this is a helpfully elastic category. We should not become unduly focused on express references to what the narrator-as-character happens to see, for much of the act of seeing is displaced onto other focalizing characters as they move through the storyworld, characters who mimic or restage or improve upon or relocate the author's originary autoptic experiences. This equips the narrator to co-opt the mass of crusaders, or at least significant sub-sections of them, in the articulation of the narrative's thematic preoccupations, which can now be embedded in and expressed through the crusaders' experiences in 'real time', the narrative now, rather than merely projected back onto the action as exercises in narratorial hindsight. Even the Solinus-inspired sequences in the *De expugnatione* ultimately serve to ground the crusaders' awareness of conditions in the Iberian peninsula, and by extension the justice of their intervention in its affairs, in their own perceptions.

The *De expugnatione* anticipates some of the texts that we shall consider in later chapters in its particular concern with the theme of Christian unity; the narrator regularly gestures to this ideal in subsuming his individual gaze within collective acts of perception. Seeing is made communal in order to enact and reify the ideal of Christian accord. The thematic orientation of the *De profectione* is somewhat more idiosyncratic in view of the narrator's anti-Greek fixations. But as we have seen, the hostility to the Byzantines in general and to the emperor in particular translates into a narrative arc that doubles up as a learning curve thanks to the parallelism between experience and reading that the narrator makes a point of introducing early in the text. As we have noted, this learning process is principally flagged by means of verbs expressing discovery and realization, but that there is an important visual component to this process is often implied, as when, for example, the two French envoys confront a changed Emperor Manuel. In both texts, therefore, seeing is not simply something that characters do; it is programmatic. Without labouring the point unduly, it would be fair to say these two narratives represent the most sophisticated historiographical visions among the texts that we are considering. As we turn to Ambroise's history of the Third Crusade, therefore, we need to establish whether the handling of autopsy and visual perception in the *De expugnatione* and *De profectione* is a function of the narrative craft, form and content of these particular texts, or has correspondences in other genres and other approaches to the narration of a crusade expedition.

3

The Third Crusade: Ambroise's *Estoire de la Guerre Sainte* and Points of Comparison and Contrast

The history of the Third Crusade known as the *Estoire de la Guerre Sainte* (*c.*1195), which is almost certainly to be attributed to an Ambroise who is named no fewer than nine times over the course of the text, commands attention as an eyewitness history for two reasons. It lies at the intersection of important developments in later twelfth-century western historiography; and the text is noteworthy for its supple, multifaceted and creative fashioning of eyewitness authority. As this chapter will argue, eyewitnessing is closely bound up in several of the *Estoire*'s self-authorizing moves. These are, most notably: the construction of the narrator as a close and informed observer; the interplay between individual narratorial perception and attention to collective agency; the co-opting of the reader's or listener's visual imagination in the act of following the narrative; the distribution of focalizing roles, with a particular emphasis on that of King Richard I of England; and, perhaps most importantly, the translation of the immersive experience of participating in the crusade expedition into a number of visually rich diegeses that do not merely punctuate the action in the nature of attention-grabbing vignettes but also programmatically aid the reader's understanding of the story as a whole. In other words, the narrator's ability to speak authoritatively about the course of the crusade is not simply the sum of multiple individual acts of informed and reflective visual perception, significant as these are; it is also a function of his inclusion within numerous collective experiences in which visual sensation is brought to the fore. In this way, and to an even greater degree than the two texts examined in the previous chapter, the *Estoire* represents an abstracting out of individual eyewitness into a collective experiential register.

Before we examine the *Estoire* in detail, it is useful to set it in its closely contemporary context. The two narratives of the Second Crusade that we considered above exemplify the challenges posed when one source of necessity dominates our understanding of a given sequence of events. With the Third Crusade (1187–92) we enter a notably fuller evidentiary landscape characterized by a greater number of narratives that were either written by eyewitness participants or were informed, to varying degrees, by eyewitness testimony.[1]

[1] There is unfortunately no modern scholarly book-length study of the Third Crusade in English. The events of 1187–92 are, of course, described in detail in the many

For example, Roger of Howden, one of the most important English chroniclers in the final third of the twelfth century, accompanied King Richard on crusade before leaving Acre early, in August 1191, probably under instructions to keep a weather eye on King Philip II of France, who had recently sailed for home after solemnly undertaking not to harm Richard's interests on his return to the west.[2] Roger's accounts in his *Gesta Regis* and in his later *Chronica* of Richard's outward voyage and of events during the few weeks he himself spent at Acre are consequently full and detailed, though they do not make direct reference to his eyewitness. In contrast, his treatment of the course of the crusade after that point is noticeably less precise and in places looks padded.[3] A significant number of the English ecclesiastical and secular elite went on the crusade, which meant that the recollections of survivors were available to those chroniclers who did not themselves take part. For example, Richard of Devizes would seem to have based his telling of the earlier parts of the crusade on one or more eyewitnesses' memories, whereas his account of the later stages is less well informed.[4]

From as early as the First Crusade there survives a well-known body of epistolary evidence, letters written by participants back to the west: some contain fairly detailed and extensive narratives of the progress of the expedition, and in most cases they seem to have been intended for distribution beyond their immediate addressees.[5] It is likely that there were more such newsletters that

---

general histories of the crusade movement: see e.g. H. E. Mayer, *The Crusades*, trans. J. Gillingham, 2nd edn (Oxford, 1988), pp. 137–51; J. Richard, *The Crusades, c.1071–c.1291*, trans. J. Birrell (Cambridge, 1999), pp. 216–31; J. S. C. Riley-Smith, *The Crusades: A History* (New Haven, 2005), pp. 137–46; C. J. Tyerman, *God's War: A New History of the Crusades* (London, 2006), pp. 375–474.

[2] See J. Gillingham, 'Roger of Howden on Crusade', in his *Richard Coeur de Lion: Kingship, Chivalry and War in the Twelfth Century* (London, 1994), pp. 141–53.

[3] See *Gesta Regis Henrici Secundi* [formerly attributed to Benedict of Peterborough], ed. W. Stubbs, 2 vols (RS 49; London, 1867), ii, *passim*; *Chronica*, ed. W. Stubbs, 4 vols (RS 51; London, 1868–71), iii, *passim*. Among the incidents recounted during the 'eyewitness' phase of the crusade, perhaps the best known is Richard's encounter with Joachim of Fiore at Messina: *Gesta Regis*, ii, pp. 151–5; *Chronica*, iii, pp. 75–86. It is probable that Roger journeyed to Rome on royal business at some point during Richard's stay in Sicily: J. Gillingham, *Richard I* (New Haven, 1999), p. 138 n. 57

[4] Richard of Devizes, *Chronicon*, ed. and trans. J. T. Appleby (London, 1963), pp. 14–17, 19–25, 26, 27–8, 35–9, 42–5, 46–8, 52–3, 58, 73–84. See also Appleby's comments, pp. xvii–xviii. The transition between the relatively detailed and more schematic treatments occurs around the departure of Philip II from Acre, pp. 52–3, suggesting that Richard's best informant(s) left around the same time, perhaps in circumstances similar to those of Roger of Howden.

[5] See *Epistulae et chartae ad historiam primi belli sacri spectantes: Die Kreuzzugsbriefe aus den Jahren 1088–1100*, ed. H. Hagenmeyer (Innsbruck, 1901), esp. nos. 4, 8, 10, 12, 15–18, 21, pp. 138–40, 144–6, 149–52, 153–5, 156–74, 176–7; part trans. M. C. Barber and K. Bate, *Letters from the East: Crusaders, Pilgrims and Settlers in the*

have not survived. Around the time of the Third Crusade the volume of correspondence sent to western Europe either by crusaders or Franks who lived in Outremer seems to have been even greater, with the result that much of it fed into the historiographical interest that the crusade stimulated. Consequently, one sees the emergence of composite texts that were compiled by writers in the west but incorporated, by means of extensive close copying, adaptation or abridgement, materials produced by participants in events. The most significant example of this subgenre is the *Historia de expeditione Friderici imperatoris* (The History of the Expedition of the Emperor Frederick), our single most important narrative source for the response to the crusade appeal in Germany, the progress of the substantial expedition led by the emperor Frederick Barbarossa until his death in Asia Minor in June 1190, and the fate of the remnants of the expedition under the leadership of Barbarossa's son Frederick of Swabia, who himself died outside Acre in January 1191.[6] The *Historia de expeditione* has been shown to be a complex composite, incorporating and adapting material found in various newsletters from the east, including, perhaps, letters sent by Barbarossa himself, as well as a *memoria*, or memorandum, of the march through Asia Minor (up to a point just before the emperor's death) written by Tageno, dean of Passau in Bavaria.[7] Similarly, a second important narrative of the German crusade, the *Historia Peregrinorum* (History of the Pilgrims) is a composite compiled around 1200 on the basis of an early recension of the *Historia de expeditione* different from the version that survives, as well as newsletter materials.[8]

12th–13th Centuries (Crusade Sources in Translation, 18; Farnham, 2010), pp. 15–17, 18–21, 22–38.

[6] 'Historia de expeditione Friderici imperatoris', ed. A. Chroust, *Quellen zur Geschichte des Kreuzzuges Kaiser Friedrichs I.* (MGH Scriptores rerum Germanicarum, ns 5; Berlin, 1928), pp. 1–115; trans. G. A. Loud, *The Crusade of Frederick Barbarossa: The History of the Expedition of the Emperor Frederick and Related Texts* (Crusade Texts in Translation, 19; Farnham, 2010), pp. 33–134. The main body of the text is devoted to the expedition led by Barbarossa and, in less detail, its difficult onward progress under Frederick of Swabia. A briefer but not insubstantial concluding sequence tracks such events and processes as the subsequent conduct of the crusade in its Anglo-French phase, Richard I's captivity in Germany, and various impacts of the crusade upon the empire. The last datable event that is mentioned took place in 1196, and the text would seem to have been compiled very soon thereafter, most probably before the death of Barbarossa's successor Henry VI in September 1197. See Loud's helpful introductory remarks in *Crusade of Frederick Barbarossa*, pp. 1–7. The final compiler may have been an Austrian cleric named Ansbert.

[7] *Crusade of Frederick Barbarossa*, pp. 1–7. Tageno died in Tripoli in the autumn of 1190.

[8] *Crusade of Frederick Barbarossa*, pp. 7–8; 'Historia Peregrinorum', ed. Chroust, *Quellen zur Geschichte*, pp. 116–72; trans. Loud, *Crusade of Frederick Barbarossa*, pp. 135–47 (a translation of the first part of the text, up to the emperor's departure from Germany).

It is important to note that the difference between composite narratives and the sort of single-author texts with which this book is concerned is only one of degree, not of kind. Self-declared single-authored works of any length and complexity would necessarily have drawn upon a range of written and oral sources; the question was simply the extent to which the author was able or willing to superimpose substantive, thematic, structural and stylistic unity on materials assembled by various means. (It is noteworthy that one of the main clues as to the composite nature of the *Historia de expeditione* is stylistic, in particular shifts in rhythmic *cursus*, the sequencing of the stressed and unstressed syllables of the final words of each sentence in patterns chosen from a menu of possibilities, the choices functioning as a form of authorial 'signature'.) Perhaps the most important decision that confronted the creator of a single-authored eyewitness work was how to effect a double move: the construction of the narratorial persona vis-à-vis the story to be narrated; and the making of choices regarding the extent to which the details of the storyworld are authenticated either by appeal to the narrator's experience understood as a singularity – the experience, that is, of the detached observer in the manner of a 'lone reporter' – or by means of narratorial immersion in perceptual collectivities, within which the 'I' might in principle persist as a locus of seeing and understanding and can even be brought to the fore at various junctures, but is for the most part subsumed within an apprehending and focalizing 'we'. As we shall see, the *Estoire* is predominantly a skilful exercise in the collectively oriented approach. The staking out of direct eyewitness authority shades into an expansive and inclusive sense of participation and is alert to the experiences of others so as not to be constrained by the limitations of one person's observations. In this way, an emphasis on collective action and perception is effected over the course of the text. We have seen something similar in the Second Crusade narratives, but the *Estoire* represents a more intensive and sustained articulation of this narratorial strategy.

Points of Comparison and Contrast

Two closely contemporary texts, offering contrasting perspectives on many aspects of the Third Crusade, help to triangulate the *Estoire*'s particular mobilization of eyewitness authority and participant experience. They are worth considering in some detail as points of comparison and contrast. One is the *Narratio de itinere navali peregrinorum Hierosolymam tendentium et Silviam capientium, A.D. 1189* (The Story of the Sea Voyage of Those who Were Journeying to Jerusalem and Captured Silves in 1189). This much underrated text, which deserves more scholarly attention than it has received, is an account of the first stages of a voyage to the Holy Land undertaken by a fleet of northern German and other north-western European ships in response to the preaching of the cross.[9] Sailing from Bremen in April 1189, the original fleet of eleven ships stopped at various English ports and added local naval forces to their number; Flemish contingents mentioned at several points in the text may have joined them there if they had not done so earlier.[10] Leaving Dartmouth towards the end of May, the crusaders reached Lisbon in early July.[11] There they discovered that the members of another flotilla of northern European vessels, sailing four or five weeks ahead of them, had been co-opted by the Portuguese to assist in an attack on the Muslim fortress of Alvor in the Algarve. The attack had met with success and the inhabitants had been massacred. The later arrivals were similarly invited by King Sancho I, the son of the Afonso Henriques whom we met in the previous chapter, to participate in a campaign in the same region, this time against a more ambitious target, the town of Silves.[12] After a siege of a little over six weeks during which the northerners seem to have borne the brunt of the fighting – the *Narratio* suggests that the local Portuguese forces offered little or no meaningful assistance[13] – the town surrendered on 3 September.[14] After some wrangling over the division of spoils, and once repairs to the ships had been made, the

[9] 'Narratio de Itinere Navali Peregrinorum Hierosolyman Tendentium et Silviam Capientium, A.D. 1189', ed. C. W. David, *Proceedings of the American Philosophical Society,* 81 (1939), 591–676. David's edition, at 610–42, is generally superior to that found in 'Narratio itineris navalis ad Terram sanctam', ed. Chroust, *Quellen zur Geschichte*, pp. 179–96. As David, 'Narratio', 610 n. 1 explains, the title given to the work – there is none such in the single surviving manuscript – is of his own devising as an improvement upon those coined by Gazzera, who discovered the manuscript in 1837 and was the first to edit it, and Chroust. There is an excellent English translation in Loud, *Crusade of Frederick Barbarossa*, pp. 193–208.

[10] The text does not explicitly state that English contingents joined the fleet at this stage, but this is suggested by its statement that at Sandwich 'people joined us here and elsewhere', and by a later reference to English among the forces besieging Silves: 'Narratio', 611, 623, trans. Loud, *Crusade of Frederick Barbarossa*, pp. 193, 199.

[11] The translation of 'Narratio', 612 in Loud, *Crusade of Frederick Barbarossa*, p. 194 omits the sentence referring to Dartmouth, and consequently has the fleet leaving English waters from Yarmouth.

[12] The *Narratio* states that the earlier fleet was composed of forces from 'our empire' and Flanders: 'Narratio', 616, trans. Loud, *Crusade of Frederick Barbarossa*, p. 196. See also *Chronica Regia Coloniensis*, ed. G. Waitz (MGH Scriptores rerum Germanicarum in usum scholarum, 18; Hanover, 1880), pp. 142–3; Lambertus Parvus, 'Annales', *MGH SS*, 16, p. 649, which states that the force comprised Frisians, Danes, Flemings and men from Cologne and Liège. See also David's helpful appendix on the Alvor campaign in 'Narratio', 663–6.

[13] 'Narratio, 629–30, trans. Loud, *Crusade of Frederick Barbarossa*, p. 203. Cf. the Portuguese commander's misplaced doubts about the crusaders' ability to take Silves: 'Narratio', 619, trans. Loud, *Crusade of Frederick Barbarossa*, p. 197. The suggestion that the royal forces present at the siege contributed nothing to it is also found in Ralph of Diceto, *Opera Historica*, ed. W. Stubbs, 2 vols (RS 68; London, 1876), ii, p. 66.

[14] For the Silves campaign, see the useful account in S. Lay, *The Reconquest Kings of*

fleet continued on its way. The *Narratio* then takes the crusaders as far as the southern French coast. According to another source, Book I of the *Itinerarium Peregrinorum et Gesta Regis Ricardi*, which is, however, somewhat unclear on this point, the northerners in due course pressed on to Acre, where they made an important contribution to the Christian cause even though they suffered grievous casualties in the process.[15]

The exact date of the *Narratio*'s composition is unclear, but it was definitely written close to events.[16] The author, who is not named, was almost certainly a

---

Portugal: Political and Cultural Reorientation on the Medieval Frontier (Basingstoke, 2009), pp. 155–7.

[15] 'Itinerarium peregrinorum', ed. H. E. Mayer, *Das Itinerarium peregrinorum: Eine zeitgenössische englische Chronik zum dritten Kreuzzug in ursprünglicher Gestalt* (MGH Schriften, 18; Stuttgart, 1962), pp. 308–9; trans. H. J. Nicholson, *Chronicle of the Third Crusade: A Translation of the Itinerarium Peregrinorum et Gesta Regis Ricardi* (Crusade Texts in Translation, 3; Aldershot, 1997), pp. 73–4. The mention of Danes and Frisians in a leading role within the fleet (cf. n. 12 above), subsequently augmented by English and Flemish contingents inspired by their example, as well as the statements that the inhabitants of Silves were slaughtered (which they were not) and that a bishop was elected (which was the case at Silves but not Alvor), suggests that the author was conflating the experiences of the Alvor and Silves fleets. The whole of this passage presents grave problems of chronology, moreover, for its position in the narrative would seem to suggest that the fleet mentioned by the *Itinerarium* arrived at Acre in early September 1189, either with or immediately before James of Avesnes, who we know took part in a battle between the Christians besieging Acre and Saladin's forces on 4 October: see *The Conquest of Jerusalem and the Third Crusade: Sources in Translation*, trans. P. W. Edbury (Crusade Texts in Translation, 1; Aldershot, 1996), pp. 81–2, 170. According to the *Narratio*'s itinerary of its fleet's movements after leaving Silves, however, it was still at the opposite end of the Mediterranean, sailing east into the Straits of Gibraltar, at the end of September. It is therefore probable that it was the Alvor fleet, plus subsequent additions, that the author of Book I of the *Itinerarium* or an informant saw in 1189, and that the conflation with the Silves expedition occurred when ships from that fleet arrived later, probably early in the 1190 sailing season. Cf. Mayer's comments in *Das Itinerarium peregrinorum*, p. 309 nn. 4–5. For conflations of the two fleets in other texts, see David's remarks in 'Narratio', 664–6.

[16] At the point at which the crusade fleet is described reaching Lisbon, the narrator observes that the city had been captured forty-four years earlier: 'Narratio', 616, trans. Loud, *Crusade of Frederick Barbarossa*, p. 196. Chroust, *Quellen zur Geschichte*, p. ci and David, 'Narratio', 598–9, 616 n. 88 interpret this as a straightforward authorial or scribal error for forty-two years, the correct interval between the conquest of Lisbon and the arrival there, in July 1189, of the fleet that is the subject of the text. The possibility of eyeslip involving a nearby Roman numeral is suggested by the fact that twenty-four is given a few lines later for the number of vessels that the northerners encountered at Lisbon in addition to their own eleven. The use of the present tense ('Haec Ulixbona...ante quadraginta et IIII^{or} annos a peregrinis nostris capta...subiacet dominio [regis] Portugalensis'), however, suggests that the narrator – who is conspicuously precise and seemingly quite accurate with numbers and dates elsewhere – means

cleric and came from or identified closely with northern Germany.[17] There is no dedicatory epistle or other contextualizing front-matter to reveal why he wrote and for whom. It is possible that the text had its origins in a memorandum that narrated the fleet's progress as far as the western Mediterranean and was intended for circulation back home in northern Germany. That ships made log-like records of their movements – either as a matter of routine maritime practice or for commemorative reasons linked to the particular experience and demands of the crusade – is suggested by the sheer amount of geographical detail, especially concerning Spain and the western Mediterranean coast, that is included by Roger of Howden in his account of the very similar route taken by another northern crusade fleet, that assembled by King Richard I, in 1190. Roger did not travel east with that fleet, but he would have encountered it when it re-established contact with Richard I at Messina in September of that year; and he must have consulted a detailed written itinerary that had been drawn up during the voyage, in addition

---

the interval to be that between the conquest of 1147 and his own narratorial now. This would suggest, if forty-four is in fact the intended figure, that the author was writing in 1191 (or perhaps 1192, given that Lisbon fell quite late in 1147, in October), as first suggested by F. Kurth, 'Der Anteil niederdeutscher Kreuzfahrer an den Kämpfen der Portugiesen gegen die Mauren', *Mitteilungen des Instituts für Österreichische Geschichtsforschung: Ergänzungsband*, 8 (1911), 164–5. If so, it is likely that he was writing before he received news of the recapture of Silves by the Almohads in July 1191. An earlier date of composition, however, would seem to be suggested by the fact that the narrative as we have it ends quite abruptly but not unneatly with the crusaders reaching Montpellier and Marseilles, and this may be its intended conclusion, in possible support of which is the fact that there is unused blank space on the final folio of the surviving manuscript: 'Narratio', 642. The last date supplied by the text is 29 September, at which point the fleet is still west of the Straits of Gibraltar, having just left Cadiz and finding itself driven by adverse winds towards Tarifa. Nineteen further days of sailing are mentioned up to the point that the fleet reaches Marseilles; this must underrepresent the total duration, allowing for lay-overs: 'Narratio', 640–2, trans. Loud, *Crusade of Frederick Barbarossa*, pp. 207–8. It is therefore unlikely that the fleet could have reached the southern French coast before the last week of October, by which time continuing the voyage to Palestine over the winter months would have been impractical. It is thus possible that the *Narratio* was written, while events were still fresh in the author's mind, in or near Marseilles over the winter of 1189–90.

[17] The point of departure for the fleet is said to be Bremen, which thereby serves as the jumping-off point for the narrative proper; and the deaths of two men from that city are particularly noted: 'Narratio', 610–11, 618, trans. Loud, *Crusade of Frederick Barbarossa*, pp. 193, 196. Silves is compared to Goslar, and the width of the Tagus at Lisbon is measured against that of the Elbe at Stade: 'Narratio', 616, 619, trans. Loud, *Crusade of Frederick Barbarossa*, pp. 195, 197. Other references, however, speak in terms of a broader German or imperial identification: 'Narratio', 616, trans. Loud, *Crusade of Frederick Barbarossa*, p. 196 ('naves de nostro imperio et de Flandria'); 618, trans. Loud, *Crusade of Frederick Barbarossa*, p. 196 ('miliare Teutonicum'); 623, trans. Loud, *Crusade of Frederick Barbarossa*, p. 199 ('nos de regno Teutonico').

to speaking to participants about the chequered history of their various interventions in Portuguese affairs.[18] It is possible that the germ of the *Narratio* was a similar record of the fleet's movements, expanded and revised to accommodate an account of the siege of Silves and the events surrounding it. However, the text's conventional prefatory remarks about the importance of recording events for posterity, and its situating of the gathering of the fleet in the general context of the response to the preaching of the crusade, both moves that would have been redundant and overblown in a straightforward newsletter, suggest that the author or reviser of the text in its surviving form was aiming for a self-standing historiographical exercise.[19]

The fleet that took part in the conquest of Silves was only one of a number of such naval forces, big and small, that assembled in response to the preaching of the crusade.[20] But it is the actions of the Silves forces that most obviously recall the circumstances of the conquest of Lisbon in 1147. Indeed, the *Narratio* itself establishes a close connection between the two campaigns by remarking that the taking of Lisbon had been the work of *peregrini nostri*.[21] It is possible, though very unlikely, that the author had read the *De expugnatione Lyxbonensi*; if he had come across any written account of the events of 1147 it would probably have been one of the variants of the Lisbon Letter. There is one tantalizing intersection with the *De expugnatione* in the narrator's remark, immediately after he has reported the fleet's arrival at Lisbon, that at the nearby castle of Sintra mares conceive from the wind, the resultant foals proving very swift but never living beyond the age of eight; the former of these two observations is very close to a statement made by the *De expugnatione* reworking Solinus.[22] This would not seem to be a case of direct borrowing, however, but rather a matter of name- or

[18] Roger of Howden, *Chronica*, iii, pp. 42–51. The list-like sequence describing the fleet's movements past Lisbon at pp. 46–51 is absent from Roger's original account of its voyage in *Gesta Regis*, ii, pp. 115–22.

[19] 'Narratio', 610, trans. Loud, *Crusade of Frederick Barbarossa*, p. 193.

[20] The narrator implies that the fleet of eleven ships that he says left Bremen should not be considered the totality of those ('quibusdam') who chose to undertake their pilgrimage by sea: 'Narratio', 610, trans. Loud, *Crusade of Frederick Barbarossa*, p. 193.

[21] 'Narratio', 616, trans. Loud, *Crusade of Frederick Barbarossa*, p. 196. See also 'Narratio', 642, trans. Loud, *Crusade of Frederick Barbarossa*, p. 208 ('tempore quo Ulixbona a nostris est capta'), which establishes that *nostri* is to be understood in contrast to the southern European forces (Pisans and Genoese are singled out) that took Tortosa around the same time. For the conquest of Tortosa, see N. Jaspert, '*Capta est Dertosa, clavis Christianorum*: Tortosa and the Crusades', in J. P. Phillips and M. Hoch (eds), *The Second Crusade: Scope and Consequences* (Manchester, 2001), pp. 90–110; J. P. Phillips, *The Second Crusade: Extending the Frontiers of Christendom* (New Haven, 2007), pp. 261–3.

[22] 'Narratio', 616, trans. Loud, *Crusade of Frederick Barbarossa*, pp. 195–6; *De expugnatione*, p. 92. See above, pp. 152–3.

place-recognition, the trotting out of what in the decades since the conquest of Lisbon and its opening up to Christian maritime contacts must have become a clichéd word-association. Elsewhere in the text of the *Narratio* the narrator displays an interest in the cultic, political and human geography of the Iberian peninsula, as well as an awareness of the impact of his and the Alvor fleets on the Portuguese Christians' military situation, but he does so without recourse to the Solinus-esque lore beloved of the *De expugnatione*.

The *Narratio* differs from the *De expugnatione* more subtly in its handling of the question of leadership, although there are indications that the organization of the two expeditions was not dissimilar; the 1189 fleet may even have drawn directly on the example of 1147 in matters of self-regulation, given that Dartmouth was its port of departure from English waters and would seem to have been a pre-arranged rendezvous point.[23] In the previous chapter we saw that the *De expugnatione* walks a fine line between acknowledging the leadership roles of prominent figures such as Hervey de Glanvill and Saher of Archelle and affirming a sense of collective agency, as programmatically anticipated in the Dartmouth Rules. In contrast, as a matter of narratorial design or as a reflection of the actual composition of the fleet's personnel – probably a combination of the two – the *Narratio* makes no mention of individual leaders. Nor is explicit reference made to contracted and sworn regulations, although it is highly likely that the fleet assembled, retained its cohesion and absorbed new arrivals on such a basis. That there was some such regulatory framework is suggested by the fact that the fleet is at one point in the text described in terms redolent of a military unit, while there are also references to *magistri* and *magistratus* with powers of command.[24] In addition, at several junctures the *Narratio* speaks of acts of decision-making and strategizing in ways that suggest mechanisms to identify and pursue collective goals as well as to negotiate as a single body with the Portuguese king and his lieutenants.[25] Ralph of Diceto, who seems to have been quite well informed

[23] See 'Narratio', 612, trans. Loud, *Crusade of Frederick Barbarossa*, p. 194: 'Ibi [Dartmouth] inventis quibusdam sociis, mane dimissa Anglia versus Britanniam processimus.'

[24] 'Narratio', 617 (where a galley from Tuy joins their *contubernium*), 621, 632, trans. Loud, *Crusade of Frederick Barbarossa*, pp. 196, 198, 204.

[25] 'Narratio', 618–19, 621 (a decision is reached, 'consilium inivimus', to attack the following day), 626 (a collective decision to persist with the siege is made: 'nostri decreverunt communiter diutius hostes Christi impugnare'), 627, 628 (King Sancho tries to secure the northerners' consent to the terms of surrender that he has negotiated: 'consensum rex extorquere a peregrinis sategit'), 631–2, 633 (the Portuguese commander fails to secure the crusaders' 'communem assensum' to his suggestion that they prolong their stay in order to take part in a campaign against Faro), trans. Loud, *Crusade of Frederick Barbarossa*, pp. 197, 198, 201, 202, 204, 205. See also the references to members of the fleet as *socii* in 'Narratio', 612, 613, trans. Loud, *Crusade of Frederick Barbarossa*, p. 194; and David's remarks, 'Narratio', 603–4.

about the fleet's adventures, provides further evidence that the crusaders were sufficiently well organized and self-regulating to be able to plan purposively on the basis of consensus and to adapt flexibly to new opportunities. He notes that the crews of the ships that had assembled 'from northern parts' entered into a formal agreement (*foedus*) with the English whom they encountered at Dartmouth;[26] and a measure of legal formality in the fleet's interactions with the Portuguese is implied by Ralph's statement that three bishops stood surety for the *pactum* concerning the division of spoils to which King Sancho himself swore.[27]

As is suggested by the varying figures for the numbers of ships that one encounters even within this single text, and in light of the long distances that the fleets travelled as well as the difficulties of co-ordination and communication that they faced once out to sea, the composition of the large northern fleets that were brought into being by the Third Crusade must have been constantly shifting. There would have been fluctuations of numbers caused by enforced lay-overs for repairs and reprovisioning, time spent waiting for stragglers, and losses and defections, as well as dispersals because of storms; the scattering of flotillas because of bad weather in the Bay of Biscay seems to have been a recurrent problem. The effect of the *De expugnatione* and the *Narratio* is, however, to transcend at least some of the fluidity that must have attended such collective endeavours in practice. They do so by dwelling on the theme of corporate identity and cohesion and, where required by the plot, its vulnerability to fracture: first by the simple expedient of shifting the naval forces to land-based military operations, where they are relatively static and necessarily occupy a restricted space over an extended period; and second by focusing on acts of collective agency

[26] *Opera Historica*, ii, pp. 65–6. As an indication of the accuracy of Ralph's sources of information, the total for the force at Silves that he gives, 3,500 (p. 66), is the same figure supplied by 'Narratio', 630, trans. Loud, *Crusade of Frederick Barbarossa*, p. 203 for the northerners' numbers at the start of the siege. Ralph states (p. 66) that 13,000 inhabitants of Silves were still alive when the city surrendered; the equivalent figure in 'Narratio', 629, trans. Loud, *Crusade of Frederick Barbarossa*, p. 203 is 15,800. On the other hand, Ralph's figure for the size of the fleet when it left Dartmouth, thirty-seven ships, is significantly higher than the eleven which the *Narratio* insists comprised the original force, though the addition of English and perhaps Flemish forces would account for at least some of the difference; while his total of thirty-seven for the galleys, in addition to several other vessels, contributed by the king of Portugal (p. 65) is greater than the twenty-four ships, presumably local vessels, some of them recently back from the expedition against Alvor, that the *Narratio* states the northerners came upon on their arrival at Lisbon: 'Narratio', 616, trans. Loud, *Crusade of Frederick Barbarossa*, p. 196 (which incorrectly has forty-four ships).

[27] *Opera Historica*, ii, pp. 65–6. The *Narratio* makes direct reference to this *prima convencio* with the Portuguese only retrospectively, when its terms are revisited after the surrender of the city: 'Narratio', 631–2, trans. Loud, *Crusade of Frederick Barbarossa*, pp. 204–5.

that are directed towards clearly identified goals. (The actors in the *De expugnatione* and *Narratio* are, indeed, among the most purposeful and motivated, in plot terms, in all crusade literature.) One way to explain the subject group's conspicuous goal-directedness was to link it back to the institutional framework within which the fleet was originally assembled and organized: by means of such a device, all the subsequent action in effect becomes a progressive working through of this inaugural motif.

Although there are various clues pointing towards such a framework in the *Narratio*, however, the text's thematic emphases lie elsewhere. The clearest demonstrations of its preference are the absence of a passage equivalent to that which sets out some of the Dartmouth Rules in the *De expugnatione*; and the very perfunctory manner in which the *Narratio* deals with Sancho I's invitation to take part in the campaign against Silves and the decision to accept it. This latter is in stark contrast to the extended wooing of the 1147 crusaders by the bishop of Oporto and Afonso Henriques that we saw is a central plot element in the *De expugnatione*, a crux which forces the crusaders to confront questions of their collective purpose and the nature of their responsibilities both to one another and to the wider crusade enterprise. In the *Narratio* it is, if anything, simply the desire to emulate the example set by the Alvor fleet a few weeks earlier that motivates the new arrivals.[28] If, then, the Silves fleet is, institutionally and organizationally speaking, a relatively hazy entity – at least by the standards set by the *De expugnatione* – we shall see that the *Narratio* nonetheless emphasizes the crusaders' cohesion by other means, drawing sustained attention to the unified quality of their actions and experiences. This is a discursive positioning in which the construction of the narratorial voice proves to be key.

Within the *Narratio* interventions by the narrator by means of verbs in the first person singular are very few, although there is one important exception to this rule, self-highlightingly placed at the very beginning of the text in its prefatory remarks. Here the narrator announces himself in insisting that his straightforward account of what took place is a matter of deliberate design in the interests of clarity: 'multiformes eventus...simpliciter explicare decrevi'.[29] The note of considered planning sounded by the verb *decrevi* alerts the reader to the idea that there is a single, and reflective, intelligence guiding the narration of events; by extension the reader is primed to expect that if the narrator retreats from overt individual participation in the storyworld, this is to be construed as a deliberate move. Thereafter in the body of the text, and by way of a brief reminder wrapped up in a formulaic utterance, the first person singular resurfaces just once, in a slightly disingenuous disavowal of knowledge (which is immediately qualified) about why the Muslim defenders of Silves chose to throw some of their dead

[28] 'Narratio', 617, trans. Loud, *Crusade of Frederick Barbarossa*, p. 196.
[29] 'Narratio', 610, trans. Loud, *Crusade of Frederick Barbarossa*, p. 193.

outside the town walls.[30] Apart from these two instances, the *Narratio*'s use of the first person, which is much in evidence throughout the text and is in many sequences the dominant means by which the action is narrated, is always in the plural.

As was noted in the previous chapter, the narratorial focus on co-ordinated movement and collective purpose lends itself to the use of the first person plural in the *De expugnatione*'s narration of the fleet's passage from Dartmouth to Lisbon. It is therefore unsurprising that the *Narratio* adopts a similar approach, and by means of much the same lexical set. Without pausing to clarify whom exactly the reader should understand by 'we', the text moves immediately from its prefatory and contextualizing remarks to a long and concentrated sequence of verbs in the first person plural in order to narrate the departure and progress of the fleet. The emphasis throughout is on what all the crusaders achieve.[31] The use of the first person plural easily extends from the passage of the fleet to second-order group actions undertaken during it, such as the celebration of Pentecost and a pilgrimage to Santiago de Compostela.[32] And it likewise carries over into the narration of the siege itself. Although the transition from sea to land, and from collective movement to more complex forms of group action and interaction in a much more stationary and confined environment, is signalled by a greater layering of verb forms, with frequent intercutting between the first and third persons plural, the focus on the crusaders as primary agents is sustained. In large part this is because the inertia that the narrator attributes to the Portuguese means that they take little active part in the siege operations and fighting. Additionally, it is noteworthy that the preponderance of the first person plural reintensifies once the siege is over and the crusaders resume their voyage.[33]

In this way, the narrator firmly aligns himself with the crusade force viewed as a single entity. There are, however, some indications in the text that gradations of value lie underneath the surface attention to the actions of *nos* and *nostri*. Thus, there is a suggestion that the precipitate actions of some of the crusaders, first in manhandling and despoiling Muslims as they leave the town even though they

[30] 'Narratio', 622, trans. Loud, *Crusade of Frederick Barbarossa*, p. 198.

[31] For example, the opening sequence, 'Narratio', 611, trans. Loud, *Crusade of Frederick Barbarossa*, p. 193 reads: 'iter movimus…velificavimus…venimus…transsivimus'.

[32] 'Narratio', pp. 612 ('Pentcosten…celebravimus'), 615 ('limina sancti Iacobi… visitavimus'); trans. Loud, *Crusade of Frederick Barbarossa*, pp. 194, 195. See also 'Narratio', 611, trans. Loud, *Crusade of Frederick Barbarossa*, p. 193 ('in Lundonia navim comparavimus').

[33] E.g. 'Narratio', 632 ('naves conscendimus et lente versus mare processimus'), 632 ('moram in portu fecimus'), 635 ('portum Silvie exivimus'), 638 ('in salo fluctu-avimus'), 639 ('velis innisi ventorum adversitate impediamur'), 640 ('prospero cursu has civitates transsivimus'), trans. Loud, *Crusade of Frederick Barbarossa*, pp. 205, 206, 207.

are protected by the terms of surrender, and then with respect to the division of booty (albeit as a reaction to pressure from the Portuguese), help to create the conditions in which King Sancho is able to leave the northerners with much less than was originally agreed.[34] There are also moments in which the composite nature of the crusade army is allowed to emerge. For example, the narrator makes a point of including the detail that it was English members of the expedition who killed a 'Saracen' in full view of his besieged coreligionists ('in oculis eorum qui obsessi erant') and in so doing triggered the tit-for-tat torture and killing of three Christian captives, once more performed for the benefit of the communal gaze ('nobis videntibus'). This negative mention is the only reference to English participants in the siege army, in fact.[35] In a similar vein, the narrator singles out members of the Flemish contingent for censure at two points: for introducing the 'vexation of dissension' ('molestia dissensionis') in wishing to withdraw from a hard-won forward position; and for selling wheat to the Portuguese contrary to the agreed arrangements for the division of the spoils found in Silves.[36]

There are also hints of strategic disagreements within the crusade army, even as the text mostly insists on the crusaders' unanimity and shared sense of purpose. In reviewing the progress of the siege once it is over, the narrator concedes that the majority of the crusade force had at some unspecified point or points become discouraged and therefore wanted to leave, though it is implied that this was the result of their having been unduly influenced by the Portuguese soldiers' reluctance to persevere.[37] Divisions also surface at a few specific moments. Once the crusaders have quit Silves and resumed their voyage, there is an attempt to launch an opportunist assault on Tarifa, further east along the southern coast of the Iberian peninsula, but the fact that agreement cannot be reached, along with bad weather and the absence of part of the fleet, aborts the undertaking.[38] Similarly, in listing the places that the fleet passes once it has left Silves, the narrator makes a rare appeal to counterfactual argument in stating that the whole region, the Algarve, would have been easily captured but for the king's hatred – which is not further explained, but is at least consonant with the negative representations of the Portuguese found at earlier points in the text – and what is allusively termed the 'execrable rush of some of our people'.[39]

[34] 'Narratio', 628–9, 631–2, trans. Loud, *Crusade of Frederick Barbarossa*, pp. 202–3, 204–5.

[35] 'Narratio', 623, trans. Loud, *Crusade of Frederick Barbarossa*, p. 199.

[36] 'Narratio', 623–4, 632, trans. Loud, *Crusade of Frederick Barbarossa*, pp. 199, 204. Cf. 'Narratio', 627, trans. Loud, *Crusade of Frederick Barbarossa*, p. 202, where a Portuguese threat to abandon the siege stirs up a great 'perturbationis molestia'.

[37] 'Narratio', 629–30, trans. Loud, *Crusade of Frederick Barbarossa*, p. 203.

[38] 'Narratio', 639–40, trans. Loud, *Crusade of Frederick Barbarossa*, p. 207.

[39] 'Narratio', 636, trans. Loud, *Crusade of Frederick Barbarossa*, p. 206: 'quorundam nostrum [*recte* nostrorum] execranda festinatio': my translation. For the one other

It would be going too far to suppose that these remarks reveal a principled disagreement over the nature of their vocation between those crusaders who prioritized war against the infidel, wherever opportunities for it might present themselves, and those who foregrounded the notion of pilgrimage to the Holy Land, for the sense of 'rush' is probably to be explained by the fact that it was already September and it would therefore have been uncertain whether the fleet still had time in that year's sailing season to reach the eastern Mediterranean. But the narrator's comments at least suggest the potential for the sorts of policy disagreements that are brought to the surface of the *De expugnatione*, as we have seen, but are largely occluded in the *Narratio*.[40]

Nonetheless, the efficacy of concerted (and divinely favoured) endeavour is the text's dominant theme. Contrastive binaries between the northerners and their Muslim foes and Portuguese allies – the latter more so than the former – do much more narrative work than internal divisions and conflicts of interest. In all this the narrator scrupulously effaces suggestions of focalization specific to an individual observer. The crusaders' self-awareness, perceptions and achievements are conspicuously those of the group as a whole.[41] It is significant that in the passage that most obviously breaks with the emphasis on communal agency, or at least has the potential to do so, when a lone knight bravely exposes himself to enemy fire as he advances to the town wall in order to dislodge the cornerstone of a tower, this figure is not named; instead, his individual heroics are promptly reabsorbed into the machinery of group effort with the narrator's remark that he was from Galicia and had served as the pilot of one of the ships, and that his actions inspired others to finish off the undermining of the tower.[42] The text's emphasis upon collective action elides into collective experience: the crusaders learn of matters that affect them as a unit, even in those situations, such as when refugees from Silves describe what conditions were like within the besieged town, where only a fraction of the total numbers of the army could have been directly involved.[43]

counterfactual in the text, see 'Narratio', 627, trans. Loud, *Crusade of Frederick Barbarossa*, p. 201.

[40] See above, pp. 135, 136, 145, 147–8.

[41] E.g. 'Narratio', 622 ('possedimus civitatem inferiorem'), 631 ('Capta civitate soli nos Franci possedimus eam'), trans. Loud, *Crusade of Frederick Barbarossa*, pp. 198, 204.

[42] 'Narratio', 624, trans. Loud, *Crusade of Frederick Barbarossa*, pp. 199–200. Cf. the narrator's failure to name the field commander of the Portuguese forces, the *princeps milicie [regis]*, though this is a detail that must have been widely known: 'Narratio', 619, 633, trans. Loud, *Crusade of Frederick Barbarossa*, pp. 197, 205.

[43] E.g. 'Narratio', 611 ('tres naves ex collisione super arenas perdidimus'), 613 ('novem dies in alto fluctuantes exegimus'), 614 ('Ibidem invenimus archam reppletam diversis magna veneratione dignis et sanctorum reliquiis'), 616 ('Ibi invenimus naves XXIIII^{or}'), 629 ('vix invenimus vivos ducentos'), trans. Loud, *Crusade of Frederick*

The focus on collective experience also shades into assertions of collective emotion and morale. Thus, for example, the narrator emphasizes the shared grief caused by the sight of three Christian captives suspended upside down from the walls: 'We sorrowfully lamented the death of our men, but were by this roused to wage war more fiercely.'[44] Similarly, we are informed that after the disappointment of a failed assault on 22 July, which had led the crusaders to burn part of the town that they had already captured out of sheer frustration, later that same day they took heart and their warlike resolve returned, emboldening them to move their camp to a more forward position.[45] There are several details in the narrative which one suspects must have been grounded in the author's own personal observations, and which in other hands might have been recounted as autobiographical reminiscences, but are nonetheless routed through collective focalization: for example, the appearance of flying fish, probably in fact dolphins, in the Bay of Biscay, and the sighting of 'two candles' during a storm, perhaps an incidence of St Elmo's Fire.[46] Similarly, the narrator's detailed attention to the condition and behaviour of a Muslim escapee from Silves – he jumps over the wall, then buries his face in the water he is given, such is his extreme thirst – implies that the author was an eyewitness to this particular incident. But if so, this is not explicitly stated.[47]

There are relatively few direct references in the text to acts of visual perception, but it is significant that those that are introduced similarly reinforce the theme of collective agency and experience. Most of the situations in which the narrator uses 'we saw' (*vidimus*) or similar constructions involve a communal ship-to-shore gaze upon aspects of the physical, political and human geography that the fleet encounters, such as stretches of rugged coastline, high inland peaks, the deserted remains of Alvor and the reactions of Muslims on a beach in anticipation of an

---

Barbarossa, pp. 193, 194, 196, 203. For collective acts of discovery, see 'Narratio', 616–17 concerning the very large number of those slain at Alvor ('sicut veraciter audivimus'), 622 for the news that those Muslims who had been first to flee back into the city during the Christian attack on the lower walls were executed by their leader ('[nuntiatum] nobis erat'), 628 on reports of escapees about conditions in the city ('plures Sarraceni fuga elapsi ad nos venerunt dicentes'), 629 on reports of freed Christian captives ('sicut nobis retulerunt'), trans. Loud, *Crusade of Frederick Barbarossa*, pp. 196, 198, 202, 203.

44 'Narratio', 623, trans. Loud, *Crusade of Frederick Barbarossa*, p. 199: 'Unde lacrimosa compassione doluimus et ad bellandum magis exasperati sumus.'

45 'Narratio', 622–3, trans. Loud, *Crusade of Frederick Barbarossa*, p. 199: 'Concepta igitur spe frustrati, inconsulcius quam deceret, districtis animis, captam civitatem, quantum potuimus, concremavimus…Sed eodem die resumptis animis et bellandi constancia, castra iuxta murum capte urbis posuimus.' Cf. the reference to the crusaders returning to camp after battle 'communiter leti': 'Narratio', 625, trans. Loud, *Crusade of Frederick Barbarossa*, p. 200.

46 'Narratio', 613, trans. Loud, *Crusade of Frederick Barbarossa*, p. 194.

47 'Narratio', 626, trans. Loud, *Crusade of Frederick Barbarossa*, p. 201.

attack.[48] Similarly, while there are few narrated acts of seeing over the course of the siege operations, it is noteworthy that the siege begins in an act of collective perception as the crusaders drop anchor in a position that affords a clear view of Silves. That night, the inhabitants of the town light numerous fires, whereupon the crusaders do the same, effectively matching visual impression for visual impression: 'Our people were joyful, and not deterred by the fact that they saw that the place was extremely strongly fortified.'[49] It is significant that at the one point in the text in which the Portuguese Christians collectively function as focalizers, they do so out of character, contrary to the prevailing tone of disjunction between themselves and the crusaders, as they cast an appreciative eye on the northerners' achievement in undermining a tower and overcoming resistance by the defenders:

> A host of the enemy manned these battlements, but the Lord gave strength to our men and struck fear into them, so that they all fled as one, while the king and his men on the other side of the hill were enormously thrilled by the spectacle of this action [*huius rei spectaculo*] and offered praises to express their great admiration of our people.[50]

The most lingering and reflective gaze in the text is again a collective act. In a sequence redolent of passages in the *De expugnatione* in which the narrator evokes the desperate plight of the Muslim inhabitants of Lisbon after its fall,[51] we are told that those defeated at Silves present a pitiful sight:

> The next morning they were led out more kindly from the three gates, and then we saw for the first time how weak they were, for they were extremely thin and could barely walk. Many were crawling; others were helped by our men, while some were lying in the squares, either dead or barely alive, and there was an awful smell from the bodies of both men and of brute animals in the city.[52]

In this way the protagonists' most sustained, penetrative and reflective act of focalization is in the service of the text's clear insistence on the actions and achievements of what it terms *totus exercitus noster*.[53]

[48] 'Narratio', 615, 617, 639, 641, trans. Loud, *Crusade of Frederick Barbarossa*, pp. 195, 196, 207, 208.
[49] 'Narratio', 619, trans. Loud, *Crusade of Frederick Barbarossa*, p. 197: translation revised.
[50] 'Narratio', 624–5, trans. Loud, *Crusade of Frederick Barbarossa*, p. 200: translation revised.
[51] *De expugnatione*, pp. 178, 180.
[52] 'Narratio', 629, trans. Loud, *Crusade of Frederick Barbarossa*, p. 203.
[53] See 'Narratio', 626, trans. Loud, *Crusade of Frederick Barbarossa*, p. 201.

The other narrative source that serves as a helpful point of comparison and contrast with Ambroise's *Estoire* is *al-Nawādir al-Sultāniyya wa'l-Mahāsin al-Yūsufiyya* (usually rendered in English as 'The Rare and Excellent History of Saladin'), a monograph on the sultan Saladin's career between 1187, the year of his greatest victories over the Latins in the East, and 1193, the year of his death, by Bahā' al-Dīn Ibn Shaddād.[54] Bahā' al-Dīn (1145–1234) was a noted religious scholar and jurist who entered Saladin's service in 1188, first as *qādī al-'askar*, or judge of the army, and thereafter in a number of positions of responsibility. The trust placed in him by the Ayyubid elite is indicated by the fact that he frequently acted as a go-between between Saladin and members of his family and as a political mediator.[55] The narratorial stance of the *Nawādir* differs from that of the *Narratio* in important respects. In the first place, the action is dominated by the central protagonist. Although there are several other individuals who play significant roles, most conspicuously members of Saladin's family when acting as his lieutenants, and ample space is also allowed for collective agents in the narration of the military activity that takes up a large part of the text, the focus consistently, and insistently, remains on Saladin throughout. In this connection, it has been suggested that the *Nawādir*'s laudatory biographical approach draws some of its inspiration from the mirror-of-princes tradition in Arabic literature as well as the *manāqib*, a genre devoted to expatiating on an individual's moral qualities.[56]

In narratological terms, such a firm foregrounding of Saladin's actions in the storyworld translates into a dominant role for him as focalizer. The range of Saladin's focalization is noteworthy: it encompasses the shrewd and fair-minded assessment of other parties' motivations, which proves a useful skill in the sultan's handling of the sometimes delicate relations with members of his family and the emirs on whose political and military support he relies; and, in light of the narrative's emphasis on military affairs, it includes the ability to anticipate, appraise and react to sometimes fast-moving tactical situations as well as a superior strategic vision, even though this is sometimes compromised in order to accommodate the needs of the emirs and the rank-and-file. At a higher order of focalization, Saladin also inspires and embodies the text's ideological programme in his devotion to *jihad*. Indeed, Bahā' al-Dīn makes a point of stating that around the time that he entered Saladin's service, he presented his new master with a treatise that he had written on this subject. As Bahā' al-Dīn further notes, Saladin received many such works – writing on his favourite topic

[54] Bahā' al-Dīn Ibn Shaddād, *The Rare and Excellent History of Saladin or al-Nawādir al-Sultāniyya wa'l-Mahāsin al-Yūsufiyya*, trans. D. S. Richards (Crusade Texts in Translation, 7; Aldershot, 2002).

[55] *Rare and Excellent History*, pp. 135, 145, 187–8, 190, 201, 202, 233–4, 237.

[56] D. S. Richards, 'A Consideration of Two Sources for the Life of Saladin', *Journal of Semitic Studies*, 25 (1980), 51–4.

must have been a good way to earn his favour – but this statement is nonetheless one of the most significant remarks in the whole text, for it sets up the narrator as more than simply an intelligent observer of the events taking place around him; he is also conspicuously well equipped to 'read' Saladin in the light of the ideological programme that scaffolds the narration.[57] Additionally, although at several junctures the narrator switches to the first person and inserts himself as a character into the storyworld, the element of autobiographical recall that this introduces seldom gets in the way of the primary attention on Saladin: there are no analepses concerning Bahā' al-Dīn's life before he became attached to Saladin's household, nor are there more than a few, brief cut-aways to a life led in a private space detached from the public domain of warfare, politics and diplomacy that Saladin dominates.[58] On the other hand, the narrator-as-character's entry into the diegesis and his interactions with the sultan are sufficiently frequent to become a signature motif that enhances the authority of the text.

Bahā' al-Dīn's monograph is one of a number of works of Arabic historiography that are either focused on Saladin, and so by extension on the events surrounding the Third Crusade, or situate his career and achievements within a wider chronological and geographical frame of reference. The richness of this body of material is such that the Third Crusade is probably the major crusading enterprise for which there is the best equipoise between eyewitness narratives from the opposing sides. There must have been many occasions when, for example, Ambroise and Bahā' al-Dīn were no more than a few hundred yards apart, observing fundamentally the same sequence of events, though of course they brought very different cultural assumptions both to their apperception and their subsequent narrativization of what took place. The confluence of the Muslim and Latin Christian source bases for the Third Crusade is such that they not only match one another quite closely with respect to the timing and sequence of major events and the whereabouts and actions of the main protagonists at numerous junctures, they also retail the same sort of incidents, including anecdotes that serve no major plot purpose but which have some noteworthy or illustrative quality. Such shared details, functioning as mnemonic hooks, speak to the ability of both sides' collective memories to fasten onto similar incidents and to develop similar instincts about the manner in which discrete events, even the seemingly trivial, concretized and exemplified larger strands of experience and perception.

Within the Arabic historiography dealing with the events leading up to the Third Crusade and the crusade itself, two authors other than Bahā' al-Dīn stand out. One is Ibn al-Athīr (1160–1223), whose well-known *al-Kāmil fi'l-ta'rīkh*,

[57] *Rare and Excellent History*, p. 28. See also p. 81.

[58] See e.g. Bahā' al-Dīn's brief mention of his withdrawing to his own tent between periods of attendance on Saladin: *Rare and Excellent History*, p. 211.

or 'The Complete Work of History', is a universal chronicle of Muslim history from the Creation to the present day.[59] Ibn al-Athīr was a member of a family with traditions of administrative service to the Zankid dynasty, under whose aegis Saladin had originally risen to prominence but which he later opposed. There is no evidence that Ibn al-Athīr ever served Saladin directly, though other former Zankid followers made the transition to supporting Saladin after the death of Nūr al-Dīn in 1174. Indeed, there is an element of criticism in his treatment of the sultan. Although it is difficult to detect the 'notorious' bias against Saladin that Sir Hamilton Gibb found in the *Kāmil*, there is certainly disapproval of Saladin's failure to capture Tyre when the momentum of his conquests was at its greatest after his victory at Hattin, thereby leaving the Franks a toehold on the Levantine coast. There are also suggestions that the sultan could fall prey to poor advice, sometimes mismanaged resources, and misread his followers' morale.[60] Ibn al-Athīr was interested in events across the Muslim world, from India to north Africa and Spain; he notes, for example, the fall of Silves and its recapture by the Almohads in 1191.[61] But the focus of the *Kāmil* for the period of Saladin's conquests and the Frankish reaction is, as in most of the text as a whole, on the Levantine world. Much of his treatment of this period is, as Gibb observed, derivative – he drew heavily on two works by the third author to be considered here, 'Imād al-Dīn – but it also includes original material.[62]

In addition to consulting the memories of people in his circle,[63] Ibn al-Athīr was able to draw on his direct experience for a period of several months in

[59] See *The Chronicle of Ibn al-Athīr for the Crusading Period from al-Kamīl fi'l-ta'rīkh*, trans. D. S. Richards, 3 vols (Crusade Texts in Translation, 13, 15, 17; Aldershot, 2006–8), i, pp. 1–5.

[60] *Chronicle of Ibn al-Athīr*, ii, pp. 328, 337–8, 365, 368, 380. But for a more positive appraisal, see *ibid.*, ii, pp. 408–9. See H. A. R. Gibb, 'The Arabic Sources for the Life of Saladin', *Speculum*, 25 (1950), 58–72; and the somewhat different verdict in D. S. Richards, 'Ibn al-Athīr and the Later Parts of the *Kāmil*: A Study of Aims and Methods', in D. O. Morgan (ed.), *Medieval Historical Writing in the Christian and Islamic Worlds* (London, 1982), pp. 76–108.

[61] *Chronicle of Ibn al-Athīr*, ii, pp. 381–2.

[62] For Ibn al-Athīr's debt to 'Imād al-Dīn, see Gibb, 'Arabic Sources', 60–70; Richards, 'Ibn al-Athīr', p. 91. For his use of earlier historians, see also H. A. R. Gibb, 'Notes on the Arabic Materials for the History of the Early Crusades', *Bulletin of the School of Oriental Studies*, 7 (1935), 745–54.

[63] See e.g. *Chronicle of Ibn al-Athīr*, ii, p. 395, in which details of Saladin's meeting with the Seljuq prince Mu'izz al-Dīn, in the autumn of 1191, reach him via 'someone I trust'; ii, p. 399, where the account of the Franks' interception of a large caravan from Egypt in June 1192, an event that is made much of in both Christian and Muslim sources, includes a passage of quoted testimony from 'one of our associates, with whom we had sent something to Egypt for trading and who had travelled back in this caravan'. Cf. the mentions in *Chronicle of Ibn al-Athīr*, ii, p. 364 of the (unfortunately undeveloped) reminiscences of a Muslim who had formerly served the Franks and

1188 during which, as he tells us, he was 'in Syria with Saladin's army with the intention of serving in the *jihad*'.[64] This autopsy translates into narrative sequences that are fuller than elsewhere in the text's treatment of Saladin's last years: for example, the siege of the Frankish castle of Bourzey (Hisn Barziyya), which occupied Saladin's forces for only a few days in August 1188, is the subject of an extended sequence.[65] This siege, however, like the rest of the narration of Saladin's military activities, is related in the third person by a narrator who is largely detached, while intradiegetic self-insertions into the storyworld in the first person tend to be limited to visually striking but minor anecdotes. For example, the narrator reports that at Bourzey he observed a Frankish woman operating a trebuchet – a fascination with Frankish warrior women is a recurrent motif in Muslim accounts of the Third Crusade and the campaigns that preceded it – and also witnessed one of the besiegers narrowly avoiding being struck by a large stone.[66] Even when drawing upon his own or others' personal experiences, therefore, Ibn al-Athīr's narrator is, if not on the margins of events, content to circle the action and capture something of its mood. As he notes of his narrative of the siege of Acre (at which he was almost certainly not present): 'I shall give an account of the great days to avoid being over long and because the others were minor engagements of limited forces, which it is not necessary to mention.'[67] Lacking the closeness to Saladin's person that to differing extents animates the narrativization of events by Bahā' al-Dīn and 'Imād al- Dīn, Ibn al-Athīr's eyewitness makes only a limited contribution to the strategies of a writer who was practised in the mobilization of written sources and whose chronological and geographical perspectives extended far beyond his own time and place.

The third major Muslim historian of Saladin's conquests and the Frankish reaction is 'Imād al-Dīn al-Isfahānī (1125–1201), who entered Saladin's service as a secretary (*kātib*) in the mid 1170s and remained in that position until the sultan's death.[68] An accomplished rhetorician and stylist, 'Imād al-Dīn wrote

had travelled as far as Rome, and a Frankish captive's remarks about his personal experience of the religious fervour that drove crusade recruitment.

[64] *Chronicle of Ibn al-Athīr*, ii, p. 357.

[65] *Chronicle of Ibn al-Athīr*, ii, pp. 349–52. For this siege, see M. C. Lyons and D. E. P. Jackson, *Saladin: The Politics of the Holy War* (University of Cambridge Oriental Publications, 30; Cambridge, 1982), p. 289. See also H. N. Kennedy, *Crusader Castles* (Cambridge, 1994), pp. 79–84.

[66] *Chronicle of Ibn al-Athīr*, ii, pp. 350, 351. For the Muslim historians' fascination with Christian female fighters, actual or imagined, see H. J. Nicholson, 'Women on the Third Crusade', *Journal of Medieval History*, 23 (1997), 335–49, esp. 337–42, 347–9.

[67] *Chronicle of Ibn al-Athīr*, ii, p. 365.

[68] Gibb, 'Arabic Sources', 59–60, 70–1; Richards, 'Consideration of Two Sources', 47–50, where he is described (48) as 'the quintessential *kātib*'; *idem*, "Imād al-Dīn al-Isfahānī: Administrator, Litterateur and Historian', in M. Shatzmiller (ed.), *Crusaders and*

two major historical works concerning recent events. The *al-Barq al-shāmī* ('The Syrian Lightning') focuses on the careers of Nūr al-Dīn and Saladin, but unfortunately only survives in its original form in two parts, covering the years 1177–80 and 1182–4, though the remainder is indirectly accessible through extracts and abridgements made by thirteenth-century writers. It has been observed that the extant original portions of the *Barq* reveal that it was autobiographical in much of its emphasis, with accounts of the author's professional activities, his correspondence and personal circumstances interwoven into a narrative of public affairs.[69] The work which is more immediately useful for purposes of comparison and contrast is, however, *al-Fath al-qussī fī' l-fath al-qudsī* ('The Conquest of Syria and Palestine'), a tightly focused monograph about the final years of Saladin's career, specifically the period between the preliminaries to the battle of Hattin in 1187 and the aftermath of Saladin's death in 1193.[70] The text is fully extant: it was completed quite close to events, no later than 1199, and in an earlier incarnation may have been intended for presentation to Saladin himself.

At several points the *Fath* constructs a narrator who is not only well positioned to observe Saladin frequently and closely, but also to interact with him on a personal level. For example, in his account of the panicked efforts to strengthen the defences of Jerusalem in January 1192, when it was believed that Richard I's forces were preparing to besiege the city, the narrator remarks that he played a part in keeping Saladin's spirits up and demonstrated his own concern by himself helping to carry stones.[71] He is also among those who offer Saladin consolation when setbacks occur.[72] This proximity to Saladin is reinforced by mentions of eyewitness experience, both that of the individual narrator, as when he sees arrows flying close by the sultan in battle, and as part of a collective gaze, as when an unspecified 'we', probably to be understood as those people of importance in and around Saladin's high command, feel distress when presented with the visible evidence that Acre has fallen to the Christians.[73] It also translates into access to informants who were closer to the principals and to the centre of the action than were those people with arresting but peripheral anecdotes to tell who were consulted by Ibn al-Athīr.[74]

Muslims in Twelfth-Century Syria (The Medieval Mediterranean, 1; Leiden, 1993), pp. 133–46.

[69] Gibb, 'Arabic Sources', 59–60; Richards, 'Consideration of Two Sources', 49.

[70] 'Imād al-Dīn al-Isfahānī, *Conquête de la Syrie et de la Palestine par Saladin*, trans. H. Massé (Documents relatifs à l'histoire des croisades, 10; Paris, 1972). See Richards, 'Consideration of Two Sources', 49–50, 60–1.

[71] *Conquête de la Syrie et de la Palestine*, p. 357.

[72] E.g. *Conquête de la Syrie et de la Palestine*, p. 319.

[73] *Conquête de la Syrie et de la Palestine*, pp. 152, 318. Cf. p. 286 for the sight of prisoners in Saladin's presence.

[74] See e.g. *Conquête de la Syrie et de la Palestine*, p. 304: two Muslims who had

Although the narrator insists that he will limit his report to what he saw, overt appeals to eyewitness experience in order to authenticate statements are quite few. It is true that in a number of scenes, although the narrator's presence or eyewitness observation is not explicitly invoked, there is a notably rich visual element that suggests that this was meant to be understood as the result of close and attentive observation, even if not necessarily on the part of the narrator himself.[75] But this is not typical of the manner in which the action is narrated as a whole. And far from functioning as a roving eye on events, the narrator's main appearances within the storyworld, including his personal encounters with Saladin, tend to cluster around situations related to his professional duties as *kātib*.[76] It is significant that when the narrator states that Saladin paid him the honour of inviting him to sit next to him at a meal attended by many important emirs, he does so in terms that suggest that such public, politically charged proximity to the sultan's person was not a routine occurrence.[77] In a revealing passage that speaks to his relationship with Saladin, and thus by extension his positioning relative to the world of military, diplomatic and political affairs within which Saladin moves throughout the text, the narrator assumes the persona of someone who was privy to all the sultan's secrets and always knew who was and was not in the sultan's favour, but who worked most effectively as a mediator behind the scenes.[78] This positioning underscores the text's means of self-authentication: the narrator-as-character is able to make interventions in the diegesis and appeal to autopsy, but these are optional and occasional strategies, moments of nuance in a text that does not routinely rely on them as validating devices.

Bahā' al-Dīn's approach is quite different. He and 'Imād al-Dīn were well acquainted with one another, perhaps even good friends, and, as Richards has demonstrated, he drew upon the *Fath* when writing the *Nawādir*; this debt is especially evident for the period up to around mid 1191, after which there

disguised their faith while they were servants of Richard's sister Joanna, when she was married to William II of Sicily, use the opportunity provided by her travelling east with her brother to escape and present themselves to Saladin.

[75] E.g. *Conquête de la Syrie et de la Palestine*, p. 312, reporting the story of a genie-like Frank who fights in an agile and confident manner, so many arrows sticking into his armour that he resembles a hedgehog, until he is struck by a flask of Greek Fire and his body burns to a crisp. Cf. the use of the same hedgehog simile, here applied to Richard I, by Ambroise: *The History of the Holy War: Ambroise's Estoire de la Guerre Sainte*, ed. and trans. M. J. Ailes and M. C. Barber, 2 vols (Woodbridge, 2003), ll. 11594–8, trans. p. 185.

[76] See e.g. their exchange concerning the suitability of silver ornamentation on a writing case: *Conquête de la Syrie et de la Palestine*, p. 433.

[77] *Conquête de la Syrie et de la Palestine*, p. 374. The *Barq*, in contrast, constructs an image of easy familiarity and trust between Saladin and 'Imād al-Dīn: Richards, "Imād al-Dīn al-Isfahānī', pp. 138–40.

[78] *Conquête de la Syrie et de la Palestine*, p. 432.

is a greater concentration of apparently original material.[79] Even when the substantive and thematic overlaps are notably close, however, and Bahā' al-Dīn's memory of an incident may have been jogged, or reconfigured, by reading about it in the *Fath*, there are significant differences of approach. These result from the *Nawādir*'s much greater emphasis on eyewitness experience in constructing a narrator who is not only frequently close to Saladin's person and information networks, but also situates himself within the storyworld as an inquisitive collector of data – in implied anticipation, that is, of his writing of the text itself. For example, both Imād al-Dīn and Bahā' al-Dīn mention their riding out to view the aftermath of a Muslim victory in battle on 25 July 1190.[80] In Imād al-Dīn's version, they view the mutilated and despoiled Frankish corpses and come upon a crying Christian woman who had been mortally wounded in the fighting. This prompts them to reflect on the scene before they return to their tents. In Bahā' al-Dīn's treatment, however, his interest in the moment is less meditative, and greater precision is duly introduced:

> I waded into the carnage there on my mount and strove to count them, but they were so many and so heaped up that I was unable to. I caught sight of two dead women amongst them. An eyewitness told me that he saw four women taking part in the battle. Two of them were taken prisoner.[81]

This attention to the quantifiable results of the battle is reiterated a few lines later, when we learn that the narrator is in fact motivated by a debate concerning the number of enemy casualties, and is using his own autopsy and that of others to reach a definitive answer:

> There was a dispute about the number of their slain. Some said 8,000, others 7,000, but nobody made an estimate less than 5,000. I witnessed five rows of them, the first at al-'Adīl's tents and the last at the enemy's tents. I met an intelligent soldier making his way between the rows of the dead and counting them. I asked him, 'How many have you counted?' He replied, 'Up to here 4,060 odd.' He was in the third row, having counted two, but the rows that he had done were more numerous than those left.[82]

[79] Richards, 'Consideration of Two Sources', 54–64.

[80] *Rare and Excellent History*, p. 119; *Conquête de la Syrie et de la Palestine*, pp. 239–40. It is noteworthy that 'Imād al-Dīn mentions Bahā' al-Dīn's presence alongside him, but the reverse is not the case. See also 'Imād al-Dīn's reference to the two men conversing as they travel with Saladin to Jerusalem: *Conquête de la Syrie et de la Palestine*, pp. 354–5.

[81] *Rare and Excellent History*, p. 119.

[82] *Rare and Excellent History*, pp. 119–20. Cf. p. 126 for similar concerns about discrepancies between estimates of numbers.

Likewise, both texts recount an incident in 1191 in which Saladin interrogates a very old Christian captive, one of a party of forty-five brought to him from Beirut, and allows him to return to the Frankish camp, at the same time refusing the request of some of his sons to be allowed to kill one of the other prisoners.[83] Although Bahā' al-Dīn's account is clearly based closely on that in the *Fath*, he introduces the fact that he was an eyewitness to the interview, and was the one who passed on the sons' request. Indeed, Saladin's stated reasoning for his clemency, that he did not want the sons to grow accustomed to the casual shedding of blood, is taken from 'Imād al-Dīn, but in the *Nawādir* it is cued by Bahā' al-Dīn himself asking Saladin for an explanation of his decision.[84]

A similar difference of emphasis emerges from the two texts' treatments of one of the best known anecdotes during the siege of Acre, when Saladin magnanimously reunites a frantic Frankish mother with her infant, who has been snatched from her by Muslim marauders. In 'Imād al-Dīn's account of the incident, the emphasis is on Saladin's clemency,[85] whereas Bahā' al-Dīn develops the scene by both inserting himself into the action in a way that makes him immediately stand out – 'She came to him when he [Saladin] was riding on Tell al-Kharrūba with me and a great crowd was attending upon him' – and by drawing attention to his eyewitnessing of the moving moment when the baby is produced and handed over to its mother: '...the woman...took it, wept mightily, and hugged it to her bosom, while people watched and wept also. I was standing there amongst the gathering.'[86] In a similar vein, the two texts register different reactions to the Muslims' destruction of the fortifications of Ascalon in September 1191, a move reluctantly entered into in order to deny the Franks a forward base from which to threaten Egypt. For 'Imād al-Dīn, his gaze is reflective as he rides around the city and contemplates the themes of transience and ruined splendour.[87] For Bahā' al-Dīn, in contrast, his autopsy is directed to much more prosaic matters:

[83] *Rare and Excellent History*, pp. 144–5; *Conquête de la Syrie et de la Palestine*, pp. 287–8.

[84] Cf. the two accounts of the circumstances in which Saladin came to acquire a prized falcon that had belonged to King Philip II of France; the narrator of the *Nawādir* insists on his own close observation of the bird – 'To my eyes its colour was a dazzling white' – whereas there is no such direct eyewitness support in the *Fath*: *Rare and Excellent History*, p. 146; *Conquête de la Syrie et de la Palestine*, p. 290.

[85] *Conquête de la Syrie et de la Palestine*, pp. 294–5.

[86] *Rare and Excellent History*, pp. 147–8; see also the same incident recounted at p. 37. Cf. the greater personal element introduced into Bahā' al-Dīn's account of a meeting with al-'Adīl, Saladin's brother: *Rare and Excellent History*, p. 187; *Conquête de la Syrie et de la Palestine*, pp. 349–50. Again, 'Imad al-Dīn mentions Bahā' al-Din's presence alongside him but not vice versa.

[87] *Conquête de la Syrie et de la Palestine*, pp. 346–7.

> It was very strongly built, so much so that in places it was nine cubits thick, even ten in some. One of the masons mentioned to the sultan, when I was present, that the thickness of the tower they were undermining was a spear's length...It [another part of the fortifications marked for demolition] was a vast tower, overlooking the sea like an impregnable fortress. I went to inspect it and saw that its construction was the most solid that one could imagine, on which pickaxes would have no effect.[88]

At the point in the narrative that corresponds to Bahā' al-Dīn's entry into Saladin's service, in June 1188, the narrator remarks: 'All that I have related before this date is just my narrative of what I have heard from eyewitnesses I trust. From this date on I shall only record what I witnessed or what I was told by people I trust, which is tantamount to eyewitness.'[89] On one level these are wholly conventional claims, but in the *Nawādir* they express a programmatic ambition that is realized in the text more consistently than in the other works that we have examined. One means to this end is to draw attention to those relatively few occasions when eyewitness observation was restricted or impossible;[90] the inference is that the narration of most of the action is securely grounded in the narrator's eyewitness experience, while every effort has been made to ensure that the remainder has a similarly authentic experiential basis.[91] A second technique is to be selective: the autoptic gaze is not indiscriminate, instead complementing and reinforcing the narrator's emphasis on his routine physical proximity to Saladin and the easy relationship between them. At a number of points the narrator presents himself as someone with whom Saladin is willing to share private thoughts, such as his reservations about the truce agreed with the Christians in September 1192 and his musings about the possibility of taking the fight across the Mediterranean to Europe.[92] In addition, there is close, even intimate, observation of Saladin commanding his forces and in the thick of battle.[93] And the narrator places himself in numerous situations that do double

[88] *Rare and Excellent History*, p. 180.

[89] *Rare and Excellent History*, pp. 81–2; cf. the similar remarks at p. 38. See also the remark attributed to Frederick of Swabia, 'For gaining knowledge there is nothing like seeing for oneself': p. 129.

[90] See *Rare and Excellent History*, pp. 94, 157, 225.

[91] See *Rare and Excellent History*, p. 107: 'This is a battle that I did not witness because I was away on my travels. Of earlier battles I observed what a person of my sort is able to observe, but I gained a knowledge of the rest comparable to that of a participant.' Cf. the narrator's hint that he was practised in the careful observation of battles: *Rare and Excellent History*, p. 93.

[92] *Rare and Excellent History*, pp. 29, 231–2.

[93] E.g. *Rare and Excellent History*, pp. 88, 118, 138 (Saladin is observed weeping mid-battle out of frustration that he cannot engage the enemy), 171 ('I saw him actually riding among the skirmishers as the enemy's arrows flew past him'), 175.

duty as demonstrations of some of the ways in which Saladin came by intelligence and showed off his political craft to friends and enemies alike, and as opportunities for the narrator to enter the action in circumstances that enable him to be positioned close to Saladin while also coming by information for his own purposes. The parading of prisoners before Saladin, a recurrent motif, is one such situation, meeting Frankish nobles, spies and deserters another.[94]

In this way the text is a blend of memoir and third-person narrative, the greater attention to the latter element consistent with its sustained focus on Saladin as principal protagonist. The passage which comes closest to a concentrated sequence of autobiographical reminiscence is revealing. The lengthy account of the Muslim assault on Jaffa and its last-minute relief by Richard I, in late July/ early August 1192, begins with a standard recounting of the Muslim siege in the third person. The narrator's own gaze is only introduced to reinforce an illustrative detail, albeit in a manner that draws the reader's attention to the narrator's particular visual acuity: two Franks put up a conspicuously bold resistance in a breach in the wall and one is struck by a missile, whereupon the other takes his place 'faster than one could wink, so that only a sharp-eyed man could tell there was any difference'.[95] At the point at which the taking of the city is nearly complete, there is a shift of emphasis towards Bahā' al-Dīn's own actions and reactions to events once he finds himself among those ordered to clear the citadel of the remaining Franks. The Franks have already surrendered but there is a danger that they might be tempted to change their minds now that a naval relief force has been sighted.[96] Bahā' al-Dīn's greater visibility within the diegesis is reinforced by his own eyewitness perception. Thus, in one of the text's richest evocations of the visual qualities of a scene, Richard I is described landing on the shore:

> The first galley to deliver its men on land was his. He was red-haired, his tunic was red and his banner was red, as was his device. In a short time all the men from the galleys had disembarked in the harbour. All this went on before my eyes.[97]

[94] *Rare and Excellent History*, pp. 26, 35, 128, 139, 144, 144–5, 168–9, 173, 194, 231. Not all intelligence so gathered was reliable: see p. 183 for the incorrect report of two Frankish captives that Philip II of France had died. For other occasions in which Bahā' al-Dīn is with Saladin when information arrives, see pp. 32, 117, 121, 208. Bahā' al-Dīn also makes occasional reference to his examination of physical objects presented to Saladin: see e.g. p. 131, where he scrutinizes the iron head of a captured Frankish battering ram; see also pp. 143, 152.

[95] *Rare and Excellent History*, p. 219. Cf. p. 220 for the suggestion that Bahā' al-Dīn was involved in discussions about the conduct of the siege.

[96] *Rare and Excellent History*, pp. 220–2.

[97] *Rare and Excellent History*, pp. 222–3. He also mentions (p. 222) that a Frank jumped

Significantly, and somewhat in the manner of the closing of a ring narrative, the autobiographical element recedes once Bahā' al-Dīn gallops back to the sultan and whispers the news of Richard's arrival in his ear, thereby in effect restoring to Saladin the role of principal focalizer that the narrator-as-character had temporarily assumed when he was thrown into the middle of unusually fast-moving and visually striking events – his fifteen minutes of fame, so to speak, in the public space that is normally dominated by his hero.[98] In this sequence, as in much of the *Nawādir*, one encounters the skilful interplay of four mutually reinforcing validating strategies that differ from the approach exemplified by the *Narratio*: the foregrounding of the agency and focalization of a central individual figure; the placing of the narrator in personal proximity to that figure within the storyworld, and so by extension the granting of privileged narratorial access to the counsels of the great and a sympathetic understanding of, or even some participation in, political and military decision-making; narratorial interventions as actor in the storyworld that closely align with and are motivated with reference to the actions of the principals; and recurrent explicit (and numerous implicit) invocations of eyewitness experience. The *Nawādir* and the *Narratio* thus represent contrasting sets of possibilities for an eyewitness narrator whose aim is to tell the story of large-scale events while also acknowledging at least some of the motivating forces behind them and exploring the extent to which they are guided by human purposes. As we shall see, Ambroise's *Estoire de la Guerre Sainte* steers a middle course between these poles, the subtleties of its mobilization of autoptic experience and narratorial immersion in the diegesis reflecting, in part, both its generic novelty and its ambitious narrative scope.

Ambroise's *Estoire de la Guerre Sainte*

The Third Crusade was the first major crusading expedition to catch a vogue for historical writing in verse and in the vernacular, specifically Old French, that had been gradually developing since the middle decades of the twelfth century.[99] Crucially, this emergent genre was sufficiently well established by the 1190s to suggest itself as a suitably prestigious and reverent form for the narration of public events of great significance in which the workings of the divine will were

down from the citadel onto the beach in order to alert Richard's fleet to the fact that the Christian position in Jaffa was not entirely lost; this detail corresponds quite closely to Ambroise's account of the same scene: *Estoire*, ll. 11076–89, trans. p. 179.

[98] *Rare and Excellent History*, p. 223.

[99] See P. Damian-Grint, *The New Historians of the Twelfth-Century Renaissance: Inventing Vernacular Authority* (Woodbridge, 1999). See also the same author's 'Truth, Trust, and Evidence in the Anglo-Norman *Estoire*', in C. Harper-Bill (ed.), *Anglo-Norman Studies XVIII: Proceedings of the Battle Conference 1995* (Woodbridge, 1996), pp. 63–78.

in evidence, while at the same time it had not hardened into an inflexible template constraining form and content. The freedom that this afforded Ambroise energizes the text, and makes the *Estoire* a particularly interesting test case for examining the ways in which well-established forms of narratorial self-positioning and mobilization of autopsy migrate into new generic environments. With the benefit of hindsight, we know that the generation after the Third Crusade would see the emergence of Old French prose histories, both accounts of contemporary events – as exemplified by the narratives of the Fourth Crusade that are the subject of the next chapter – and translations and adaptations of works concerning the more remote past, which would to a large extent supersede the vernacular verse historiographical form. It is important, however, not to treat Ambroise's text as simply a transitional moment in a trajectory leading to something else, or as in some way a failed experiment.[100] Ambroise was attempting to produce a work that was serious-minded and innovative as well as monumental in scope, qualities that reflected the importance that he and his anticipated readers and listeners attached to the memory of the Third Crusade.[101]

The *Estoire* was a product of the same Anglo-Norman cultural space in which Old French verse historiography had been pioneered. At first it took the form of

[100] Cf. Gabrielle Spiegel's perhaps too sweeping judgement that 'by the end of the twelfth century an expanding body of literate laymen nurtured a growing suspicion of poeticized history': *Romancing the Past: The Rise of Vernacular Prose Historiography in Thirteenth-Century France* (Berkeley, 1993), p. 12.

[101] Ambroise's text has attracted a good deal of scholarly interest in recent decades. Valuable studies include C. Croizy-Naquet, 'Deux répresentations de la troisième croisade: l'*Estoire de la guerre sainte* et la *Chronique d'Ernoul et de Bernard le Trésorier*', *Cahiers de civilisation médiévale*, 44 (2001), 313–27; *eadem*, 'Les figures du jongleur dans l'*Estoire de la guerre sainte*', *Le moyen Âge*, 104 (1998), 229–56; *eadem*, 'Merveille et miracle dans l'*Estoire de la guerre sainte* d'Ambroise: éléments de définition d'un genre', in F. Gingras, F. Laurent, F. Le Nan and J.-R. Valette (eds), *'Furent les merveilles pruvees et les aventures truvees': Hommage à Francis Dubost* (Paris, 2005), pp. 177–92; M. J. Ailes, 'Ambroise's *Estoire de la Guerre sainte* and the Development of a Genre', *Reading Medieval Studies*, 34 (2008), 1–19; G. Schirato, 'Forme narrative del discorso storico: I modelli letterari dell'*Estoire de la Guerre Sainte* di Ambroise', *Studi Medievali*, 3rd ser., 51 (2010), 95–151. For a useful discussion of the socio-political framework in which the text was produced and to which it speaks, see C. Hanley, 'Reading the Past Through the Present: Ambroise, the Minstrel of Reims and Jordan Fantosme', *Mediaevalia*, 20 (2001), 263–81, esp. 265–73. For the text's treatment of matters of interest to military historians, see P. Ménard, 'Les combattants en Terre sainte au temps de Saladin et de Richard Coeur de Lion', in J. Paviot and J. Verger (eds), *Guerre, pouvoir et noblesse au Moyen Âge: Mélanges en l'honneur de Philippe Contamine* (Paris, 2000), pp. 503–11. See also C. Croizy-Naquet, 'Légende ou histoire? Les assassins dans l'*Estoire de guerre sainte* d'Ambroise et dans la *Chronique d'Ernoul et de Bernard le Trésorier*', *Le moyen âge*, 117 (2011), 237–57.

what have been termed 'dynastic' histories, treatments of the distant past that drew upon written sources as well as oral tradition. The foremost surviving examples are Geffrei Gaimar's *Estoire des Engleis*, Wace's *Roman de Brut* and *Roman de Rou*, and Benoît de Sainte-Maure's *Chronique des ducs de Normandie*.[102] A significant extension of the genre into closely contemporary history was signalled by Jordan Fantosme's *Chronicle*, which deals with the great rebellion against Henry II of England in 1173–4.[103] Although Jordan declares that his focus is on Henry II, his narrative in fact largely concentrates on just one of the theatres of war in which the rebellion against the king was fought out, the Anglo-Scottish borderlands. This was the setting of one of the principal turning points in the whole rebellion, the capture of the Scottish king William the Lion at Alnwick in July 1174; and this event is consequently the climax of Jordan's narrative. Despite significant differences in terms of prosody, length and subject matter, Fantosme's history is the closest surviving analogue to Ambroise's *Estoire*. There is no evidence that Ambroise had read it or heard it performed, but this is not altogether unlikely if, as some scholars argue, the *Chronicle* was written for the Anglo-Norman royal court. If so, the *Chronicle*'s use of an eyewitness narrator inserted into the storyworld (albeit at only a few points in the action) may have been one of Ambroise's sources of inspiration, alongside Latin crusade histories in which similar narratorial self-positionings are adopted.[104]

[102] In addition to Damian-Grint, *New Historians*, see e.g. J. Blacker, *The Faces of Time: Portrayal of the Past in Old French and Latin Historical Narrative of the Anglo-Norman Regnum* (Austin, TX, 1994); E. Albu, *The Normans in Their Histories: Propaganda, Myth and Subversion* (Woodbridge, 2001), pp. 215–39; C. Urbanski, *Writing History for the King: Henry II and the Politics of Vernacular Historiography* (Ithaca, NY, 2013).

[103] Jordan Fantosme, *Chronicle*, ed. and trans. R. C. Johnston (Oxford, 1981). The secondary literature on this text is extensive: see e.g. I. Macdonald, 'The Chronicle of Jordan Fantosme: Manuscripts, Author, and Versification', in *Studies in Medieval French Presented to Alfred Ewert in Honour of his Seventieth Birthday* (Oxford, 1961), pp. 242–58; A. Lodge, 'Literature and History in the Chronicle of Jordan Fantosme', *French Studies*, 44 (1990), 257–70; M. Strickland, 'Arms and the Men: War, Loyalty and Lordship in Jordan Fantosme's Chronicle', in C. Harper-Bill and R. Harvey (eds), *Medieval Knighthood IV: Papers from the Fifth Strawberry Hill Conference 1990* (Woodbridge, 1992), pp. 187–220; P. E. Bennett, 'La Chronique de Jordan Fantosme: épique et public lettré au XIIe siècle', *Cahiers de civilisation médiévale*, 40 (1997), 37–56; L. Ashe, *Fiction and History in England, 1066–1200* (Cambridge, 2007), pp. 81–120; G. Rector, '"Faites le mien desir": Studious Persuasion and Baronial Desire in Jordan Fantosme's *Chronicle*', *Journal of Medieval History*, 34 (2008), 311–46.

[104] See Jordan Fantosme, *Chronicle*, ll. 575–80, p. 44 (a clear narratorial alignment with the value system of the baronial class loyal to Henry II); l. 890, p. 66 (explicit mention of narratorial absence from one of the theatres of war); l. 1142, p. 84 (personal experience of the effects of William the Lion's campaigning in Northumberland); ll. 1153–4, p. 86 (exercise of discretion in not naming a baron who sided with William

The *Estoire* is the fullest and most complete eyewitness account of the Anglo-French contribution to the Third Crusade.[105] There has been a long scholarly debate about its relationship to a Latin prose narrative of much the same series of events, the *Itinerarium Peregrinorum et Gesta Regis Ricardi.* A popular view used to be that the *Estoire* was derived from the *Itinerarium Peregrinorum*, or that they both drew on a common source.[106] Certainly their plot arcs and action-by-action sequencing are very close in many places. This emboldened Gaston Paris, Ambroise's first modern editor, to use the *Itinerarium Peregrinorum* to attempt reconstructions of the content of passages in the *Estoire* where he suspected there were lacunae.[107] It is now generally accepted, however, that the *Estoire* was the principal written source for Books II–VI (of six) of the *Itinerarium Peregrinorum*, which is a compilation made by Richard de Templo, prior of Holy Trinity in London, around 1220.[108] Book I is also in the nature of a compilation of material from different sources, but its main narrative element, which takes the story of the crusade up to November 1190, would seem to have been based on an eyewitness account, probably by an English crusader, of the period before the arrival of the kings of France and England at Acre, during which time various parties of English and other crusaders had been making their way east and joining the Christian forces besieging the city. Book I is based on an originally free-standing text which Hans Mayer, whose groundbreaking work began to resolve the uncertainties surrounding the textual history and transmission of the *Itinerarium Peregrinorum*, labelled IP1; this is known to have

---

the Lion); ll. 1768–9, p. 132 (assertion of autoptic authority); l. 1804, p. 134 (presence as eyewitness at the climactic moment, the capture of William the Lion).

[105] It is, for example, drawn upon extensively in the best modern account of the course of the Third Crusade: Gillingham, *Richard I*, pp. 123–221.

[106] For older verdicts, see K. Norgate, 'The "Itinerarium Peregrinorum" and the "Song of Ambrose"', *English Historical Review*, 25 (1910), 523–47; J. G. Edwards, 'The *Itinerarium Regis Ricardi* and the *Estoire de la Guerre Sainte*', in J. G. Edwards, V. H. Galbraith and E. J. Jacob (eds), *Historical Essays in Honour of James Tait* (Manchester, 1933), pp. 59–77.

[107] See *L'estoire de la guerre sainte: Histoire en vers de la troisième croisade (1190–1192)* (Paris, 1897), pp. lxvii–lxxvi.

[108] See Mayer in *Das Itinerarium peregrinorum*, esp. pp. 7–51, 80–102, 107–51. Mayer's arguments concerning the authorship of IP1, which he attributed to an English Templar, were revised by H. Möhring, 'Eine Chronik aus der Zeit des dritten Kreuzzugs: das sogenannte *Itinerarium peregrinorum* 1', *Innsbrucker Historische Studien*, 5 (1982), 149–62. For an excellent summary of the whole debate surrounding the *Itinerarium*, as well as helpful remarks concerning the composite quality of IP1, see Nicholson in *Chronicle of the Third Crusade*, pp. 6–15. See also the useful overview in Schirato, 'Forme narrative', 96–8. The discussion of the relationship between the *Estoire* and the *Itinerarium* in F. Vielliard, 'Richard Coeur de Lion et son entourage normand: Le témoignage de l'*Estoire de la guerre sainte*', *Bibliothèque de l'École des chartes*, 160 (2002), 7–8, 10–12 is much less convincing.

circulated as a discrete work. It is probable that the compiler of IP1 was also English, and he may indeed have been the author of his principal source narrative, in other words a participant in the crusade. The last word has not been said on the subject, however; in particular, the morphology of IP1/Book I in its various iterations merits further investigation, as does the question of its sources.[109] For our present purposes, it is sufficient to note that the *Estoire* is not a derivative text as used to be believed, at least not in substantial part, and may therefore be read as what it purports to be, a predominantly eyewitness account written by a participant in the Third Crusade.

In its surviving form – the single extant manuscript copy, which is from the later thirteenth century, clearly has lacunae and shows other signs of scribal disarrangement of the text – the *Estoire* comprises 12,313 octosyllabic lines in rhymed couplets.[110] The story it tells begins with the trigger for the Third Crusade, the disasters that befell the Latin East in 1187, first with the calamitous defeat at Hattin and the loss of the relic of the True Cross, and then the fall of Jerusalem and other places to Saladin's forces. In the account of western Europe's response to the terrible news, the reaction of Duke Richard of Aquitaine, soon to become king of England, is emphasized, a foretaste of his centrality to the action thereafter.[111] We follow Richard's preparations for the crusade, his assumption of royal power on Henry II's death in 1189, his departure in 1190, and the quite drawn-out progress of his journey to the east. The narrative offers extended treatments of Richard's two significant interventions in Mediterranean politics: his stay in Sicily over the autumn and winter and into the spring of 1190–1, and his conquest of Cyprus from its Byzantine ruler, Isaac Komnenos, in May 1191. Richard is then delivered to Acre, in June 1191, some weeks after the arrival there of his fellow crusader and rival, Philip II of France.[112] The kings' arrivals at

[109] The edition in Mayer, *Das Itinerarium peregrinorum*, pp. 241–357 is of what he argues is the original form of IP1. For the whole text, one still needs to consult *Itinerarium Peregrinorum et Gesta Regis Ricardi*, ed. W. Stubbs, *Chronicles and Memorials of the Reign of Richard I*, vol. 1 (RS 38:1, London, 1864). Nicholson's translation in *Chronicle of the Third Crusade* is of the Stubbs text.

[110] The figure is that reached in the Ailes and Barber edition: see *Estoire*, i, p. 199. Different editorial approaches to clear and suspected lacunae and other textual disarrangements lead to different totals: Gaston Paris, in the first modern critical edition, *L'estoire de la guerre sainte*, col. 332, arrives at 12,352.

[111] Richard is the first named individual to be shown taking the cross, and is described as the first great noble to do so: *Estoire*, ll. 59–64, trans. p. 30. (All references to the *Estoire de la Guerre Sainte* are by line number as per the sequence established in the first volume of the Ailes and Barber edition and translation, while the accompanying page extents refer to the corresponding points in the modern English translation in the second volume.)

[112] For the *Estoire*'s treatment of Richard as its principal hero, see M. J. Ailes, 'Heroes of War: Ambroise's Heroes of the Third Crusade', in C. Saunders, F. Le Saux and N.

Acre trigger the narrative's most extended and detail-rich analepsis, amounting to about one sixth of the whole text: this recounts the earlier progress of the siege of Acre, which had been begun almost two years earlier as a desperate gambit on the part of Guy of Lusignan, the king of Jerusalem, but which, thanks to the arrival of various groups of western reinforcements, then became the sharp end of the Christian efforts to salvage something from the collapse of Outremer at Saladin's hands.[113] It is highly likely that Ambroise arrived at Acre with Richard's fleet, so in the absence of eyewitness experience it is likely that he drew on the recollections of English veterans of the siege for this portion of the text.

As the narrative of the backstory of the siege returns to the point where the western kings arrive at Acre, Ambroise's main plot arc, what he terms his 'matter', is resumed. After this, the most significant departure from the primary focus on Richard is a substantial sequence (ll. 11865–12158) towards the end of the text that recounts the experiences of those groups of crusaders who, under the terms of the truce agreed between Richard and Saladin in September 1192, were permitted to visit Jerusalem as unarmed pilgrims. Richard was not among them. Consequently, the narrative – the author would seem to have been in the second of the three groups that made the journey to the Holy City – decouples itself from the king and shifts into a more devotional register. This switch is characterized by a foregrounding of the pilgrims' collective experiences and is signposted by a greater use of the first person plural than at any earlier point in the text. The focus on Richard is, however, briefly but emphatically resumed in order to reach closure, the text concluding with the king's departure from Palestine in October 1192. The final scene is of Richard gazing upon the Palestinian shore as he sails away, and expressing his wish to return, though this noble sentiment is immediately undercut by irony, in that the reader is reminded that at that poignant moment Richard was unaware of the grave challenges that he would face in the next few years, specifically his long captivity in Germany, the unpopular measures taken to raise his ransom, and the attacks launched on his French lands by Philip II.[114] These references, and the apparent absence of knowledge of Richard's death, in 1199, suggest that the text was written at some point between 1194, when Richard

Thomas (eds), *Writing War: Medieval Literary Responses to Warfare* (Cambridge, 2004), pp. 29–48, esp. 37–47. See also Schirato, 'Forme narrative', 116–17, 119–20, 128–32. For the text's use of Philip II as a foil to Richard, see B. J. Levy, 'Pèlerins rivaux de la 3e Croisade: les personnages des rois d'Angleterre et de France, d'après les chroniques d'Ambroise et d'"Ernoul" et le récit anglo-normand de la *Croisade et Mort Richard Coeur de Lion*', in D. Buschinger (ed.), *La croisade: réalités et fictions. Actes du Colloque d'Amiens 18–22 mars 1987* (Göppinger Arbeiten zu Germanistik, 503: Göppingen, 1989), pp. 143–55, esp. 145–50. See also Hanley, 'Reading the Past', 265–7, 268–9, 270–1.

[113] The analepsis occupies ll. 2383–4544, trans. pp. 66–94.

[114] *Estoire*, ll. 12255–99, trans. p. 193.

was released from captivity, and 1199, most probably around 1195/6, by which point Richard had done much to reverse Philip's gains, a comeback of which the narrator is aware.[115] Other than this concluding prolepsis, there are only a few references to events after the conclusion of the crusade, mostly plaintive remarks about Philip II's opportunistic and envious exploitation of Richard's absence to chip away at his power in France, the harm that this had done to Normandy, and Prince John's scheming against his brother.[116] This too suggests a date of composition around the mid 1190s, at a time when we can imagine that the crusade was still being actively discussed and debated and its ramifications were still unclear.[117]

Who was the author?[118] The text supplies the name Ambroise no fewer than nine times; the references, all in the third person, are concentrated in the first half of the text, but there is no stylistic or structural reason to suspect that the *Estoire* is the work of more than one person.[119] Attempts to differentiate between the author of the *Estoire* and Ambroise as the writer of an anterior text, which the later author used as a source, are wholly unconvincing.[120] The clearest indication that mentions of 'Ambroise' are to be understood as authorial self-references is to be found in the use of deixis in connection with what is, significantly, the first occurrence of the name: 'Ambroise dit, qui fist cest livre' ('Says Ambroise, who made *this* book').[121] Ambroise was most probably from Normandy, possibly the region around Évreux. His status has been the subject of some debate. Gaston Paris was persuaded that he was a jongleur, or failing that someone who made his living from writing, and this view is still held by a number of scholars.[122] Marianne

[115] *Estoire*, ll. 12295–9, trans. p. 193.

[116] *Estoire*, ll. 820–9, 1162–4, 9408–35, trans. pp. 42, 47, 159. See also *Estoire*, ll. 8857–86, trans, p. 152 for the idea that the false belief that Richard was responsible for Conrad of Montferrat's assassination led to his German captivity. For anticipations of future events that take place within the temporal range of the narrative, see *Estoire*, ll. 4525–6, trans. p. 94 (death of the count of Flanders); ll. 5344–50, trans. p. 106 (Duke Henry of Burgundy's future borrowing of funds from Richard); ll. 5389–92, trans. p. 106 (the Christians' ignorance that they are being strung along in negotiations concerning the return of the True Cross); ll. 8062–3, trans. p. 140 (Richard's destruction of the fortifications of Ascalon).

[117] For Richard's largely successful efforts to reverse his losses to Philip II and confront other challenges to his authority, see Gillingham, *Richard I*, pp. 283–320.

[118] For a helpful discussion, see Ailes and Barber's introduction in *Estoire*, ii, pp. 1–3.

[119] *Estoire*, ll. 171, 728, 2397, 3221, 3728, 4554, 4822, 5913, 6005, trans. pp. 32, 41, 66, 78, 84, 94, 99, 113, 114.

[120] See Vielliard, 'Richard Coeur de Lion', 11–12.

[121] *Estoire*, l. 171: my translation. The narrator is remarking on the wisdom of fulfilling one's vows promptly, in contrast to the experience of Henry II who took the cross but died before he could go on crusade.

[122] *L'estoire de la guerre sainte*, pp. vi–x.

Ailes has, however, made a strong case for supposing that he was a cleric with a good education in rhetoric and is perhaps, given the relative rarity of his name, to be identified with the *clericus* Ambroise who is recorded singing at King John and Queen Isabella's coronation at Westminster in October 1200. In light of the considerable amount of attention paid in the *Estoire* to the festivities surrounding Richard's coronation in September 1189, and the narrator's insistence on his eyewitness participation in them, this is a very attractive suggestion.[123]

Further support for clerical authorship comes in the form of an unusual, and for this reason self-highlighting, break in the normal narration of the action when, in the latter part of the text and with half an eye cast forward to future criticism of the king's failure to take Jerusalem, a dispirited Richard is button-holed by a chaplain named William of Poitiers, who reminds him of his past achievements in order to persuade him to persist in his efforts.[124] As Ailes has observed, this lengthy run-through of Richard's deeds, heightened by the use of direct discourse and multiple appeals to remember directed at Richard personally ('Reis, remenbre', 'Reis, recorde'), amounts to a *mise-en-abyme* of the whole narrative. For although William begins with examples of Richard's prowess that predate the crusade, most of what he says recalls the king's journey east and his actions in Palestine.[125] It is further noteworthy that, plot-wise, the priest's intervention is motivated by the sight of Richard acting very atypically in both diegetic and narratological terms. He is no longer the active, vocal leader that appears elsewhere in the text, but is instead glimpsed sitting in his tent in gloomy silence; he has, moreover, surrendered his usual role of perspicacious and astute focalizer, in that the priest has to alert him to the rumours circulating in the army that he is intending to leave for home. William clearly functions as the narrator's surrogate, for he is the one character who intradiegetically articulates, in microcosm, the text's larger narrative project. That this role is given to a cleric is therefore significant.[126]

[123] *Estoire*, ii, p. 2. See Ailes, 'Ambroise's *Estoire*', 2–3, and for the author's facility with learned rhetorical devices *ibid.*, 9–16. On the author's status, see also C. Croizy-Naquet, 'Les festivités dans l'*Estoire de la guerre sainte* d'Ambroise', *Le moyen âge*, 108 (2002), 80–2, revising somewhat her endorsement of Paris's verdict in her 'Les figures', esp. 229–30. For Richard's coronation festivities, see *Estoire*, ll. 190–210, trans. p. 32.

[124] *Estoire*, ll. 9528–655, trans. pp. 160–2. The narrator adds (ll. 9656–64, trans. p. 162) that the effect of this 'sermon' was to clarify Richard's thinking. Its position in the narrative would place the exchange, if historical, in early June 1192.

[125] Ailes, 'Ambroise's *Estoire*', 12–15; *eadem*, 'Heroes of War', pp. 45–6.

[126] It is also noteworthy that part of the warrant that William claims for addressing Richard in such frank terms is that he already knew him from his time as count of Poitiers, i.e. duke of Aquitaine: l. 9575, trans. p. 161. Cf. the exclusively clerical slant of the shadow authorship evoked when the narrator observes of the siege of Acre before

Because, at least as far as the surviving evidence indicates, Ambroise was, alongside Fantosme, innovative in his use of vernacular verse to narrate very recent events, the *Estoire* has largely attracted the attention of literary scholars with a view to identifying its generic influences. The persistence of Paris's belief that the author was a jongleur has validated an approach that situates the text in relation to the two principal genres in late-twelfth-century Old French literature, the *chanson de geste* and romance. Of these two, the question of indebtedness to the *chanson de geste* form has attracted more attention in light of the martial orientation of, and epic resonances within, the *Estoire*'s storyworld. Scholarly verdicts differ as to the extent to which Ambroise drew upon the *chanson de geste* tradition, and this is unsurprising given both the length and complexity of the work and the fact that one can appeal to several different indicators of possible generic influence, such as style, prosody, structure, plot situations, motifs, figuration, and characterization and character motivation.[127] Certainly, there are numerous indications of a familiarity with certain *chansons de geste*.[128] On the other hand, this influence is not pervasive and does not dominate the content and form of the text. The choice of prosody and structure would have announced to practised listeners and readers of vernacular texts that some distancing was intended, for octosyllabic rhyming couplets were used in a number of Old French genres but not in *chansons de geste*, nor is the text divided into *laisses*; by extension, there is no looping and repetition of the action along the lines of that found in *laisses similaires*.[129]

---

the kings' arrival that 'No priest nor cleric nor deacon could tell or relate the great hardships and martyrdom that the Christians suffered': *Estoire*, ll. 2943–6, trans. p. 74.

[127] For a convincingly guarded verdict as to the influence of *chansons de geste* on the *Estoire*, see Ailes, 'Ambroise's *Estoire*', esp. 3–9, 16–17. See also the nuanced discussion of Ambroise's selective mobilization and adaptation of epic motifs and narrative structures in Schirato, 'Forme narrative', esp. 102–33. For a more traditional view, see Croizy-Naquet, 'Deux représentations', 321–5, 327.

[128] See e.g. the comparison made between the treacherous Isaac Komnenos and Ganelon, the character who betrays Roland and his companions in the *Song of Roland*: *Estoire*, ll. 1384–5, trans. p. 50; the belief that Geoffrey of Lusignan's prowess in battle made him the most praiseworthy knight since Roland and Oliver: ll. 4658–60, p. 96; and the statement that no one at Roncesvalles conducted himself as well as did Richard at Jaffa: ll. 11175–8, trans. p. 180. See also the reference to Agoland, a Saracen king who features in the *Chanson d'Aspremont*: ll. 515–16, trans. p. 37.

[129] Partial exceptions to the absence of passages resembling *laisses similaires* are two sequences of thematically linked anecdotes that are strung together by means of repeated opening or concluding refrains: see *Estoire*, ll. 3516–764, 4309–406, trans. pp. 82–4, 91–2. It is noteworthy that these sequences occur in the extended analepsis concerning the siege of Acre before the arrival of Richard I, in which there is a good deal of padding and much of the narrator's attention is directed towards anecdotes that illustrate the central theme of the army's sufferings as well as associated preoccupations including, in the second of these sequences, criticism within the army of Conrad of Montferrat's inactivity.

A comparison with the closely contemporary *Chanson d'Antioche*, which Ambroise may possibly have known in some form, immediately indicates that he could have pushed his material much closer towards the 'standard' *chanson de geste* model if his aim had been solely to decant the story of the crusade into a vernacular epic idiom.[130] Indeed, just as the sermon directed by William of Poitiers to Richard represents a staging within the diegesis of the narrator's main thematic concerns, so the distancing of the text from the *chanson de geste* form is itself enacted within the storyworld when we are told that Richard's court at Lyons-la-Forêt over Christmas 1189 was a solemn affair: the king's attention is directed to the serious business of co-ordinating arrangements for the upcoming crusade with Philip II of France, and as a result 'there was little singing of epic songs'.[131] In contrast to the *Estoire*'s epic resonances, somewhat less scholarly attention has been paid to the influence of romance, though it has been convincingly argued that the construction of the narrator owes something to romance tradition, which favoured a more interventionist, mediating narratorial presence, 'stage-managing' the action and offering editorializing comments on it, than was typical of narrators in *chansons de geste*.[132] Again, however, one needs to differentiate between influences, strategically and selectively applied to the text, which one certainly sees in the *Estoire*, and close adherence to one dominant generic template, which is absent from it.

An unfortunate side effect of the scholarly focus on the *Estoire*'s place in vernacular literary history has been a relative neglect of the possible influence of Latin historiography, in particular crusade narratives. Studies of Ambroise that, quite correctly, see his text as a blend of genres have nonetheless tended to set up a stark opposition between the subtle play of vernacular literary influences and Ambroise-the-eyewitness-participant's raw confrontation with the experience of the Third Crusade, which, when not in self-consciously vernacular literary mode, the author, it is supposed, aspired to recount in strictly factual and accurate terms. Moreover, the question of the possible influence of Latin historiography would

[130] See *La Chanson d'Antioche: chanson de geste du dernier quart du XIIe siècle*, ed. and trans. B. Guidot (Champion classiques moyen âge, 33; Paris, 2011); trans. S. B. Edgington and C. Sweetenham, *The Chanson d'Antioche: An Old French Account of the First Crusade* (Crusade Texts in Translation, 22; Farnham, 2011).

[131] *Estoire*, l. 250, trans. p. 33: 'Mais poi i ot chanté de geste'. Cf. the distancing achieved in ll. 4173–96, trans. pp. 89–90, where the narrator contrasts his own ability to tell the truth about the crusaders' sufferings at Acre with his uncertainty concerning the truth-status of the deeds of figures such as Alexander, Tristan, Arthur, and Charlemagne, in other words characters who metonymically stand for romances and 'the old epic tales of which jongleurs make so much' ('vielles chançons de geste / Dont jugleür font si grant feste').

[132] For the narrative voice and other traces of romance influences in the *Estoire*, see Schirato, 'Forme narrative', 100–2, 133–50.

once have seemed redundant, for the author of the *Estoire* was believed to have been a jongleur, and jongleurs were supposedly detached from learned textual culture. Indeed, Paris believed that Ambroise knew no Latin.[133] Although still influential, Paris's reasoning vis-à-vis the status of the author now seems strained, to say the least: the author must have been a non-combatant, so the argument goes, and because there were only two main categories of non-combatants on the Third Crusade, priests and jongleurs, the absence of evidence of learning in the text means that the author could not have been a cleric and was therefore a jongleur. Paris's thesis was based on old-fashioned assumptions about the rigid separation of opposites in medieval culture – lay and clerical, vernacular and Latinate, uneducated and learned, unarmed poor pilgrims and rich crusading knights – which no longer stand up to close scrutiny.[134] There is, in fact, more than a whiff of the 'simple knight' who allegedly wrote the *Gesta Francorum* in Paris's conjuring forth of the jongleur-as-author.

If, however, the author of the *Estoire* was a cleric, as is likely, and especially if he was someone with the education and connections of a trained *cantor* who could be entrusted with singing at a coronation in Westminster, it is highly probable that he would have had access to and read Latin works of history, including histories of earlier crusades. One possibility would have been Robert the Monk's *Historia Iherosolimitana*, which was the mostly widely circulated account of the First Crusade in the twelfth century and seems to have been especially in vogue around the time of the Second and Third Crusades.[135] Another is Baldric of Bourgueil's *Historia Ierosolimitana*, which, as Steven Biddlecombe's research has shown, was much better known than used to be supposed, especially in Normandy and elsewhere in north-western France.[136] The difficulty lies in identifying clear evidence of the influence of works such as these – especially given that Latin crusade historiography had itself been sensitive to epic influences from the First Crusade onwards.[137] Ambroise's receptivity to Latin historiographical models is

[133] *L'estoire de la guerre sainte*, pp. vii–viii.

[134] But cf. C. B. Bouchard, *'Every Valley Shall Be Exalted': The Discourse of Opposites in Twelfth-Century Thought* (Ithaca, NY, 2003).

[135] Robert the Monk, *The Historia Iherosolimitana*, ed. D. Kempf and M. G. Bull (Woodbridge, 2013), pp. xlii–xlvii.

[136] Baldric of Bourgueil, *The Historia Ierosolimitana*, ed. S. Biddlecombe (Woodbridge, 2014), pp. lxx–lxxiii, lxxix–lxxx, lxxxi–lxxxiv, xciii–xciv, xcviii–xcix.

[137] See e.g. *Estoire*, ll. 10635–54, trans. p. 174, which unfavourably contrasts the conduct of some of those on the Third Crusade with those on the First. Ailes, *Estoire*, ii, p. 174 n. 677 suggests that the achievements of the first crusaders were known to Ambroise from the *Chanson d'Antioche*, and this is supported by the narrator's reference in the same passage to the celebratory function of song (*chançon*) in crusade contexts, as well as by his mention of the taking of Antioch as the First Crusade's signature achievement. But his knowledge of the First Crusade may also have derived from Latin narratives in which the southern Italian Norman leaders whom he mentions were central figures. Cf.

a topic that merits further investigation. For our present purposes it is sufficient to note that the probable, if difficult to isolate, influence of Latin historiography on the *Estoire* confirms that this is a text that resists narrow genre constraints. This in turn has important implications for the freedom which we shall see the author enjoyed to fashion a narratorial persona around his participation in the crusade.

How, then, is the narrator constructed? It is a common reaction, when presented with a highly competent, even assured and skilful, literary production, to suppose that it is unlikely to have been the author's first attempt at writing. But if Ambroise had written Old French or Latin works before the *Estoire*, these are not known to have survived; and the narrator does not stake any of his authority on his being a practised writer. In any event, there had been nothing in recent memory to match the scope, significance and cultural impact of the Third Crusade. This meant that it sufficed to emphasize authorial autopsy as the basis of the *Estoire*'s claim on the reader's or listener's attention. An important sequence early in the text, reminiscent of the lavish *mises-en-scène* of elite spaces in romances' loving stagings of courtly life, establishes this position particularly clearly. It uses repetition of the verb *veoir* not only to assert the narrator's eyewitness status in relation to that specific scene, but also to set up an expectation that similar moments of close autoptic scrutiny will punctuate the narration to follow, and so by extension that eyewitness participation will authenticate at least a significant portion of all the subsequent action. This is the coronation feast scene that has already been noted:

> Little time passed before he had himself crowned in London. There I saw great gifts given and I saw such gifts of food that no one could tell how much nor keep account of it. Never in all my life did I see a court served in a more courtly manner [*Cort plus cortoisement servie*]; I saw such rich vessels in that most lovely hall. I saw the tables so laden that they could not be counted. But why should I give you a long account of this? Each of you knows what it means, what a great court can be held by him who holds England.[138]

The lingering gaze within what is presented as a familiar milieu, along with the easy, allusive address to a 'you' equally *au fait* with that world, establishes the narrator as someone comfortably at home in courtly environments, especially the royal court. It follows that the narrator will be competent thenceforth to perceive actions and to frame judgements in line with a corresponding set of courtly

the narrator's identification with the Norman conquerors of southern Italy and Sicily as 'our ancestors': *Estoire*, ll. 615–18, trans. p. 39.

[138] *Estoire*, ll. 190–204, trans. p. 32. For a discussion of the narrative functions of the several feasts and courtly festivities that feature in the text, see Croizy-Naquet, 'Les festivités', 61–80.

values.[139] If Richard I himself cannot be the sole protagonist and focalizer – which would be extremely difficult to sustain over such a long text and given the scale and complexity of the events that comprise what is termed the 'matter' (*matire*) of the crusade – then the narrator is setting up an expectation that he will find, as necessary, individual and collective surrogates for Richard to extend and confirm the aristocratic slant of the narrative.

It is sometimes suggested that, in addition to his fascination with the workings of knightly culture, the narrator also demonstrates a particular concern for the sufferings and frustrations of the poor rank-and-file crusaders.[140] There is some evidence to support this reading.[141] But the biographist move that is sometimes made as a result – that sympathy of this sort reveals the author's own relatively humble social status and his intention to act as some sort of spokesman for the powerless within the crusade army – is an unnecessary carry-over from Paris's approach to the question of authorship. It is important to see the Janus-like perspective on the narrator's part – engaged with the actions and values of Richard and other members of the aristocratic elite while alive to the anxiety and vulnerability of the poorer crusaders – in the context of the narrative's principal aim. This emerges from a consideration of the conflicts that energize the plot of the *Estoire*. On a surface level, the text's principal agon is obviously the war waged between the Christians and Muslims; this binary confrontation is complemented by the conflicts that Richard enters into in Sicily and Cyprus against Christians who are tantamount to Muslim surrogates, as well as by the tensions between Richard and Philip II that spread to their respective supporters. But underneath all this there is a further plot conflict, one that turns on the question of Jerusalem. As the text's parting shot of Richard's wistful sailing away from Palestine reinforces, for the narrator the Third Crusade is unfinished business.

[139] See e.g. the account of Richard's courtly reception of Guy of Lusignan at their first meeting: *Estoire*, ll. 1717–31, trans. p. 55. See also the use of the metaphor of jousting with respect to one-on-one combat during battle: *Estoire*, ll. 1560–1, 7558–69, trans. pp. 53, 134. For Richard as the performer *par excellence* of *chevaleries* and *pröesces*, see *Estoire*, ll. 11615–18, trans. p. 185. Cf. the exchange when an armed cleric, Hugh de la Mare, urges Richard to retreat from a Greek force during the Cyprus campaign; Richard's reply is, 'Sir clerk, concern yourself with your writing and come out of the fighting; leave chivalry to us, by God and Saint Mary': *Estoire*, ll. 1604–13, trans. p. 53.

[140] E.g. Croizy-Naquet, 'Deux répresentations', 314.

[141] See esp. the account of the contrasting circumstances, by late 1190, of the rich and poor among the forces besieging Acre: *Estoire*, ll. 4089–100, trans. p. 88. See also *Estoire*, ll. 4197–220, trans. p. 90. In the account of the crusaders' pilgrimage to Jerusalem, the narrator implies that he was among those who travelled on foot rather than with those on horseback: *Estoire*, ll. 11997–12006, trans. p. 189. But cf. the emphasis upon the care of the poor by the rich in *Estoire*, ll. 4407–56, trans. pp. 92–3. See also the hint of snobbishness towards lower-class people in *Estoire*, ll. 2908–10, trans. p. 74.

Jerusalem was still not recaptured, a point driven home by the inclusion of the group pilgrimage sequence. Apart from the rather different case of the analepsis concerning the siege of Acre, which is motivated by a desire to fill out the backstory of the crusade for clarity's sake because the arrival of the kings' forces represented the intensification of a pre-existing struggle, the pilgrimage section is the text's most extended break from the deeds-of-Richard orientation of the narrative as a whole. The contrast between the two sequences is effectively that between the reasons why hopes were raised by Richard's arrival in Palestine and the disappointment of those hopes, a disjunction which enables the crusade rank-and-file to serve as a kind of purist, devout chorus frustrated by the fact that its many sufferings have not been rewarded by the conquest of Jerusalem.

The rank-and-file's perspective is, however, balanced, and even exposed as unrealistic, by passages that express an appreciation of the severe tactical difficulties that militated against a strike against Jerusalem, as well as a strategic understanding of the value of directing the crusaders' energies towards consolidation of the surviving Latin footholds in Outremer with a view to exerting military pressure on Egypt, the key to the regional dominance that would best secure the Latins' long-term security.[142] Far from appearing in the text in order to enable the narrator to drop hints about his own circumstances and sympathies, therefore, the poorer crusaders and their stubborn attachment to the idea of capturing Jerusalem serve to cement the narrator's credentials as someone equipped to understand and navigate the ultimately unresolvable tensions within the crusade while always doing justice to its, and especially Richard's, achievements.[143] Moreover, because, in the narrator's estimation, suffering was so commonplace and severe, the rank-and-file are those elements within the crusade army who routinely get to enact the close connection between collective perception and experience that we shall see forms a central part of the narrator's self-validation. As the narrator observes very close to the end of the text:

> Just as the martyrs who leave this world suffer different martyrdoms for God, so, if I dare say it, did those who undertook this pilgrimage suffer in different ways, endure different events. But many ignorant people say repeatedly, in their folly, that they achieved nothing in Syria since Jerusalem was not conquered. But they have not inquired into the business. They criticize what they do not

[142] See esp. Richard's detailed and judicious reply to those urging a push towards Jerusalem in *Estoire*, ll. 10128–83, trans. p. 168. See also the defence, against implied critics, of Richard's agreement to the concluding truce with Saladin: *Estoire*, ll. 11718–67, trans. p. 186–7.

[143] Cf. the narrator's celebration of the golden mean in one of his most overt ethical remarks: *Estoire*, ll. 8746–9, trans. p. 150: 'It is right that one should know and hear and one can know in truth, that no one should rejoice too much in joy, nor should any mourn too much in mourning.'

> know and where they did not set their feet. But we who were there saw it; we saw this and knew it, and just as we had to suffer, so we must not lie about others who suffered for the love of God, as we saw with our own eyes.[144]

To what extent did this emphasis on eyewitness perception accommodate other ways of learning about events? And did the experiential basis of true understanding of the crusade extend to the vicarious experience of reading and hearing about others? An important clue is provided by the word *estoire*, and its variant *estorie*, which is the text's preferred term for a narrative. In his study of the appearances of this word in twelfth-century vernacular historiography, Peter Damian-Grint has argued that, within this particular generic discourse, *estoire* was understood to mean 'a (vernacular) narrative of past events, presented as true, and whose authenticity is attested by an authority'.[145] Some of the use of *estoire* by Ambroise is consistent with this definition, though whether all or most of the instances of it refer to an actual written source is another matter. There are some references that seem, at least on the surface, to suggest that the author made use of written source materials, including narrative accounts. For example, when commenting upon Raymond of Tripoli's culpability in the events leading up to the battle of Hattin, the narrator observes that 'later he was to die shamefully because of it [his treacherous dealings], as the account tells us' ('com l'estorie reconte').[146] Raymond died in late 1187, more than three years before Ambroise arrived in the East, so the reference could conceivably be to an account of events in the Latin East around that time.[147] Similarly, when Count Henry of Champagne and other envoys journey from Acre to Tyre in April 1192 in order to offer Conrad of Montferrat the crown of Jerusalem, we are informed that 'The history tells us reliably that he [Conrad] had such joy in his heart' ('Si dit l'estoire finement / Qu'il ot tel joie en son corage').[148] Here the narrator sets up a contrast by stating a few lines earlier that he saw the envoys depart, the implication being that his knowledge of the start and conclusion of their mission was necessarily based on different kinds of information.[149]

[144] *Estoire*, ll. 12181–200, trans. p. 192: translation slightly revised.

[145] P. Damian-Grint, '*Estoire* as Word and Genre: Meaning and Literary Usage in the Twelfth Century', *Medium Aevum*, 66 (1997), 189–206, definition at 198. See also *idem*, *New Historians*, pp. 254–8.

[146] *Estoire*, ll. 2482–3, trans. p. 67.

[147] See also *Estoire*, l. 2739, trans. p. 71: 'So goes the tale that does not falter' ('Si dist l'estoire qui ne ceste'): the context is Guy of Lusignan's celebration of the arrival in the east of his brother Geoffrey in 1189, again long before Ambroise was there himself. Also *Estoire*, l. 3531, trans. p. 82: 'as the history tells us in truth' ('Ço dit l'estorie en verité'), concerning the large number of catapults within Acre at a point in the siege before Richard's arrival.

[148] *Estoire*, ll. 8713–14, trans. p. 149.

[149] *Estoire*, l. 8695, trans. p. 149.

On the other hand, most of the text's mentions of *estoire*, and of synonyms such as *livre* and *escripture*, involve self-reference, some unambiguously, others probably so. Damian-Grint observes of the twelfth-century vernacular historiographical corpus as a whole that references to source materials outnumber self-references, but that the eyewitness authors, Fantosme and Ambroise, buck this trend.[150] Many of the *Estoire*'s self-references are unambiguous: for example, 'Ambroise, the writer of this book, says that';[151] 'One day something happened that Ambroise relates in his writings';[152] 'according to the tale I tell';[153] 'this is where the story ends'.[154] Other mentions introduce an element of ambiguity but are probably also self-references, especially those that refer to incidents in and around the area where the narrator is himself situated.[155] Two further points about the use of *estoire* and its synonyms in the text are worthy of emphasis. First, references to such terms are not concentrated in the analepsis concerning the pre-Richard stages of the siege of Acre, where we would expect the gaps in Ambroise's eyewitness knowledge to have been greatest; they are distributed quite evenly across the whole text. True, the narrator remarks of himself at the point at which the analepsis is introduced that 'He did not see any of this [the earlier action]; I only know what I have read.'[156] But the emphasis here is clearly on the admission of the absence of eyewitness experience, not on what were actually used as sources in its stead; what it was that was read is not specified, and it is therefore tempting to conclude that *leü* was simply chosen as a neat contrast to *veü* in order to create a snappy rhyme. In any event, the English and Norman veterans of the siege whom Ambroise encountered at Acre are likely to have been his principal sources of information for the period 1189–91, not a written record.

Second, many of the appeals to *estoire* and similar terms reinforce details that are incidental to the main plot, even exotic, trivial or redundant: for example, we

[150] Damian-Grint, '*Estoire* as Word and Genre', 192–5.

[151] *Estoire*, l. 171, trans. p. 32: 'Ambroise dit, qui fist cest livre'.

[152] *Estoire*, ll. 3727–8, trans. p. 84: 'Un jor avint une aventure – / Ço conte Ambroise en s'escripture'.

[153] *Estoire*, l. 11237, trans. p. 180: 'Selonc l'estoire que jo di ci'.

[154] *Estoire*, l. 12305, trans. p. 194: 'l'estoire en [i]tel point fine': translation slightly revised.

[155] E.g. *Estoire*, l. 9411, trans. p. 159: 'He who tells the story says that' ('Si dit cil qui l'estorie traite'); l. 11383, trans. p. 182: 'The tale tells truly' ('Si dit l'estoire finement'). See also ll. 928–31, trans. p. 44 where the narrator expresses doubts whether the *estoire* can definitively pronounce that Philip II was acting treacherously in his dealings with Tancred of Lecce in Sicily, whereas popular belief was confident that this was the case, the implication being that *estoire* here signifies his own record which formally maintains higher standards of proof, while it is also hinted for good measure that the rumours were quite possibly true. Cf. the contrast between the authority of *livres* and *fable* at ll. 7120–3, trans. p. 128.

[156] *Estoire*, ll. 2401–2, trans. p. 66: 'Kar il n'en aveit rien veü / Fors tant come jo en ai leü.'

are told that it took two men to arm one particularly destructive enemy catapult 'according to the written word';[157] two hundred snakes were loaded onto a Muslim supply ship at Beirut 'according to the written tale' as well as, for good measure, 'the word of someone who helped in putting them there';[158] and 'the tale tells truly' that Henry of Champagne fought on horseback at Jaffa.[159] There is one possible glimpse of Ambroise consulting written materials in the observation that a clerk had kept a list of the higher-status casualties during and after the siege of Acre;[160] the narrator implies that he had had sight of this document in stating that the number of archbishops, bishops, counts and lords 'is found and written in the account, written in his hand'.[161] As so described this document would seem to resemble the casualty list that Roger of Howden inserted into his *Gesta Regis* and, in an abbreviated form, his *Chronica*; this list is unlikely to have originated with Roger, for many of the entries in it died before his arrival in the east.[162] If, as seems quite possible, Ambroise had sight of a version of this list, it would have interesting implications for his access to the circle of clerics in and around Richard I's household and to the documents that they produced. But for our immediate purposes, the important point is that this reference, however intriguing, is unusual in a text that is generally shy of identifying what, if any, written sources it used.[163] The use of such sources is gestured towards from time to time, but they do not play a significant role in the narrator's staking out of his authority.

It follows that the bulk of the material in the text, to the extent that it has an experiential basis, is grounded in a combination of direct, individual eyewitness perception and forms of collective experience in which the narrator participates but which is not overtly filtered through his individual gaze, as well as information supplied by others. With respect to the last of these, the *Estoire* refers to, or implies the existence of, oral informants far more frequently than it gestures towards the idea of written sources. It is important to remember that the large

[157] *Estoire*, l. 3541, trans. p. 82: 'sulunc la letre'. The rhyme is with *metre* used of the act of placing the stone in the sling. Cf. l. 7531, trans. p. 134: 'according to the book' ('ço dit li livres') of some of the details of a skirmish in December 1191.

[158] *Estoire*, ll. 2177–8, trans. p. 63: 'Ce conte l'estoire e la letre / E cil quis a metre': translation slightly revised.

[159] *Estoire*, l. 11383, trans. p. 182: 'Si dit l'estoire finement'.

[160] *Estoire*, ll. 5575–7, trans. p. 109: 'Dont uns clers escrist le conte, / De toz cels qui en l'ost mururent / [E] qui auques renomé furent'.

[161] *Estoire*, ll. 5582–3, trans. p. 109: 'En la letre trova e dist / El fol qui de sa main escrist'.

[162] Roger of Howden, *Gesta Regis*, ii, pp. 147–50; *Chronica*, iii, pp. 87–9. Although Howden's totals are substantially fewer than the figures of forty counts and 500 lords cited by Ambroise, he lists five archbishops compared with the *Estoire*'s six.

[163] Cf. the mention of the papal crusade appeal in terms which would seem to suggest some knowledge of the bull *Audita tremendi*: *Estoire*, ll. 43–52, trans. pp. 29–30.

majority of statements made in the text are not pegged to any source; they are simply presented as the informed utterances of a narrator who is fashioned to seem, if not omniscient, then certainly deeply knowledgeable and reliable. Nor are certain types of information or storyworld detail source-tagged particularly often, as if they represented particular challenges to the narrator's ability to come by knowledge of what was happening around him. Some of the details so sourced are incidental to the plot, even quite trivial in themselves.[164] It follows that all references to sources are in the nature of optional padding, often in the interests of well-worked rhyme. Nonetheless, the sheer number of references to oral informants of some sort suggests that this is a significant part of the narrator's self-fashioning. In this, the effect is cumulative and tonal, the narrator building up a picture of his receptivity to a variety of sources of information ranging from hearsay – the buzz of a military camp – to precise and well-informed briefings by informants whose eyewitness perception he is willing to treat as equivalent to his own.

Many of the constructions that express the acquisition of knowledge by the narrator are imprecise: they do not invoke a particular location or occasion, nor hint at the narrator's circumstances. The information simply seems to enter the storyworld under its own propulsion.[165] At a significant number of junctures, however, the narrator positions himself in relation to the circulation of news and the gaining of information. There are, for example, points in the text in which the narrator sets himself up as the representative or spokesperson of communal understandings. Lamenting the death of James of Avesnes, for example, the narrator remarks that the failure of some, specifically the count of Dreux and his men, to come to James's aid in his final moments was the subject of 'much talk' ('grand parlance') in the army.[166] The narrator then hints at a sense of obligation vis-à-vis an emergent collective memory in stating that 'I have heard so many speak ill of this that the history [i.e. the present text] cannot deny it.'[167] (It is probably the case, however, that the narrator would have included an account of James's death anyway, given that he is identified several times as a conspicuous and praiseworthy hero; in addition, his death cues the most developed *planctus*-type

[164] E.g. *Estoire*, l. 1687, trans. p. 55: Isaac Komnenos's translator 'whom I heard called John' ('Qui jo oï apeler Johan'); l. 2863, trans. p. 73: the fact that certain arrivals at Acre come from Denmark, the [Welsh?] Marches and Cornwall is attested by the words of 'one who knows well' ('Ço dist tels qui bien le saveit'); l. 5771, trans. p. 111: a man-at-arms who fought resolutely even though badly injured was called Evrart, 'so they told us' ('ce nos conterent': translation amended).

[165] E.g. 'l'en dist': *Estoire*, l. 628, trans. p. 39; 'ço conta l'em': l. 7601, trans. p. 135.

[166] *Estoire*, ll. 6644–8, trans. p. 122.

[167] *Estoire*, ll. 6649–50, trans. p. 122: 'Sin oï l'en tant gent mesdire / Que l'estorie nel puet desdire.' (Here *estorie* must be an example of self-reference.)

lament in the text.)[168] The narrator also appeals to the beliefs of 'the people' in the context of appearing not to make direct accusations of treacherous conduct against major figures while implicitly endorsing the popular conviction that they were culpable; we have seen this strategy of indirection used of Philip II's actions in Sicily, and it is also applied to Raymond of Tripoli's alleged betrayal of Guy of Lusignan.[169]

Elsewhere there are occasional appeals to the argument that the narrator cannot lie because it would run counter to the recollections of the other observers of a given scene, as if these were a matter of secure and incontestable group memory.[170] Otherwise, the narrator favours constructions that imply not common belief or the circulation of camp-fire rumour but more candid and specific acts of briefing in which the information is either directed to him individually or as a member of a group of auditors. The nature and composition of such groups, as invoked by *nos*, are never specified, and in some instances may simply be a case of the editorial 'we', but for the most part the reader/listener is invited to picture the narrator coming by news within small and attentive gatherings, not simply as one member of the whole crusade army.[171] Those who pass on information are seldom identified by name – the few exceptions, mentions of aristocrats who were participants in the action that is being reported rather than outside observers of it, seem to be cases of name dropping[172] – but in several instances the trustworthiness of the witness is affirmed in terms redolent of the language of many historiographical

[168] See *Estoire*, ll. 2848–59, trans. pp. 72–3, where James is compared favourably to Alexander, Hector and Achilles; ll. 3046–7, trans. p. 75; ll. 6170–1, trans. p. 116; ll. 6623–50, trans. pp. 121–2. For James as a hero of the narrative, see also Ailes, 'Heroes of War', pp. 30–3.

[169] *Estoire*, ll. 2507, trans. p. 68: 'Mais li poeples puis recorda'.

[170] See e.g. *Estoire*, l. 6279, trans. p. 117 of the heavy and murderous raining down of arrows at Arsuf: 'many would know if I were lying' ('Ço sevent plus[or] si ge ment').

[171] In a number of cases Ailes's translation suggests that information was communicated to the narrator alone, 'me', whereas the text is clear that he is to be understood as one of a group of listeners, *nos*: *Estoire*, l. 5771, trans. p. 111: 'so they told us' ('ce nos conterent'); l. 9839, trans. p. 164: 'so we have been told' ('ço nos conta l'am'). For the narratorial 'we', see e.g. ll. 8648–9, trans. p. 148: 'as we bore witness and have told you' ('...comm nos veïmes, / E come nos le vos deïmes').

[172] *Estoire*, ll. 8684–91, trans. pp. 148–9: Stephen of Turnham recalls the names of some of the envoys acting for the treacherous Conrad of Montferrat whom he encountered in Jerusalem when on an embassy to Saladin; ll. 9999–10002. trans, p. 166: Baldwin of Carew relates that he witnessed the decapitation of the man who had just given him his horse in battle.

prefaces.[173] Several such informants are described as eyewitnesses or as having been present at a given event.[174]

For all that the narrator regularly declares his reliance on informants, however, direct eyewitness observation is more frequently invoked. In this way, it serves as an important prop of the text's claims to authority. The narrator is aided by the imprecision that almost always attends his positioning and line of sight relative to the action that is being observed. There are several passages in which one can infer the presence of Ambroise-as-character within a group that is granted agency, especially when we come across the first person plural, which the narrator uses quite sparingly. But Ambroise does not make any intervention in the storyworld as a named individual. Instead, the narrator is to be mostly imagined floating close to the action and casting an informed, and unobstructed, gaze upon it. Disavowals of knowledge and expressions of uncertainty tend towards the conventional in mostly referring to names and numbers. What seem to be concessions on the narrator's part do the work of reality effects in that they mimic the boundaries that eyewitnesses to an event are typically prepared to acknowledge, thereby drawing an implied distinction between an accurate and retrievable mnemonic core and dispensable peripheral details.[175] As Damian-Grint has argued, these are powerful validating devices that reinforce the narrator's truth claims by ring-fencing those areas of knowledge where he is willing to concede occasional uncertainty.[176]

[173] E.g. *Estoire*, l. 704, trans. p. 41: 'according to one who should be believed' ('Si dist tels qui nos fist a croire'); l. 2863, trans. p. 73: 'so says one who knows well' ('Ço dist tels qui bien le saveit'); ll. 8015–16, trans. p. 140: 'as we are told by those who know the truth' ('Issi come[e] cil nos conterent / Qui saveient le verité'); l. 10416, trans. p. 171: 'One who knew the situation said that' ('Si dit cil qui puis sot lor estre'). Cf. those informants who are well qualified by virtue of having counted enemy casualties in circumstances redolent of Bahā' al-Dīn's investigations: ll. 6613–14, trans. p. 121: 'Those who were there [in the aftermath of the battle of Arsuf] said that they counted' ('Si distrent cil qui i alerent / Qui des Sarazins mort conterent').

[174] E.g. *Estoire*, l. 677, trans. p. 40: 'With them [Kings Richard and Philip] was he who recounted this tale' ('Si fud o lui quil reconta') – a possible self-reference; l. 3573, trans. p. 82: 'Those who were there saw' ('Ço virent ço qui illoc erent'); l. 3616, trans. p. 83: 'He who told me about this saw' ('Si vit cil quil me reconta'); l. 8275, trans. p. 143: 'those who were there tell' ('Car cil redistrent q*ui* i fure*nt*'); l. 8908, trans. 152: 'He from whom I received this tells' ('Si dit cil aprés que jel di').

[175] For professions of ignorance or uncertainty as to numbers, see e.g. *Estoire*, ll. 470–6, trans. p. 36 (the numbers of those who perished when a bridge over the Rhône collapsed); l. 736, trans. p. 41 (the number of Lombards cut down by Richard); l. 3829–30, trans. p. 85 (the number of siege engines built outside Acre); l. 6592, trans. p. 121 (the number of Turks killed by William des Barres and his men at Arsuf). For ignorance of names, see e.g. *Estoire*, ll. 884–5, trans. p. 43; ll. 9284–5, trans. p. 157; and virtually the same formulation at ll.10903–4, trans. p. 177.

[176] Damian-Grint, *New Historians*, pp. 166–8.

There are a few passages in which Ambroise the individual perceiving agent nudges towards breaking the fourth wall and intradiegetically entering the scene that he is constructing. For example, when we are told that a spy named Bernard, most probably an eastern Christian, and two companions report to Richard's camp, the narrator would seem to be including himself in a group of onlookers marvelling at the spies' ability to pass themselves off as the enemy: 'I swear to you that I never saw anyone look so like Saracens nor speak their language better with people listening.'[177] In addition, there is a handful of moments in the narrative in which the narrator as an actor within the diegesis permits himself to be situated quite precisely. It is significant, however, that the clearest such scene involves the unusually constricting environment of a ship that is with one part of Richard I's fleet as it nears Acre. Once the narrator is on dry land, in contrast, he is able to roam freely in the grey area between intradiegetic involvement and detached observation. Triangulations and deictic shifters that situate the narrator's line of sight, and so by extension plant him in a specific location at a given moment, are few and imprecise, typically involving nothing more than positioning to the left and right of a putative but unspecified reference point.[178] The narrator's free-floating quality is enhanced by the fact that he seldom tracks his own personal movements; almost all the text's seemingly autobiographical content is embedded in collective action and perception.[179] Nor is there a favoured social nexus within which the narrator is immersed as his default social environment, such as a particular lord's household; the range of 'we' in the text extends from the total Latin Christian world to the English crusade army in contradistinction to the French, but it does not shrink down to more specific collectivities – part of the reason why the text offers so little in the way of a biographical 'fix' on Ambroise the author.[180] There is a cumulative sense that the narrator's primary

[177] *Estoire*, ll. 10248–51, trans. p. 169: translation slightly revised.

[178] See e.g. *Estoire*, ll. 7417–18, trans. p. 132 (the Turks attack 'from the right and from the left'); ll. 9293–4, trans. p. 157 (one of the banners raised on the walls of Darum, that belonging to Andrew of Chauvigny, is placed 'to the right'); l. 9783, trans. p. 163 (Richard has his tent pitched uphill and to the right of his main force); ll. 10414–15, trans. p. 171 (the Turks are pursued 'to the right and to the left'); ll. 10681–2, trans. p. 174 ('The French were on the left and the king and his men on the right'); ll. 11408–10, trans. p. 183 ('The knights were on the left, towards St Nicholas, along the strand, against the Saracen race'); ll. 12020–1, trans. pp. 189–90 (the pilgrims walk to Mount Calvary 'on the right').

[179] E.g. *Estoire*, l. 518, trans. p. 37 ('we found', *trovames,* the people of Messina evil); ll. 1500–9, trans. p. 52 (some of the account of the amphibious assault on Limassol is narrated in the first person plural, including the remark 'We, however, better understood the business of war').

[180] It is noteworthy that the first instances of the first person plural in the narrative are of maximal extent, referring to collective responsibility ('nostre surfaite folie') throughout Christendom for the disasters of 1187: *Estoire*, ll. 11–19, trans. p. 29.

area of eyewitness experience is first Acre and then the movements of Richard's army, but the boundaries between direct and indirect experience are not sharply drawn. Events in Tyre, for example, are at one point recounted in terms that nudge towards the appearance of autoptic knowledge even though it is unlikely that Ambroise the historical actor visited the city at that particular moment given the text's close attention to the experiences of Richard I's army around the same time.[181]

As noted earlier, the narrator reinforces the transition from his extended analepsis on the past history of the siege of Acre to the narrative now, as Richard I arrives in Outremer, by stating that henceforth his treatment of the *estorie* and *materie* will be governed by 'what he can remember of the story of how Acre was taken, as he saw it with his own eyes'.[182] The transition is redolent of Bahā' al-Dīn's self-conscious assertion of eyewitness authority once the action reaches the point at which he entered Saladin's service.[183] For the narrator of the *Estoire*, however, his newly reacquired eyewitness gaze is less focused on the figure of Richard than is that of the narrator of the *Nawādir* on Saladin. What the narrator therefore 'sees' shades beyond the accumulation of specific observed moments towards impressions and judgements closer to the ancient Greek sense of autopsy as understanding born of experience. That is to say, perception itself becomes part of the experience that the narrator shares with his fellow crusaders, not something detached from it; and it is the cumulative force of this immersive seeing-while-doing, or rather seeing-as-doing, that grants the narrator much of his authority.

That said, the narrator first stakes a claim to visual acuity and perceptiveness in relation to specific moments or occasions, the essential building blocks of his larger autoptic competence. It is significant that two of the explicit mentions of Ambroise (which, as we have seen, are all in the third person) refer to his witnessing of events – the Lombards' flight during the English storming of Messina, and a Turk's efforts to destroy two of the king of France's siege engines – while others do similar work by reinforcing the notion of direct experience.[184] It is also significant that early in the text there is a run of visually rich set-pieces that set up the narrator's gaze as conspicuously

[181] The narrator states that 'we saw' the two men who had just murdered Conrad of Montferrat: *Estoire*, l. 8826, trans. p. 151. This may, however, be a scribal error: see trans. p. 151 n. 568.

[182] *Estoire*, ll. 4560–2, trans. p. 94: 'De ço quil en vient a memoire / E coment Acre fud eüe, / Si com il vit a sa veüe.'

[183] See above, pp. 209–10, 214–19.

[184] *Estoire*, l. 728, trans. p. 41 ('Si vit Ambroises a icel hore'); l. 4822, trans. p. 99 ('Que Ambroises vit cele foie'). Cf. the bearing of witness concerning tarantulas that plagued the crusade army: 'En testimonie en trai Ambroise': *Estoire*, l. 5913, trans. p. 113. See also the declaration of certainty as to the time of day when the army was readying to move: 'Ço solt Ambroise enfin sanz falte': *Estoire*, l. 6005, trans. p. 114.

observant and reflective. One is Richard I's coronation feast, as noted above. This is preceded by an account of Archbishop Joscius of Tyre's pleas for help for the Latin East to Kings Philip II and Henry II at Gisors (in January 1188). In a scene reminiscent of Odo of Deuil's evocation of the crush and discomfort at St-Denis when Louis VII set out for the east, the narrator neatly maps mass enthusiasm for the crusade onto his own impressions and their in-the-moment sensory correlates:

> There you might have seen knights running up eagerly to take the cross. They did not seem a downhearted people. I saw there such a large press around the bishops, the archbishops and the abbots (may God help me and protect them) and so many people rushing forward that, with the great heat (may no one ever demand a greater), they were nearly suffocated.[185]

Later, the attentive gaze, attuned to courtly environments, that was brought to bear upon Richard's coronation feast is mobilized once more during the 1190 Christmas celebrations in Mategrifon, the castle that the king has built as his base of operations in Sicily. Note the repetition of the act of seeing and the practised, scrutinizing gaze in the service of informed evaluation:

> So a great celebratory feast was held on the day of the Nativity. Truly King Richard had it announced that all should come and celebrate the feast with him...I was present at the feasting in the hall and I saw no dirty table-linen, nor wooden chalice or bowl. Rather I saw there rich vessels, embossed, with images cast on them, and richly set with precious stones, not in any way paltry. I saw there such good service that everyone had what he wanted. It was a good and honourable feast as is appropriate for such a festival; I have not, it seems to me, seen so many rich gifts given at once as King Richard gave then, handing over to the king of France and to his people vessels of gold and silver.[186]

The sense of an assured narratorial eye that these set-pieces help to establish is carried over into the action once Richard and his army reach Palestine. It is characterized by an ability to pick out particular scenes, some of them visually striking in themselves or reinforced by reality effects or simile, such as when Richard and his companions pitch in to help carry catapult beams along the sandy beach at Darum, 'their faces sweating...[and] weighed down like a horse or a beast of burden'.[187] Beyond such single moments, the narrator's gaze

[185] *Estoire*, ll. 144–54, trans. pp. 31–2.
[186] *Estoire*, ll. 1077–81, 1088–1105, trans. p. 46.
[187] *Estoire*, ll. 9175–81, trans. p. 156: translation slightly revised. Cf. the reference to the joyful return of a spy to Richard's camp: *Estoire*, ll. 9809–12, trans. p. 164.

extends outwards to recurrent events,[188] and from there to evidence of patterns of behaviour, abstractions and collective moods.[189] Over the course of the text the narrator shifts from a preference for the first person singular to the first person plural to express acts of seeing in which he is involved. The extent of the 'we' within which the narrator is thereby embedded is never specified, and in many instances, when an event presents itself to the gaze of the crusaders *en masse*, specificity would be impossible or superfluous. Nonetheless, the plot contexts suggest that verbs of perception in the first person plural are not cases of a 'royal we' but are intended to express a collective act, just as we saw above that the text's references to coming by information typically imply a collective receipt of news.[190]

It is noteworthy that the most pronounced cluster of *veïsmes/veïmes*, 'we saw', in the text occurs towards the end in the narrator's account of the pilgrims' journey to Jerusalem and the holy sites that they visited in the city, a sequence within which the collective nature of the pilgrims' devotional acts and of their emotional reactions is particularly emphasized.[191] Although there is some important action that remains to be played out after the pilgrimage sequence, as we have seen, the narrator effectively signs off as an eyewitness in his own right at this point, thereby reasserting the fact that his individual gaze, while made evident at several junctures, has been broadly subsumed within the collective perceptions that he feels qualified to articulate.[192] The narrator thus seeks to establish that, for all his visual acuity and elite cultural situatedness, he brings no privileged or idiosyncratic perception to the act of seeing the crusade unfold before him. Consequently, he is at the service of, and sensitive to, communal perceptions. At one point, for example, he stresses that his enthusiastic evocation

[188] E.g. *Estoire*, ll. 9106–8, trans. p. 155: 'Many times we saw there came to the king of England messengers who brought him trouble': translation revised. Cf. the mention of the witnessing of the departure of messengers for Tyre: *Estoire*, ll. 8694–5, trans. p. 149. See also the remark that 'we often saw when we were encamped, in the evening… that the French went apart from the other men and pitched camp by themselves, aside': *Estoire*, ll. 10614–19, trans. p. 173.

[189] E.g. *Estoire*, l. 9494, trans. p. 160: 'There I saw the army full of joy' ('La vi l'ost tote esleïcee'). Cf. the reference to narratorial perception, voiced in the third person ('Que cil vit qui l'estoire trove'), of conditions within the army in *Estoire,* ll. 7072–4, trans. p. 128.

[190] See e.g. the reinforcing 'with our own eyes' ('a nos oilz') in an observation of Richard I's movements and actions: *Estoire*, l. 10914, trans. p. 177.

[191] *Estoire,* ll. 11987–12066, esp. ll. 11989, 11992, 12006, 12007, 12027, 12031, 12049, trans. pp. 189–90.

[192] Other eyewitnesses on whom the narrator draws are likewise situated within collective responses: see e.g. the reference to those who were besieged within Jaffa reporting ('Si conterent cil qui la furent') the dire circumstances that they faced after they agreed to surrender: *Estoire*, ll. 11024–47, trans. p. 178.

of Richard's prowess in battle is not mere flattery 'for so many men see his fine blows that they make me dwell on them'.[193] Likewise, he insists that the sight of Richard's departure from Palestine would have elicited the same reaction in any viewer:

> Anyone who witnessed [*Qui lors veïst*] his leave-taking would have seen the people in tears, following him and praying for him, lamenting [the loss of] his prowess, his deeds of valour and his generosity...Then you would have seen many men weep and the king, who was also distressed, without delay set to sea.[194]

The narrator makes use of two devices, conventional in themselves but highlighted by dint of repetition, in order to emphasize the visual quality of the crusade and his own receptivity to it. The first is hyperbole, many instances of which have a visual component. Often there is an evaluative dimension, the narrator thereby suggesting that he or whoever else is stated or implied to be viewing at a given moment is capable of penetrating beneath surface details in order to form judgements about characters' mental states as well as to make pertinent comparisons with similar scenes. The narrator's own gaze is permitted hyperbolic judgement with reference to implied life experiences that predate the crusade: of Richard's coronation feast, which we have seen functions as an early marker of the narrator's eyewitness competence, he observes, 'Never in all my life ('Në onques ne vi en ma vie') did I see a court served in more courtly a manner; I saw such rich vessels in that most lovely hall';[195] and the formula is all but repeated ('Onq[ue]s ne vi tele en ma vie') with respect to the sight of Richard's fleet when it had reached Messina.[196] Although the narrator makes further appeals to his personal experience and appraisals,[197] he mostly opens out the hyperbolic perception in ways that parallel his sharing out of focalization in general. Thus hyperbole is clearly attached to seeing in the first person plural,

193 *Estoire*, ll.10427–30, trans. p. 171: 'Car tantes genz ses biaus cops virent / Que sor ço arester me firent': translation slightly revised.

194 *Estoire*, ll. 12238–42, 12249–52, trans. pp. 192–3. Cf. the remark that anyone who saw the array of the crusade army would have judged it a *grant affaire*: *Estoire*, ll. 5860–1, trans. p. 112.

195 *Estoire*, ll. 195–8, trans. p. 32.

196 *Estoire*, ll. 539–40, trans. p. 38.

197 See e.g. of the riches to be found on Cyprus, 'I have not seen any like them anywhere else I have been': *Estoire*, l. 2075 trans. p. 61. But note that this statement is principally made in the service of a pun on *seie*, 'silk' and 'have been'. See also *Estoire*, ll. 9023–5, trans. p. 154, where it is noted of the marriage in Tyre between Count Henry of Champagne and the widow of the recently murdered Conrad of Montferrat that there was joy 'such as I believe I shall never see nor hear in my whole life', which seems to imply authorial autopsy.

creating the sense of each member of the group reacting in unison to a given perception.[198] In addition, it extends still further to suggest a communal response, on behalf of which the narrator effectively serves as a spokesman. The generalizing thrust is typically accentuated by appeal to a generic observer or by the use of the passive voice, the narrator's favoured means to frame hyperbolic remarks. Thus of a sea battle off Tyre around March 1190, which Ambroise the historical actor could not have witnessed in person, it is noted that 'Never was such a battle seen. No man ever witnessed such a fight.'[199]

This opening out of perception further permits the narrator to blur the boundaries between the evaluations that he himself introduces to guide the narratee's response and the reactions of the actors themselves in the midst of the action. For them, hyperbole does much of the work of expressing their own reactions, in this doubtless mimicking the exaggerated terms in which people often report close shaves, noteworthy experiences or striking sights in conversational discourse. The narrator shows that he is aware of this tendency in others but is happy to build it into his own evaluative programme. Thus, when the Christian army is confronted by the Turks near Tell Kurdana in November 1190, we are told:

> When they looked around them they saw all the Turks in the world, or so it seemed to them [*Ço lor fud vis*], surrounding them, besieging their army. The land was so covered with them, beyond and behind, to the left and the right, that the army wished itself elsewhere. Never were such people seen.[200]

Hyperbolic group perception is so typical of the storyworld that it extends to the enemy. When Richard arrives at Acre, there is an outpouring of collective relief and joy among the Christians which, when perceived by the Turks, leads to a back and forth of perception and reaction:

[198] E.g. *Estoire*, ll. 1744–5, trans. p. 56 of galleys arriving at Limassol 'so well armed and equipped that we had never seen such in our lives' ('Ne vit l'em tels en noz vies').

[199] *Estoire*, ll. 3318–19, trans. p. 79: 'Ne fud tel bataille veüe, / N'om ne la vit de sa veüe'. For other examples of the passive voice in conjunction with hyperbolic assertions, see e.g. *Estoire*, l. 417, trans. p. 36: 'Tel merveille ne fud veüe'; l. 4626, trans. p. 95: 'Ainc n'en eürent tant veüz'; ll. 7772–3, trans. p. 137: 'Que onques puis que Deus fist le siecle / Ne fud gent veüe si tenicle'; l. 8549, trans. p. 147: 'Si ne cuit c'onques fust veüe'; l. 9730, trans. p. 163: 'Si ne cuit mie c'unques fust veüe'; l. 11535, trans. p. 184: 'Onques tele ne fud veüe'. For the generic observer, see also the narrator's remark concerning the progress of Richard's army before the battle of Arsuf that 'I do not think that any man saw or would ever see in any place' a finer order of march ('Si ne cuit pas que nus hom voie, / Ne qu'en un liu nul ost veïst / Plus bel errer que illoc feïst'): *Estoire*, ll. 6095–7, trans. p. 115.

[200] *Estoire*, ll. 4016–23, trans. pp. 87–8

> I think you would never have seen, anywhere you might go, such lights and candles so that it seemed to [*Estoit avis que*] the Turks in the opposing army that the whole valley was ablaze. When they heard of the arrival of the king on whose account the celebrations were held they gave the impression of great excitement [*Par semblant lores s'esbaudirent*].[201]

It is also such a potent device that its range of reference extends back into the distant past, overcoming the narrator's general reluctance to refer to times before the events that he narrates.[202] In all these ways, hyperbole draws attention to the crusade as spectacle, while normalizing the narrator's frequent exaggerations by situating them within a collective mood, what amounts to a culture of expectation and perception among the participants themselves that readily accommodates the striking and the remarkable.

The second, and more important, device involves interjections that co-opt the narratee's visual imagination by means of *veïssiez* ('you would have seen'). As Damian-Grint has observed, this is a formula that evokes the form and tone of the oral delivery of epic.[203] In *chansons de geste* it often involves invitations to linger imaginatively over a poignant but essentially static scene, such as a battlefield once the fighting has ceased. There are some similar *mises-en-scène* in the *Estoire*, including loving evocations of aristocratic bearing, chivalric display and martial aptitude,[204] but it is noticeable that the great majority of cases have

[201] *Estoire*, ll. 2369–77, trans. p. 66. Cf. the emir Sanguin of Aleppo's observation to Saladin about Richard that 'We've never seen anyone like him' ('Onques mes nul tel ne veïmes'): *Estoire*, l. 6818, trans. p. 124: translation revised.

[202] Thus of the bloody nature of one battle the narrator remarks, 'There you might have seen such a slaughter of Turks, such as was never seen in the days of our ancestors ('Tel ne vit l'em el tens nostre aive'): *Estoire*, ll. 10475–6, trans. p. 172. Cf. the almost identical formulation used of the fine military display of Richard's army as it marches from Ascalon: *Estoire*, l. 9750, trans. p. 163.

[203] Damian–Grint, *New Historians*, pp. 146–9. See also Schirato, 'Forme narrative', 112–15.

[204] E.g. *Estoire*, ll. 5728–43, trans. p. 111: 'There you would have seen chivalry, the finest of young men, the most worthy and most elite that were ever seen, before then or since. There you would have seen so many confident men, with such fine armour, such valiant and daring men-at-arms, renowned for their prowess. There you would have seen so many pennoncels on shining, fine lances; there you would have seen so many banners, worked in many designs, fine hauberks and good helmets; there are not so many of such quality in five kingdoms; there you would have seen a people on the march who were much to be feared.' For similar 'mood' montages, see *Estoire*, ll. 4619–30, trans. p. 95; ll. 8735–45, trans. p. 150. Cf. one of the narrator's more conventional mobilizations of the device in the depiction of the aftermath of Richard's defeat of Isaac's forces at Limassol: *Estoire*, ll. 1638–42, trans. p. 54: 'The battle was hard fought and fierce. You would have seen so many horses lying there, hauberks and swords and lances and pennoncels and cognisances. Horses, with their burdens, stumbled.'

a pronounced dynamic element: that is to say, as the action moves quickly the narratee must work to keep up with the narrator, tracking plot connections and actors' motivations in the act of updating what is imaginatively reconstructed.[205] It is significant that the *veïssiez* device is initially deployed in the first of the set-pieces by means of which the narrator evokes the crusade's beginnings, as knights scramble to take the cross at Gisors in January 1188.[206] This occurs within a passage in which the narrator also mentions his own individual and collective eyewitness of Archbishop Joscius of Tyre's appeals to Kings Philip II and Henry II and of the mass enthusiasm that it elicited. Elsewhere, sequences are developed by means of the repetition of this device. For example, in the early part of the siege of Acre, the Christians try to dig themselves in though constantly harried by the enemy:

> There you might have seen in a short space of time more than five hundred thousand arrows handed from the diggers to those who were defending them. There you might have seen bold and courageous men on both sides. There you might have seen men keel over, fall and be disembowelled, great blows exchanged until night parted them.[207]

Most of the narrator's mobilizations of the *veïssiez* formula respond to its epic resonance by referring to scenes of armed conflict. The text's longest battle narrative, its account of the battle of Arsuf in September 1191, makes full use of the motif, and the same is true of several other combat sequences.[208] The device is, however, extended to other types of scene, particularly moments of collective emotional tension.[209] To some extent the formula is used to direct the narratee's imaginative gaze away from the broad sweep of the action, and to

[205] See the helpful observations of Schirato, 'Forme narrative', 113–14.

[206] 'There you might have seen knights running up eagerly to take the cross' ('La veïssiez chevaliers cure / E crosier sei par ahatie'): *Estoire*, ll. 144–5, trans. p. 31.

[207] *Estoire*, ll. 3104–13, trans. p. 76. Cf. *Estoire*, ll. 3785–90, trans. p. 85; ll. 4948–69, trans. pp. 100–1.

[208] *Estoire*, ll. 6084–759, trans. pp. 115–23. See esp. ll. 6119–20, 6158–9, 6216–20, 6318–19, 6360, 6454, 6474–5, 6485–7, 6495–501, 6505–13, 6538–9, 6549–50, 6578–80, 6707–12, trans. pp. 116, 117, 118, 119, 120, 121, 122. For a similar concentration in the scaled-down context of a skirmish, see *Estoire*, ll. 9948–10061, trans. pp. 166–7, esp. ll. 9974–81, 10010, 10017–24, 10031–6. See also the account of Richard's attack on a rich caravan in June 1192: *Estoire*, ll. 10285–536, trans. pp. 170–2, esp. ll. 10423–6, 10431–2, 10452–3, 10463–8, 10475–6, 10481–510.

[209] E.g. *Estoire*, ll. 7640–2, trans. p. 135 (collective joy and the desire to perform worthy deeds); ll. 8344–5, trans. p. 144 (mass distress at discord within the army); ll. 8832–3, trans. p. 151 (universal mourning for Conrad of Montferrat); ll. 9002–5, trans. p. 153 (the elite of Tyre urge Henry of Champagne to marry Conrad of Montferrat's widow); ll. 10603–5, trans. p. 173 (sorrow at the delay in pressing on towards Jerusalem); l. 12249, trans. p. 193 (mass weeping at Richard's departure).

linger briefly on tangential but quirky or striking details: for example, the furious rage of the Turks when they see Christian reinforcements arriving at Acre;[210] the rough treatment meted out by Christian women on the crew of a Turkish galley that is forced to beach at Acre;[211] and starving aristocrats reduced to grazing on grass.[212] The principal thrust of the *veïssiez* motif is, however, to emphasize the crusaders' collective purpose and their capacity for concerted action. Although there is some acknowledgement of the crusade's other sensory aspects – for example, the stench of dead bodies, the thunderous noise of the Turkish drums, and the howls of the dying[213] – these mentions almost always take the form of complements within sequences in which the visual quality of a given scene is emphasized by means of character focalization and the recruitment of the narratee's ability to picture events.[214] It is noteworthy that the narrator tends to pack similes that have a clear visual dimension or which invite visualization into such passages.[215] And the narrator draws the narratee's attention by means of this device both to specific episodes and recurrent behaviours, thereby reasserting his ability to see patterns, to identify connections and, where warranted, to offer generalizations.[216] Many of the *veïssiez* sequences relate to events – such as during the earlier parts of the siege of Acre – which Ambroise the historical actor could not have witnessed himself.[217] So this is not a device that particularly attaches itself to the visual quality and mnemonic texture of eyewitness recall as such. But it does function as a clear analogue of the narrator's eyewitness perception, an insistence that the visual is the primary resource for achieving an understanding of the crusade.

[210] *Estoire*, ll. 2866–7, trans. p. 73. See also *Estoire*, l. 6360, trans. p. 118.

[211] *Estoire*, ll. 3304–9, trans. p. 79.

[212] *Estoire*, ll. 4251–6, trans. p. 90.

[213] *Estoire*, ll. 3088–93, trans. p. 76; ll. 4639–41, trans. p. 95; l. 6514, trans. p. 120.

[214] See also *Estoire*, ll. 6225–31, trans. p. 117.

[215] E.g. *Estoire*, l. 1546, trans. p. 53 (the crusaders attack the Greeks and Armenians in Cyprus like lions); l. 10438, trans. p. 171 (the Muslims flee before Richard like sheep who have seen a wolf). Cf. *Estoire*, ll. 3267–9, trans. p. 78: 'Then you might have been reminded of the scrabbling of ants coming out of an anthill in all directions' ('Adonc vos peüst sovenir / De formiz ki de formilliere / S'en issent devant e deriere'); ll. 5699–700, trans. p. 110: 'There you would have seen them [the Turks] coming, like rain from the mountains' ('Lors les veïssiez esploveir / Des montaines…'). For the text's use of metaphor and simile, see Schirato, 'Forme narrative', 123–6.

[216] See e.g. the description of the sorrowful departures of those who had taken the cross, which itself draws upon preaching tropes, in *Estoire*, ll. 327–38, trans. pp. 34–5. See also the evocations of the trench warfare-like conditions during the siege of Acre: *Estoire*, ll. 3094–113, trans. p. 76.

[217] Cf. the account of the departures of the French contingents before the rendezvous at Vézelay, processes which Ambroise is very unlikely to have seen for himself: *Estoire*, ll. 287–302, trans. pp. 33–4.

A similar foregrounding of the visual as epistemological tool is evident in the narrator's accumulation and intensification of gazes that simultaneously penetrate the storyworld from without and criss-cross it from within. That is to say, references to the narratee's imaginative recreation of a scene often accompany particular concentrations of character focalization. Usually more is involved than the simple 'stacking' of perceptions; scenes are energized by this means. The convergence of gazes happens too frequently to be an incidental feature; it is a clear strategy to stake out the narrator's capacities as a mediator between the participants' experience and the comprehension of the reader/listener. For example, character perceptions and appeals to the narratee's imagination (principally visual but with some aural reinforcement) join forces with the narrator's use of figurative and evaluative language in an account of the crusaders' landing at Limassol:

> Our crossbowmen attacked, and there were among them those who would not miss! First they fired upon the boatmen, who were not learned in warfare. They hurt and injured so many of those in the galleys that they jumped into the sea, four by four. Then you could see one fighting another. Then were their galleys taken and put with our snacks. The archers and the bowmen fired thick and fast, forcing the Greeks to move their position. Then you might have heard our men baying as they had bayed at us before we had moved. From both sides came firing and hurling [of missiles] and the oarsmen moved forward while it rained bolts and arrows wherever they went. The strand and the shore were covered with these wild people. There you might have seen a bold undertaking and men learned in war. When the king saw his companions struggling to reach land he leapt into the sea from his skiff and, reaching the Greeks, attacked them. All the others leapt in after him and the Grifons defended themselves, but our men went along the shore striking and overcoming them. There you might have seen arrows flying and Greeks dying and being killed. They forced them into the town, striking them down, striking blows. They went after them like lions, striking at them and at their horses.[218]

Similarly, the perceptions of witnesses to a feat of arms by Earl Robert of Leicester, complemented by a rare mention of spatial orientation, nudge the

[218] *Estoire*, ll. 1510–47, trans. pp. 52–3. Cf. the frequency with which the narratee's gaze complements a choric focalization of the action on the part of the Turks: e.g. *Estoire*, ll. 2351–82, trans. p. 66; ll. 4637–57, trans. pp. 95–6; ll. 5697–700, trans. p. 110. For the cultural frame of the text's use of the word *grifon* (and the variant *grifonaille*) to refer to the Greeks, see L. Diggelmann, 'Of Grifons and Tyrants: Anglo-Norman Views of the Mediterranean World during the Third Crusade', in L. Bailey, L. Diggelmann and K. M. Phillips (eds), *Old Worlds, New Worlds: European Cultural Encounters, c.1000–c.1750* (Late Medieval and Early Modern Studies, 18; Turnhout, 2009), pp. 11–30.

narratee's visualization of the scene towards an appreciation of its ethical dimension:

> There you would have seen the count of Leicester holding firm, striking to the left and to the right, until two horses had been killed under him. There were there men who will repeat that they have never seen greater valour in a man of his age, nor better bar none than those who came to his rescue that day.[219]

The text's visual regime further emerges, as one would expect, in its use of focalization. In a text of such length, it is unsurprising that the role of focalizer is shared around a wide range of characters and types of plot situation.[220] Many of the narrator's mobilizations of character gazes are imaginative evocations of the transformative effects of sight within the storyworld, what it is like to see and be seen. For example, a convergence of the narratee's invited gaze and those of witnesses to the crusaders' departure reinforces the emotional content of the experience by implicitly evoking the ways in which grief might be manifested:

> There you could see so great a movement of people, so many pouring in from all parts, such a company to send them off and such sadness at their departure that those who were accompanying them nearly broke their hearts with sorrow.[221]

Similarly, character gazes are not simply directed onto a scene but can also have an effect on those within the storyworld, as when the Saracens scrutinize those crusaders who are allowed to go on pilgrimage to Jerusalem:

> When the Saracens saw them they looked at them, eyeing them in such a way that I truly tell you there was not in that company one man so bold that he would not have happily been back at Tyre or back at Acre.[222]

For all that the narrator is willing to share focalization duties around, however, he shows a clear preference for Richard I, whose perceptions and understandings of the world are built into the storyworld far more frequently than those of Louis VII in Odo of Deuil's *De profectione*. This is all the more noteworthy in that the narrator of the *Estoire* does not sit on Richard's shoulder, nor does he volunteer

[219] *Estoire*, ll. 7575–83, trans. p. 134. Cf. the concentration of gazes in Conrad of Montferrat's death scene: *Estoire*, ll. 8832–42, trans. p. 151.

[220] See e.g. the Muslims' incomprehension and fear at their first sight of a windmill, one which was built by the Germans outside Acre in 1190: *Estoire*, ll. 3220–7, trans. p. 78. See also the story ('bele aventure') of the Genoese who spots the shining helmets of an approaching Turkish force and raises the alarm: *Estoire*, ll. 11347–57, trans. p. 182.

[221] *Estoire*, ll. 297–302, trans. p. 34.

[222] *Estoire*, ll. 11929–34, trans. p. 189.

moments of autobiographical recall that would show off his proximity to the centres of power within the crusade army. This is not to say that the flesh-and-blood Ambroise was never close, literally or figuratively, to Richard: we simply cannot tell. But his narratorial persona is not granted intimate access to the king along similar lines to Bahā' al-Dīn's close tracking of Saladin. Nonetheless, the narrator presumes to be able to penetrate Richard's acts of apperception and to find there quick thinking, shrewd judgement and strategic and tactical awareness superior to those of any other character. This happens so frequently over the course of the text that the narrator's relationship with, even reliance upon, Richard as focalizer can be said to transcend the many individual moments of visual acuity and intelligence on the king's part; he is recruited as the narrator's most trusted coadjutor in the acts of seeing and understanding. And the relationship works both ways, for the king's apperceptual sharpness exemplifies the high level of visual acuity which the reader/listener is invited by the narrator to mobilize in order to gain an imaginative appreciation of the experience of being part of the crusade.

Even when, as is typically the case, Richard is surrounded by others, his individual gaze is often highlighted. For example, as he and his forces first approach Cyprus, where his sister Joanna is in danger and some of his men have been mistreated, he displays the ability to perceive the different elements of a complex situation. Note the way in which the narrator's evaluative language shades towards indirect speech or thought on Richard's part, thereby assimilating their two perspectives:

> When the king, who had arrived in the port, learned of the perfidy, of the trials of his men, when he saw the dromond in which his sister was awaiting him in terror, when he saw the shore covered with the perfidious Greeks, he had no desire to hunt out Saracens worse than these.[223]

Similarly, as the English fleet nudges down the Syrian and Palestinian coast in May-June 1191, it is Richard whose gaze encapsulates the crusaders' collective experience:

> As quickly as a running stag he travelled across the sea. Then he saw Margat, on the coast of the land rightfully belonging to God. After Margat he saw Tortosa, which was also sited on the tumultuous sea. He quickly passed Tripoli, Infré and Botron and then saw Gibelet, with the tower of its castle. Before Sidon, near Beirut, the king noticed a ship full of Saladin's men.[224]

[223] *Estoire*, ll. 1425–32, trans. p. 51.

[224] *Estoire*, ll. 2127–39, trans. p. 62. Cf. Richard's acute gaze from aboard ship earlier in the voyage: *Estoire*, ll. 1332–4, trans. p. 50. See also his ability to revise his plans in light of his perception of changing circumstances: e.g. *Estoire*, ll. 1932–3, trans. p. 59.

Likewise, it is Richard whose first sight of Acre is emphasized, the narrator's evaluations blending with his own while, for good measure, the narratee's invited recreation of the scene is added to the mix:

> Then he saw Acre, clearly exposed, with the flower of the world encamped around it. He saw the slopes and the mountains, the valleys and the plains, covered with Turks and tents and men who had it in their hearts to harm Christianity, all there in very great numbers. He saw the tents of Saladin and those of his brother Saphadin, so near to our Christian army that the pagans pressed upon them...The king looked and studied, continually drawing up and re-drawing his plans. When he came near to the shore there you would have seen all the nobility of the army, behind the king of France, coming eagerly to meet him; many there were who came to greet him.[225]

Whereas other individual characters tend to focalize the patently obvious, such as when Isaac Komnenos sees that his defeated men are no match for Richard's troops, and Guy of Lusignan discovers that the people of Tyre have closed their gates to shut him out,[226] Richard's focalization is typically more penetrative and forward-looking.[227] Significantly, perhaps, among the other characters it is Saladin whose perceptions come closest to matching Richard's level of insight.[228] There are, it is true, moments in which Richard's perceptiveness fails him or his limitations are exposed: we have seen that William of Poitiers's pep-talk to him is motivated by an uncharacteristic inability on the king's part to read the mood of his army; and one of his final focalizing acts is to recognize the gap between his ambition and achievement when he sees how badly he has been let down by all those around him.[229] But the king's central role of focalizer *par excellence* is nonetheless restored and reaffirmed in his final scene, as his ship sails away and he looks back towards shore, promising to return as he does so.[230]

[225] *Estoire*, ll. 2308–20, 2327–33, trans. p. 65. Cf. Richard's awareness of his central importance to the prosecution of the crusade when Philip II leaves for home: *Estoire*, ll. 5351–4, trans. p. 106.

[226] *Estoire*, ll. 1643–5, trans. p. 54; ll. 2704–5, trans. p. 70.

[227] See e.g. Richard's superior strategic understanding in his speech to those who wish to press on towards Jerusalem: *Estoire*, ll. 10128–83, trans. p. 168.

[228] E.g. *Estoire*, ll. 5160–2, trans. p. 103. Cf. the text's most sustained collective focalization of their situation on the Muslims' part in *Estoire*, ll. 5064–88, trans. pp. 102–3. For the text's treatment of Saladin and his brother 'Saphadin' (al-'Adīl), see M. J. Ailes, 'The Admirable Enemy? Saladin and Saphadin in Ambroise's *Estoire de la guerre sainte*', in N. J. Housley (ed.), *Knighthoods of Christ: Essays on the History of the Crusades and Knights Templar, Presented to Malcolm Barber* (Aldershot, 2007), pp. 51–64.

[229] *Estoire*, ll. 11718–22, trans. p. 186.

[230] *Estoire*, ll. 12255–63, trans. p. 193.

Richard I is the most conspicuous individual agent in all the Christian texts that we are examining in this book. He is, moreover, the individual whose own gaze and powers of understanding are most salient with respect to the motivation of action and the movement of the plot. What the narrator sees Richard doing and the manner in which Richard sees the world of the crusade around him powerfully align with the text's ethical system. Richard is the narrator's most trusted and effective surrogate within the storyworld; and it is therefore significant that his visual acuity and perceptiveness are emphasized in numerous places. For all that Richard stands out in this respect, however, the narrator's stagings of action and his interactions with the narratee predominantly amount to invitations to imagine scenes of collective agency and concerted purpose. To this important extent, the narrator moves away from the kind of focus on the individual leader that we saw characterizes some contemporary treatments of Saladin; and, while his admiration for Richard in particular and his attachment to heroic tropes and chivalric *mises-en-scène* in general militate against the sort of exclusive attention to communal agency that we saw animates the *Narratio*, purposive group action is the text's principal action mode. It is possible that the circumstances of the flesh-and-blood author Ambroise while on the crusade immersed him, more than any other of our authors, in the sort of small-group collective memory environments that we considered in Chapter 1. This can only be speculation. But the narrator leaves many clues that his eyewitness is to be treated as purposeful and well honed.[231] For example, when conceding that he was not present at the battle of Hattin, he draws attention to some of the categories of experience that he uses

[231] One indication of narratorial acuity is the inclusion of reality effect-like details that instantiate and authenticate the narrator's observant perception of the storyworld: e.g. *Estoire*, ll. 1616–18, trans. p. 53 (forty, or at most fifty, knights accompany Richard into battle); ll. 9288–90, trans. p. 157 (the detail that one of the banners raised on the walls of Darum, that belonging to Stephen of Longchamp, was badly damaged); ll. 9764–8, trans. p. 163 (two men, a knight and a man-at-arms, die of snake bites on the same day and close to one another); ll. 10561–4, trans. p. 173 (the appearance and taste of roasted camel meat); l. 10771, trans. p. 175 (Saladin's forces include at least 106 emirs – the figure serves a rhyme). See also the numerous counterfactuals that underscore the narrator's shrewd understanding of cause and effect as they work themselves out over both the shorter and longer terms: e.g. *Estoire*, ll. 5027–32, trans. p. 102 (Acre would have been taken had more people been aware of a bold Pisan assault); ll. 5384–5, trans. p. 106 (Richard would have recovered God's heritage if he had not been undermined by the envy of others); ll. 5946–55, trans. pp. 113–14 (Richard would have done great deeds of valour in an engagement were it not for others' laziness); ll. 6651–4, trans. p. 122 (at Arsuf the Christians would have inflicted an even heavier defeat had they fought in better order); ll. 7431–3, trans. p. 132 (Richard would have reconquered the land had he not been hindered by those who stole from his treasury); ll. 7784–95, trans. p. 137 (Jerusalem could have been taken had the crusaders known of the Turks' weakness).

to organize his perceptions, where he directs his gaze when circumstances so permit, and by extension the type of informants he routinely seeks out when his own autopsy is lacking: 'I do not know who struck whom, who escaped and who perished. I was not present at the battle.'[232]

Likewise, the narrator's gaze is acute and informed but not idiosyncratic, which means that his eyewitness informants are in principle capable of the same ethical discernment that he brings to bear on his *matire*. Thus, in the account towards the end of the text of the treacherous treatment of the Christians who surrender at Jaffa, the narrator implies that the reactions of those present, presumably his informants, were consonant with his own set of values to the extent that they too can invoke the *veïssiez* formula. At the same time, the narrator's attention to the visual quality of the event and his evocation of the scene's highly charged emotional content reinforce his own ability to capture scenes and to understand the perceptions of those caught up in them, albeit this is a self-awareness bound up in conventional discourses of Christian devotion and sacrifice:

> Those who were there have said that there you might have seen a piteous sight before the tower in the Toron, for, condemned to death, they were afraid. There you might have seen men weep and go down on their knees to worship, to make their confession and say their *mea culpa*...They awaited their martyrdom. We can say in truth that tears were shed there which pleased God for they came from the distress of death and the depth of their hearts which yearned for Him.[233]

Similarly, in an important staging of the importance of the gaze – in a scene significantly constructed to show Richard off well relative to Philip II – the narrator suggests that all those within his storyworld, even the members of amorphous and temporary collectivities that are mobilized only briefly in order to perform a single narrative function, are equipped to form judgements on the basis of what they see. When Philip sails into Messina, in September 1190, many people gather to be presented with the spectacle of his royal arrival, but he disappoints on two counts: he has come in only a single vessel, and he disembarks away from the crowd to avoid the crush.[234] Richard's contrasting arrival, a week later, more than meets the crowd's expectations:

> When King Richard arrived, then there were just as many on the shore who sought to see him, both wise men and frivolous, who had never seen him and who wished to see him on account of his valour. He came with such pomp that

[232] *Estoire*, ll. 2550–2, trans. p. 68.
[233] *Estoire*, ll. 11025–32, 11038–44, trans. p. 178.
[234] *Estoire*, ll. 573–80, trans. p. 38.

> the whole sea was covered by galleys full of competent people, fighters, bold of countenance, with little pennoncels and with banners…Those who saw the procession said that this was how a king should enter [*itels reis deveit venir*], a king to hold his land well. But the Grifons were angry and the Lombards grumbled because he came into their city with such a fleet and such pomp and circumstance.[235]

The narrator points the contrast with reference to his most significant mention of proverbial wisdom and general knowledge. Richard acted the part of the great lord in conformity to the proverb 'As I see you so I perceive you'.[236] The force of this dictum extends beyond the immediate context of proper regal deportment and the visible performance of power to embrace the narrator's entire project. For although the narrator's acuity extends to hearing, it is sight that dominates the construction of his storyworld.[237]

Some qualifications are in order. As we have seen, the narrator's eyewitness perception is not laboured, nor indeed is it mentioned over quite long stretches of text; and as we have also seen it typically has a free-floating quality that does not drop the narrator into precisely delineated and oriented space and place. Additionally, many sequences that we may suspect draw upon some element of eyewitness recall are not so tagged, while a number of scenes that the author could not have witnessed are narrated as if he did or might have done.[238] The

[235] *Estoire*, ll. 581–92, 598–604, trans. pp. 38–9. This scene and the manner of its telling represent one of the most significant intersections, at the level of the discrete, anecdotal narrative unit, between the *Estoire* and closely contemporary Latin historiographical texts favourable to Richard, which suggests that the arrival at Messina quickly became a well-rehearsed set-piece in the pro-Angevin collective memory. Richard of Devizes, *Chronicon*, p. 16 highlights the visual and aural impression made by the arrival of Richard's force, the fact that large crowds gathered to see the king, and the favourable comparison that they themselves made with Philip II's arrival a week earlier. Roger of Howden likewise draws attention to the impressive sights and sounds of Richard's arrival, and to the appreciative gaze of the local people – now joined as focalizers by Philip II and his entourage – but does not make the contrast between the two kings explicit: *Gesta Regis*, ii, pp. 125–6; *Chronica*, iii, p. 55.

[236] *Estoire*, l. 570, trans. p. 38: 'Tel te voi te[l] t'espeir'. Ailes renders *espeir* as 'regard', which nicely captures the dual sense of physical perception and opinion. But 'perceive' perhaps better expresses the idea of a verdict born of visual impression. See A. Hindley, F. W. Langley and B. J. Levy (eds), *Old French-English Dictionary* (Cambridge, 2000), s.v. *espoir*. For the narrator's appeals to proverbial wisdom elsewhere, see e.g. *Estoire*, ll. 964–5, trans. p. 44 to the effect that jealousy is a constant source of discord.

[237] See e.g. *Estoire*, ll. 6020–1, trans. p. 114 for the narrator's observation that he heard the name of a formidable emir who died in battle. This emir's death is also reported by Bahā' al-Dīn, one of the several interesting overlaps between the two texts: *The Rare and Excellent History*, p. 171.

[238] E.g. *Estoire*, ll. 449–80, trans. p. 36 (the collapse of a bridge over the Rhône); ll.

narrator's few references to the workings of his and others' memories are not all attendant upon or emphasize the act of eyewitnessing.[239] But for all these caveats, the *Estoire* stakes out a powerful position as an eyewitness text whose narrator skilfully interweaves his own gaze and those of his characters with the imaginative resources of his narratee, and by extension those of the reader or listener.

1284–97, trans. p. 49 (a description of the ruinous state of Rhodes); ll. 5640–55, trans. p. 110 (the differences between Christian and Muslim equipment and tactics).

[239] See e.g. *Estoire*, l. 2952, trans. p. 74, where the statement that 'I recall ['me membre'] one particular day, a Friday' refers to events during the siege of Acre before Richard's, and Ambroise's, arrival there, and, if it is anything more than a fill in the interests of prosody and rhyme, must gesture towards the author's memory of being told about the incident concerned. When we move into possible eyewitness recall, moreover, memory is typically invoked with respect to minor details such as dates: *Estoire*, ll. 5222–4, trans. p. 104; ll. 9860–1, trans. 164. But cf. the reference to the workings of memory, and its direct link to eyewitnessing, in the important transitional passage in which the narrative resumes the subject of Richard's arrival at Acre after the lengthy analepsis on the earlier history of the siege: *Estoire*, ll. 4551–62, trans. p. 94. See also the insistence that memory is a guarantee against mendacity: *Estoire*, ll. 8069–71, trans. p. 140.

4

Geoffrey of Villehardouin's and Robert of Clari's Narratives of the Fourth Crusade

The sources for the Fourth Crusade are as rich as for the Third, if not richer.[1] In addition to charter evidence for departing crusaders and newsletters sent home by some of the leading figures in the crusade army, we have several letters to and from Pope Innocent III as well as an apologia, the *Gesta Innocentii Papae*, written in 1206, which amongst other aspects of the pope's pontificate up to that point addresses his handling of the problems that the crusade had presented.[2] In addition, there are formal records of some of the treaties and agreements that scaffold the story of the crusade, and narrative accounts that were either written by an eyewitness or capture the reminiscences of a former participant.[3] The invaluable balancing function performed in the case of the Third Crusade by authors close to Saladin is, for the Fourth, principally assumed by a major

[1] For the events of the Fourth Crusade, the best accounts in English are D. E. Queller and T. F. Madden, *The Fourth Crusade: The Conquest of Constantinople*, 2nd edn (Philadelphia, 1997); J. P. Phillips, *The Fourth Crusade and the Sack of Constantinople* (London, 2004); and C. J. Tyerman, *God's War: A New History of the Crusades* (London, 2006), pp. 501–60. See also M. Angold, *The Fourth Crusade: Event and Context* (Harlow, 2003), which has many thoughtful remarks on both the long-term background to the crusade and its consequences. For the crusade's antecedents see in addition M. Angold, 'The Road to 1204: The Byzantine Background to the Fourth Crusade', *Journal of Medieval History*, 25 (1999), 257–78.

[2] 'Gesta Innocentii PP. III.', *PL*, 214, cols. xvii–ccxxviii. Many of the most important sources are helpfully assembled in translation in *Contemporary Sources for the Fourth Crusade*, trans. A. J. Andrea with B. E. Whalen (The Medieval Mediterranean, 29; Leiden, 2000). For the many letters from Innocent III's register that bear on the crusade, see pp. 7–176. For overviews of the source base, see A. J. Andrea, 'Essay on Primary Sources', in Queller and Madden, *Fourth Crusade*, pp. 299–313; Angold, *Fourth Crusade*, pp. 7–22.

[3] For several of the important agreements that were made before, during and shortly after the crusade, see *Urkunden zur älteren Handels- und Staatsgeschichte der Republik Venedig mit besonderer Beziehung auf Byzanz und die Levante*, ed. G. L. F. Tafel and G. M. Thomas, 3 vols (Vienna, 1856–7), i, nos. 89–93, 119–21, 123, pp. 358–73, 444–501, 512–15. For a valuable study of the importance of formal agreements in determining the course of the crusade, see T. F. Madden, 'Vows and Contracts in the Fourth Crusade: The Treaty of Zara and the Attack on Constantinople in 1204', *International History Review*, 15 (1993), 441–68.

Byzantine historian, Niketas Choniates, a high-ranking member of the aristocracy of service in the imperial government who was directly affected by the crusaders' capture and sack of Constantinople in April 1204.[4] Choniates's account of this turn of events is a famous set-piece that has done much to set the tone of modern sensibilities about the crusade's moral bankruptcy and negative cultural legacy.[5]

There are significant gaps in the evidence, nonetheless. Crucially, there is no closely contemporary historiographical coverage from a Venetian perspective, an imbalance that undoubtedly contributed to the dim view of Venice's involvement in the crusade that characterized a great deal of scholarship in the nineteenth and twentieth centuries. It is only in recent decades that a more balanced assessment of the Venetian role has emerged, thanks to the work of scholars such as Donald Queller and Thomas Madden. We now have a better appreciation of the enormous costs that Venice incurred in building and equipping the large fleet that it contracted to supply for the crusaders, and of the various ways in which the Venetians' reactions to events as they unfolded constantly came back to the implications and consequences of this central fact. We have also become more suspicious of outmoded assumptions about the separation of classes and mutually exclusive value systems within medieval society – assumptions that saw in the fourth crusaders 'feudal', chivalrous, financially and strategically naïve aristocratic man-children stumbling into a fateful cultural collision with the Venetians' world of cold bourgeois calculation and pursuit of self-interest. Nevertheless, the absence of a clear contemporary Venetian voice is a reminder of the ways in which the distribution of historiographical evidence unavoidably inflects our understanding of events.[6]

[4] Niketas Choniates, *Historia*, ed. J. L. van Dieten, 2 vols (Corpus Fontium Historiae Byzantinae, Series Berolinensis, 11; Berlin, 1975); trans. H. J. Magoulias, *O City of Byzantium, Annals of Niketas Choniates* (Detroit, 1984). For Choniates and his work, see P. Magdalino, 'Aspects of Twelfth-Century Byzantine *Kaiserkritik*', *Speculum*, 58 (1983), 326–46; A. Kazhdan and S. Franklin, *Studies on Byzantine Literature of the Eleventh and Twelfth Centuries* (Cambridge, 1984), pp. 256–86; J. Harris, 'Distortion, Divine Providence and Genre in Nicetas Choniates's Account of the Collapse of Byzantium 1180–1204', *Journal of Medieval History*, 26 (2000), 19–31; W. Treadgold, *The Middle Byzantine Historians* (Basingstoke, 2013), pp. 422–56; A. Simpson, *Niketas Choniates: A Historiographical Study* (Oxford, 2013). See also A. Simpson, 'Niketas Choniates: the Historian', in A. Simpson and S. Efthymiadis (eds), *Niketas Choniates: A Historian and a Writer* (Geneva, 2009), pp. 13–34.

[5] For modern condemnation of the Fourth Crusade, see most [in]famously the comment by Steven Runciman in his *A History of the Crusades*, 3 vols (Cambridge, 1951–4), iii, p. 130: 'There was never a greater crime against humanity than the Fourth Crusade.' That this comment was made less than a decade after the end of the Second World War is, to say the very least, curious.

[6] See the pertinent observation by Angold, *Fourth Crusade*, p. 19 that 'it is easy to blame the Venetians, on the grounds that they pleaded, so to speak, the fifth amendment'. For

Within the western historiographical corpus, two texts have traditionally stood out: the narratives of Geoffrey of Villehardouin and Robert of Clari.[7] These are the two longest tellings of the events of the Fourth Crusade and its aftermath.[8] Both

later Venetian sources bearing on the crusade, see T. F. Madden, 'The Venetian Version of the Fourth Crusade: Memory and the Conquest of Constantinople in Medieval Venice', *Speculum*, 87 (2012), 311–44. See also S. Marin, 'Between Justification and Glory: The Venetian Chronicles' View of the Fourth Crusade', in T. F. Madden (ed.), *The Fourth Crusade: Event, Aftermath, and Perceptions: Papers from the Sixth Conference of the Society for the Study of the Crusades and the Latin East, Istanbul, Turkey, 25–29 August 2004* (Crusades Subsidia, 2; Aldershot, 2008), pp. 113–21. Cf. the valuable Venetian orientation in Madden's account of the Fourth Crusade and the beginnings of the Latin empire of Constantinople in his *Enrico Dandolo and the Rise of Venice* (Baltimore, 2003), pp. 117–94. For the treatment of the Venetians in other western sources, see D. E. Queller and I. B. Katele, 'Attitudes Towards the Venetians in the Fourth Crusade: The Western Sources', *International History Review*, 4 (1982), 1–36.

[7] Geoffrey of Villehardouin, *La conquête de Constantinople*, ed. and trans. E. Faral, 2nd edn, 2 vols (Les classiques de l'histoire de France au moyen âge, 18–19; Paris, 1961) [hereafter *Conquête*. Note that references are to section and page extents but not to volume; volume 1 contains §§1–205, volume 2 §§206–500]; trans. C. Smith, *Joinville and Villehardouin, Chronicles of the Crusades* (London, 2008), pp. 5–135 [hereafter 'trans.']; Robert of Clari, *La Conquête de Constantinople*, ed. and trans. P. Noble (British Rencesvals Publications, 3; Edinburgh, 2005) [henceforth RC]. This supersedes the familiar but much looser translation in Robert of Clari, *The Conquest of Constantinople*, trans. E. H. McNeal (Medieval Academy Reprints for Teaching, 36; Toronto, 1996). For another recent edition of Clari's text, see *La conquête de Constantinople*, ed. and trans. J. Dufournet (Champion classiques moyen âge, 14; Paris, 2004). The Italian translation by A. M. Nada Patrone, *La conquista di Costantinopoli (1198–1216): Studio critico, traduzione e note* (Collana storica di fonti e studi, 13; Genoa, 1972), has a useful introduction, although it attaches too much significance to Clari's personality and his 'temperamento piccardo' (p. 68).

[8] The two texts are, unsurprisingly, often considered in combination: see e.g. the important study by G. Jacquin, *Le style historique dans les recits français et latins de la quatrième croisade* (Geneva, 1986). See also J. Dufournet, *Les écrivains de la IVe croisade: Villehardouin et Clari*, 1 vol. in 2 (Paris, 1973), which discusses Villehardouin at greater length than Clari. Peter Noble makes a number of perceptive remarks in his 'The Importance of Old French Chronicles as Historical Sources of the Fourth Crusade and the Early Latin Empire of Constantinople', *Journal of Medieval History*, 27 (2001), 399–416, though he focuses more on the differences between Villehardouin's and Clari's texts than on their areas of overlap. For Villehardouin in particular, see J. M. A. Beer, *Villehardouin: Epic Historian* (Études de philologie et d'histoire, 7; Geneva, 1968). Although Villehardouin is the better known figure, Clari has attracted as much scholarly interest in recent decades: see e.g. P. F. Dembowski, *La chronique de Robert de Clari: Etude de la langue et du style* (University of Toronto Romance Series, 6; Toronto, 1963); C. P. Bagley, 'Robert de Clari's *La Conquête de Constantinople*', *Medium Aevum*, 40 (1971), 109–15; A. Varvaro, 'Esperienza e racconto in Robert de Clari', in R. Antonelli *et al.* (eds), *Miscellanea di studi in onore*

are eyewitness accounts, broadly understood.[9] Both are pioneering exercises in the use of Old French prose as the medium for the writing of the history of recent affairs, further evidence of the important role of the crusades as a forcing-ground of historiographical experiment in the twelfth and thirteenth centuries. Although the two works would seem to have been conceived and executed independently of one another – Clari was aware of Villehardouin, but as a prominent figure within the crusade host, probably not as a chronicler in the making[10] – they are typically considered together. This is in some ways unfortunate, because each tends to be used to draw attention to the supposed deficiencies of the other. Clari, it is often argued, supplies the perspective of that much-loved but elusive figure the 'simple knight': he lacks the grasp of detail available to Villehardouin as a major actor in the diplomatic and military endeavours of the crusade's leadership, but by the same token he has no need for the evasions and obfuscations that many have suggested characterize Villehardouin's attempts to sanitize the story of the

---

di Aurelio Roncaglia a cinquant'anni dalla sua laurea, 1 vol. in 4 (Modena, 1989), iv, pp. 1411–27 (a particularly perceptive analysis); G. Jacquin, 'Robert de Clari, témoin et conteur', in J.-C. Aubailly, E. Baumgartner, F. Dubost, L. Dulac and M. Faure (eds), *Et c'est la fin pour quoy sommes ensemble: Hommage à Jean Dufournet*, 1 vol. in 3 (Nouvelle bibliothèque du moyen âge, 25; Paris, 1993), ii, pp. 747–57; U. Mölk, 'Robert de Clari über den vierten Kreuzzug', *Romanistisches Jahrbuch*, 61 (2011), 12–22.

[9] There are several other western narratives that, while shorter than those by Villehardouin and Clari, were written by, or were based on the memories of, eyewitnesses, and make an important contribution to our understanding of the crusade. The most substantial is Gunther of Pairis, *Hystoria Constantinopolitana*, ed. P. Orth (Spolia Berolinensia, 5; Hildesheim, 1994); trans. A. J. Andrea, *The Capture of Constantinople: The 'Hystoria Constantinopolitana' of Gunther of Pairis* (Philadephia, 1997). Gunther did not take part in the crusade but drew upon the memories of his abbot, Martin. Gunther's text is, *inter alia*, one of a number written to record and legitimize the translation of Byzantine relics to the west in and after 1204: for this subgenre see D. M. Perry, *Sacred Plunder: Venice and the Aftermath of the Fourth Crusade* (University Park, PA, 2015), esp. pp. 77–134. The *Devastatio Constantinopolitana* is an informative eyewitness account, possibly the work of a German cleric: ed. A. J. Andrea, 'The *Devastatio Constantinopolitana*, A Special Perspective on the Fourth Crusade: An Analysis, New Edition, and Translation', *Historical Reflections*, 19 (1993), 107–29, 131–49; also trans. Andrea, *Contemporary Sources*, pp. 205–21. As with the Third Crusade, there is evidence that newsletters were sent by participants to the west; the most significant, amounting to a substantial historiographical exercise in its own right, was written on behalf of one of the major lords on the crusade, Hugh of St-Pol, soon after the crusaders had succeeded in ousting the Byzantine emperor Alexios III and putting Alexios IV on the throne in July 1203, and would seem, on the basis of the variants that survive, to have been sent to several recipients: see Andrea, *Contemporary Sources*, pp. 177–201, with references to editions of the extant variants.

[10] See RC, c. 1, p. 4; c. 6, p. 8.

Fourth Crusade in favour of the vested interests with which he identified.[11] The contrast between the two works, however, though warranted to some extent, can be overstated. Whereas Clari is usually typed as a representative of a particular class, the relative abundance of biographical information about Villehardouin as an individual has encouraged a 'fix' on his particular circumstances as a historical actor, which in turn has led to biographist, even in some cases psychologizing, readings of his *La Conquête de Constantinople*. It is, however, a better move to focus on the internal workings of Villehardouin's text, within which, as we shall see, questions of eyewitnessing and visual perception fold into larger issues of narratorial construction, choices of substantive and thematic emphasis, and ethical orientation. From this perspective, the differences between Villehardouin's and Clari's renderings of events do not seem quite so pronounced, though we shall find that each has distinctive approaches to the challenge of narrating the Fourth Crusade.

Geoffrey of Villehardouin

Villehardouin's history has long enjoyed the status of being the single most important piece of evidence for the course of the Fourth Crusade. Whereas Clari and other eyewitness and second-hand writers are able to enrich our picture of the whole and sometimes zoom in on particular incidents that Villehardouin overlooks or downplays, their contribution on these scores is generally uneven. Villehardouin, it seems, supplies the indispensable rhythm track to the telling of the Fourth Crusade. His narrative more than any other source enables a detailed reconstruction of events to be attempted and argued over. To a greater extent than is the case with any other piece of evidence, therefore, interpretations of the *Conquête* have become wrapped up in larger judgements about the ethics of the Fourth Crusade's achievement and legacy. The reasons why this is so expose some of the inconsistencies to be found in scholarly and popular engagements with the past when it is looked upon as a site of moral value: historical actors are treated as ethical subjects whose characters and behaviour may, and some would argue should, be assessed in openly evaluative terms. The Fourth Crusade, in particular the crusaders' sack of Constantinople, is one of a number of historical events and processes – the massacre of the Muslim and Jewish inhabitants of Jerusalem by the first crusaders in July 1099 is another – that has traditionally invited overt expressions of disapproval. The Fourth Crusade troubled earlier generations of scholars confident in the superiority of western values; and it has equally lent

[11] See e.g. the verdicts of Queller and Madden, *Fourth Crusade*, pp. 43–4, and of Andrea, 'Essay on Primary Sources', pp. 302–3.

itself to censure in more recent, self-critical and introspective times.[12] It is not necessary to enter into the large debate about what, if any, degrees of moralizing judgementalism are appropriate to modern-day historiographical discourses in their various academic and popular registers. It is, however, important to note that historians' moralizing tends to be highly selective and uneven in its choice of targets, largely because it is a matter of convention. To take just one example from the Third Crusade, scholars often worry about, or feel they must argue around, the propriety of the massacre of two thousand or more Muslim prisoners, on Richard I's orders, outside Acre in August 1192, whereas little comment is occasioned by the slaying of – if the figure supplied by the *Narratio de itinere navali peregrinorum Hierosolymam tendentium et Silviam capientium* is to be believed – more than twice that number of Muslims when the fleet of northern third crusaders that sailed ahead of the *Narratio*'s principals captured the fortress of Alvor in May or June 1189.[13]

This is not to minimize the human and material costs of the Fourth Crusade, nor to derogate from its continuing role as a site of painful collective memory in Greek Orthodox tradition. But it helps to explain why Villehardouin's narrative, as the principal western 'voice' on the crusade, was for a long time a particularly burdened text. Omissions, signs of selectivity and partiality, and choices of emphasis easily assumed a dark significance, whereas these same features would, when found in other examples of twelfth- and thirteenth-century historiography, simply be tolerated as what is to be expected of sources written in cultural environments very different from our own – part and parcel, that is, of the inescapable gappiness and alterity of the medieval historiographical record. This acutely mistrustful handling of Villehardouin paid insufficient regard to the innovative nature of his choice of vernacular prose as his medium, nor did it make due allowance for the hit-and-miss quality that one is bound to find in texts that have an experimental, pioneering edge and no convenient generic framework to fall back on. Villehardouin's bad faith was also an easy target. Thus past generations of scholars, many of them persuaded that the diversion of the Fourth

[12] For a thoughtful assessment of the severity of the sack of Constantinople, see Angold, *Fourth Crusade*, pp. 100–1, 111–13. See also the detailed account in Queller and Madden, *Fourth Crusade*, pp. 193–200.

[13] 'Narratio de Itinere Navali Peregrinorum Hierosolyman Tendentium et Silviam Capientium, A.D. 1189', ed. C. W. David, *Proceedings of the American Philosophical Society,* 81 (1939), 616–17; trans. G. A. Loud, *The Crusade of Frederick Barbarossa: The History of the Expedition of the Emperor Frederick and Related Texts* (Crusade Texts in Translation, 19; Farnham, 2010), p. 196. The text's figure of about 5,600 seems too high for the number of inhabitants of Alvor, which is described as a castle, though those killed most probably included refugees from other places. For the massacre outside Acre and reactions to it, see J. Gillingham, *Richard I* (New Haven, 1999), pp. 166–71.

Crusade to Constantinople was the result of a conspiracy, debated the question of Villehardouin's sincerity.[14] Was his account a cover-up? Failing that, was he the dupe of cleverer forces within the crusade leadership whose manipulation of events in pursuit of their own agendas he failed to see?

The debate over Villehardouin's sincerity has died down in recent decades, but to a large extent only because the once standard explanation of the Fourth Crusade's conquest of Constantinople as the result of a conspiracy has lost ground to the now more popular 'chain of accidents' theory, not because of a methodological rejection of the debate's biographist premises, nor thanks to any thoroughgoing re-examination of the *Conquête* as cultural artefact and historiographical experiment.[15] Recent historians' verdicts on the *Conquête* have generally taken a more positive view of the veracity of much of its substantive content; they correctly point out that at many points the information it supplies is corroborated by documentary and other narrative sources.[16] This welcome rehabilitation, however, carries with it the risk of an under-appreciation of the text, the scholarly utility of which can appear to be most securely grounded if the author is regarded as an honest but unimaginative observer, self-serving or forgetful in some places to be sure, but not egregiously so, and fundamentally committed to telling the truth within the narrow conceptual parameters afforded

[14] See esp. E. Faral, 'Geoffroy de Villehardouin: La question de sa sincérité', *Revue historique*, 177 (1936), 530–82. For healthy scepticism about the value of the sincerity debate, see J. M. A. Beer, *In Their Own Words: Practices of Quotation in Early Medieval Writing* (Toronto, 2014), pp. 39–40.

[15] For the view that the diversion of the crusade was the result of a conspiracy hatched by the doge Enrico Dandolo and the Venetians, see e.g. J. Godfrey, *1204: The Unholy Crusade* (Oxford, 1980). For a critique of Godfrey's position and the similar views of other scholarly and popular writers, see T. F. Madden, 'Outside and Inside the Fourth Crusade', *International History Review*, 17 (1995), 729–33, 734–7. For a more positive, and more convincing, view of the Venetians' policies and actions, see D. E. Queller and G. W. Day, 'Some Arguments in Defense of the Venetians on the Fourth Crusade', *American Historical Review*, 81 (1976), 717–37; D. E. Queller and T. F. Madden, 'Some Further Arguments in Defense of the Venetians on the Fourth Crusade', *Byzantion*, 62 (1992), 433–73. For a thoughtful discussion of the conspiracy-versus-accident question, see R.-J. Lilie, 'Zufall oder Absicht? Die Ablenkung des vierten Kreuzzugs nach Konstantinopel: repetita lectio', in P. Piatti (ed.), *The Fourth Crusade Revisited: Atti della Conferenza Internazionale nell'ottavo centenario della IV Crociata 1204-2004, Andros (Grecia), 27-30 maggio 2004* (Atti e documenti, 25; Vatican City, 2008), pp. 129–44. For longer-term factors that played into the conquest, see J. Harris, 'The Problem of Supply and the Sack of Constantinople', in *ibid.*, pp. 145–54. S. Neocleous, 'Financial, Chivalric or Religious? The Motives of the Fourth Crusaders Reconsidered', *Journal of Medieval History*, 38 (2012), 183–206 attempts to sift through the different sorts of pressures and challenges that the crusade faced.

[16] See Queller and Madden, *Fourth Crusade*, p. 18; Andrea, 'Essay on Primary Sources', pp. 299–302; Angold, *Fourth Crusade*, pp. 11–13.

to him. This characterization has a good deal to commend it, but it needs to be nuanced. The discussion of Villehardouin in this chapter will not attempt a full re-reading of the *Conquête*, but it will suggest that an examination of the place of eyewitness perception and testimony, seen within the larger context of the narratorial persona that the text creates and the narrator's staking out of his authority, aids an appreciation of Villehardouin's achievement and of some of the subtleties of his narrative craft.

The classification of Villehardouin's text as an 'eyewitness' source has traditionally been the main foundation of the value that is attached to it. This has never been challenged. For Edmond Faral, who produced what remains the best edition of the *Conquête*, Villehardouin bore witness to all, or at least nearly all, the events from start to finish of his narration.[17] Other scholars have emphasized the same quality. Colin Morris, for example, claims that '[h]is narrative is confined to events at which he himself had been present', and that this was the result of 'his policy of confining himself to eye-witness experiences'.[18] This is demonstrably an overstatement, however, for there are numerous episodes narrated in the *Conquête* at which Villehardouin could not have been present or was probably not so. The narrator, moreover, seldom situates himself precisely in relation to the location of an event so as to state or imply a specific line-of-sight gaze upon the playing out of the action. It is true, as we shall see, that there are several sequences in which Villehardouin the character is expressly placed within the storyworld, but these are surrounded by much longer stretches of text in which he is not mentioned. As a matter of inference, we may suspect with greater or lesser degrees of confidence that Villehardouin the historical actor was indeed a participant in several of the events that these 'blank' sequences narrate, but that is a quite separate question from Villehardouin's presence within the text's diegesis as a character.

In addition, the fact that the narrator does not routinely share with the reader when he was *not* present at a given event, nor state how he came by his information in such cases, means that it is deceptively easy to exaggerate the range of Villehardouin-the-historical-eyewitness's mobility and first-hand experience.[19]

[17] *Conquête*, i, p. xiii: 'De tous les événements qu'il a raconté, ou presque, depuis le commencement jusqu'à la fin, il a été le temoin.'

[18] C. Morris, 'Geoffroy de Villehardouin and the Conquest of Constantinople', *History*, 53 (1968), 24–34, quotations at 25, 32; cf. the remarks at 33, 'He always wrote supremely as an eye-witness, and avoided reporting episodes at which he had not been present', and 34, 'a careful concentration upon what was actually seen and heard' informed by 'an honest intention to preserve for posterity the great events which he had witnessed'. See also Beer, *In Their Own Words*, p. 39: 'He [Villehardouin] was proud of his eyewitness experience.'

[19] See e.g. the claim in P. J. Archambault, *Seven French Chroniclers: Witness to History* (Syracuse, NY, 1974), p. 28 that 'He seems to have been an eye witness to those

For much of the action on which scholars tend to concentrate, that is to say the progress of the Fourth Crusade as a military venture, Villehardouin defaults to the status of a presumed eyewitness simply because his narrative concentrates so tightly on the movement of the crusade army as a unit. Cut-aways to other agents and locations are few. What is consistently emphasized is the image of a cohesive and compact crusade host, even though it is threatened by dissenters; those who fractured the all-important unity by either avoiding the rendezvous at Venice and making their own way east, or quitting the army once it was in motion, are described in very negative terms.[20] Between the crusade fleet's departure from Venice and the successful assault on Constantinople, therefore, Villehardouin-the-character is implicitly embedded in pretty much all the action.[21] But that does not necessarily make him an effective eyewitness to all that transpired during that time.

In addition, any assessment of the *Conquête* as an eyewitness source has to be based on a reading of the whole text. Because the sequence of events that reached a climax in April 1204 tends to attract more scholarly attention than the subsequent emergence of various Latin successor polities in parts of the

---

moving sermons preached by the hermit Fulk of Neuilly'. The narrative's account of Fulk's preaching, with which it opens, makes no reference to authorial autopsy: *Conquête*, §1, p. 2, trans. p. 5.

[20] For Villehardouin's hostility to those who avoided the rendezvous at Venice, quit the main crusade force over the course of its travels, or, as he saw it, undermined the army's unity, see *Conquête*, §36, pp. 36–8, trans. p. 12; §§49–51, pp. 52–4, trans. pp. 16–17; §57, pp. 58–60, trans. p. 18; §67, p. 68, trans. p. 20; §81, p. 82, trans. p. 23; §85, p. 86, trans. p. 24; §§95–7, pp. 94–8, trans. pp. 26–7; §109, pp. 110–12, trans. p. 30; §231, p. 32, trans. p. 61. See Dufournet, *Les écrivains*, i, pp. 57–9; N. R. Hodgson, 'Honour, Shame and the Fourth Crusade', *Journal of Medieval History*, 39 (2013), 232–5. Villehardouin's belief that those who pressed on to the Holy Land or defected achieved little of substance would seem to have been more than an expression of ill-will in that it had some basis in fact: see Queller and Madden, *Fourth Crusade*, pp. 48, 52, 92–4. See also D. E. Queller, T. F. Compton and D. A. Campbell, 'The Fourth Crusade: The Neglected Majority', *Speculum*, 49 (1974), 441–65. For a very different perspective, one that endorses the actions of Simon de Montfort and the abbot of Vaux-de-Cernay, two of those whose departures from the crusade Villehardouin notes, see Peter of Vaux-de-Cernay, *Hystoria Albigensis*, c. 106, ed. P. Guébin and E. Lyon, 3 vols (Paris, 1926–39), i, pp. 106–11; trans. W. A. Sibly and M. D. Sibly, *The History of the Albigensian Crusade* (Woodbridge, 1998), pp. 57–9. See also M. Zerner-Chardavoine and H. Piéchon-Palloc, 'La croisade albigeoise, une revanche: Des rapports entre la quatrième croisade et la croisade albigeoise', *Revue historique*, 267 (1982), 3–18.

[21] This was a period of about eighteen months which in text time corresponds to the interval between §75, p. 76, trans. p. 22 (the departure from Venice in October 1202) and §255, p. 60, trans. p. 68 (the distribution of Constantinople's spoils, which concludes the sequence on the capture of Constantinople and the crusaders' immediate reactions to their success in April 1204). This amounts to a little more than a third of the total length of the text.

Byzantine world, it is easy to overlook the fact that the *Conquête* does not stop at the fall of Constantinople. Far from it: the narrative of the capture of the city and its immediate aftermath concludes just past the text's mid-way point.[22] It might be expected that the sequence that immediately follows, on the election and coronation of Count Baldwin of Flanders as the new emperor in May 1204, would offer itself as a significant liminal, transitional moment, but if it was experienced as such by those who took part, this is not registered by any narratorial reflection or break in narrative rhythm.[23] The election of Baldwin, moreover, emerges as a natural progression from what precedes it in that it effectively plays out a script with which the reader/listener has already been made familiar; we have by this stage been informed in some detail of the terms of the agreement that the crusade's leaders had reached concerning the electoral process to be followed should they gain control of Constantinople, as well as the arrangements for the distribution of booty and lands.[24]

If there is a shift in tone around this point, a sense of a turning point in the crusaders' affairs, it emerges from the narrator's disapproval of the greed that motivated the hoarding of booty from Constantinople in defiance of the arrangements for the pooling of resources: henceforth, we are told in what amounts to a veiled prolepsis hinting at setbacks to come, the Lord began to love the crusaders less because they abandoned the loyalty that had characterized their behaviour up to that point.[25] Although a sense of moral diminishment is thereby set up to hang over all that follows, this does not in the event emerge as a major thematic emphasis in the second half of the narrative, over the course of which the ethical orientation of the narration remains governed by the aristocratic value system that has been much in evidence in the first half and which continues to motivate action and to ground the awarding of praise or blame.[26] It is important to note that the story stuff that appears in the second half of the text is not significantly disfavoured when it comes to the density of the text time devoted to it relative to its real-time duration: it covers the approximately three and a half years between Baldwin's election and the death of the former crusade leader Boniface of Montferrat in October 1207, the event with which the narrative concludes.[27]

[22] As measured as a proportion of the 500 paragraph-like sections into which the text is conventionally divided.

[23] *Conquête*, §§256–63, pp. 60–70, trans. pp. 69–71.

[24] *Conquête*, §§234–5, pp. 34–6, trans. pp. 62–3.

[25] *Conquête*, §§253–4, pp. 56–60, trans. p. 68. See also §303, pp. 110–12, trans. p. 82 in which the narrator criticizes those whose greed led them to exploit the lands assigned to them unjustly, thereby alienating the Greek population.

[26] For the aristocratic value set played out in the text, see Hodgson, 'Honour, Shame and the Fourth Crusade', 220–39, esp. 228–39.

[27] For the choice of ending and the closure that it effects, see Jacquin, *Le style historique*, pp. 40–1.

It is likely that the text was written, or completed, within one or two years of this final date.

Nonetheless, the latter half of the *Conquête* is sometimes treated as a lesser accomplishment, almost an afterthought; Archambault, for example, labels it 'a frequently tedious but lucid account' and 'a dry enumeration of sieges, battles, and conquests'.[28] There is, however, no evidence that Villehardouin originally meant the text to achieve closure with the events of April and May 1204 and then resumed the narrative of subsequent affairs at some later point. Nor does the manuscript tradition – which is substantially fuller than those of the other texts that this book considers – suggest that copyists and their intended readers discriminated between a more important and engaging first half and a second half of only narrow, specialist interest.[29] For our purposes, what is particularly noteworthy about the narrative in the *Conquête*'s latter half is that, in attempting to track the various attempts by the Latin secular elite to establish control of the dispersed lordships assigned to them, and to deal with the variety of threats that they faced, the narrator has to abandon the conveniently tight narrative focus that the crusade army had provided up to the capture of Constantinople.[30]

The challenge is in part met by tolerating gaps and uneven coverage, for once most of the Latin elite fans out to make good on the distribution of its regional lordships, a number of imbalances in the narrator's treatment become evident. There is a clear Constantinople-centric favouring of the priorities of Baldwin and his brother Henry, who succeeds him first as regent, then as emperor; more attention is paid to events in Thrace than across the Sea of Marmora in Asia Minor; Boniface of Montferrat, whose main sphere of interest was some distance from Constantinople in and around Thessaloniki in north-eastern Greece, receives relatively little attention, despite the fact that the historical Villehardouin appears to have been close to him and the narrator speaks of him warmly;[31] and there is very little on the Venetian settlement, Venice's lordship over certain towns only receiving mention as an incidental detail when the flow of the action passes through these places. Nonetheless, some attempt is made to capture the sheer geographical spread of the Latins' energies, as well as the ways in which success or failure in one place could have consequences in others.[32] This is especially

[28] Archambault, *Seven French Chroniclers*, pp. 26, 38.

[29] See *Conquête*, i, pp. xxxvii–xxxix.

[30] For the establishment of Latin lordships in areas taken from the Byzantines, see P. Lock, *The Franks in the Aegean, 1204–1500* (London, 1995), pp. 35–60.

[31] For Villehardouin's positive view of Boniface, which we are told was reciprocated, see esp. *Conquête*, §41, pp. 40–2, trans. p. 13; §265, pp. 70–2, trans. p. 71; §283, p. 92, trans. p. 76; §285, p. 94, trans. p. 77; §500, p. 314, trans. p. 135.

[32] See esp. *Conquête*, §460, p. 276, trans. p. 124, where the narrator remarks 'that at no time have any people ever been so burdened by war, for they were scattered among so many different places'. For Villehardouin's intercutting between multiple plot points,

well brought out in what is probably the text's most sustained and skilfully crafted patterning of action around a recurrent theme, its account of the various setbacks in different parts of the Latin empire that one after another postpone Emperor Henry's plans in 1207 to lead his forces to relieve Adrianople.[33] To the extent, then, that the narrator's attention is fragmented and dispersed over a large geographical area in the latter half of the *Conquête*, this further undermines the text's already exaggerated claims to eyewitness status.

As the foregoing discussion reveals, it is important to remember that, as we have seen in relation to other texts, a reading of the *Conquête* presents us with four Geoffrey of Villehardouins: the narrator, that is the shadowy anthropomorphic presence behind the narratorial voice; Villehardouin the character within the narrated action; Villehardouin the author of the *Conquête*; and Villehardouin the flesh-and-blood historical actor who is attested by a good deal of independent evidence as well as by much of the substantive content of the *Conquête* itself.[34] There is arguably a fifth presence, Villehardouin the implied author, but this much-debated category of analysis is less important for our immediate purposes.[35] At the risk of some over-simplification, it is fair to say that historical analysis of the *Conquête* mostly stages a conversation between the first and fourth figures, while the distinction between the first and third is typically collapsed. The central question has been: how does one get from the voice in the text to the mindset, value system, intentions, subterfuges and actions of Villehardouin the historical actor, and beyond him to those of the other historical figures caught up in the events of the Fourth Crusade? Again at the risk of over-simplification, literary readings have tended to foreground the relationship between the first and third figures. Here the operative question becomes: what may attending to the narratorial voice contribute to an understanding of Villehardouin the historically situated author, his reasons for the innovative use of vernacular prose, his intentions for the text as a communicative act, his stylistic and rhetorical skillset, and his possible exposure to formative cultural influences such as the literary milieu of the court of the counts of Champagne? The dynamic between the first and second categories, the narrator and Villehardouin the character within the storyworld of the text, has received a good deal less attention. For our purposes, however, this is the key to understanding the extent to which, and in what ways, the *Conquête* may be understood as an 'eyewitness' narrative.

---

see Jacquin, *Le style historique*, pp. 533–6. For such interlacing, see also R. Hartman, *La quête et la croisade: Villehardouin, Clari et le* Lancelot en prose (New York, 1977), pp. 87–94.

[33] *Conquête*, §§461–90, pp. 276–304, trans. pp. 124–32.

[34] For the historical Villehardouin, see esp. J. Longnon, *Recherches sur la vie de Geoffroy de Villehardouin, suivis du catologue des actes des Villehardouin* (Bibliothèque de l'École des Hautes Études, fasc. 276; Paris, 1939).

[35] For the implied author, see above, pp. 54–5.

What sort of narrator emerges in the text? The principal means by which a narrator usually announces him- or herself overtly, the use of the first person singular, is relatively little deployed. At the very beginning, initial indications that a guiding narratorial presence will be in the business of inserting itself into the narration emerge in references to Fulk of Neuilly 'of whom I speak to you' and the crusade indulgence 'such as I will describe to you'.[36] The degree of narratorial self-reference that these remarks seem to anticipate is not sustained, however. Insertions of the telling 'I' thereafter are few and seldom serve to introduce commentary or to flag major plot junctures or thematic emphases;[37] most are of the routine type that we have encountered in Ambroise's *Estoire de la Guerre Sainte* to express uncertainty as to numbers and an inability or unwillingness in the interests of narrative economy to list all of the names of those involved in a given event.[38] Often they appear in formulaic disavowals of the

[36] *Conquête*, §1, p. 2, trans. p. 5 ('dont je vos di'); §2, p. 4, trans. p. 5 ('tel con je vos dirai'): translations revised.

[37] For the fairly few cases of professed narratorial ignorance or uncertainty as to matters of plot substance, see e.g. *Conquête*, §203, p. 208, trans. pp. 54–5 (ignorance – 'ne sai quex genz' – as to which group was responsible for starting a highly destructive fire in Constantinople after a brawl between Greeks and Latins); §247, p. 48, trans. p. 66 (likewise ignorance as to who was responsible – 'ne sai quels genz' – for a further fire in the city); §271, p. 78, trans. p. 73 (uncertainty as to the number of days – 'ne sai quanz jorz' – Alexios IV and the future Alexios V were together at Mosynopolis before the former was taken prisoner by the latter); §277, p. 84, trans. p. 74 (ignorance as to whose advice – ' Ne sai par cui conseil' – persuaded Emperor Baldwin to campaign towards Thessaloniki despite Boniface of Montferrat's protestations that this infringed his rights as its lord, a significant and damaging fracture in their political relationship); §479, p. 294, trans. p. 129 (ignorance as to how – 'Ne sai comment' – Theodore Lascaris's admiral Stirione became aware of the approach of Latin forces). It is noteworthy that the same kinds of ignorance and uncertainty are often expressed by means of other constructions: see e.g. §204, pp. 208–10, trans. p. 55 ('ne vos porroit nus conter'); §249, p. 52, trans. pp. 66–7 ('ne couvient mie parler'); §263, p. 68, trans. p. 71 ('ne couvient mie a parler'). See also the third-person circumlocution concerning a knight's possible responsibility for a particular defeat in §484, p. 298, trans. pp. 130–1: 'The composer of this history is not sure whether this is true of false' ('Cil qui ceste ystoire traita ne seut s'il fu a tort ou a droit').

[38] E.g. *Conquête*, §10, p. 14, trans. p. 7: 'and many others whose names I do not know' ('et maint autre dont je ne sai pas les nons'); §114, p. 116, trans. p. 31: 'I cannot give you the names of all those involved in this affair' ('Je ne vos puis mie toz cels nomer qui a ceste ouvre faire furent'); §168, p. 168, trans. p. 44: 'I cannot begin to recount to you all the blows, wounds and deaths suffered there' ('Tolz les cops et tols les bleciez et toz les mors ne vos pui mie raconter'). It is significant that exactly the same sorts of shortcuts and qualifications are often made by means of constructions that do not use the first person singular: e.g. §183, p. 186, trans. p. 49: 'It is impossible to describe their joy' ('de la joie ne convient mie a parler'); §192, p. 194, trans. p. 51; 'It is impossible even to begin to describe all the saints' relics' ('Des saintuaires ne convient mie a parler'); §204, p. 210, trans. p. 55: 'No one could tell you' ('ne vos porroit nus conter').

ability to go into the complexities of the debate in a given meeting, followed by a succinct statement of what the meeting eventually decided.[39] In addition, the narratorial 'I' does not become an intradiegetic participant in its own storyworld, with the result that its knowledge of people and events is seldom expressly tagged as based on experience.[40]

By extension, there is no attempt implicitly to collapse the distance between the narrator and Villehardouin-the-character by depicting the latter actively engaged in the gathering of data or attempting the kind of after-the-fact autopsy that was valued by ancient historians. It is significant that on the few occasions in which the text expressly refers to those who supply information, the giving of their testimony is presented as though it were in the nature of a general bearing of witness unto the world, not a specific conversation or briefing at which Villehardouin happened to be present; and in thematic terms the complexity of the events so reported reduces in a clichéd manner to elite individuals conforming to the ethical standards that the narrator expects from members of the aristocracy.[41] In a formal but important sense, therefore, the *Conquête* cannot be categorized as an 'autobiographical' work or as a memoir. Certain types of information are supplied that seem to have functioned at some level as mnemonic scaffolding for the author, such as the regular punctuation of the action by obituary notices

[39] *Conquête*, §20, p. 22, trans. p. 9: 'I cannot tell you all the arguments that were put forward' ('Totes les paroles qui la furent dites et retraites ne vos puis mie raconter'); §30, p. 30, trans. p. 11: 'I cannot recount to you all the fine and fitting words the doge said' ('Des paroles qui li dux dist, bones et belles, ne vos puis tout raconter'). It is noteworthy that after these examples early in the narrative, the first person singular drops away from the numerous further instances of the narrator shortcutting what was said in councils and other debates: see e.g. §117, p. 120, trans. p. 32; §147, p. 148, trans. p. 39; §234, p. 34, trans. p. 62; §298, p. 106, trans. p. 80; §423, p. 236, trans. p. 114.

[40] Cf. Beer, *In Their Own Words*, pp. 43–4 for the unconvincing argument that the 'I' within the narrative represents the figure of an 'oral reader', presumably a performer of the text of the *Conquête*, whom Villehardouin-the-author interjects between himself and the anticipated audience. Villehardouin's 'I' is far more straightforwardly to be interpreted as one manifestation of the narratorial voice, an effect which solely exists *within* the text.

[41] See *Conquête*, §332, p. 142, trans. p. 89 regarding a damaging Greek sortie against James of Avesnes's forces besieging Corinth, and James's efforts to save his followers: 'People who were present at this event have given faithful witness that it was through his good conduct that they were rescued' ('et bien li porterent tesmoing cil qui la furent, qui per son bien faire furent rescols'); §360, p. 168, trans. p. 96 concerning survivors' reports of the disastrous defeat at the battle of Adrianople in April 1205, during which Emperor Baldwin was taken prisoner, never to be seen again: 'People who were present that day have given faithful witness that no knight ever defended himself better than he did' ('et bien tesmoignent cil qui la furent que onques mes cors de chevaliers mielz ne se defendi de lui').

of elite figures, sometimes with mention of their place of burial,[42] and details of where on his body a certain named, which is to say high-status, individual received a mortal blow or was injured in battle – the most recurrent type of reality effect, in fact, in a text in which such precise details are fairly rare.[43] But the narrator's memory is never expressly invoked. Almost all the information at his disposal simply appears available to him as a body of self-evident knowledge.

If a perceiving, experiencing, knowledge-acquiring and self-consciously recollecting narratorial 'I' is only a very muted presence within the text, the narrator's voice and the authority it claims are, however, substantially reinforced by a number of other devices. One is the sense of the narrator's and narratee's shared immersion in the unfolding of the plot as conveyed by the use of the first person plural *lairons*, 'we shall leave', in constructions that announce jumps in the focus of attention.[44] This device is especially common in the latter part of the text, where the narrator frequently cuts between the actions of various individuals and groups dispersed across the Franks' several areas of operation. A second way in which the narratorial presence is amplified is by appeals to the text-as-book as a source of authority.[45] None of the ambiguities that attach to Ambroise's references to books and writings applies here: in the *Conquête* the book is

[42] E.g. *Conquête*, §37, p. 38, trans. p. 12 (Theobald of Champagne); §46, pp. 46–8, trans. pp. 14–15 (Geoffrey of Perche); §73, p. 74, trans. p. 21 (Fulk of Neuilly); §124, p. 126, trans. p. 33 (Guy of Coucy); §200, p. 204, trans. p. 54 (Matthew of Montmorency); §206, p. 6, trans. p. 55 (Abbot Simon of Loos); §262, p. 68, trans. p. 71 (Odo the Champenois of Champlitte); §290, p. 98, trans. p. 78 (John of Noyon, Baldwin of Flanders's chancellor); §291, p. 100, trans. p. 78 (Peter of Amiens, Guy of Mauchicourt and Giles of Aunoi); §300, p. 108, trans. p. 81 (Renier of Mons); §332, p. 142, trans. p. 89 (Dreux of Étrœungt); §334, p. 144, trans. p. 90 (Hugh of St-Pol); §388, p. 198, trans. p. 104 (the doge Enrico Dandolo). See also the mentions of the deaths of two (named) knights in Constantinople, and of Baldwin of Flanders's wife Marie while en route to join her husband: §302, p. 110, trans. p. 82; §§317–18, pp. 124–6, trans. p. 85. For longer casualty lists, see §361, p. 170, trans. p. 96; §409, p. 222, trans. p. 110.

[43] See below, pp. 282–3.

[44] *Conquête*, §51, p. 54, trans. p. 17: 'Or vos lairons de cels'; the same formulation appears in §232, p. 32, trans. p. 62; §324, p. 132, trans. p. 87; §380, p. 188, trans. p. 102. See also §347, p. 156, trans. p. 93: 'Or lairons de Renier de Trit, si revendrons a l'empereour Baudoin'; §398, p. 208, trans. p. 107: 'Or lairons de Henri…ici, si dirons de Johannisse'; §402, p. 212, trans. p. 108: 'Or lairons de Phynepople et de Renier de Trit…si revenrons a Henri'; §455, p. 270, trans. p. 123: 'Or lairons de cez, si dirons de Tyerri de Los'. For such transitions in Villehardouin's history and similar texts, see Jacquin, *Le style historique*, pp. 81–91; Beer, *Villehardouin*, pp. 40–2.

[45] *Conquête*, §99, p. 98, trans. p. 27: 'Et tant vos retrait li livres'; §114, p. 118, trans. p. 31: 'si que li livre testimoigne bien'; §129, p. 130, trans. p. 34: 'ne vos contera mie li livres'; §201, p. 204, trans. p. 54: 'dont li livre ore se taist'; §231, p. 32, trans. p. 61: 'Et bien tesmoigne li livres'; §236, p. 38, trans. p. 63: 'et bien tesmoigne li livres'; §345, p. 154, trans. p. 92: 'Or conte li livres une grant mervoille'. Cf. §141, p. 142, trans. p. 37; §361, p. 170, trans. p. 96; §367, p. 176, trans. p. 98; §376, p. 184, trans. p. 100;

straightforwardly a surrogate for, or extension of, the narrator, a secure source of knowledge that is itself equipped to 'testify'.[46] A third device, and the most important, is the frequent use of apostrophes to the narratee by means of the verb *savoir*, 'to know', either as an infinitive with a modal verb in the construction *poez savoir*, 'you may know',[47] or more directly as an imperative in the form *sachiez*.[48] The latter is the more common; *sachiez* is, in fact, the attention-grabbing word with which the text begins.[49] The effect of this frequent direct address to the narratee is to simulate the candour of a conversational exchange within a group of intimates.[50]

These interjections mostly serve to introduce background details and amplifying glosses that enhance faith not only in the narrator's fund of knowledge but also his ability to select and arrange appropriate details from the extensive body of data presumed to be available to him, and to anticipate the queries of attentive readers or listeners as they follow the plot.[51] In several instances the apostrophes shade from the simply explanatory and expansive towards evaluative commentary.[52] Some make reference to the emotional content of scenes and thus, albeit

§409, p. 222, trans. p. 110, in which the references to the book mimic the reluctance or inability of the first-person narrator to provide a complete account.

[46] For a somewhat different approach to the text's references to itself as book, see Beer, *In Their Own Words*, pp. 45–6. See also M. Buda, 'Early Historical Narrative and the Dynamics of Textual Reference', *Romanic Review*, 80 (1989), 1–17 for the argument that the mentions of the book are evidence of an authenticating strategy in which seeing and writing are treated as closely equivalent forms of validation.

[47] *Conquête*, §104, p. 104, trans. p. 28; §128, p. 130, trans. p. 34; §192, p. 194, trans. p. 51; §255, p. 60, trans. p. 68.

[48] E.g. *Conquête*, §2, p. 2, trans. p. 5; § 3, p. 4, trans. p. 5; §39, p. 40, trans. p. 13; §89, p. 90, trans. p. 25; §151, p. 150, trans. p. 39; §211, p. 10, trans. pp. 56–7; §238, p. 38, trans. p. 63; §320, p. 128, trans. p. 86; §436, p. 248, trans. p. 117; §460, p. 276, trans. p. 124.

[49] *Conquête*, §1, p. 2, trans. p. 5: the opening sentence alerts the narratee to the preaching of Fulk of Neuilly, which is dated with reference to the reigns of Pope Innocent III and Kings Philip of France and Richard of England.

[50] But see C. Aslanov, 'Aux sources de la chronique en prose française: entre déculturation et acculturation', in T. F. Madden (ed.), *The Fourth Crusade: Event, Aftermath, and Perception: Papers from the Sixth Conference of the Society for the Study of the Crusades and the Latin East, Istanbul, Turkey, 25–29 August 2004* (Crusades Subsidia, 2; Aldershot, 2008), p. 149, arguing that the use of *savoir* is more formal in that it mimics the style of address in letters and charters.

[51] E.g. *Conquête*, §151, p. 150, trans. 39 (the presence of many fine knights in a battalion); §159, p. 158, trans. p. 42 (the fact that the chain across the entrance to the Golden Horn controlled access for everyone); §202, p. 206, trans. p. 54 (the degree of Greek submission to Emperor Baldwin, and the extent of the Bulgarian ruler Ioannitsa's conquest of Byzantine territory); §238, pp. 38–40, trans. p. 63 (the fact that the crusaders' losses were greater than those of the Greeks in the assault on Constantinople on 9 April 1204).

[52] E.g. *Conquête*, §39, p. 40, trans. p. 13 (Duke Odo of Burgundy made a bad choice in

in a limited way, gesture towards the actors' subjective self-awareness, capacity for anticipation, collective mood and shared experientiality, aspects which are routinely lost in the narrator's generally straightforward narration of action sequences.[53] Other examples serve to cue associations that are not explicitly spelled out for the reader or listener but nonetheless have the potential to guide understanding of characters and their actions.[54] In a number of cases evaluative language, which on the surface represents a narratorial assessment made after the fact, nudges towards evocations of the sentiments of those involved at the time, in effect a double focalization; this is especially evident in references to danger and risk.[55]

The use of *savoir* in these ways is significant because the text's presentation of action in itself tends towards the singulative, punctual, linear and tightly

---

rejecting the offer to replace Theobald of Champagne on the crusade); §104, p. 104, trans. p. 28 (it was only thanks to God's love that the army held together while at Zara); §332, p. 142, trans. p. 89 (God's help permitted the Franks besieging Corinth to turn near-defeat to victory). Cf. the use of 'oiez', 'hear', to introduce the reflection that the Franks' abandonment of Rodosto, which precipitated an avoidable catastrophe, was unnecessary given the site's defensive strength: §416, p. 228, trans. p. 112. The narrator's judgement that there was a pattern to Ioannitsa's ruthless destruction of captured cities and castles and his treatment of their inhabitants is reinforced by the repetition of 'sachiez' in §§420–1, pp. 232–4, trans. p. 113. See also the tone of special pleading introduced by the repetition of 'sachiez' and equivalent terms in the passage dealing with the distribution of spoils after the capture of Constantinople, a problematic and contentious matter that the narrator chooses to acknowledge while nonetheless drawing attention to how well the arrangements did in fact work: §§254–5, pp. 58–60, trans. p. 68.

[53] E.g. *Conquête*, §31, p. 32, trans. p. 11 (the shedding of many tears); §89, p. 90, trans. p. 25 (the greatest cause for grief); §100, p. 100, trans. p. 27 (men's hearts know no peace – one of the text's most lyrical moments); §128, p. 130, trans. p. 34 (no man was so tough that his flesh did not tremble); §181, p. 182, trans. p. 48 (no man was so brave he did not feel relieved); §225, p. 24, trans. p. 60 (comforting reassurance is provided by the offer of spiritual rewards); §345, p. 156, trans. p. 93 (deserters are little mourned); §368, p. 176, trans. p. 98 (the fear and expectation of future disaster on the part of those who fled the defeat at Adrianople); §411, p. 224, trans. p. 111 (collective distress in Constantinople); §432, p. 246, trans. p. 116 (everyone interprets Ioannitsa's withdrawal from Demotika as a great miracle); §475, p. 290, trans. p. 128 (Ioannitsa's withdrawal from Adrianople is considered a great miracle).

[54] See e.g. *Conquête*, §3, pp. 4–6, trans. p. 5, where 'sachiez' prefaces the information that Theobald of Champagne and Louis of Blois were aged twenty-two and twenty-seven, respectively, when they took the cross, thereby evoking associations of youthful virility and enthusiasm.

[55] E.g. *Conquête*, §157, p. 156, trans. p. 41 (pride in the crusaders' amphibious landing near Constantinople in July 1203); §160, p. 160, trans. p. 42 (James of Avesnes is in danger when fiercely attacked and wounded in the face); §181, p. 182, trans. p. 48 (God has never delivered a people from so great a danger); §436, pp. 248–50, trans. p. 117 (those going on a rescue mission face great danger).

sequential. Like begets like in the narrator's handling of action: that is to say, actions arranged in paratactic sequence, which is very common, tend to be of similar types and similar orders of scale and consequentiality, and there is little zooming in and out. There is likewise little dwelling on characters' mental operations, with the result that character motivation mostly involves the reaction to an immediate stimulus as it presents itself in the plot chain, not the playing out of longer-term ambitions or the demonstration of permanent attributes. In these circumstances, the use of *savoir* becomes the narrator's principal mechanism to step outside the relentless beat of the narrative rhythm in order to introduce some measure of reflection and to guide the reader/listener's responses, albeit in predominantly conventional directions.[56]

In these ways, then, the narrator's authority is built up without emphasizing either a homodiegetic or heterodiegetic 'I'. The principal effect is to facilitate the separation of narrator and Villehardouin the character that is a central element, indeed the signature contrivance, of the *Conquête*'s narrative strategy. As is well known, Villehardouin the character within the *Conquête*'s storyworld is always introduced in the third person. The reasons for this detached form of self-reference are not altogether clear. It has been plausibly suggested that it was a means to enhance confidence in the text's veracity, especially in light of the fact that the novelty of the vernacular prose form as applied to contemporary history would have denied the reader or listener a familiar horizon of expectations by means of which to gauge the text's authority.[57] On the other hand, if the first-person narrator had been inserted more fully into the action, thereby making the work much more overtly autobiographical, then it is likely that this too would now be interpreted as a validating device. It is possible that the technique of self-reference in the third person was inspired by Caesar's *Commentaries*, knowledge of which Villehardouin may have acquired at second hand from someone with better Latin than he himself probably possessed. (It is important to remember, however, that Caesar's works were routinely misattributed to another author in the medieval period, although some writers seem to have been aware of the author's

[56] For similar narratorial interventions without the use of *savoir*, most of them also embodying a double focalization that both evokes the participants' own experiences and appraisals of their situation, and articulates narratorial evaluations after the fact, see e.g. *Conquête*, §163, p. 164, trans. p. 43 (the Greeks' failure to engage a far smaller Latin force comes as a great surprise ['mult grant merveille']); §256, pp. 60–2, trans. p. 69 (the inevitability that there would be competition for the imperial title); §351, p. 160, trans. p. 94 (the company of mounted sergeants at the battle of Adrianople was less effective than it should have been); §412, p. 226, trans. p. 111 (Ioannitsa's force was so large that it was nothing less than a marvel ['merveille']); §414, p. 226, trans. p. 111 (the mortality at Apros was a marvel ['merveille']); §429, p. 242, trans. p. 116 (it was perilous for so few to campaign against so many).

[57] See Aslanov, 'Aux sources de la chronique', pp. 146–7.

actual identity.) The fact that an interest in Roman history was developing among the writers and audiences of Old French texts around this time is suggested by, for example, *Li Fet des Romains*, composed only a few years after Villehardouin was writing, between 1211 and 1214. A compilation and adaptation of all the works of Roman history known to the author, *Li Fet des Romains* was intended to cover the same range as Suetonius's *Twelve Caesars*, that is up to Domitian, but in the event it did not get past Caesar, whose *Bellum gallicum* and *Bellum civile* were among its principal sources.[58] If the *Commentaries* were known to Villehardouin, and if he was aware of the author's true identity – both big ifs – then a link is not out of the question, although it is important to bear in mind that Caesar the character is all but omnipresent throughout the *Commentaries* and is the consistent centre of interest, whereas, as we shall see, Villehardouin the character is an irregular presence within the storyworld of the *Conquête*, his appearances mostly limited to discrete and concentrated bursts of action.

The *Conquête* does not have a preface or dedication which might have clarified the question of authorship for the reader or listener; whether there originally was such front matter that is no longer preserved in the surviving manuscript witnesses is unclear. In practice, of course, it is highly likely that a medieval reader or listener would have come to the *Conquête* with some idea of the identity of the author even without the wealth of background historical knowledge that a modern reader unavoidably brings to the text. It is noteworthy, nonetheless, that when it comes to the express flagging up of authorial identity, the name of the author is not announced until §120, about a quarter of the way into the text, at a point in the action at which the crusaders have already travelled beyond Venice and Zara and are well on their way to Constantinople:

> Geoffrey, the marshal of Champagne – who dictated this work without ever knowingly telling a lie, and was present at all the councils – gives sure witness [*bien testimoigne*] that such a beautiful thing [the crusade fleet leaving Corfu on 24 May 1203] was never seen.[59]

This is the first of five broadly similar affirmations, distributed fairly evenly over the course of the text, which to some extent close the distance between the narratorial voice, Geoffrey the character and Geoffrey the author.[60] Their contribution to the text's self-validation in the round should not be exaggerated, however. While two of these interjections seek to reinforce points that address some of

[58] *Li Fet des Romains: compilé ensemble de Saluste et de Suetoine et de Lucan*, ed. L.-F. Flutre and K. Sneyders de Vogel, 2 vols (Paris, 1935–8). See Beer, *In Their Own Words*, pp. 69–103.

[59] *Conquête*, §120, p. 122, trans. pp. 32–3: translation slightly revised.

[60] See *Conquête*, §174, p. 176, trans. p. 46; §218, pp. 16–18, trans. p. 58; §250, p. 52, trans. p. 67; §460, p. 276, trans. p. 124.

the narrative's principal substantive and thematic emphases, namely the great extent of the booty won in the conquest of Constantinople, and the fact that the Franks in the incipient Latin empire were hugely burdened by war because their energies were dispersed across a large number of places,[61] the others concern details of more topical interest bearing upon precise plot junctures that are similar to many others found over the course of the narrative: the fact that more than forty witnesses reported to Villehardouin that they had seen the Venetians' banner of St Mark planted on one of the towers on the walls of Constantinople during the assault on the city on 17 July 1203, and the observation that the Venetians acquitted themselves well in warding off the danger posed by Byzantine fire ships drifting across the Golden Horn, an attack that took place on 1 January 1204.[62]

It is unlikely, then, that these passages are meant to be read as conspicuous narratorial signposts to which the reader or listener is encouraged to attach heightened importance. Nor is there a particularly pronounced emphasis on autobiographical experience or a mnemonic resonance lurking beneath the surface of the narrative at these points. It is true that in some of these passages there is a measure of attention to the visual that is not typical of the text as a whole.[63] The sequence quoted above concerning the fleet's departure from Corfu, which is described as such a beautiful thing ('si bele chose') to behold, is followed by the statement that the vessels' sails extended as far as the eye could see, a sight which lifted the spirits of those present.[64] Similarly, the passage concerning the banner of St Mark, which stresses the fact that multiple witnesses honestly reported what *they* saw, is preceded, in a manner redolent of Ambroise's bundling of complementary and mutually reinforcing gazes,[65] first by the Venetians' sight of the banner as it is moved from the doge's galley onto land, and then an invitation to the narratee, by means of the apostrophizing 'veïssiez', to visualize a remarkable assault ('assault merveillox').[66] But it is important to note that the verbs that are found in these passages to express the act of bearing witness ('testimoigne'/'tesmoigne') are also used in a more depersonalized manner with respect to the utterances of 'the book'.[67] In other words, the narrator does not emphasize the epistemological importance of eyewitness as part of the larger project of gaining knowledge and

[61] *Conquête*, §250, p. 52, trans. p. 67; §460, p. 276, trans. p. 124.

[62] *Conquête*, §174, p. 176, trans. p. 46; §218, pp. 16–18, trans. p. 58. For these events, see Queller and Madden, *Fourth Crusade*, pp. 123–4, 158; Phillips, *Fourth Crusade*, pp. 174–6, 218–20.

[63] See below, pp. 281–92.

[64] *Conquête*, §120, p. 122, trans. p. 33.

[65] See above, pp. 248–9.

[66] *Conquête*, §174, p. 176, trans. p. 46.

[67] E.g. *Conquête*, §114, p. 118, trans. p. 31: 'li livre testimoigne bien'; §231, p. 32, trans. p. 61: 'bien tesmoigne li livres'. See also §236, p. 38, trans. p. 63; §464, p. 280, trans. p. 125.

understanding of the storyworld, nor the particular acuity and accuracy of his or others' gazes.

If, then, the narrator is a quite reticent presence as a site of authority, what of Villehardouin the character within the storyworld? Here several significant interventions are made. They are not so frequent or extended as to dominate the action except in certain short bursts of narrative, nor are they such that the overall plot would break down if they were absent. That is so say, they do not represent a coherent and joined-up sequence of autobiographical reminiscence smuggled into, or superimposed over, a host 'public' narrative of the crusade expedition and the beginnings of the Latin empire. These interventions do, however, amount to more than solipsistic indulgences or tokenistic self-references. Villehardouin the character enters the storyworld in order to personify and enact expressions of some of the text's principal thematic preoccupations: specifically, the importance of the crusaders' alliance with the Venetians; the need for the crusade host to be unified; the legitimacy of the crusaders' actions, in particular their correct reading of the behaviour and motivations of the Byzantine political elite; and the ethical standards expected of members of the aristocracy, most notably loyalty, quick thinking and personal courage. In this connection, it is significant that Villehardouin the character first appears in the text in an unhighlighted manner that stresses his participation alongside many of his peers in a large and corporate endeavour: his name is embedded among those of other members of the Champenois contingent within the long roll-call of high-status northern French and Flemish crusaders' names that anchors the beginning of the narrative.[68]

Thereafter, Villehardouin appears performing a number of roles in the plot, chief among them that of diplomatic envoy and negotiator.[69] The first and best known of the embassies in which he participates is, of course, that which entered into the fateful negotiations with Venice in the spring of 1201 concerning the size and cost of the fleet that Venice contracted to place at the crusaders' disposal.[70] The long account of this mission in the *Conquête* illustrates a tension that will run through several of Villehardouin's subsequent appearances in the plot. His individual agency is highlighted at several points, as when, with the agreement of the other five envoys, it is he who addresses the doge and the large number of Venetians assembled in St Mark's.[71] But for the most part he functions as part of a

[68] *Conquête*, §§3–10, pp. 4–14, trans. pp. 5–7. The principal crusaders from Champagne are listed in §5, Villehardouin appearing exactly mid-way, i.e. twelfth in a list of twenty-three names.

[69] See Dufournet, *Les écrivains*, i, pp. 160–5.

[70] *Conquête*, §§11–32, pp. 14–34 trans. pp. 7–11. For this embassy and the crucial question of the terms that it agreed with Venice, see Queller and Madden, *Fourth Crusade*, pp. 9–20; Phillips, *Fourth Crusade*, pp. 55–77.

[71] *Conquête*, §27, p. 28, trans. p. 10. The character's standing out from the crowd is

group in full conformity with its collective actions and intentions – such as when the speech to the Venetians is followed by the statement that 'Immediately the six envoys knelt at the feet of the Venetians, weeping heavily'.[72] Villehardouin the character's willingness to act in the group interest is clearly a theme that the narrator seeks to emphasize. It is noteworthy that in many of the instances in which Villehardouin is temporarily thrust into a position of prominence within the storyworld, the fact that he is acting at the behest of others is expressly mentioned. For example, we are told that Villehardouin was chosen for another of his diplomatic missions, that undertaken with Hugh of St-Pol to Pavia in order to persuade a vacillating Count Louis of Blois that he should commit to travelling east via Venice, doubtless in reality a much more fraught and knife-edge moment than the amount of space that the text devotes to it would seem to suggest.[73] Similarly, he is one of four envoys, alongside Matthew of Montmorency and two Venetians, chosen by the crusade leadership to sound out the situation in Constantinople after the flight of Emperor Alexios III from the city and the resumption of the imperial throne by his brother Isaac II in July 1203;[74] and he is one of three French nobles later sent into the city to remind Alexios IV of the formal promises that he had made to the crusade leaders in return for their help in restoring him to his rightful inheritance.[75]

There is one important exception to this recurrent presentation of Villehardouin as the dutiful and reliable lieutenant of the crusade's, and subsequently of the Latin empire's, high command.[76] This concerns his efforts to save the remnants of the Frankish army after its disastrous defeat at the hands of the Bulgarian ruler Ioannitsa's forces at the battle of Adrianople on 14 April 1205. According to the *Conquête*, it is Villehardouin who salvages something from the wreckage by

reinforced by the use of direct discourse. Note, however, the motif of seeking the assent of one's peers before acting as spokesman, which is also evident in the account of the former of Villehardouin's two embassies into Constantinople: §186, pp. 188–90, trans. p. 50. See also §144, p. 144, trans. p. 38 and §213, p. 12, trans. p. 57, where the agreed spokesman is Conon of Béthune, the individual who comes closest to functioning as Villehardouin's *alter ego* in the narrative.

[72] *Conquête*, §28, p. 28, trans. p. 10: 'Mantenant li .vi. message s'agenoillent a lor piez mult plorant'.

[73] *Conquête*, §53, pp. 54–6, trans. p. 17: 'A cel message fu esliz li cuens Hues de Sain Pol et Joffrois li marechaus de Champaigne'.

[74] *Conquête*, §184, pp. 186–8, trans. p. 49: 'Li consels as barons et as contes fu tels, et celui al duc de Venise, que il envoieroient messaiges…Eslit furent li message…'.

[75] *Conquête*, §211, p. 10, trans. p. 56: 'A cel message fu esliz…'. For similar instances bearing on Villehardouin's military as well as diplomatic roles, see §268, p. 76, trans. p. 72; §283, p. 92, trans. p. 76; §296, p. 104, trans. p. 80; §343, p. 152, trans. p. 92; §354, p. 164, trans. p. 95; §457, p. 272, trans. p. 123.

[76] For Villehardouin the character's reputation for reliability among the elite, see esp. *Conquête*, §283, p. 92, trans. p. 76.

efficiently organizing and leading the surviving Franks' retreat over the course of several days until they reach the relative safety of the coastal town of Rodosto.[77] Not only is this the longest sequence in the narrative in which Villehardouin the character is to the fore, he moves through and, insofar as circumstances permit, controls the diegetic space and the other actors in it in a far more dominant and proactive manner than hitherto. This newly acquired centrality to the plot – albeit in a role that is thrust upon Villehardouin *faute de mieux* because the battle has just removed two of the principals, Emperor Baldwin and Louis of Blois, to whom he has routinely deferred in previous interactions – is registered in various ways. First and foremost, Villehardouin focalizes more acutely and more often than at any other point. Indeed, his taking charge of the situation begins in an act of perception and understanding as the nature and scale of the defeat become clear to him: 'When Geoffrey, marshal of Champagne, who was keeping guard in front of one of the gates of Adrianople, saw what had happened he set out as soon as he could with as many men as he could muster.'[78] Thereafter, his usual role as the willing deputy of others is strikingly reversed as he takes control of the situation; he issues commands ('manda') to Manassiers of L'Isle, hitherto regularly presented as a near-equal when engaged alongside Villehardouin in a variety of military and diplomatic tasks;[79] and at one point he even tells ('manda' again) the doge what to do.[80] When the retreat begins, with Villehardouin assuming the all-important task of covering the rear, the narrator makes a point of insisting that no one gets left behind.[81] Villehardouin's authority, moreover, is explicitly acknowledged by other Franks encountered during the retreat: 'Sir', they ask, 'what do you want us to do?'[82]

It is tempting to see this sequence as a moment of self-aggrandizing autobiographical reminiscence, or perhaps wishful thinking, breaking through the surface of a narrative that is routinely focused on the corporate decision-making and collective agency of a group of leaders in which Villehardouin plays a significant but second-string role. Viewed in this way, the retreat from Adrianople effectively becomes Villehardouin's 'finest hour' as an individual actor. But the foregrounding of Villehardouin the character's actions is also a narratorial device to draw attention to the disastrous nature of the defeat and its significance for the

[77] *Conquête*, §§362–6, 369–75, pp. 170–6, 178–84, trans. pp. 96–100.

[78] *Conquête*, §362, p. 170, trans. pp. 96–7. See also §373, p. 182, trans. p. 99 for his realization that the headlong flight was tiring the horses.

[79] *Conquête*, §362, p. 170, trans. p. 97. For Villehardouin's earlier interactions with Manassiers, see §151, p. 150, trans. p. 39; §268, p. 76, trans. p. 72; §283, p. 92, trans. p. 76; §287, pp. 94–6, trans. p. 77; §§343–4, pp. 152–4, trans. p. 92; §354, p. 164, trans. p. 95; §356, p. 166, trans. p. 95.

[80] *Conquête*, §364, p. 172, trans. p. 97.

[81] *Conquête*, §366, p. 174, trans. p. 98.

[82] *Conquête*, §372, p. 180, trans. p. 99.

future of the Latin empire; to this extent, Villehardouin is simply the man with the right qualifications who happened to be on the spot, that member of the fast-shrinking roll call of veterans of the crusade who is called upon to demonstrate the qualities of tactical good sense, bravery and steadfast command that would be expected of any high-status figure in those circumstances. It is significant that Villehardouin's domination of the action and his centrality to the plot quickly fade once his moment of decisive crisis-management has passed. There is a transitional passage in which the emperor Baldwin's brother Henry of Hainaut rides to Rodosto and meets Villehardouin and the doge. There the three men discuss how they should proceed. And at that point the baton of narrative focus is handed over: Henry is recognized as the regent for his brother, whose fate after his capture during the battle is still unknown, and from this point onwards it is Henry who becomes the narrator's centre of attention as he throws himself into shoring up the Frankish position.[83]

If the sequence on the retreat from Adrianople, as well as the treatment of some aspects of the embassies in which Villehardouin had a role, are the exceptions to the general rule that the text nudges only slightly towards autobiography, are there nonetheless indications that Villehardouin the character is permitted greater experiential depth and mnenomic capacity than other actors? In other words, does the narrator smuggle into the text traces of personal experience and memory that could in principle be tracked back to the circumstances of Villehardouin the author? There are some passages in which one might suspect that a particular scene-specific authorial recollection is at play in sequences in which Villehardouin is participating in the action. For example, the text supplies the detail that as the envoys entered Constantinople on the first of the two embassies into Constantinople in which Villehardouin took part, in July 1203, their route between the gate through which they entered the city and the Blachernae palace was lined by 'Englishmen and Danes bearing battle-axes', that is to say members of the Varangian Guard; and we are further told that once the envoys reached the palace and encountered Emperor Isaac, the throng was so great 'that one could barely turn around'.[84] In the account of the second embassy to the imperial court some months later, the purpose of which was to confront Alexios IV with demands for the payments he had promised, there is likewise a possible element of specific recall in a reference to the sort of human detail that the narrator seldom

[83] *Conquête*, §§383–6, pp. 192–4, trans. p. 103. That Henry is clearly in charge is soon demonstrated thereafter: §§402–3, pp. 212–16, trans. pp. 108–9.

[84] *Conquête*, §185, p. 188, trans. p. 49. For the Varangian Guard at the time of the Fourth Crusade and its role in imperial politics, see S. B. Blöndal and B. S. Benedicz, *The Varangians of Byzantium* (Cambridge, 1978), pp. 163–6. For this mission, see Queller and Madden, *Fourth Crusade*, pp. 132–3.

mentions, when we are told that the faces of Alexios and the shocked Byzantine courtiers registered anger where before they had shown kindness.[85]

There are also some indications of emotional responses to specific situations that arguably have an autobiographical basis. For example, the envoys in the same fraught encounter with Alexios IV and his court make a swift exit and feel great relief when they reach the safety of the city gate; the description of their escape as a 'grant mervoille' seems to register their own focalization as they reflect on their lucky getaway at least as much as it does the narrator's assessment of their predicament after the fact.[86] Similarly, the narrator observes that when the Frankish forces, which include Villehardouin, approach Adrianople in what will prove to be the build-up to the fateful battle, their act of focalization – '[they] found the city very well garrisoned; they saw the banners of Ioannitsa, king of Vlachia and Bulgaria, above the walls and towers' – and the paucity of their own numbers make them feel great anxiety ('grant mesaise').[87] Likewise, Villehardouin individually experiences a similar reaction ('grand souci') during the retreat from Adrianople as he ponders the possibility that Ioannitsa's victorious forces will pursue and catch up with the Franks, in which case – the narrator deploys one of his infrequent counterfactuals to emphasize the element of danger – they would all be lost.[88] And when Frankish forces, Villehardouin in command of the vanguard, are on campaign towards Demotika, which Ioannitsa is besieging, we are told that they are afraid, not only because of the fact that their numbers are fewer than those of the enemy, but also because the local Greek population might go over to Ioannitsa's side.[89]

One should not, however, attach too much importance to these possible glimpses into the recollected personal experiences and emotional reactions of Villehardouin the historical actor. These moments are few when considered in relation to the whole length of the text; and the very limited role that, as we have noted, is assumed by the narratorial voice in the first person singular militates against these experiences being expressly tagged as vivid personal memories. It is true that Villehardouin the character feels personal anxiety at the thought of being caught by Ioannitsa's forces, as we have noted, but this sort of individuation of experience is specific to the atypical foregrounding of Villehardouin as an actor that we have seen characterizes the narrator's handling of the retreat from Adrianople. Elsewhere Villehardouin is immersed within communal expressions

[85] *Conquête*, §215, p. 14, trans. p. 57. For this embassy, see Queller and Madden, *Fourth Crusade*, pp. 154–5.

[86] *Conquête*, §216, p. 14, trans. pp. 57–8.

[87] *Conquête*, §350, p. 160, trans. p. 94: translation slightly revised.

[88] *Conquête*, §371, p. 180, trans. p. 99.

[89] *Conquête*, §§430–1, pp. 242–4, trans. p. 116.

of anxiety, grief or elation in a manner consistent with his overarching adhesion to the motivations and behaviours of collectives over the course of the narrative.[90]

It is noteworthy, moreover, how readily descriptions of scenes in which we might suspect an element of context-specific personal recall, in relation to both visual details and mental states, slip into conventional and clichéd language, much of it inspired by the tropes of courtly romance. It is often supposed that Villehardouin the author was deeply influenced by epic *chansons de geste*,[91] but less attention has been paid to the fact that the *Conquête* frequently calls forth human and physical landscapes, and moves Villehardouin the character and others through them, in a manner that is reminiscent of romances and *lais*.[92] The quick and easy travelling of long distances by means of the phrase 'They rode on day after day' recalls the seemingly effortless traversing of the landscape by knights in such tales.[93] Additionally, in the latter half of the text, in which much of the action involves the Latins moving back and forth across Thrace and other areas of insecure Latin control, there are several evocations of pleasing romance-like landscapes that seem to jar with the narrative's relentless attention to military action and its mood of constant vulnerability in a threatening and scarcely subdued foreign land.[94] In conformity to this romance inflection, even

[90] See e.g. the collective delight experienced by both the liberators and the liberated when a rescue party led by Villehardouin comes to the aid of Renier of Trit, who has been doggedly holding out in a remote and vulnerable fortress: *Conquête*, §438, p. 252, trans. p. 118: 'si firent grant joie li uns a l'autre'.

[91] Villehardouin's indebtedness to the *chanson de geste* form is most fully explored in Beer, *Villehardouin*, esp. pp. 31–56.

[92] Several romance motifs are, for example, evident in one of the text's rare capsule narratives which deals with the adventures of Villehardouin's nephew, also named Geoffrey of Villehardouin, in the Peloponnese during the Frankish land-grab. It is noteworthy that this is the nearest thing to Villehardouin family memory that the text offers. The younger Geoffrey, a 'very worthy, very valiant, and an able knight', is blown onto a foreign shore, enters the service of a conveniently to-hand, obliging and beneficent local lord, and passes up the offer of service to Boniface of Montferrat in order to pursue his adventurous ambitions in the Peloponnese, where he and his superior William of Champlitte succeed against great numerical odds and secure the submission of many local people. See *Conquête*, §§325–30, pp. 134–40, trans. pp. 87–9. For this sequence, see Jacquin, *Le style historique*, pp. 517–19.

[93] See *Conquête*, §32, p. 32, trans. p. 11: 'et chevauchierent par lor jornees'; §35, p. 36, trans. p. 12: 'chevaucha…par ses jornees'. Note that the subject of the verb in the first example is the group of six envoys returning from Venice, Villehardouin among them, while the subject in the second is Villehardouin alone returning from this embassy to Champagne. See also the similar constructions, all of which relate to the movement of groups that include Villehardouin, in §284, p. 92, trans. p. 76; §297, p. 104, trans p. 80; §298, p. 106, trans. p. 80; §457, p. 272, trans. p. 123.

[94] E.g. *Conquête*, §432, p. 246, trans. p. 116: Henry on campaign in 1206 reaches Adrianople and sets up camp (close, it should be noted, to the site of the bloody Frankish defeat one year earlier) 'in the most beautiful meadows in the world, along

autopsy amidst the splendours of the Byzantine court reduces to the sort of cliché appropriate to that genre: thus, when Villehardouin and the other envoys arrive on the second, which is to say the more fraught, embassy into Constantinople, we are blandly informed that the wife of Emperor Isaac was 'a beautiful and good woman' and that 'this court certainly appeared to be that of a powerful prince'.[95] In a similar manner, when Villehardouin is part of an embassy sent to meet Emperor Henry's future bride, Boniface of Montferrat's daughter, and escort her to Constantinople, we simply learn that when they encountered her she was 'both very virtuous and very beautiful'.[96]

Undeveloped or formulaic evocations of scenic detail, lacking apparent autoptic precision and texture, are found elsewhere in the text. When, for example, we are told that it was very pleasant on the day after the crusade fleet arrived at Zara in November 1202 – 'the weather was particularly fine and clear' – we might initially suspect that this is a mnemonic hook on which hangs the author's recollections of that particular event, time and place, until we discover that the only subsequent references to fair weather conditions over the course of the narrative also relate to signpost moments in the itinerary of the fleet, and that we are therefore dealing with convention, a 'fill' cued by idea association.[97] Similarly,

the riverbank there' ('sor les plus bels prez del munde sor la riviere'); §433, p. 246, trans. p. 117: after pursuing Ioannitsa for five days, the Franks encamp 'in a pleasant spot by a castle called Fraïm' ('sor un bel leu, a un chastel que on appelle le Fraïm'); §435, p. 248, trans. p. 117: a few days later the Franks set up camp 'in a most beautiful valley' ('en une mult bele valee'); §486, p. 300, trans. p. 131: in 1207, on campaign in Asia Minor, Henry encamps outside Nicomedia 'in a most attractive riverside meadow at the foot of the mountain' ('en une mult bele praerie, sor un flum, par devers la montaigne'); §496, p. 310, trans. p. 134: Henry's meeting with Boniface of Montferrat later that year near İpsala is held 'in a most beautiful meadow' ('en une mult bele praerie').

95 *Conquête*, §212, pp. 10–12, trans. p. 57: 'bele dame et bone', 'mult sembla bien cort a riche prince'. We are similarly told during the earlier embassy to the court that the empress was beautiful ('mult bele dame') and that the ladies of the court were richly attired ('si richement acesmees que eles ne pooient plus'): §185, p. 188, trans. p. 49.

96 *Conquête*, §458, p. 272, trans. p. 123: 'mult ere et bone et bele'. Cf. the statement that the Frankish barons were saddened by the death of Emperor Baldwin's wife Marie, while *en route* to Constantinople, because they 'very much wanted her to be their lady ('il la desiroient mult avoir a dame'): §318, p. 126, trans. p. 85. See also the report that when, after the fall of Constantinople, Boniface of Montferrat and his men took possession of the Great Palace (the Bucoleon), they discovered there 'many of the most noble women in the world' ('li plus des haltes dames del munde'): §249, p. 50, trans. p. 66.

97 *Conquête*, §78, p. 78, trans. p. 22: 'fist mult bel jor et mult cler'. Cf. §119, p. 122, trans. p. 32 concerning the fleet's departure from Corfu: 'li jors fu bels et clers, et li venz dolz et soés'; §156, p. 154, trans. p. 40 concerning the fleet sailing across the Bosphorus to Constantinople: 'li matins fu biels, aprés le solei un poi levant'. For this motif, see Jacquin, *Le style historique*, pp. 277–9.

mentions of the expressive, gestural content of scenes in which Villehardouin the character is said to be present or may be assumed to be so, in particular the plaintive dropping to one's knees and the copious shedding of tears, might appear to capture episodic memories of important and emotionally charged interactions, but again they slide towards the highly conventional, articulations, that is, of a routine and expected way of acting.[98] And while there are some references scattered across the text that might possibly be grounded in authorial eyewitness recall of distinctive details – for example, that the knight Eustace of Le Marchais wore only a gambeson (padded jacket), an iron cap and a shield in one particular skirmish with Byzantine forces; that a knight hanged for theft was strung up with his shield still hanging around his neck; that Hugh of St-Pol's gout affected his knees and feet; and that Emperor Henry was sitting down to a meal, with Villehardouin and others in attendance, when a messenger arrived with urgent news[99] – the narrative as a whole is generally sparing in its use of such reality effects. Moreover, one again finds a drift towards convention and repetition in the selection of such details. This is especially evident in the recurrent mentions of where on their bodies high-status individuals were injured, sometimes fatally. These references would seem to be the results of routine conversational queries, after the fact, about matters of particular interest to men of Villehardouin's class – the answers, in effect, to 'So, who got it, and where?'[100]

It is noteworthy, and not altogether surprising, that the most detailed scholarly investigation to date of the role of sight in the *Conquête*, by Paul Archambault, is also one of the most damning assessments of the text as a historiographical exercise.[101] According to Archambault, Villehardouin structured his acts of visual perception selectively and narrowly. His aim was to exclude most of the pertinent detail from his field of vision in the interests of avoiding awkward questions about the diversion of the crusade, and in order to simplify the world into neat binaries, especially the contrast between those who valued the unity of the crusade army and duly stuck it out through thick and thin, and those crusaders who either avoided the Venice rendezvous or subsequently left the army in order to make their own way east. In this view, moreover, Villehardouin lacked any aesthetic sense and regarded visual description as wasted effort: indifferent to

[98] See e.g. *Conquête*, §28, p. 28, trans. p. 10; §31, p. 32, trans. p. 11; §43, p. 44, trans. p. 14; §67, p. 68, trans. p. 20; §§116–17, pp. 118–20, trans. p. 32.

[99] *Conquête*, §168, p. 170, trans. p. 44; §255, p. 60, trans. p. 68; §314, p. 122, trans. pp. 84–5; §§465–6, p. 280, trans. p. 126. See also §68, p. 68, trans. p. 20: during the crowd scene in St Mark's a cross is sewn onto a large cap for the doge to ensure maximum visibility.

[100] See e.g. *Conquête*, §90, p. 90, trans. p. 25; §359, p. 168, trans. p. 96; §392, p. 202, trans. p. 105; §396, p. 206, trans. p. 106; §483, p. 298, trans. p. 130; §499, p. 312, trans. p. 135.

[101] Archambault, *Seven French Chroniclers*, pp. 25–39.

nuance and the revealing detail, he was 'attentive to reality not in order to see it, but to act upon it', and his visual memory was poor. Whereas a writer such as Froissart would have bombarded the reader with sensitively observed visual details had he found himself in the same circumstances, even the splendid opportunities for a lingering, awestruck gaze presented by Venice and Constantinople were wasted on Villehardouin.[102] Archambault's interpretation relies on a highly questionable psychologizing approach: his assumption, that is, that the *Conquête* grants us access, via its lexical idiosyncrasies, tone and omissions, to the historical Villehardouin's personality, his moral compass, the limitations of his memory, his fantasies and his general psychological state.[103] But one can also applaud the basic intuition that informs Archambault's approach: that what are at stake in the text's mobilization of the visual are questions of thematic and substantive emphasis, structural choices, the manner in which experience is rendered, and narratorial (Archambault would say 'authorial') self-construction. There would also seem to be some truth to the argument that the *Conquête*'s diegeses are, on the whole, less richly realized than those constructed by many comparable narrative histories; these include Robert of Clari's account of the Fourth Crusade, as we shall see. To what extent, then, does Archambault's critique of the *Conquête*'s impoverished engagement with the visual isolate a significant feature of the narrative?

There is indeed a good deal of evidence for the very limited use of the visual in fashioning the storyworld and communicating it to the reader or listener. We have already encountered a passage, concerning the Venetians' assault on the walls of Constantinople on 17 July 1203, in which the narrator's construction of the visual aspects of a scene is reinforced both by the gaze of some of the participants and an apostrophe to the narratee to picture the remarkable ('merveillox') attack. But this layering of the visual quality of the diegesis by means of the bundling of gazes is in fact unusual, in stark contrast to its recurrent use in Ambroise's *Estoire de la Guerre Sainte*.[104] There are, moreover, few invitations to visualize a scene by means of *veïssiez* and *peüssiez voir* ('you could have seen'), again unlike the *Estoire*: most invite the picturing of collective and purposeful action, for example when the crusaders disembark at Zara and unload their horses and tents; the gathering of a throng of knights and sergeants leading fine warhorses when news spreads that the future Alexios IV has joined the crusade army on Corfu; when the leaders conduct an open-air meeting on horseback, surrounded

[102] Archambault, *Seven French Chroniclers*, esp. pp. 28–31, 33–4, 35–7, 39.

[103] See e.g. Archambault's assertion that Villehardouin's participation in the embassy to Venice gave him, as a mere lord, an opportunity to play-act the power and status of a count: 'One imagines him during that scenic if arduous trip [his return journey]... wrapped entirely in thoughts of power and prestige': *Seven French Chroniclers*, p. 29. Cf. p. 27: 'Villehardouin was intelligent enough to be a scoundrel.'

[104] *Conquête*, §174, p. 176, trans. p. 46.

by many knights mounted on fine horses; and ship-borne mangonels bombarding the walls of Constantinople along with the firing of crossbows and bows.[105] There are only a few other such instances, and the aristocratic, chivalric focus of several of the limited number of examples that we do have suggests where the narrator is most concerned to draw the reader's or listener's selective attention.[106] Only two such apostrophes invite a more lingering, imaginative gaze on objects, though one of these concerns the important matter of the booty seized as Constantinople is taken.[107]

In a similar manner, there are many examples of hyperbole in the text, to the extent that it functions as one of the principal means by which the narrator introduces evaluative remarks, but only a small minority of these instances involve claims concerning the storyworld's visual aspects.[108] In other words, the narrator does not routinely exploit this device as a way of enriching the diegesis through exaggeration or caricature.[109] Likewise, the narrator generally deploys a very narrow and formulaic range of terms to evoke the appearance and experience

[105] *Conquête*, §78, p. 78, trans. pp. 22–3; §112, p. 114, trans. p. 31; §147, p. 148, trans. p. 39; §172, p. 174, trans. p. 46.

[106] See e.g. *Conquête*, §371, p. 180, trans. p. 99: the shedding of tears and the wringing of hands when a group of knights learn of the loss of Emperor Baldwin and Louis of Blois at Adrianople; §466, p. 282, trans. p. 126: Constantinople swarming with Venetians, Pisans and other mariners as preparations are made to cross to Asia Minor on a rescue mission, in which they are joined by fully-armed knights.

[107] *Conquête*, §61, p. 64, trans. p. 19: the many beautiful gold and silver dishes that are carried to the doge as the crusade leaders try to pay back as much of their debt as possible; §244, p. 46, trans. p. 65: Greeks struck down during the storming of Constantinople and horses, palfreys, mules and other things taken as booty.

[108] See e.g. *Conquête*, §29, p. 28, trans. p. 10: 'no man had ever seen one [the uproarious crowd reaction in St Mark's when the doge agrees to the envoys' request] greater' ('que onques plus grant ne vit nus hom'); §56, p. 58, trans. p. 18: 'no one has ever seen an army more impressive or with so many combatants' ('Onques de tant de gent nus hom plus bele ne vit'); *ibid.*: 'The fleet they had prepared was so well equipped and handsome that no Christian man has ever seen another more handsome or better equipped' ('Et li navies que il orent appareillé fu si riches et si bels que onques nus hon crestïens plus bel ne plus riche ne vit'); §217, p. 16, trans. p. 58: as the Byzantine fire ships burn 'it seemed as if the whole world was on fire' ('il sembloit que tote la terre arsist'); §263, p. 70, trans. p. 71: the Bucoleon palace, as the site of Baldwin's coronation feast, was 'as splendid as any ever seen' ('que onques plus riches ne fu veüz'): translation slightly amended.

[109] For the text's wider use of hyperbole, see e.g. *Conquête*, §37, p. 38, trans. p. 12: grief 'greater than that ever shown for any other man'; §65, p. 66, trans. p. 20: 'you are joined with the finest men in the world in the most noble endeavour anyone has ever undertaken'; §130, pp. 130–2, trans. p. 35: 'the most pressing business and the most perilous enterprise any men have ever undertaken'; §419, p. 232, trans. p. 113: 'no man has ever heard of destruction on this scale'. Such examples could be multiplied. For hyperbole in the *Conquête*, see also Beer, *Villehardouin*, pp. 110–14.

of place and space. For example, the palace at Chalcedon is blandly described by means of routine hyperbole: it is 'one of the most beautiful and charming palaces any eyes might ever have seen'.[110] Elsewhere the narrator's adjectives of choice to capture the quality of a place are for the most part simply *bel*, *bon* and *riche*;[111] while evocations of walled cities and castles merely ring a few changes on the themes of strength, size and wealth.[112] A limited lexical range does not necessarily preclude sensitive handling of the distinctive qualities of different places, and even some ability to capture the moment-by-moment specificity of lived experience and impression, but in the *Conquête*'s case the narrator prefers to settle for predictable human landscapes that betray the guiding influence of formula, cliché and prettified romance diegesis, and for this reason throw up few surprises.

That said, there are some passages in which the narrator seems to be alive to visual impact and situates this within the storyworld by means of the staging of attentive and collective gazes. It is noteworthy that it is in such passages that a doubling up of the narrator's own judgement with the reactions implied by character focalization in the immediate narrative moment is most in evidence. For example, when the crusaders first see the strength of Zara's fortifications, we are informed that they are quite astonished ('il se merveillerent'); when the Franks are confronted outside the walls of Constantinople by troops led by Alexios III, 'it appeared as if the entire plain was covered with enemy battalions'; and when the crusaders launch what will be their successful assault on the city, on 12 April 1204, the inhabitants, emboldened by their beating back of the attack that had been attempted three days earlier, mass on the defences in such a way that 'all one could see along the walls and towers was people'.[113] The narrator never

[110] *Conquête*, §134, pp. 134–6, trans. p. 36: 'uns des plus biax et des plus delitables que onques oel peüssent esgarder'. Cf. the remark concerning Zara that 'you would have sought a finer, stronger, more impressive city in vain' ('por noïent demandesiez plus bele ne plus fort ne plus riche'): §77, p. 78, trans. p. 22.

[111] E.g. *Conquête*, §123, p. 124, trans. p. 33; §125, p. 126, trans. p. 34; §135, p. 136, trans. p. 36; §141, p. 142, trans. p. 37; §280, p. 88, trans. p. 76; §428, p. 240, trans. p. 115. For the range of adjectives used in the *Conquête*, see the helpful list in Beer, *Villehardouin*, pp. 122–3, and for his limited descriptive vocabulary *ibid.*, pp. 100–4.

[112] E.g. *Conquête*, §279, p. 86, trans. p. 75: the castle of Demotika is 'mult bel et mult fort et mult riche'; §280, p. 88, trans. 75: the castle of Christopolis is 'uns des plus forz del munde'; §320, p. 128, trans. p. 86: Appolonia has 'une des plus forz chastiaus'; §330, p. 140, trans. p. 89: the castle of Kalamata is 'mult...forz et bials'; §350, p. 160, trans. p. 94: Adrianople is 'mult fort et mult riche et mult plaine de gent'; §415, p. 228, trans. p. 111: Rodosto is 'mult...riche et forz et granz'; §428, p. 240, trans. p. 115: Bizöe is 'mult...bone et forz'.

[113] *Conquête*, §77, p. 78, trans. p. 22; §179, p.180, trans. p. 47: 'Il sembloit que tote la campaigne fust coverte de batailles'; §241, p. 42, trans. p. 64: 'sor les murs et sors les tors ne paroient se genz non'.

positions himself in such a way that he has his own distinctive line of sight on the action. This is, significantly, emphasized in the first of the passages in which Villehardouin is announced as author of the work: the bearing of witness as to the beauty of the sight as the fleet sails from Corfu is in the first instance expressed as an individual act ('bien testimoigne Joffrois li mareschaus de Champaigne'), but the underlying experience is then swiftly generalized when we are told that the sails stretched out as far as the eye could see, and that this vista prompted a collective feeling of joy ('li cuer des hommes s'en esjoïssoient').[114]

There are also some indications, albeit relatively few, that the narrator is willing to register the impact that the visual environment could make on his actors. Almost all the instances of focalization in the text involve the apprehension of short-term changes that motivate some form of immediate, often urgent, response: that is to say, the act of seeing or otherwise apprehending itself is not stressed relative to the reaction that it elicits.[115] It is unsurprising, therefore, that several of these examples of short-term focalization involve the rapid back-and-forth of combat, as commanders, soldiers and those caught up in the fighting swiftly react to changes in their circumstances.[116] There are, however, a handful of more sustained gazes in which the act of seeing is itself a significant part of the action chain. For example, when the electors emerge to announce the result of the imperial election held after the fall of Constantinople, the narrator emphasizes the importance of the occasion and the tension it generated by promising the narratee that 'you may be assured that they were being watched by a throng of men who wanted to discern the result of the election'.[117] Perhaps the most striking example of the collective gaze participating in, and inviting an evaluation of, the narrated action concerns the crusade leaders' reactions, from their camp across the Golden Horn, to the sight of the large and highly destructive fire that broke out in Constantinople in August 1203. Villehardouin the historical actor was

[114] *Conquête*, §120, p. 122, trans. pp. 32–3.

[115] For the fairly few instances of focalization involving considered appraisals of longer-term, strategic factors, see e.g. *Conquête*, §209, p. 8, trans. p. 56: the barons grow to appreciate Alexios IV's true intentions; §296, p. 104, trans. p. 79: Emperor Baldwin comes to understand that a dispute with Boniface of Montferrat is ill advised; §333, pp. 142–4, trans. p. 90: on perceiving that the Franks' forces are dispersed, the Greeks enter into treacherous dealings with Ioannitsa; §399, pp. 208–10, trans. p. 107: Ioannitsa realizes that further gains are not possible in his current campaign; §422, pp. 234–6, trans. pp. 113–14: the Greeks realize that Ioannitsa is not honouring the agreements made with them, and that he therefore poses a grave danger to Adrianople and Demotika.

[116] E.g. *Conquête*, §137, p. 138, trans. p. 36; §139, p. 140, trans. p. 37; §174, p. 176, trans. p. 46; §180, p. 182, trans. p. 48; §233, pp. 32–4, trans. p. 62; §331, pp. 140–2, trans. p. 89; §406, p. 218, trans. p. 109.

[117] *Conquête*, §260, p. 66, trans. p. 70: 'Or poez savoir qu'il furent de maint home esgardé, et por savoir quels li eliscions seroit'.

almost certainly among the shocked spectators; the passage is therefore likely to be informed by autobiographical episodic memory, but even so the individual experience is subsumed within an emphasis upon perceptions that are shared in a like manner by all the high-status observers:

> When they saw this the barons of the army, who were encamped on the other side of the port, were deeply saddened [*furent mult dolent*] and felt great pity [*mult en orent grant pitié*] as they watched those noble churches and fine palaces crumble and fall, and the broad streets of merchants' shops engulfed by flames. And there was nothing more they could do.[118]

Some appreciation of the crusaders' curiosity about their surroundings and the exercise of their gaze is evident in the narrator's remark that, once Isaac II's restoration and Alexios IV's entry into Constantinople in July 1203 meant that the Latins had fairly free access to the city, many of them went on sightseeing trips to view its palaces, churches and great riches.[119] An understanding of the force of the collective gaze further emerges from the text's most developed visual set-piece, the moment when Constantinople comes into view for the first time as the crusade fleet sails east along the northern coast of the Sea of Marmora. Again, the assurance volunteered to the narratee flags up the significance of the occasion for those involved, while the fact that the participants' act of perception elicits a physical response, a type of detail not found anywhere else in the text, highlights the experiential dimension in a way that the bland adjectives on their own could not:

> Now you may be assured that those who had never seen it before gazed at Constantinople for a long time, barely believing that there was such a great city in all the world. They saw its high walls and mighty towers, with which the city was completely encircled, as well as the fine palaces and tall churches, of which there were so many that none could believe it if he did not see it with his own eyes, the length and breadth of the city, which is the sovereign of all others. And know that there was no one there so bold that his flesh did not shudder, which should come as no surprise, for never was such a great project undertaken by so many [or perhaps 'so few'] people since the creation of the world.[120]

[118] *Conquête*, §203, p. 208, trans. p. 55: translation slightly revised. For this highly destructive fire, see T. F. Madden, 'The Fires of the Fourth Crusade in Constantinople, 1203–1204: A Damage Assessment', *Byzantinische Zeitschrift*, 84/5 (1992), 74–84, 87, 91–3; Queller and Madden, *Fourth Crusade*, pp. 145–7.

[119] *Conquête*, §192, p. 194, trans. p. 51.

[120] *Conquête*, §128, p. 130, trans. p. 34: translation revised. For the unclear reading concerning the crusaders' numbers, see *Conquête*, i, p. 131 n. 3.

The slight hint of narratorial distancing from the category of 'those who had never seen it before' ('qui ne l'avaient jamais vue') suggests that a subtle distinction is being attempted between the visual impact that Constantinople makes on first-time viewers and the fuller understanding of it, its people, its political culture and the values it represents that comes with greater familiarity. (It is indeed possible that Villehardouin the historical actor had already had some experience of the city during his travels when, as seems probable, he took part in the Third Crusade.)[121]

As we shall see, Robert of Clari's narrative of the Fourth Crusade also has an account of the impression made by the sight of Constantinople, part of a full and layered exploration of the visual quality of the text's storyworld.[122] In contrast, the fleet's first glimpse of Constantinople in the *Conquête* sets up an expectation of attention to the visual aspects of the diegesis that the remainder of the text largely frustrates. For just this one moment, the narrator, in company with the crusaders *en masse*, chooses to linger on the act of seeing as an activity in itself, thereby signalling to the reader or listener that more such passages could have been included had the narrator so chosen. The implication is that the text's relative inattention to the visual aspects of its *mise-en-scène* is deliberate, in that it serves the greater interest of relentlessly driving the action, *qua* action, ever forward.[123] Perhaps there is, therefore, some merit in Archambault's argument that the *Conquête* treats the visible world principally as so many sites of potential achievement and acquisition. Some support for this comes from the passage just quoted, in that a hint of anachronism may be present in the narrator's observation that the onlookers shuddered when their thoughts turned from the physical scale of Constantinople to the size of their undertaking. This implies that they were already imagining what it would take to besiege and storm the city; in other words, they were anticipating the events of July 1203 and more particularly April 1204, whereas in later June 1203, as the fleet approached the city, the crusade's leaders were almost certainly still thinking along the same lines as when they had sold the Constantinople 'diversion' to the army some weeks earlier, namely, that a show of force would suffice to trigger one of the palace coups that they knew were a regular feature of Byzantine political life, whereupon the rights of the imperial claimant Alexios would be duly and fairly painlessly vindicated. The turning point was in fact to take place a few days later, when the prince Alexios, flanked by the doge and Boniface of Montferrat, was paraded for the benefit of the city's populace on a galley manoeuvred close to the sea walls, but

[121] For the question of Villehardouin's participation in the Third Crusade, see Longnon, *Recherches sur la vie*, pp. 59–63.

[122] See below, pp. 329–30, 331–2.

[123] Cf. Jacquin, *Le style historique*, pp. 423–32. For Villehardouin's treatment of events, see *ibid.*, pp. 505–11.

to no avail.[124] The *Conquête* relates this episode in a studied, low-key manner, stoically maintaining that the people of Constantinople professed not to recognize Alexios because of their fear of his uncle Alexios III's regime.[125] In reality, this was something of a debacle that forced the crusade leadership to recognize that they had misjudged the political temper of the city and had badly overestimated the leverage that their having the prince Alexios in tow afforded them. Such a nuance, turning on fine chronological discriminations, abrupt shifts of perspective and major revisions of plans, is, however, lost in the *Conquête*'s treatment: in June 1203 the crusaders see Constantinople, and form their judgements of it, in much the same terms as they would in April 1204.

There are a few countervailing indications, however, that the narrator of the *Conquête* is capable of mobilizing the visual in subtle and meaningful ways, even if this is seldom a priority for him. In the latter part of the text, that devoted to the early years of the Latin empire, there are several sequences in which various Franks fail to recognize one another. In every instance this misrecognition occurs in moments of crisis: a force of knights and sergeants moving up from Constantinople mistakes those fleeing after the battle of Adrianople for Greeks; in the mood of panic after the defeat at Adrianople, Henry of Hainaut mistakenly believes, when he first spots a group of knights and sergeants led by Villehardouin's nephew Anseau of Courcelles, that it is a Greek force, while Anseau's company makes the same mistake *vice versa*; and when Renier of Trit, holed up in an isolated and exposed Frankish position in Stenimaka, catches sight of a relief column, which is under Villehardouin's command, he is unsure who it is, and his first reaction is one of apprehension as he convinces himself that it is a force of Greeks intent on besieging the castle.[126] This narrative device seems to be more than just a filler. Nor is it simply a means to introduce suspense, a quality that the narrator seldom builds into action sequences. Instead, it uses mistaken visual perception as a metaphor for the uncertainty and panic felt by the beleaguered Latins in a hostile environment, a human landscape where one has to work especially hard to differentiate between friend and foe.

A similar intuition that attention to the visual presents interesting opportunities for the literal and figurative to work off one another is evident in the narrator's account of the form of execution that the Franks devised for the former emperor Alexios V Mourtzouphlos after he had been captured towards the end of 1204: he was to be taken to the top of a column and forced to jump off it 'in

[124] Queller and Madden, *Fourth Crusade*, pp. 113–14; Phillips, *Fourth Crusade*, pp. 163–5.

[125] *Conquête*, §§145–6, pp. 146–8, trans. pp. 38–9. For Clari's version of the same episode, see RC, c. 41, p. 50.

[126] *Conquête*, §370, p. 178, trans. p. 99; §383, p. 192, trans. p. 103; §437, p. 250, trans. p. 118.

front of all the people, since it was right that everyone should see high justice ['halte justise'] being done'. The execution does not disappoint as a spectacle; we are told that the people of the city 'flocked to see such a remarkable sight ['merveille']', while Mourtzouphlos's body plays its full part by shattering on impact.[127] On the whole, however, the potential for sight to become a vehicle for metaphorical evocations of the Latins' understandings of their new world, their insecurities and their attempts to appropriate and control their environment, is not realized. As is often the case, the narrator offers tantalizing glimpses of greater conceptual depth, imagination and sophistication than he is generally prepared to deliver.[128]

Villehardouin the character is, as we have seen, expressly present in some of the action, and implicitly so in much of the remainder. To that, in itself limited, extent Villehardouin the historical actor may be said to have been an 'eyewitness' to at least some aspects of much of the action that is narrated in the text. In places, the simple thickness of the description of certain incidents and sequences seems, at least on the surface, to be a function of authorial autopsy. But it is important to maintain the distinction between where we situate the historical Villehardouin in real space and time, and the narrator's positioning vis-à-vis the storyworld as it is called forth in the narrative. As stated above, the narrator does not set himself up as a roving investigative eye, nor does he routinely appeal to individual experience and individual memory. The rare moments of lingering gaze encountered in the evocation of the sight of Constantinople – albeit this is a passage narrowly constrained by a very limited repertoire of descriptive and evaluative terms – and in the barons' looking across at the burning city hint at a largely unrealized potential for building the visual into explorations of the crusaders' experiences. Likewise, the few occasions in which the physical act of seeing shades into the figurative gesture towards a capacity for thinking with metaphor that is in the end little exploited. As always seems to be the case with Villehardouin, it is important to differentiate clearly between what we would like the *Conquête* to deliver as an 'eyewitness' source and what it actually says.[129]

[127] *Conquête*, §307, pp. 114–16, trans. p. 83. Other accounts confirm the currency of the pun on the idea of 'high justice', which suggests that it was part of the official rhetoric that surrounded the event, an execution which was devised and staged with both its visibility and its symbolic resonances in mind: RC, c. 109, p. 126; Gunther of Pairis, *Hystoria Constantinopolitana*, c. 20, p. 165, trans. Andrea, *Capture of Constantinople*, pp. 115–16. The column was that of Theodosius the Great situated in the Tauros, one of the city's main fora.

[128] For the limited use of simile and metaphor in the *Conquête*, see Beer, *Villehardouin*, pp. 107–8.

[129] It is curious, for example, that Villehardouin omits any mention of his having met Boniface of Montferrat on his return journey from the embassy to Venice, although it is highly probable that he did so. He does, however, mention running into the crusader

There are, to be sure, gaps and kinks in the plot: Villehardouin the author was, after all, crafting a long and detailed narrative, featuring a large number of characters and situations, in a pioneering generic idiom. But for the most part the *Conquête*'s story logic holds up extremely well within the explanatory parameters, the assumptions about cause and effect and about human motivation, that it brings to bear on its world. The plot of the *Conquête* is driven by a set of irreducible aristocratic values that do not need to be justified for the audience, simply played out in the action. These include fear of shame and its corollary sensitivity to reputation, the virtue of loyalty to one's group and to one's superiors, the sacrosanct quality of all formal agreements ranging from treaties and sworn contracts to crusade vows and the obligations of a vassal to his lord, and a rather imprecise but nonetheless recurrent and important value within the narrator's taxonomy of aristocratic ethics, which is the need to achieve things. Other aristocratic values emerge as they are cued by the needs of the story at a given point. Taken together, they suffice to propel the plot of the *Conquête*, both its whole story arc and its many sub-sequences large and small. These values frequently lend themselves to illustration – in a sense this is what the *Conquête* is *for* – and to that extent there is always the potential for visual reinforcement. But in practice this proves an optional extra that the narrator selects quite rarely. The visual is not central to the workings of the narrator's ethical system, and this, in conjunction with a breakneck narrative rhythm of action heaped upon action, helps to explain the relatively small contribution made by eyewitnessing and character focalization to the creation and authentication of the *Conquête*'s storyworld. Indeed, on a strict reading of the narrative, one that does not rush to conflate the various Villehardouins that we have identified, the *Conquête* is scarcely to be categorized as an 'eyewitness' text at all.

Robert of Clari

Robert of Clari's *La Conquête de Constantinople* is the account of the Fourth Crusade that most obviously invites comparison with Villehardouin's text. Like Villehardouin's narrative, the *Conquête* represents a pioneering exercise in the use of French vernacular prose as the medium for the writing of closely contemporary history.[130] Clari, however, wrote, or dictated, his work in his native Picard dialect

Walter of Brienne. See *Conquête*, §§32–5, pp. 32–6, trans. pp. 11–12; Queller and Madden, *Fourth Crusade*, pp. 21–2.

[130] For a thoughtful and stimulating study of Clari's work, which seeks to synthesize its historical and literary dimensions, see. S. Kinoshita, *Medieval Boundaries: Rethinking Difference in Old French Literature* (Philadelphia, 2006), pp. 139–75. Kinoshita's analysis is, however, undermined by her heavy reliance on the oddly old-fashioned,

rather than Francien, which was gaining prominence as the prestige literary form of French. This has implications for our understanding of the nature and range of Clari's intended audience; it is perhaps unsurprising that the text survives in only one known manuscript, dating from about 1300, which was probably produced at the abbey of Corbie. The author's toponym, Clari, is conventionally rendered in the form in which it appears in the text; it has been identified as Cléry-les-Pernois, near Amiens.[131] Robert the author is almost certainly the 'Robillard of Clari' who is recorded in an inscription on a reliquary from Corbie as having presented the abbey with various relics that had formerly been in the chapel of the imperial palace in Constantinople. This is said to have taken place 'when Baldwin, count of Flanders, was emperor', which would suggest that Clari probably returned to Picardy in 1205 and certainly no later than 1206. It has been suggested that the *Conquête* was conceived as a kind of companion piece or complement to the gift of the relics to Corbie.[132] But, if so, it is not directly akin to the several *translationes* that were written about the movement of Byzantine relics to the west in and after 1204, in that no specific mention of the Corbie relics is made in the narrative, nor are the circumstances of Robert's acquisition of them recounted. The *Conquête* in its surviving form could not have been completed before 1216 (the year of the death of Emperor Henry of Constantinople, mentioned in the penultimate chapter), so if a copy was indeed presented to the monks of Corbie, which seems perfectly plausible, this would most probably have been by way of reinforcing the connection that had been forged by the gift of the relics a decade or so earlier.

Exactly when the *Conquête* was written is unclear, but it is likely that the bulk of the text, that dealing with events up to 1205, was produced within a few years of this last date, after which a miscellany of relatively brief chapters concerning events in the Latin empire and the reign of Emperor Henry (1206–16) was added in one or more tranches as the author came by the information.[133] The narrator

essentializing and monolithic term 'feudal' in relation to all aspects of Latin aristocratic experience, whence 'feudal politics', 'feudal crises', 'feudal mentality', 'feudal society', 'feudal ideals', 'feudal categories', 'feudal outrage', 'feudal loyalties' and so on. This results in an exaggeration of western European aristocratic culture's innumeracy, naivety, brittleness and lack of sophistication vis-à-vis the challenges of conceptual adaptation that the Fourth Crusade presented. Likewise, to speak (p. 163) of 'the political, social, and epistemological chaos unleashed by the Fourth Crusade' is a clear overstatement.

[131] For what is known of the historical Robert, see *La conquista*, trans. Nada Petrone, pp. 3–6, citing G. Boudon, 'Robert de Clari en Aminois, chevalier, auteur d'une chronique de la IVe croisade (1202–1216)', *Bulletin de la Société des antiquaires de Picardie*, 19 (1895–7), 700–34. Also *Conquest*, trans. McNeal, pp. 4–6.

[132] Dembowski, *La chronique*, p. 74; *La conquista*, trans. Nada Petrone, pp. 17–18, 63–4.

[133] The miscellany of briefer remarks occupies RC, cc. 113–19, pp. 130–2. It has been suggested that the main body of the text was written in two discrete stages:

announces his basic aim at the very start of the text: 'This is the beginning of the story of those who conquered Constantinople; we will tell you later who they were and the reason why they went there.'[134] Details about the author, however, as well as a fuller statement of the text's purpose, are reserved for an *explicit* that takes up the final chapter. Here we are informed that we have been told the truth of 'how Constantinople was conquered and how Baldwin the count of Flanders was emperor and succeeded by his brother, the lord Henry'.[135] In fact, the text substantially exceeds this self-description, principally by means of analepses, two of which are substantial, which supply some of the background to the crusade, as well as a quite detailed description of various buildings and sites in Constantinople, the fullest such account in any surviving western crusade narrative.[136]

At first blush, the *Conquête* seems to promise a narration that will closely resemble the structure and content of Villehardouin's version of events: it has a similar opening on the origins of the crusade, one that also highlights the impact of Fulk of Neuilly's preaching, and it too supplies the names of prominent crusaders listed by French region.[137] Thereafter, however, the two texts go their separate ways. While some historians express a clear preference for Villehardouin's narrative as a source, given that the author was in an excellent position to come by accurate information, as against the more marginal Robert, seemingly reliant on gossip, ill-informed impression and speculation, there is in fact a good case for arguing that Robert's text is the more artfully crafted and considered piece of writing. It provides an explanation of events that relies less than does Villehardouin's telling on the relentless machinery of sequential action and moment-by-moment cause and effect. And it nudges a little further into explorations of cultural collisions, conflicts between competing value systems and other structural factors.[138] As we shall see, as part of this project actors' gazes

Dembowski, *La chronique*, p. 68 n. 14; Dufournet, *Les écrivains*, ii, pp. 342–3. This has not received general scholarly support, however, and for our purposes there is no evidence of it in the text's construction of the narratorial voice.

[134] RC, c. 1, p. 2: translation revised.

[135] RC, c. 120, p. 132: translation revised.

[136] For a detailed discussion of the two substantial analepses and other digressions in the narrative, see Jacquin, *Le style historique*, pp. 300–35. For the description of Constantinople, see below, pp. 329–30, 331–2.

[137] RC, c. 1, pp. 2–4.

[138] There are numerous references in the text to suggest that the narrator is alive to the larger forces influencing the course of the crusade and to the various difficult choices that confronted the leaders. See e.g. RC, c. 13, p. 16: the doge has equipped fifty galleys at his own expense; c. 16, pp. 18–20: the crusaders at Zara are fully aware that the moneys already spent as well as future expenses and the need for provisions preclude their reaching Egypt or Syria directly; c. 32, p. 38: the pretender Alexios is shown to be pliable in his eagerness to accommodate the leaders' wishes and so makes

within the storyworld play an important role in directing themselves to scenes in which ideas and values are concretized by virtue of their being played out in visible forms.

As noted above, comparisons between Villehardouin's and Clari's versions of the Fourth Crusade and its aftermath have tended to accentuate their differences as historical records thanks to an emphasis upon the contrasts between the two authors' respective backgrounds and personal circumstances. Whereas Villehardouin, in this view, offers a top-down vision of events driven by a self-justifying, self-exculpatory agenda, Clari comes at his material from the perspective of an ordinary knight with no such baggage. This, it is supposed, makes him a representative, indeed the spokesman, of a group that in many respects felt itself socially and culturally attuned to the aristocratic cadre that ran the crusade and dominated the carving up of the Latin empire in and after 1204, but was detached from it in matters of policy and strategic decision-making – to that extent, therefore, a group more acted upon than acting in the general sweep of events.[139] As a corollary, Clari's knightly status has traditionally been adduced to explain many of his text's stylistic, structural and thematic features, for example, the use of parataxis and other straightforward forms of coordination to fashion a simple one-thing-after-another narrative rhythm, the limited lexical range, and an apparent predilection for anecdote.[140] Similarly, Clari's relatively low social status – and *relatively* should be emphasized – has been linked to the recurrent theme of wonder that is encountered in the text, especially in one of its most interesting and unusual sections, the description of several of the noteworthy sights to be found in Constantinople.[141] In this view, a country-bumpkinesque, somewhat infantile provincial of very limited cultural range and experience suddenly found himself confronted by the visual richness and sophistication of a large, complex

large promises; c. 33, pp. 38–40: awareness of the logistical pressures on the crusade army; c. 68, p. 84: some knowledge of the arrangements governing the election of the new emperor and the division of the empire.

[139] See Dembowski, *La chronique*, p. 124: 'C'est le récit de la croisade telle qu'elle a été connue par les centaines de chevaliers et les milliers de fantassins qui y prirent part.' For Dufournet, *La conquête de Constantinople*, pp. 12, 18, 34, Robert is variously 'un bon représentant du monde des petits chevaliers', 'un bon représentant de la petite chevalerie, au nom de laquelle il parle', and 'un bon échantillon de la petite chevalerie des XIIe et XIIIe siècles'. For Noble, RC, p. xxvii, 'Clari is a spokesman for a section of society rarely heard from amongst medieval writers, namely the poor knights.' See also Noble, 'Importance of Old French Chronicles', 410, 413, 416; Jacquin, *Le style historique*, pp. 381–4.

[140] For coordination in Clari's history and comparable texts, see Jacquin, *Le style historique*, pp. 178–84. For Clari's vocabulary, see Dembowski, *La chronique*, pp. 60–84, esp. 75–9; *La conquista*, trans. Nada Petrone, pp. 35–8; Dufournet, *Les écrivains*, ii, pp. 362–6.

[141] For the theme of wonder in the text, see Varvaro, 'Esperienza e racconto', p. 1412.

and alien urban environment; and the limitations of the text duly reflect the fact that his vocabulary, aesthetic sensibility and general cognitive assumptions were unequal to the challenge of such a collision.[142]

Some recent appraisals of Clari's *La Conquête de Constantinople* have tended to be more positive, however, while not altogether abandoning the image of the author as an innocent abroad.[143] True to the distinction between author and narrator that runs through this study, the following analysis will not foreground Clari's biographical circumstances, about which we know very little anyway. It examines, instead, the ways in which the narrator of the text aligns his value system with the behaviour of certain social groups either represented in the crusade army or encountered by the crusaders. We shall see that the ethical orientations that result from this alignment, and the manner in which they are played out, or performed, in specific incidents and sequences, help to explain the narrator's choices of story material and the linkages that he fashions between discrete blocks of action, in other words the operating logic of his storyworld. This in turn serves as a useful point of entry into the text's treatment of the visual and of visual perception, which we shall see is in many respects more sophisticated than that informing Villehardouin's narrative universe.

Although our attention will thus be on the narrator of the *Conquête*, some initial remarks of a biographical nature are nonetheless in order because they speak to the class bias that many commentators have detected in the text – a slant that potentially has a bearing on the sort of narratorial voice that we find there and on our reading of the narrator's ethical positioning and thematic preoccupations. We therefore need to consider the case for Clari's class allegiances. Obviously, the argument that Clari the simple knight saw the world, and wrote about it, as a simple knight would have done is wholly circular. But it is striking how often the meagre evidence that we have about Robert beyond the text itself is pressed into service to support this notion. Following Boudon's researches in the late nineteenth century into the charter evidence for Clari's family and its landed

[142] See e.g. Suzanne Fleischmann's verdict on Clari in 'On the Representation of History and Fiction in the Middle Ages', *History and Theory*, 22 (1983), 297: 'the attraction of his chronicle for the modern reader lies principally in his vivid *personal* reactions to events in which he took part, and the almost childlike wonder with which he depicts the splendors of the Orient'. For Archambault, *Seven French Chroniclers*, pp. 27–8, Clari's narrative is a 'brief chronicle…wrapped in a shroud of insuperable ignorance' while Clari himself is 'a lackluster and solipsistic figure' characterized by 'engaging stupidity'.

[143] See e.g. Dembowski, *La chronique*, p. 8: 'Nous croyons que Robert n'est pas un simple chevalier qui relate ses expériences personelles, mais plutôt un simple chevalier nanti de prétentions d'historiographe, c'est-à-dire, de prétentions littéraires indéniables.' See also *ibid.*, pp. 118–22. Cf. the nuanced verdict in Varvaro, 'Esperienza e racconto', pp. 1411, 1412–13, 1425–6.

holdings, it has become axiomatic that Robert was of very limited means, as if the modest fief for which evidence happens to survive represented the sum total of his and his family's assets.[144] Robert's first documentary appearance is as a witness, alongside his father Gilo, in a charter of May 1202 in which the future fourth crusader Peter of Amiens, 'about to set out on pilgrimage to Jerusalem', confirms testamentary dispositions that he had made two years earlier in favour of the Premonstratensian abbey of St-Jean, Amiens.[145] This suggests that Robert was an important member of Peter's vassal network on the eve of their departure on crusade and was close to his lord, who unsurprisingly features prominently and favourably in the *Conquête*.

In any event, the exact extent of Clari's family resources back home in Picardy would have mattered less and less as the crusade wore on and as men of his class confronted harsh economic realities. As initial cash reserves ran down, and as the horses brought from home died off, as almost all of them surely did, any measure of personal autonomy that these assets secured would have melted away, with the result that even knights of quite substantial status and means would, sooner rather than later, have become wholly dependent on the resources of lordly patrons. We know very little about the operation of lordship and patronage networks within crusade armies – this is a subject that merits further research – but it is reasonable to suspect that by dint of crusaders' detachment from their familiar environments, traditional sources of income and domestic support networks over long periods, and because of the very straitened, hand-to-mouth conditions which they typically confronted, aristocratic homosocial bonds of loyalty and interdependence were, if anything, strengthened.[146] There would have been a kind of reversion to the early medieval model of the tight household *comitatus* clustered around a central lord-as-provider. The division of the lay aristocratic participants of the crusade into two categories, the 'high' and rich as against the 'poor knights', which we shall see is a significant structuring device in the *Conquête*, should therefore be regarded as a reflex of the experience of the crusade itself, rather than as a notion transplanted from what would in fact have been much more layered and complex social structures back home in north-western Europe. In the *Conquête*'s vision of the Fourth Crusade, the interactions between these two groups, where they harmonize and where they misfire, become indices of the expedition's success as

[144] See Boudon, 'Robert de Clari en Aminois', 700–34; *idem*, 'Documents nouveaux sur la famille de Robert de Clari', *Bulletin de la Société des antiquaires de Picardie*, 20 (1899), 372–9.

[145] *La conquista*, trans. Nada Petrone, p. 4.

[146] Cf. M. G. Bull, 'The Historiographical Construction of a Northern French First Crusade', *Haskins Society Journal*, 25 (2013), 35–55. See also, for the First Crusade, the discussion of lordship networks in J. France, 'Patronage and the Appeal of the First Crusade', in J. P. Phillips (ed.), *The First Crusade: Origins and Impact* (Manchester, 1997), pp. 5–20.

an ethical undertaking. As we shall see, the narrator is not an outsider looking in or up; he is positioned as an insider completely at home in the value system that major lords and their knightly followers are presumed to share – and, at least most of the time in the *Conquête*'s storyworld, *do* in fact share.

The 'high men' or 'barons' that form the crusade's upper aristocratic register in the *Conquête* are mentioned numerous times, an indication of the narrator's principal focus on them and their central role in the plot. The composition of this group is not clearly delineated, though one or two narratorial asides and contextual details cumulatively lend it some shape. In a rare parenthetical expansion early in the text, the narrator glosses his reference to 'the richest/most powerful men' ('li plus rike homme') by adding that these are those who carry banners.[147] And as the crusade fleet leaves Venice bound for Zara, we are informed that the leading men ('haus homes') were those who had their own ships for themselves and their followers ('gent') as well as transports to carry their horses.[148] The important defining role of military leadership implied by these remarks extends to actual combat, in which 'li haut homme' function as field commanders, their own names sufficing to identify the units that they direct.[149] The most characteristic narrative roles that this group performs, however, often in conjunction with the doge Enrico Dandolo, are strategic planning within the crusade's governing council and the conducting of diplomatic exchanges.[150] Albeit within the constraints of a narrow lexical set, the text tries to ring the changes on the terms used for this group, which is variously labelled 'les barons croisiés', 'li haut homme croisié', 'li haut baron', 'li haut', 'barons', and 'li haut baron de l'ost', among other permutations.[151] In a few constructions it would appear that an attempt is made to differentiate within this group between the senior leaders, those of comital rank or its close equivalent, and the rest.[152] But elsewhere, where two elements are mentioned, these appear

147 RC, c. 1, p. 4: 'et si portoient baniere'.

148 RC, c. 13, pp. 14–16: '[e]t cascuns des haus homes avoit se nef a lui et a se gent et sen uissier a ses chevax mener'.

149 See e.g. RC, c. 44, p. 54; c. 47, p. 58.

150 E.g. RC, c. 5, p. 8; c. 8, p. 10; c. 15, p. 18; c. 39, p. 48; c. 41, p. 50; c. 44, p. 54; c. 62, p. 76; c. 64, p. 76; c. 65, p. 78; c. 78, p. 96; c. 80, p. 96; c. 93, p. 110; c. 98, p. 116; c. 109, p. 126.

151 E.g. RC, c. 8, p. 10; c. 15, p. 18; c. 30, p. 36; c. 32, p. 38; c. 41, p. 50; c. 52, p. 64; c. 78, p. 96. Cf. c. 33, p. 42, where 'li haut baron de le tere' is used of the major barons of Outremer.

152 See RC, c. 2, p. 6: 'li conte et li haut baron' summon 'tous les haus hommes' who have taken the cross; c. 58, p. 72: 'tout li conte et li haut homme de l'ost'; c. 60, p. 72: 'li conte et tout li haut homme de l'ost et li Venicien'; c. 62, p. 76: Alexios V sends word to the count of Flanders, the count of Blois, the marquis (Boniface of Montferrat) 'et a tous les autres haus barons'; c. 93, p. 110: 'tout li conte et tout li haut home'.

to be simply pairings of synonyms rather than attempts to make fine distinctions between different aristocratic ranks.[153]

Within the text's storyworld, the 'high men' stand apart from the rest of the crusade army by virtue of their plot functions and the amount of narrative space that they are afforded. Their principal binary positioning is relative to a group that the text identifies as 'li povre chevalier de l'ost' or 'povres chevaliers'.[154] It is in terms of his being a member of this class of 'poor knights' that Clari's authorial self-fashioning is usually explained. But while there are certainly points in the narrative in which the relationship between the powerful leaders and their knightly followers becomes strained, the overall significance of these moments of antagonism should not be exaggerated. Nor should we overstate the narrator's identification with the poor knights as some especially self-conscious and cohesive grouping. In this context, it is noteworthy how circuitously the text goes about establishing the author's identity, and by extension his categorization as one of the 'poor knights'. The result is that a first-time reader or listener needs to get to the very end of the text to be in a position to tie the various threads together.

First, towards the beginning of the work one finds listed those 'riques hommes' and 'povres' who performed conspicuous feats of arms on the crusade. Among those in the latter category is 'the priest Aleaumes of Clari in the Amiénois'. The fact that his home region is specified, and more particularly the addition of a clause that expands upon his prowess – 'who was very brave and achieved many daring feats' – whereas the names around him are simply listed, suggest that the narrator is hinting at some particular prominence or significance for this individual. But at this stage we are told nothing more specific.[155] Next, Aleaumes surfaces for the first time in the plot at a critical moment in the crusaders' assault on Constantinople on 12 April 1204, bravely wriggling through a hole in the city wall to confront the defenders inside, despite the efforts of his anxious brother, Robert of Clari, to pull him back from danger. Robert is here identified as a knight ('chevalier'), but the narrator volunteers no self-identification at this stage. For the purposes of the narrative moment, Robert is simply one actor amongst many others in a fast-moving scene, his motivations implicitly established by his close blood relationship to Aleaumes, who is firmly the focus of the narrator's attention.[156] Finally, in the epilogue that concludes the text, the author is announced

[153] E.g. RC, c. 13, p. 14: 'Li barom et li haut homme croisié', in implied contrast to 'tout chil de l'ost'; c. 14, p. 16: 'li baron et li haut homme'; c. 80, p. 96: 'li haut homme, li rike homme'.

[154] E.g. RC, c. 80, pp. 96–8; c. 81, p. 98. Cf. c. 93, p. 110, where the doge speculates, seemingly in the spirit of invoking an extreme limit case, that a 'povre chevalier' could be elected emperor.

[155] RC, c. 1, p. 4: 'Aleaumes de Clari en Aminois li clers, qui molt y fu preus et mult y fist de hardement et de proesches'.

[156] RC, cc. 75–6, pp. 92–4.

as 'Robert of Clari, knight'.[157] This drip-feeding of information makes for an interesting exercise in piecing together the identity of the author from clues dispersed across the text; but it does not amount to a ringing narratorial alignment with the class of poorer knights.

In any event, the poorer knights are less a narrative agent consistently visible within the action than a vested interest that emerges from time to time, specifically when the crusade's leadership, in the narrator's view, fails in its responsibilities to its followers. A first discordant note is sounded very soon after the fall of Constantinople, when the leaders take prompt possession of the best houses in the city without the knowledge of 'the lower ranks ['le menue gent'] and the poor knights of the army'; this is said to be the point at which the high men began to betray their subordinates, to show bad faith and to abandon a sense of camaraderie ('compaingnie').[158] Later, the powerful ('rikes hommes') defraud the rest of the army, including the knights and sergeants, of many of the precious objects that should by rights have been included in the agreed communal pooling of Constantinople's pillaged riches.[159] And further injustice is visited upon those who served under Emperor Baldwin in Thrace in the summer of 1204 when they return to Constantinople to discover that they have been deprived of their lodgings in a carving up of the city's resources that has disregarded their interests; we are not told explicitly that knights were among those so mistreated, but this is to be assumed in light of the narrator's earlier remarks about houses.[160]

In view of the fact that Robert the historical actor most probably took part in the Thrace campaign, for we are told that his lord Peter of Amiens died during it,[161] these observations and those about earlier injustices would seem to take on an implied but potent autobiographical colouring, thereby appearing, on the face of it, to be the embittered recollections of someone who believed that he and those like him had been much less well rewarded for their efforts than they deserved. Such has been the common scholarly reading of the text and of its author's ultimate verdict upon the crusade, a view that seems to be powerfully confirmed by the text's insistence that the crushing defeat at Adrianople in 1205 was God's vengeance upon the leaders 'for their pride and for the bad faith which they had shown to the lower ranks of the army ['le povre gent de l'ost']', as well as for 'the horrible sins which they had committed in the city after they had captured it'. These 'oribles pekiés' would seem to be a reference not to the sack of Constantinople and the mistreatment of its inhabitants, which the narrator

[157] RC, c. 120, p. 132: 'ROBERS DE CLARI, li chevaliers'.
[158] RC, c. 80, pp. 96–8.
[159] RC, c. 81, p. 98.
[160] RC, c. 105, p. 122.
[161] RC, c. 103, p. 120.

scarcely registers as in any way problematic, but to the unfair sharing out of the city's wealth among its higher-status Latin conquerors.[162]

One should not, however, exaggerate the extent to which this sense of grievance, with its associated suggestion of class antagonism driving the poor knights to make common cause with the no-less-mistreated social levels beneath them, serves as a leitmotif of the whole text.[163] Several of the leadership's potentially divisive actions do not attract adverse narratorial comment, for example when it keeps the rank and file in the dark about the diversion of the crusade army to Zara.[164] Similarly, even after a sour note has been entered concerning the distribution of dwellings and moveable wealth in Constantinople, the text's account of the corresponding arrangements for the granting of fiefs in the new Latin empire is upbeat, implying that it was appropriate to make the allocations in descending order according to rank, and acknowledging that due allowance was made for the sizes of lords' followings and thus the extent of their responsibilities towards their men.[165] Moreover, the nearest that the text comes to mentioning how Clari the historical actor was himself personally affected in the distribution of resources – via the person of his brother Aleaumes, who here becomes a kind of surrogate – involves the satisfactory resolution of initial difficulties thanks to the equitable and fair-minded exercise of lordly judgement in a spirit of mutual respect and co-operation. When the barons decide that they should at least make a division of the more commonplace precious items collected in Constantinople, in effect the domestic silverware, Aleaumes of Clari objects that he has not received the amount allocated to a knight even though he owns a horse and a hauberk and has performed conspicuous feats of arms. Count Hugh of St-Pol, a member of the inner core of the crusade's leadership, personally attests to Aleaumes's stature

[162] RC, c. 112, pp. 128–30. For the text's rather cursory treatment of the acquisition of the city and its resources, which makes no mention of its impact upon the Greek population other than the disingenuous assertion that 'no harm was done to rich or to poor', see cc. 80–1, pp. 96–8.

[163] It is arguable that the account of the barons' petitioning the emperor Baldwin for lands and titles in RC, c. 111, p. 128 serves to draw attention to their individual and collective greed. The word that the narrator uses for each block of territory so requested is 'kingdom' ('roiaume'), as if to convey the barons' overreaching ambition. But the sequence's very unadorned paratactical structure and the absence of overt narratorial judgement would seem to weaken the force of such an interpretation.

[164] RC, c. 13, p. 14. The subsequent diversion of the crusade to Constantinople likewise attracts no unfavourable comment, even though we know from Villehardouin that Clari's lord Peter of Amiens was among those who opposed the project during the stand-off on Corfu between those for and against: see *Conquête*, §114, p. 116, trans. p. 31. Note that what is described as the first act of lordly betrayal only takes place much later, in the aftermath of the conquest of Constantinople: RC, c. 80, p. 98: '[E]t tresdont commenchierent il a traïr le menue gent, et a porter leur male foi et compaingnie'.

[165] RC, c. 107, pp. 124–6.

and achievements and accordingly awards him his knightly due.[166] Hugh was a close relative of Robert's, and almost certainly Aleaumes's, lord Peter of Amiens. In what looks like some system for redress organized along existing lordship, kinship and regional lines – Aleaumes was appealing to the lord and kinsman of his own lord in what was probably a specifically Picard forum – there is a satisfying restoration of harmony and reciprocal respect between lord and knight, their *compaingnie* grounded in a shared aspiration to be known for *fait d'armes* and *proeches* and expressed through the proper playing out of social roles within familiar hierarchical frameworks.[167]

The narrator's belief that a shared aristocratic value system transcended the tensions between lords and knights that arose from their exposure to extraordinary temptations further emerges from an anecdote placed near the end of the narrative. At first glance, this story seems misplaced, properly belonging among the concluding chapters that we have seen record bits and pieces about the affairs of the Latin empire that came to Robert's attention after he had returned home to Picardy, most probably in 1205.[168] But it is in fact situated a little before these final chapters, punctuating the narrative of the discord between the newly elected Emperor Baldwin and Boniface of Montferrat in 1204. Having reported that Baldwin's forces returned to Constantinople after campaigning in Thrace, to be confronted with the loss of their lodgings as we have seen, the narrator abruptly announces that he has forgotten to relate an incident ('aventure') that happened to Peter of Bracieux (or Bracheux), who has by this point emerged as the narrative's

166 RC, c. 98, p. 116.

167 For the known crusaders from St-Pol and the Amiénois, see J. Longnon, *Les compagnons de Villehardouin: Recherches sur les croisés de la quatrième croisade* (Hautes études médiévales et modernes, 30: Geneva, 1978), pp. 195–207.

168 As noted above, there is general scholarly agreement that there is a discernible transition in the latter stages of the text between the fairly detailed 'participant' portion of the narrative and a series of far sketchier notices extending up to 1216, the year of Emperor Henry's death recorded in RC, c. 119, p. 132. The cut-off point between the two narrative registers is difficult to isolate precisely: c. 112, pp. 128–30 offers a fairly full account of the battle of Adrianople in April 1205, but it is arguable that it would have been still fuller had Robert himself been present, especially given the narrator's remarks about its symbolic resonance. Noble, RC, p. 141 n. 165 makes the plausible suggestion that Robert was among those who Villehardouin mentions sailed home to western Europe in five large Venetian vessels in the spring of 1205; although begged to stay both by the Latin leaders remaining in Constantinople and by the survivors of the battle of Adrianople in Rodosto, they turned a deaf ear to all entreaties: *Conquête*, §§376–9, pp. 184–8, trans. pp. 100–1. It should be noted that Hugh of St-Pol had died in early 1205, further weakening Robert's connection to the embryonic Latin settlement after Peter of Amiens's death the previous year. From c.113, p. 130 the telescoping and simplification of events clearly signal that Robert was reliant on hearsay reaching him in Picardy.

foremost exemplar of martial virtues.[169] This anecdote concerns an exchange between Peter and Ioannitsa's Vlachs and Cumans, who had heard about his reputation for *boine chevalerie*, during which Peter appeals to the Trojan descent myth to argue for the legitimacy of the French conquests of Byzantine territory as the vindication of long-dormant ancestral rights.[170] The encounter is said to have taken place during a campaign led by Emperor Henry, Baldwin's brother and successor, whereas at the conclusion of this episode the main narrative returns to Baldwin's arrival back in Constantinople in 1204.[171]

One's first reaction is to suspect that the anecdote has become misplaced at some point in the transmission of the text, and that it originally belonged among the miscellaneous concluding chapters. But its positioning is probably original: the chapter is fuller and more circumstantial than are those in the concluding section; and the interjection 'we had forgotten to relate' ('aviemes evlié a conter') flags up that the narrator is aware that this is in the nature of a break from the normal narrative flow. The anecdote serves to mitigate the note of divisiveness sounded by the dispute between Baldwin and Boniface by abruptly inserting into the middle of it a probably apocryphal incident featuring the crusade's most well-known chivalric 'star'. Peter is presented here as someone who personifies chivalric achievement to the extent that even the Latins' barbaric enemies recognize as much.[172] And he articulates a legitimation of the French conquests that now seems far-fetched, of course, but at least represents an attempt to fashion a unifying political ideology for the members of the Frankish elite as they carve out lordships for themselves in the remnants of the Byzantine empire.

The core aristocratic value system that the narrator endorses has various interlocking components, each of which is staged at one or more points in the plot: the importance of achievement and the recognition of it by both peers and appreciative external observers, good lordship, largesse, loyalty, bravery and martial prowess, the fear of treachery and of disgrace (a common theme), the legitimacy of vengeance (another particularly recurrent theme), and the justice of rightful

[169] See RC, c. 1, p. 4; c. 55, p. 68; c. 74, p. 90; c. 75, p. 92; c. 78, p. 94. See also Dufournet, *Les écrivains*, ii, pp. 374–7; Hodgson, 'Honour, Shame and the Fourth Crusade', 229–30. For Peter, see also Longnon, *Les compagnons*, pp. 91–8.

[170] RC, c. 106, pp. 122–4. See Varvaro, 'Esperienza e racconto', p. 1425.

[171] Henry was appointed regent in 1205 when Baldwin's fate after his capture at Adrianople was unknown; and he was crowned emperor in August 1206, once the news that Baldwin had been put to death by his captors became generally accepted. For the purposes of dating this incident, if indeed it has a basis in fact, this may not, however, be a distinction that Robert fully understood. Ioannitsa was killed in the autumn of 1207.

[172] Cf. the recognition of the Franks' accomplishments by the sultan of Iconium; RC, c. 52, pp. 64–6.

claims to an inheritance.[173] In addition, the narrator positions himself as someone who is fully attentive to, and competent to pronounce upon, these qualities and norms, which are presented as self-evident and widely shared cultural reference points. Thus, when at the beginning of the text we are supplied with the names of various *riques hommes* and *povres* who performed the most notable feats of arms, the implication is that they are ranked on the basis of criteria that people applied during the crusade; that is to say, what constitute *proesches* and *armes* and the means to make fine discriminations between different levels of achievement are universal and obvious measures duly applied to themselves by the aristocratic members of the crusade host while in the thick of the action, not simply or mainly a matter of personal narratorial judgement after the fact.[174] For our purposes, this adhesion to a unifying aristocratic code is particularly important because it informs the narrator's ethical positioning, which in turn modulates both the narratorial gaze upon the storyworld and the gazes of actors within it.

In the *explicit* the narrator stakes his authority firmly to the fact that he was present and to his sensory perception, both of which grant him access to the truth:

> Now you have heard the truth...which is the testimony of one who was there, who saw it and heard it [*que chis qui i fu et qui le vot et qui l'oï le tesmongne*]... And he has had the truth put in writing of how it was conquered. And although he may not have described the conquest so finely [*si belement*] as many good tellers of tales would have done, nevertheless he has told nothing but the truth. And he has omitted very many things that are true because he cannot remember them all.[175]

Several aspects of this passage invite comment. The repetition of the idea of truth (*verité*) is a form of emphasis that is found elsewhere in the text, almost

[173] For treachery and disgrace, see e.g. RC, c. 17, p. 20; c. 25, p. 32; c. 25, p. 34; c. 34, p. 44; c. 47, p. 60; c. 48, p. 60; c. 60, p. 72; c. 61, p. 74; c. 62, p. 76; c. 73, p. 88; c. 101, p. 120; c. 109, p. 126. For the text's warm endorsement of the propriety of vengeance, see e.g. RC, c. 13, p. 14; c. 14, p. 16; c. 33, p. 40; c. 33, p. 42; c. 39, p. 48; c. 62, p. 76. For the insistence on the importance of rightful inheritance, see RC, c. 39, p. 48.

[174] RC, c. 1, p. 4: Peter of Bracieux is mentioned first as 'the one who did the greatest feats amongst both the rich and the poor' ('che fu chis de povres et de rikes qui plus y fist de proesches'). The succeeding names are not explicitly ranked, but the implication that some descending scale of achievement is to be understood emerges from the fact that Henry of Hainaut, the brother of Count Baldwin of Flanders and himself a future emperor of Constantinople, only comes eighth in the list of nine *rikes*, while Robert's brother Aleaumes of Clari (though the reader does not yet know of their relationship) is thirteenth of the fifteen *povres*. Cf. Kinoshita, *Medieval Boundaries*, pp. 142–3, unconvincingly arguing that Aleaumes is nonetheless given 'pride of place'.

[175] RC, c. 120, pp. 132–4. For a thoughtful discussion of Clari's *explicit*, see Jacquin, *Le style historique*, pp. 44–7. See also Varvaro, 'Esperienza e racconto', pp. 1426–7.

a signature device. Claims of stylistic inadequacy appear routinely in the prefaces of medieval texts, but the particular variant of the humility topos that is set up here, the insistence on there being an inverse relationship between literary embellishment and the truthful reporting of war, anticipates a trope that would in later centuries become a clichéd assertion in countless military memoirs. Indeed, the veteran who captures the raw experience of conflict most effectively and most truthfully in simple but sincere prose remains a type in modern culture, and we therefore need to be careful not to retroject the assumptions that attach to it back onto Clari. Once again, the phantom of the 'simple knight' looms.

Two further aspects related to this insistence on truth and stylistic simplicity are noteworthy. First, a clear contrast with Villehardouin emerges. As we have seen, one element of the authority carved out by Villehardouin's narrator involves his having been a member of the crusade's leadership team and having attended its councils. This sets up a narratorial persona who is assumed to be equipped to collate information from multiple sources and, by extension, can discriminate between them, at least at some rudimentary level.[176] This implied hierarchy or variety of sources of knowledge is not available to the narrator of the *Conquête*, with the result that there is a flattening but also broadening effect in his baldly stated reliance on what he has seen and heard. The narrator's epistemological purchase on the world of the crusade and the emergent Latin empire is less specific than is the case in Villehardouin's text, but it is also opened up to a potentially fuller range of sights and sounds.

Second, the referent of *i* in 'qui i fu' is open ended and imprecise: where exactly is Clari's 'there', and what sorts of events and actions could he see and hear in or from it? The narrator's unspecified and apparently wide-ranging presence, his 'thereness', seems to lay ambitious claim to a kind of roving autopsy activated by keen senses and anchored by a good memory; though the narrator gestures

[176] In those cases in which the status and circumstances of the author so permitted, it seems that claims to both eyewitness participation in events in general and having been privy to the counsels of the great in particular soon became formulaic in vernacular histories. See, for example, the prefatory remark of Henry of Valenciennes, to a large extent Villehardouin's continuator: *Histoire de l'empereur Henri de Constantinople*, ed. J. Longnon (Documents relatifs à l'histoire des croisades, 2; Paris, 1948), §501, pp. 27–8: 'Car Henris vit oell a oell toz les fais qui la furent, et sot toz les consaus des haus homes et des barons.' Cf. a slightly later vernacular history concerning events in the east: Philip of Novara, *Mémoires, 1218–1243*, ed. C. Kohler (Les classiques français du moyen âge, 10; Paris, 1913), I (97), p. 5; trans. J. L. La Monte and M. J. Hubert, *The Wars of Frederick II Against the Ibelins in Syria and Cyprus* (New York, 1936), p. 61: 'Phelipe de Nevaire, quy fu a tous les fais et conseils, et qui mainte fois esté amés des bons pour le voire dire et haïs des malvais, vous en dira la verité, aucy come en touchant les homes et les grans fais.'

towards the limits of what he can recall, the gaps he concedes are ones of quantity not quality, and the implication is, therefore, that enough has been remembered to make a full, coherent and truthful telling of events possible. As we shall see, in some respects the position staked out in the *explicit* corresponds quite closely to the ways in which the narrator selects and organizes his material in the body of the narrative. In other respects, however, the claims to personal autopsy prove to be overstated, while the underlying insistence on eyewitnessing itself as an authenticating device is nonetheless retained. The gap between the two, as in some of the other works that we have examined but to a greater extent, is closed by transposing engagement with matters of perception and understanding of the world from the narrator himself to focalizing actors within the storyworld.

What roles does the narrator play vis-à-vis the narration? The action of the *Conquête* is narrated solely in the third person, while the narrator announces himself sufficiently often by means of the first person to effect a formal temporal separation from the inhabitants of the storyworld in their moment-by-moment navigation of their experience. In other words, there is none of the bridging between the narrative now and the narratorial now that we have found in other texts' mobilizations of the first person plural. The first person plural is sometimes used, but only editorially of the narrator and interchangeably with the singular. It is simply a question of ringing the changes, and no shift or modulation of the narratorial persona is implied by it; there are no shadowy comrades or coadjutors or subgroups of the crusade host lurking within the 'we'.[177] In either guise, singular or plural, the narrator does not play a homodiegetic role in the action. It is true that a character named Robert of Clari does feature at one important juncture as a member of the group that attempts to force an entry through Constantinople's walls during the assault on 12 April 1204, but as we have seen this name has not yet been announced to the reader or listener as that of the author. Moreover, the narrator is at pains to introduce the character of Robert in a seemingly casual, disinterested manner, as if merely adding some incidental and minor detail to a narrative sequence that is really about his brother: as he puts it, 'now there was there a knight, who was his [Aleaumes's] brother, and Robert of Clari was his name'.[178] By virtue of being absent from the storyworld, the narrator does not himself get to fix his gaze upon it as a character; Robert of Clari the historical actor was doubtless 'there' in relation to many of the action sequences narrated by the text, but a corresponding situatedness is denied the narrator.

[177] See e.g. RC, c. 92, p. 108, where the first person singular ('que je vous ai chi acontées) and plural ('nous ne vous poons mie aconter') are used in close proximity and do very similar work. For similar pairings, see also c. 81, p. 98; c. 98, p. 116. Cf. Mölk, 'Robert de Clari', 215–16.

[178] RC, c. 76, p. 92: '[s]i avoit illuec un chevalier, .i. sien frere, Robers de Clari avoit a non': translation revised.

Consequently, the narrator's prime function is as organizer of the telling, signposting shifts of focus, recapitulating and anticipating.[179] This is particularly in evidence at the beginning and end of analepses and other interruptions of the main narrative flow.[180] The narrator does not make many interventions by way of judging the actors' behaviour or qualifying his own understanding of such matters as cause and motivation, though there are a few interesting exceptions.[181] Similarly, his relatively few disavowals of knowledge are routine disclaimers with respect to names or totals.[182] Interestingly, there is a brief gesturing towards a deeper sense of narratorial incapacity when the narrator is confronted with the marvels to be seen in Constantinople; describing that part of Hagia Sophia where the Gospels were read, he informs us that it was so richly and finely wrought ('si rikes et si nobles') that 'I cannot describe to you how it was made'.[183] Even so, the narrator's reactions to Constantinople's wonders for the most part draw on the standard ways in which disavowals of narratorial knowledge tend to be expressed.[184]

[179] E.g. RC, c. 1, p. 2: 'Aprés si nommerons'; c. 1, p. 4: 'que nous avons ichi nommés'; c. 30, p. 36: 'dont nous avons parlei par devant'; c. 44, p. 54: 'comme je vous ai chi conté'; c. 52, p. 64: 'comme nous vous dirons aprés', which also appears in c. 80, p. 98; c. 64, p. 76: 'com jou vous ai par devant dit'; c. 94, p. 112: 'com je vous dirai'; c. 98, p. 116: 'dont je vous ai parlé par devant' and 'comme nous vous avons dit par devant'. The construction 'com[me] je vous ai dit' is especially common: e.g. c. 55, p. 68; c. 66, p. 82; c. 81, p. 98.

[180] See e.g. RC, c. 18, p. 20; c. 29, p. 36; c. 33, p. 40; c. 39, p. 48; c. 65, p. 78; c. 66, p. 80.

[181] E.g. RC, c. 65, pp. 78–80: the leaders act unwisely in rejecting Ioannitsa's offer of an alliance; c. 66, p. 80: the narrator expresses the belief, rather than simply states as a fact, that the crusaders' defeat of Alexios V Mourtzouphlos was the result of his illegitimate appropriation of the icon of Our Lady that the Greeks traditionally carried into battle; c. 81, p. 98: the narrator's judgement ('au mien ensient') is mobilized to buttress the hyperbolic claim that the wealth found in Constantinople exceeded the combined riches of any forty other cities elsewhere in the world.

[182] E.g. RC, c. 1, p. 4: 'nous n'en savons le nombre', which recurs in c. 112, p. 128; c. 1, p. 4: 'nous avons nous mie tous chiaus nommés'. The formula 'nous ne vous savons mie tous nommer' appears regularly in the early part of the text: see c. 1, p. 2; c. 1, pp. 2–4; c. 1, p. 4.

[183] RC, c. 85, p. 104: 'nous ne le vous sariemes mie descrire com fais il estoit'. Cf. the more impersonal note sounded in the remarks in the same chapter, with respect to a thaumaturgic tube attached to the great doors of Hagia Sophia, that 'no one knew what metals it was made of', while a silver tabernacle over the altar 'was so rich no one could reckon the amount it was worth': translation slightly revised.

[184] See RC, c. 82, p. 100: so many relics are found in one chapel, Our Lady of Pharos, that 'I could not tell you them all nor tell the whole truth'; c. 92, p. 108: some of the marvels ('mervelles') of Constantinople are described whereas others 'I cannot tell you about'; c. 92, p. 110: 'as for the other Greeks, both high and low, poor and rich, and the size of the city, the palaces, the other wonders ['mervelles'] which are there I will give up telling you about them'.

Are there nonetheless passages in the narrative in which we might suspect the operation of eyewitness memory in its fullest, episodic sense? As we have already observed with respect to other texts, we need to be extremely careful: just as bald and brief accounts of given events do not prove absence of autopsy,[185] more fully realized scenes, the inclusion of circumstantial details and overt attention to the visual cannot be treated as *prima facie* evidence of the contrary.[186] That said, there are certainly several moments of visual richness and density that on the face of it seem to suggest some basis in personal, autoptic memory. For example, when reporting that the crusaders, while camped on the Lido, were overjoyed to learn that the doge had suggested a way out of the debt with which they were burdened, the narrator states:

> So that night they celebrated so much that there was no one so poor that he did not carry many lights, and they carried great torches of candles high on their lances around their quarters and inside so that it seemed as if the whole army was ablaze [*que che sanloit que tote l'os fust esprise*].[187]

The text as a whole is sparing in its use of figurative language, so the use of a simile in this passage looks like an attempt to capture the impression made on someone who was directly observing this moment. A similar attempt to evoke the effect of a striking visual scene is evident in the narrator's account of the departure of the crusade fleet from Venice: 'it seemed as if the whole sea was

[185] It is likely that Robert was present at, or at the very least knew people who could narrate in detail, the major assembly, which he places at Corbie, at which those who had negotiated the contract with Venice reported back to the northern French crusade leadership. This event is, however, treated quite briefly within a sequence that compresses the chronology and simplifies the events leading up to the crusaders' departure for the east: RC, c. 8, p. 10. The meeting at Corbie is not mentioned by Villehardouin, but it is likely that Clari's version of events has a basis in fact: see Queller and Madden, *Fourth Crusade*, pp. 24, 46–7.

[186] See e.g. RC, cc. 21–2, p. 28 for a well-realized scene – as the future emperor Isaac II overcomes his would-be murderer, takes his horse and rides to Hagia Sophia brandishing his bloody sword and calling out to bystanders – that we can be sure Robert did not witness, both because he was almost certainly not in Constantinople in 1185 and because it never took place. For other cases in which authorial autopsy is impossible or extremely unlikely, see e.g. c. 25, p. 34 for precise details of the violence done to the emperor Andronicos's body by the people of Constantinople; and c. 33, pp. 42–4, for a dramatic but wholly fictitious scene in which Queen Sybilla of Jerusalem hands the crown back to her former husband Guy of Lusignan. In c. 19, p. 24, in a reference to events that would have taken place back in 1179, the French king and his people marvel at the opulence of a Byzantine embassy.

[187] RC, c. 12, p. 14: translation slightly revised.

billowing and blazing with the ships which they were sailing and from the great joy which they were displaying'.[188]

Likewise, similes that speak to direct experience of the visual impact of a scene feature in the account of how the party led by Peter of Amiens forced its way into Constantinople during the successful assault on 12 April 1204. When the attackers make an opening in a disused postern gate and peer into the city, we are told that they are confronted with the sight of so many people that it seems as if half the world were there.[189] Then Aleaumes of Clari wriggles through the hole in the wall and charges the enemy with a knife, with the result that he makes them flee before him 'like cattle'.[190] We are, in addition, given some very specific and incidental information in this sequence: that Aleaumes crawled through the breach in the wall on all fours, while his brother Robert tried to pull him back by grabbing hold of his foot; and that there were ten knights among the party of sixty that made this attack.[191] In this account, then, the language of impression and seeming appearance, in conjunction with trivial but precise details, would seem to suggest that we are getting close to the personal recollections of Robert the eyewitness. After all, this incident amounts to the historical Clari's fifteen minutes of fame within the parameters of the plot of his own narrative.

But, once again, we need to exercise caution: as we shall see, Robert the character plays only a minor role in this extended sequence, over the course of which several actors, some physically close to Robert and presumably observable by him but others not, perceive events in an intricate criss-cross of gazes and acts of focalization.[192] Autoptic, episodic memory undoubtedly contributes to the telling of these events, but it does not drive the manner of their narration nor expressly authenticate the significance that the narrator attaches to them. In a similar vein, we might surmise that the details in the quite fully narrated scene in which the army nervously awaits the result of the imperial election in May 1204, probably the most effective building up of suspense in the whole narrative, as well as the attention that the text pays to the sumptuous appearance of Emperor Baldwin's coronation robes and all the paraphernalia of that occasion, have some basis in authorial eyewitness recall.[193] But it is the significance of these events

[188] RC, c. 13, p. 16: 'si sanla bien que le mers formiast toute et qu'ele fust toute enbrasee des nes qu'il menoient et de le grant goie qu'il demenoient'.

[189] RC, c. 75, p. 92: 'que sanloit que demis li mondes i fust'.

[190] RC, c. 76, pp. 92–4: 'si les faisoit aussi fuir devant lui comme bestes'. Cf. c. 75, p. 92 for the slightly earlier remark, with respect to this same group assault, that as they hack at the postern gate through which they will soon gain entry, the attackers are so heavily bombarded with stones from above that it seems they might be buried under them ('que il sanloit enaises k'il y fussent enfoï es pierres').

[191] RC, c. 76, pp. 92, 94.

[192] See below, pp. 324–6.

[193] RC, c. 95, pp. 112–14; cc. 96–7, pp. 114–16.

for the embryonic Latin empire that is the narrator's principal concern, not the parading of personal reminiscence. As is almost always the case, the line between details that we can ascribe to actual episodic memory and those that function as reality effects is very unclear.

There is, therefore, no straightforward correlation between the likelihood that the historical Robert of Clari took part in a given piece of action and the dropping of autoptic markers into the narration. A case in point is the account of the French crusaders' manoeuvrings against Alexios III's forces that formed part of the assault on Constantinople on 17 July 1203 (the Venetians were simultaneously launching a seaborne attack from the Golden Horn).[194] This is one of the most extended set-pieces in the whole narrative. It captures the French lords and knights engaged in the sort of activity that best allows them to parade their sense of dignity, identity and social status: not hacking through postern gates or fighting it out on siege towers, but lined up in massed mounted squadrons positioned ahead of supporting infantry units.[195] The text highlights the deployment of these battalions, each formed along regional lines and identified by their respective noble leaders, in that this is the only moment in the plot in which the high-status crusaders get to conduct themselves in close alignment with the schematic of the crusade's aristocratic membership, the parading of names region by region, with which the narrative begins.[196] The historical Robert of Clari almost certainly took part in this action, as a member of the squadron ('batalle'), the second in line, that was under the command of Hugh of St-Pol and Peter of Amiens; and it is consequently tempting to read the account as that of someone caught up in the thick of things.[197] In particular, the reference to the appointment of two well-respected men in each squadron to issue moment-by-moment commands, and the mention of the orders that they were to give, 'Set spurs!' and 'Trot!', point to both a detailed understanding of cavalry command structures and direct experience of this particular engagement.[198]

All is not as it seems, however. As Alberto Varvaro has noted, the most fully narrated armed confrontation in the whole text is in fact an anticlimactic non-battle, for, after some initial squaring up, Alexios III's troops lose their nerve

[194] RC, cc. 44–9, pp. 54–64. For this assault, see Queller and Madden, *Fourth Crusade*, pp. 122–8; Phillips, *Fourth Crusade*, pp. 173–82.

[195] Henry of Hainaut's later skirmish with the forces of Alexios V Mourtzouphlos is also a partly mounted engagement but on a smaller scale involving only a portion of the French forces: RC, c. 66, pp. 80–2. For this clash of arms, see Queller and Madden, *Fourth Crusade*, pp. 165–7; Phillips, *Fourth Crusade*, pp. 228–31.

[196] RC, c. 1, pp. 2–4.

[197] RC, c. 45, p. 56.

[198] It emerges a little later that the two such commanders in the Hugh of St-Pol/Peter of Amiens squadron are Peter himself and Eustace of Canteleux: RC, c. 47, p. 60.

and prefer not to come to blows with the French.[199] Moreover, the burden of Clari's account involves a dispute between, on the one side, Baldwin of Flanders, who perceives the dangers posed to the French position by the larger Byzantine force and duly pulls his men back, and, on the other, Hugh of St-Pol and Peter of Amiens, who wish to press home the attack and accuse Baldwin of acting shamefully. In what amounts to a restaging of the tension between the brave Roland and the wise Oliver, the narrator's sympathies seem to lie squarely with Hugh and Peter: their squadron, presumably with the historical Robert of Clari riding in its midst, functions as a sort of chorus parroting its leaders' criticism of Baldwin and urging Hugh and Peter to take up the vanguard position that has been vacated.[200] The narrator further emphasizes his taking of sides by means of multiple converging and judgemental focalizations: those French guarding the camp and observing the unfolding action express their support for Hugh and Peter, while admiring ladies and maidens look on from the walls of Constantinople. Moreover, Baldwin's own people reprove him, going as far as to threaten defiance, and this spurs him to rejoin the others.[201] In the event, however, the French advance stalls, each leader losing the initiative and finding himself obliged to seek guidance from the others. The French make a tactical error in putting too much distance between themselves and their camp, and a canal obstructs their progress.[202] After all the bravado and the promise of derring-do, then, it is Baldwin's reading of the situation and his cautious approach that actually end up being vindicated. It is reasonable to suppose that some measure of eyewitness recollection runs through this passage. But the staging of conflicting aristocratic values, with perhaps a hint of criticism of the leaders' eventual, and literal, *impasse*, is what is principally at stake, not an illustration of personal autoptic experience.

The traditional scholarly picture of Clari as something of an *ingénu* tends to encourage a compensating image of him as a wide-eyed innocent abroad in the world of the Fourth Crusade and Latin empire; what he lacks in historiographical sophistication and access to detailed, accurate information, it is supposed, he at least partly makes up for in an ability, however crude, to translate recalled moments of raw perception into words on the page. Whence, for example, the small but arresting visual details in the text, such as the manner in which the Venetians drew lots to determine who would sail with the crusade fleet.[203] But the lengthy sequence devoted to the non-battle of 17 July 1203 suggests that narrative craft and the exploration of conflicts of values matter more to the narrator than the

[199] Varvaro, 'Esperienza e racconto', pp. 1412–14.

[200] RC, c. 47, p. 60: 'si disent tot ensanle que li cuens de Flandres faisoit grant honte qui retornoit'.

[201] RC, cc. 47–8, pp. 60–2.

[202] RC, c. 48, p. 62.

[203] RC, c. 11, p. 12.

recording of vivid personal memories. In a similar vein, a seemingly proto-anthropological description of the Cumans under Ioannitsa's command looks at first sight like the recollections of a curious observer, Clari himself or an informant, struck by an unusual cultural collision.[204] This may well be part of the story: the details that the narrator picks out, such as the Cumans' dairy and meat diet, their use of felt tents as dwellings, their pastoralism, and their effectiveness as hard-riding horsemen, intriguingly anticipate some of the characteristics, vis-à-vis a broadly similar steppe culture, that would be noted some decades later by the first Latin visitors to the Mongol world. But the true pay-off of these remarks, even though they simply seem to be dropped in *obiter* to help pad out the relative lull in the action between the restoration of Isaac II and Alexios IV and the coming to power of Alexios V Mourtzouphlos, emerges later, when the disastrous defeat at Adrianople is explained by the fact that the French badly misread the appearance of Ioannitsa's Cuman forces and so fatally underestimated the threat that they posed.[205] Again, narrative craft, not immediate eyewitness experience for its own sake, informs the inclusion of material.

Nonetheless, there is within Clari's text a great deal of attention both to the visual dimensions of the storyworld and to acts of perception – page for page, and consistently across the narrative as opposed to concentrations in clusters, noticeably more so than is the case with Villehardouin's *Conquête* and the other works that we have considered. Clari's characters are involved in a great deal of seeing and learning. In the absence of a central figure who dominates the action, focalization is shared around widely, although there is some favouring of the doge, Enrico Dandolo, in keeping with the positive image that the narrator constructs of him as reflective, adaptable and decisive.[206] In a similar manner, the French barons are placed in several situations in which their perceptions and awareness propel the action and motivate shifts in direction.[207] That said, the barons do not dominate the storyworld, at least not in the ways that focalization could potentially make available to them. Although their reading of the world and

[204] RC, c. 65, p. 78.

[205] RC, c. 112, p. 128.

[206] See e.g. RC, c. 11, p. 12; c. 12, p. 14; c. 14, p. 18; c. 17, p. 20. Cf. the lively, and no doubt largely invented, scene in which Dandolo vigorously and earthily reproves Alexios IV for failing to honour his agreements with the Latins: c. 59, p. 72. A possible, if muted and indirect, note of criticism is sounded towards the end of the text, when the narrator reports that the doge and the other Venetians opposed the election of Henry of Hainaut as emperor. However, the apparent triviality and inconsequentiality of their stated reasons for doing so – they wanted possession of a famous and richly fashioned icon of Our Lady that the Greeks had especially venerated – reinforces the imprecision of this episode, which is part of the 'afterthought' sequence written some time after Clari had returned to France: c. 114, p. 130.

[207] E.g. RC, c. 57, p. 70; c. 59, p. 72; c. 62, p. 76; c. 100, p. 118; c. 104, p. 120.

the values that inform their reactions to it substantially align with those of the narrator, the only dissonances appearing in the criticisms that we noted earlier, the narration of events is not for the most part filtered through their consciousness. One possible interpretation of the narrator's variegated approach to focalization might be that he is suggesting that the crusade was, crudely, a mess: conspicuously perspicacious individuals such as the doge might attain moments of clarity and correctly anticipate future outcomes, but overall none of the principal actors was ever in true control of events. This is an attractive hypothesis, though it perhaps rests on an over-reading of the narrator's handling of motivation and the sweep of events, and an over-estimation of the text's subtlety.

A more plausible explanation is to be found in the narrator's scene-by-scene adumbration of the action, in particular the staging of interactions between characters and of the ways in which information reaches them so as to make them revise their understandings, plans and ambitions. For the most part, and putting to one side the occasional supervenient workings of the divine will and what Bagley has aptly termed the 'feeling that there is some kind of destiny at work in their [the crusaders'] expedition', the text's regime of causation is quite simple.[208] Events are not the product of convergent multiple factors. They are triggered by single operative causes, the logic of which is taken as self-evident and readily available to the understanding of the actors *in medias res* as well as to the narrator after the fact. Consequently, it is largely the job of focalizers in the text simply to recognize these straightforward cause-and-effect mechanisms and to anticipate their implications for themselves and others. This is the case to greater or lesser extents in all the texts that we have examined, but it is an especially pronounced feature of Clari's narrative strategy, one that sits comfortably alongside, but is not simply a reflex of, the tightly sequential, blow-by-blow recounting of the action that characterizes much of the narrative delivery.

A prime illustration of this approach is an extended sequence early in the text which does much to guide the reader's or listener's expectations about the ways in which the remainder of the action will be narrated. This concerns the back and forth of negotiations that persuade Boniface of Montferrat to join the crusade's leadership after the death of one of the original leaders, Theobald of Champagne. What is particularly striking about this sequence is the way in which

[208] Bagley, 'Robert de Clari's *La Conquête*', 110–11. Examples of the (fairly rare) irruption of divine power into the storyworld include the manner in which Isaac II is saved when Andronicos tries to shoot him: RC, c. 23, p. 30 (the belief that an angel thwarted Andronicos's attempt is stated later at c. 25, p. 34); the miraculous ability ('par miracle de Dieu') of the bishop of Soissons's ship to manoeuvre up against Constantinople's seawall during the assault of 12 April 1204: c. 74, p. 90; divine protection of Andrew of Dureboise, the first Frenchman to force his way onto the wall, during the same assault: c. 74, p. 90; and St Demetrius's hand in the death of Ioannitsa: c. 116, p. 130.

its story logic requires no prior knowledge on the part of the principals: this is on the surface a world without pre-planning, intimations and suspicions, without anticipation, expectation, deduction, inference or guesswork. Thus the barons assemble at Soissons after Theobald's death and, seemingly spontaneously, agree to approach Boniface; their reasoning is not explained.[209] Messengers duly reach Boniface, who is 'very surprised that the barons of France had summoned him'.[210] He journeys to France, specifically Soissons again, having sent the (apparently very coy or uncommunicative) messengers on ahead, and is lavishly received by his hosts. Only at this point does Boniface ask the barons why he has been summoned, is informed of Theobald's death, and is begged to join the enterprise, whereupon, after some reflection, he takes the cross.[211]

Boniface's journey of discovery is still not done, however, for only after he has been ceremoniously given the cross by the bishop of Soissons, and has been handed the large amount of cash that Theobald had collected for use on the crusade, does he think to ask the barons, 'Where do you want to go and which Saracen territory is it your intention to reach?'[212] When told that the plan is to hire a fleet to sail to Alexandria or 'Babylon' (Cairo), he simply expresses his agreement, and then proposes that ambassadors be sent to Venice, Pisa or Genoa, a suggestion with which the barons, seemingly unaware up to this point of the potential usefulness of the Italian maritime cities to their cause, happily concur. Similar story-telling machinery is in evidence a little later, when the crusade's leaders begin to work through the implications of their continuing indebtedness to the Venetians after the fall of Zara. Only at the point at which the doge makes the suggestion that the crusade could easily solve its supply problems in Greece does Boniface stand up and recall that over the previous winter, at the court of the German king, Philip of Swabia, he had encountered Isaac II's disinherited son Alexios, the future Alexios IV, who, he suggests, could usefully serve as the crusaders' point of entry into Constantinople and its resources.[213]

As always, it is important to distinguish between the modern historical reconstruction of actors' actions and motivations to which passages such as these may contribute, and the ways in which a narrative propels its characters through the storyworld of its own devising. The apparent naivety, lack of curiosity, and inability to make mental connections that at first sight characterize the crusade leaders' interactions in these sequences are, historically speaking, extremely

[209] RC, c. 3, p. 6.

[210] RC, c. 3, p. 6: 'si se merveilla molt de chou que li baron de Franche l'avoient mandé'.

[211] RC, c. 4, pp. 6–8.

[212] RC, cc. 4–5, p. 8: translation revised.

[213] RC, c. 17, p. 20. For Boniface meeting Alexios at Philip of Swabia's court at Hagenau over Christmas 1201, see J. Folda, 'The Fourth Crusade, 1201–3: Some Reconsiderations', *Byzantinoslavica*, 26 (1965), 277–90; Queller and Madden, *Fourth Crusade*, pp. 33, 35–6.

implausible, to put it mildly, and are for the most part contradicted by the evidence of other sources.[214] An advocate of the conspiracy-theory view of the crusade's diversion to Constantinople might argue that in the second of the two passages that we have noted, Clari is dropping hints that Enrico Dandolo and Boniface were in cahoots, their apparently spontaneous suggestion, in the doge's case, and recollection, in Boniface's, no more than charades to dupe the other crusade leaders. But it is not necessary to appeal to some implicit friction between what Clari says took place and what he knew, or must have known, 'really' happened, for this scene proceeds in a way consistent with the story logic that runs through the whole text in its privileging of characters' perceptions and cognition in the immediate narrative now.

That said, it is true that the narrator acknowledges in places that cause and effect can play out over longer intervals. This is particularly evident in the two lengthy analepses that occupy much of the earlier part of the text, before the main action has reached Constantinople. The first, which begins immediately after Boniface recalls meeting the imperial pretender Alexios, relates affairs in Byzantium since the final years of the reign of Manuel I Comnenos (d. 1180) and centres on the fall of the emperor Andronicos, the coming to power of Isaac II (1185) and his subsequent usurpation at the hands of his brother Alexios III (1195). (The narrator himself does not supply these dates or other specific markers, and temporal imprecision hangs over the whole sequence.) The second analepsis mostly concerns the activities of Boniface of Montferrat's brother Conrad between 1187 and 1192 – again, the narrator supplies no clear chronological orientation either in absolute date terms or in relation to the narrative now of the Fourth Crusade – in Byzantium, where he is poorly treated despite his excellent service to an (unnamed) emperor in overcoming a dangerous rival, and then in the Latin East, where he saves Tyre from Saladin, repulses Guy of Lusignan and becomes king of Jerusalem, only to be murdered by the Assassins. These sequences contain complex narratives; they occupy eleven and nearly six of the text's 120 chapters, respectively, and in terms of length amount to about a sixth of the whole work.[215]

The stated purpose of these interruptions of the main plot is to supply useful background. The first analepsis is cued by the initial mention of the pretender Alexios, which prompts the narrator to announce that he will break off talking about the pilgrims and the fleet and turn to Alexios and his father Isaac and how they came to be caught up in the story of the crusade; at the conclusion of

[214] Clari's most glaring error in this sequence is to place the embassy to Venice after Boniface had been recruited to join the crusade: see RC, cc. 5–6, p. 8; Queller and Madden, *Fourth Crusade*, pp. 9–20, 25–31.

[215] RC, cc. 18–28, pp. 20–36; cc. 33–8, pp. 40–8. The second analepsis begins a few sentences into the long c. 33.

the sequence, the narrator likewise wraps up by stating that the foregoing has explained how Isaac came to power and the circumstances in which his son fetched up in Germany, which neatly closes the ring narrative because this is, of course, where Boniface has some pages earlier said that he first came upon Alexios.[216] The second analepsis is triggered by the narrator's belief that Boniface was particularly vocal in arguing for the crusade's rerouting to Constantinople, an aim which is explained with reference to his hatred for the Byzantine emperor because of some past wrong ('mesfait'). Similarly, at the conclusion of the flashback the narrator back-announces, 'Now I have told you the misdeed for which the marquis of Montferrat hated the emperor of Constantinople and why he was putting more effort into going to Constantinople and urging it more strongly than anyone else.'[217]

While the first analepsis is on the surface a quite straightforward exercise in contextual scene-setting, the second is more intriguing in that, in speaking to one crusader's personal motivations, it implies that the narrator understood both that past experience could have a possible bearing on crusaders' attitudes and behaviour, and that Boniface himself brought a distinctive and personal appreciation of his place in the play of long-term cause and effect to his decision to participate in the expedition. The explanatory force of this analepsis is weak, however, both in relation to our knowledge of the actual historical circumstances and in terms of its own internal logic. The emperor on the throne whom Conrad would have encountered when he went to Constantinople (in 1187) would not have been Alexios III, as the narrative implies, but the very Isaac II whose rights Boniface is apparently so keen to vindicate by means of the crusade.[218] The sequence also does a poor job of explaining why Boniface would nurse such vengeful feelings. Yes, Conrad is badly treated by the Byzantine emperor, but he lives to fight another day, very successfully in fact. And why does the narrator then include at some length Conrad's post-Byzantium adventures in Outremer, filling the sequence out still further with some additional background on the recent history of the Latin East, unless in some poorly worked-through way Conrad's death at the hands of the Assassins in 1192 is to be regarded as a remote but appreciable consequence of his mistreatment in Constantinople? It is, moreover, noteworthy that Boniface's vengefulness does not resurface as a motivating force later on in the text. Indeed,

[216] RC, c. 18, p. 20; c. 29, p. 36.

[217] RC, c. 33, p. 40; c. 39, p. 48.

[218] As already noted, at the beginning of the sequence the narrator states, c. 33, p. 40, that Boniface wished to avenge an injury ('mesfait') 'which the emperor of Constantinople, who was ruling the empire, had done him' ('que li empereres de Coustantinoble, qui l'empire tenoit, li avoit fait'). The relative clause would seem to be redundant unless *tenoit* pertains to the narrative now of Boniface's vengeful sentiments at that particular point in the crusade – that is, the reference is to someone who was reigning at that time, namely Alexios III, but is no longer emperor in the narratorial now.

Boniface is not someone on whom the narrator particularly dwells thereafter, at least not until the concluding chapters on the embryonic Latin empire, where the treatment of him is far from positive.[219] And while the crusaders do indeed come to assume a posture of righteous vengefulness vis-à-vis the Byzantines, and this becomes a central strand of their self-justification and motivation in Clari's rendering, this is in the first instance to vindicate the future Alexios IV's rightful inheritance, and later to avenge his and his father's murders, not as instruments of Boniface's personal agenda.

The two analepses are subtle and fascinating exercises in story-telling, anticipating many of the themes and plot tensions that will subsequently emerge in the main narrative. The first part of the first sequence, for instance, which recounts how Emperor Manuel contrives a showdown between his Greek courtiers and the Frenchmen in his service in order to lay bare the formers' pusillanimity, both sets up the superior martial abilities of the French over the Greeks as a cultural given and shows that the French belong in the Byzantine world.[220] These stories must have drawn on multiple sources: there are numerous folkloric motifs in the two sequences, such as the literally rags-to-riches change of fortune experienced by Isaac, the quick thinking of resourceful heroes, the timely interventions of helper figures, and the parts played by forest and water in the *mises-en-scène*. It is reasonable to suspect that lively stories told by the Latin population of Constantinople was one source of inspiration, as well as perhaps a *chanson de geste* recounting the deeds of Conrad. In these ways, even though they are embedded in the narration of the main action, the analepses announce their separation from it. Although, then, the second analepsis nudges towards an interesting individuation of character motivation – in other words, Boniface's implied focalization of his goals and circumstances takes in multiple, supposedly connected events that stretch back over several years – it does not establish a pattern for the narrator to follow vis-à-vis the story of the crusade proper. That is to say, the analepses stand in contrastive relation to the rest of the text so as to highlight the narrative's story-telling craft and ambition. The narrator is simply showing off. They do not establish a regime of long-term causation and actor focalization that significantly complicates the text's predominant attention, when

[219] See RC, cc. 99–101, pp. 118–20; cc.103–5, pp. 120–2; c. 110, pp. 126–8; cc. 115–16, p. 130.

[220] RC, c. 18, pp. 20–2. Cf. the manner in which the discussion, in the first analepsis, concerning the best way to stage Andronicos's execution anticipates the debate about how Alexios V Mourtzouphlos should be put to death: c. 25, p. 34; c. 109, p. 126. See also the anticipation of the crusaders' justification of their actions in April 1204 in Isaac II's willingness, by way of acknowledging the role of the people of Constantinople in his rapid ascent to power, to allow them to break into the two imperial palaces and to reward themselves by looting the treasures that they find there: c. 24, pp. 30–2.

narrating the main plot arc, to the narrative now and the immediate perceptual awareness of characters in such moments.[221]

Because the narrator highlights characters' moment-by-moment experiences, and tends to introduce operative causes only at points of immediate plot need, it follows that a particular onus is placed upon the circumstances in which characters perceive and act upon changes in their circumstances and environment. One notable illustration of this within the workings of the plot is the movement of messengers between principals. This is so recurrent a motif that on a biographist reading one might be tempted to speculate that the historical Robert of Clari had himself performed this role, thereby predisposing him to give his fellow-messengers their narrative due. Certainly, a messenger (*message*) in this storyworld is more than just a courier or go-between: there are proper protocols, even courtly scripts, governing their proper reception;[222] their status, trappings and deportment can attract the admiring gaze of onlookers in their own right;[223] and they are invariably reliable and authoritative.[224] They even have a place in a compact and fast-moving scene, shuttling between the French leaders during the 'non-battle' of 17 July 1203.[225] Tempting as it might be, however, to imagine that the text's interest in messengers is an extension of Robert the author's personal experience, we should focus instead on its function as a story-telling device. The messengers help to slow down, and in some cases to formalize and solemnify, the action at moments of learning and discovery. Their use complements the device, which is also found in Villehardouin, whereby the recipient of a message does not immediately articulate his reaction to it but delays his response, thereby

[221] See e.g. RC, c. 41, p. 50, where Alexios III seems to be unaware of the crusade before it arrives on his doorstep.

[222] See the reception of the envoys to Venice on their return to France and the treatment of their Venetian companions: RC, c. 8, p. 10. See also the fair welcome – 'et molt fist biau sanlant as messages' – given by the future Alexios IV to the crusaders' envoys to Philip of Swabia's court: c. 30, p. 36.

[223] See RC, c. 19, p. 24: 'So the emperor [Manuel] sent his messengers to France, who were very high-ranking men and they went in great state; never did anyone see people going in greater or more noble state than they did, so that the king of France and his people marvelled at the great splendour which the messengers displayed.' Cf. the two splendidly accoutred knights sent by the crusade leaders to Philip of Swabia's court: c. 30, p. 36; and similarly the two high-ranking and richly equipped knights sent by Emperor Henry to Ioannitsa's successor Boril: c. 116, p. 132.

[224] See RC, c. 22, p. 30: 'When Isaac was crowned, the news went up and down until Andronicos knew about it…nor could he ever believe it until he sent out his messengers. When the messengers got there [Hagia Sophia], they saw that it was certainly true; so they went straight back to the emperor and said: "Sire, it is all true."' Cf. the ability of *messages* to locate the future Alexios III in a Saracen prison and negotiate his release: c. 26, p. 34. See also Alexios III's immediate reaction on learning of the crusaders' arrival, which is to send messengers: c. 41, p. 50.

[225] RC, c. 47, p. 60.

doubling the number of staged encounters that the imparting of the information requires.[226]

A corollary of the regular movement of messengers through the storyworld is the frequency with which characters learn by hearing. There is more of this device in Clari's text, page for page, than in any of the other works that we have considered, in large part a consequence of the narrator's careful policing of his story logic when he wants to move information across barriers or over long distances, or to suggest that a communicative act was not reducible to a single interaction.[227] Sometimes, hearing is the straightforward accompaniment of face-to-face meetings with messengers and other expressly identified interlocutors;[228] but it extends to situations, many involving the Byzantines, in which the informant is not specified or cannot be inferred from the story logic, or in which the information is to be understood as coming from multiple sources, as in the spread of rumour.[229]

Important as hearing is, however, to the ways in which the characters learn about their world, it is predominantly by means of sight that the narrator actualizes the short-term horizons of perception and understanding that we have seen dominate the characters' mind stuff in their action-by-action progress through the plot. The narrator seldom makes generalizations about recurrent events or identifies patterns of experience.[230] The result is an emphasis upon discrete and specific moments of action in which the actors' perceptions are to the fore. Consequently, most of the characters' focalization functions in relation to their immediate circumstances and is what motivates their reactions to events.[231]

[226] See e.g. Boniface of Montferrat's reaction to the messengers bearing the crusade leaders' summons: RC, c. 3, p. 6.

[227] See e.g. RC, c. 62, p. 76, where the barons learn of Alexios Mourtzouphlos's coup against Alexios IV from a message attached to an arrow shot from the city.

[228] E.g. RC, c. 30, p. 36; c. 33, p. 42; c. 59, p. 72; c. 80, p. 96; c. 94, p. 112; c. 100, p. 118.

[229] E.g. RC, c. 21, p. 24: Manuel learns of Andronicos's abduction of his sister, and then Andronicos hears reports ('oï dire') of Manuel's death; c. 21, p. 26: Andronicos hears that three survivors of his purge of the Byzantine elite are members of the Angeloi family; cc. 50–1, p. 64: Alexios III is told by the citizens of Constantinople that they will desert him unless he saves them from the Franks; c. 52, p. 64: the sultan of Iconium hears tell ('oï dire') of the crusaders' achievements; c. 67, p. 82: Alexios V hears the Greeks' criticism of his failure to defeat the Franks.

[230] But see the summary account of the crusaders passing the winter of 1202–3: RC, c. 16, pp. 18–20. The narrator's observation that many of the relatives of departing crusaders grieved is more likely to have been inspired by a topos of crusade preaching than based on direct observation of several such moments: c. 9, p. 10.

[231] Among numerous examples, see e.g. RC, c. 25, p. 32: Isaac II sees and then confronts Andronicos; c. 71, p. 86: the Greek defenders of Constantinople hurl down large stones when they see the attackers using siege engines; c. 75, p. 92: the attackers in siege towers do not move when they see the great throng of defenders on and below the

A clear example is the text's account of the fire ships that the Byzantines twice sent across the Golden Horn: the swift and effective counter-measures taken by the Venetians to protect their vessels are motivated by their acute acts of perception, which the narrator emphasizes by departing from his standard verb for seeing, *vire*.[232]

The narratorial focus upon the moment of apperception is tightened still further by the many references to characters' emotional responses to what they see. The stock example of this found in innumerable texts is, of course, the situation in which one side in an armed encounter flees before the other; if not expressly stated, feelings of terror are routinely to be inferred. There are several such moments in Clari's text.[233] But the narrator pushes beyond this cliché to depict affective reactions in a variety of interactions. The emotional taxonomy at the narrator's disposal is limited and predictable, but it manages to evoke a range of mental states that the reader or listener would readily surmise were expressed in visible ways. Thus in moments of focalization we encounter sadness and dismay;[234] anger;[235] joy and elation;[236] discomfort;[237] shock;[238] and outrage and sorrow.[239] Emotional reactions, or at least the implied emotional component of more complex responses, are also one of the few means by which the narrator acknowledges the possibility of variety and

---

wall; c. 108, p. 126: on seeing the captured Alexios V, Emperor Baldwin has him put in prison.

232 RC, c. 60, p. 74: 'Quant s'aperchoivent li Venicien'; 'quant li Venicien les raperchurent'. For the fire ships, see Queller and Madden, *Fourth Crusade*, pp. 157–8.

233 E.g. RC, c. 18, p. 22; c. 22, p. 28; c. 33, p. 42; c. 43, p. 52; c. 66, pp. 80–2; c. 76, p. 94; c. 78, p. 94. Cf. the variant fright response in which characters are immobilized: c. 45, pp. 56–8.

234 See e.g. RC, c. 3, p 6 for the text's most elaborate evocation of grief: when the crusaders learn of Theobald of Champagne's death, 'they were very sad, dismayed and distressed' ('si en furent molt dolent et molt corchié et molt esmari'). Cf. Andronicos's reaction to the sight of Isaac in Hagia Sophia: 'When he saw him, he was very upset' ('Quant il le vit, si en fu molt dolens'), and a moment later when his bow string breaks 'he was very dismayed and distressed' ('il en fu molt esmaris et molt esperdus'): c. 23, p. 30. See also c. 71, p. 86; c. 72, p. 86.

235 E.g. RC, c. 11, p. 12: when the doge and Venetians see the shortfall in the crusaders' payment of their debt 'they were very angry' ('si furent tout corchié'). See also c. 33, p. 44; c. 99, p. 118; c. 104, p. 120.

236 E.g. RC, c. 12, p. 14: 'they were overjoyed and fell at his [the doge's] feet with joy ('si en furent molt lié et se il caïrent as pies de goie'). See also c. 27, p. 36; c. 31, p. 38.

237 RC, c. 33, p. 42: 'When the marquis [Conrad] heard the news, he felt very uncomfortable' ('Quant li marchis oï ches nouveles, si ne fu mie a aise').

238 RC, c. 48, p. 62: 'they were so taken aback and shocked' ('furent si abaubi et si esbahi'). See also c. 74, p. 90.

239 RC, c. 100, p. 118: 'they were outraged and very annoyed' ('si en eurent molt grant engaingne et molt grant duel').

difference within groups, which otherwise tend to be treated as homogeneous units that unproblematically assume collective positions.[240] The temporal reach of characters' focalization occasionally extends beyond immediate reactions to some assessment of their longer-term needs. In most of these cases, however, a clear visual basis to what leads them to such judgements is implied by the characters' positioning within the diegesis at that particular juncture. In other words, 'to see that' (*vire que*) is to be understood as securely grounded in the actual act of seeing itself.[241]

The importance of the apprehending gaze extends into sequences in which perception and reaction are not simply devices with which to situate characters in a given narrative moment. They energize scenes, in the process gesturing towards their experiential quality. In this context, it should be noted that, in contrast to Ambroise and Villehardouin, Clari makes no use of the formula 'you would have seen' to co-opt the narratee's imaginative resources in the fleshing out of scenes; in other words, the onus is placed squarely on the gazes of the characters within the storyworld to achieve this vivifying effect for themselves. It is useful to quote some of these passages at length in order to capture something of their narrative 'sway', the movement of perception back and forth between sets of actors, typically when placed in situations of crisis or conflict. For example, in the analepsis that recounts the recent history of Byzantium, the emperor Andronicos attempts to flee Constantinople when he is ousted by Isaac II, but his boat is caught in a fierce storm that drives it back towards the city. There follows an exchange between Andronicos and his people that dramatizes their awareness of their predicament through the staging of multiple gazes, as well as by means of utterances that are strictly speaking redundant in rehearsing what is already known to themselves and to the reader/listener:

> When they saw that they were beached and could not continue, Andronicos said to his people: 'Lords, see where we are.' They looked and saw for certain [*virrent bien*] that they had come back to Constantinople, so they said to

[240] RC, c. 11, p. 12: some Venetians respond enthusiastically to the doge's suggestion that half their number should join the crusade fleet, whereas others demur; c. 62, p. 76: the barons differ in their reactions to the news of Alexios IV's death.

[241] E.g. c. 10, p. 10: the crusaders see that they cannot all lodge in the city of Venice; c. 12, p. 14: the doge sees, presumably on the basis of visual and other evidence, that the crusaders cannot fully discharge their debt; c. 14, p. 18: on seeing the siege engines set up outside their city, the people of Zara realize that they cannot resist; c. 28, p. 36: the tutor to the future Alexios IV sees the danger posed by Alexios III's coup; c. 34, p. 44: Guy of Lusignan sees that he is shut out of Tyre and changes course to Acre; c. 36, p. 46: Conrad of Montferrat appreciates the severity of the famine in Tyre; c. 57, p. 70: the barons who stay in Constantinople while others campaign with Alexios IV see that Isaac II is not paying the moneys owed to them; c. 79, p. 96: when the Greeks see that Alexios V has fled the city, they elect Laskers (Constantine Lascaris) emperor.

> Andronicos: 'My lord, we are dead, for we have come back to Constantinople.' When Andronicos heard this, he was dismayed for he did not know what to do.[242]

The emphasis upon visual apprehension, even at the expense of the repetition of information that has already been supplied, carries forward into the sequence that immediately follows. Indirect discourse capturing the terms of the companions' outburst adds to the several references to the act of seeing and further fixes the reader's or listener's attention upon the characters' moment-by-moment perceptions and reactions in the narrative now:

> They replied that they could not go any further, even if someone were to cut off their heads. When they saw that in no way could they go any further, they took Andronicos, the emperor, and led him to an inn and hid him behind the barrels. The innkeeper and his wife looked carefully at these people and were definitely of the opinion that they were followers of Andronicos, the emperor, with the result that when the wife of the innkeeper went by chance amongst the barrels to see that they were properly closed, looking all around she saw Andronicos behind the barrels with all his imperial robes, and she recognized him perfectly.[243]

Sight also facilitates fast-moving scenes in which characters must react to sudden changes and opportunities with particular dexterity. For example, in the same lengthy analepsis on the vicissitudes of the Byzantine imperial throne, sight, either stated or implied by the presence of visually striking props and a sense of close physical interaction, saves Isaac Angelos, who has just seized the moment and killed the henchman whom the emperor Andronicos had sent to murder him. He is propelled towards his imperial destiny as his perception of the possibilities available to him progressively enlarges. Isaac works his way through the crowd towards Hagia Sophia, in the process inaugurating the relationship with the people of Constantinople that will soon play a significant role in his becoming emperor:

> When the men at arms and the people who were with the steward saw that the young man had cut through the steward in this way, they took to flight. When the young man saw that they were fleeing, he took the horse of the steward whom he had killed, mounted it and brandished his sword which was all bloody...All along the route he called out for mercy to the people who were in the streets, who were all dismayed by the uproar which they had heard.[244]

[242] RC, c. 25, p. 32.
[243] RC, c. 25, p. 32: translation slightly revised.
[244] RC, c. 22, p. 28. For the decisive role played by the people of the city in elevating Isaac

In a similar manner, sight drives a remarkable cascading of perceptions and reactions as the defenders see that the crusaders have gained a foothold on the walls of Constantinople during the assault on 12 April 1204. Andrew of Dureboise leads the way, the reader/listener invited to picture the posture and bearing that he presents to his opponents in one of the multi-storey wooden towers that the defenders have recently erected along the walls:

> And when he was upright, he drew his sword. When they saw him standing up, they were so taken aback and were so frightened that they fled down a storey. When those on that storey saw that the men from the floor above were running away, they vacated that storey, nor did they dare stay there any longer. [More Latins follow Andrew's lead.] ...And when those on the other storeys down below saw that the tower was filling up with Franks, they were so frightened that none of them dared stay; instead they abandoned the tower completely.[245]

In a number of sequences, sight is not simply something that equips actors to understand their immediate environment; it expressly forms part of the self-awareness that they bring to their action, the ultimate aim of the narrator being to reconcile conflicting gazes and to harmonize them within a single and coherent view of the unfolding situation. For instance, much of the agon that drives the interactions between the French leaders during the 'non-battle' of July 1203 involves competing acts of vision. On the advice of some of his followers, Baldwin of Flanders withdraws his squadron, which forms the French vanguard, for fear that it will become cut off from the crusaders' camp.[246] This manoeuvre is spotted by those leading the formations behind him and a back and forth of gazes ensues, the experiential quality of the moment once again accentuated by character rehearsal of the obvious as well as by the use of direct and indirect discourse:

> When the squadron of the count of St-Pol and the lord Peter of Amiens saw the count of Flanders retreat, they all said together that the count of Flanders was acting very shamefully in retreating as he had the vanguard. And they all said: 'Lord, lord, the count of Flanders is retreating! Since he is withdrawing, he is leaving you the vanguard. For God's sake let us take it!' So the barons agreed together and said that they would take the van. When the count of Flanders saw

to the throne, see c. 22, pp. 28–30; c. 24, pp. 30–2. For a similarly fast-paced scene shot through with acts of visual perception and prompt reaction, in this instance the confrontation between Conrad of Montferrat and the Byzantine rebel Vernas (Alexios Branas), see c. 33, pp. 40–2. See also the battle scenes in c. 66, pp. 80–2 and c. 71, p. 86.

[245] RC, c. 74, p. 90: punctuation of translation slightly amended.

[246] RC, c. 47, pp. 58–60.

> that the count of St-Pol and the lord Peter of Amiens were not turning back, he sent a messenger to them to ask them to turn back.[247]

There follows a toing and froing of messengers, after which the formation led by Hugh of St-Pol and Peter of Amiens presses on towards the Byzantine position. And when those in the French camp perceive what is happening, the direction in which they point their gaze and their exhortation to others to share it play out their support of Hugh's and Peter's actions as against those of Baldwin: 'and all those in the camp who had remained behind began to shout after them: "Look, look! ['Veés, veés!'] The count of St-Pol and the lord Peter of Amiens are going to engage the enemy… Look! ['Veés!']"'[248]

It is perhaps unsurprising that one of the most intense and sustained mobilizations of sight in order to energize an action sequence occurs in the passage that we have already encountered in which the party of crusaders under Peter of Amiens, Robert's brother Aleaumes to the fore, force their way into Constantinople by opening up a hole in a disused postern gate.[249] As we noted earlier, it is superficially tempting to suppose that the concentration of gazes and visual markers that is a pronounced feature of this sequence relates in some way to Robert's autopsy. That is to say, as Robert composed his work, his episodic recall of that slice of the narrated action in which he was most personally and actively involved – though, as we have seen, the narrator does not expressly make the identification between author and actor – activated visually rich memories that were duly worked into the fabric of the narrative. This is the sort of supposition that we often make when we encounter authors-as-characters placed particularly close to events; references to sensory awareness are easily read as markers of autobiographical reminiscence rising to the surface of the text. It is indeed possible that some of the gazes in the sequence have a basis in specific autobiographical memories on Robert's part, in particular that suggested by the reference to the attackers' own impressions when they finally open up an aperture and peer through into the city beyond: 'they looked through and saw so many people of all ranks that it seemed ['que sanloit'] that half the world was there, so that they did not dare risk entering there'.[250] But, as noted above, we should not make too much of this moment of apparent autoptic immediacy, for the image of the intrepid attackers looking into the city and their hyperbolic reactions to what they see are arguably reality effects, just like, perhaps, the detail that Peter grabs Aleaumes by the foot as he tries to crawl through the gap on all fours.[251]

[247] RC, c. 47, p. 60: translation slightly revised.
[248] RC, c. 47, p. 60: translation slightly revised.
[249] RC, cc. 75–7, pp. 92–4.
[250] RC, c. 75, p. 92: translation slightly revised.
[251] RC, c. 76, p. 92.

This moment is, moreover, part of a longer and more complex sequence involving slices of action and multiple gazes in which Robert the character is not directly implicated, and in which Robert the historical actor could not have been consistently and closely involved. The sequence begins just after the assault on the walls mentioned above. Peter of Amiens realizes that the crusaders' attack is in danger of stalling (he 'saw that the men in the towers were not advancing'),[252] and he conceives the idea of leading his followers onto the sliver of land between the sea and the foot of the walls. They look around, spot the bricked-up postern and set to work on it with various tools. Making a hole, they look within, as we have seen. Then Aleaumes, whom the narrator has just informed us already has a track record of brave deeds second only to Peter of Bracieux, takes over.[253] Realizing that no one else has the nerve to enter, he does so himself. Once inside, Aleaumes focalizes the defenders' efforts at resistance and reacts in a suitably bold and odds-defying manner, the mismatch between his dagger and the huge missiles launched at him bordering on the comedic: 'When he was inside a really large number of those Greeks ran at him. And the ones on top of the walls began to throw down enormous stones. When the priest saw this, he took out his knife and charged them, making them all flee before him like cattle.'[254] He then urges Peter of Amiens to follow him in by describing the scene as it presents itself to his gaze: 'I can see that they are in great disarray and are turning in flight.'[255]

At this juncture, the focalization of the defenders briefly takes over: we are told that they are so terrified by the sight of Peter's party forcing an entry into the city that they abandon a large section of the city wall. Then a further shift of focalization is effected, cuing the narrator's signature back and forth of gazes in the playing out of the sequence: Alexios V, positioned nearby, sees that Peter of Amiens's force is on foot and makes a pretence of attacking; Peter sees this and encourages his people to resist; Alexios then sees that the crusaders are going to stand firm and so withdraws to his tent; Peter in his turn sees this and orders a group of his men to force open one of the city's gates. Then those outside see that the gate has been opened and begin to enter the city. Alexios now resumes

[252] RC, c, 75, p. 92: 'vit que chil qui estoient es tours ne se mouvoient'.

[253] RC, c. 75, p. 92. The mention of Aleaumes's feats of arms in the capture of the 'tower of Galata' ('tor de Galatha') is sometimes taken to refer to the narrative now of the assault being led by Peter of Amiens on 12 April 1204, as if this were the name of that part of the city wall under attack. This is incorrect. The reference is to the crusaders' successful assault, on 5 July 1203, on the tower on the other side of the Golden Horn that guarded the defensive chain across the mouth of the inlet, an episode that the text has in fact already mentioned: cc. 43–4, pp. 52–4. For this earlier attack and its strategic significance for the crusaders, see Queller and Madden, *Fourth Crusade*, pp. 114–18; Phillips, *Fourth Crusade*, pp. 166–70.

[254] RC, c. 76, pp. 92–4.

[255] RC, c. 76, p. 94: translation revised.

the role of focalizer: seeing the Franks pouring in he flees so precipitously that he abandons his tents and jewels (which subsequently fall to Peter of Bracieux as a kind of implied reward for his status as the most accomplished warrior in the army). Then the remaining defenders on the walls see that the Franks are inside and that Alexios has fled, and they too run off, whereupon this breathless sequence is concluded with the narrator's concise remark that 'in this way was the city taken'.[256]

This striking passage is modulated throughout by characters' perceptions and the understandings they form as a consequence. The spatial orientations that the narrator supplies in order to build up the diegesis are fairly sparse: there is simply the top-to-bottom alignment of the attackers by the postern and the defenders on the walls, and the within-without of the city space. But the multiple gazes in the sequence work like lines of sight shooting across the diegetic space and binding it and the action together. In addition, in this sequence the workings of sight contribute to a well-wrought hour-glass structure: we begin with the progress of the general assault on the city; Peter of Amiens's gaze initiates the process of narrowing the action down to the deeds of his party at the postern; thereupon Aleaumes's gaze moves as he moves from outside to inside the city, and the narrator's focus of attention moves with him; Peter's perceptions follow suit as he resumes his focus upon the needs and progress of the overall assault; and Alexios's reactions to what he sees confirm that the scale of the action has broadened once again, for now nothing less than the success of the whole assault and the Latins' gaining control of the city are at stake. Sight is the connective tissue between the various plot cruxes in this complex sequence. And it is the deft use of visual focalization to effect a fast-paced narrative glissando, from large to small to large again, that best explains the apparently 'autobiographical' details in the postern scene, not particularly vivid personal recollections breaking, as it were, the narrative plane.

Given that characters' motivations in the narrative are so closely linked to stimuli in their immediate environment, it is unsurprising that several sequences do not merely depend on this mechanism in order to propel the action forward but actually stage the manner in which sight functions as a means of discovery and a route to correct understanding. One striking example involves the text's most direct and self-highlighting foray into forms of *mise-en-scène* and character deportment redolent of chivalric romance. Although the 'non-battle' of July 1203 does not involve an actual clash of arms in the narrator's telling, it is nonetheless used to depict aristocratic values being visibly acted out.[257] This is affirmed by

[256] RC, cc. 76–8, p. 94. What immediately follows switches tack to the crusaders' longer-term approach to securing control of the city.

[257] Cf. Varvaro, 'Esperienza e racconto', pp. 1413–14.

the fact that the Franks' manoeuvres are the object of approving gazes that evoke the viewing of a tournament:

> And the ladies and the maidens of the palace had come up to the windows and other people from the city, both women and young girls, had climbed on the city walls to watch that squadron ride past and the emperor [Alexios III] on the other side, and they were saying to each other that it looked as if ours were made up of such very handsome angels, because they were so richly armed and their horses so finely caparisoned.[258]

It is also noteworthy that some of the moments in the text in which characters are confronted with the frustration of their plans, or when an ironic distance is set up between their perceptions and intentions and the reader or listener's knowledge of how matters will turn out, involve contested understandings of the meaning of a scene. The most revealing example is the incident that we have seen is also narrated in Villehardouin's *Conquête*, when the doge parades the pretender Alexios to those gathered on the walls of Constantinople, only to be met by ignorance and indifference.[259] Unlike Villehardouin, however, Clari repeats the plot device when he has Boniface of Montferrat display his wife Maria, the widow of Isaac II, and her two children by her former husband to those assembled on the walls of Adrianople. Eventually an old man recognizes Maria but neatly undermines Boniface's ambitions to exploit his wife's and her children's imperial background to gain Greek support by insisting on a precondition for the townspeople's submission that, in its near-impossibility, amounts to an act of confident defiance: 'Go to Constantinople and have him [one of the children] crowned. And when he has sat on the throne of Constantine, and we know that, then we will do with him what we should.'[260]

Other misfires of visual perception have major plot repercussions. In the text's account of the disastrous battle of Adrianople, the Franks' haughty misreading of the Cumans' appearance, dressed as they are in animal skins, is immediately followed by the Cumans' devastating and deadly charge; the consequences of

[258] RC, c. 47, p. 60. Subsequently, when the emperor retreats into the city, the *dames*, *demiseles* and others reprove him severely for his failure to engage so few Franks with the large force under his command: c. 48, p. 62.

[259] RC, c. 41, p. 50. Cf. *Conquête*, §§145–6, pp. 146–8, trans. pp. 38–9.

[260] RC, c. 101, p. 120. On a third occasion, however, the act of parading evidence before walls has its desired effect when the people of Constantinople are shown the icon of Our Lady that the crusaders have captured in battle, thereby exposing Alexios V Mourtzouphlos's attempts to cover up this fact: RC, cc. 66–7, p. 82. Cf. Villehardouin's version of this incident in *Conquête*, §228, p. 28, trans. p. 61, which emphasizes the importance that the Greeks attached to the icon but does not mention the Franks' parading of it.

the Franks' misjudgement are visited upon them without delay.[261] And in the sequence on the history of the Latin East within the analepsis concerning Conrad of Montferrat, a visual misfire is actually contrived: a plan is devised to thwart the Saracens' naval blockade of Tyre by staging a break-out that the enemy, it is correctly anticipated, will misinterpret because they will react precipitously to what they see.[262] When the Christian scheme succeeds and the Saracens are defeated, the fact that they have misread the situation is further emphasized by the sheer impotence of the gaze of one of their number, their leader no less, once the fact that they have fallen into a trap becomes clear. The narrator adds a striking scene of helpless viewing from afar which is oddly reminiscent of Thucydides's remarkable treatment of the naval battle off Syracuse that we noted in the Introduction.[263] Although Clari could not have known of this passage in Thucydides, the staging, lines of sight and character reactions are strikingly similar:

> And Saladin watched all this, lamenting all too bitterly, pulling his beard and tearing his hair in grief, for he could see his people being cut up before his eyes and was unable to help them. When he had lost his fleet, he broke camp and went away.[264]

In most of Clari's text most of the time actors' perceptions are attuned to the narrator's construction of the storyworld; the understandings they form and the inferences they draw seem to be a matter of common sense within the parameters of the story logic, and they are typically vindicated by the way in which events play out. But as these examples illustrate, the narrator is also drawn to visual misfires that dramatize the importance of sight in his characters' world. Nowhere is this staged with greater pathos and irony than when Alexios V prematurely celebrates the Greeks' repulse of the assault on Constantinople on 9 April 1204, aggressively inviting the gaze of his subjects in order to gain their approval of him as their deliverer, while apparently unaware that the crusaders will, of course, soon be back:

> When Mourtzouphlos saw that the pilgrims had withdrawn, he began to have his drums and trumpets sounded and to make an exceedingly loud noise and summoned his people and began to say: 'See [*Vées*], lords, am I not a good emperor? You have never had such a good emperor. Haven't I done well? We have no reason to fear them; I will have them all hanged and disgraced.'[265]

[261] RC, c. 112, p. 128.
[262] RC, cc. 36–7, pp. 46–8.
[263] See above, pp. 13–14.
[264] RC, c. 37, p. 48.
[265] RC, c. 71, p. 86: translation revised.

Scholarly assessments of the narrative's visual confrontation with the people and places that the crusaders encounter rightly draw particular attention to its description of Constantinople and its wonders, which occupies a substantial portion of the text.[266] Although the sequence in which some of the major buildings and other notable sites in the city are described makes no sense as an actual itinerary, it is clear that many of the narrator's remarks must have some basis in direct personal observation. Ruth Macrides has, moreover, made a good case for supposing that Clari was not the naïve tourist fed tall tales by local guides as he wandered, wide eyed and gullible, through Constantinople's cityscape, as has often been supposed; rather, he was a discriminating and reflective observer.[267] True, the vocabulary at the narrator's disposal to register the aesthetic qualities of what is encountered is extremely limited. But there seems to be some thoughtful attention to the ways in which the residents of the city themselves understood and explained their environment, as evidenced for example by their interpretation of supposedly prophetic inscriptions on various monuments. There is also something of an idealized quality about the description of the city, for although this passage is placed after the text's account of the fall of Constantinople in April 1204, it would have perhaps made better sense to have inserted it after the restoration of Isaac II and the coronation of Alexios IV in July 1203, after which the crusaders had relatively easy access to the city and its sights. The description does not seem to take into account the enormous damage that was done to Constantinople in and before April 1204, in particular by three hugely destructive fires. For, as Varvaro argues, the text essentially treats the city as a prize that redounds to the glory of those who had conquered it.[268]

However much Clari the historical actor would have had opportunities to familiarize himself with Constantinople, however, the description of the city in the text is not narrated as a series of personal reminiscences. While there is some interesting attention to the city as a space existing in past time, and also some elements that are described with reference to specific moments of discovery on

[266] RC, cc. 82–92, pp. 100–10. For this passage, see R. J. Macrides, 'Constantinople: The Crusaders' Gaze', in R. J. Macrides (ed.), *Travel in the Byzantine World: Papers from the Thirty-Fourth Spring Symposium of Byzantine Studies, Birmingham, April 2000* (Society for the Promotion of Byzantine Studies Publications, 10; Aldershot, 2002), pp. 193–212, esp. 195–6, 197–211. See also P. Schreiner, 'Robert de Clari und Konstantinopel', in C. Sode and S. Takács (eds), *Novum Millennium: Studies on Byzantine History and Culture Dedicated to Paul Speck* (Aldershot, 2001), pp. 337–56. Cf. the insightful remarks of Varvaro, 'Esperienza e racconto', pp. 1420–3; Mölk, 'Robert de Clari', 217–19.

[267] Macrides, 'Constantinople', esp. pp. 199–210.

[268] Varvaro, 'Esperienza e racconto', pp. 1421–3. For the three fires that cumulatively did enormous damage to the city, in July 1203, August 1203 (this was especially destructive) and April 1204, see Madden, 'Fires of the Fourth Crusade', 72–93.

the Franks' part, there is no mention of the circumstances in the author's own recent past when he saw the buildings, objects and monuments that attract the narrator's attention. In addition, scholars have paid insufficient attention to a series of connected passages in the text before the Constantinople sequence which, in anticipating it, draws much of its sting. Here we find the text's deftest interweaving of its structural, thematic and substantive strands. The aptly chosen hook is the crusade fleet, for as it progresses from Venice to Constantinople it grants the narrator a number of opportunities to stage confrontations in which characters' reactions to its impressive appearance – as well as its auditory qualities – are emphasized. First the fleet departs from Venice itself, the sensations of those present emphasized in one of the text's most direct and expansive evocations of the quality of lived experience in the narrative now:

> The galley in which he [the doge] was was all scarlet [*vermeille*], and it had an awning spread above him of scarlet silk; for there were four silver trumpets sounding in front of him and drums which throbbed joyfully, and all the important men, the priests and laymen, the great and the lowly, showed such great joy at the sailing that never was there such joy nor was such a fleet seen or heard, and so the pilgrims made all the priests and clerics climb up to the poops of the ships to sing *Veni creator spiritus*. Everyone, high and low, wept with the emotion and the great joy that they were feeling. And when the fleet sailed from the harbour of Venice...it was the most beautiful sight to see since the beginning of the world...When they were out to sea, they spread their sails and their banners were hung high on the fighting tops of the ships with their standards, so that it seemed as if the whole sea was billowing and blazing with the ships that they were sailing and from the great joy that they were displaying.[269]

This passage does not simply seek to capture the sense of anticipation and excitement of a one-off and unrepeatable moment as the great undertaking gets under way. Because the fleet functions as a spectacle unto itself, further stagings of the impression that it makes on observers are possible. Sure enough, almost immediately the first to be impressed are the citizens of Pola, one of the cities on the Adriatic under Venice's control, where the fleet takes on fresh supplies. Note how the narrator presumes to speak confidently and knowledgeably about the populace's collective reaction, which is highlighted by the use of indirect speech. Note also the manner in which the reading of exterior, empirical evidence and the making of qualitative judgements are rolled together:

> If they [the crusaders] had been joyful and celebrating greatly earlier, they were celebrating as much or even more, so that the townspeople wondered very

[269] RC, c. 13, p. 16: translation slightly revised.

much at the great joy and at the great fleet and the great nobility [*nobleche*] that they showed. And indeed they said, and it was true, that such a fine [*biaus*] and powerful [*rikes*] fleet had never been seen or assembled in any land as was gathered there.[270]

The fear subsequently felt by the people of Zara when they see the 'great fleet' is dealt with succinctly, without expatiating further on the visual impression that it made on them.[271] Similarly, what is actually there to be perceived when the pretender Alexios joyfully sees the crusade ships for the first time off Corfu is only implied.[272] But when the fleet reaches Constantinople, the narrator ramps up its visual impact once more, his repetitions gaining in emphasis what they lose in nuance:

> When the whole fleet and all the vessels were together, they decked out and decorated their vessels so beautifully that it was the most beautiful sight to see in the world. When the people of Constantinople saw this fleet, which was so richly adorned, they looked on in wonder. And they climbed on the walls and on the houses to behold this marvel. And those in the fleet gazed at the size of the city, which was so long and wide that they were overcome with amazement.[273]

A little later, after the abortive displaying of the prince Alexios from aboard the doge's galley and as the crusaders mass for an attack, it is the Greeks' reactions to the sight of the Latins, rather than the reciprocated gaze, which is once again emphasized by the narrator's reference to their experience:

> When the citizens saw this great fleet and navy and they heard the noise of the trumpets and the tabors, which were making such a din, they all armed themselves and climbed on to the houses and the rooftops of the city. It seemed to them that the whole sea and the land trembled and that the sea was completely covered by ships.[274]

By the time, therefore, that we are told, in a rather abrupt insertion of a narrative passage into the description of Constantinople, that the pilgrims marvelled at the size of the city, its palaces, abbeys and wonders, and especially at Hagia Sophia and its riches, this has already been more than counterbalanced by references to the visual impression that the Latins made on the Greeks.[275] Not

[270] RC, c. 13, p. 16: translation slightly revised.
[271] RC, c. 14, p. 16.
[272] RC, c. 31, p. 38.
[273] RC, c. 40, pp. 48–50: punctuation slightly revised.
[274] RC, c. 42, p. 52: punctuation slightly revised.
[275] RC, c. 84, p. 102.

that Constantinople falls short as a source of great wonder: the Franks are said, for example, to have marvelled at the Hippodrome, or 'Games of the Emperor' ('Jus l'Empereeur'), clearly something beyond their previous experience. But the old-fashioned image of uncouth barbarians at large amidst the wonders of a superior civilization needs to be set aside.[276] In Clari's telling, the crusaders contrive, command and appreciate their own spectacle as well as perceiving that of their eventual opponents; and ultimately they are the victors in the contest of the spectacular, for their spectacle resides in their fleet and thus in their military power and the value system that undergirds it. Their spectacle, moreover, speaks to the crusaders' domination of the narrative now and the agency and movement that express that domination, in contrast to the ways in which Constantinople is experienced by a visitor – as a residue of past achievements, the site of prophetic anticipations of the coming of the Latins, and the passive, static recipient of the crusaders' appropriating gaze.

The two accounts of the Fourth Crusade by Geoffrey of Villehardouin and Robert of Clari have a good deal in common beyond the fact that they are both 'eyewitness sources' in the conventional sense of that term. In both, the ethical alignment of their narratives amounts to close adhesion to the value system of the northern French aristocracy. As we have seen, the argument that Clari was exercised by a fracture between the noble elite and the so-called 'poor' knights is certainly exaggerated.[277] What one finds are simply narratorial expressions of regret that there were some moments of injudicious lordship which threatened the usually harmonious relationship between the elite and the lesser knights who depended on their patronage. If anything, the values that the two groups share are accentuated in order to enhance the image of unity asserting itself whenever disunity threatens.[278] Villehardouin's text, too, aligns itself consistently and unambiguously with aristocratic views of the world. In a few places the narrator seems to suggest that he is attuned to the experience of the whole crusade host and can consequently speak to its collective mood.[279] But it is overwhelmingly

[276] RC, c. 90, pp. 106–8.

[277] Cf. Dufournet, *Les écrivains*, ii, pp. 378–80; Mölk, 'Robert de Clari', 220–2.

[278] See e.g. the even-handed treatment of Simon de Montfort and Enguerrand of Boves when they choose not to participate in the attack on Zara in RC, c. 14, p. 18, in contrast to the negative judgement on them and others in the same situation in *Conquête*, §§109–10, pp. 110–12, trans. p. 30. See also the verdict on the crusade placed in the mouth of the sultan of Iconium to the effect that the crusaders' achievements were characterized by conspicuous aristocratic virtue and prowess ('molt grant barnage et molt grant proeche'): RC, c. 52, pp. 64–6.

[279] See e.g. *Conquête*, §225, p. 24, trans. p. 60, where the narrator observes that the clergy's reassurances that fighting the Greeks was just and earned spiritual reward for those who fell 'was a great comfort to the barons and the pilgrims'.

an aristocratic collective understanding, in an aristocratic idiom, that he articulates.[280] This is brought out particularly clearly early in the text in the consonance between a narratorial judgement, reinforced by a quite rare counterfactual, and the stated sentiments of the crusade leaders. In praising the Venetians for keeping to their side of the contract agreed in 1201 and expressing regret that many crusaders evaded their responsibilities, the narrator expostulates:

> Oh! What great damage was done when the others who went to different ports did not go to Venice! Christendom would certainly have been exalted and the land of the Turks laid low! The Venetians had fulfilled their side of the agreement very well and more besides [*et plus assez*].[281]

A few sentences later the barons themselves repeat exactly the same sentiments, the force of their argument increased by the use of direct speech:

> 'Sirs, the Venetians have upheld our agreement to the letter and have done more besides [*et plus assez*], but we do not have nearly enough people to pay them what we owe with fees of passage. This is the fault of those who went to other ports.'[282]

This repetition primes the reader to situate the narrator's ethical positioning in all that follows in this close alignment with the perspectives of the crusade's leadership.

To a large extent because of their adhesion to the collective values of the aristocracy, neither narrator chooses to stand out from the crowd as an intradiegetic, gaze-directing, information-acquiring individual actor at large within the storyworld. But it is in the manner in which the two texts work with, or around, this shared narratorial reticence that they begin to go their separate ways. For Villehardouin, the use of third-person self-reference formally excludes the possibility of a first-person homodiegetic gaze on the action, and by extension precise line-of-sight orientations in relation to the action as it unfolds. Likewise, it is participation in the crusade's decision-making councils, not autopsy in itself, that the narrator singles out as the principal basis of his authority. The narrator

[280] Cf. the repetition of the idea that the crusade's leaders were just below the level of kings: 'the most exalted of men without crowns' ('li plus haut home qui soient sanz corone'): *Conquête*, §16, p. 18, trans. p. 8; 'the best of men among those who do not wear crowns' ('la meillor gent qui soient sanz corone'): §143, p. 142, trans. p. 37. It is noteworthy that these descriptions are especially validated by being placed in the mouths of two high-ranking outsiders, the doge Enrico Dandolo and the emperor Alexios III, respectively.

[281] *Conquête*, §57, p. 58, trans. p. 18.

[282] *Conquête*, §59, p. 60, trans. p. 18.

wants to be noted for his candour, but to share the means by which he came by information, at least outside the baronial councils, is not a priority. Moreover, Villehardouin the character does not function as a privileged site of focalization; and even in the most sustained sequence in which he is, relatively briefly, central to the plot, during the retreat from Adrianople, he is not granted any greater experiential depth or autoptic acuity than those accorded others in similar predicaments elsewhere in the narrative. There are a few suggestions of personal episodic memory adding to the texture of certain scenes, but these are neither very common nor emphasized. In the same way, reality effects that mimic the specificity of episodic recall are infrequent, and the use of hyperbole does not as a rule extend to the visual. The potential for interesting reflection on the Latins' perceptions of their new environment is glimpsed in the motif of the misidentification of friendly forces, but this is little developed.

Significantly, too, the narrator's allegiance to the crusade as a corporate exercise does not incline him to sublimate the individual gaze within collective understandings. There are some passages in the *Conquête* which suggest a potential to linger on scenes and to evoke the crusaders' visual experiences, for example in acknowledging the impulse to go sight-seeing in Constantinople: 'Now you may know that many people from the army went to look at Constantinople, its sumptuous palaces, its many impressive churches and it great riches, of which no other city ever had as many.'[283] But this is not a recurrent device over the course of the narrative. Archambault's verdict on Villehardouin that 'his visual memory remains poor, rough, and discolored' has some merit, therefore, though it transposes onto the person of the author remarks that properly apply to the narrator's modest exploitation of the visual in the fashioning of the storyworld.[284] Of the mental capacities of Villehardouin the historical actor we can know nothing, and while the narrative craft on show in the *Conquête* has many limitations, we do not need to appeal to supposed personal shortcomings to account for them.[285] The hints in the text that a fuller engagement with the crusade's visual dimension could have been attempted reveal that its relative absence is a matter of narrative strategy. Jeanette Beer captures the position well when she ascribes Villehardouin's 'astonishing lack of physical description' to an emphasis on

[283] *Conquête*, §192, p. 194, trans. p. 51.

[284] *Seven French Chroniclers*, p. 39.

[285] See e.g. *Conquête*, §§380–1, 385, pp. 188, 190, 194, trans. pp. 102, 103, in which the narrator misses the opportunity to express or imply a sense of irony or to sound a note of criticism when 20,000 slow-moving Armenians, whom Henry of Hainaut has brought over to Thrace from Asia Minor after they had helped him against the Greeks, are left behind in his desire to react quickly to news of the disaster at Adrianople and are then all captured or killed by local people, even though Henry had been 'confident that they would be able to make their own way in safety and had no reason to be fearful'.

action that limits graphic detail to what is immediately required by the plot or is embedded in the choice of action verb.[286] Just as Villehardouin the historical actor's autopsy in relation to the totality of events narrated in the *Conquête* tends to be exaggerated because insufficient attention is paid to the multiplication of the foci of attention in the latter half of the text dealing with the emergent Latin empire, so the impact of narratorial autopsy and character focalization is more restricted than in any other text included in this study.

As we have seen, Clari's *explicit* stakes out an authority grounded in the fact of participation in the crusade and in autopsy, in contrast to Villehardouin's narrower emphasis upon knowledge of how the crusade was run. Before this concluding statement, however, as we read the body of the narrative we find ourselves confronted by the same sort of challenge that is presented by Villehardouin in matching 'flashbulb'-like details to the possible workings of authorial episodic memory, given the absence of a perceiving and experiencing intradiegetic narrator at large in the storyworld. It is arguable that, compared with Villehardouin, there is a greater density of autoptic memory informing the choice of throwaway detail and the manner in which it is built into the text: witness, for example, the narrator's observation that ten herons (probably in fact storks) nested on the equestrian statue of Heraclius (*recte* Justinian) on a column near Hagia Sophia.[287] But it is always hazardous to attach too much significance to such apparent autoptic traces. We are on firmer ground, however, in distinguishing between Clari's and Villehardouin's approaches to the visual in four key respects. First, Clari's narrator is much more attuned to the notion that the experience of going on crusade translated, at certain times at any rate, into visually vivid or otherwise striking scenes. This is registered at several junctures. For example, when the French barons encounter someone who is identified as the 'king of Nubia', his physical appearance and the remarkable story of long-distance pilgrimage that he tells are such that the barons stare at him in astonishment.[288] Similarly, when Alexios III's soldiers catch sight of a makeshift force of cooks and grooms thrown together in order to strengthen the Frankish line before the non-battle of 17 July 1203, they are paralyzed by fear because the appearance of these irregulars is so hideous.[289] Second, just as Clari's family memory of the crusade, as embodied by his brother Aleaumes, concentrates on receiving fair judgement from one senior lord and fighting conspicuously bravely alongside another, we need to get away from the traditional image of Clari the 'simple knight', whatever that actually means. In particular, we should put aside the notion of Clari as an innocent abroad; this is untenable in light of the text's

[286] *Villehardouin*, pp. 98–103.
[287] RC, c. 86, p. 104. Cf. Dembowski, *La chronique*, pp. 113–14.
[288] RC, c. 54, pp. 66–8. See Kinoshita, *Medieval Boundaries*, pp. 158–60.
[289] RC, c. 45, pp. 56–8.

description of Constantinople, which suggests a discriminating eye as well as an appreciation of the fact that places and spaces do not reduce to their surface appearances, but are, rather, animated and made explicable by the ways in which people interact with them, the stories that are told about them, and the reactions that they elicit in the viewer.

Third, Clari's narrative engages much more fully with sight, and also to some extent hearing, as the means by which characters gain understandings of their world and of the movement of events. As the narration of the way in which Boniface of Montferrat was co-opted into the crusade's leadership illustrates, the foregrounding of characters' acts of discovery is accentuated by an emphasis on the narrative now as the operative horizon of experience. In the relative absence of prior understandings and long-term perspectives – the main apparent exception, Boniface's long-standing grudge against Byzantium, is, revealingly, poorly motivated in being opaque about why Boniface actually nursed his vengeful feelings – sight becomes the principal epistemic resource that characters have at their disposal as they move through the storyworld. Fourth, and related to this, in several sequences of the narrative verbs of seeing are densely concentrated: sight criss-crosses the action and animates it. For, as Alberto Varvaro suggests, the visual ultimately functions as an index of the crusaders' achievement, which the narrator equates with display and appearance.[290] The contest of spectacle is won by the crusaders over the Byzantines; and the spectacular becomes a central element of the project announced at the beginning of the text, to tell 'the story of those who conquered Constantinople'.[291] The most pointed contrast between Villehardouin's and Clari's accounts of the Fourth Crusade, then, is that between, on the one hand, a notionally 'eyewitness' text that in fact downplays the visual and, on the other, a narrative that creatively builds it into its ethical programme and plot design.

[290] Varvaro, 'Esperienza e racconto', pp. 1413–19.
[291] RC, c. 1, p. 2.

Conclusion

Eyewitnessing is deeply ingrained in our understanding of the world. To repeat a point made in the Introduction, this is not to detract from those for whom sight plays little or no part in their sensory purchase on their environment. As the numerous figurative extensions of the semantic range of light and sight in many languages reveal, however, there are powerful associations between the act of seeing and the means by which people form understandings of the world. This connection extends into the reasons why the study of people in the past is interesting, for, irrespective of the cultural differences that separate past societies from our own, we trust that historical actors lived in states of moment-by-moment sensory experience and self-awareness closely akin to our own. If they did not, the study of history would shade into primatology. Although there is evidence to suggest that parts of the brain's neural network physically configure themselves in response to experiential influences in the first years of development – in other words, the brain is to some degree 'wired' by its ambient culture – what remains physiologically common to us as a species is much more significant. The span of recorded human history scarcely registers on the evolutionary timescale. We may therefore suppose that historical actors were prone to the same 'sins' of misperception and misremembering that so much recent research has found in modern subjects. The ethnocentricity and culture-specific assumptions that critics see embedded in some of this research should be noted, but the larger point remains valid. Historians' belief in the alterity of people in the past is a widespread article of faith, but alterity is not an absolute value, and lessons drawn from experiments conducted on modern subjects, if due caution is applied, may be projected back in time.

As much as anything, the cognitive and social psychological research traditions surveyed in Chapter 1 introduce a note of healthy scepticism into our often unexamined faith in the veracity, accuracy and amplitude of eyewitness evidence. This is salutary in itself. But beyond that, what are we to do with this scepticism? This body of research does not enable the historian to revisit a given declarative utterance in an eyewitness source and pronounce that it is the product of a perceptual or mnemonic misfire, any more than a research psychologist can tell a court that a particular witness *must* be in error when she says she recognizes the accused. We are only permitted to deal in possibilities. That said, some of these possibilities are suggestive, notably where the questions posed by psychological researchers have overlapped with matters of interest to sociologists in examining smaller-scale collective memory, that is the mnemonic back-and-forth that takes place within face-to-face groups. As we have seen, it is difficult to do anything more than suggest some of the human environments in which the authors of our sample texts participated in this kind of transactive memory-formulation. But we may be confident that they did, and that this had a fundamentally important influence on the content and structure of the narratives they wrote.[1] Whereas the word 'eyewitness' tends to conjure up an image of a more or less observant individual self-consciously detached to some extent from the action that is being perceived, even if she or he is right in the thick of things, a better definition of the word, in a historiographical context, might be someone who may be presumed to have participated in one or more transactive memory environments as a corollary of her or his participation in an event or series of events that the transactive group or groups in question understood as a discrete and significant collective experience.

The texts studied here are a small sample of a very large category of historical narratives that have traditionally been evaluated and deployed as transmitters of the sort of reliable eyewitness evidence that lends itself to the reconstruction of events. This has been their fundamental function. But two problems emerge. First, although questions about the relationship of a flesh-and-blood author to the events that his text narrates are regularly posed – did Villehardouin really see such-and-such? – they are almost always unanswerable. Villehardouin the historical actor was 'there' in relation to the Fourth Crusade, but exactly where at any given point is usually unknown and unknowable. And in any event, how elastic is the notion of 'there', in both spatial and temporal terms, before Villehardouin's eyewitness status begins to fade? Second, we have seen that many prologues in medieval works of history, like their ancient forerunners, show a sensitivity to the value of eyewitness evidence, both the author's own and that supplied by others. But there is more often than not a noticeable slippage between the methodological commitment to autopsy articulated in a prefactory statement of intent and the validation of the narrative's substantive content in the body of the text. For these two reasons, it is better to turn to the internal workings of eyewitness texts for evidence of autopsy at work.

The central argument of this book is that narratology offers a useful heuristic. It is not a *Verfremdungseffekt* that destabilizes familiar narrative sources, but a way of supplementing the habits of close reading that medieval historians already bring to these sorts of materials. In particular, narratology's separation of the historical author from the figure of the narrator – the intermediate notion of the implied reader is not without interest but is less important for our particular purposes – opens up a space in which we do not need to lock any and all articulations and suggestions of autopsy into the author's supposed biographical circumstances. Not only does such a biographist approach invariably lead to

[1] Cf. J. Prager, *Presenting the Past: Psychoanalysis and the Sociology of Misremembering* (Cambridge, MA, 1998), esp. pp. 55, 59–60, 70–1.

circular argumentation sooner or later, it runs up against the same sort of problem that frustrates a trial lawyer when a psychologist called as an expert witness refuses to say that, yes, the witness definitely did have a clear and uninterrupted view of the event at issue, has formed a precise and uncontaminated memory of it, and has articulated that memory without omissions, confabulations, exaggerations or any other type of distortion. The autoptic flesh-and-blood author may or may not be dimly visible through the text at certain points. But the narrator has the great merit of being ever-present. And the manner in which he or she – or it – constructs an analogical relationship to the experiences of the author is what is ultimately at stake when those experiences are transposed onto the narrator's various functions as teller, focalizer, interpreter and organizer of the story matter. The working through of this analogical relationship is really what permits us to characterize the result as an 'eyewitness source'.

Our sample texts narrate much the same sorts of basic subject matter: long journeys, armed conflict, the work of leadership, large groups of people thrown together in unfamiliar and often stressful environments. But no two construct their narratorial personae in the same way. If they have one thing in common, it is that they do not as a rule prioritize the experience of an individual perceiving agent who is voiced in the first person singular and who serves as the principal centre of narrative interest. This sort of intradiegetic presence maximally closes the distance between the narrator and the self-as-character – though there will always be some separation, at the very least a brief temporal gap between the narrated now and the narratorial now, and often reflections and judgements made after the fact as well as the introduction of information that was unavailable to the experiencing self *in medias res*. Some of our texts adopt this strategy in a relatively few places. But it is perhaps significant that the technique is most in evidence in the two texts that are culturally detached from our main sample, the Saladin monographs. Among the Christian texts, the fullest separation of the narratorial voice from an individual locus of perception is found in the account of the Silves campaign; although a narratorial 'I' emerges at a couple of points, there is elsewhere a near-total immersion of that 'I' within a collectively experiencing and focalizing 'we'. In Villehardouin's *Conquête* another distancing device is evident in the use of the third person to refer to Villehardouin the character; even in the sequence concerning the aftermath of the battle of Adrianople in which this character and his agency are most in evidence, initiating action and focalizing, the separation of actor and narrator is sustained.[2] In a similar manner, although we as modern readers necessarily bring to Clari's account of the Fourth Crusade the knowledge that permits us to foreshorten the distances between Clari the author, Clari the character and Clari the anthropomorphic projection of the narratorial

[2] Cf. P. Lejeune, 'Autobiography in the Third Person', *New Literary History*, 9 (1977), 27–50.

voice, the text itself keeps these different elements at arm's length throughout. In other texts we have seen more flexible approaches: an experiencing 'I' and a remembering 'I', either in conjunction or alone, may sometimes pierce the fourth wall, inserting themselves into a storyworld in which they have occasional 'walk-on' parts even though they are not routinely counted among the principals. This does not, however, play a decisive role in their construction of the narrative instance, which is typically either absorbed by the collective 'we' or set apart from the action by means of the use of the third person.

When thinking about possible directions for future research, it is important to remember that our chosen texts occupy a quite narrow thematic, substantive and chronological bandwidth, even though there is significant internal variety in terms of form and language. To what extent, then, do other texts construct similar narratorial voices? Do the challenges of narrating a crusade expedition place particular demands on the narrator, or do our texts participate in wider patterns of narratorial positioning? A supposition that has run underneath this study's discussion of its target narratives, but which cannot be tested with reference to them alone, is that even though any direct connection between the flesh-and-blood eyewitnessing author and the content of his or her text is far more problematic, and tenuous, than is usually supposed, one nonetheless encounters strategies to evoke, mimic or sublimate the author's autoptic experiences and memories. These include set-piece diegeses characterized by concentrations of visible detail; appeals to the narratee to create a scene in the mind's eye; the energizing of sequences of action by means of a criss-cross of gazes; the use of the verb 'to see' and close equivalents in plot-dynamic contexts in which characters' actions are motivated by some re-evaluation of their circumstances; and, perhaps most importantly, the distribution of focalizing functions. None of these devices is specific to autoptic texts. Stay-at-home medieval authors were at liberty to have their characters focalize and change a course of action on the basis of what they perceive; they might also pause over scenic details or apostrophize the narratee in order to co-opt his or her imaginative resources.[3] Is there, nonetheless, across the range of so-called eyewitness sources a relatively greater density of such devices? Might this be explained as an indirect, even veiled, but nonetheless potentially effective 'planting' of authorial autoptic experience into the machinery of the narrative and the workings of its storyworld? And if this is the case, are such second-order traces of authorial autopsy to be understood principally as validating moves in a subtler key than the sort of 'I was there' assertions to be found in some historiographical prologues? Or do they also subserve other authorial strategies?

[3] Cf. Nancy Partner's verdict on Orderic Vitalis's 'compulsive attraction to directly rendered speech, and the headlong plunge into the dramatized scene, the impersonated voice, the you-are-there effect': 'Medieval Histories and Modern Realism: Yet Another Origin of the Novel', *Modern Language Notes*, 114 (1999), 859–60.

Another area that would repay further investigation is the place of the first person plural in historiographical narratives.[4] We have seen that most of the target texts use it to greater or lesser extents, passages in the account of the Silves campaign amounting to the limit case within our corpus. The stock interpretation of the first person plural in such contexts is that it is a reflection, or an attempt to capture, aspects of lived actuality, specifically a sense of collective cohesion and identity, a *Wirgefühl*, within a given group. But even if the usage can, in part at any rate, be linked to circumstances outside the text, it is still a matter of choice and strategy. The narratorial instance is free to detach itself from the group by foregrounding the first person singular – thereby standing out from the crowd, so to speak – or alternatively to step back by confining itself to the third person, even in passages of action in which the self-as-character implicitly or explicitly participates. There is often, moreover, a particular ideological element at play in the first person plural – the hope or belief that the subjects of 'we' are not only capable of collective agency but also possess a self-awareness that extends to a consciously shared ownership of 'we-ness'. This is clearly evident in our corpus at various junctures, but to what extent is it also present in other historiographical texts?

The first person plural is a flexible instrument: we have seen, for example, how its shifting acceptations respond to the emergence of fractures among the crusaders in the *De expugnatione Lyxbonensi*. But it also raises important questions. 'We' is normally taken to mean a collective subject, 'I + they', whose group agency can assume various forms – for example, individual actors performing the same action in unison, as in 'We travelled to Jaffa', or engaging in a variety of actions that work towards a single goal, as in 'We built a siege tower'. It is a commonplace of numerous disciplines from psychiatry to oral history that a subject's self-report with respect to a given action typically differs in matters of lexis, density of detail, ascribed motivation and assumed consequence from the manner in which she or he narrates the performance of exactly the same sort of action by a third party. In narratives such as ours, does the 'I' or the 'they' modulate the terms in which action on the part of 'we' is conceived? Does the 'I' enlarge itself into a 'we' made in its own image? Or does it efface its individuality in arrogating to itself others' actions and mental states of which it has no direct experience? Additionally, does the first person plural map effectively onto statements of collective perception and apperception? The premise that seems to run through our sample texts is that the crusade army that fights together focalizes together; but it is a bold move to corral matters of sensory perception and cognitive operation into the same narrative machinery that goes to work on

[4] See U. Margolin, 'Telling Our Story: On "We" Literary Narratives', *Language and Literature*, 5 (1996), 115–33; *idem*, 'Telling in the Plural: From Grammar to Ideology', *Poetics Today*, 21 (2000), 591–618; A. Marcus, 'A Contextual View of Narrative Fiction in the First Person Plural', *Narrative*, 16 (2008), 46–64.

people walking down the road or building a siege tower. We have seen the effects that our texts strive for in extending group agency into matters of focalization, but are these present in other narratives, or are different approaches evident?

A third area that would benefit from further research is the chunking of action in medieval eyewitness texts. 'Chunking' is a slightly clumsy but useful term of art in action theory, the study of what may be said to cause human action and of the terms in which it may accurately be described and understood.[5] We have seen the inescapable hold of language in matters of perception, memory and narration. Action theory supplies one route into understanding this hold and working through its consequences. A stock illustration of some of the concerns of action theory involves imagining a school-age girl walking along a pavement at 8.30 on a weekday morning. If we ask the question 'What is she doing?', one response might be 'She is alternately swinging her arms and legs in an ambulatory motion'; another might be 'She is getting an education'. Both are correct. But the obvious answer, 'She is going to school', falls somewhere inbetween. This is the same sort of response that a lawyer cross-examining a witness would be looking for; and it is the sort of information that as a rule we want and expect from eyewitness authors, either to permit a reconstruction of events in a similar action register or to build up towards synthesizing and interpretive remarks. But what makes the third answer seem 'natural'? The girl's physical movements are the same for all the descriptions, after all. What are we *seeing* when we see the girl in motion?[6]

The fact that the girl's going to school seems to capture what is happening most satisfactorily has something to do with the ways in which we project mental states, goals and self-awareness onto other people; and it also reflects the importance of scripts and schemata as a form of social 'shorthand' that allows us to manage and navigate the complexities of the world. Both of these factors are at play in eyewitness narratives: the ascription to characters of sensory and cognitive capacities, and the placing of action within more or less clichéd frames of reference such as the 'battle script' or the 'travel script'.[7] The chunking of action in texts such as ours would therefore repay further investigation. It does

[5] See D. Herman, 'Action Theory', in D. Herman, M. Jahn and M.-L. Ryan (eds), *Routledge Encyclopedia of Narrative Theory* (Abingdon, 2005), pp. 2–3. See also the lucid observations in L. Doležel, *Heterocosmica: Fiction and Possible Worlds* (Baltimore, 1998), pp. 55–7. Cf. C. Ginet, *On Action* (Cambridge, 1990); L. Valach, R. A. Young and M. J. Lynam, *Action Theory: A Primer for Applied Research in the Social Sciences* (Westport, CT, 2002), esp. pp. 3–43.

[6] See the valuable overview of key issues in J. M. Zacks and B. Tversky, 'Event Structure in Perception and Cognition', *Psychological Bulletin*, 127 (2001), 3–21.

[7] Cf. E. A. Heinemann, 'Network of Narrative Details: The Motif of the Journey in the *Chanson de Geste*', in H. Scholler (ed.), *The Epic in Medieval Society: Aesthetic and Moral Values* (Tübingen, 1977), pp. 178–92.

not just come down to the lexical choices made word by word and phrase by phrase, but also extends to matters of character motivation, plot architecture and sequencing. We have seen that eyewitness memory often lends itself to moments of experience akin to the short scenes contrived by psychological researchers – the tightly-bound slice of life that has the potential to translate into flashbulb-like recall.[8] But in what ways might eyewitnessing extend into a narrative's larger structural and thematic programmes, even though one cannot 'see' abstractions?[9] Further text-by-text investigation into this question is needed in order to explore the variety of ways in which what an eyewitness author 'sees' may be said to translate into narrative content on the page.

The narrators of at least most of our target texts strive to evoke or mimic the texture of lived experience at given points in their storyworlds. Experience is an emerging area of scholarly interest, though its lessons for the analysis of texts such as ours are yet to be fully explored.[10] Monika Fludernik has even argued that narrative may essentially be defined as 'mediated experientiality'.[11] In a recent important study, Jonas Grethlein has examined the ways in which Thucydides's history of the Peloponnesian war tries to capture what it felt like for the historical actors caught up in the flow of events, unable to know what would happen next and alive to a range of possible outcomes.[12] Thucydides's narrative devices do not entirely map onto those found in medieval works of history, though there are several correspondences, so further research along the lines suggested by Grethlein would be welcome. In thinking about the experiential 'capture' that may be present in texts such as ours, it is important to remember that experiences do not reduce to what happens to people in the narrative now and what it

[8] Cf. A. Hollingsworth, 'Memory for Real-World Scenes', in J. R. Brockmole (ed.), *The Visual World in Memory* (Hove, 2009), pp. 89–116.

[9] For an interesting examination of the relationship between memory for particular events and memory for and evaluation of larger life patterns, which has parallels to the relationship between the micro and the macro levels in narrative, see D. K. Thomsen, 'There Is More to Life Stories than Memories', *Memory*, 17 (2004), 445–57. See also the important study of the place of short, free-standing anecdotes within more elaborate historical narratives in L. Gossman, 'Anecdote and History', *History and Theory*, 42 (2003), 143–68. Cf. J. D. Evans, 'Episode in Analysis of Medieval Narrative', *Style*, 20 (1986), 126–41; P. Haidu, 'The Episode as Semiotic Module in Twelfth-Century Romance', *Poetics Today*, 4 (1983), 655–81.

[10] See D. Carr, *Experience and History: Phenomenological Perspectives on the Historical World* (Oxford, 2014).

[11] M. Fludernik, *An Introduction to Narratology*, trans. P. Häusler-Greenfield and M. Fludernik (Abingdon, 2009), pp. 12–13, 20–30.

[12] J. Grethlein, 'Experientiality and "Narrative Reference", With Thanks to Thucydides', *History and Theory*, 49 (2010), 315–35. See also the same author's *Experience and Teleology in Ancient Historiography: 'Futures Past' from Herodotus to Augustine* (Cambridge, 2013).

might have 'felt like' in a historical actor's moment-by-moment consciousness; as Joan Scott has argued, subjects do not merely come by experiences, they may be said to be constituted by them.[13] The implication of Scott's argument is that eyewitness texts do not simply strive for certain autoptic-esque effects; they also have the potential to contribute to our understanding of medieval notions of subjectivity and identity.

Grethlein's exploration of experience in Thucydides is inspired by what he argues is a growing scholarly dissatisfaction with the postmodernist axiom that reality is nothing more than an artefact of language. Although this present study has avoided postmodernist readings of the sample texts in favour of elements of a structuralist approach of an older vintage, it has suggested ways in which both the lessons of cognitive and social psychological research and narratological categories of analysis destabilize many of the biographist shortcuts and assumptions about the homologies between source content and historical event that are often applied to texts such as ours. But where does this leave the uses to which eyewitness narratives may be put? The drift of a good deal of research into medieval historiography in recent years has been to bypass the relationship between the world-making and the world-reflecting properties of texts; more attention is paid to the ways in which medieval works of history plugged into larger circuits of thought such as theology. But the demands of reconstructionist historiography are not going away. What is at stake is nicely illustrated by a rather unfair attack by Noah Guynn on Donald Queller and Thomas Madden for what he claims is their naivety in transposing details culled from Villehardouin into their own narrative of the Fourth Crusade. As Guynn puts it: 'For medieval chroniclers (including Villehardouin), the truth of temporal events derives not from factual reporting but from the instantiation of universal, theological paradigms.'[14] Guynn is in fact wrong on this specific point, for, as is well known, medieval theories of reading encouraged close attention to literal meanings as well as to higher-order interpretations. He is also off the mark in his larger assumption that what Queller and Madden are doing is illegitimate and tendentious. One may disagree with their mobilization of Villehardouin at various specific junctures, but their basic approach, one that underpins numerous works on the history of the crusades and many other areas of medieval history, is entirely valid. This is so for two reasons.

The first was mentioned in Chapter 1: that however much a narrative of events is likely to have fallen victim detail by detail to the sorts of sins of perception and memory that we have identified, it is as often as not kept within quite wide but

[13] J. W. Scott, 'The Evidence of Experience', *Critical Inquiry*, 17 (1991), 773–97.

[14] N. D. Guynn, 'Rhetoric and Historiography: Villehardouin's *La Conquête de Constantinople*', in W. Burgwinkle, N. Hammond and E. Wilson (eds), *The Cambridge History of French Literature* (Cambridge, 2011), pp. 102–10, quotation at pp. 106–7.

nonetheless effective tramlines by the demands of plot coherence. Indeed, how plot exerts this disciplining effect in historical texts – for example, thanks to expectations about character consistency, the scripts that succinctly motivate action sequences, and the narrator's control over the storyworld – is a large subject that would repay further investigation. The second reason is that one emerges from a reading of eyewitness texts such as our corpus, not with a residual postmodernist scepticism that nothing that actually happened is accessible through them, but in fact with a renewed faith in the ways in which medieval people very often did try, and tried hard, to 'tell it like it was', in the process reposing trust in the evidentiary value of their own sensory experiences and memories as well as those of others.[15] As we have seen, we need to be much more careful than we sometimes are in converting the narrative articulations of those experiences and memories into modern historiographical idiom; more qualifications of confidence in given statements, and a reduction of the number of propositions that we label as true, or probably so, are in order. But historical reconstruction proceeding on amber is still historical reconstruction. It is therefore hoped that this book contributes to debates about the ways in which we may satisfactorily combine close, methodologically wide-ranging reading of our narrative sources with a renewed sense that the past is, at least sometimes, recoverable because it was lived by real, sensate, perceiving, self-aware people – which is to say, by eyewitnesses.

[15] Cf. the valuable observations of P. Lamarque, 'On Not Expecting Too Much from Narrative', *Mind and Language*, 19 (2004), 397–400 on the absence of an inherent anti–realism in narrative. See also G. Strawson, 'Against Narrativity', *Ratio*, ns 17 (2004), 444.

Bibliography

Primary Sources

Aelred of Rievaulx, 'Relatio de Standardo', ed. R. Howlett, *Chronicles of the Reigns of Stephen, Henry II and Richard I*, vol. 3 (RS 82:3; London, 1886), pp. 181–99; trans. J. P. Freeland, *Aelred of Rievaulx: The Historical Works*, ed. M. L. Dutton (Cistercian Fathers Series, 56; Collegeville, MN, 2008), pp. 245–69.

Agnellus of Ravenna, *Liber pontificalis ecclesiae Ravennatis*, ed. D. M. Deliyannis (CCCM 199; Turnhout, 2006); trans. D. M. Deliyannis, *The Book of Pontiffs of the Church of Ravenna* (Washington, DC, 2004).

Akutagawa, Ryūnosuke, *Rashōmon and Seventeen Other Stories*, trans. J. Rubin with an introduction by H. Murakami (London, 2006).

Ambroise, *The History of the Holy War: Ambroise's Estoire de la Guerre Sainte*, ed. and trans. M. J. Ailes and M. C. Barber, 2 vols (Woodbridge, 2003); *L'estoire de la guerre sainte: Histoire en vers de la troisième croisade (1190–1192)*, ed. G. Paris (Paris, 1897).

'Annales Sancti Disibodi', ed. G. Waitz, *MGH SS*, 17, pp. 4–30.

Anonymi Gesta Francorum et aliorum Hierosolimitanorum, ed. H. Hagenmeyer (Heidelberg, 1890).

Asser, *Life of King Alfred*, ed. W. H. Stephenson, rev. edn (Oxford, 1959); trans. S. Keynes and M. Lapidge, *Alfred the Great: Asser's* Life of King Alfred *and Other Contemporary Sources* (Harmondsworth, 1983), pp. 65–110.

Astronomer, 'Vita Hludovici Imperatoris', in *Thegan, Die Taten Kaiser Ludwigs/ Astronomus, Das Leben Kaiser Ludwigs*, ed. and trans. E. Tremp (MGH Scriptores rerum Germanicarum in usum scholarum, 64; Hanover, 1995), pp. 278–555; trans. A. Cabaniss, *Son of Charlemagne: A Contemporary Life of Louis the Pious* (Syracuse, NY, 1961).

Bahā' al-Dīn Ibn Shaddād, *The Rare and Excellent History of Saladin or al-Nawādir al-Sultāniyya wa'l-Mahāsin al-Yūsufiyya*, trans. D. S. Richards (Crusade Texts in Translation, 7; Aldershot, 2002).

Baldric of Bourgueil, *The Historia Ierosolimitana*, ed. S. Biddlecombe (Woodbridge, 2014).

Bede, *Ecclesiastical History of the English People*, ed. and trans. B. Colgrave and R. A. B. Mynors (Oxford, 1969).

La Chanson d'Antioche: chanson de geste du dernier quart du XIIe siècle, ed. and trans. B. Guidot (Champion classiques moyen âge, 33; Paris, 2011); trans. S. B. Edgington and C. Sweetenham, *The Chanson d'Antioche: An Old French Account of the First Crusade* (Crusade Texts in Translation, 22; Farnham, 2011).

'Chronica Adefonsi Imperatoris', ed. A. Maya Sánchez, in E. Falque Rey, J. Gil and A. Maya Sánchez (eds), *Chronica Hispana saeculi XII* (CCCM 71; Turnhout, 1990), pp. 109–248; trans. S. Barton and R. Fletcher, *The World of the Cid: Chronicles of the Spanish Reconquest* (Manchester, 2000), pp. 148–263.

'Chronica Gothorum', *Portugaliae Monumenta Historica, Scriptores*, vol. 1 (Lisbon, 1856), pp. 5–17.

Chronica Regia Coloniensis, ed. G. Waitz (MGH Scriptores rerum Germanicarum in usum scholarum, 18; Hanover, 1880).

La Chronique de Saint-Maixent 751–1140, ed. and trans. J. Verdon (Les classiques de l'histoire de France au moyen âge, 33; Paris, 1979).

The Conquest of Jerusalem and the Third Crusade: Sources in Translation, trans. P. W. Edbury (Crusade Texts in Translation, 1; Aldershot, 1996).

Contemporary Sources for the Fourth Crusade, trans. A. J. Andrea with B. E. Whalen (The Medieval Mediterranean, 29; Leiden, 2000).

Devastatio Constantinopolitana, ed. A. J. Andrea, 'The *Devastatio Constantinopolitana*, A Special Perspective on the Fourth Crusade: An Analysis, New Edition, and Translation', *Historical Reflections*, 19 (1993), 107–29, 131–49; also trans. A. J. Andrea with B. E. Whalen, *Contemporary Sources for the Fourth Crusade* (The Medieval Mediterranean, 29; Leiden, 2000), pp. 205–21.

Eadmer, 'Historia Novorum in Anglia', in *Historia Novorum in Anglia et Opuscula Duo*, ed. M. Rule (RS 81; London, 1884), pp. 1–302; trans. G. Bosanquet, *Eadmer's History of Recent Events in England* (London, 1964).

Einhard, *Vie de Charlemagne*, ed. and trans. M. Sot, C. Veyrard-Cosme *et al.* (Les classiques de l'histoire au moyen âge, 53; Paris, 2015); trans. D. Ganz, *Einhard and Notker the Stammerer: Two Lives of Charlemagne* (London, 2008), pp. 15–44.

Encomium Emmae Reginae, ed. and trans. A. Campbell with a supplementary introduction by S. Keynes (Cambridge, 1998).

Epistulae et chartae ad historiam primi belli sacri spectantes: Die Kreuzzugsbriefe aus den Jahren 1088-1100, ed. H. Hagenmeyer (Innsbruck, 1901); part trans. M. C. Barber and K. Bate, *Letters from the East: Crusaders, Pilgrims and Settlers in the 12th–13th Centuries* (Crusade Sources in Translation, 18; Farnham, 2010), pp. 15–38.

Erchempert, 'Historia Langobardorum Beneventanorum', ed. G. H. Pertz and G. Waitz, *MGH Scriptores rerum Langobardicarum et Italicarum saec. VI-IX* (Hanover, 1878), pp. 231–64.

De expugnatione Lyxbonensi: The Conquest of Lisbon, ed. and trans. C. W. David, rev. J. P. Phillips (New York, 2001); *A Conquista de Lisboa aos Mouros: Relato de um Cruzado*, ed. and trans. A. A. Nascimento with an introduction by M. J. V. Branco (Lisbon, 2001).

Falco of Benevento, *Chronicon Beneventanum: Città e feudi nell' Italia dei Normanni*, ed. and trans. E. D'Angelo (Testi mediolatini con traduzione, 9; Florence, 1998); trans. G. A. Loud, *Roger II and the Creation of the Kingdom of Sicily* (Manchester, 2012), pp. 130–249.

Li Fet des Romains: compilé ensemble de Saluste et de Suetoine et de Lucan, ed. L.-F. Flutre and K. Sneyders de Vogel, 2 vols (Paris, 1935–8).

Fredegar, *The Fourth Book of the Chronicle of Fredegar with its Continuations*, ed. and trans. J. M. Wallace-Hadrill (London, 1960).

Fulcher of Chartres, *Historia Hierosolymitana (1095–1127)*, ed. H. Hagenmeyer (Heidelberg, 1912); trans. M. E. McGinty in E. Peters (ed.), *The First Crusade: The Chronicle of Fulcher of Chartres and Other Source Materials*, 2nd edn (Philadelphia, 1998), pp. 47–101 [Book I].

Galbert of Bruges, *De multro, traditione, et occisione gloriosi Karoli comitis Flandriarum*, ed. J. Rider (CCCM 131; Turnhout, 1994); trans. J. Rider, *The Murder, Betrayal, and Slaughter of Glorious Charles, Count of Flanders* (New Haven, 2013).

Geoffrey Malaterra, *De rebus gestis Rogerii Calabriae et Siciliae comitis et Roberti Guiscardi ducis fratris eius*, ed. E. Pontieri (Rerum Italicarum Scriptores, 5:1; Bologna, 1927–8); trans. K. B. Wolf, *The Deeds of Count Roger of Calabria and Sicily and of His Brother Duke Robert Guiscard* (Ann Arbor, MI, 2005).

Geoffrey of Monmouth, *The History of the Kings of Britain*, ed. M. D. Reeve, trans. N. Wright (Woodbridge, 2007).

Geoffrey of Villehardouin, *La conquête de Constantinople*, ed. and trans. E. Faral, 2nd edn, 2 vols (Les classiques de l'histoire de France au moyen âge, 18–19; Paris, 1961); trans. C. Smith, *Joinville and Villehardouin, Chronicles of the Crusades* (London, 2008), pp. 5–135.

Gerald of Wales, *Expugnatio Hibernica: The Conquest of Ireland*, ed. and trans. A. B. Scott and F. X. Martin (Dublin, 1978).

Gesta Francorum et aliorum Hierosolimitanorum, ed. and trans. R. M. T. Hill [with R. A. B. Mynors] (London, 1962).

'Gesta Innocentii PP. III.', *PL*, 214, cols. xvii–ccxxviii.

Guibert of Nogent, *Autobiographie*, ed. and trans. E.-R. Labande (Les classiques de l'histoire de France au moyen âge, 34; Paris, 1981); trans. P. J. Archambault, *A Monk's Confession: The Memoirs of Guibert of Nogent* (University Park, PA, 1996).

—— *Dei Gesta per Francos*, ed. R. B. C. Huygens (CCCM 127A; Turnhout, 1996); trans. R. Levine, *The Deeds of God through the Franks* (Woodbridge, 1997).

Gunther of Pairis, *Hystoria Constantinopolitana*, ed. P. Orth (Spolia Berolinensia, 5; Hildesheim, 1994); trans. A. J. Andrea, *The Capture of Constantinople: The 'Hystoria Constantinopolitana' of Gunther of Pairis* (Philadephia, 1997).

Helmold of Bosau, *Cronica Slavorum*, ed. B. Schmeidler (MGH Scriptores rerum Germanicarum in usum scholarum, 32; Hanover, 1937); trans. F. J. Tschan, *The Chronicle of the Slavs* (New York, 1935).

Henry of Huntingdon, *Historia Anglorum*, ed. and trans. D. E. Greenway (Oxford, 1996).

Henry of Valenciennes, *Histoire de l'empereur Henri de Constantinople*, ed. J. Longnon (Documents relatifs à l'histoire des croisades, 2; Paris, 1948).

Herodotus, [*The Histories*], ed. and trans. A. D. Godley, 4 vols (Loeb Classical Library, 117–20; Cambridge, MA, 1920–5); trans. R. Waterfield, *The Histories*, with introduction and notes by C. Dewald (Oxford, 1998).

'Historia de expeditione Friderici imperatoris', ed. A. Chroust, *Quellen zur Geschichte des Kreuzzuges Kaiser Friedrichs I.* (MGH Scriptores rerum Germanicarum, ns 5; Berlin, 1928), pp. 1–115; trans. G. A. Loud, *The Crusade of Frederick Barbarossa: The History of the Expedition of the Emperor Frederick and Related Texts* (Crusade Texts in Translation, 19; Farnham, 2010), pp. 33–134.

'Historia Peregrinorum', ed. A. Chroust, *Quellen zur Geschichte des Kreuzzuges Kaiser Friedrichs I.* (MGH Scriptores rerum Germanicarum, ns 5; Berlin, 1928), pp. 116–72; part trans. G. A. Loud, *The Crusade of Frederick Barbarossa: The History of the Expedition of the Emperor Frederick and Related Texts* (Crusade Texts in Translation, 19; Farnham, 2010), pp. 135–47.

'Historia Turpini', in *Liber Sancti Jacobi: Codex Calixtinus*, ed. W. M. Whitehill, G. Prado and J. C. García, 3 vols (Santiago de Compostela, 1944), i, pp. 301–48; trans. K. R. Poole, *The Chronicle of Pseudo-Turpin* (New York, 2014).

Hugo Falcandus, *La Historia o Liber de Regno Sicilie e la Epistola ad Petrum Panormitane Ecclesie Thesaurium*, ed. G. B. Siragusa (Fonti per la storia d'Italia, 22; Rome, 1897); trans. G. A. Loud and T. Wiedemann, *The History of the Tyrants of Sicily by 'Hugo Falcandus' 1154–69* (Manchester, 1998).

David Hume, *An Enquiry Concerning Human Understanding: A Critical Edition*, ed. T. L. Beauchamp (Oxford, 2000).

Ibn al-Athīr, *The Chronicle of Ibn al-Athīr for the Crusading Period from al-Kamīl fi'l-ta'rīkh*, trans. D. S. Richards, 3 vols (Crusade Texts in Translation, 13, 15, 17; Aldershot, 2006–8).

'Imād al-Dīn al-Isfahānī, *Conquête de la Syrie et de la Palestine par Saladin*, trans. H. Massé (Documents relatifs à l'histoire des croisades, 10; Paris, 1972).

'Indiculum Fundationis Monasterii Beati Vincenti Vlixbone', in *A Conquista de Lisboa aos Mouros: Relato de um Cruzado*, ed. and trans. A. A. Nascimento with an introduction by M. J. V. Branco (Lisbon, 2001), pp. 178–201.

Isidore of Seville, *Etymologiarum sive Originum Libri XX*, ed. W. M. Lindsay, 2 vols (Oxford, 1911); trans. S. A. Barney, W. J. Lewis, J. A. Beach and O. Berghof with M. Hall, *The Etymologies of Isidore of Seville* (Cambridge, 2006).

'Itinerarium peregrinorum', ed. H. E. Mayer, *Das Itinerarium peregrinorum: Eine zeitgenössische englische Chronik zum dritten Kreuzzug in ursprünglicher Gestalt* (MGH Schriften, 18; Stuttgart, 1962), pp. 241–357.

Itinerarium Peregrinorum et Gesta Regis Ricardi, ed. W. Stubbs, *Chronicles and Memorials of the Reign of Richard I*, vol. 1 (RS 38:1, London, 1864); trans. H. J. Nicholson, *Chronicle of the Third Crusade: A Translation of the Itinerarium Peregrinorum et Gesta Regis Ricardi* (Crusade Texts in Translation, 3; Aldershot, 1997).

John Kinnamos, *Epitome rerum ab Ioanne et Alexio Comnenis gestarum*, ed. A. Meineke (Corpus Scriptorum Historiae Byzantinae, 23; Bonn, 1836); trans. C. M. Brand, *Deeds of John and Manuel Comnenus by John Kinnamos* (New York, 1976).

John of Salisbury, *Historia Pontificalis*, ed. and trans. M. Chibnall (London, 1956).

Jordan Fantosme, *Chronicle*, ed. and trans. R. C. Johnston (Oxford, 1981).

Josephus, *The Jewish War*, ed. and trans. H. St. J. Thackeray, 3 vols (Loeb Classical Library, 203, 210, 487; Cambridge, MA, 1997); trans. G. A. Williamson, *The Jewish War*, rev. E. M. Smallwood (Harmondsworth, 1981).

Lambertus Parvus, 'Annales', *MGH SS*, 16, pp. 645–50.

Lampert of Hersfeld, 'Libelli de institutione Herveldensis ecclesiae quae supersunt', in *Lamperti monachi Hersfeldensis opera*, ed. O. Holder-Egger (MGH Scriptores rerum Germanicarum in usum scholarum, 38; Hanover, 1894), pp. 341–54.

Lethald of Micy, 'Liber miraculorum S. Maximini abbatis Miciacensis', *PL*, 137, cols. 795–824.

Letters from the East: Crusaders, Pilgrims and Settlers in the 12th–13th Centuries, trans. M. C. Barber and K. Bate (Crusade Sources in Translation, 18; Farnham, 2010).

Liudprand of Cremona, 'Antapodosis' and 'Relatio de legatione Constantinopolitana', in *Die Werke Liudprands von Cremona*, ed. J. Becker, 3rd edn (MGH Scriptores rerum Germanicarum in usum scholarum, 41; Hanover, 1915); trans. P. Squatriti, *The Complete Works of Liudprand of Cremona* (Washington, DC, 2007).

Lucian, 'How To Write History', in *Lucian: A Selection*, ed. and trans. M. D. MacLeod (Warminster, 1991), pp. 198–246.

'Narratio de Itinere Navali Peregrinorum Hierosolyman Tendentium et Silviam Capientium, A.D. 1189', ed. C. W. David, *Proceedings of the American Philosophical Society*, 81 (1939), 591–676; trans. G. A. Loud, *The Crusade of Frederick Barbarossa: The History of the Expedition of the Emperor Frederick and Related Texts* (Crusade Texts in Translation, 19; Farnham, 2010), pp. 193–208. Also 'Narratio itineris navalis ad Terram sanctam', ed. A. Chroust, *Quellen zur Geschichte des Kreuzzuges Kaiser Friedrichs I.* (MGH Scriptores rerum Germanicarum, ns 5; Berlin, 1928), pp. 179–96.

Niketas Choniates, *Historia*, ed. J. L. van Dieten, 2 vols (Corpus Fontium Historiae Byzantinae, Series Berolinensis, 11; Berlin, 1975); trans. H. J. Magoulias, *O City of Byzantium, Annals of Niketas Choniates* (Detroit, 1984).

Odo of Deuil, *De profectione Ludovici VII in orientem*, ed. and trans. V. G. Berry (New York, 1948).

Odorannus of Sens, *Opera Omnia*, ed. and trans. R.-H. Bautier, M. Gilles, M.-E. Duchez and M. Huglo (Sources d'histoire médiévale, 4; Paris, 1972).

Orderic Vitalis, *Ecclesiastical History*, ed. and trans. M. Chibnall, 6 vols (Oxford, 1968–80).

Otto of Freising and Rahewin, *Gesta Frederici seu rectius Cronica*, ed. F.-J. Schmale, trans. A. Schmidt (Ausgewählte Quellen zur deutschen Geschichte des Mittelalters, 17; Darmstadt, 1965); trans. C. C. Mierow, *The Deeds of Frederick Barbarossa* (Medieval Academy Reprints for Teaching, 31; Toronto, 1994).

Peter Abelard, *Historia Calamitatum*, ed. J. Monfrin, 4th edn (Paris, 1978); trans. B. Radice, *The Letters of Abelard and Heloise*, rev. M. T. Clanchy (London, 2003), pp. 3–43.

Peter of Vaux-de-Cernay, *Hystoria Albigensis*, ed. P. Guébin and E. Lyon, 3 vols (Paris, 1926–39); trans. W. A. Sibly and M. D. Sibly, *The History of the Albigensian Crusade* (Woodbridge, 1998).

Philip of Novara, *Mémoires, 1218–1243*, ed. C. Kohler (Les classiques français du moyen âge, 10; Paris, 1913); trans. J. L. La Monte and M. J. Hubert, *The Wars of Frederick II Against the Ibelins in Syria and Cyprus* (New York, 1936).

Polybius, *The Histories*, ed. and trans. W. R. Paton, rev. F. W. Walbank and C. Habicht, 6 vols (Loeb Classical Library, 128, 137–8, 159–61; Cambridge, MA, 2010–12); trans. R. Waterfield, *The Histories*, with introduction and notes by B. McGing (Oxford, 2010).

Prologues to Ancient and Medieval History: A Reader, ed. J. Lake (Readings in Medieval Civilizations and Cultures, 17; Toronto, 2013).

Ralph of Diceto, *Opera Historica*, ed. W. Stubbs, 2 vols (RS 68; London, 1876).

Richard of Devizes, *Chronicon*, ed. and trans. J. T. Appleby (London, 1963).

Robert of Clari, *La Conquête de Constantinople*, ed. and trans. P. Noble (British Rencesvals Publications, 3; Edinburgh, 2005); also *La conquête de Constantinople*, ed. and trans. J. Dufournet (Champion classiques moyen âge, 14; Paris, 2004). See also *The Conquest of Constantinople*, trans. E. H. McNeal (Medieval Academy Reprints for Teaching, 36; Toronto, 1996); *La conquista di Costantinopoli (1198–1216): Studio critico, traduzione e note*, trans. A. M. Nada Patrone (Collana storica di fonti e studi, 13; Genoa, 1972).

Robert the Monk, *The Historia Iherosolimitana*, ed. D. Kempf and M. G. Bull (Woodbridge, 2013); trans. C. Sweetenham, *Robert the Monk's History of the First Crusade: Historia Iherosolimitana* (Crusade Texts in Translation, 11; Aldershot, 2005).

Rodulfus Glaber, *Opera*, ed. and trans. J. France, N. Bulst and P. Reynolds (Oxford, 1989).
Roger of Howden, *Gesta Regis Henrici Secundi* [formerly attributed to Benedict of Peterborough], ed. W. Stubbs, 2 vols (RS 49; London, 1867).
—— *Chronica*, ed. W. Stubbs, 4 vols (RS 51; London, 1868–71).
Solinus, *Collectanea rerum memorabilium*, ed. T. Mommsen (Berlin, 1895).
The Song of Roland, ed. and trans. G. J. Brault, 2 vols (University Park, PA, 1978).
Suger, 'Epistolae Sugerii abbatis S. Dionysii', *RHGF*, 15, pp. 483–532.
—— 'Gesta Suggerii Abbatis' [= *De Rebus in Administratione sua Gestis*], in *Oeuvres*, ed. and trans. E. Gasparri, 2 vols (Les classiques de l'histoire de France au moyen âge, 37 and 41; Paris, 1996–2001), i, pp. 54–154.
—— 'De glorioso rege Ludovico, Ludovici filio', in *Oeuvres*, ed. and trans. E. Gasparri, 2 vols (Les classiques de l'histoire de France au moyen âge, 37 and 41; Paris, 1996–2001), i, pp. 156–77.
—— *Vie de Louis VI le Gros*, ed. and trans. H. Waquet, 2nd edn (Les classiques de l'histoire de France au moyen âge, 11; Paris, 1964); trans. R. C. Cusimano and J. Moorhead, *The Deeds of Louis the Fat* (Washington, DC, 1992).
Thietmar of Merseburg, *Chronicon*, ed. R. Holtzmann (MGH Scriptores rerum Germanicarum, ns 9; Berlin, 1935); trans. D. A. Warner, *Ottonian Germany: The* Chronicon *of Thietmar of Merseburg* (Manchester, 2001).
Thucydides, *History of the Peloponnesian War*, ed. and trans. C. Forster Smith, 4 vols (Loeb Classical Library, 108–10, 169; Cambridge, MA, 1928–30); trans. M. Hammond, *The Peloponnesian War*, with an introduction and notes by P. J. Rhodes (Oxford, 2009).
Urkunden zur älteren Handels- und Staatsgeschichte der Republik Venedig mit besonderer Beziehung auf Byzanz und die Levante, ed. G. L. F. Tafel and G. M. Thomas, 3 vols (Vienna, 1856–7).
We Saw Lincoln Shot: One Hundred Eyewitness Accounts, ed. T. L. Good (Jackson, MS, 1995).
William of Jumièges, Orderic Vitalis, and Robert of Torigni, *Gesta Normannorum Ducum*, ed. and trans. E. M. C. van Houts, 2 vols (Oxford, 1992–5).
William of Malmesbury, *Gesta Regum Anglorum*, ed. and trans. R. A. B. Mynors, R. M. Thomson and M. Winterbottom, 2 vols (Oxford, 1998–9).
—— *Historia Novella*, ed. and trans. K. R. Potter (London, 1955).
William of Poitiers, *The Gesta Guillelmi*, ed. and trans. R. H. C. Davis and M. Chibnall (Oxford, 1998).
William of St-Denis, 'Le dialogue apologétique du moine Guillaume, biographe de Suger', ed. A. Wilmart, *Revue Mabillon*, 32 (1942), 80–118.
Wipo, 'Gesta Chuonradi II. Imperatoris', in *Die Werke Wipos*, ed. H. Bresslau, 3rd edn (MGH Scriptores rerum Germanicarum in usum scholarum, 61; Hanover, 1915), pp. 1–62; trans. T. E. Mommsen and K. F. Morrison, 'The

Deeds of Conrad II', in *Imperial Lives and Letters of the Eleventh Century*, ed. R. L. Benson (New York, 1962), pp. 52–100.

Secondary Works

Abbott, H. P., *The Cambridge Introduction to Narrative*, 2nd edn (Cambridge, 2008).

Adams, F., and K. Aiziwa, *The Bounds of Cognition* (Malden, MA, 2008).

Adorno, R., 'The Discursive Encounter of Spain and America: The Authority of Eyewitness Testimony in the Writing of History', *William and Mary Quarterly*, 3rd ser., 49 (1992), 210–28.

Ailes, M. J., 'Early French Chronicle – History or Literature?', *Journal of Medieval History*, 26 (2000), 301–12.

—— 'Heroes of War: Ambroise's Heroes of the Third Crusade', in C. Saunders, F. Le Saux and N. Thomas (eds), *Writing War: Medieval Literary Responses to Warfare* (Cambridge, 2004), pp. 29–48.

—— 'The Admirable Enemy? Saladin and Saphadin in Ambroise's *Estoire de la guerre sainte*', in N. J. Housley (ed.), *Knighthoods of Christ: Essays on the History of the Crusades and Knights Templar, Presented to Malcolm Barber* (Aldershot, 2007), pp. 51–64.

—— 'Ambroise's *Estoire de la Guerre sainte* and the Development of a Genre', *Reading Medieval Studies*, 34 (2008), 1–19.

Ainsworth, P., 'Contemporary and "Eyewitness" History', in D. M. Deliyannis (ed.), *Historiography in the Middle Ages* (Leiden, 2003), pp. 249–76.

Albu, E., *The Normans in Their Histories: Propaganda, Myth and Subversion* (Woodbridge, 2001).

Andrea, A. J., 'Essay on Primary Sources', in D. E. Queller and T. F. Madden, *The Fourth Crusade: The Conquest of Constantinople*, 2nd edn (Philadelphia, 1997), pp. 299–313.

Angold, M., 'The Road to 1204: The Byzantine Background to the Fourth Crusade', *Journal of Medieval History*, 25 (1999), 257–78.

—— *The Fourth Crusade: Event and Context* (Harlow, 2003).

Archambault, P. J., *Seven French Chroniclers: Witness to History* (Syracuse, NY, 1974).

Ash, M. A., 'Academic Politics in the History of Science: Experimental Psychology in Germany, 1879–1941', *Central European History*, 13 (1980), 255–86.

Ashe, L., *Fiction and History in England, 1066–1200* (Cambridge, 2007).

Aslanov, C., 'Aux sources de la chronique en prose française: entre déculturation et acculturation', in T. F. Madden (ed.), *The Fourth Crusade: Event, Aftermath, and Perception: Papers from the Sixth Conference of the Society *for the Study of the Crusades and the Latin East, Istanbul, Turkey, 25–29 August 2004* (Crusades Subsidia, 2; Aldershot, 2008), pp. 143–65.

Assmann, A., 'Transformations between History and Memory', *Social Research*, 75 (2008), 49–72.

Baddeley, A. D., *Human Memory: Theory and Practice*, rev. edn (Hove, 1997).

—— *Essentials of Human Memory* (Hove, 1995).

Bagley, C. P., 'Robert de Clari's *La Conquête de Constantinople*', *Medium Aevum*, 40 (1971), 109–15.

Bal, M., *Narratology: Introduction to the Theory of Narrative*, 3rd edn (Toronto, 2009).

Baragwanath, E., *Motivation and Narrative in Herodotus* (Oxford, 2008).

Barthes, R., 'Introduction to the Structural Analysis of Narratives', in his *Image, Music, Text*, trans. S. Heath (London, 1977), pp. 79–124.

—— 'The Reality Effect', in his *The Rustle of Language*, trans. R. Howard (Berkeley, 1989), pp. 141–8.

Bartlett, F. C., *Remembering: A Study in Experimental and Social Psychology* (Cambridge, 1932).

Basden, B. H., D. R. Basden, S. Bryner and R. L. Thomas III, 'A Comparison of Group and Individual Remembering: Does Collaboration Disrupt Retrieval Strategies?', *Journal of Experimental Psychology: Learning, Memory, and Cognition*, 23 (1997), 1176–89.

Basden, B. H., D. R. Basden and S. Henry, 'Costs and Benefits of Collaborative Remembering', *Applied Cognitive Psychology*, 14 (2000), 497–507.

Becklen, R., and D. Cervone, 'Selective Looking and the Noticing of Unexpected Events', *Memory & Cognition*, 11 (1983), 601–8.

Beer, J. M. A., *Villehardouin: Epic Historian* (Études de philologie et d'histoire, 7; Geneva, 1968).

—— *Narrative Conventions of Truth in the Middle Ages* (Études de philologie et d'histoire, 38; Geneva, 1981).

—— *In Their Own Words: Practices of Quotation in Early Medieval Writing* (Toronto, 2014).

Behrman, B. W., and S. L. Davey, 'Eyewitness Identification in Actual Criminal Cases: An Archival Analysis', *Law and Human Behavior*, 25 (2001), 475–91.

Bekerian, D. A., and J. M. Bowers, 'Eyewitness Testimony: Were We Misled?', *Journal of Experimental Psychology: Learning, Memory, and Cognition*, 9 (1983), 139–45.

Bell, B. E., and E. F. Loftus, 'Degree of Detail of Eyewitness Testimony and Mock Juror Judgments', *Journal of Applied Social Psychology*, 18 (1988), 1171–92.

Belli, R. F., 'Color Blend Retrievals: Compromise Memories or Deliberate Compromise Responses?', *Memory & Cognition*, 16 (1988), 314–26.

Bennett, M., 'Military Aspects of the Conquest of Lisbon, 1147', in J. P.

Phillips and M. Hoch (eds), *The Second Crusade: Scope and Consequences* (Manchester, 2001), pp. 71–89.

Bennett, P. E., 'La Chronique de Jordan Fantosme: épique et public lettré au XIIe siècle', *Cahiers de civilisation médiévale*, 40 (1997), 37–56.

Bensmaia, R., 'Reality Effect', in D. Herman, M. Jahn and M.-L. Ryan (eds), *Routledge Encyclopedia of Narrative Theory* (Abingdon, 2005), p. 492.

Berkowitz, S. R., and N. L. Javaid, 'It's Not You, It's the Law: Eyewitness Memory Scholars' Disappointment with *Perry v. New Hampshire*', *Psychology, Public Policy, and Law*, 19 (2013), 369–79.

Bernstein, D. M., and E. F. Loftus, 'How To Tell if a Particular Memory Is True or False', *Perspectives on Psychological Science*, 4 (2009), 370–4.

Bernsten, D., 'Flashbulb Memories and Social Identity', in O. Luminet and A. Curci (eds), *Flashbulb Memories: New Issues and New Perspectives* (Hove, 2009), pp. 187–205.

Bernsten, D., and D. K. Thomsen, 'Personal Memories for Remote Historical Events: Accuracy and Clarity of Flashbulb Memories Related to World War II', *Journal of Experimental Psychology: General*, 134 (2005), 242–57.

Betz, A. L., J. J. Skowronski and T. M. Ostrom, 'Shared Realities: Social Influence and Stimulus Memory', *Social Cognition*, 14 (1996), 113–40.

Binet, A., *La suggestibilité* (Paris, 1900).

Black, J. B., and G. H. Bower, 'Story Understanding as Problem-Solving', *Poetics*, 9 (1980), 223–50.

Blacker, J., *The Faces of Time: Portrayal of the Past in Old French and Latin Historical Narrative of the Anglo-Norman Regnum* (Austin, TX, 1994).

Blank, H., 'Remembering: A Theoretical Interface Between Memory and Social Psychology', *Social Psychology*, 40 (2009), 164–75.

Bliese, J. R. E., 'Aelred of Rievaulx's Rhetoric and Morale at the Battle of the Standard, 1138', *Albion*, 20 (1988), 543–56.

Bloch, M., *The Historian's Craft*, trans. P. Putnam with an introduction by J. R. Strayer (Manchester, 1954).

Blöndal, S. B., and B. S. Benedicz, *The Varangians of Byzantium* (Cambridge, 1978).

Bluck, S., and T. Habermas, 'The Life Story Schema', *Motivation and Emotion*, 24 (2000), 121–47.

Bodner, G. E., E. Musch and T. Azad, 'Reevaluating the Potency of the Memory Conformity Effect', *Memory & Cognition*, 37 (2009), 1069–76.

Bohannon III, J. N., 'Flashbulb Memories for the Space Shuttle Disaster: A Tale of Two Theories', *Cognition*, 29 (1988), 179–96.

Booth, W. C., *The Rhetoric of Fiction*, 2nd edn (Chicago, 1983).

Bornstein, B. H., and S. D. Penrod, 'Hugo Who? G. F. Arnold's Alternative Approach to Psychology and Law', *Applied Cognitive Psychology*, 22 (2008), 759–68.

Bouchard, C. B., *'Every Valley Shall Be Exalted': The Discourse of Opposites in Twelfth-Century Thought* (Ithaca, NY, 2003).

Boudon, G., 'Robert de Clari en Aminois, chevalier, auteur d'une chronique de la IVe croisade (1202–1216)', *Bulletin de la Société des antiquaires de Picardie*, 19 (1895–7), 700–34.

—— 'Documents nouveaux sur la famille de Robert de Clari', *Bulletin de la Société des antiquaires de Picardie*, 20 (1899), 372–9.

Bournazel, É., *Louis VI le Gros* (Paris, 2007).

Boyd, B., *On the Origin of Stories: Evolution, Cognition, and Fiction* (Cambridge, MA, 2009).

Bradfield, A. L., G. L. Wells and E. A. Olson, 'The Damaging Effect of Confirming Feedback on the Relation Between Eyewitness Certainty and Identification Accuracy', *Journal of Applied Psychology*, 87 (2002), 112–20.

Bradley, P. J., 'Irony and the Narrator in Xenophon's *Anabasis*', in E. I. Tylawsky and C. G. Weiss (eds), *Essays in Honor of Gordon Williams* (New Haven, 2001), pp. 59–84.

Brewer, M. B., and W. Gardner, 'Who Is This "We"? Levels of Collective Identity and Self-Representation', *Journal of Personality and Social Psychology*, 71 (1996), 83–93.

Brodersen, K., 'Mapping Pliny's World: The Achievement of Solinus', *Bulletin of the Institute of Classical Studies*, 54 (2011), 63–88.

—— 'A Revised Handlist of Manuscripts Transmitting Solinus' Work', in K. Brodersen (ed.), *Solinus: New Studies* (Heidelberg, 2014), pp. 201–8.

Bronzwaer, W., 'Mieke Bal's Concept of Focalization: A Critical Note', *Poetics Today*, 2 (1981), 193–201.

Brown, A. D., A. Coman and W. Hirst, 'The Role of Narratorship and Expertise in Social Remembering', *Social Psychology*, 40 (2009), 119–29.

Brown, E. A. R., 'Saint-Denis and the Turpin Legend', in J. Williams and A. Stones (eds), *The* Codex Calixtinus *and the Shrine of St. James* (Jakobus-Studien, 3; Tübingen, 1992), pp. 51–88.

Brown, R., and J. Kulik, 'Flashbulb Memories', *Cognition*, 5 (1977), 73–99.

Buckhout, R., 'Eyewitness Testimony', *Scientific American*, 231:6 (1974), 23–31.

Buda, M., 'Early Historical Narrative and the Dynamics of Textual Reference', *Romanic Review*, 80 (1989), 1–17.

Bull, M. G., 'The Eyewitness Accounts of the First Crusade as Political Scripts', *Reading Medieval Studies*, 36 (2010), 23–37.

—— 'The Relationship between the *Gesta Francorum* and Peter Tudebode's *Historia de Hierosolymitano Itinere*: The Evidence of a Hitherto Unexamined Manuscript (St. Catherine's College, Cambridge, 3)', *Crusades*, 11 (2012), 1–17.

—— 'The Historiographical Construction of a Northern French First Crusade', *Haskins Society Journal*, 25 (2013), 35–55.

—— 'Narratological Readings of Crusade Texts', in A. J. Boas (ed.), *The Crusader World* (Abingdon, 2016), pp. 646–60.
—— 'Eyewitness and Medieval Historical Narrative', in E. S. Kooper and S. Levelt (eds), *The Medieval Chronicle 11* (Leiden, 2018), pp. 1–22.
Bur, M., *Suger, abbé de Saint-Denis, régent de France* (Paris, 1991).
Bynum, C. W., 'Did the Twelfth Century Discover the Individual?', *Journal of Ecclesiastical History*, 31 (1980), 1–17; expanded in her *Jesus as Mother: Studies in the Spirituality of the High Middle Ages* (Berkeley, 1982), pp. 82–109.
Cam, H. M., 'An East Anglian Shire-Moot for Stephen's Reign', *English Historical Review*, 39 (1924), 568–71.
Carmichael, L., H. P. Hogan and A. A. Walter, 'An Experimental Study of the Effect of Language on the Reproduction of Visually Perceived Form', *Journal of Experimental Psychology*, 15 (1932), 73–86.
Carr, D., *Experience and History: Phenomenological Perspectives on the Historical World* (Oxford, 2014).
Carrard, P., *Poetics of the New History: French Historical Discourse from Braudel to Chartier* (Baltimore, 1992).
Chatman, S., *Story and Discourse: Narrative Structure in Fiction and Film* (Ithaca, NY, 1978).
—— 'Characters and Narrators: Filter, Center, Slant, and Interest-Focus', *Poetics Today*, 7 (1986), 189–204.
—— *Coming to Terms: The Rhetoric of Narrative in Fiction and Film* (Ithaca, NY, 1990).
Chibnall, M., *The World of Orderic Vitalis* (Oxford, 1984).
Christianson, S.-Å, 'Flashbulb Memories: Special, But Not So Special', *Memory & Cognition*, 17 (1989), 435–43.
Chrobak, Q. M., and M. S. Zaragoza, 'Inventing Stories: Forcing Witnesses to Fabricate Entire Fictitious Events Leads to Freely Reported False Memories', *Psychonomic Bulletin and Review*, 15 (2008), 1190–5.
—— 'When Forced Fabrications Become Truth: Causal Explanations and False Memory Development', *Journal of Experimental Psychology: General*, 142 (2013), 827–44.
Cioffi, C. A., 'The Epistolary Style of Odo of Deuil in his "De Profectione Ludovici VII in Orientem"', *Mittellateinisches Jahrbuch*, 23 (1988), 76–81.
Cizek, A., 'L'Historia comme témoignage oculaire: Quelques implications et conséquences de la définition de l'historiographie chez Isodore de Séville', in D. Buschinger (ed.), *Histoire et littérature au moyen âge: Actes du Colloque du Centre d'Études Médiévales de l'Université de Picardie (Amiens 20–24 mars 1985)* (Göppinger Arbeiten zur Germanistik, 546; Göppingen, 1991), pp. 69–84.
Clark, A., and D. Chalmers, 'The Extended Mind', *Analysis*, 58 (1998), 7–19.
Clifford, B., 'A Critique of Eyewitness Research', in M. M. Gruneberg, P. E.

Morris and R. N. Sykes (eds), *Practical Aspects of Memory* (London, 1978), pp. 199–209.

Coady, C. A. J., *Testimony: A Philosophical Study* (Oxford, 1992).

Cobley, P., *Narrative* (Abingdon, 2001).

Cohen, G., and M. A. Conway (eds), *Memory in the Real World*, 3rd edn (Hove, 2008).

Cohn, D., *The Distinction of Fiction* (Baltimore, 1999).

Colegrove, F. W., 'Individual Memories', *American Journal of Psychology*, 10 (1899), 228–55.

Coman, A., A. D. Brown, J. Koppel and W. Hirst, 'Collective Memory from a Psychological Perspective', *International Journal of Politics, Culture, and Society*, 22 (2009), 125–41.

Coman, A., D. Manier and W. Hirst, 'Forgetting the Unforgettable Through Conversation: Socially Shared Retrieval-Induced Forgetting of September 11 Memories', *Psychological Science*, 20 (2009), 627–33.

Connerton, P., *How Societies Remember* (Cambridge, 1989).

Constable, G., 'The Second Crusade as Seen by Contemporaries', *Traditio*, 9 (1953), 213–79; revised version in his *Crusaders and Crusading in the Twelfth Century* (Farnham, 2008), pp. 229–309.

—— 'The Crusading Project of 1150', in B. Z. Kedar, J. S. C. Riley-Smith and R. Hiestand (eds), *Montjoie: Studies in Crusade History in Honour of Hans Eberhard Mayer* (Aldershot, 1997), pp. 67–75.

—— 'A Further Note on the Conquest of Lisbon in 1147', in M. G. Bull and N. J. Housley (eds), *The Experience of Crusading I: Western Approaches* (Cambridge, 2003), pp. 39–44.

Conway, M. A., *Flashbulb Memories* (Hove, 1995).

—— 'Memory and the Self', *Journal of Memory and Language*, 53 (2005), 594–628.

Conway, M. A., and L. Jobson, 'On the Nature of Autobiographical Memory', in D. Bernsten and D. C. Rubin (eds), *Understanding Autobiographical Memory: Theories and Approaches* (Cambridge, 2012), pp. 54–69.

Conway, M. A., J. A. Singer and A. Tagini, 'The Self and Autobiographical Memory: Correspondence and Coherence', *Social Cognition*, 22 (2004), 491–529.

Cowley, E., 'Remembering the Impressions of Others as Our Own: How Post-experience Decisions can Distort Autobiographical Memory', *Applied Cognitive Psychology*, 20 (2006), 227–38.

Croizy-Naquet, C., 'Les figures du jongleur dans l'*Estoire de la guerre sainte*', *Le moyen âge*, 104 (1998), 229–56.

—— 'Deux répresentations de la troisième croisade: L'*Estoire de la guerre sainte et* la *Chronique d'Ernoul et de Bernard le Trésorier*', *Cahiers de civilisation médiévale*, 44 (2001), 313–27.

—— 'Les festivités dans l'*Estoire de la guerre sainte* d'Ambroise', *Le moyen âge*, 108 (2002), 61–82.

—— 'Merveille et miracle dans l'*Estoire de la guerre sainte* d'Ambroise: éléments de définition d'un genre', in F. Gingras, F. Laurent, F. Le Nan and J.-R. Valette (eds), *'Furent les merveilles pruvees et les aventures truvees': Hommage à Francis Dubost* (Paris, 2005), pp. 177–92.

—— 'Légende ou histoire? Les assassins dans l'*Estoire de guerre sainte* d'Ambroise et dans la *Chronique d'Ernoul et de Bernard le Trésorier*', *Le moyen âge*, 117 (2011), 237–57.

Cubitt, G., *History and Memory* (Manchester, 2007).

Cuc, A., J. Koppel and W. Hirst, 'Silence Is Not Golden: A Case for Socially Shared Retrieval-Induced Forgetting', *Psychological Science*, 18 (2007), 727–33.

Cuc, A., Y. Ozuru, D. Manier and W. Hirst, 'On the Formation of Collective Memories: The Role of a Dominant Narrator', *Memory & Cognition*, 34 (2006), 752–62.

Culler, J., *Structuralist Poetics: Structuralism, Linguistics and the Study of Literature* (London, 1975).

—— *The Literary in Theory* (Stanford, 2007).

Curci, A., O. Luminet, C. Finkenauer and L. Gisle, 'Flashbulb Memories in Social Groups: A Comparative Test-Retest Study of the Memory of French President Mitterand's Death in a French and a Belgian Group', *Memory*, 9 (2001), 81–101.

Currie, G., *Narratives and Narrators: A Philosophy of Stories* (Oxford, 2010).

Cutler, B. L., and S. D. Penrod, *Mistaken Identification: The Eyewitness, Psychology, and the Law* (Cambridge, 1995).

Cutler, B. L., S. D. Penrod and T. K. Martens, 'The Reliability of Eyewitness Identification: The Role of System and Estimator Variables', *Law and Human Behavior*, 11 (1987), 233–58.

Damian-Grint, P., 'Truth, Trust, and Evidence in the Anglo-Norman *Estoire*', in C. Harper-Bill (ed.), *Anglo-Norman Studies XVIII: Proceedings of the Battle Conference 1995* (Woodbridge, 1996), pp. 63–78.

—— '*Estoire* as Word and Genre: Meaning and Literary Usage in the Twelfth Century', *Medium Aevum*, 66 (1997), 189–206.

—— *The New Historians of the Twelfth-Century Renaissance: Inventing Vernacular Authority* (Woodbridge, 1999).

Darby, D., 'Form and Context: An Essay in the History of Narratology', *Poetics Today*, 22 (2001), 829–52.

Davidson, J., 'The Gaze in Polybius' *Histories*', *Journal of Roman Studies*, 81 (1991), 10–24.

Davis, B., R. Anderson and J. Walls (eds), *Rashomon Effects: Kurosawa,* Rashomon *and Their Legacies* (Routledge Advances in Film Studies, 44; Abingdon, 2016).

Dembowski, P. F., *La chronique de Robert de Clari: Etude de la langue et du style* (University of Toronto Romance Series, 6; Toronto, 1963).
Denery II, D. G., *Seeing and Being Seen in the Later Medieval World: Optics, Theology and Religious Life* (Cambridge, 2005).
Dewald, C. J., *Thucydides' War Narrative: A Structural Study* (Berkeley, 2005).
Diggelmann, L., 'Of Grifons and Tyrants: Anglo-Norman Views of the Mediterranean World During the Third Crusade', in L. Bailey, L. Diggelmann and K. M. Phillips (eds), *Old Worlds, New Worlds: European Cultural Encounters, c.1000–c.1750* (Late Medieval and Early Modern Studies, 18; Turnhout, 2009), pp. 11–30.
Dodd, D. H., and J. M. Bradshaw, 'Leading Questions and Memory: Pragmatic Constraints', *Journal of Verbal Learning and Verbal Behavior*, 19 (1980), 695–704.
Doležel, L., *Heterocosmica: Fiction and Possible Worlds* (Baltimore, 1998).
—— *Possible Worlds of Fiction and History: The Postmodern Stage* (Baltimore, 2010).
Douglass, A. B., and N. Steblay, 'Memory Distortion in Eyewitnesses: A Meta-Analysis of the Post-identification Feedback Effect', *Applied Cognitive Psychology*, 20 (2006), 859–69.
Doyle, J. M., *True Witness: Cops, Courts, Science, and the Battle Against Misidentification* (New York, 2005).
Dudukovic, N. M., E. J. Marsh and B. Tversky, 'Telling a Story or Telling it Straight: The Effects of Entertaining Versus Accurate Retellings on Memory', *Applied Cognitive Psychology*, 18 (2004), 125–43.
Dufournet, J., *Les écrivains de la IVe croisade: Villehardouin et Clari*, 1 vol. in 2 (Paris, 1973).
—— 'Robert de Clari, Villehardouin et Henri de Valenciennes, juges de l'empereur Henri de Constantinople. De l'histoire à la légende', in *Mélanges de littérature du moyen âge au XXe siècle offerts à Mademoiselle Jeanne Lods*, 1 vol. in 2 (Collection de l'École Normale Supérieure de Jeunes Filles, 10; Paris, 1978), pp. 183–202.
Echterhoff, G., E. T. Higgins and S. Groll, 'Audience-Tuning Effects on Memory: The Role of Shared Reality', *Journal of Personality and Social Psychology*, 89 (2005), 257–76.
Echterhoff, G., E. T. Higgins and J. M. Levine, 'Shared Reality: Experiencing Commonality with Others' Inner States About the World', *Perspectives on Psychological Science*, 4 (2009), 496–521.
Echterhoff, G., and W. Hirst, 'Thinking About Memories for Everyday and Shocking Events: Do People Use Ease-of-Retrieval Cues in Memory Judgments?', *Memory & Cognition*, 34 (2006), 763–75.
Echterhoff, G., S. Lang, N. Krämer and E. T. Higgins, 'Audience-Tuning

Effects on Memory: The Role of Audience Status in Sharing Reality', *Social Psychology*, 40 (2009), 150–63.

Edgington, S. B., 'The Lisbon Letter of the Second Crusade', *Historical Research*, 69 (1996), 328–39.

—— 'Albert of Aachen, St Bernard and the Second Crusade', in J. P. Phillips and M. Hoch (eds), *The Second Crusade: Scope and Consequences* (Manchester, 2001), pp. 54–70.

—— 'The Capture of Lisbon: Premeditated or Opportunistic?', in J. T. Roche and J. M. Jensen (eds), *The Second Crusade: Holy War on the Periphery of Latin Christendom* (Outremer, 2; Turnhout, 2015), pp. 257–72.

Edmiston, W. F., 'Focalization and the First-Person Narrator: A Revision of the Theory', *Poetics Today*, 10 (1989), 729–44.

Edmonds, D., and J. Eidinow, *Wittgenstein's Poker: The Story of a Ten-Minute Argument Between Two Great Philosophers* (London, 2001).

Edwards, D., and D. Middleton, 'Joint Remembering: Constructing an Account of Shared Experience Through Conversational Discourse', *Discourse Processes*, 9 (1986), 423–59.

Edwards, D., and J. Potter, 'The Chancellor's Memory: Rhetoric and Truth in Discursive Remembering', *Applied Cognitive Psychology*, 6 (1992), 187–215.

Edwards, J. G., 'The *Itinerarium Regis Ricardi* and the *Estoire de la Guerre Sainte*', in J. G. Edwards, V. H. Galbraith and E. J. Jacob (eds), *Historical Essays in Honour of James Tait* (Manchester, 1933), pp. 59–77.

Ellis, H. D., 'Practical Aspects of Face Memory', in G. L. Wells and E. F. Loftus (eds), *Eyewitness Testimony: Psychological Perspectives* (Cambridge, 1984), pp. 12–37.

Emmott, C., *Narrative Comprehension: A Discourse Perspective* (Oxford, 1997).

Engel, S., *Context Is Everything: The Nature of Memory* (New York, 1999).

Epp, V., *Fulcher von Chartres: Studien zur Geschichtsschreibung des ersten Kreuzzuges* (Studia humaniora, 15; Düsseldorf, 1990).

Erll, A., *Memory in Culture*, trans. S. B. Young (Basingstoke, 2011).

Evans, J. D., 'Episode in Analysis of Medieval Narrative', *Style*, 20 (1986), 126–41.

Faral, E., 'Geoffroy de Villehardouin: La question de sa sincérité', *Revue historique*, 177 (1936), 530–82.

Farris, W. W., *Heavenly Warriors: The Evolution of Japan's Military, 500–1300* (Harvard East Asian Monographs, 157; Cambridge, MA, 1992).

Fentress, J., and C. Wickham, *Social Memory* (Oxford, 1992).

Ferzoco, G. P., 'The Origins of the Second Crusade', in M. Gervers (ed.), *The Second Crusade and the Cistercians* (New York, 1992), pp. 91–9.

Fischhof, B., 'Hindsight ≠ Foresight: The Effect of Outcome Knowledge on Judgment Under Uncertainty', *Journal of Experimental Psychology: Human Perception and Performance*, 1 (1975), 288–99.

Fleischmann, S., 'On the Representation of History and Fiction in the Middle Ages', *History and Theory*, 22 (1983), 278–310.

Fling, F. M., *The Writing of History: An Introduction to Historical Method* (New Haven, 1920).

Flori, J., *Chroniqueurs et propagandistes: Introduction critique aux sources de la première croisade* (Hautes études médiévales et modernes, 98; Geneva, 2010).

Flower, M. A., *Xenophon's* Anabasis, *or* The Expedition of Cyrus (Oxford, 2012).

Fludernik, M., 'Histories of Narrative Theory (II): From Structuralism to the Present', in J. Phelan and P. J. Rabinowitz (eds), *A Companion to Narrative Theory* (Oxford, 2005), pp. 36–59.

—— *An Introduction to Narratology*, trans. P. Häusler-Greenfield and M. Fludernik (Abingdon, 2009).

Folda, J., 'The Fourth Crusade, 1201–3: Some Reconsiderations', *Byzantinoslavica*, 26 (1965), 277–90.

Foot, S., 'Remembering, Forgetting and Inventing: Attitudes to the Past in England at the End of the First Viking Age', *Transactions of the Royal Historical Society*, 6th ser., 9 (1999), 185–200.

—— 'Finding the Meaning of Form: Narrative in Annals and Chronicles', in N. F. Partner (ed.), *Writing Medieval History* (London, 2005), pp. 88–108.

Forey, A. J., 'The Failure of the Siege of Damascus in 1148', *Journal of Medieval History*, 10 (1984), 13–23.

—— 'The Siege of Lisbon and the Second Crusade', *Portuguese Studies*, 20 (2004), 1–13.

Fornara, C. W., *The Nature of History in Ancient Greece and Rome* (Berkeley, 1983).

Foster, J. K., *Memory: A Very Short Introduction* (Oxford, 2009).

France, J., 'Patronage and the Appeal of the First Crusade', in J. P. Phillips (ed.), *The First Crusade: Origins and Impact* (Manchester, 1997), pp. 5–20.

—— 'Logistics and the Second Crusade', in J. H. Pryor (ed.), *Logistics of Warfare in the Age of the Crusades: Proceedings of a Workshop held at the Centre for Medieval Studies, University of Sydney, 30 September to 4 October 2002* (Aldershot, 2006), pp. 77–93.

Frisch, A., 'The Ethics of Testimony: A Genealogical Perspective', *Discourse*, 25 (2003), 36–54.

—— *The Invention of the Eyewitness: Witnessing and Testimony in Early Modern France* (Chapel Hill, NC, 2004).

Führer, J., 'Französisches Königreich und französisches Königtum in der Wahrnehmung der zeitgenössischen Historiographie: Suger von Saint-Denis und Guillaume de Nangis', in N. Kersken and G. Vercamer (eds), *Macht und Spiegel der Macht: Herrschaft in Europa im 12. und 13. Jahrhundert vor dem Hintergrund der Chronistik* (Deutsches Historisches Institut Warshau, Quellen und Studien, 27; Wiesbaden, 2013), pp. 199–218.

Gabbert, F., A. Memon and K. Allan, 'Memory Conformity: Can Eyewitnesses Influence Each Other's Memories for an Event?', *Applied Cognitive Psychology*, 17 (2003), 533–43.

Galbraith IV, S., *The Emperor and the Wolf: The Lives and Films of Akira Kurosawa and Toshiro Mifune* (New York, 2001).

Gardiner, J. M., 'Episodic Memory and Autonoetic Consciousness: A First-Person Approach', in A. Baddeley, J. P. Aggleton and M. A. Conway (eds), *Episodic Memory: New Directions in Research* (Oxford, 2002), pp. 11–30.

Garraghan, G. J., *A Guide to Historical Method*, ed. J. Delanglez (New York, 1946).

Garrett, B. L., *Convicting the Innocent: Where Criminal Prosecutions Go Wrong* (Cambridge, MA, 2011).

Garry, M., and H. Hayne (eds), *Do Justice and Let the Sky Fall: Elizabeth F. Loftus and Her Contributions to Science, Law, and Academic Freedom* (Mahwah, NJ, 2007).

Garry, M., C. G. Manning, E. F. Loftus and S. J. Sherman, 'Imagination Inflation: Imagining a Childhood Event Inflates Confidence That it Occurred', *Psychonomic Bulletin and Review*, 3 (1996), 208–14.

Garzke Jr, W. H., D. K. Brown, A. D. Sandiford, J. Woodward and P. K. Hsu, 'The *Titanic* and the *Lusitania*: A Final Forensic Analysis', *Marine Technology*, 33 (1996), 241–89.

Gasparri, F., *Suger de Saint-Denis: Abbé, soldat, homme d'État au XIIe siècle* (Paris, 2015).

Genette, G., *Narrative Discourse: An Essay in Method*, trans. J. E. Lewin (Ithaca, NY, 1980).

—— *Narrative Discourse Revisited*, trans. J. E. Lewin (Ithaca, NY, 1988).

—— *Paratexts: Thresholds of Interpretation*, trans. J. E. Lewin (Literature, Culture, Theory, 20; Cambridge, 1997).

Gerrie, M. P., L. E. Belcher and M. Garry, '"Mind the Gap": False Memories for Missing Aspects of an Event', *Applied Cognitive Psychology*, 20 (2006), 689–96.

Gerrig, R. J., *Experiencing Narrative Worlds: On the Psychological Activities of Reading* (New Haven, 1993).

Gibb, H. A. R., 'Notes on the Arabic Materials for the History of the Early Crusades', *Bulletin of the School of Oriental Studies*, 7 (1935), 739–54.

—— 'The Arabic Sources for the Life of Saladin', *Speculum*, 25 (1950), 58–72.

Gillingham, J., 'Roger of Howden on Crusade', in his *Richard Coeur de Lion: Kingship, Chivalry and War in the Twelfth Century* (London, 1994), pp. 141–53.

—— *Richard I* (New Haven, 1999).

—— 'The English Invasion of Ireland', in his *The English in the Twelfth Century: Imperialism, National Identity and Political Values* (Woodbridge, 2000), pp. 145–60.

—— 'Henry of Huntingdon and the Twelfth-Century Revival of the English Nation', in his *The English in the Twelfth Century: Imperialism, National Identity and Political Values* (Woodbridge, 2000), pp. 123–44.

Ginet, C., *On Action* (Cambridge, 1990).

Godfrey, J., *1204: The Unholy Crusade* (Oxford, 1980).

Gordon, R., N. Franklin and J. Beck, 'Wishful Thinking and Source Monitoring', *Memory & Cognition*, 33 (2005), 418–29.

Gossman, L., 'Anecdote and History', *History and Theory*, 42 (2003), 143–68.

Gottschalk, L., *Understanding History: A Primer of Historical Method*, 2nd edn (New York, 1969).

Gransden, A., 'Prologues in the Historiography of Twelfth-Century England', in D. T. Williams (ed.), *England in the Twelfth Century: Proceedings of the 1988 Harlaxton Symposium* (Woodbridge, 1990), pp. 55–81.

Grant, L., *Abbot Suger of St-Denis: Church and State in Early Twelfth-Century France* (London, 1998).

Gray, V. J., 'Xenophon', in I. J. F. de Jong, R. Nünlist and A. M. Bowie (eds), *Narrators, Narratees, and Narratives in Ancient Greek Literature* (Studies in Ancient Greek Narrative, 1; Leiden, 2004), pp. 129–46.

Greenberg, M. S., D. R. Westcott and S. E. Bailey, 'When Believing Is Seeing: The Effects of Scripts on Eyewitness Memory', *Law and Human Behavior*, 22 (1998), 685–94.

Greenblatt, S., *Marvelous Possessions: The Wonder of the New World* (Chicago, 1991).

Greene, E., 'Whodunit? Memory for Evidence in Text', *American Journal of Psychology*, 94 (1981), 479–96.

Greenwald, A. G., 'The Totalitarian Ego: Fabrication and Revision of Personal History', *American Psychologist*, 35 (1980), 603–18.

Grethlein, J., 'Experientiality and "Narrative Reference", with Thanks to Thucydides', *History and Theory*, 49 (2010), 315–35.

—— 'Xenophon's *Anabasis* from Character to Narrator', *Journal of Hellenic Studies*, 132 (2012), 23–40.

—— *Experience and Teleology in Ancient Historiography: 'Futures Past' from Herodotus to Augustine* (Cambridge, 2013).

Guynn, N. D., 'Rhetoric and Historiography: Villehardouin's *La Conquête de Constantinople*', in W. Burgwinkle, N. Hammond and E. Wilson (eds), *The Cambridge History of French Literature* (Cambridge, 2011), pp. 102–10.

Haber, L., and R. N. Haber, 'Criteria for Judging the Admissibility of Eyewitness Testimony of Long Past Events', *Psychology, Public Policy, and Law*, 4 (1998), 1135–59.

Haber, R. N., and L. Haber, 'Experiencing, Remembering and Reporting Events', *Psychology, Public Policy, and Law*, 6 (2000), 1057–97.

Habermas, T., 'Identity, Emotion, and the Social Matrix of Autobiographical

Memory: A Psychoanalytic Narrative View', in D. Bernsten and D. C. Rubin (eds), *Autobiographical Memory: Theories and Approaches* (Cambridge, 2012), pp. 33–53.
Haidu, P., 'The Episode as Semiotic Module in Twelfth-Century Romance', *Poetics Today*, 4 (1983), 655–81.
Halbwachs, M., *On Collective Memory*, ed. and trans. L. A. Coser (Chicago, 1992).
Hale, M., *Human Science and Social Order: Hugo Münsterberg and the Origins of Applied Psychology* (Philadelphia, 1980).
Hall, D. F., E. F. Loftus and J. P. Tousignant, 'Postevent Information and Changes in Recollection for a Natural Event', in G. L. Wells and E. F. Loftus (eds), *Eyewitness Testimony: Psychological Perspectives* (Cambridge, 1984), pp. 124–41.
Hanley, C., 'Reading the Past Through the Present: Ambroise, the Minstrel of Reims and Jordan Fantosme', *Mediaevalia*, 20 (2001), 263–81.
Harari, Y. N., 'Eyewitnessing in Accounts of the First Crusade: The *Gesta Francorum* and Other Contemporary Narratives', *Crusades*, 3 (2004), 77–99.
—— 'Scholars, Eyewitnesses, and Flesh-Witnesses of War: A Tense Relationship', *Partial Answers: Journal of Literature and the History of Ideas*, 7 (2009), 213–28.
—— 'Armchairs, Coffee, and Authority: Eye-witnesses and Flesh-witnesses Speak About War, 1100–2000', *Journal of Military History*, 74 (2010), 53–78.
Harley, E. M., K. A. Carlsen and G. R. Loftus, 'The "Saw-It-All-Along" Effect: Demonstrations of Visual Hindsight Bias', *Journal of Experimental Psychology: Learning, Memory, and Cognition*, 30 (2004), 960–8.
Harris, C. B., H. M. Paterson and R. I. Kemp, 'Collaborative Recall and Collective Memory: What Happens When We Remember Together', *Memory*, 16 (2008), 213–30.
Harris, J., 'Distortion, Divine Providence and Genre in Nicetas Choniates's Account of the Collapse of Byzantium 1180–1204', *Journal of Medieval History*, 26 (2000), 19–31.
—— *Byzantium and the Crusades* (London, 2003).
—— 'The Problem of Supply and the Sack of Constantinople', in P. Piatti (ed.), *The Fourth Crusade Revisited: Atti della Conferenza Internazionale nell'ottavo centenario della IV Crociata 1204-2004, Andros (Grecia), 27-30 maggio 2004* (Atti e documenti, 25; Vatican City, 2008), pp. 145–54.
Hartman, R., *La quête et la croisade: Villehardouin, Clari et le* Lancelot en prose (New York, 1977).
Hawkins, S. A., and R. Hastie, 'Hindsight: Biased Judgments of Past Events After the Outcomes Are Known', *Psychological Bulletin*, 107 (1990), 311–27.
Head, T. F., *Hagiography and the Cult of the Saints: The Diocese of Orléans, 800–1200* (Cambridge, 1990).

Heider, F., and M. Simmel, 'An Experimental Study of Apparent Behavior', *American Journal of Psychology*, 57 (1944), 243–59.

Heine, S. J., D. R. Lehman, H. R. Markus and S. Kitayama, 'Is There a Universal Need for Positive Self-Regard?', *Psychological Review*, 106 (1999), 766–94.

Heinemann, E. A., 'Network of Narrative Details: The Motif of the Journey in the *Chanson de Geste*', in H. Scholler (ed.), *The Epic in Medieval Society: Aesthetic and Moral Values* (Tübingen, 1977), pp. 178–92.

Henige, D., *Historical Evidence and Argument* (Madison, WI, 2005).

Herbers, K., *Der Jakobuskult des 12. Jahrhunderts und der "Liber Sancti Jacobi": Studien über das Verhältnis zwischen Religion und Gesellschaft im hohen Mittelalter* (Historische Forschungen, 7; Wiesbaden, 1984).

Herkommer, E., *Die Topoi in den Proömien der römischen Geschichtswerke* (Stuttgart, 1968).

Herman, D., *Story Logic: Problems and Possibilities of Narrative* (Lincoln, NE, 2004).

—— 'Action Theory', in D. Herman, M. Jahn and M.-L. Ryan (eds), *Routledge Encyclopedia of Narrative Theory* (Abingdon, 2005), pp. 2–3.

—— 'Storyworld', in D. Herman, M. Jahn and M.-L. Ryan (eds), *Routledge Encyclopedia of Narrative Theory* (Abingdon, 2005), pp. 569–70.

—— 'Histories of Narrative Theory (I): A Genealogy of Early Developments', in J. Phelan and P. J. Rabinowitz (eds), *A Companion to Narrative Theory* (Oxford, 2005), pp. 19–35.

Herman, D., M. Jahn and M.-L. Ryan (eds), *Routledge Encyclopedia of Narrative Theory* (Abingdon, 2005).

Herman, D., J. Phelan, P. J. Rabinowitz, B. Richardson and R. Warhol, *Narrative Theory: Core Concepts and Critical Debates* (Columbus, OH, 2012).

Herman, L., and B. Vervaeck, *Handbook of Narrative Analysis* (Lincoln, NE, 2005).

Higgins, E. T., and W. S. Rhodes, '"Saying Is Believing": Effects of Message Modification on Memory and Liking for the Person Described', *Journal of Experimental Social Psychology*, 14 (1978), 363–78.

Higham, P. A., 'Believing Details Known To Have Been Suggested', *British Journal of Psychology*, 89 (1998), 265–83.

Hill, D., *An Atlas of Anglo-Saxon England* (Oxford, 1981).

Hindley, A., F. W. Langley and B. J. Levy (eds), *Old French-English Dictionary* (Cambridge, 2000).

Hirst, W., A. Cuc and D. Wohl, 'Of Sins and Virtues: Memory and Collective Identity', in D. Bernsten and D. C. Rubin (eds), *Understanding Autobiographical Memory: Theories and Approaches* (Cambridge, 2012), pp. 141–57.

Hirst, W., and G. Echterhoff, 'Creating Shared Memories in Conversation: Toward a Psychology of Collective Memory', *Social Research*, 75 (2008), 183–216.

—— 'Remembering in Conversations: The Social Sharing and Reshaping of Memories', *Annual Review of Psychology*, 63 (2012), 55–79.

Hirst, W., and D. Manier, 'Towards a Psychology of Collective Memory', *Memory*, 16 (2008), 183–200.

Hirt, E. R., H. E. McDonald and K. D. Markman, 'Expectancy Effects in Reconstructive Memory: When the Past Is Just What We Expected', in S. J. Lynn and K. M. McConkey (eds), *Truth in Memory* (New York, 1998), pp. 62–89.

Hoch, M., 'The Choice of Damascus as the Objective of the Second Crusade: A Re-evaluation', in M. Balard (ed.), *Autour de la première croisade* (Byzantina Sorboniensia, 14; Paris, 1996), pp. 359–69.

Hockett, H. C., *The Critical Method in Historical Research and Writing* (New York, 1955).

Hodgson, N. R., 'Honour, Shame and the Fourth Crusade', *Journal of Medieval History*, 39 (2013), 220–39.

Hollingsworth, A., 'Memory for Real-World Scenes', in J. R. Brockmole (ed.), *The Visual World in Memory* (Hove, 2009), pp. 89–116.

Hornblower, S., 'Narratology and Narrative Techniques in Thucydides', in S. Hornblower (ed.), *Greek Historiography* (Oxford, 1994), pp. 131–66.

Howell, M. C., and W. Prevenier, *From Reliable Sources: An Introduction to Historical Methods* (Ithaca, NY, 2001).

Howes, M. B., and G. O'Shea, *Human Memory: A Constructivist View* (San Diego, 2014).

Huglo, M., 'Les chants de la *missa Greca* de Saint-Denis', in J. Westrup (ed.), *Essays Presented to Egon Wellesz* (Oxford, 1966), pp. 74–83.

Hunyadi, Z., 'Hungary and the Second Crusade', *Chronica*, 9–10 (2011), 55–65.

Hyman, I. E., T. H. Husband and F. J. Billings, 'False Memories of Childhood Experiences', *Applied Cognitive Psychology*, 9 (1995), 181–97.

Hyman, I. E., and J. Pentland, 'The Role of Mental Imagery in the Creation of False Childhood Memories', *Journal of Memory and Language*, 35 (1996), 101–17.

Jackson, P., 'William of Rubruck in the Mongol Empire: Perception and Prejudices', in Z. von Martels (ed.), *Travel Fact and Travel Fiction: Studies on Fiction, Literary Tradition, Scholarly Discovery and Observation in Travel Writing* (Brill's Studies in Intellectual History, 55; Leiden, 1994), pp. 54–71.

Jacoby, L. L., C. Kelley, J. Brown and J. Jasechko, 'Becoming Famous Overnight: Limits on the Ability to Avoid Unconscious Influences of the Past', *Journal of Personality and Social Psychology*, 56 (1989), 326–38.

Jacquin, G., *Le style historique dans les recits français et latins de la quatrième croisade* (Geneva, 1986).

—— 'Robert de Clari, témoin et conteur', in J.-C. Aubailly, E. Baumgartner, F. Dubost, L. Dulac and M. Faure (eds), *Et c'est la fin pour quoy sommes ensemble: Hommage à Jean Dufournet*, 1 vol. in 3 (Nouvelle bibliothèque du moyen âge, 25; Paris, 1993), ii, pp. 747–57.

Jahn, M., 'Frames, Preferences, and the Reading of Third-Person Narratives: Towards a Cognitive Narratology', *Poetics Today*, 18 (1997), 441–68.

—— 'Focalization', in D. Herman, M. Jahn and M.-L. Ryan (eds), *Routledge Encyclopedia of Narrative Theory* (Abingdon, 2005), pp. 173–7.

—— 'Focalization', in D. Herman (ed.), *The Cambridge Companion to Narrative* (Cambridge, 2007), pp. 94–108.

Jamison, E., 'Some Notes on the *Anonymi Gesta Francorum*, with Special Reference to the Norman Contingent from South Italy and Sicily in the First Crusade', in *Studies in French Language and Mediaeval Literature Presented to Professor Mildred K. Pope* (Manchester, 1939), pp. 183–208.

Janson, T., *Latin Prose Prefaces: Studies in Literary Conventions* (Studia Latina Stockholmiensia, 13; Stockholm, 1964).

Jaspert, N., '*Capta est Dertosa, clavis Christianorum*: Tortosa and the Crusades', in J. P. Phillips and M. Hoch (eds), *The Second Crusade: Scope and Consequences* (Manchester, 2001), pp. 90–110.

Jay, M., *Downcast Eyes: The Denigration of Vision in Twentieth-Century French Thought* (Berkeley, 1993).

Jesch, T., and M. Stein, 'Perspectivization and Focalization: Two Concepts – One Meaning? An Attempt at Conceptual Differentiation', in P. Hühn, W. Schmid and J. Schönert (eds), *Point of View, Perspective, and Focalization: Modeling Mediation in Narrative* (Narratologia, 17; Berlin, 2009), pp. 59–77.

Johanek, P., 'Die Wahrheit der mittelalterlichen Historiographen', in F. P. Knapp and M. Niesner (eds), *Historisches und fiktionales Erzählen im Mittelalter* (Schriften der Literaturwissenschaft, 19; Berlin, 2002), pp. 9–25.

John, S., 'Historical Truth and the Miraculous Past: The Use of Oral Evidence in Twelfth-Century Latin Historical Writing on the First Crusade', *English Historical Review*, 130 (2015), 263–301.

Johnson, A., *The Historian and Historical Evidence* (Port Washington, NY, 1926).

Johnson, M. K., S. Hashtroudi and D. S. Lindsay, 'Source Monitoring', *Psychological Bulletin*, 114 (1993), 3–28.

Jong, I. J. F. de, *A Narratological Commentary on the Odyssey* (Cambridge, 2001).

—— *Narrators and Focalizers: The Presentation of the Story in the* Iliad, 2nd edn (London, 2004).

—— *Narratology and Classics: A Practical Guide* (Oxford, 2014).

Kazhdan, A., and S. Franklin, *Studies on Byzantine Literature of the Eleventh and Twelfth Centuries* (Cambridge, 1984).

Keen, S., *Narrative Form*, 2nd edn (Basingstoke, 2015).

Kempshall, M., *Rhetoric and the Writing of History, 400–1500* (Manchester, 2011).
Kennedy, H. N., *Crusader Castles* (Cambridge, 1994).
Kindt, T., and H.-H. Müller, *The Implied Author: Concept and Controversy* (Narratologia, 9; Berlin, 2006).
Kindt, T., and H.-H. Müller (eds), *What Is Narratology? Questions and Answers Regarding the Status of a Theory* (Narratologia, 1; Berlin, 2003).
Kinoshita, S., *Medieval Boundaries: Rethinking Difference in Old French Literature* (Philadelphia, 2006).
Kopietz, R., G. Echterhoff, S. Niemeier, J. H. Hellmann and A. Memon, 'Audience-Congruent Biases in Eyewitness Memory and Judgment', *Social Psychology*, 40 (2009), 138–49.
Kostick, C., 'A Further Discussion on the Authorship of the *Gesta Francorum*', *Reading Medieval Studies*, 35 (2009), 1–14.
Koziol, G., 'England, France, and the Problem of Sacrality in Twelfth-Century Ritual', in T. N. Bisson (ed.), *Cultures of Power: Lordship, Status, and Process in Twelfth-Century Europe* (Philadelphia, 1995), pp. 124–48.
Kraus, C. S., 'Caesar's Account of the Battle of Massilia (*BC* 1.34–2.22): Some Historiographical and Narratological Approaches', in J. Marincola (ed.), *A Companion to Greek and Roman Historiography* (Chichester, 2011), pp. 371–8.
Kurosawa, A., *Something Like an Autobiography*, trans. A. E. Bock (New York, 1983).
Kurth, F., 'Der Anteil niederdeutscher Kreuzfahrer an den Kämpfen der Portugiesen gegen die Mauren', *Mitteilungen des Instituts für Österreichische Geschichtsforschung: Ergänzungsband*, 8 (1911), 131–252.
Lakoff, G., and M. Johnson, *Metaphors We Live By*, rev. edn (Chicago, 2003).
Lamarque, P., 'On Not Expecting Too Much from Narrative', *Mind and Language*, 19 (2004), 393–408.
Lapina, E., '"Nec signis nec testis creditur…": The Problem of Eyewitnesses in the Chronicles of the First Crusade', *Viator*, 38 (2007), 117–39.
Lay, S., 'Miracles, Martyrs and the Cult of Henry the Crusader in Lisbon', *Portuguese Studies*, 24 (2008), 7–31.
—— *The Reconquest Kings of Portugal: Political and Cultural Reorientation on the Medieval Frontier* (Basingstoke, 2009).
—— 'The Reconquest as Crusade in the Anonymous *De expugnatione Lyxbonensi*', in J.-J. López-Portillo (ed.), *Spain, Portugal and the Atlantic Frontier of Medieval Europe* (The Expansion of Latin Europe, 1000–1500, 8; Farnham, 2013), pp. 123–30.
Le Fanu, M., *Mizoguchi and Japan* (London, 2005).
Leary, M. R., 'Hindsight Distortion and the 1980 Presidential Election', *Personality and Social Psychology Bulletin*, 8 (1982), 257–63.

Leichtman, M. D., Q. Wang and D. B. Pillemer, 'Cultural Variations in Interdependence and Autobiographical Memory: Lessons from Korea, China, India, and the United States', in R. Fivush and C. A. Haden (eds), *Autobiographical Memory and the Construction of a Narrative Self: Developmental and Cultural Perspectives* (Mahwah, NJ, 2003), pp. 73–97.

Lejeune, P., 'Autobiography in the Third Person', *New Literary History*, 9 (1977), 27–50.

Lendon, J. E., 'Historians Without History: Against Roman Historiography', in A. Feldherr (ed.), *The Cambridge Companion to the Roman Historians* (Cambridge, 2009), pp. 41–61.

Levy, B. J., 'Pèlerins rivaux de la 3e Croisade: les personnages des rois d'Angleterre et de France, d'après les chroniques d'Ambroise et d'"Ernoul" et le récit anglo-normand de la *Croisade et Mort Richard Coeur de Lion*', in D. Buschinger (ed.), *La croisade: réalités et fictions. Actes du Colloque d'Amiens 18-22 mars 1987* (Göppinger Arbeiten zur Germanistik, 503: Göppingen, 1989), pp. 143–55.

Lilie, R.-J., *Byzantium and the Crusader States 1096–1204*, trans. J. C. Morris and J. E. Ridings (Oxford, 1993).

—— 'Zufall oder Absicht? Die Ablenkung des vierten Kreuzzugs nach Konstantinopel: repetita lectio', in P. Piatti (ed.), *The Fourth Crusade Revisited: Atti della Conferenza Internazionale nell'ottavo centenario della IV Crociata 1204-2004, Andros (Grecia), 27-30 maggio 2004* (Atti e documenti, 25; Vatican City, 2008), pp. 129–44.

Lindberg, D. C., *Studies in the History of Medieval Optics* (London, 1983).

Lindner, R. P., 'Odo of Deuil's *The Journey of Louis VII to the East*: Between *The Song of Roland* and Joinville's *Life of Saint Louis*', in J. Glenn (ed.), *The Middle Ages in Text and Texture: Reflections on Medieval Sources* (Toronto, 2011), pp. 165–76.

Lindsay, D. S., 'Misleading Suggestions Can Impair Eyewitnesses' Ability to Remember Event Details', *Journal of Experimental Psychology: Learning, Memory, and Cognition*, 16 (1990), 1077–83.

—— 'Autobiographical Memory, Eyewitness Reports, and Public Policy', *Canadian Psychology*, 48 (2007), 57–66.

Lindsay, D. S., B. P. Allen, J. C. K. Chan and L. C. Dahl, 'Eyewitness Suggestibility and Source Similarity: Intrusions of Details from One Event into Memory Reports of Another Event', *Journal of Memory and Language*, 50 (2004), 96–111.

Lindsay, D. S., and M. K. Johnson, 'The Eyewitness Suggestibility Effect and Memory for Source', *Memory & Cognition*, 17 (1989), 349–58.

Linton, M., 'Transformations of Memory in Everyday Life', in U. Neisser (ed.), *Memory Observed: Remembering in Natural Contexts* (New York, 1982), pp. 77–91.

Livermore, H., 'The "Conquest of Lisbon" and its Author', *Portuguese Studies*, 6 (1990), 1–16.

Lock, P., *The Franks in the Aegean, 1204–1500* (London, 1995).

Lodge, A., 'Literature and History in the Chronicle of Jordan Fantosme', *French Studies*, 44 (1990), 257–70.

Loftus, E. F., 'Leading Questions and the Eyewitness Report', *Cognitive Psychology*, 7 (1975), 560–72.

—— 'Shifting Human Color Memory', *Memory & Cognition*, 5 (1977), 696–9.

—— 'The Reality of Repressed Memories', *American Psychologist*, 48 (1993), 518–37.

—— *Eyewitness Testimony*, rev. edn (Cambridge, MA, 1996).

—— 'Planting Misinformation in the Human Mind: A 30-Year Investigation of the Malleability of Memory', *Learning and Memory*, 12 (2005), 361–6.

Loftus, E. F., J. M. Doyle and J. E. Dysart (eds), *Eyewitness Testimony: Civil and Criminal*, 5th edn (New Providence, NJ, 2013).

Loftus, E. F., and K. Ketcham, 'The Malleability of Eyewitness Accounts', in S. M. A. Lloyd-Bostock and B. R. Clifford (eds), *Evaluating Witness Evidence: Recent Psychological Research and New Perspectives* (Chichester, 1983), pp. 159–71.

—— *Witness for the Defense: The Accused, the Eyewitness, and the Expert Who Puts Memory on Trial* (New York, 1991).

—— *The Myth of Repressed Memory: False Memories and Allegations of Sexual Abuse* (New York, 1994).

Loftus, E. F., D. G. Miller and H. J. Burns, 'Semantic Integration of Verbal Information into a Verbal Memory', *Journal of Experimental Psychology: Human Learning and Memory*, 4 (1978), 19–31.

Loftus, E. F., and J. C. Palmer, 'Reconstruction of Automobile Destruction: An Example of the Interaction Between Language and Memory', *Journal of Verbal Learning and Verbal Behavior*, 13 (1974), 585–9.

Longnon, J., *Recherches sur la vie de Geoffroy de Villehardouin, suivis du catologue des actes des Villehardouin* (Bibliothèque de l'École des Hautes Études, fasc. 276; Paris, 1939).

—— *Les compagnons de Villehardouin: Recherches sur les croisés de la quatrième croisade* (Hautes études médiévales et modernes, 30; Geneva, 1978).

Loraux, N., 'Thucydides Is Not a Colleague', in J. Marincola (ed.), *Greek and Roman Historiography* (Oxford, 2011), pp. 19–39.

Loud, G. A., 'The Genesis and Context of the Chronicle of Falco of Benevento', in M. Chibnall (ed.), *Anglo-Norman Studies XV: Proceedings of the XV Battle Conference and of the XI Colloquio Medievale of the Officina di Studi Medievali 1992* (Woodbridge, 1993), pp. 177–98.

—— 'Some Reflections on the Failure of the Second Crusade', *Crusades*, 4 (2005), 1–14.

Luminet, O., 'Models for the Formation of Flashbulb Memories', in O. Luminet and A. Curci (eds), *Flashbulb Memories: New Issues and New Perspectives* (Hove, 2009), pp. 51–76.
Lyons, M. C., and D. E. P. Jackson, *Saladin: The Politics of the Holy War* (University of Cambridge Oriental Publications, 30; Cambridge, 1982).
Macdonald, I., 'The Chronicle of Jordan Fantosme: Manuscripts, Author, and Versification', in *Studies in Medieval French Presented to Alfred Ewert in Honour of his Seventieth Birthday* (Oxford, 1961), pp. 242–58.
Mack, A., and I. Rock, *Inattentional Blindness* (Cambridge, MA, 1998).
Macrides, R. J., 'Constantinople: The Crusaders' Gaze', in R. J. Macrides (ed.), *Travel in the Byzantine World: Papers from the Thirty-Fourth Spring Symposium of Byzantine Studies, Birmingham, April 2000* (Society for the Promotion of Byzantine Studies Publications, 10; Aldershot, 2002), pp. 193–212.
Madden, T. F., 'The Fires of the Fourth Crusade in Constantinople, 1203–1204: A Damage Assessment', *Byzantinische Zeitschrift*, 84/5 (1992), 72–93.
—— 'Vows and Contracts in the Fourth Crusade: The Treaty of Zara and the Attack on Constantinople in 1204', *International History Review*, 15 (1993), 441–68.
—— 'Outside and Inside the Fourth Crusade', *International History Review*, 17 (1995), 726–43.
—— *Enrico Dandolo and the Rise of Venice* (Baltimore, 2003).
—— 'The Venetian Version of the Fourth Crusade: Memory and the Conquest of Constantinople in Medieval Venice', *Speculum*, 87 (2012), 311–44.
Magdalino, P., 'Aspects of Twelfth-Century Byzantine *Kaiserkritik*', *Speculum*, 58 (1983), 326–46.
—— *The Empire of Manuel I Komnenos, 1143–1180* (Cambridge, 1993).
Malle, B. F., and J. Knobe, 'The Folk Concept of Intentionality', *Journal of Experimental Social Psychology*, 33 (1997), 101–21.
Marchello-Nizia, C., 'L'historien et son prologue: Forme littéraire et stratégies discursives', in D. Poirion (ed.), *La chronique et l'histoire au moyen âge: Colloque des 24 et 25 mai 1982* (Paris, 1984), pp. 13–25.
Marcus, A., 'A Contextual View of Narrative Fiction in the First Person Plural', *Narrative*, 16 (2008), 46–64.
Margolin, U., 'Telling Our Story: On "We" Literary Narratives', *Language and Literature*, 5 (1996), 115–33.
—— 'Telling in the Plural: From Grammar to Ideology', *Poetics Today*, 21 (2000), 591–618.
—— 'Focalization: Where Do We Go from Here?', in P Hühn, W. Schmid and J. Schönert (eds), *Point of View, Perspective, and Focalization: Modeling Mediation in Narrative* (Narratologia, 17; Berlin, 2009), pp. 41–57.
Marin, S., 'Between Justification and Glory: The Venetian Chronicles' View

of the Fourth Crusade', in T. F. Madden (ed.), *The Fourth Crusade: Event, Aftermath, and Perceptions: Papers from the Sixth Conference of the Society for the Study of the Crusades and the Latin East, Istanbul, Turkey, 25–29 August 2004* (Crusades Subsidia, 2; Aldershot, 2008), pp. 113–21.

Marincola, J., *Authority and Tradition in Ancient Historiography* (Cambridge, 1997).

—— 'Genre, Convention, and Innovation in Greco–Roman Historiography', in C. S. Kraus (ed.), *The Limits of Historiography: Genre and Narrative in Ancient Historical Texts* (Leiden, 1999), pp. 281–324.

Marnette, S., *Narrateur et points de vue dans la littérature française médiévale: Une approche linguistique* (Bern, 1998).

—— 'Narrateur et points de vue dans les chroniques médiévales: une approche linguistique', in E. S. Kooper (ed.), *The Medieval Chronicle: Proceedings of the 1st International Conference on the Medieval Chronicle, Driebergen/ Utrecht 13–16 July 1996* (Costerus New Series 120; Amsterdam, 1999), pp. 174–90.

—— 'The Experiencing Self and the Narrating Self in Medieval Chronicles', in V. Greene (ed.), *The Medieval Author in Medieval French Literature* (Basingstoke, 2006), pp. 117–36.

Marsh, E. J., 'Retelling Is Not the Same as Recalling', *Current Directions in Psychological Science*, 16 (2007), 16–20.

Marsh, E. J., M. L. Meade and H. L. Roediger III, 'Learning Facts from Fiction', *Journal of Memory and Language*, 49 (2003), 519–36.

Marsh, E. J., and B. Tversky, 'Spinning the Stories of our Lives', *Applied Cognitive Psychology*, 18 (2004), 491–503.

Marsh, E. J., B. Tversky and M. Hutson, 'How Eyewitnesses Talk About Events: Implications for Memory', *Applied Cognitive Psychology*, 19 (2005), 531–44.

Marsh, L., A. J. Barnier, J. Sutton, C. B. Harris and R. A. Wilson, 'A Conceptual and Empirical Framework for the Social Distribution of Cognition: The Case of Memory', *Cognitive Systems Research*, 9 (2008), 33–51.

Mayer, H. E., *The Crusades*, trans. J. Gillingham, 2nd edn (Oxford, 1988).

Mayr-Harting, H., 'Odo of Deuil, the Second Crusade and the Monastery of Saint-Denis', in M. A. Meyer (ed.), *The Culture of Christendom: Essays in Medieval History in Commemoration of Denis L. T. Bethell* (London, 1993), pp. 225–41.

—— 'Liudprand of Cremona's Account of his Legation to Constantinople and Ottonian Imperial Strategy', *English Historical Review*, 116 (2001), 539–56.

McCloskey, M., and M. S. Zaragoza, 'Misleading Postevent Information and Memory for Events: Arguments and Evidence Against Memory Impairment Hypotheses', *Journal of Experimental Psychology: General*, 114 (1985), 1–16.

Meade, M. L., and H. L. Roediger III, 'Explorations in the Social Contagion of Memory', *Memory & Cognition*, 30 (2002), 995–1009.

Memon, A., and D. B. Wright, 'Eyewitness Testimony and the Oklahoma Bombing', *The Psychologist*, 12 (1999), 292–5.

Ménard, P., 'Les combattants en Terre sainte au temps de Saladin et de Richard Coeur de Lion', in J. Paviot and J. Verger (eds), *Guerre, pouvoir et noblesse au Moyen Âge: Mélanges en l'honneur de Philippe Contamine* (Paris, 2000), pp. 503–11.

Michotte, A., *The Perception of Causality*, trans. T. R. Miles and E. Miles (London, 1963).

Middleton, D., and D. Edwards, 'Conversational Remembering: A Social Psychological Approach', in D. Middleton and D. Edwards (eds), *Collective Remembering* (London, 1990), pp. 23–45.

Migueles, M., and E. García-Bajos, 'Selective Retrieval and Induced Forgetting in Eyewitness Memory', *Applied Cognitive Psychology*, 21 (2007), 1157–72.

Möhring, H., 'Eine Chronik aus der Zeit des dritten Kreuzzugs: das sogenannte *Itinerarium peregrinorum* 1', *Innsbrucker Historische Studien*, 5 (1982), 149–62.

Mölk, U., 'Robert de Clari über den vierten Kreuzzug', *Romanistisches Jahrbuch*, 61 (2011), 12–22.

Morris, C., 'Geoffroy de Villehardouin and the Conquest of Constantinople', *History*, 53 (1968), 24–34.

—— *The Discovery of the Individual 1050–1200* (Medieval Academy Reprints for Teaching, 19; Toronto, 1987).

—— 'The *Gesta Francorum* as Narrative History', *Reading Medieval Studies*, 19 (1993), 55–71.

Mortimer, R., 'The Family of Ranulf de Glanville', *Bulletin of the Institute of Historical Research*, 54 (1981), 1–16.

Münsterberg, H., *On the Witness Stand: Essays on Psychology and Crime* (New York, 1908).

Naus, J. L., 'Negotiating Kingship in France at the Time of the Early Crusades: Suger and the *Gesta Ludovici Grossi*', *French Historical Studies*, 36 (2013), 525–41.

—— *Constructing Kingship: The Capetian Monarchs of France and the Early Crusades* (Manchester, 2016).

Neisser, U., 'John Dean's Memory: A Case Study', *Cognition*, 9 (1981), 1–22.

—— 'Snapshots or Benchmarks?', in U. Neisser (ed.), *Memory Observed: Remembering in Natural Contexts* (New York, 1982), pp. 43–8.

Neisser, U., and R. Becklen, 'Selective Looking: Attending to Visually Specified Events', *Cognitive Psychology*, 7 (1975), 480–94.

Neisser, U., and L. K. Libby, 'Remembering Life Experiences', in E. Tulving and F. I. M. Craik (eds), *The Oxford Handbook of Memory* (Oxford, 2000), pp. 315–32.

Nelles, W., 'Getting Focalization into Focus', *Poetics Today*, 11 (1990), 365–82.

Nelson, K., and R. Fivush, 'Socialization of Memory', in E. Tulving and F. I. M. Craik (eds), *The Oxford Handbook of Memory* (Oxford, 2000), pp. 283–95.

Nenci, G., 'Il motivo dell'autopsia nella storiografia greca', *Studi classici e orientali*, 3 (1955), 14–46.

Neocleous, S., 'Byzantine-Muslim Conspiracies against the Crusades: History and Myth', *Journal of Medieval History*, 36 (2010), 253–74.

—— 'Financial, Chivalric or Religious? The Motives of the Fourth Crusaders Reconsidered', *Journal of Medieval History*, 38 (2012), 183–206.

Nevins, A., *The Gateway to History* (Boston, 1938).

Nicholson, H. J., 'Women on the Third Crusade', *Journal of Medieval History*, 23 (1997), 335–49.

Nieragden, G., 'Focalization and Narration: Theoretical and Terminological Refinements', *Poetics Today*, 23 (2002), 685–97.

Niskaken, S., 'The Origins of the *Gesta Francorum* and Two Related Texts: Their Textual and Literary Character', *Sacris Erudiri*, 51 (2012), 287–316.

Noble, P., 'The Importance of Old French Chronicles as Historical Sources of the Fourth Crusade and the Early Latin Empire of Constantinople', *Journal of Medieval History*, 27 (2001), 399–416.

Norgate, K., 'The "Itinerarium Peregrinorum" and the "Song of Ambrose"', *English Historical Review*, 25 (1910), 523–47.

Oeberst, A., and J. Seidemann, 'Will Your Words Become Mine? Underlying Processes and Cowitness Intimacy in the Memory Conformity Paradigm', *Canadian Journal of Experimental Psychology*, 68 (2014), 84–96.

Olick, J. K., 'Collective Memory: The Two Cultures', *Sociological Theory*, 17 (1999), 333–48.

Otter, M., *Inventiones: Fiction and Referentiality in Twelfth-Century English Historical Writing* (Chapel Hill, NC, 1996).

—— 'Functions of Fiction in Historical Writing', in N. F. Partner (ed.), *Writing Medieval History* (London, 2005), pp. 109–30.

Páez, D., G. Bellelli and B. Rimé, 'Flashbulb Memories, Culture, and Collective Memories: Psychosocial Processes Related to Rituals, Emotions, and Memories', in O. Luminet and A. Curci (eds), *Flashbulb Memories: New Issues and New Perspectives* (Hove, 2009), pp. 227–45.

Pagden, A., *Eyewitness Encounters with the New World: From Renaissance to Romanticism* (New Haven, 1993).

—— '*Ius et Factum*: Text and Experience in the Writings of Bartolomé de Las Casas', in S. Greenblatt (ed.), *New World Encounters* (Berkeley, 1993), pp. 85–100.

Paivio, A., 'The Mind's Eye in Arts and Science', *Poetics*, 12 (1983), 1–18.

Partner, N. F., *Serious Entertainments: The Writing of History in Twelfth-Century England* (Chicago, 1977).

—— 'Medieval Histories and Modern Realism: Yet Another Origin of the Novel', *Modern Language Notes*, 114 (1999), 857–73.

Pasupathi, M., L. M. Stallworth and K. Murdoch, 'How What We Tell Becomes What We Know: Listener Effects on Speakers' Long-Term Memory for Events', *Discourse Processes*, 26 (1998), 1–25.

Paul, N. L., *To Follow in Their Footsteps: The Crusades and Family Memory in the High Middle Ages* (Ithaca, NY, 2012).

Payne, D. G., M. P. Toglia and J. S. Anastasi, 'Recognition Performance Level and the Magnitude of the Misinformation Effect in Eyewitness Memory', *Psychonomic Bulletin and Review*, 1 (1994), 376–82.

Pelling, C. B. R., 'Seeing Through Caesar's Eyes: Focalisation and Interpretation', in J. Grethlein and A. Rengakos (eds), *Narratology and Interpretation: The Content of Narrative Form in Ancient Literature* (Berlin, 2009), pp. 507–26.

Perry, D. M., *Sacred Plunder: Venice and the Aftermath of the Fourth Crusade* (University Park, PA, 2015).

Phelan, J., 'Why Narrators Can Be Focalizers – and Why It Matters', in W. van Peer and S. Chatman (eds), *New Perspectives on Narrative Perspective* (Albany, NY, 2001), pp. 51–64.

Phillips, J. P., *Defenders of the Holy Land: Relations Between the Latin East and the West, 1119–1187* (Oxford, 1996).

—— 'St Bernard of Clairvaux, the Low Countries and the Lisbon Letter of the Second Crusade', *Journal of Ecclesiastical History*, 48 (1997), 485–97.

—— 'Ideas of Crusade and Holy War in *De expugnatione Lyxbonensi* (The Conquest of Lisbon)', in R. N. Swanson (ed.), *The Holy Land, Holy Lands, and Christian History* (Studies in Church History, 36; Woodbridge, 2000), pp. 123–41.

—— 'Odo of Deuil's *De profectione Ludovici VII in Orientem* as a Source for the Second Crusade', in M. G. Bull and N. J. Housley (eds), *The Experience of Crusading I: Western Approaches* (Cambridge, 2003), pp. 80–95.

—— *The Fourth Crusade and the Sack of Constantinople* (London, 2004).

—— *The Second Crusade: Extending the Frontiers of Christendom* (New Haven, 2007).

Pillemer, D. B., 'Flashbulb Memories of the Assassination Attempt on President Reagan', *Cognition*, 16 (1984), 63–80.

—— *Momentous Events, Vivid Memories: How Unforgettable Moments Help Us Understand the Meaning of Our Lives* (Cambridge, MA, 2000).

—— '"Hearing the News" versus "Being There": Comparing Flashbulb Memories and Recall of First-Hand Experiences', in O. Luminet and A. Curci (eds), *Flashbulb Memories: New Issues and New Perspectives* (Hove, 2009), pp. 125–40.

Pitcher, L., *Writing Ancient History: An Introduction to Classical Historiography* (London, 2009).

Polan, D., *Pulp Fiction* (London, 2000).

Poly, J.-P., and É. Bournazel, *The Feudal Transformation 900–1200*, trans. C. Higgitt (New York, 1991).

Prager, J., *Presenting the Past: Psychoanalysis and the Sociology of Misremembering* (Cambridge, MA, 1998).

Prince, G., 'Narrative Analysis and Narratology', *New Literary History*, 13 (1982), 179–88.

—— 'On Narrative Studies and Narrative Genres', *Poetics Today*, 11 (1990), 271–82.

Prince, S., *The Warrior's Camera: The Cinema of Akira Kurosawa*, rev. edn (Princeton, 1999).

Purkis, W. J., *Crusading Spirituality in the Holy Land and Iberia c.1095–c.1187* (Woodbridge, 2008).

Purves, A. C., *Space and Time in Greek Narrative* (Cambridge, 2010).

Queller, D. E., T. F. Compton and D. A. Campbell, 'The Fourth Crusade: The Neglected Majority', *Speculum*, 49 (1974), 441–65.

Queller, D. E., and G. W. Day, 'Some Arguments in Defense of the Venetians on the Fourth Crusade', *American Historical Review*, 81 (1976), 717–37.

Queller, D. E., and I. B. Katele, 'Attitudes Towards the Venetians in the Fourth Crusade: The Western Sources', *International History Review*, 4 (1982), 1–36.

Queller, D. E., and T. F. Madden, 'Some Further Arguments in Defense of the Venetians on the Fourth Crusade', *Byzantion*, 62 (1992), 433–73.

—— *The Fourth Crusade: The Conquest of Constantinople*, 2nd edn (Philadelphia, 1997).

Radstone, S., and B. Schwarz (eds), *Memory: Histories, Theories, Debates* (New York, 2010).

Rector, G., '"Faites le mien desir": Studious Persuasion and Baronial Desire in Jordan Fantosme's *Chronicle*', *Journal of Medieval History*, 34 (2008), 311–46.

Remensnyder, A. G., *Remembering Kings Past: Monastic Foundation Legends in Medieval Southern France* (Ithaca, NY, 1995).

Rensick, R. A., J. K. O'Regan and J. J. Clark, 'To See or Not To See: The Need for Attention to Perceive Changes in Scenes', *Psychological Science*, 8 (1997), 368–73.

Reuter, T., 'The "Non-Crusade" of 1149–50', in J. P. Phillips and M. Hoch (eds), *The Second Crusade: Scope and Consequences* (Manchester, 2001), pp. 150–63.

Reysen, M. B., 'The Effects of Social Pressure on Group Recall', *Memory & Cognition*, 31 (2003), 1163–8.

Richard, J., *The Crusades, c.1071–c.1291*, trans. J. Birrell (Cambridge, 1999).

Richards, D. S., 'A Consideration of Two Sources for the Life of Saladin', *Journal of Semitic Studies*, 25 (1980), 46–65.

—— 'Ibn al-Athīr and the Later Parts of the *Kāmil*: A Study of Aims and Methods', in D. O. Morgan (ed.), *Medieval Historical Writing in the Christian and Islamic Worlds* (London, 1982), pp. 76–108.
—— "Imād al-Dīn al-Isfahānī: Administrator, Litterateur and Historian', in M. Shatzmiller (ed.), *Crusaders and Muslims in Twelfth-Century Syria* (The Medieval Mediterranean, 1; Leiden, 1993), pp. 133–46.
Richie, D. (ed.), *Focus on Rashomon* (Englewood Cliffs, NJ, 1972).
—— (ed.) *Rashomon: Akira Kurosawa, Director* (Rutgers Films in Print, 6; New Brunswick, NJ, 1987).
—— *The Films of Akira Kurosawa*, 3rd rev. edn (Berkeley, 1998).
Rider, J., *God's Scribe: The Historiographical Art of Galbert of Bruges* (Washington, DC, 2001).
—— '"Wonder with Fresh Wonder": Galbert the Writer and the Genesis of the *De multro*', in J. Rider and A. V. Murray (eds), *Galbert of Bruges and the Historiography of Medieval Flanders* (Washington, DC, 2009), pp. 13–35.
Riggsby, A. M., *Caesar in Gaul and Rome: War in Words* (Austin, TX, 2006).
Riley-Smith, J. S. C., *The First Crusade and the Idea of Crusading* (London, 1986).
—— *The Crusades: A History* (New Haven, 2005).
Rimmon-Kenan, S., *Narrative Fiction: Contemporary Poetics*, 2nd edn (Abingdon, 2002).
Riniolo, T. C., M. Koledin, G. M. Drakulic and R. A. Payne, 'An Archival Study of Eyewitness Memory of the *Titanic*'s Final Plunge', *Journal of General Psychology*, 130 (2001), 89–95.
Roalfe, W. R., *John Henry Wigmore: Scholar and Reformer* (Evanston, IL, 1977).
Roche, J. T., 'Conrad III and the Second Crusade: Retreat from Dorylaion?', *Crusades*, 5 (2006), 85–97.
Roediger III, H. L., and K. B. McDermott, 'Distortions of Memory', in E. Tulving and F. I. M. Craik (eds), *The Oxford Handbook of Memory* (Oxford, 2000), pp. 149–62.
Rogers, R., *Latin Siege Warfare in the Twelfth Century* (Oxford, 1992).
Rood, T. C. B., *Thucydides: Narrative and Explanation* (Oxford, 1998).
Rosado Fernandes, R. M., 'O vento, as éguas de Lusitânia e os autores grecos e latinos', *Euphrosyne*, 12 (1984), 53–77.
Rowe, J. G., 'The Origins of the Second Crusade: Pope Eugenius III, Bernard of Clairvaux and Louis VII of France', in M. Gervers (ed.), *The Second Crusade and the Cistercians* (New York, 1992), pp. 79–89.
Rozier, C. C., D. Roach, G. E. M. Gasper and E. M. C. van Houts (eds), *Orderic Vitalis: Life, Works and Interpretations* (Woodbridge, 2016).
Rubenstein, J., 'Putting History to Use: Three Crusade Chronicles in Context', *Viator*, 35 (2004), 131–68.

—— 'What Is the *Gesta Francorum*, and Who Was Peter Tudebode?', *Revue Mabillon*, ns 16 (2005), 179–204.

Rubin, D. C., 'The Basic Systems Model of Autobiographical Memory', in D. Bernsten and D. C. Rubin (eds), *Understanding Autobiographical Memory: Theories and Approaches* (Cambridge, 2012), pp. 11–32.

Rubin, D. C., and M. Kozin, 'Vivid Memories', *Cognition*, 16 (1984), 81–95.

Runciman, S., *A History of the Crusades*, 3 vols (Cambridge, 1951–4).

Russo, L., 'Oblia e memoria di Boemondo d'Altavilla nella storiografia normanna', *Bulletino dell'Istituto storico italiano per il medio evo*, 106 (2004), 137–65.

Ryan, M.-L., 'The Narratorial Functions: Breaking Down a Theoretical Primitive', *Narrative*, 9 (2001), 146–52.

Sacks, O., *The Man Who Mistook His Wife for a Hat* (London, 1986).

Sanna, L. S., N. Schwarz and E. M. Small, 'Accessibility Experiences and the Hindsight Bias: I Knew It All Along Versus It Could Never Have Happened', *Cognition*, 30 (2002), 1288–96.

Sato, T., *Kenji Mizoguchi and the Art of Japanese Cinema*, trans. B. Tankha, ed. A. Vasudev and L. Padkaonkar (Oxford, 2008).

Schacter, D. L., *Searching for Memory: The Brain, the Mind, and the Past* (New York, 1996).

—— *The Seven Sins of Memory: How the Mind Forgets and Remembers* (Boston, 2001).

Scheck, B., P. J. Neufeld and J. Dwyer, *Actual Innocence: Five Days to Execution, and Other Dispatches from the Wrongly Convicted* (New York, 2000).

Schepens, G., *L'autopsie dans la méthode des historiens grecs du Ve siècle avant J.-C.* (Verhandelingen van de Koninklijke Academie voor Wetenschappen, Letteren en Schone Kunsten van België. Klasse der Letteren, 93; Brussels, 1980).

—— 'Travelling Greek Historians', in M. G. Angeli Bertinelli and A. Donati (eds), *Le vie della storia: Migrazioni di popoli, viaggi di individui, circolazione di idee nel Mediterraneo antico. Atti del II Incontro Internazionale di Storia Antica (Genova 6–8 ottobre 2004)* (Serta antiqua et mediaevalia, 9; Rome, 2006), pp. 81–102.

—— 'History and *Historia*: Inquiry in the Greek Historians', in J. Marincola (ed.), *A Companion to Greek and Roman Historiography* (Chichester, 2011), pp. 39–55.

—— 'Some Aspects of Source Theory in Greek Historiography', in J. Marincola (ed.), *Greek and Roman Historiography* (Oxford, 2011), pp. 100–18.

Schirato, G., 'Forme narrative del discorso storico: I modelli letterari dell'*Estoire de la Guerre Sainte* di Ambroise', *Studi Medievali*, 3rd ser., 51 (2010), 95–151.

Scholl, B. J., and P. D. Tremoulet, 'Perceptual Causality and Animacy', *Trends in Cognitive Sciences*, 4 (2000), 299–309.

Schooler, J. W., and T. Y. Engstler-Schooler, 'Verbal Overshadowing of Visual

Memories: Some Things Are Better Left Unsaid', *Cognitive Psychology*, 22 (1990), 36–71.

Schooler, J. W., D. Gerhard and E. F. Loftus, 'Qualities of the Unreal', *Journal of Experimental Psychology: Learning, Memory, and Cognition*, 12 (1986), 171–81.

Schreiner, P., 'Robert de Clari und Konstantinopel', in C. Sode and S. Takács (eds), *Novum Millennium: Studies on Byzantine History and Culture Dedicated to Paul Speck* (Aldershot, 2001), pp. 337–56.

Schudson, M., 'Dynamics of Distortion in Collective Memory', in D. L. Schacter *et al.* (eds), *Memory Distortion: How Minds, Brains, and Societies Reconstruct the Past* (Cambridge, MA, 1995), pp. 346–64.

Schultz, J. A., 'Classical Rhetoric, Medieval Poetics, and the Medieval Vernacular Prologue', *Speculum*, 59 (1984), 1–15.

Schuster, B., 'The Strange Pilgrimage of Odo of Deuil', in G. Althoff, J. Fried and P. J. Geary (eds), *Medieval Concepts of the Past: Ritual, Memory, Historiography* (Cambridge, 2002), pp. 253–78.

Scott, J. W., 'The Evidence of Experience', *Critical Inquiry*, 17 (1991), 773–97.

Shafer, R. J. (ed.), *A Guide to Historical Method*, 3rd edn (Homewood, IL, 1980).

Shaw III, J. S., L. M. Appio, T. K. Zerr and K. E. Pontoski, 'Public Eyewitness Confidence Can Be Influenced by the Presence of Other Witnesses', *Law and Human Behavior*, 31 (2007), 629–52.

Simon, G., 'Untersuchungen zur Topik der Widmungsbriefe mittelalterlicher Geschichtsschreiber bis zum Ende des 12. Jahrhunderts', *Archiv für Diplomatik*, 4 (1958), 52–119; 5/6 (1959–60), 73–153.

Simons, D. J., and C. F. Chabris, 'Gorillas in Our Midst: Sustained Inattentional Blindness for Dynamic Events', *Perception*, 28 (1999), 1059–74.

Simons, D. J., and D. T. Levin, 'Failure to Detect Changes to People During a Real-World Interaction', *Psychonomic Bulletin and Review*, 5 (1998), 644–9.

Simpson, A., 'Niketas Choniates: the Historian', in A. Simpson and S. Efthymiadis (eds), *Niketas Choniates: A Historian and a Writer* (Geneva, 2009), pp. 13–34.

—— *Niketas Choniates: A Historiographical Study* (Oxford, 2013).

Smith, A. M., 'What Is the History of Medieval Optics Really About?', *Proceedings of the American Philosophical Society*, 148 (2004), 180–94.

Smith, V. L., and P. C. Ellsworth, 'The Social Psychology of Eyewitness Accuracy: Misleading Questions and Communicator Expertise', *Journal of Applied Psychology*, 72 (1987), 294–300.

Snyder, M., and S. W. Uranowitz, 'Reconstructing the Past: Some Cognitive Consequences of Person Perception', *Journal of Personality and Social Psychology*, 36 (1978), 941–50.

Souyri, P. F., *The World Turned Upside Down: Medieval Japanese Society*, trans. K. Roth (London, 2002).

Spiegel, G. M., *Romancing the Past: The Rise of Vernacular Prose Historiography in Thirteenth-Century France* (Berkeley, 1993).

—— 'History, Historicism, and the Social Logic of the Text', in her *The Past as Text: The Theory and Practice of Medieval Historiography* (Baltimore, 1997), pp. 3–28.

—— 'History as Enlightenment: Suger and the *Mos Anagogicus*', in her *The Past as Text: The Theory and Practice of Medieval Historiography* (Baltimore, 1997), pp. 163–77.

Sporer, S. L., 'Lessons from the Origins of Eyewitness Testimony Research in Europe', *Applied Cognitive Psychology*, 22 (2008), 937–57.

Stanzel, F. K., 'Teller-Characters and Reflector-Characters in Narrative Theory', *Poetics Today*, 2 (1981), 5–15.

Stephenson, P., *Byzantium's Balkan Frontier: A Political Study of the Northern Balkans, 900–1204* (Cambridge, 2000).

Stern, W., 'Realistic Experiments', in U. Neisser (ed.), *Memory Observed: Remembering in Natural Contexts* (New York, 1982), pp. 95–108.

Sternberg, M., *The Poetics of Biblical Narrative: Ideological Literature and the Drama of Reading* (Bloomington, IN, 1985).

Stone, C. B., A. J. Barnier, J. Sutton and W. Hirst, 'Building Consensus About the Past: Schema Consistency and Convergence in Socially Shared Retrieval-Induced Forgetting', *Memory*, 18 (2010), 170–84.

Strawson, G., 'Against Narrativity', *Ratio*, ns 17 (2004), 428–52.

Strickland, M., 'Arms and the Men: War, Loyalty and Lordship in Jordan Fantosme's Chronicle', in C. Harper-Bill and R. Harvey (eds), *Medieval Knighthood IV: Papers from the Fifth Strawberry Hill Conference 1990* (Woodbridge, 1992), pp. 187–220.

Suard, F., 'Constantinople dans la littérature épique française jusqu'au XIVe siècle', in L. Nissim and S. Riva (eds), *Sauver Byzance de la barbarie du monde: Gargnano del Garda (14-17 maggio 2003)* (Quaderni di Acme, 65; Milan, 2004), pp. 91–112.

Sutton, J., 'Distributed Cognition: Domains and Dimensions', *Pragmatics & Cognition*, 14 (2006), 235–47.

—— 'Between Individual and Collective Memory: Coordination, Interaction, Distribution', *Social Research*, 75 (2008), 23–48.

Talarico, J. M., and D. C. Rubin, 'Flashbulb Memories Result from Ordinary Memory Processes and Extraordinary Event Characteristics', in O. Luminet and A. Curci (eds), *Flashbulb Memories: New Issues and New Perspectives* (Hove, 2009), pp. 79–97.

Tapper, C., and R. Cross, *Cross and Tapper on Evidence*, 12th edn (Oxford, 2010).

Thomas, H. M., *The English and the Normans: Ethnic Hostility, Assimilation, and Identity 1066–c.1220* (Oxford, 2003).

Thompson, R. G., 'Collaborative and Social Remembering', in G. Cohen and M. A. Conway (eds), *Memory in the Real World*, 3rd edn (Hove, 2008), pp. 249–67.

Thomsen, D. K., 'There Is More to Life Stories than Memories', *Memory*, 17 (2009), 445–57.

Thomson, R. M., *William of Malmesbury* (Woodbridge, 1987).

Throop, S. A., *Crusading as an Act of Vengeance, 1095–1216* (Farnham, 2011).

—— 'Christian Community and the Crusades: Religious and Social Practices in the *De expugnatione Lyxbonensi*', *Haskins Society Journal*, 24 (2012), 95–126.

Tolan, M. J., *Narrative: A Critical Linguistic Introduction* (London, 1988).

Trankell, A., *Reliability of Evidence: Methods for Analyzing and Assessing Witness Statements* (Stockholm, 1972).

Treadgold, W., *The Middle Byzantine Historians* (Basingstoke, 2013).

Trites, A. A., *The New Testament Concept of Witness* (Society for New Testament Studies Monograph Series, 31; Cambridge, 1977).

Tuan, Y.-F., 'Language and the Making of Place: A Narrative-Descriptive Approach', *Annals of the Association of American Geographers*, 81 (1991), 684–96.

Tuckey, M. R., and N. Brewer, 'The Influence of Schemas, Stimulus Ambiguity, and Interview Schedule on Eyewitness Memory over Time', *Journal of Experimental Psychology: Applied*, 9 (2003), 101–18.

Tulving, E., *Elements of Episodic Memory* (Oxford Psychology Series, 2; Oxford, 1983).

—— 'Memory and Consciousness', *Canadian Psychology*, 26 (1985), 1–12.

Tversky, B., and E. J. Marsh, 'Biased Retellings of Events Yield Biased Memories', *Cognitive Psychology*, 40 (2000), 1–38.

Tyerman, C. J., *England and the Crusades 1095–1588* (Chicago, 1988).

—— *God's War: A New History of the Crusades* (London, 2006).

Tyler, S. A., 'The Vision Quest in the West, or What the Mind's Eye Sees', *Journal of Anthropological Research*, 40 (1984), 23–40.

Urbanski, C., *Writing History for the King: Henry II and the Politics of Vernacular Historiography* (Ithaca, NY, 2013).

Valach, L., R. A. Young and M. J. Lynam, *Action Theory: A Primer for Applied Research in the Social Sciences* (Westport, CT, 2002).

van Houts, E. M. C., 'Genre Aspects of the Use of Oral Information in Medieval Historiography', in B. Frank, T. Haye and D. Tophinke (eds), *Gattungen mittelalterlicher Schriftlichkeit* (ScriptOralia, 99; Tübingen, 1997), pp. 297–311.

—— *Memory and Gender in Medieval Europe, 900–1200* (Basingstoke, 1999).

van Koppen, P. J., and S. K. Kochun, 'Portraying Perpetrators: The Validity of Offender Descriptions by Witnesses', *Law and Human Behavior*, 21 (1997), 661–85.

Varvaro, A., 'Esperienza e racconto in Robert de Clari', in R. Antonelli *et al.* (eds), *Miscellanea di studi in onore di Aurelio Roncaglia a cinquant'anni dalla sua laurea*, 1 vol. in 4 (Modena, 1989), iv, pp. 1411–27.

Vielliard, F., 'Richard Coeur de Lion et son entourage normand: Le témoignage de l'*Estoire de la guerre sainte*', *Bibliothèque de l'École des chartes*, 160 (2002), 5–52.

Villegas-Aristizábal, L., 'Revisiting the Anglo-Norman Crusaders' Failed Attempt to Conquer Lisbon *c.* 1142', *Portuguese Studies*, 29 (2013), 7–20.

von Martels, Z., 'Turning the Tables on Solinus' Critics: The Unity of Contents and Form of the *Polyhistor*', in K. Brodersen (ed.), *Solinus: New Studies* (Heidelberg, 2014), pp. 10–23.

von Sybel, H., *Geschichte des ersten Kreuzzugs* (Düsseldorf, 1841).

Vornik, L. A., S. J. Sharman and M. Garry, 'The Power of the Spoken Word: Sociolinguistic Cues Influence the Misinformation Effect', *Memory*, 11 (2003), 101–9.

Wagenaar, W. A., and J. Groeneweg, 'The Memory of Concentration Camp Survivors', *Applied Cognitive Psychology*, 4 (1990), 77–87.

Wall, P. M., *Eye-witness Identification in Criminal Cases* (Springfield, IL, 1965).

Walsh, R., 'Who Is the Narrator?', *Poetics Today*, 18 (1997), 495–513.

Waubert de Puiseau, B., A. Assfalg, E. Erdfelder and D. M. Bernstein, 'Extracting the Truth from Conflicting Eyewitness Reports: A Formal Modelling Approach', *Journal of Experimental Psychology: Applied*, 18 (2012), 390–403.

Weldon, M. S., 'Remembering as a Social Process', in D. L. Medin (ed.), *The Psychology of Learning and Motivation: Advances in Research and Theory: Volume 40* (San Diego, 2001), pp. 67–120.

Weldon, M. S., and K. D. Ballinger, 'Collective Memory: Collaborative and Individual Processes in Remembering', *Journal of Experimental Psychology: Learning, Memory, and Cognition*, 23 (1997), 1160–75.

Wells, G. L., 'Applied Eyewitness-Testimony Research: System Variables and Estimator Variables', *Journal of Personality and Social Psychology*, 36 (1978), 1546–57.

—— 'What Do We Know About Eyewitness Identification?', *American Psychologist*, 48 (1993), 553–71.

Wells, G. L., and A. L. Bradfield, '"Good, You Identified the Suspect": Feedback to Eyewitnesses Distorts Their Reports of the Witnessing Experience', *Journal of Applied Psychology*, 83 (1998), 360–76.

Wertsch, J. V., *Voices of Collective Remembering* (Cambridge, 2002).

—— 'Collective Memory', in P. Boyer and J. V. Wertsch (eds), *Memory in Mind and Culture* (Cambridge, 2009), pp. 117–37.

Wertsch, J. V., and H. L. Roediger III, 'Collective Memory: Conceptual Foundations and Theoretical Approaches', *Memory*, 16 (2008), 318–26.

White, H., 'The Historical Text as Literary Artifact', in his *Tropics of Discourse: Essays in Cultural Criticism* (Baltimore, 1978), pp. 81–100.

—— 'The Value of Narrativity in the Representation of Reality', in his *The Content of the Form: Narrative Discourse and Historical Representation* (Baltimore, 1987), pp. 1–25.

—— 'Historical Emplotment and the Problem of Truth in Historical Representation', in his *Figural Realism: Studies in the Mimesis Effect* (Baltimore, 1999), pp. 27–42.

Whitehead, A., *Memory* (London, 2009).

Wigmore, H., 'Professor Muensterberg and the Psychology of Testimony: Being a Report of the Case of Cokestone *v.* Muensterberg', *Illinois Law Review*, 3 (1909), 399–445.

Wilson, R. A., *Boundaries of the Mind: The Individual in the Fragile Sciences: Cognition* (Cambridge, 2004).

—— 'Collective Memory, Group Minds, and the Extended Mind Thesis', *Cognitive Processing*, 6 (2005), 227–36.

Wolf, K. B., 'Crusade and Narrative: Bohemond and the *Gesta Francorum*', *Journal of Medieval History*, 17 (1991), 207–16.

Wood, G., 'The Knew-It-All-Along Effect', *Journal of Experimental Psychology: Human Perception and Performance*, 4 (1978), 345–53.

Woodman, A. J., *Rhetoric in Classical Historiography: Four Studies* (London, 1988).

Wright, D. B., 'Recall of the Hillsborough Disaster over Time: Systematic Biases of "Flashbulb" Memories', *Applied Cognitive Psychology*, 7 (1993), 129–38.

—— 'Causal and Associative Hypotheses in Psychology: Examples from Eyewitness Testimony Research', *Psychology, Public Policy, and Law*, 12 (2006), 190–213.

Wright, D. B., E. F. Loftus and M. Hall, 'Now You See It; Now You Don't: Inhibiting Recall and Recognition of Scenes', *Applied Cognitive Psychology*, 15 (2001), 471–82.

Wright, D. B., and S. L. Schwartz, 'Conformity Effects in Memory for Actions', *Memory & Cognition*, 38 (2010), 1077–86.

Wright, D. B., G. Self and C. Justice, 'Memory Conformity: Exploring Misinformation Effects When Presented by Another Person', *British Journal of Psychology*, 91 (2000), 189–202.

Yarmey, A. D., *The Psychology of Eyewitness Testimony* (New York, 1979).

Yarmey, A. D., and H. P. Tresillian Jones, 'Is the Psychology of Eyewitness Identification a Matter of Common Sense?', in S. M. A. Lloyd-Bostock and B. R. Clifford (eds), *Evaluating Witness Evidence: Recent Psychological Research and New Perspectives* (Chichester, 1983), pp. 13–40.

Yoshimoto, M., *Kurosawa: Film Studies and Japanese Cinema* (Durham, NC, 2000).

Yuille, J. C., and J. L. Cutshall, 'A Case Study of Eyewitness Memory of a Crime', *Journal of Applied Psychology*, 71 (1986), 291–301.

Zacks, J. M., and B. Tversky, 'Event Structure in Perception and Cognition', *Psychological Review*, 127 (2001), 3–21.

Zaragoza, M. S., R. F. Belli and K. E. Payment, 'Misinformation Effects and the Suggestibility of Eyewitness Memory', in M. Garry and H. Hayne (eds), *Do Justice and Let the Sky Fall: Elizabeth F. Loftus and Her Contributions to Science, Law, and Academic Freedom* (Mahwah, NJ, 2007), pp. 35–63.

Zaragoza, M. S., and S. M. Lane, 'Source Misattribution and the Suggestibility of Eyewitness Memory', *Journal of Experimental Psychology: Learning, Memory, and Cognition*, 20 (1994), 934–45.

Zerner-Chardavoine, M., and H. Piéchon-Palloc, 'La croisade albigeoise, une revanche: Des rapports entre la quatrième croisade et la croisade albigeoise', *Revue historique*, 267 (1982), 3–18.

Index